SOCIAL DEVIANCE
BEING, BEHAVING, AND BRANDING

DAVID A. WARD
Clemson University

TIMOTHY J. CARTER
James Madison University

ROBIN D. PERRIN
Pepperdine University

ALLYN AND BACON
Boston   London   Toronto   Sydney   Tokyo   Singapore

Dedicated to:

Leslie and David
Kaye, Jeff, and Jon
Cindy and Jacob

Vice President, Publisher: Social Sciences Susan Badger
Senior Editor: Karen Hanson
Editorial Assistant: Sarah Dunbar
Production Coordinator: Marjorie Payne
Editorial-Production Service: Chestnut Hill Enterprises, Inc.
Cover Administrator: Linda Dickinson
Cover Designer: Suzanne Harbison
Composition Buyer: Linda Cox
Manufacturing Buyer: Louise Richardson

Library of Congress Cataloging-in-Publication Data

Ward, David Andrew
    Social Deviance : being, behaving, and branding / David A. Ward,
Timothy J. Carter, Robin D. Perrin.
        p.   cm.
    Includes bibliographical references (p.   ) and index.
    ISBN 0-205-13752-0 (acid-free paper)
    1. Deviant behavior.   I. Carter, Timothy J.   II. Perrin, Robin D.
III. Title
HM291.W26   1994
302.5'42—dc20   93-19695
                                                                         CIP

PHOTO CREDITS   Chapter 1, UPI/Bettmann; Chapter 2, AP/Wide World Photos;
Chapter 3, Ellis Herwig/The Picture Cube; Chapter 4, Spencer Grant/Stock, Boston;
Chapter 5, John Coletti/The Picture Cube; Chapter 6, Frank Siteman/The Picture
Cube; Chapter 7, UPI/Bettmann Newsphotos; Chapter 8, Ira Kirschenbaum/Stock,
Boston; Chapter 9, John Maher/The Picture Cube; Chapter 10, James R. Holland/
Stock, Boston; Chapter 11, Rhoda Sidney/Stock, Boston; Chapter 12, UPI/Bettmann;
Chapter 13, Michael Hayman/Stock, Boston; Chapter 14, AP/Wide World Photos.

CONTENTS

PREFACE

Our collective impression after having taught undergraduate courses in social deviance over the past two decades is that students are good at memorizing various theories and facts about deviance, but are less adept at *thinking* about deviance. To provoke students to think about deviance (or any other substantive area in sociology) is clearly the greatest challenge facing all of us who teach at the undergraduate level. Accordingly, this is our attempt to provide a pedagogy that will challenge students to do as much conceptualizing as they do memorizing. We seek to achieve this aim in a number of separate, but interrelated, ways.

First, the text conceptualizes each form of deviance examined from two points of view: the objectivist conception (deviance is norm-violation), and; the subjectivist conception (deviance is a definition). While other texts make a similar distinction, usually in the opening chapter, they do not apply both conceptions to the differing forms of deviance examined in later chapters. Rather, one or the other conception is chosen and adopted throughout the remainder of the text. This leaves the student with the misconception that the abandoned conception is somehow less worthy than the one chosen. But as we know, each conception of deviance can tell us something about the phenomenon under study. Second, within each conception (whether objectivist or subjectivist), both macro and micro level theories relevant to the form of deviance in question are presented in a concise way. Third, for each theory presented, available empirical research is reviewed with an eye toward evaluating the validity of the theory. Fourth, with this approach, the student is taught that the answer to the question "What is Deviance?" depends on one's conception and, further, when asked to provide an explanation (theory) for a given type of deviance, the student is provoked to ask "What is your conception of the kind of deviance being considered?"

Thus, the text underscores the importance of connecting conceptions of deviance with theories of deviance. If deviance is conceptualized in objectivist terms, then the theories reviewed will be theories designed to explain why people engage in norm-violating acts. By the same token, if deviance is conceptualized in subjectivist terms, then the theories reviewed will be theories about how deviance definitions are created and differentially applied to groups or persons.

Throughout the text, we seek a balanced examination of different types of deviance from both the objectivist and subjectivist points of view. Moreover, each chapter follows a similar organization in hopes of increasing readability and improving retention. Thus, each chapter includes the following sections: (1) What is deviance? This section examines the form of deviance considered in the chapter from both the objectivist and subjectivist points of view; (2) Who are the Deviants? This section presents current information of the sociodemographic correlates of the form of deviance considered in the chapter, (3) What Causes Deviance? This section presents applicable sociological theories of the form of deviance in question and reviews available research relevant for assessing the viability of the theory; (4) What is the prevailing social policy regarding each form of deviance examined? This section analyzes the social and political processes by which a form of deviance has become an aspect of public policy; and (5) What are the treatment approaches and measures of social control surrounding a particular type of deviance? This section presents popular treatment strategies for each form of deviance contained in the text.

We are indebted to many anonymous reviewers whose scholarly criticisms and insightful suggestions throughout the many revisions of the manuscript have been invaluable. We owe special thanks to Mark Stafford of Washington State University, Ed Bolander of Western Kentucky University and Mervin White of Clemson University for their critical commentary from the very beginning, and for sticking with us to the end.

Chapter 1

What is Deviance?

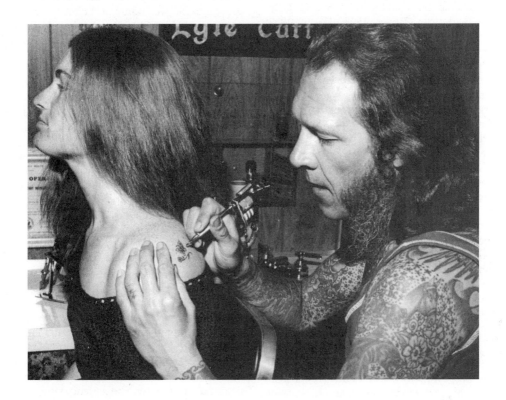

"THE BOY WHO DIVORCED HIS PARENTS"

Shawn Russ is finally at peace. Now living with his adoptive parents, George and Lizabeth Russ, Shawn has the love and affection he has sought all his life. Blessed with eight siblings, Shawn has begun to feel like part of the family.

Despite his present joy, Shawn's past was scarred by an abusive alcoholic father and a drug-dependent mother. When Shawn was just four, his mother separated from his father. But, a short visit with his father turned into nearly five years of moving around the country with Shawn often sleeping in the car (Tippet, 1993:204). By 1989, Shawn (then Gregory) was back with his mother. But, after only a brief stay, his mother realized she couldn't care for him so Gregory was again placed in foster care and then moved to Lake County Boys Ranch in Orlando, Florida.

George Russ, an Orlando attorney, visited the Boys Ranch where he met Gregory. George and Lizabeth Russ became his foster parents only later to have Gregory's mother seek renewed custody of her son through the courts. Gregory, who by that time had changed his name to Shawn, refused to return to his mother and, with the help of George Russ, sought to divorce his biological parents. Following intense court proceedings, Shawn was granted his wish and became the legally adopted son of the Russ family. The drama of a child obtaining a divorce from his biological parents set a national precedent—no child had ever taken such an extreme path before.

"THE PREPPY MURDER"

Jennifer Levin, the 19-year-old daughter of a successful New York real estate broker, had everything going for her. Rich family, a recent graduate from the $9,000-a-year Baldwin School, voted "best looking" in her class, readying herself for a well-financed college career, Jennifer Levin had it all (*Washington Post*, 1986:A6). She had it all, that is, until she met and became irresistibly attracted to Robert Chambers. Six feet four inches tall, unusually handsome, Chambers was not rich but moved in the social circles of the upper crust. Like Levin, Robert Chambers had been to the finest prep schools. But his academic career appeared to be all but over when he was expelled from Boston University before the end of his first semester.

Though their academic careers differed, their social life-styles bore marked similarities. Both Levin and Chambers frequented Dorrian's Red Hand bar where large crowds of "preps" would converge to drink, get high, and meet the beautiful people. It was at Dorrian's that Jennifer first met Robert Chambers. And, on an August night in 1986, she was back looking for him again. Further, according to a close girlfriend, Levin "wanted to go home with Chambers that night." Jennifer spotted Chambers through the crowd and, as the night grew into the wee hours of the morning, Jennifer Levin and Robert Chambers left for a walk in New York's Central Park (*Washington Post*, 1986:A6).

It was about 4 a.m. on that misty August night in 1986 when Levin and Chambers made their way behind the Metropolitan Museum of Art. Just two hours later, Jennifer Levin's body was found beneath a tree, half-naked, twisted, and battered (*Washington Post*, 1986:A6). Across the road sat Robert Chambers, his face and stomach bleeding from scratches. His hands were marked with open wounds. After approximately seven hours of questioning by the Central Park precinct police, Chambers admitted that he accidentally killed Jennifer Levin when, according to Chambers, she had molested him.

While there were 1,582 homicides in New York City in 1986, none so deeply captivated the public as the killing of Jennifer Dawn Levin on that dark and eerie night in August of 1986 (*Washington Post*, 1986:A6). Eleven months later, a jury was to deadlock over the verdict. The issue was whether Chambers intended to kill or merely intended to inflict physical harm. The jury at a impasse, Chambers's lawyer Jack Litman and prosecutor Linda Fairstein came to terms for a plea bargain—first-degree manslaughter. The sentence would amount to 5 to 15 years in prison. The parents of Jennifer Levin and the general public were outraged! Had Robert Chambers gotten away with murder?

"WHEN COPS BECOME CROOKS"

At 41, Brian O'Regan had settled into being a respected and well-integrated member of the New York Police Department

(N.Y.P.D.) at the 77th Precinct in Brooklyn. Having returned to the department after working a few years for the Broward County Sheriff's Department outside Miami, Brian was to receive a total of eight citations for excellent duty or bravery during his notable career (*New York Times*, 1986:1).

Everything seemed to be going Brian's way until he was suspended from duty following an investigation into departmental corruption. When he failed to surrender on Thursday morning, November 6, 1986, for arraignment on charges of stealing money and drugs and then reselling them, Brian O'Regan had apparently chosen a path of desperation and eventual suicide.

It had come to light from the investigation by the Internal Affairs Division of the N.Y.P.D. that over a dozen police officers, many having served more than ten years with the force, had become deeply involved in the trafficking of narcotics. It seemed that the very key to effective law enforcement in such areas as "The Alamo" (the name copes had given to the crime-ridden Bedford-Stuyvesant area of New York) was to become the vehicle for graft, corruption, and dope dealing among some of the most respected men on the force. That key to both effective law enforcement and eventual corruption was the building of intimate, personal relationships with the street people of the area. Although such intimate relationships are used by the police to uncover criminal activities, they can have corrupting influences and offer criminal opportunities, which became the doom of Brian O'Regan.

Having failed to appear for the arraignment in which he and partner Officer William Gallagher were to be charged with drug stealing and dealing, O'Regan checked into a modest one-story motel on County Road 39 outside the city. Later, he was found face up on the bed, fully clothed, with a .25-caliber pistol in his right hand. Next to his body were handwritten notes. The chief spokesperson for the department, Commissioner McCillion, said the notes were "not suicide notes, as such," but described the officer's "thoughts about several things, including the 77th Precinct and the police department" (*New York Times*, 1986:36).

The suicide of Brian O'Regan was a profound human tragedy. An illustrious career before him, he was caught in a web of deceit, betrayal, and corruption that eventually led to his destruction. A central question is now being asked by concerned administrators of law enforcement across the nation. Will the money, power, and eventual corruption connected to illegal drug trafficking threaten to destroy the credibility and effectiveness of law enforcement agencies everywhere? The question raises an important sociological issue. And many people (laypersons, judges, and political leaders alike) believe that the answer may well shape the course of the nation's justice system for decades to come.

CONCEPTIONS OF DEVIANCE

The separate events described at the beginning of this chapter are examples of what sociologists study when they seek to understand the world of deviance. While these events involving kinds of people and kinds of behaviors may give us an initial clue as to what constitutes deviance, the sociologist demands more than a simple list of such events to answer the question: "What is deviance?" What is required is a fairly abstract conceptual definition that will capture the many varieties of people and behaviors thought to be instances of deviance. In constructing such a conceptual definition, the sociologist tries to identify the things that are *common* to each kind of person or behavior considered deviant. For instance, if it could be shown that a large number of the kinds of people or behaviors considered deviant appear to evoke disapproval among those who may witness them, then part of one's conceptual definition of deviance would include a statement such as: "Deviance is a personal attribute or a behavior that results in social disapproval from others."

Aspects of Social Interaction

In the following two sections of this chapter, we will examine two alternative conceptions of deviance. To make the distinctions between the competing conceptions clear, we will compare and contrast them in terms of three aspects of social interaction that are considered more or less central to an understanding of deviance. These aspects of social interaction include *actors and their acts, norms,* and *societal reactions.* Before we consider the alternative ways of conceptualizing deviance, let us briefly examine the nature of these three aspects of human social interaction.

It may offend common sense to suggest that deviance has something to do with how people act. As Albert Cohen put it over 20 years ago, deviance involves "knavery, skulduggery, cheating, unfairness, crime, sneakiness, malingering, cheating, cutting corners, immorality, dishonesty, betrayal, graft, corruption, wickedness, and sin" (1966:1). Also suggesting that deviance has something to do with how people act, Alexander Liazos (1972:109) contended that we should turn away from the narrow definition of deviance that only includes "nuts, sluts, and 'preverts' " to a broader definition that would include corporate and governmental deviance. Whether it is "crime in the streets" or "crime in the suites," it is quite typical when we think of deviance to think in terms of how people act.

But the way people behave, or how they act, may not be the only reason for classifying them or their behaviors as deviant. For example, Dinitz, Dynes, and Clarke (1975) defined midgets, dwarfs, giants, sinners, heretics, bums, tramps, hippies, and bohemians as deviant. If we analyze their definition, it becomes clear that some of the things they define as deviant are not acts but kinds of people. Midgets, dwarfs, and giants are not doing anything wrong. They are considered deviant for the way they are, not for what they have done. That conditions of being may be considered deviant is most dramatically shown by a now-classic illustrative case cited by Goffman (1961) in his work *Stigma.* The case, in the form of a letter, is drawn from a book entitled *Miss Lonelyhearts* (1933:2), written by Nathanael West. The letter begins, "Dear Miss Lonelyhearts:"

> *I am sixteen years old now and I dont know what to do and would appreciate it if you could tell me what to do. When I was a little girl it was not so bad because I got used to the kids on the block making fun of me, but now I would like to have boy friends like the other girls and go out on Saturday nites, but no boy will take me because I was born without a nose—although I am a good dancer and have a nice shape and my father buys me pretty clothes.*
>
> *I sit and look at myself all day and cry. I have a big hole in the middle of my face that scares people even myself so I cant blame the boys for not wanting to take me out. My mother loves me, but she crys terrible when she looks at me. What did I do to deserve such a terrible bad fate? . . . Papa says he doesnt know, but that maybe I did something in the other world before I was born or that maybe I was being punished for his sins. I dont believe that because he is a very nice man. Ought I commit suicide?*
>
> *Sincerely yours,*
> *Desperate*

To be sure, some persons are considered deviant because they have committed criminal or deviant acts. But for others (as in the case of "Dear Miss Lonelyhearts"), deviance arises merely from a condition of being. To make things a little more complicated, people may be regarded as deviant not because of their physical characteristics (their condition of being) but because they have been branded by others as a "fag," "slut," "whore," "pimp," "nurd," or some other insidious label. In these cases, the deviant public identity stems from the stigmatizing reactions of others.

Whether people are regarded as deviant because of what they have done, a condition of being, or a stigmatizing label affixed by others, good definitions of deviance should reflect the fact that people, as well as behaviors, may be regarded as deviant by ordinary people in everyday situations.

We suggested earlier that conceptions of deviance may be compared in terms of three aspects of social interaction. We have considered both being and behaving. Taken together, they may be considered as one aspect of human social interaction. Here, we turn to the second aspect of social interaction, norms. Simply put, norms are rules of conduct; they are the "shoulds" and "shouldn'ts" of society. "Roll the toilet paper counterclockwise" may be thought of as a norm. "Don't pick, blow, or otherwise dislodge any substance from your nose in a social gathering" is a norm. "Don't cheat on a classroom exam" is an example of a norm. In each case, a statement about what people should or shouldn't do is made. Norms may also relate to states of being. "Don't be too fat!" is a norm. "Don't be too skinny!" is a norm. Each is a statement indicating desirable or undesirable states of being.

More formally, norms are shared expectations for behavior or being and shared evaluations of behavior or being. Expectations refer to how people will act or be. Evaluations refer to how people *should* act or be (Meier, 1981). How "shared" an expectation or evaluation must be before it is considered a norm is a difficult issue to resolve and one that we will address in later pages.

Many scholars view norms as central to an understanding of what deviance is. Deviance is seen as behavior or being that breaks the rules. No rules, no rule breakers. You just can't have deviance without norms, some scholars would contend. While this idea appears reasonable enough, not all sociologists agree. One source of the disagreement stems from the difficulty in knowing exactly how, and under what circumstances, a particular norm applies. Consider the norm: "Thou shalt not kill." If one violates this rule, has deviance occurred? In general, yes, but ponder the following situations. Harry Malone's wife is brain dead, kept alive only by artificial means. Harry, under severe distress for over

nine months and against the avowed policy of the hospital, pulls the plug and allows his wife to die. Has Harry committed an act of deviance? Now consider an additional case. John Sax hears a noise in the middle of the night. Creeping through the dining room, he spots what he believes to be a robber. Taking his double-barreled shotgun from the mantel, he unloads two rounds into his wife's upper body. She, by all indications from the autopsy, was returning from the kitchen where she had consumed two glasses of water. Has John committed an act of deviance?

In either of these two examples, it is difficult to conclude that the norm "Thou shalt not kill" has been violated because the norm does not stipulate the endless circumstances that could arise to render the norm inapplicable. Given this kind of dilemma, are norms really useful in defining deviance? As we shall see, the answer depends upon the way one conceptualizes deviance—an issue we will address in the next section.

The third aspect of social interaction that serves to distinguish competing ways of defining deviance is *societal reactions*. This concept embraces all of the ways in which society responds to individuals or their acts when deviance is known or suspected. One category of societal reactions is formal sanctions. In this context, the term *sanctions* refers to punishments usually designed to control actual or suspected deviance. *Formal sanctions* refers to punishments administered by the state or other acknowledged institutions of society, such as, fines, prison sentences, and execution by lethal injection or hanging. Other state sanctions may emanate from institutional psychiatry. Examples include placement in a mental institution, involuntary treatment for alcoholism or drug abuse, and a frontal lobotomy. Sanctions administered by formal agencies of social control most often carry with them a stigma. The person who has served time in prison is labeled an "ex-con." The person who has been a patient in a psychiatric institution is branded "mentally ill" or, less sensitively, "nuts." These labels are verbal statements that define persons or actions as deviant. They are stigmatizing in that they tend to discredit a person and cause social audiences to impute evil or otherwise disrespectable motives and intentions to the labeled individual.

Stigmatizing labels are not only aspects of the formal sanctioning process. They arise from informal sanctions as well. *Informal sanctions* come from unofficial sources such as peer groups, work groups, and members of a community. Again, the purpose is to control deviance or suspected deviance. Ridicule, peer disapproval, ostricism, criticism, and interpersonal hostility are types of informal sanctions. Taken together, informal and formal sanctions, with their accompanying stigmatizing labels, constitute the bulk of societal reactions. In very concrete terms, a person may engage (or at least be perceived to have engaged) in a behavior that violates somebody's norm. Society reacts in the form of informal and formal sanctions. The reaction often carries a label that verbally defines the behavior as an instance of deviance or the person as a kind of deviant. In this way, societal reactions may be considered essential in defining deviance as a social phenomenon. Whether societal reactions *are* considered crucial in defining deviance depends upon which conception of deviance one adopts, as we shall soon discover.

In summary, whether acts or actors, norms, or societal reactions are considered critical in defining deviance depends upon one's conception. Different conceptions emphasize different combinations of the three aspects of social interaction. We now turn to an examination of two alternative conceptions of deviance. We will present each conception in terms of how it emphasizes or neglects the three aspects of social interaction. To simplify our presentation, we will

first examine each conception in terms of how it defines deviance. *Deviance* refers to acts. Then, we will analyze each conception in terms of how deviants are defined. *Deviants* refers to people.

The Objectivist Conception

The objectivist conception defines deviance as *norm-violating behavior*. Consider the following objectivist definitions of deviance:

> Merton:
> *Deviant behavior refers to conduct that departs significantly from the norms set for people in their social statuses (1966:805).*

> Kaplan:
> *Deviant behavior . . . is the failure of a person to conform to the specified normative expectations of one or more of the specified groups in which the individual holds membership (1975:4).*

> Cohen:
> *. . . behavior which violates institutionalized expectations—that is, expectations that are shared and recognized as legitimate within a social system (1955:62).*

In light of these definitions, deviance is seen as "objectively given" (Rubington and Weinberg, 1987). To suggest that deviance is objective is to claim that researchers (or anyone else) can identify an act of deviance by comparing that act with readily available, scientifically measurable norms. Norms serve as an objective standard by which deviant behavior may be discovered. Table 1–1 depicts the way in which the objectivist conception defines deviance (acts) in terms of the three aspects of social interaction. The only factors held to be central to the objectivist conception are behavior and norms. Societal or audience reactions are ignored. To suggest, as we do in Table 1–1, that the objectivist conception makes both behavior and norms central in defining deviance is consistent with the generally recognized assertion that few, if any, behaviors are deviant in and of them-

TABLE 1.1   Objectivist Conception of Deviance in Terms of Three Aspects of Social Interaction.

BEHAVIOR	NORMS	SOCIETAL REACTIONS
Acts that violate norms are instances of deviance.	Norms are rules of conduct. They are the objective measuring rods for evaluating acts as being either instances of conformity or deviance.	Audience reactions are not central to an objectivist definition of deviance.

selves. While early social pathologists accepted the notion that certain behaviors were inherently deviant, most modern objectivists no longer hold to this absolutist view. They recognize and affirm that behaviors may only be considered deviant against the background of cultural norms. Indeed, one of the chief proponents of the objectivist conception, Robert Merton, considers it utterly obvious that an act is deviant only when it violates cultural norms: "It is blatantly true and trivial: namely, the statement that behavior cannot be considered 'deviant' unless there are social norms from which that behavior departs. It seems banal and safe to stipulate: no rule, no rule-violating behavior" (Merton, 1966:827).

The objectivist conception suggests that we can identify deviant behavior with reference to norms. But can the same thing be said about deviant statuses or identities? As we have suggested earlier, if the term *deviance* may be reserved for acts, then we may reserve the term *deviants* for people. How, then, do people come to be socially regarded as deviant? There are really two ways: either because their condition of being violates social norms regarding ideal conditions of being (for example, someone with no nose) or because their acts (real or imagined) have caused social audiences to publicly define them as a kind of person who is morally blemished. Here, labeling may include brands such as "pimp," "whore," "kook," "pervert," "slut," or "drunk." Because the objectivist conception does not consider societal reactions as central to defining deviance, the conception is only relevant for understanding the deviant status in terms of conditions of being. The objectivist conception of deviants is depicted in Table 1–2.

Conditions of being, such as blindness, dwarfism, and facial disfigurement, may be conceptualized as deviant because these conditions violate norms regarding "ideal" conditions of being. The idea that there are societal norms regarding states of being is suggested by Goffman's notion of "identity norms" (1963:128). Identity norms are "depictions of 'ideal persons,' shared beliefs as to what individuals ought to be (behaviorally and otherwise)" (Stafford and Scott, 1986:81). Goffman suggests that, at least in the United States, the ideal person is one who is "young, married, white, urban, northern, heterosexual Protestant father of college education, fully employed, of good complexion, weight, and height, and a recent record in sports" (Goffman, 1963:128). While many of us may not agree that any or all of these attributes are ideal, our disagreement does not negate the assertion that *some* ideal standards of being are widely shared by members of American society.

Evaluating the Objectivist Conception. The first difficulty with the objectivist conception relates to problems surrounding the definition and measurement of norms. This is somewhat ironic because those who embrace

TABLE 1.2   Objectivist Conception of Deviants in Terms of Three Aspects of Social Interaction.

CONDITIONS OF BEING	NORMS	SOCIETAL REACTIONS
This includes physical deformities, racial characteristics, and the like.	There are norms that specify "ideal" conditions of being	Societal reactions are not part of the objectivist conception of being deviant.

the objectivist conception have long argued that the primary virtue of the approach is its "objectivity." What they mean is that norms are objective standards against which we can compare behavior or being. If the behavior or state of being violates the objective standard (norm), then it is an instance of deviance or deviants. But are norms abstract standards that can be readily identified and objectively determined? If the answer should turn out to be no, then the objectivist conception is faced with the embarrassing predicament of defining deviance or deviants in terms of a concept (norm) that is itself vague and without readily identifiable empirical referents (Gibbs, 1981).

 As noted earlier, norms really have two aspects. First, norms are shared expectations for behavior or being. Second, norms are shared evaluations of behavior or being. In both cases, however, norms are always defined as "shared." But what does it mean to claim that expectations for (or evaluations of) behavior or being are shared? How "shared" does an expectation (or evaluation) have to be for it to be a norm? Just considering deviance (acts) for a moment, let us suppose that a sociologist decided to survey a random sample of people in the United States to determine their opinions (evaluation) about some behavior, for instance, marijuana use. What kind of results would the survey have to produce to enable the sociologist to conclude that opinions about pot use are shared? Would all of the respondents have to express the same opinion, or would it only take about 75 percent? Would 51 percent be enough? How does

one draw the line? Obviously, any answer is arbitrary (Gibbs, 1981:11).

A second criticism relates to the recognition that norms are abstract ideals that may not be easily applied in concrete situations. We alluded to this problem in connection with our discussion of norms at the outset of this chapter. Suppose it were established that all members of a group or society disapproved of a behavior in the abstract. Would they continue to disapprove if the conditions under which the behavior occurred were to change? For example, it is entirely conceivable that all of the members of a group or society may strongly disapprove of smoking pot. Accordingly, marijuana use would reasonably be considered deviance. But would members continue to disapprove if an individual were to use marijuana to relieve the discomfort associated with chemotherapy? The answer is "probably not." And this is the point. Because there are so many situations in which any given norm would have to be qualified, it is questionable whether the concept of norm as an abstract ideal is really useful as a standard for defining an act as an instance of deviance in concrete situations. And, to the extent that the objectivist conception of deviance is predicated on the concept of norm, the conception is all the more dubious (Gibbs, 1981:12).

The third criticism of the objectivist conception is its tendency to ignore power differentials in the identification of norms (Gibbs, 1981:13). For expectations and evaluations to constitute a norm, must all or most of the members of a society agree in their expectations or evaluations, or is it sufficient that only a few very powerful people agree? Gibbs, in commenting on sociologists' attempts to identify the norms about marijuana use through social surveys, makes the following observation:

> Suppose that one respondent in the survey is a wealthy senator and another is a skid-row bum, the conventional survey practice [in an attempt to identify norms] would assign equal weight to their normative opinions, but that practice is debatable. Granted that power is a fuzzy notion, in this instance one respondent clearly has more power than the other. Insofar as there is a marijuana norm, the senator would surely have more opportunities to alter the norm through legislative action (Gibbs, 1981:13)

Here, Gibbs is really hinting at a theoretical question: Does power influence the making of norms? Since conceptions are not theories (and therefore not amenable to empirical tests), why does the issue of "differential power" present a challenge to the objectivist *conception* of deviance? Can't deviance still be defined as norm-violation irrespective of where norms come from? Strictly speaking, the answer is yes, if one is willing to count an opinion about, say, marijuana use, as a norm even if it is held by only two or three very powerful members of a society of millions!

In the past, objectivists were not inclined to allow norms to be defined by such a small consensus. Primarily influenced by the structural-functionalist perspective in sociology, traditional objectivists held that society was characterized by relatively high levels of normative consensus (Merton, 1939). Normative consensus was achieved through adequate socialization of members to society's norms. From this perspective, it seems quite reasonable to conceptualize deviance as norm violation. But what if society is not characterized by normative consensus? What if *normative conflict* best depicts the fabric of society?

Would it still be reasonable to define deviance as acts that violate norms? What norms? Whose norms?

Here the objectivist conception appears to lose credibility, unless its proponents are willing to define deviance as the violation of norms of the members of society who count more, have more power, and can, therefore, impose their norms upon the less powerful members of society. Most objectivists appear reluctant to go this far.

But even if objectivists were to concede that some normative opinions count more, and they were willing to take this into consideration in defining deviance, we are still left with the difficulty of identifying the norms.

> Even if an empirically applicable definition of power could be formulated, the relative importance of different kinds of power (e.g., political, economic) is not likely to be approximately the same for evaluations of all types of behavior; and there is no prospect of assigning "power weights" to each normative opinion (Gibbs, 1981:21).

Given these difficulties in defining norms when differential power is taken into consideration, it is not surprising that very few (if any) objectivists "explicitly stipulate that only evaluations of conduct endorsed by the powerful members of a social unit are norms" (Gibbs, 1981:21). Even so, ignoring power differentials when identifying norms seems highly unrealistic. Indeed, this is the position held by those objectivists who identify themselves as neo-Marxists. Their contention is that norms (and particularly formal., legal norms) are not necessarily shared by members of society, but are *imposed* on the majority by a powerful minority in an attempt to protect their property interests. More on this later.

A fourth criticism of the objectivists conception centers on its inability to lend insight into how deviance (a person's action) gets transformed into deviant (a person's social identity). This shortcoming relates to the failure of the objectivist view to make societal or audience reactions central to the definition of deviance. As we noted earlier, audience reactions can be formal, as in the case of legal punishments by official agents of social control, or informal, as in the case of peer disapproval or peer rejection. In both cases, the individual who is the target of such reactions is responded to, singled out, and often publicly defined (labeled) as one who is deviant. Since it is possible for one to be publicly defined as deviant even though he or she may not have actually violated any norm (the so-called bum rap), then it follows that others' negative responses (audience reactions) are often the single determining factor in whether a person will be publicly regarded as deviant. As we shall see in the next section, one of the major contentions of the subjectivist conception of deviance is that audience reactions in the form of sanctions and labels may be *differentially* applied to alleged "offenders," and it is this differential application that often defines some individuals as socially deviant.

The Subjectivist Conception

The subjectivist conception defines deviance as an act (real or imagined) that has been labeled "deviance" by a social audience. Accordingly, societal reactions are the ultimate means for identifying deviance. The importance of studying the reactions of others in understanding how deviance is socially "created" is dramatized in Becker's (1963:9) well-known typology. Table 1–3 shows a cross-classification of the actual behavior of an actor and the labels attached to that behavior by others. We may recall that one of the assumptions of the objectivist conception is that the reactions of others are irrelevant in defining deviance. The only relevant factor in determining deviance is how people act in relation to norms. Becker's deviance typology makes clear the potential shortcoming of

this objectivist position. Making others' reactions central, Becker shows that there is not always a perfect correspondence between what an actor objectively does and how his or her behavior will be defined (labeled) by others. This lack of correspondence exists for both "secret deviance" and the "falsely accused."

Our analysis of Becker's typology of deviance suggests that the subjectivist conception shifts the focus of attention away from the behavior of the alleged norm-violator and toward the reactions of the audience that, either directly or indirectly, bears witness to it. Consider the following subjectivist definitions of deviance:

> *Kitsuse:*
> Forms of behavior per se *do not differentiate deviants from non-deviants; it is the responses of the conventional and conforming members of the society who identify and interpret behavior as deviant which sociologically transform persons into deviants (1962:253).*

> *Erikson:*
> *Deviance is not a property* inherent in *certain forms of behavior; it is a property conferred upon those forms by the audiences which directly or indirectly witness them. Sociologically, then, the critical variable in the study of deviance is the social audience . . . . (1962:308).*

> *Becker:*
> *From this point of view, deviance is* not *a quality of the act a person commits, but rather a consequence of the application by others of rules and sanctions to an "offender." The deviant is one to whom that label has successfully been applied; deviant behavior is behavior that people so label (1963:9).*

According to the subjectivist conception, then, deviance is not "objectively given" but "subjectively problematic" (Rubington and Weinberg, 1987). That is, the subjective viewpoints (interpretations) of the social audience must be taken into account in order to understand how an alleged norm-violation be-

---

TABLE 1.3 Becker's Typology of Deviance.

		Others' Labels	
		Conformity	Deviance
Actor's Behavior	Conformity	Conformity	Falsely accused
	Deviance	Secret Deviance	Pure Deviance

---

comes publicly regarded as an instance of deviance, or how an alleged norm-violator becomes socially regarded as deviant. Table 1–4 depicts the subjectivist conception of deviance (acts) in terms of three aspects of social interaction: behavior, norms, and societal reactions.

If we push the subjectivist conception to its extreme, societal or audience reactions are the central factors in defining an act as an instance of deviance. The application of sanctions and labels to a perceived violation of ill-defined, and often weakly shared, norms serves to create deviance.

If acts may be identified as instances of deviance on the basis of societal reactions, does the same hold true for how persons come to be publicly regarded as deviant? From the subjectivist viewpoint, societal or audience reactions socially stigmatize a person, giving him or her a deviant status. Thus, the deviant is a person so labeled. As Becker observed:

The question is raised: "What kind of person would break such an important rule?" and the answer is given: "One who is different from the rest of us, who cannot or will not act as a moral human being and therefore might break other important rules" (Becker, 1963:34).

Consistent with Becker's observations, Table 1–5 depicts the subjectivist conception of deviants. Whether one is considering deviance (acts) or deviants (persons), it is societal or audience reactions that identify them as nonconforming. No societal or audience reaction, no deviance or deviants!

Evaluating the Subjectivist Conception As we have seen, the subjectivist defines deviance as a label. It is not the act, but societal reaction that defines deviance. For this conception of deviance to remain viable, it must be able to point to instances in the real world that constitute deviance according to the definition. Put in question form, what *kind* and *intensity* of reaction is required before an

---

TABLE 1.4 Subjectivist Conception of Deviance in Terms of Three Aspects of Social Interaction.

BEHAVIOR	NORMS	SOCIETAL REACTIONS
Norm-violating acts are not deviance unless they are discovered and labeled as deviance.	Norms are not the ultimate measuring rod for identifying deviance. However, norms may guide societal reactions in response to actual or perceived rule breaking.	Societal reactions are the ultimate measuring rod for identifying deviance. Deviance is an act so labeled.

TABLE 1.5   Subjectivist Conception of Deviants in Terms of Three Aspects of Social Interaction.

DEVIANT SOCIAL IDENTITY	NORMS	SOCIETAL REACTIONS
Deviant identities are labels affixed to some persons by social audiences.	Norms may serve to guide audience reactions but only in concrete situations.	It is audience reactions in the form of stigmatizing labels that designate a person as a kind of deviant.

act is considered an instance of deviance? Must the reaction involve formal sanctions by courts and cops, or will informal sanctions by peers and pals do? Does the intensity of the reaction have to be outrage, or will simple disapproval be enough? If the subjectivist conception were empirically applicable (that is, if it helped identify deviance or deviants in the real world), then independent observers would be able to classify the types of reactions (both in terms of kind and intensity) that will identify an act as an instance of deviance or a person as a deviant. At this point, any criteria stipulating the kind and intensity of audience reactions necessary to define acts as deviance or persons as deviants would appear arbitrary at best (Gibbs, 1981:27).

A second, and somewhat related, criticism stems from an apparent tendency among subjectivists to ignore norms in the definition of deviance. Though norms may serve to guide societal reactions once an act (real or imagined) is *perceived* by social audiences as one of deviance, norms are not central in defining deviance. Only societal reactions do that. The tendency among subjectivists to avoid norms springs most likely from the many problems norms create for those who adhere to an objectivist conception. But if subjectivists do not concede that there are generally shared norms stipulating whether particular acts are right or wrong, then logical difficulties arise that make their conception troublesome. For instance, why would audiences react unless they perceived that a rule has been broken? Unless reactions are purely random (some-

thing a subjectivist does not accept) then it is difficult to understand why audiences react in the absence of a consideration of norms (Meier, 1981:7). How can a reaction (for instance, an accusation) constitute a label unless others who witness the reaction share a belief (norm) that the accusation signifies something blameworthy, bad, or otherwise deviant? (Gibbs, 1981:28). In other words, how do we know that a label such as "queer" denotes deviance unless we consider norms?

A third criticism of the subjectivist approach relates to the concept of "secret deviants" as advanced by Becker (1963). We may recall from Becker's typology of deviance that secret deviance is an instance of rule breaking that has not been discovered or publicly labeled. While Becker's typology dramatized the importance of distinguishing between what people actually do in terms of rule breaking and how their acts are perceived and labeled by others, it is clear that the notion of secret deviance contradicts the subjectivist conception of deviance. The critics say: "Is it possible to have *secret* deviance when the subjectivist conception defines deviance only in terms of others' reactions?" If deviance is a public label, then secret deviance is logically impossible.

A fourth criticism of the subjectivist conception is that it ignores the possibility that the norm-violating act may *cause* the deviant label. As Akers has noted, "The label does not create the behavior in the *first place*. People can and do commit deviant acts because of the particular contingencies and circumstances in their lives, quite apart from or in combination with the labels others apply to them" (1968:463). The subjectivist seems to be suggesting that people are going around minding their own business when along come the biased police or psychiatrists to slap them with a deviant label! But as Nettler has argued, "some people *are* more crazy than others; we can tell the difference; and calling lunacy a name does not cause it" (1974:894).

A final criticism of the subjectivist conception derives from the apparent denial by the subjectivist that a real deviant act has occurred if the perpetrator has not been publicly labeled "deviant." Consider the following example: John raped Mary on their first date. Mary fell into a deep state of depression and was forced to leave college just prior to graduation. Terrified of the publicity, Mary has not told anyone that the rapist was John. John has finished college and is now employed in a major corporation. No one has ever become aware of John's actions. He has not been labeled. Given these facts, is it reasonable to suggest that no deviance was committed simply because no labeling has occurred?

Consider another possibility: Jane has been using cocaine for years. Now, she deals coke to maintain her habit. Last month, Jane sold crack to her girlfriend Sue. Sue overdosed and died of a heart attack. Jane has not been discovered as the source of the cocaine. Jane leaves town and escapes detection. Given these facts, is it reasonable to conclude, as the subjectivist seems to contend, that no deviance has occurred? If, in both examples, the answer is no, then the subjectivist conception of deviance must be considered deficient.

SUMMARY OF THE COMPETING CONCEPTIONS

According to the objectivists, deviance is behavior that violates social norms. Societal reactions are not central to the objectivist

conception, because they are viewed as *following* deviance, not defining it. On the other hand, subjectivists define deviance in terms of societal reactions. Deviance is a definition (label) applied to acts by social audiences. Deviance is behavior so labeled.

In terms of deviants, the objectivist conception is only applicable to individuals regarded as deviant because of their conditions of being. The subjectivist conception, on the other hand, is relevant for grasping the process whereby persons who commit acts of deviance get transformed into persons who are socially defined as deviant. For the subjectivist, audience reactions affix deviant identities to persons.

Each of the conceptions has its strengths and weaknesses. A strength of the objectivist conception is that it defines deviance apart from societal reactions. Therefore, *undetected* (as well as detected) deviance is "true" deviance from this point of view. Further, since societal reactions are conceptualized as distinct from deviance, the objectivist definition may suggest how societal reactions might influence deviance as is found, for example, in statements of the "deterrence doctrine," which we will examine in Chapter 2.

The major weakness of the objectivist conception relates to difficulties in the definition and measurement of norms. For the objectivist, norms are "out there." They serve as objective measuring rods for defining deviance. But the definition of norms as "shared" implies that society is characterized by a fairly widespread consensus as to what constitutes a moral or immoral act. The issue of just what constitutes sufficient consensus persists as a problem for the objectivist conception. Even with this criticism, the objectivist conception appears useful when it comes to a consideration of consensus deviance. *Consensus deviance* refers to acts that violate norms shared by most people in society and for which there are fairly uniform societal reactions. For example, most people agree that murder is wrong, that rape of a four-year-old child is criminal, and that mothers or fathers should not have sex with their children.

A strength of the subjectivist conception is the insight that societal reactions are critical in defining some categories of deviance and deviants. In terms of deviance, it is possible for acts to be inaccurately perceived and misinterpreted by social audiences. Even so, audiences may treat the act as deviance, thereby making it deviance for those who witness the labeling event. This suggests that the bum rap, or what Becker (1963:9) calls the "falsely accused," is an important category for sociological studies of deviance—a category not recognized by the objectivist conception. Further, the subjectivist conception, in emphasizing societal reactions, points out how deviants may derive from the differential application of rules to offenders (actual or accused). Here, the issue centers on the process whereby only certain individuals among the total population of rule breakers get selected to be included in the social category designated as deviant (Becker, 1963). The issue turns on how definitions of acts as deviance get transformed into definitions of persons as deviants.

In spite of these strengths, a potential weakness of the subjectivist view is its tendency to bypass norms in defining deviance. To avoid the problems confronted by the objectivists (who make norms central to their definition), the subjectivists define deviance solely in terms of societal reactions. But why do audiences react unless they collectively perceive that a rule has been violated? How do we know that a label such as "fag," "tramp," "head," or "sick" denotes deviance unless the label reflects shared beliefs (norms) about desirable or undesirable conduct? These are questions that appear to threaten the viability of the subjectivist view of deviance.

CONCEPTIONS AND THEORIES

Conceptions of deviance are abstract definitions of what deviance *is*. Theories are sets of ideas that seek to explain *why* deviance occurs. The difference between conceptions and theories should not be confused. Hence, it is meaningful to speak of a conception of deviance (for example, objectivist versus subjectivist) and then recommend a theory of deviance based on that conception. Logically, if one conceptualizes deviance in subjectivist terms, one is likely to propose a theory that explains how definitions of deviance are created and applied. On the other hand, if one conceptualizes deviance in objectivist terms, then one is likely to propose a theory that attempts to explain the cause of behaviors that violate social norms. As you will learn in Chapters 2 and 3, exceptions to this link between conceptions and theories are rare, but they nonetheless exist.

Throughout Chapters 2 and 3, we will examine a variety of theories that purport to explain deviant behavior, deviance definitions, or both. To guide our analysis of these theories, we will adopt the classification scheme shown in Table 1–6. In the scheme, theories are categorized according to whether they define deviance objectively or subjectively and whether they focus on macro-level social structures or micro-level social processes. Some who accept the objectivist conception develop theories aimed at explaining differing *rates* of norm-violating behavior between broad categories within society. These theories invoke structural and cultural factors to account for the observed differences. Hence, such theories may be referred to as macro-theories of deviance. Other objectivist theories seek to explain the interactional processes whereby single individuals acquire and maintain deviant behavioral patterns. Such theories may be referred to as micro-theories of deviance. Therefore, it is meaningful to speak of *macro-objectivist* theories and *micro-objectivist* theories. Both are trying to explain norm-violating behaviors, but one seeks explanation in terms of large-scale social forces while the other focuses on processes at the level of human interaction.

TABLE 1.6 Examples of Theories Reflecting Varying Conceptions of Deviance at Differing Levels of Analysis.

	OBJECTIVIST	SUBJECTIVIST
Macro-Level	Strain theories	Interest group theories
Micro-Level	Social learning theories	Labeling theories

As in the case of the objectivist conception, there are subjectivist theories that focus primarily on large-scale social forces while others concentrate primarily on interaction processes at the individual level. Whether at the macro- or micro-level, the questions are often the same: "How are deviance definitions created, and how are they applied to offenders?" Interest group theorists tend to focus on the creation and application of deviance definitions at the macro-level, while labeling theorists concentrate on these processes at the micro-level. It is reasonable, then, to speak of *macro-subjectivist* and *micro-subjectivist* theories.

As you read through Chapters 2 and 3, you will develop a more comfortable grasp of the classification scheme and the way it may help you distinguish between various theories. While the scheme may assist us in keeping different things different, it is not without its shortcomings. Any such classification scheme may distort a particular theory by acting as if the theory is a pure representation of the category within which it is placed. Even so, if within some classification scheme, there are more similarities than differences among same placed theories and more differences than similarities among different placed theories, then the scheme gains in conceptual defensibility. Ultimately, however, its defensibility hinges on its usefulness in organizing our thoughts about deviance phenomena.

ASSUMPTIONS AND THEORIES

Theories can be distinguished on the basis of how they conceptualize deviance and on the basis of whether they concentrate on macro- or micro-level phenomena. They can also be distinguished by underlying assumptions they make regarding the nature of human actors, more specifically, whether human beings are endowed with free will or whether their behavior is determined by forces beyond conscious choice.

Though not always true, most theories designed to explain norm-violation (and therefore conceptualize deviance in objectivist terms) have as an underlying assumption the idea that human behavior is *determined*. To suggest that human behavior (including norm-violating behavior) is determined, is to accept the belief that behavior is *caused* by events that precede it. As the argument goes, human behavior is not random, but patterned. Patterns of human conduct are believed to exist because social and cultural forces are exerting irresistible influences over human actors. In its extreme form, the deterministic assumption implies that the human actor really has no choice in the matter. If social and cultural factors cause human behavior and all the relevant factors could be identified, variations in behavior (including deviant behavior) could be perfectly explained.

To find theories that suggest that human actors are endowed with free will, we are led more in the direction of those theories that we have categorized as subjectivist. For example, some statements of labeling theory are inclined to incorporate elements of free will in their theoretical arguments about the origin of deviance. Even so, the admission of free will in labeling theories should not be interpreted as a blanket rejection of determinism. Most

TABLE 1.7   Whether an Act Will Be Considered as Crime, Deviance, or Both.

	VIOLATION OF FORMAL LAWS	VIOLATION OF INFORMAL NORMS	SANCTIONS AS FORMAL LEGAL PUNISHMENTS	SANCTIONS AS INFORMAL SOCIAL DISAPPROVAL
I. Crime is deviance.	yes	yes	yes	yes
II. Crime is not deviance.	yes	no	yes	no
III. Deviance is not crime.	no	yes	no	yes

subjectivist theories, including labeling theory, tend more toward what has come to be called "soft-determinism." The notion suggests that human actors are neither totally free nor totally determined. Large-scale structural conditions confront each actor with an objective reality that, in good measure, narrows the alternatives for choice. On the other hand, no society appears capable of eliminating every possible alternative for conduct. Given alternatives, individuals must make choices. This seems true, as many a political martyr would attest, even if the choice is death.

CRIME AND DEVIANCE

We are now comfortable with the observation that the answer to the question, "What is deviance?" depends upon the way it is conceptualized. For the objectivist, deviance is an act. For the subjectivist, deviance is a label. In this section, we will explore the similarities and differences between crime and deviance. At least at the intuitive level, most of us recognize a connection between crime and deviance. But when are crime and deviance different and when are they the same?

Table 1–7 will help us in making distinctions between the two. It distinguishes between crime and deviance as norm-violation in terms of whether an act violates a formal law or an informal norm *and* whether the violation is met by legal sanctions or informal social disapproval. As may be seen, the con-

nection between crime and deviance has three interesting possibilities. The first possibility suggests that there are acts that will be considered as crimes and instances of deviance simultaneously. Here, a person engages in an act (for example, forcible rape) that violates formal laws and is subject to legal sanctions if discovered. Further, the act is disapproved of by the informal social audiences that may become aware of it. Therefore, crime is considered deviance when acts violate legal norms, are subject to legal punishments, and are met with informal social disapproval. The most evident examples of acts that are considered crimes and also instances of deviance are murder, rape, child molestation, and other serious offenses.

The second possibility in Table 1–7 is that an act is a crime but is not considered deviance. There is a critical difference between this act and an act that is considered an instance of both crime and deviance, because we find an absence of social disapproval for the act. Clearly, driving 80 miles per hour in a 55-mile-per-hour speed zone is of this type. While not a felony, the act is nonetheless a crime. But, as everyone who has broken speed laws knows, the act is not widely regarded as a case of deviance. The reason, of course, is that the informal social reaction to such an offense is extremely mild, if not total indifference. As another example, some states have laws that make oral sex with one's spouse a criminal offense. But as married people who reside in such states are aware, such sexual activity (even if known by others) is not regarded as deviance. Informal norms simply do not prohibit such behavior. The critical distinction between crimes that are considered deviance and crimes not regarded as deviance lies, then, in the degree of informal social disapproval for the act.

The third possibility, acts which are instances of deviance but not instances of crime, are behaviors that violate only the informal norms of the group. Further, informal social disapproval is the only source of sanction. A number of behaviors may come to mind: bad manners at the dinner table, staring at people, passing gas in a formal setting, bad breath, getting too drunk at a party, cheating, and the like.

THE STUDY OF DEVIANCE AND UNDERSTANDING SOCIETY

In this section, we want to analyze how the study of deviance might explain how society is possible. For example, will the study of deviance also inform us about conformity, a fundamental process in the maintenance of social order? Will the study of deviance help us better understand how power and conflict operate within society? Might the study of deviance lead us to better understand the nature of norms—those shared expectations for, or evaluations of, behavior or being? All of these are critical questions that may be posed as we seek to grasp how the study of deviance might inform us about the structure and functioning of society—how social order is possible.

The Functions of Deviance

One hundred years ago, Emile Durkheim published his now influential book, *The Division of Labor in Society* (Durkheim, 1893). In this and related works, Durkheim emphasized the importance of social solidarity as a fundamental process that holds society together. He was also interested in what happens when social solidarity is weakened. For example, in his now classic work entitled *Suicide,* he studied how solidarity influenced rates of suicide (Durkheim, 1897).

A related interest of Durkheim's, set forth in his *The Rules of Sociological Method* (Durkheim, 1893), was how groups actually "create" deviance to maintain "healthy" levels of solidarity. In this connection, and perhaps somewhat ironically, he persuasively argued that deviance in society can actually increase levels of social solidarity! This occurs, according to Durkheim, in at least two related ways. First, deviance serves to define the boundaries between acceptable and unacceptable behavior. Periodically, the boundary lines between deviance and conformity become blurred to the point where members of society are unclear about what is acceptable behavior and what is not. When this occurs, societies will single out types of behaviors that threaten the social order. In doing so, the deviant behaviors are identified as that which is to be avoided. Accordingly, the difference between deviance and conformity is dramatized to the more conventional members of society.

In addition to clarifying the boundaries that define acceptable and unacceptable behaviors, the presence of deviance in society may increase the conforming members' commitment to conventional norms. This occurs when the deviant is punished for norm-violation. The conforming members of society never feel a greater sense of social solidarity than when they stand united against the common threat of deviance. Punishing the deviant reinforces majority commitment to conventional norms. In this way, deviance is not pathological for society, but a normal part of all social systems. Durkheim's insight has shown how the study of deviance can inform us about an important aspect of social order—social solidarity.

Durkheim's thesis suggests that deviance

is normal and serves certain functions for society. In his argument, deviance serves the function of increasing social solidarity or cohesion. Other, more contemporary, scholars have also explored the various ways in which deviance may be functional (rather than harmful) for society. In each case, the aim is always to trace the implications of deviance for the larger social order. For example, Davis (1971:347) has made the argument that prostitution may actually contribute to marital stability! By directing the sexual energies of men toward "disreputable" women and away from "respectable" women, Davis implies that prostitution serves to maintain the traditional institution of the family.

Also suggesting that deviance may have positive functions for society, Merton (1957) contends that political machines in large urban areas, though often corrupt and tied to organized crime, are better able to meet the social and material needs of the members of the community. For example, while a family in need of assistance would have to go through considerable red tape to receive help from a federal or state agency, a political "boss" merely has to pick up the phone and have the district "captain" take care of the family's needs. Of course, this is done in exchange for votes on election day. Nonetheless, the political machine is far more efficient than governmental agencies and, therefore, serves the function "of humanizing and personalizing all manner of assistance to those in need" (Merton, 1957:128). Such activity on the part of the political machine may also contribute to the cohesion and solidarity of the neighborhood and community even though the social institution of "political bossism" is often corrupt.

Deviance and Social Control

As our preceding discussion has shown, the study of deviance often leads to a greater understanding of the structure and functioning of the larger society. The study of deviance has also widened our knowledge of the process of social control. In an attempt to prevent or contain deviance, societies develop large-scale social arrangements, which sociologists refer to as institutions of social control. The criminal justice system, which includes the police, courts, and jails, is an example of an institution of social control. While not often recognized as such, certain areas of modern medicine such as institutional psychiatry, which includes psychiatrists, drugs, and mental hospitals, is another example of an institution of social control.

All institutions of social control exist to maintain the social order. But as we shall learn in the following chapters, consensus theories differ radically from conflict theories as to how social order is achieved. The consensus perspective views social order as arising from normative consensus. Therefore, students of deviance who subscribe to this perspective will view social control institutions as existing to protect the generally agreed-upon norms held by a majority of the members of society. By contrast, the conflict perspective sees social order as *imposed* by the more powerful members of society. Coercion, not consensus, assures order and stability. Accordingly, scholars of deviance who tend to make this assumption view institutions of social control as existing not to protect the interests of all, but to defend and protect the value and material interests of the powerful.

Contemporary sociologists interested in a conflict approach to deviance are not the first to point to the implications of conflict for the structure and functioning of society (we would have to go back to Marx and Simmel for that). They have, nonetheless, helped to sharpen our understanding of the centrality of power and conflict in relation to the question of social control. For the conflict theorist, deviance is a political phenomenon. This means that deviance is a definition created by the powerful to protect their values and interests in society. Since groups in society are constantly competing for scarce resources, the powerful must control the powerless by defining as deviance or criminal those behaviors that threaten the interests of the powerful. From the perspective of conflict theories, social control agencies, such as the criminal justice system and institutional psychiatry, are viewed as mechanisms of the powerful to control the powerless. The conflict theorist's study of deviance, therefore, has given us an alternative conception of the purpose of social control mechanisms in society.

SUMMARY

We began this chapter by asking the question, "What is deviance?" We quickly learned that the answer to the question depends upon which conception of deviance one adopts.

Two major and competing conceptions of deviance were considered: the objectivist and subjectivist. To highlight their differences, we compared these conceptions in terms of three different aspects of social interaction: behavior or being, norms, and societal reactions. *Norms* are shared expectations and evaluations for behavior. *Societal reactions* involve all the ways in which social audiences (including groups, communities, and entire societies) respond to acts believed to violate social rules or actors believed to have committed rule-violating acts. Often, societal reactions take the form of sanctions. *Sanctions* are punishments designed to control deviance. *Formal sanctions* emanate from those officially authorized to administer punishments. *Informal sanctions* are unofficial sanctions such as peer disapproval.

In comparing the competing conceptions, we sought to determine whether a particular conception considered each aspect of social interaction as either critical or trivial in defining deviance and deviants. *Deviance* refers to acts, whereas *deviants* refers to persons. The objectivist conception defines deviance (acts) as norm-violating behavior. Hence, only behavior and norms are aspects of the objectivist conception. In terms of deviants (persons), the objectivist conception appears to be restricted only to a consideration of conditions of being. How deviance (a person's action) becomes transformed into deviant (a person's social identity) is best understood from the subjectivist conception.

The subjectivist conception views deviance as a definition applied to some acts (real or imagined). In its extreme form, behavior is either less relevant or largely irrelevant in conceptualizing deviance. What is relevant are societal or audience reactions. From the viewpoint of the subjectivist conception, the application of sanctions (which involves labeling and stigmatizing) is a central process in socially creating deviance, and in creating the deviant as a publicly recognized social status.

By distinguishing between macro- and micro-level theories of deviance, we were able to construct a classification scheme within which various contemporary theories of deviance may be placed. *Macro-objectivist theories* attempt to explain differences in rates of norm-violation between various social categories within society. *Micro-objectivist theories* focus on the social factors involved in producing or inhibiting norm-violation at the individual level of analysis. Strain theories are examples of macro-objectivist theories. Social learning theories are examples of micro-objectivist theories. Both are examined in Chapter 2.

Likewise, we may distinguish between macro- and micro-subjectivist theories. *Macro-subjectivist theories* attempt to identify the social, economic, and political forces involved in the construction of deviance definitions. Interest group theories are examples of macro-subjectivist theories. *Micro-subjectivist theories* concentrate on the social-psychological processes by which social audiences formulate deviance definitions and apply them to acts or individuals who are suspected of rule breaking. Labeling theories are examples of micro-subjectivist theories. Both macro- and micro-subjectivist theories are examined in Chapter 3.

In addition to categorizing theories according to how they define deviance (objectivist versus subjectivist) and what level of analysis they employ (macro versus micro), we may categorize theories as to their assumptions regarding the nature of human action. While not always true, objectivist theories assume that human behavior is *determined*. While not always true, subjectivist theories assume that human beings are capable of at least a modicum of *free will*. While this distinction is justified, many theories fall somewhere in between by adopting a "soft-determinism" position.

Additional discussion in this chapter surrounded the differences and similarities between crime and deviance. *Crime is deviance* when the violation of criminal laws also involves the violation of informal social norms. Murder, rape, and armed robbery fit here. *Crime is not deviance* if the violation of criminal laws is not a breach in the social mores. The commission of certain sex acts between spouses may be illegal in some states, but these acts are not considered instances of deviance. In fact, one may be considered deviant if he or she *doesn't* engage in such acts! *Deviance is not crime* if the violation of informal social norms does not violate formal laws.

In the final section of this chapter, we turned to the question of how the study of deviance might increase our understanding of the larger social order. We saw, from the initial insights of Durkheim, that the study of deviance may contribute to our understanding of social solidarity. Moreover, we saw that conflict theories of deviance could lead to a new understanding of institutions of social control. Instead of protecting the values, norms, and interests of everyone, institutions of social control may actually operate to protect only the interests of the more powerful members of society.

GLOSSARY

Conceptions   Abstract definitions of what deviance *is*.

Crime   Acts that violate formal, legal norms (laws). Not all crime is deviance, and not all deviance is crime.

Determinism   An assumption that human behavior, including deviance, is caused by antecedent social and cultural factors.

Deviance   It depends on one's conception. If one adopts an objectivist conception of deviance, *deviance* refers to acts that violate norms. By contrast, if one subscribes to a subjectivist conception, deviance is a label affixed to acts (real or imagined) by a social audience. In either case, *deviance* refers to acts.

Deviants   Persons assigned a deviant status by social audiences (subjectivist) or persons devalued because they violate norms regarding ideal conditions of being (objectivist). In either case, *deviants* refers to persons.

Formal sanctions   Sanctions that emanate from those officially authorized to administer punishments.

Free will   An assumption that human behavior, including deviance, is the result of human choice.

Informal sanctions   Unofficial sanctions, such as peer disapproval.

Macro-objectivist theories   Theories that seek to explain differences in rates of norm-violation between various social categories within society.

Macro-subjectivist theories   Theories that seek to identify the social, economic, and political forces involved in the construction of deviance definitions.

Micro-objectivist theories   Theories that focus

on the social factors involved in producing or inhibiting norm-violation at the individual level of analysis.

Micro-subjectivist theories Theories that focus on how informal social audiences create and apply deviance definitions and how these definitions may affect the self-concepts and behaviors of those defined as deviant.

Norms Shared expectations and evaluations for behavior.

Sanctions Punishments designed to control deviance.

Societal reactions All of the ways in which social audiences (including groups, communities, and entire societies) respond to acts believed to violate social rules or actors believed to have committed rule-violating acts.

Soft-determinism An assumption that, while much of deviance is caused by social and cultural factors, there is always room for human choice. Soft-determinism is a midway position between total determinism and total voluntarism (free will).

Theories Theories of deviance are sets of ideas that seek to explain *why* deviance occurs.

SUGGESTED READINGS

Becker, Howard S. *Outsiders.* New York: Free Press, 1963. In this now classic statement of the subjectivist conception of deviance, Becker underscores the importance of social audiences in the creation of deviance definitions.

Birenbaum, Arnold, and Edward Sagarin. *Norms and Human Behavior.* New York: Praeger, 1976. In this well-written paperback, the authors examine the many issues surrounding the definition of deviance and approach its explanation and control from both objectivist and subjectivist points of view.

Gibbs, Jack P. *Norms, Deviance, and Social Control: Conceptual Matters.* New York: Elsevier, 1981. This is perhaps the most incisive treatment of the problem of defining deviance. Both objec-

tivist and subjectivist (what Gibbs calls "normativist" and "reactivist") conceptions are presented and systematically evaluated. For the student interested in a more advance treatment of the conceptual issues surrounding the study of deviance.

Rubington, Earl, and Martin S. Weinberg. *Deviance: The Interactionist Perspective.* 5th Ed. Macmillan, 1987. In this collection of interesting and readable articles, the authors show the different ways in which subjectivists examine varying types of deviance.

REFERENCES

Akers, Ronald L. "Problems in the Sociology of Deviance: Social Definition and Behavior." *Social Forces* 46 (1968): pp. 461–476.

Becker, Howard W. *Outsiders.* New York: Free Press, 1963.

Cohen, Albert K. *Delinquent Boys: The Culture of the Gang.* Glencoe, Ill. Free Press, 1955.

———. *Deviance and Control.* Englewood Cliffs, N.J.: Prentice-Hall, 1966.

Davis, Kingsley. "Sexual Behavior." *Contemporary Social Problems.* Eds. Robert K. Merton and Robert Nisbet. 3rd ed. New York: Harcourt Brace Jovanovich, 1971.

Dinitz, Simon, Russell Dynes, and Alfred Clarke Eds. *Deviance: Studies in Definition, Management, and Treatment.* 2nd ed. New York: Oxford University Press, 1975.

Durkheim, Emile. *Division of Labor in Society.* Trans. George Simpson. Glencoe, Ill.: Free Press, 1947. Originally published in French in 1893.

———. *The Rules of the Sociological Method.* Trans. J. A. Spaulding and George Simpson. New York: Free Press, 1964. Originally published in 1893.

———. *Suicide.* Trans. J. A. Spaulding and George Simpson. Glencoe, Ill.: Free Press, 1964. Originally published in French in 1897.

Erikson, Kai T. "Notes on the Sociology of Deviance." *Social Problems* 9 (1962): pp. 307–314.

Gibbs, Jack P. *Norms, Deviance, and Social Control: Conceptual Matters.* New York, Elsevier, 1981.

Goffman, Erving. *Stigma.* Englewood Cliffs, N.J.: Prentice-Hall, 1963.

Kaplan, Howard B. *Self-Attitudes and Deviant Be-*

havior. Pacific Palisades, Calif.: Goodyear, 1975.

Kitsuse, John I. "Societal Reaction to Deviant Behavior." *Social Problems* 9 (1962): pp. 247–256.

Liazos, Alexander. "The Poverty of the Sociology of Deviance: Nuts, Sluts, and Preverts." *Social Problems* 20 (1972): pp. 103–120.

Marx, Karl, and Friedrich Engels. *The Communist Manifesto.* Baltimore: Penguin, 1969. Originally published in German in 1848.

Meier, Robert F. "Norms and the Study of Deviance: A Proposed Research Strategy." *Deviant Behavior* 3 (1981): pp. 1–25.

Merton, Robert K. "Social Problems and Sociological Theory" *Contemporary Social Problems.* Eds. Robert K. Merton and Robert Nisbet. 2nd ed. New York: Harcourt Brace and World, 1966: pp. 775–827.

———. *On Theoretical Sociology.* New York: Free Press, 1957: p. 128.

Nettler, Gwynn "On Telling Who's Crazy." *American Sociological Review* 39 (1974): pp. 892–912.

Purdum, Todd S. "Missing Indicted Officer Found Dead in Motel" *New York Times*, Saturday, November 8, 1986: pp. 1, 36.

Simmel, Georg. *The Sociology of Georg Simmel.* Trans. Kurt Wolf. New York: Free Press, 1964. Originally published in 1905.

Rubington, Earl, and Martin S. Weinberg *Deviance: The Interactionist Perspective.* 5th ed. Macmillan, 1987: pp. 3–5.

Tippet, Sarah "I've Got The Family I Always Wanted," *Ladies Home Journal* April (1993): 150, 204.

Hornblower, Margot, "A Murder Among Manhattan's Elite," *Washington Post*, Saturday, August 30, 1986: p. A6.

West, Nathanael. *Miss Lonelyhearts.* New York: New Directions, 1933: p. 2.

Chapter 2

Objectivist Theories of Deviance

"ONE DOCTOR DOWN"

From the viewpoint of abortion-rights activists, the killing of Dr. David Gunn, an abortion clinic physician at Pensacola, Florida, is simply the culmination of many years of harassment, vandalism, and violence against clinics all across the nation (Lacayo, 1993:46)

Upon hearing of Gunn's murder at the hands of antiabortion activist, Michael Griffen, B.J. Isaacson-Jones was shaken—but not surprised. At the clinic located in St. Louis where she is president, members of her staff always drive cautiously during their trips home from work. They often take different routes every evening to avoid establishing a pattern that could make them vulnerable to attack. Clinic mail is opened only by those staff members with special training by bomb and arson experts to detect suspicious envelopes or packages (Lacayo, 1993:46).

Clinic workers are not the only targets of antiabortion activists; their children are targets as well. Lisa Merritt, a counselor at an abortion clinic in Melbourne, Florida, tells how her 13-year-old son, Justin, was lured by two antiabortion proponents into a trip to Burger King after they had deceived him into believing they were going to be his new neighbors. Once at the Burger King, Justin was asked if he was aware that "both he and his mother were going to burn in hell." As the two antiabortion activist tried to get Justin to provide names of patients at his mother's clinic, Justin got wise. He bolted from his seat, and ran home (Lacayo, 1993:47).

The antagonism that exists between antiabortion and pro-choice activists is expected to produce even further acts of violence—even more killings. This chapter seeks to understand why people break rules. As we shall see, sociologists have developed a number of theories that sensitize us to the fact that norm-violation is often an outgrowth of involvement in groups whose beliefs and values stand in opposition to formal laws as well as informal norms.

MACRO-OBJECTIVIST THEORIES

Macro-objectivist theories focus on large-scale social arrangements in seeking explanation for behavior. These theories attempt to explain differences in rates of norm-violation between broad social categories in society. The focus is not on individuals but on categories of individuals who share similar social circumstances. It is differences in social circumstances that are hypothesized to account for differences in rates of norm-violating behavior.

Strain Theories

Strain theories of deviance attempt to explain differing rates of norm-violation by pointing to inconsistencies in the social structure, culture or, both. These theories propose that various aspects of the social and cultural structure can get out of kilter, thereby creating stresses and strains on certain groups in society. This strain serves to motivate group members to violate the norms of society. Hence, the motivation for deviance is located in society rather than in individual psychology. All strain theories appear to assume that members of society would prefer to conform. Individuals are pushed toward norm-violating behavior only because of undue strain stemming from their circumstance in society.

Anomie Theory. In the mid-nineteenth century, Emile Durkheim (1964) conducted his now classic study of suicide. He took an extreme sociological approach. One of his conclusions was that some types of suicide were related to the degree of social integration of groups. For example, he accounted for differences in suicide rates between Catholics and Protestants by examining differences in the social integration of the respective religions. Durkheim also theorized about other types of suicide. Each type was related to different social conditions in society. For example, he called one type "anomic" suicide. *Anomie* is a state of normlessness. According to Durkheim, it is brought about by a sudden breakdown in the norms that regulate human behavior. A sudden breakdown in norms often accompanies abrupt social changes like a stock market crash. When a state of anomie, or normlessness, occurs, individual aspirations and appetites spin out of control. This condition, Durkheim argued, influenced an increase in the rate of anomic suicide.

Modern sociologists have used Durkheim's ideas about anomie and suicide to explain other forms of deviant behavior. Robert K. Merton (1938) is generally regarded as the chief spokesperson for the anomie approach among contemporary deviance theorists. He has extended Durkheim's ideas about anomie to explain differences in rates of crime and deviance between various social categories in U.S. society.

Merton begins with the observation that Americans have been socialized to value the accumulation of wealth. Success, ambition, and making it materially are valued goals in our culture. Merton refers to these values as *culturally defined success goals.* Along with these success goals, the culture also defines the acceptable and legitimate ways of achieving them. One who works hard and makes sacrifices can eventually reach the American Dream of material success. Merton refers to these culturally approved ways of achieving success goals as *institutionalized means.* They are the respectable, non-deviant, ways of reaching the valued ends of U.S. society. The problem is that these two aspects of the culture are not always in balance. Americans tend to overemphasize winning and success but underemphasize *how* they win or succeed. Honoring the ultimate goals without equal respect for the institutionalized means results in an inconsistency in our culture.

According to Merton, different social segments of our society respond to this inconsistency between goals and means in different ways. A key variable in predicting these different responses (or what Merton calls "modes of adaptation") is social class position. Not all social classes have equal opportunities for achieving success goals. Because of discrimination, members of the lower classes and certain racial and ethnic minorities suffer "opportunity blockage." They are denied equal access to the culturally approved means for achieving success goals. The strain that results from blocked opportunities causes individuals to question the legitimacy of the traditional, institutionalized means. They begin to think of other, often illegal, ways to succeed. When this occurs, respect for the traditionally accepted means of achieving goals begins to crumble. Norms become weakened to the point at which they no longer regulate the methods people use to obtain success. A state of normlessness, or anomie, may be the result. Hence, Merton has attributed the high crime rates among the lower classes to this breakdown in the culturally approved avenues for achieving success in American society.

Table 2–1 shows the principal ways that individuals respond to the relationship between cultural goals and legitimate means. Anomie leads to what Merton calls the "innovator" mode of adaptation. The table shows that innovators continue to accept the goal of material success but reject the conventional means. Included in the innovator category are the thief, pimp, prostitute, organized drug dealer and others who are seeking success goals through illegal, innovative, means. According to Merton, innovators tend to be located in the lower classes, because members of the lower classes are more likely to experience blocked opportunities.

The innovator is the most relevant type of adaptation when considering criminal deviance. Table 2–2 depicts the factors involved in leading to criminal deviance, or innovation.

While the innovator is the most relevant type of adaptation when considering criminal deviance, the other modes of adaptation also deserve our attention because they are often useful for understanding certain forms of noncriminal deviance. *Ritualism* is typified by a rigid adherence to rules prescribing the proper way of doing things. All of the emphasis is on the means, not the ends. *Overconfor-*

TABLE 2.1 Merton's Types of Modes of Adaptation.

MODES OF ADAPTATION		CULTURAL GOALS ARE:	INSTITUTIONAL MEANS ARE:
I.	Conformist	accepted	accepted
II.	Innovator	accepted	rejected
III.	Ritualism	ignored	accepted
IV.	Retreatism	rejected	rejected
V.	Rebellion	rejected & replaced	rejected & replaced

Adapted from Merton, 1938.

TABLE 2.2 Basic Ideas in Merton's Strain Theory.

Blocked opportunities → Strain → Weakening of → Anomie → Innovation
commitment to
norms regulating
means of goal-attainment

mity is the term often used to describe the ritualist. *Retreatism* is a mode of response in which individuals abandon both cultural goals and the institutionalized means for attaining them. They are "in the society, but not of it." Typical of this type of adaptation is the alcoholic, the drug addict, and some who are considered mentally ill. *Rebellion* is the mode of adaptation involving the rejection of both goals and means and an attempt to replace them with new goals and means. This type of adaptation is characteristic of social and political revolutionaries.

Illegitimate Opportunity Theory. In Merton's version of strain theory, motivation for criminal deviance comes from denied access to legitimate means. Cloward and Ohlin's (1960) theory extends Merton's initial insight by making access to *illegitimate* means problematic as well. Merton assumed that strained individuals would have ready access to deviant opportunities. But opportunities for deviance involve, among other things, the availability of role models from whom devi-

ant attitudes and skills may be learned *and* the opportunity to perform the deviant role once learning has taken place. Even if one is strained in the sense that Merton speaks, and has learned how to perform the deviant role, there may still be "unemployment" in the illegitimate opportunity structure—one may never get the chance to become involved in a deviant career.

Given opportunity blockage to legitimate means, it is the varying access to deviant subcultures that, for Cloward and Ohlin, determines whether strained individuals will pursue deviance and, if so, what kind of deviance will be pursued. In lower-class neighborhoods there are, according to Cloward and Ohlin, three kinds of deviant subcultures. One neighborhood may be dominated by one type of deviant subculture, while a different neighborhood may be dominated by another subculture. The *criminal* subculture provides the illegitimate opportunities that Merton assumed were readily available to all who are denied access to the legitimate opportunity structure. Being integrated into this subculture permits lower-class youth opportunities to achieve material success through theft, robbery, drug dealing, and the like. If one is not adequately integrated into the criminal subculture, however, the probability of achieving material success through criminal activity is reduced significantly.

In other neighborhoods, the *conflict* subculture may be more dominant. In these subcultures, youth are preoccupied with being bad, building a rep, and protecting their turf. Their status is dependent upon being a good street fighter, being fearless in gang wars, and being willing to take risks for the welfare of the gang. If some youth are unable to meet the physical requirements of doing battle in the streets, they will not become bona fide members of the gang.

According to Cloward and Ohlin, the *retreatist* subculture provides the final opportunity structure in the illegitimate world. We may recall that Merton conceptualized retreatists as those who neither accepted cultural goals nor the institutional means for achieving them. Believing in neither, they simply drop out. They are "in society, but not of it." Cloward and Ohlin suggest that retreatists are really "double failures." That is, many retreatists probably started out in a criminal subculture but, for various reasons, were not successful in their criminal careers. Having failed in both the legitimate and illegitimate opportunity structures, the retreatist turns to drugs and escapism.

The essential ideas of Cloward and Ohlin's illegitimate opportunity theory are depicted in Table 2–3. Cloward and Ohlin's theory may be considered an important extension of Merton's original thesis. They agree with Merton that lower-class youth experience strain due to an inconsistency between aspirations and legitimate opportunities. But whether that strain will result in criminal deviance (or in some other form of deviance), depends on the opportunity structure in the *illegitimate* world. Cloward and Ohlin are suggesting, then, that a more comprehensive theory of deviance must take account of both legitimate and illegitimate opportunities.

Status-Frustration Theory. In Merton's version of strain theory, the innovator is one who wants the goal of material success but is denied the opportunity to achieve it through socially approved means. Denied access to legitimate means, the innovator turns to delinquent activities *in pursuit of material success*. Deviant behavior, then, may be considered *utilitarian* in the sense that it is useful in obtaining the desired goal.

Albert Cohen (1955) developed his version of strain theory to account for the development of delinquent subcultures. Also, he saw a major weakness in Merton's theory: the assumption that deviant behavior was always in pursuit of societies most cherished goal—money! If this were true, Cohen speculated, then why is so much delinquent behavior literally useless as far as acquiring material wealth? For example, many delinquencies involve vandalism of schools and other buildings, stealing hubcaps from parked cars only to throw them away, and other kinds of deviance done just for kicks.

To provide an explanation of the development of delinquent subcultures and to address these nonutilitarian forms of deviance, Cohen centered his analysis on status striving within the context of the school. According

---

TABLE 2.3 Cloward and Ohlin's Illegitimate Opportunity Theory.

Strain	→	Differential illegitimate opportunities	→	Type of deviance

to Cohen, lower-class youth find that the way to achieve status in school is to meet the standards set up by their teacher's middle-class measuring rod. Such values and dispositions as verbal fluency, courtesy, respect for property, diligence and the ability to delay immediate gratification for the pursuit of long-term goals are among the personal characteristics most rewarded within the middle-class school environment. If these are the attitudinal and behavioral characteristics that lead to the achievement of status in the middle-class school system, then clearly lower-class youth will find it difficult to compete. Their family backgrounds and socialization experiences have not conditioned them to value these characteristics. Instead of achieving status, lower-class youth experience humiliation and status-frustration. As Cohen puts it:

> [D]ifferent patterns of socialization are associated with the different social classes and middle-class socialization is far more effective in training children for such success than is lower-class socialization. For this and other reasons, lower-class children are more likely to experience failure and humiliation. In brief, they are caught up in a game in which others are typically the winners and they are the losers . . . (Cohen, 1966:65).

Recognizing that many of their lower-class peers are experiencing a similar condition of status-frustration, youth from the lower classes often join together to solve this problem of adjustment. The solution is a subculture with its own competitive activities and criteria for status. As it turns out, the very things that are valued by the middle-class school system are now despised, and the things condemned by the middle class are extolled. Cohen states it this way:

> The delinquent subculture, we suggest, is a way of dealing with the problem of adjustment we have described. These problems are chiefly status problems: certain children are denied status in the respectable society because they cannot meet the criteria of the respectable status system. The delinquent subculture deals with these problems by providing criteria of status which children can meet (Cohen, 1955:121).

Setting up their own rules and criteria for status allows delinquents to achieve respectability within their own subculture. But making up one's own rules is not quite that easy. After all, the value system of the dominant middle class is, to some extent, the delinquent's value system as well.

> They have, to a certain extent, internalized its rules also. They can tell themselves that they don't really care about what people think of them . . ., but their internalized values, even if repressed, threaten always to break through and dilute their satisfaction with the alternative they have chosen (Cohen, 1966:66).

Therefore, to reinforce their choice to stick to rules they have created (rules that are in opposition to the rules of the middle class), and to make sure that their own internalized commitment to the middle-class measuring rod does not resurface, they resort to *reaction-formation*.

> They not only reject the dominant value system, but do so with a vengeance. They "stand it on its head"; they exalt its opposition; they engage in malicious, spiteful, "ornery" behavior of all sorts to demonstrate not only to others, but to themselves as well, their contempt for the game they have rejected . . . (Cohen, 1966:66).

The central ideas of Cohen's status-frustration theory are shown in Table 2–4. While Cohen's theory is similar to Merton's, in that both suggest that strain pushes individuals toward deviance, it should be noted that the causal influence is different for the two theories. For Merton, the disjuncture between aspirations and opportunities (strain) causes deviance through weakening an individual's commitment to culturally approved means. For Cohen, strain influences deviance (or deviant subcultures) by creating status-frustration, along with the idea that youth can achieve status in their own subculture by openly rejecting the values of the middle class. This theorizing permits Cohen to meaningfully address the development of deviant subcultures and nonutilitarian forms of deviance.

Evaluating Strain Theories.   Merton's anomie theory has had a powerful influence on modern deviance theory. The notion that blocked opportunities can strain the cultural norms that regulate approved means to goal attainment points to a major source of anomie. Even so, the theory has been widely criticized for concentrating only on lower-class deviance, a criticism applicable to the theories of Cloward and Ohlin and Cohen as well. White-collar offenses such as tax evasion and embezzlement are difficult to understand from the perspective of these strain theories.

Another criticism is that strain theories are motivational theories of deviance. The basic picture being presented is that people are socialized to conform. It is only because of opportunity blockage or, in the case of Cohen's theory, status-frustration that individuals are seemingly *compelled* toward a deviant way of life. If most people are basically good, the question to be answered by strain theories is, "Why did they do it?" As convincing as strain explanations appear, the motivational aspect of the theories leads to embarrassment when the phenomenon of maturational reform is considered. *Maturational reform* refers to the fact that most juvenile delinquents abandon their deviant behaviors for a more conventional life-style as they mature. This often happens when they reach a certain age, get a job, get married, and have a family. It appears that strain theories build so much strain into

people to explain "why they do it" that it is difficult to understand how they can ever "not do it"!

Additional criticism of strain theories comes from research studies that question whether norm-violation is, as strain theories suggest, a predominantly lower-class phenomenon. In the early years, strain theorists relied almost exclusively on official statistics to test their theories. From studies based on official records, a fairly consistent finding emerged; members of the lower classes and ethnic minorities showed higher *arrest* rates for criminal activity. But beginning in the late 1950s, researchers began to study deviance with the use of self-report questionnaires. This permitted sociologists to study hidden, or undetected, deviance. Among most of these studies, when self-reported deviant acts were correlated with the respondent's social class (for juveniles, the social class of their parents), little to no differences were found between class position and the incidence of undetected deviance (Nye and Short, 1957; Nye et al., 1958; Dentler and Monroe, 1961; Tittle et al., 1978).

In spite of the negative evidence noted above, the issue of whether deviance is predominantly a lower-class phenomenon has resurfaced in recent years (Braithwaite, 1981; Elliott and Ageton, 1980). It appears that one conclusion may be drawn from the more recent evidence: Whether and how social class is related to crime depends upon the type of crime considered. (See Tittle and Meier, 1990, for an alternative interpretation.) It appears that more violent personal and property crimes are disproportionately located in the lower-classes, whereas white-collar offenses such as embezzlement, corporate fraud, and

---

TABLE 2.4   Cohen's Status-Frustration Theory.

Status frustration	→	Deviant subculture	→	Reaction-Formation	→	Nonutilitarian deviance

the like, are upper-class crimes. Therefore, more recent evidence is at least consistent with the assertion that "predatory" crimes are crimes of the lower classes. If this is accepted, then strain theories are not as inconsistent with available evidence as early studies appeared to suggest.

Neo-Marxist Theories

The objectivist theories we have examined thus far tend to assume that society is characterized by normative consensus. Norms are assumed to be widely shared because they reflect the general interests of most members of society. By contrast, neo-Marxist theory provides an explanation of the assumed disproportionate amount of predatory crime in the lower classes, but rejects the assumption of normative consensus. Influenced by the writings of Karl Marx, this body of theory assumes that norms are not shared by but *imposed* on members of society by the state in an effort to protect the material (property) interests of the capitalist class.

Neo-Marxists reject the exclusive attention paid to deviance (acts) by the more traditional objectivists, such as strain theorists. They also reject the subjectivists' exclusive focus on the process whereby deviance definitions are created and applied to acts or actors by social audiences. Instead, neo-Marxists propose theories of both acts and labels. As Quinney suggests:

> The basic problem in any study of the meaning of crime is that of integrating the two sides of the crime phenomenon: placing into a single framework (1) the defining of behavior as criminal . . . and (2) the behavior of those who are defined as criminal. Thus far, the analysis of crime has focused on one side or the other, failing to integrate the two interrelated processes into one scheme (Quinney, 1977:33).

While neo-Marxist theories focus on both deviance (acts) and deviance definitions (labels), we will confine our present examina-

tion to the way in which neo-Marxist theories explain deviance (acts). In Chapter 3, we will examine the contribution this body of deviance theory has made to our understanding of how deviance definitions are created.

The New Criminology.   With the publication of *The New Criminology,* Ian Taylor, Paul Walton, and Jock Young (1973) caused many deviance theorists to reassess their ideas and move toward a conflict theory of deviance based on Marxist thought. The three British sociologists propose a theory of criminal definitions and behavior rooted in Marxist theory about class conflict in capitalist society. Their thesis is that crime cannot be fully understood unless it is viewed in a broader context—within the political economy of a society during a particular period of that society's historical development. In spite of its wide influence, *The New Criminology* does not contain the fundamental elements of a social theory of deviance. Its major contribution has been to provide the most comprehensive critique of the objectivist and subjectivist theories of crime and deviance to date. Despite this important contribution, more systematic theoretical statements of a political economy of crime have been left to others.

A Marxian Theory of Deviance.   Steven Spitzer (1975) has sketched a theory of deviance in which he contends that capitalism contains inherent contradictions that produce deviance as objective behaviors. For example, to increase profit, the industrialists must constantly seek to cut production costs by finding cheap labor. This may be done either by increasing automation, which makes human wage-earners unnecessary, or by seeking low-cost labor in foreign markets. In either case, the result is either unemployment or underemployment among a significant proportion of the labor force. Marxists refer to this part of the labor force as the *relative surplus population.* These workers, who were once needed to build the capital base of the economic system, have become expendable and, moreover, tend to drain the economic resources of society. Removed from the process of production and its material rewards, these populations threaten the social relations of economic production in capitalist societies. For example, members of the surplus population may steal from the working poor or the rich. They may refuse to work for reduced and otherwise meager wages. Moreover, from the surplus population, revolutionary groups may emerge who question the very political ideology that serves to justify the contradictions inherent in the political economy of advanced capitalism.

A second source of problem populations may be found in the contradictions that emerge from the very institutions created by the ruling class to maintain domination. Paradoxically, the consequences of these institutional arrangements are not always consistent with ruling-class interests. For example, Spitzer notes that compulsory education in the United States is a means to prepare youth for capitalist occupational roles, to transmit bourgeois values to the working classes, and to temporarily withhold large segments of the population from the labor market at any given time. However, a contradictory outcome of formal education is that students are more sensitive to the injustice and oppression suffered by the have-nots of society. Thus, education may instill in a significant segment of the population the critical capacity to question the legitimacy of the capitalist system.

Spitzer divides problem populations into two categories: social junk and social dynamite. *Social junk* refers to the passive, withdrawn and deranged sectors of problem populations. These sectors are relatively harmless, but they nevertheless threaten the social relations of production by their refusal or failure to participate in the capitalist economic system. Included here are the mentally ill, the homeless, the skid-row alcoholic, and others. *Social dynamite* refers to active groups who engage in a variety of legal and illegal attacks on capitalist relations of production. These groups include underground groups and even more visible extremist groups that seek revolutionary change in the present social, economic, and political organization of society. Social dynamite are subject to harsh legal social control.

Class, State, and Crime. In his book, *Class, State and Crime*, Richard Quinney (1977) echoes and extends Spitzer's theorizing. Quinney's central thesis is that criminal behavior and crime control (including deviance definitions and their application) stem from inherent contradictions within the capitalist mode of production. These contradictions produce a relative surplus population whose members adopt crime as a means of economic survival. Moreover, according to Quinney, crime can be a conscious force of resistance and a progressive force in the transition from capitalism to a crime-free socialist society. An example is the radical environmental movement whose members spike trees with steel bolts to prevent deforestation by the profit-oriented timber industry. The idea that crime may be a progressive force in the ultimate demise of capitalism is an extremely controversial aspect of Quinney's version of neo-Marxist theory.

Quinney conceptualizes the state (including, but not synonymous with, "the government") as a "coordinating agency" charged with the task of administering capitalist society. In the administration of capitalist society, the state is involved in facilitating capital accumulation. *Capital accumulation* involves protecting existing wealth and creating opportunities for increased wealth among the capitalist class. The state is also involved in legitimation. *Legitimation* refers to the justification of the capitalist system to the masses of oppressed workers and to the chronically unemployed surplus labor population. The legitimation function of the state often involves handouts and subsidies to the surplus population, whose numbers and misery are increasing due to capitalist accumulation. The state, as the ultimate protector of the capitalist system, must appease the powerless and attempt to convince them that economic inequality is somehow just. A complete ideology of legitimation develops. Quinney suggests that Wolfe has adequately captured this aspect of the legitimizing function of the state:

> The most important reproductive mechanism which does not involve the use of state violence is consciousness-manipulation. The Liberal state has an enormous amount of violence at its disposal, but it is often reluctant to use it. Violence may breed counter-violence, leading to instability. It may be far better to manipulate consciousness to such an extent that most people would never think of engaging in the kinds of action which could be repressed. The most perfectly repressive (though not violently so) capitalist system, in other words, would not be a police state, but the complete opposite, one in which there were no police because there was nothing to police, everyone having accepted the legitimacy of the society and all its daily consequences (Wolfe, 1971:20).

In meeting the contradictory demands of accumulation and legitimation, the state has evolved into an autonomous entity. That is, the state is not simply an instrument of the capitalist class. Quinney theorizes that the demands for accumulation by the capitalist class will cause a fiscal crisis for the state. And the state's inability to provide for the surplus population will cause a "crisis of legitimation." Given these crises, the state must become more repressive toward the working class in its regulation of the inherent class struggle between the bourgeoisie and the proletariat. Such repression begets revolt, and the state becomes the target of revolution as the class struggle has been "transposed into a political struggle" (Quinney, 1977:83). Here,

Quinney has dealt with the question critics have asked of neo-Marxists: "Where's the revolution?" According to Quinney, the classic proletarian revolutionary overthrow of the bourgeoisie predicted by Marx has been transformed into a political struggle against the state.

Quinney's conception of criminality (acts) entails crimes of both the rich and the poor, the capitalist class and the working class. There are two major types of working-class crime. *Crimes of accommodation* include predatory crimes, such as property crimes, crimes of theft, and drug dealing. Also included in the category of crimes of accommodation are personal crimes, such as murder, rape, and armed robbery. *Crimes of resistance* are the second major type of working-class crime and include sabotage or other activities directed against the work place (Quinney, 1977:59). All are crimes committed by the surplus labor population. They derive from alienation and oppression inherent in the capitalist system.

Criminality (objectively conceived) does not only exist among the working class. *Crimes of domination* are crimes committed by the capitalist class and the state in their attempt to secure the fate of the capitalist system. Crimes of domination are of two types. First, there are *crimes of economic domination*, such as various types of corporate crime. The widely publicized Savings and Loan scandals of the 1980s, in which loan officials of local S&L's would lend depositors' savings to borrowers with questionable credit in exchange for a piece of the action, are a forceful example of crimes of economic domination. Second, there are *crimes of government.* Examples include the taking of kickbacks among political officials and crimes of control such as the recent beating of Rodney King by members of the Los Angeles Police Department in the name of "law and order."

Evaluating Neo-Marxist Theories. Neo-Marxist theories of deviance have stimulated a good deal of criticism. For example, since Marx did not develop a systematic theory of deviance, the question may be asked, "Is a Marxian theory of deviance possible?" Paul Hirst has claimed that "there is no Marxist theory of deviance, either in existence, or which can be developed within orthodox Marxism" (1972:54). In fact, no sociologist of deviance has been so bold as to claim that he or she has developed a theory of deviance within orthodox Marxism. Even so, the works of Marxist criminologists draw heavily from the works of neo-Marxists. Whether neo-Marxists, from which deviance theorists draw, have accurately interpreted and applied the writings of Marx to a theory of society remains debatable.

A second criticism suggests that neo-Marxist theory oversimplifies the connection between criminal behavior and capitalism. If capitalism is the "mother of crime," why do the crime and delinquency problems vary so much from one capitalist system to another? Moreover, if capitalism is the cause of crime, why did crime and delinquency exist in the former Soviet Union (Voigt and Thornton, 1985)? In this connection, David Schichor notes that neo-Marxists are guilty of an "overpoliticization" of delinquency and crime "without paying enough attention to the criminogenic attributes of socialist social systems" (1983:93).

MICRO-OBJECTIVIST THEORIES

Unlike macro-objectivist theories, which concentrate on rates of norm-violating behavior, micro-objectivist theories focus on social processes that account for the acquisition

and maintenance of deviant behavior at the individual level. Though their final unit of analysis is the individual, micro-objectivist theories are not psychological theories. Always, the central question is, "How is individual deviance influenced by sociological forces that lie outside of the person?" The influence of the group or society remains the critical explanatory variable.

Control Theories

Pure control theories view deviance as resulting from a failure of social controls. Whereas strain theories attempt to explain why people engage in deviance, control theories focus on why people don't engage in deviance. According to control theory, the answer lies in the strength of the social ties that bind individuals to conforming society.

Our discussion of Merton's strain theory showed that commitments to legitimate means are weakened because of strain stemming from an imbalance between aspirations and expectations. In Merton's theory, strain is needed as an explanatory concept because he assumes that almost everyone wants to conform. Control theories, on the other hand, begin with a different image of the human actor. Their view is that almost everyone would choose deviant means to success because deviant means are often a lot easier than conforming means (Nye, 1958). Since control theorists do not assume that most people want to conform, they do not have to use such ideas as strain to explain why people deviate. They believe everyone would "if they dared!" (Hirschi, 1969). Therefore, pure control theories do not contain motivational

TABLE 2.5 Social Control Theory.

All have potential for deviance	→	Weakening of social controls	→	Individual released to engage in deviance

concepts. They are simply not needed since deviance is assumed. It is conformity that must be explained.

Table 2–5 shows the basic ideas of control theory. As we have said, all are assumed to have the potential for deviance. Given this potential, if there is a weakening of the social controls that prevent deviance, then norm-violation is more likely. Notice that the table characterizes individuals as being *released* to engage in deviance. Unlike strain theories, which see individuals as compelled to commit deviance due to excessive strain, control theory focuses on the social bond that *prevents* deviance. If the social bond breaks, individuals are freed to engage in deviant conduct.

Social Bonding Theory. Travis Hirschi (1969) has been one of the chief proponents of control theory in modern sociology. Hirschi refers to the social controls that tie individuals to conforming society as the *social bond.* He has identified four elements of the bond. First, *commitment* reflects an individual's "stake in conformity." According to Hirschi and other control theorists, before individuals decide to engage in deviance, they calculate what they have to lose were they to be caught. If their stake in conforming society is high (for example, good job, nice home, proud family, and good social standing in the community), the chance of committing deviance is low. On the other hand, if one has little or nothing to lose by engaging in deviance—because of low stakes in conformity—then deviance becomes more likely.

The second element of the bond is attachment. Whereas commitment refers to the way people rationally calculate the costs and rewards of their deviance, *attachment* refers to the emotional ties individuals have with conforming others. "I would just die if Mom found out." This is a statement that sounds familiar to anyone who has been privy to conversations of adolescents. The statement reflects the desire not to disappoint one's par-

ents. When young people are attached to their parents in this way, the likelihood of deviance is decreased. On the other hand, if one does not have a strong affectionate relationship with one's parents (and therefore is not so concerned about letting them down), this element of the bond is weak and deviance is more likely. Youth may be more or less attached to parents, school teachers, and religious leaders, who are important embodiments of conventional norms. The greater the attachment to these conventional others, the less the likelihood of deviance.

The third element is *involvement*, which refers to the amount of time individuals spend on conventional activities. If one is totally involved in conforming activities (for example, school, sports, church, part-time job), then there simply isn't enough time to get involved in deviance. The limitations of time itself prevent deviance from becoming part of one's role behaviors.

The final element is *belief*, which refers to how much a person believes in the moral validity of laws. Some people believe that laws exist because they are right. They represent deep moral values that should not be compromised. Others feel that laws are merely obstacles to pleasure and a quick buck! Control theorists claim that when individuals believe in the morality of laws, they are less likely to violate them. Those who do not feel this moral conviction are less restrained and, hence, have a greater chance of engaging in deviant behavior.

The most positive aspect of social bonding theory is its simplicity. It assumes that everyone is equally motivated to commit deviance. Given this potential, deviance is the result of a failure of social controls. Recall that strain theory began with a different image of the human actor. From the strain perspective, everyone would prefer to conform. Thus, strain theorists must explain why people go wrong. Their answer is strain. We saw the problem this created when strain theorists try to explain how it is possible for individuals to abandon delinquent ways for a life of conformity. This phenomenon (called maturational reform) is not as much a problem for social bonding theory. When individuals are young, their stakes in conformity are low. Hence, these weak ties release them to engage in deviance. But when they get a little older, get a job, marry, and have a family, their stakes grow stronger. Strong ties prevent deviance. From a control perspective, maturational reform is explained by weak ties then individuals are juveniles and strong ties when they are adults.

Neutralization Theory. In our discussion of strain theories, we found that both Cohen's status-frustration theory and Cloward and Ohlin's illegitimate opportunity theory were designed to explain how juveniles become involved in delinquent subcultures. The concept of a delinquent subculture suggests that some youth live out their daily lives in a social environment made up of values and norms that are in opposition to those held by the larger, conventional society (Kornhauser, 1978). It is as if a member of a delinquent subculture does not believe in conventional values and norms at all. Socialization into the "oppositional subculture" almost guarantees it.

Gresham Sykes and David Matza (1957) have criticized subcultural theories on a number of grounds and have argued that a control theory of delinquency better depicts what actually takes place in the life of the delinquent. Of the many criticisms leveled at subcultural theories, Sykes and Matza pay special attention to the following. First, they note that many delinquents, upon being caught for a deviant act, actually express guilt and remorse over having engaged in deviance. As Sykes and Matza observe, "if there existed in fact a delinquent sub-culture such that the delinquent viewed his illegal behavior as morally correct, we could reasonably sup-

pose that he would exhibit no feelings of guilt or shame at detection or confinement" (1957:665). Secondly, Sykes and Matza note that delinquents often draw a clear line between persons who can be victimized and those who cannot. The fact that the victims of delinquents are not merely chosen at random suggests that delinquents have a sense of the wrongfulness of their behavior. "When the pool of victims is limited by considerations of Kinship, friendship, Ethnic group, social class, age, sex, etc., we have reason to suspect that the virtue of delinquency is far from unquestioned" (Sykes and Matza, 1957:665). Again, the assumption held by subcultural theorists that delinquents are oblivious to conventional values and norms appears questionable.

Given the above criticisms of subcultural theories, Sykes and Matza suggest that most delinquents really do embrace the values and norms of the more conventional society. Therefore, the question to be answered is, "Why do people violate norms in which they believe?" Sykes and Matza propose their brand of control theory to answer this question. The basic idea is that individuals must somehow neutralize the bond to conventional society before they are released to engage in deviant conduct. Bonds prevent deviance. Neutralization of bonds makes deviance possible. Sykes and Matza contend that the essence of the neutralization process is that individuals verbally justify or excuse their deviance *before* they do it.

The basis upon which juveniles and adults can excuse and justify deviant actions may be found in the flexibility of social norms themselves. As Sykes and Matza note:

> [S]ocial rules or norms calling for valued behavior seldom if ever take the form of categorical imperatives. Rather, values or norms appear as qualified guides for action, limited in their applicability in terms of time, place, persons, and social circumstances. The moral injunction against killing, for example, does not apply to the enemy during combat

in time of war, although a captured enemy comes once again under the prohibition. Similarly, the taking and distributing of scarce goods in a time of acute social need is felt by many to be right, although under other circumstances private property is held inviolable. The normative system of a society, then, is marked by . . . flexibility; it does not consist of a body of rules held to be binding under all conditions (1957:666).

Indeed, because norms are flexible, many who commit criminal acts are able to avoid legal sanctions by invoking certain mitigating circumstances that legally excuse their actions. By invoking pleas such as insanity, drunkenness, self-defense, and the like, "[t]he individual can avoid moral culpability for his criminal action—and thus avoid the negative sanctions of society—if he can prove that criminal intent was lacking" (Sykes and Matza, 1957:666).

In similar fashion, the juvenile delinquent may neutralize the normative constraints of conventional society by invoking rationalizations and justifications for deviance *prior to the commission of the deviant act*. These justifications for deviance are learned in association with other delinquents. They are part of the common folklore of juvenile offenders. Thus, for Sykes and Matza, justifications that neutralize bonds to conventional society lead to deviance, not, as subcultural theorists clearly imply, "moral imperatives, values or attitudes standing in direct contradiction to those of the dominant society" (Sykes and Matza, 1957:667).

There are a number of ways that individuals can go about verbally excusing their deviance. Sykes and Matza propose five different kinds of excuse making, or what they call *techniques of neutralization*. The first technique of neutralization is *denial of responsibility*. "Insofar as the delinquent can define himself as lacking responsibility for his deviant actions, the disapproval of self or others is sharply reduced in effectiveness as a restraining influence" (Sykes and Matza, 1957:667). It is

not uncommon, in this regard, for the delinquent to blame his or her broken home, deviant companions or slum neighborhood for deviant actions. Somewhat interestingly, the delinquent is a good social scientist! Prior to the commission of a deviant act, the delinquent can invoke a virtual catalog of sociological and psychological explanations (excuses) for his or her delinquency.

The second technique of neutralization is *denial of injury*. The delinquent can justify and or rationalize his or her conduct by claiming "nobody got hurt." For example, "[v]andalism . . . may be defined by the delinquent simply as 'mischief'—after all, it may be claimed, the persons whose property has been destroyed can well afford it" (Sykes and Matza, 1957:667). *Denial of the victim* is a third technique of neutralization. Using this technique, the deviant is able to neutralize conventional norms by rationalizing that the victim of the deviant act somehow deserved it. "The injury, it may be claimed, is not really an injury; rather, it is a form of rightful retaliation or punishment. By a subtle alchemy the delinquent moves himself into the position of an avenger and the victim is transformed into a wrong-doer" (Sykes and Matza, 1957:668).

A fourth technique of neutralization is *condemnation of the condemners*. "The delinquent shifts the focus of attention from his own deviant acts to the motives and behavior of those who disapprove of his violations. His condemners, he may claim, are hypocrites, deviants in disguise, or impelled by personal spite" (Sykes and Matza, 1957:668). Finally, there is the technique of neutralization, which Sykes and Matza call an *appeal to higher loyalties*. "[I]nternal and external social controls may be neutralized by sacrificing the demands of the larger society for the demands of the smaller social groups to which the delinquent belongs such as the Sibling pair, the gang, or the friendship clique" (Sykes and Matza, 1957:668). For example, juveniles may become involved in drugs, not so much because they reject the values and norms of their parents, but because other norms held by their peers regarding drug use are believed to be more pressing or [to] involv[e] a higher loyalty.

In summarizing the way in which the various techniques of neutralization may serve to deflect the controlling power of conventional norms, Sykes and Matza observe:

> *"I didn't mean it." "I didn't really hurt anybody." "They had it coming to them." "Everybody's picking on me." "I didn't do it for myself." These slogans or their variants, we hypothesize, prepare the juvenile for delinquent acts. These "definitions of the situation" represent tangential or glancing blows at the dominant normative system rather than the creation of an ideology; and they are extensions of patterns of thought prevalent in society rather than something created* de novo *(Sykes and Matza, 1957:668).*

From the preceding discussion, we may depict Sykes and Matza's theory as shown in Table 2–6. Consistent with control theories, it is bonds to conventional society that prevent deviance. Techniques of neutralization weaken conventional ties. When bonds are weakened, deviance is made possible.

Deterrence Theory. As we saw earlier, the control aspect of Hirschi's social bonding theory centers on *extra-legal* controls such as parents, schools, and work. Deterrence theory shifts the emphasis to controls that emanate from the legal institutions of society. Hence, the emphasis is on *legal* social controls. The basic idea of the "deterrence doctrine" is that individuals will refrain from deviance because of the *fear of punishment*. Human actors are assumed to be rational in the sense that they are capable of weighing the rewards and costs (pleasure and pain) that would follow from deviant conduct. Hence, prior to engaging in a deviant act, a person will rationally calculate whether the act will result in more pleasure than pain. If it is concluded that the results of the deviant act will be predominantly painful, then it is likely that the person will not engage in norm-violation.

Deterrence theory, therefore, centers on how legal sanctions may prevent norm-violation. It is important to remember that though the theory involves sanctions (and particularly formal sanctions), it does not qualify as a subjectivist theory. Subjectivist theories concentrate of how sanctions are involved in *defining* acts as deviance or individuals as deviant. Deterrence theory, being an objectivist theory, focuses on how sanctions influence objective, norm-violating behavior.

Deterrence theorists distinguish between general and specific deterrence. *General deterrence* refers to instances in which persons in the non-offending, general population are deterred from initial deviance because they are aware that others have been punished for norm-violation. *Specific deterrence* refers to instances in which a person is deterred from future deviance as a result of having been punished for past deviant conduct. The most popular example of general deterrence is the belief among the general population that murder is deterred by executing those who have committed murder. An example of specific deterrence is the belief that a lengthy prison sentence for individuals convicted of armed robbery will decrease the likelihood that they will continue to commit armed robbery upon release from prison.

Deterrence theorists identify three proper-

TABLE 2.6 Neutralization Theory.

Bonds to conventional society	→	Techniques of neutralization	→	Weakening of bonds	→	Deviance made possible

---

TABLE 2.7   The Deterrence Doctrine.

Actual likelihood of punishment	→	Perception of punishment	→	Fear of punishment	→	Likelihood of deviance

---

ties of sanctions (punishments) that should, in theory, affect the likelihood of deviance. The first is the *certainty* of punishment. From a general deterrence perspective, the greater the *perceived* certainty of punishment, the less the chance an individual will engage in norm-violation. It is important to note that general deterrence focuses on how an individual perceives the chances of being caught and punished for deviance. Clearly, if the real likelihood of being caught for, say, cheating on a classroom exam is near zero, but a student perceives the chances to be 90 percent, then the student is likely to be deterred *irrespective of the fact that the objective probability of punishment is low.*

The second property of punishment is its *severity.* From the perspective of general deterrence, the greater the *perceived* severity of punishment, the less likely an individual is to engage in a deviant act. The third property of punishment that should affect behavior is the perceived *celerity*, or "swiftness," of punishment. From the perspective of general deterrence, if punishment is perceived to be immediate or swift, it should have a greater deterrent effect.

Table 2–7 depicts the central concepts of deterrence theory. The argument is that the actual probability of being punished for norm-violation will influence an individuals' perception of that probability. And, further, the perception of the certainty, severity, and celerity of punishment will create fear of actually being punished. And finally, fear of punishment will decrease the likelihood of deviant behavior. While all of the concepts in Table 2–7 are important, deterrence theorists tend to focus on the relationship between a person's perception of punishment and that

person's frequency of norm-violating behavior (the second and fourth concepts in Table 2–7).

The perceptions of certainty and severity of punishment may be considered separately, but it is important to understand how they combine to prevent deviance. At least in theory, the combined effects of certainty and severity of punishment should best predict behavior if their relative magnitudes are *multiplied* rather than simply added together. For example, consider whether a student will decide to shoplift an item from the school bookstore. If the student perceives that she will definitely get caught (perceived certainty) but will receive only a very mild scolding (perceived severity), then she is likely to engage in shoplifting. Or, put another way, even though she thinks the chances of being caught are great, she may not be deterred because of the mild penalty she perceives she will have to suffer. Conversely, if the same student believes that she would be sent to prison for a year if she were caught but simultaneously perceives that it is totally unlikely that she will be apprehended, then she will probably not be deterred from shoplifting.

As we noted at the beginning of our discussion of deterrence theory, whether legal punishments will deter depends upon a person's rational calculation of the consequences of her or his behavior. This is central to the debate over the deterrent effects of the death penalty. The majority of the American public and many in the legal profession believe that the death penalty deters murder in the general population. But since the deterrence doctrine assumes that individuals rationally calculate the consequences of their acts, then irrational acts or acts of extreme passion are, by the assumption of the theory, not deterrable. This is an important point because many murders are crimes of passion. For example, a significant number of homicides are committed in the context of family disputes. In such situations, emotions often run out of control. Those involved in the heat of the conflict are probably not rationally calculating what will happen to them if they should commit murder. Indeed, if a murder is committed, reason only begins to take hold after passions have subsided. But, by then, deterrence has failed. In a similar vein, certain crimes committed out of political or religious martyrdom may not be deterrable because the perpetrator is motivated less by reason than by passion.

Evaluating Control Theories. In assuming that everyone is motivated to commit deviant acts, control theorists avoid the embarrassment suffered by strain theorists when confronted with the issue of maturational reform. Even so, many critics remain uncomfortable with the claim made by control theorists that all are equally motivated to commit deviance. To assume that motivation is constant across social categories (for example, social class) appears to suggest that social structural variations in opportunities to obtain society's goals are irrelevant in explaining differences in rates of deviance. Many sociologists are unwilling to concede that structurally created stresses and strains (which are assumed to be different across the class structure) are not important for a complete understanding of deviant behavior.

In terms of empirical evidence, whether control theories are valid depends upon which brand of control theory one is talking about. In relation to social bonding theory, Hirschi (1969) has provided evidence showing that strong attachments to others, a strong commitment to conventional institutions, greater involvement in conventional activities, and deeply held beliefs in the moral validity of laws all reduce the likelihood of deviance. While other research studies have supported Hirschi's conclusions (Krohn and Massey, 1980; Wiatrowski, Griswold, and Roberts, 1981), a recent and more methodologically rigorous study by Agnew (1991) casts doubt on earlier positive findings. Specifically, Agnew found very weak support for control theory. Of the four elements of the bond, only commitment (as measured by school performance variables such as grade point averages) was related to delinquency. In fact, Agnew's analysis showed that the best predictors of future delinquency were prior delinquent involvement and deviant peer associations, findings more supportive of social learning theory.

Research on deterrence theory has been mixed (Tittle, 1980). Even so, the accumulated evidence suggests that the perceived certainty and severity of legal sanctions have at least moderate deterrent effects (Grasmick and Bursik, 1990). The research agenda over the last decade and a half has focused on the social conditions under which sanctions may deter deviant acts. For example, evidence suggests that individuals who morally condemn an act are less deterrable because they do not contemplate the act in the first place (Burkett and Ward, 1993).

The research agenda for the coming decade will likely be dominated by rational choice models of deterrence. *Rational choice models* incorporate actors' perceptions of the costs and rewards for crime, and they predict that deterrence will occur when perceived costs exceed perceived rewards. In the past, deterrence theory focused exclusively on the punishment, or cost, side of crime. Variables such as perceived certainty and severity of punishment dominated empirical research. Now, deterrence researchers are beginning to measure actors perceptions of the probability (certainty) and magnitude (intensity) of rewards for crime. In this way, a reward/cost difference can be calculated, and predictions about deterrence, based on the calculated difference, can be made (Klepper and Nagin, 1989). Thus, if a person perceives that the reward for a crime is only moderate but that the cost is extremely high then, from a rational choice perspective, the person will be unlikely to engage in the crime.

Less empirical attention has been paid to evaluating neutralization theory than to the other theories we have examined. One of the difficulties is methodological. Since the theory states that techniques of neutralization occur *prior* to deviant behavior, an adequate test of the theory requires longitudinal data. It must be shown that the various neutralization techniques precede deviance in time. Though this methodological problem is not specific to neutralization theory (it is also relevant for all control theories as well as social learning theory), no single study has adequately resolved the issue. Even so, Cressey (1953) has shown that techniques of neutralization, or what he calls "verbalizations," are important in explaining embezzlement among corporate executives. Given their commitment to conventional norms, before corporate executives could embezzle they had to rationalize their deviance or order to maintain a favorable conception of themselves. More recently, Minor (1984) used two waves of data to determine if techniques of neutralization actually precede deviance as the theory argues. His findings provide moderate support for the assertion in neutralization theory that excuse making does, indeed, precede deviance in time.

Social Learning Theories

In the 1920s, Clifford Shaw and Henry McKay (1942) conducted lengthy studies of juvenile delinquency. Their "laboratory" was the inner city of Chicago. Analysis of official arrest records for juveniles showed that the delinquency rate for inner-city youth was quite high. The important thing about this finding was that the high delinquency rate persisted *despite changes in the ethnic background of those who lived there.* Initially, Shaw and McKay theorized that the persistence of high delinquency rates resulted from social disorganization. Later, they were to abandon that concept for the idea that high rates of delinquency were the consequence of the transmission of deviant cultural traditions. They identified *cultural transmission* as the social mechanism by which deviant cultural traditions are passed from one generation to the next.

Differential Association Theory. In his theory of differential association, Edwin Sutherland (1939) attempted to make more precise the learning processes involved in deviant cultural transmission. Table 2–8 presents the major propositions of Sutherland's theory. At the center of Sutherland's theory is the *principle of differential association.* This principle (stated in proposition 6) suggests that deviance becomes more likely when a person's definitions favoring violation of the law outweigh definitions unfavorable to law violation.

The "definitions" Sutherland is referring to include attitudes toward deviance, certain rationalizations that would justify deviance, and the very motives necessary to commit deviant acts. Definitions are learned in intimate groups through the process of symbolic interaction. Whether an individual's definitions for criminality will actually outweigh definitions against criminality depends upon the nature of a person's deviant associations.

Sutherland specified four conditions that define the nature of deviant associations (proposition 7). When each condition is present, the chances increase that criminal definitions will be successfully learned. The first is the *frequency* with which one associates with deviant others. The greater the frequency, the greater the likelihood of deviance. The second deals with the intensity of one's deviant

TABLE 2.8 Propositions in Sutherland's Differential Association Theory.

1. Criminal behavior is learned.
2. Criminal behavior is learned in interaction with other persons in a process of communication.
3. The principal part of the learning of criminal behavior occurs within intimate personal groups.
4. When criminal behavior is learned, the learning includes (a) techniques of committing the crime, which are sometimes very complicated, sometimes very simple; (b) the specific direction of motives, drives, rationalizations, and attitudes.
5. The specific direction of motives and drives is learned from definitions of the legal codes as favorable or unfavorable.
6. A person becomes delinquent because of an excess of definitions favorable to violation of law over definitions unfavorable to violation of law.
7. Differential associations may vary in frequency, duration, priority, and intensity.
8. The process of learning criminal behavior by association with criminal and anticriminal patterns involves all of the mechanisms that are involved in any other learning.
9. While criminal behavior is an expression of general needs and values, it is not explained by those general needs and values, since noncriminal behavior is an expression of the same needs and values.

TABLE 2.9 Differential Association Theory.

Exposure to criminal patterns via differential association	$\rightarrow$	Learning of criminal definitions	$\rightarrow$	Deviant behavior

associations. *Intensity* refers to the degree to which one identifies with deviant others. The third condition specified by Sutherland is *priority,* the term Sutherland used to indicate how early in life deviant influences occur. Apparently, the earlier one is exposed to deviant definitions, the greater the chance that one will develop deviant behavior patterns. The fourth condition is *duration;* it refers to the length of time spent with deviant role models. Therefore, the more frequent, intense, early, and enduring one's differential associations (or differential contacts) with criminal patterns, the more likely it is that criminal behavior will result. The basic ideas contained in Sutherland's theory are shown in Table 2–9.

Sutherland's differential association theory has had a strong influence on the sociology of deviance. The idea that deviant behaviors must be learned (a systematic check forger is not born that way!) appears simple enough. As obvious as it seems, learning has not always been part of sociological theories of deviance. Even among modern theories, the concept of learning is noticeably absent. Our analysis showed no elements of learning in either Merton's strain theory or Hirschi's control theory. It is as if strain and control theorists assume that people will automatically know *how* to engage in deviant behaviors if either they are sufficiently strained or if they suffer from weak ties. This assumption is not acceptable to may sociologists of deviant behavior.

Differential Reinforcement Theory. Sutherland's differential association theory has strongly influenced contemporary theories of crime and deviance. While his original intent was to identify the learning processes involved in deviant behavior, according to more contemporary scholars of social deviance, Sutherland did not go quite far enough.

For example, Burgess and Akers (1966) have noted that Sutherland's theory remains too abstract and therefore is difficult to test. Such concepts as "definitions favorable to law-violation" are difficult to get an empirical handle on. In an attempt to bring differential association theory down to earth, Burgess and Akers reformulated Sutherland's original theory by using principles from modern-day learning theory. They contend that the principles of learning derived from operant conditioning (a learning theory pioneered in this country by psychologist B. F. Skinner) could help to recast Sutherland's initial ideas into a general, and yet testable, theory of deviance.

According to Burgess and Akers's differential-reinforcement theory, learning of deviant behaviors occurs primarily through the reinforcement of deviant behaviors and punishment of conventional behaviors (or, at least, by reinforcing deviant behaviors and failing to reinforce conventional behaviors). *Reinforcers* increase the probability that behaviors will be repeated, while *punishers* decrease the probability that behaviors will be repeated.

In addition to the concepts of reinforcement and punishment, another important concept in operant conditioning theory helps us better grasp the learning processes involved in the acquisition of deviant behavior: the concept of discriminative stimulus. A *discriminative stimulus* is a stimulus event that signals to an individual that reinforcement (or punishment) is about to occur. A discriminative stimulus, in itself, has no reinforcing value. It has merely been paired with a reinforcer in the past. For example, if a person has found that there are certain reinforcing properties in consuming alcohol and if alcohol consumption has been frequently accompanied by watching Monday night football, then watching the ball game may "call out the desire to have a drink." This occurs because watching the game sets the stage for reinforcement (getting high on booze). In this example, the televised football game may be said to act as a discriminative stimulus for drinking alcohol.

There are many different kinds of discriminative stimuli. As Burgess and Akers indicate, one of the most important is verbal stimuli, or the words and phrases people use in connection with deviant behaviors. They note that Sutherland's (1939) concept of "definitions favorable to law violation" may be understood as discriminative stimuli of the verbal kind. For example, individuals often utter certain statements that tend to justify deviant acts or to remove guilt associated with them. These utterances or "vocabularies of motive" are learned. Once learned, they may continue as discriminative stimuli, setting the stage for the commission of future deviant acts. By recasting Sutherland's concept of definitions favoring violation of the law into discriminative stimuli, Burgess and Akers believe they have made Sutherland's original statement more consistent with modern-day principles of learning.

The refinement of Sutherland's theory of differential association by Burgess and Akers is depicted in Table 2–10. The table suggests that differential reinforcement mediates the connection between differential associations and deviant behavior. In less complicated terms, the theory suggests that deviant contacts lead to deviant behavior because devi-

---

TABLE 2.10   Differential-Reinforcement Theory of Deviant Behavior.

Differential association	→	Differential reinforcement	→	Deviant behavior and learning vocabularies of motive	→	Future deviance

ant peers positively reinforce deviant conduct *and* provide the social context within which vocabularies of motive (discriminative stimuli for deviance) may be learned.

Differential Identification Theory. While Burgess and Akers have sought to reduce Sutherland's theory of differential association to principles of operant conditioning, Daniel Glaser (1956) has taken Sutherland's ideas in another direction. Rather than reduce human actors (including deviants) to the mechanistic laws of learning typically applied to rats and pigeons, Glaser argues that Sutherland's theory should be broadened to include not only individual's objective associations but their *subjective associations* as well.

To suggest that we should take into account subjective associations is to contend that human actors have inner worlds as well as outer (objective) worlds. These inner worlds include such phenomena as a person's imagination, self-other identifications, and personal (subjective) orientations about others, whether these others are real or imaginary. Here, Glaser is drawing on an important theme in symbolic interactionism. The interactionist contends that, with the acquisition of language, individuals gain the ability to take the role of the other. From this process, individuals can imagine how their behavior appears in the eyes of others even if the "others" are groups to which the individuals do not belong. It is clearly possible, therefore, that a person may be influenced by a group not necessarily by virtue of membership but by virtue of identification. Sociologists refer to groups (or others) with whom a person identifies as reference groups. Not only does one identify with a reference group, in that the group's views are taken into account in developing views of self, but reference groups serve as important frames of reference from which to see the world. In this connection, reference groups may serve to define acceptable and unacceptable lines of conduct; they provide a social backdrop for defining norms.

Thus, while Sutherland emphasized differential associations, and by implication the importance of membership groups, Glaser underscores the importance of differential identification and the centrality of reference groups. The theory of differential identification is depicted in Table 2–11.

According to Glaser, even if a person associates with deviants on a daily basis, if that person does not *identify* with them (hold them as an important reference group), then his or her behavior will probably not be influenced by the deviants. Conversely, even if a person's actual associations are predominantly conventional, if he or she subjectively identifies with a group (real or imaginary) from whose perspective deviance is justified, then deviance is more likely. As Glaser has argued:

> *The theory of differential identification, in essence, is that a* person pursues criminal behavior to the extent that he identifies with real or imaginary persons form whose perspective his criminal behavior seems acceptable. *Such a theory focuses attention on the interaction in which choice of models occurs, including the individual's interaction with himself, in rationalizing his conduct (Glaser, 1956:440).*

The concept of differential identification portrays a different image of the deviant than does either Sutherland's concept of differential association or Burgess and Akers's notion of differential reinforcement. The image they fostered is one of a passive actor whose devi-

---

TABLE 2.11 Differential Identification Theory.

Differential associations	→	Differential identification	→	Deviance

ance is, in good measure, determined. By contrast, Glaser paints a picture of the potential deviant as active in selecting reference groups to serve as models and important frames of reference for choosing deviant lines of conduct. Our discussion in Chapter 1 suggested that objectivist theories tend to view human behavior as determined. Glaser's theory of differential identification appears to be an exception to this observation.

Evaluating Social Learning Theories.   Much of criminal and deviant behavior is learned. Perhaps social learning theorists tend to overstate the importance of learning, particularly, when it comes to most delinquent acts committed by juveniles. To suggest that juveniles need to learn special skills or techniques to commit most delinquencies does not square with the relatively uncomplicated nature of the bulk of delinquent acts. Indeed, control theorists such as Hirschi (1969) and Nye (1958) passionately reject the assertion that individuals must learn deviance. They believe that, beyond a very narrow range of deviant acts for which sophisticated skills and techniques may be necessary, all delinquents have sufficient intellect and ingenuity to commit deviance.

But this should not be taken as a wholesale indictment of social learning theory. Clearly, there are many types of deviance that appear to require intensive learning. Complicated crimes, such as price-fixing, computer crimes, sophisticated stock-market schemes, and the like, are good examples of acts that require considerable learning. Often, this learning derives from differential associations. Therefore, while many acts committed by juveniles may not require extensive learning, many "adult" crimes appear to be technical and sophisticated enough that learning appears to be a necessary condition for their enactment.

The most persistent criticism of social learning theories (and particularly Suther-

land's expression of them) has been methodological. In spite of the fact that some scholars have concluded that tests of learning theory support its major hypotheses (Short, 1960), many other sociologists contend that the important concepts of learning theories are difficult to measure. Consider Sutherland's principle of differential association. Recall that the principle suggests that deviant behavior is more likely if an individual's definitions favorable to law-violation outweigh definitions unfavorable to law-violation. The concept suggests a ratio of favorable definitions divided by unfavorable definitions. But how are researchers supposed to measure these definitions? How are they to compute the ratio? The issue has not been resolved to the satisfaction of most deviance researchers.

Regarding the problem of measurement that seems to burden differential association theory, Akers (1985) feels that the reformulation of Sutherland's theory into reinforcement terms will help avoid this problem. Reinforcers appear to be more easily observable than Sutherland's "definitions" and, therefore, may remove some of the problems that inhere in Sutherland's original formulation. Despite Aker's attempt to make social learning theory more testable, and thus more scientific, there is an irony: How does one identify a reinforcer independently of behavior? To illustrate, Akers would suggest that deviance will be committed if it is reinforced. It appears that we have two variables in this statement, reinforcers and deviance. But reinforcers are stimuli (for example, peer approval) that increase the probability of deviance *by definition.* The only way one can know that a stimulus is reinforcing is to wait and observe the consequences (behavior). Since reinforcers cannot be defined independently from deviance, any statement relating deviance to reinforcers is tautological, or true by definition. If a statement is true by definition, it is not empirically falsifiable. If it is not at least potentially falsifiable, then it is not theory, but mere definition.

Though it has been difficult to measure the central concepts in Sutherland's theory, research inspired by his theory has proliferated. Typically, researchers will correlate an adolescent's report of his or her own deviance with reports of his or her friends' deviance. And, in most cases, the researcher obtains a significant correlation between the two (Warr and Stafford, 1991). But the mere correlation between peer deviance and deviance in the respondent does not necessarily provide data supportive of social learning theory. For example, and from the perspective of social bonding theory, it may be that a weakening of ties leads to deviance and that individuals involved in deviance *select* deviant peers with whom to associate. Table 2–12 depicts possible causal relationships between peer deviance, frequency of respondent deviance, and the respondent's stake in conventional society (a control theory variable).

As Table 2–12 shows, social learning theories such as Sutherland's differential association theory assert that deviant peer associations lead to deviance in the focal person and that weak stakes in conventional society are *consequences* of this process. Social bonding theory, by contrast, predicts that weak stakes in conventional society *cause* deviance in the focal person (only in the sense, of course, that weak ties release individuals to engage in deviance). In this model, deviant peer associations are a result of the "sorting and sifting" process deviants use in choosing their peer associations (Burkett and Warren, 1987). Given that there are two alternative theoretical interpretations of the relationship between peer associations and deviance, con-clusions suggesting that the relationship supports social learning theory must be interpreted with caution.

SUMMARY

Objectivist theories seek to explain norm-violating behavior. Notable among these are the *strain* theories. Merton's *anomie theory* suggests that an imbalance between cultural goals and objective opportunities to obtain them leads to deviance. Cloward and Ohlin's *illegitimate opportunity theory* points to the importance of recognizing that there are two opportunity structures: one legitimate, the other illegitimate. For them, the type of deviant behavior that follows from strain depends upon the availability of the following deviant subcultures: criminal, conflict, and retreatist.

Cohen's *status-frustration theory* attempts to account for the development of deviant subcultures and nonutilitarian forms of deviance. Lower-class youth are not as equipped to achieve status in the middle-class school environment. Humiliated and frustrated, they form their own deviant subculture, which is in direct opposition to middle-class values. Often, status is achieved by destroying property, such as vandalizing schools, even though the behavior is not utilitarian in the sense of achieving material wealth.

Neo-Marxist theories are theories of both deviance (acts) and deviance definitions (labels). In this chapter, we have considered how neo-Marxist theory accounts for deviance. In Chapter 3, we will examine how neo-Marxist theory has contributed to an understanding of the social and political process whereby deviance definitions are created.

TABLE 2.12 Bonding Versus Learning Models of Deviance.

Learning Theory:	Deviant peer associations	→	Deviance	→	Weak stakes
Bonding Theory:	Weak stakes	→	Deviance	→	Deviant peer associations

Neo-Marxist theories reject the assumption shared by strain theorists that society is characterized by normative consensus. Instead, they view society as consisting of normative diversity. Hence, norms are not shared but *imposed* upon members of society by the state in an attempt to protect the interests of the ruling class. Neo-Marxists account for lower-class crimes by pointing out that contradictions in capitalism create a *surplus labor population* that has a higher probability of engaging in *crimes of accommodation* and *crimes of resistance*. A capitalist economic system not only creates so-called predatory crimes of economic survival among the oppressed, but it creates *crimes of domination*. *Crimes of economic domination* include such corporate crimes as the violation of worker safety laws. *Crimes of government* include crimes committed by political officials and agents of social control.

Micro-objectivist theories seek to explain norm-violating behavior at the individual level. There are two popular micro-objectivist theories. *Control theories* assume that human beings are basically bad. All have the inclination to engage in deviance. The question becomes, "Why don't we all do it?" The answer provided by control theory is that strong bonds to conventional society prevent individuals from norm-violating behavior. *Social bonding theory* points to the importance of an individual's ties to conventional society in the prevention of deviance. The focus is primarily on informal social controls. Another brand of control theory is Sykes and Matza's *neutralization theory*. According to this theory, individuals utilize *techniques of neutralization* to weaken their commitments to conventional values and norms. When commitments are weakened, deviance is more likely to occur. *Deterrence theory* centers on whether legal sanctions (punishments) are effective in preventing deviance. Deterrence theorists claim that deviance will be prevented if the *perceived* certainty, severity, and celerity of punishment is high.

Sutherland's *differential association theory* is a learning theory of deviance. Individuals learn deviance definitions (attitudes and the like) from contact with deviant others. These deviance definitions increase the likelihood of norm-violating behavior. Burgess and Akers have reformulated Sutherland's theory into what they call *differential-reinforcement theory*. According to their theory, deviance is learned because it is reinforced. *Reinforcers* are stimulus events that increase the probability that a behavior will be repeated. *Punishers* are stimulus events that decrease the probability that a behavior will be repeated. If deviance is reinforced more than conformity, an individual is likely to continue to engage in norm-violating behavior. *Discriminative stimuli* are verbal justifications or excuses that lead to the expectation that deviance will be reinforced once it is committed. Past reinforcement for deviance combined with discriminative stimuli increase the likelihood that deviance will be committed in the future. Glaser's *differential identification theory* suggests that individuals are influenced to engage in deviance by those with whom they subjectively identify. Therefore, whether association with deviant others will lead to deviance depends upon the extent to which an individual identifies with deviant others.

GLOSSARY

Anomie theory   Merton's version of strain theory, stating that a disjuncture between cultural goals and objective opportunities weakens the commitment individuals have to culturally approved means to achieve goals. A weakening of commitment to cultural norms creates a state of normlessness or anomie that, in turn, increases the likelihood of criminal "innovation."

Control theories   Theories that assume that human actors are prevented from norm-violation either by informal or formal social controls.

Crimes of domination In neo-Marxist theories, crimes of the ruling class, such as corporate crime, and crimes of government, such as crimes committed by political officials. Both types of crimes of domination are to protect the capital accumulation of the ruling class.

Deterrence theory A theory proposing that human actors refrain from deviance because they fear punishment. According to the theory of general deterrence, individuals are less likely to commit deviance when they perceive that the certainty, severity, and celerity of punishment is high.

Differential association theory Sutherland's theory that individuals learn deviance definitions when their associations with deviant others outweigh their associations with conventional others. These deviance definitions, in turn, increase the likelihood that individuals will commit norm-violating acts.

Differential identification theory Glaser's theory that deviance definitions are learned from others (real or imagined) with whom one subjectively identifies.

Differential reinforcement theory Burgess and Akers's reformulation of Sutherland's differential association theory, which contends that the probability of deviance increases when it is reinforced (rewarded) by significant others.

Illegitimate opportunity theory A theory developed by Cloward and Ohlin, which states that differential opportunities exist in both the legitimate and illegitimate social structure. The forms of deviance produced by opportunity blockage in the legitimate social structure depend on opportunities in the illegitimate social structure.

Neo-Marxist theories Theories of criminal deviance based on the writings of Karl Marx to explain both deviance (acts) and deviance definitions (laws). According to

these theories, criminal acts are a result of contradictions in a capitalist economic system.

Neutralization theory Sykes and Matza's theory that individuals must break the bond to conventional values and norms *prior* to committing deviance.

Punishers Stimulus events that decrease the probability that behavior will be repeated.

Rational Choice model A model used by deterrence researchers that incorporates actors' perceptions of the costs and rewards for crime and predicts that one will be deterred only when perceived costs exceed perceived rewards.

Reinforcers Stimulus events that increase the probability that behavior will be repeated.

Social bonding theory Hirschi's brand of control theory, which argues that all individuals have the capacity to commit deviance. The crucial mechanism in preventing deviance is an individual's bond to conventional institutions, activities, and significant others.

Status frustration theory A subcultural theory of deviance developed by Cohen to partly account for nonutilitarian forms of juvenile delinquency, such as vandalism.

Surplus labor population The segment of the population in a capitalist society that has become "superfluous" to capital accumulation. Crimes of the surplus labor population are, primarily, crimes of economic survival.

Techniques of neutralization In neutralization theory, justifications or excuses that serve to neutralize the bond thereby making deviance possible.

SUGGESTED READINGS

Cloward, Richard, and Lloyd Ohlin. *Delinquency and Opportunity: A Theory of Delinquent Gangs.* New York: Free Press, 1960. Here, Cloward and Ohlin present their theory of differential opportunity. First, they review Merton's classic statement regarding opportunity blockage and deviance. Then they extend the theory to differential illegitimate opportunities and show how differential learning opportunities augment strain in the production of deviance.

Cohen, Albert. *Delinquent Boys: The Culture of the Gang.* New York: Free Press, 1955. In this important contribution to theories of deviance, Cohen contends that lower-class boys have a difficult time competing in a middle-class school environment and, because of the humiliation of failure, form a subculture whose values are in opposition to the values of the middle class. From this oppositional subculture come various forms of deviance, including nonutilitarian deviance, such as vandalism and escapist drug abuse.

Liska, Allen E. *Perspectives in Deviance.* 2nd ed. Englewood Cliffs, N.J.: Prentice-Hall, 1987. This is an excellent text summarizing the major theoretical perspectives in the sociology of deviance. In addition to providing an excellent treatment of the concepts contained within each theoretical approach, the author gives the historical context within which the theory was developed as well as biographical information on the major proponents of the theory.

REFERENCES

Agnew, Robert. "A Longitudinal Test of Social Control Theory and Delinquency," *Journal of Research in Crime and Delinquency* 28 (1991):pp. 126–156.

Akers, Ronald. *Deviant Behavior: A Social Learning Approach.* (3rd Edition.) Belmont, Calif.: Wadsworth, 1985.

Braithwaite, John. "The Myth of Social Class and Criminality Reconsidered." *American Sociological Review* 46 (1981): pp. 36–57.

Burgess, Robert, and Ronald Akers. "A Differential Association-Reinforcement Theory of Criminal Behavior," *Social Problems* 14 (1966): pp. 128–147.

Burkett, Steven, and David A. Ward. "A Note on Perceptual Deterrence, Religiously Based Moral Condemnation, and Social Control." *Criminology* 31, (1993): pp. 119–134.

Burkett, Steven, and Bruce Warren. "Religosity, Peer Associations, and Adolescent Marijuana Use: A Panel Study of Underlying Causal Structures." *Criminology* 24 (1987): pp. 109–131.

Cloward, Richard, and Lloyd Ohlin. *Delinquency and Opportunity.* New York: Free Press, 1960.

Cohen, Albert. *Delinquent Boys.* New York: Free Press, 1955.

———. *Deviance and Control.* Englewood Cliffs, N.J.: Prentice-Hall, 1966.

Cressey, Donald R. *Other People's Money.* New York: Free Press, 1953.

Dentler, Robert A., and Lawrence J. Monroe. "Social Correlates of Early Adolescent Theft." *American Sociological Review* 26 (1961): pp. 733–743.

Durkheim, Emile. *Suicide* Glencoe, Ill.: Free Press, 1964. Originally published in 1897.

Elliott, Delbert S., and Suzanne S. Ageton. "Reconciling Race and Class Differences in Self-Reported and Official Estimates of Delinquency." *American Sociological Review* 46 (1980): pp. 36–57.

Glaser, Daniel. "Criminality Theory and Behavioral Images." *American Journal of Sociology* 61 (1956): pp. 433–444.

Grasmick, Harold G., and Robert J. Bursik. "Conscience, Significant Others, and Rational Choice: Extending the Deterrence Model." *Law and Society Review* 24 (1990): pp. 837–861.

Hirschi, Travis. *Causes of Delinquency.* Berkeley, Calif.: University of California Press, 1969.

Hirst, Paul. "Marx and Engels on Law, Crime and Morality." *Economy and Society.* 6, 1972: pp. 28–56.

Klepper, Steven, and Daniel Nagin. "The Deterrent Effect of Perceived Certainty and Severity of Punishment Revisited." *Criminology* 27 (1989): pp. 721–746.

Kornhauser, Ruth. *Social Sources of Delinquency.* Chicago: University of Chicago Press, 1978.

Krohn, Marvin and James Massey. "Social Control and Delinquent Behavior: An Examination of the Elements of the Social Bond." *The Sociological Quarterly* 21, 1980: pp. 529–544.

Lacayo, Richard. "One Doctor Down, How Many More?" *Time* (1993): pp. 46–47.

Merton, Robert K. "Social Structure and Anomie."

American Sociological Review 3 (1938): pp. 672–682.

Minor, William. "Neutralization as a Hardening Process: Considerations in the Modeling of Change," *Social Forces* 62, 1984: pp. 995–1019.

Nye F. Ivan. *Family Relationships and Delinquent Behavior.* New York: Wiley, 1958.

Nye, F. Ivan, and James Short. "Scaling Delinquent Behavior." *American Sociological Review* 22 (1957): pp. 326–331.

Nye, F. Ivan, James F. Short, and Virgil Olson. "Socioeconomic Status and Delinquent Behavior." *American Sociological Review* 63 (1958): pp. 381–389.

Quinney, Richard. *Class, State and Crime.* New York: David McKay, 1977.

Schichor, David. "Socialization: The Political Aspects of a Delinquency Explanation." *Sociological Spectrum* 3 (1983): p. 93.

Shaw, Clifford, and Henry McKay. *Juvenile Delinquency in Urban Areas.* Chicago: University of Chicago Press, 1942.

Short, James F. "Differential Association as a Hypothesis: Problems of Empirical Testing," *Social Problems* 8, 1960: p. 24.

Spitzer, Steven. "Toward a Marxian Theory of Deviance." *Social Problems* 22 (1975): pp. 638–651.

Sutherland, Edwin. *Criminology.* 3rd ed. Philadelphia: Lippincott, 1939.

Sykes, Gresham M., and David Matza. "Techniques of Neutralization: A Theory of Delinquency." *American Sociological Review* 22 (1957): pp. 664–670.

Taylor, Ian, Paul Walton, and Jock Young. *The New Criminology.* New York: Harper Torchbooks, 1973.

Tittle, Charles R. *Sanctions and Deviance: The Question of Deterrence.* New York: Praeger, 1980.

Tittle, Charles R., and Robert F. Meier. "Specifying the SES/Delinquency Relationship." *Criminology* 28 (1990): pp. 271–299.

Tittle, Charles R., Wayne J. Villemez, and Douglas A. Smith. "The Myth of Social Class and Criminality." *American Sociological Review* 43 (1978): pp. 643–656.

Voight, Lydia, and William Thorton. "The Rhetoric and Politics of Soviet Delinquency: An American Perspective." *Comparative Social Research* 8 (1985): pp. 123–167.

Warr, Mark, and Mark Stafford. "The Influence of Delinquent Peers: What They Think or What They Do?" *Criminology* 29 (1991): pp. 851–866.

Wiatrowski, M.D., D. Griswold, and M. K. Roberts. "Social Control Theory and Delinquency." *American Sociological Review* 46 (1981): pp. 525–541.

Wolfe, Alan. "Political Repression and the Liberal State." *Monthly Review* 23, (1971): p. 20.

Chapter **3**

Subjectivist Theories of Deviance

"THE SUBWAY VIGILANTE"

The subway train slowed as it approached the downtown Manhattan station in New York City. The trip seemed pretty routine. Then, four black youths approached a slender male passenger and asked for the time and a match, then five dollars. The passenger, Bernhard Hugo Goetz, reportedly said, "Yes, I have five dollars for each of you." Then Goetz stood up from his subway seat and opened fire on the four teenagers with a .38 caliber silver pistol hitting each of them in the upper body (*Newsweek*, 1985:34). As the police reports would later indicate, Goetz then checked the first three to see if they were "taken care of" and next turned to the fourth who was "half sitting, half lying" on the bench. Goetz looked at the wounded youth and said, "you don't look too bad, here's another" and shot the fourth youth even a second time (*Newsweek*, 1985:50). A conductor ran to the scene and asked Goetz if he was a cop. After Goetz replied no, he turned and jumped from the subway only to disappear into the dark, damp maze of the subway system.

The four black teenagers were all hospitalized with serious injuries. Nineteen-year old Darrell Cabey had been paralyzed from the waist down after one of the bullets from Goetz silver pistol smashed his spinal cord. Cabey is now in his midtwenties and, because of the shooting, has the mental capacity of an eight year old and, according to experts, will need medical attention for the rest of his life (*New York Times*, 1989:30).

Just nine days after Bernie Goetz had dispensed his vigilante justice upon the four Manhattan youths, he turned himself in at a Concord, New Hampshire, police station. "It had to be done," he told police. "You don't know what it's like to be a victim" (*Newsweek*, 1985:34).

The social and political uproar during the aftermath of the shooting of the four youths by Goetz was to shake New York City more than "any politician has in 50 years" claimed *Daily News* columnist Jimmy Breslin (*Newsweek*, 1985:51). Breslin had been shocked by the influx of hate mail after he had written a column denouncing the action of Goetz. "Every one used the word 'nigger' or said 'Breslin is scum,' " he recalls. The support for Bernard Goetz reflected in the mail Breslin received was also evident in a national public opinion poll

conducted by *Newsweek*. The *Newsweek* poll found that 57 percent of the respondents approved of Goetz's actions when asked the question, "From what you know about the Goetz case so far, do you tend to approve or disapprove of Goetz shooting four youths on a New York subway?" Interestingly, support for Goetz ran particularly high among men (62 percent), Republicans (63 percent), suburbanites (65 percent) and those who carry guns themselves (70 percent).

The legal aspects of the case are complicated. Was Goetz acting in self-defense? If so, did the perceived threat justify the use of lethal force? Following the first grand jury investigation and trial, the verdict for Goetz was not guilty of assault or even attempted murder; guilty only of possessing an unlicensed gun! (*Newsweek*, 1987:334). There was not only applause at the verdict by Goetz supporters, but there was also condemnation and outrage. Some suggested that the verdict reflected an underlying racism in the criminal justice process. Ronald Kuby, lawyer for Darrell Cabey, who had been paralyzed from the waist down, argued, "You cannot shoot someone in the back and claim self-defense . . ." (*Newsweek*, 1985:50).

Such outrage provoked yet another grand jury investigation, which led to Goetz being charged with four counts of attempted murder, four counts of assault, one count of reckless endangerment and one count of criminal possession of a weapon. On the eve of 1989, and following two years of legal maneuvering, the final sentence was handed down: one year in jail for possessing an unlicensed gun (*New York Times*, 1989:29).

Is Bernhard Goetz a victim or villain, hero or cold-blooded killer? Though it is apparent that he (and the four black teenagers) committed criminal acts, whether Goetz will be socially regarded as deviant will hinge not just on his formal, legal conviction but on the informal social judgments of the public. "I don't think he did it," said New Yorker Barbara McConnell last week. "He would have liked to have done it—his hero would have done it. *But somehow the crime doesn't match with him* [emphasis added]" *Newsweek*, 1985:35). The inevitable question of the subjectivist lingers: Would Barbara McConnell have drawn the same conclusion if Bernhard Goetz were black and the four youths were white?

The case of the "Subway Vigilante" raises questions that go to the heart of the subjectivist conception of deviance. As the case of Bernhard Goetz has unfolded, it is clear that whether he will be socially regarded as a deviant depends less on what he did and more on who he is and what others decide to do about it. It is the reactions of social audiences that will ultimately determine the social identity of Bernhard Goetz.

Consistent with a subjectivist conception of deviance, the theories in this chapter concentrate on how deviance definitions are created and applied to behaviors or people. The creation of deviance definitions may come from several levels of social organization. Laws may be regarded as deviance definitions that derive from large-scale societal forces. The level of analysis is macro. Social organizations within society, such as police departments, mental institutions, and alcoholism and drug treatment agencies, create deviance definitions as well. Still, the level of analysis is macro. But deviance definitions may also derive from micro-level interpersonal transactions. The social audiences at this level become those with whom the branded individual interacts on a daily basis. Peers, and other informal associations, become the ones who define deviance.

MACRO-SUBJECTIVIST THEORIES

The theories that fall into this category focus on how large-scale social, economic, and political forces influence the *creation and application of deviance definitions*. The theories may

be distinguished from those in the objectivist camp because little attention is given to the social conditions that produce norm-violating behavior. A particularly interesting concern within macro-subjectivist theories is how legal norms change throughout the history of a society. Macro-subjectivists believe that legal norms (laws) change through time as some groups gain power and the ability to influence the formulation and enforcement of law.

Interest Group Theories

The first set of macro-subjectivist theories are interest group theories. *Interest group theories* focus on the social, political, and economic forces involved in the process whereby deviance definitions (including both criminal and noncriminal definitions) are created. Some interest group theories posit a conception of society as constituted of two conflicting classes—the ruling class and the working class. Still other interest group theories posit a pluralistic conception of society. According to these theories, society comprises many diverse interest groups, each with its own values and interests. When one or more of these groups is able to gain enough political power to influence the legislative process, then their interests get translated into formal law.

Capitalist Interests and Deviance Definitions. In Chapter 2, we considered how neo-Marxist theories account for deviance, objectively conceived. While most traditional and contemporary theories of deviance are either theories of deviance (acts) or deviance definitions (labels), theories based on Marxist thought are theories of both. In Chapter 2, we drew upon the words of Richard Quinney not only to emphasize that extant deviance theories exclude one or the other aspect of deviance but to call attention to the ultimate goal of neo-Marxist theory: a comprehensive understanding of both acts and labels. Quinney's words are worth reconsidering here:

> The basic problem in any study of the meaning of crime is that of integrating the two sides of the crime phenomenon: placing into a single framework (1) the defining of behavior as criminal . . . and (2) the behavior of those who are defined as criminal. Thus far, the analysis of crime has focused on one side or the other, failing to integrate the two interrelated processes into one scheme (Quinney, 197:33).

As we learned in Chapter 2, neo-Marxists account for criminality (acts) by pointing to contradictions inherent in a capitalist economic system. By the same token, deviance definitions, such as formal laws, emerge from the conflicting interests of the capitalist class and the working class. The primary function of the state, according to neo-Marxists, is to protect the capitalist system. This means that laws are created to protect the material interests of the bourgeoisie.

In terms of enforcement of these criminal definitions, the members of the bourgeoisie are protected in other ways. First, the interests of the ruling class are protected because it is difficult to prosecute them for "crimes in the suites." Second, the interests of the ruling class are protected by the criminal justice system in the name of "law and order." Hence while the capitalist class is only rarely the target of the control mechanisms of the state, the crimes of the working class (accommodation and resistance) are constantly subject to the legal sanctions of the criminal justice system.

According to Quinney, the term *criminal justice* is just a euphemism. In reality, the legal institutions of society serve the goals of the capitalist system. Laws are created in the interest of capital accumulation. Agents of the criminal justice apparatus apply legal definitions to members of the surplus population who threaten the accumulation of wealth. The state perceives certain social categories or groups as being greater threats to the perpetuation of capitalism than others.

Indeed, Spitzer (1975) has identified the social and behavioral characteristics of problem populations that quality them for "management as deviant" by the social control apparatus of the state. Examples are those who refuse to work for meager wages, those who use drugs to escape rather than to adjust, those who challenge or do not participate in schooling or traditional family life, and those who seek economic and political alternatives to the capitalist political economy. In a widely cited study, Carter and Clelland (1979) found support for Spitzer's Marxist assertion in a test of the relationship between social class position and the sentencing of juvenile offenders. They argued that the social class background of juveniles will have a greater impact on the sentencing of crimes against the "moral order" than on the sentencing of crimes against persons and property. "Moral order" offenses include status offenses, such as running away and incorrigibility, as well as victimless offenses, such as illegal alcohol and drug use and sexual misconduct. From the Marxian perspective, moral violators threaten capitalist accumulation because they are not actively involved in the economic process of producing and consuming material goods. The state cannot rely on nonlegal institutions, such as family, school, and church, to control the morality of lower-class youth. However, the state can rely on these institutions to control working-class and middle-class youth; these youth have a greater stake in the system because they have come to realize that they will profit, the way their parents have, by moral conformity. Thus, the juvenile court manages lower-class youth by imposing more severe sentences on them for moral misconduct than on their working-class and middle-class counterparts. Class bias, however, will not occur in the sentencing of youth who commit crimes against persons or property. These crimes are "direct threats to all classes" and, therefore, will be punished according to the seriousness of the offense and prior record of the offender, rather than according to the offender's class background (Carter and Clelland, 1979:100).

The Theory of Status Politics.   Marxist conflict theories view the history of society as being played out through a struggle between economic classes. The battle is one of class struggle, and class is determined by economic considerations alone. Other interest group theories that seek to explain the creation of deviance definitions view conflict as arising from a broader set of issues than mere economic interests. As Gusfield has pointed out, complex societies are not stratified solely along economic lines and social status is not linked only to economic considerations (1963:12–35). Social status (prestige) may also derive from the ability of one group to impose its religious values and general life-style upon another group. "Victory in issues of status is the symbolic conferral of respect upon the norms of the victor and disrespect upon the norms of the vanquished" (Gusfield, 1963:174). From this perspective, if the values and life-styles of certain groups threaten the status of established groups, then the established groups will attempt to pass laws that will condemn the competing life-style.

Gusfield amply characterizes this approach to understanding the creation of deviance definitions as "status politics." He is not denying the importance of economic conflict. He is contending that a purely Marxist approach does not adequately take into account the importance of prestige based on cultural phenomena, such as values and norms, to an understanding of why some groups attempt to impose their moral definitions on other groups in society (Gusfield, 1963:166–88).

Gusfield's analysis of how the American Temperance Movement influenced the passage of the Eighteenth Amendment to the constitution (which outlawed the sale and consumption of alcohol during the Prohibi-

tion Era) provides support for the idea that status politics is central to the creation of deviance definitions.

In the mid-1800s, the United States was a predominantly rural, small-town society. The values of sobriety and hard work held by the rural middle-class served as ideals to which everyone should aspire. Even though drunkenness was at odds with these values, the drinker, not his drunken comportment, posed a threat to the esteemed place held by the middle class in the status order of rural American society. The drinker was looked upon as someone to be "saved" through moral conversion to rural Protestantism.

Toward the end of the nineteenth century, however, the United States experienced a tremendous influx of immigrants from Europe. The major cities of the United States witnessed dramatic increases in population. The rapid urbanization that took place "threatened the social position of those who strongly identified their social status with dominance in the small-town image of the community" (Gusfield, 1963:80). Moreover, most of the European immigrants were Catholic, which was another threat because Protestantism had, for so long, been the dominant and most prestigious religious faith in U.S. society. Rural versus urban, Protestant versus Catholic—the stage was set for a struggle for cultural dominance in the United States in the early twentieth century.

But how did the fight for prohibition of alcohol get into the picture? As it turns out, drinking was an accepted, if not expected, part of the daily life-style of the European immigrant. Therefore, if the small-town rural American could create laws prohibiting the use of alcohol, it would serve as public testimony to the dominance of native over immigrant. In the final analysis, the Prohibition Amendment was passed. And, from the vantage point of the theory of status politics, its passage "was the high point of the struggle to assert the public dominance of old middle-class values. It established the victory of Protestant over Catholic, rural over urban, tradition over modernity . . ." (Gusfield, 1963:7).

The Functions of Manufacturing Deviance. Gusfield's theory of status politics leads to the conclusion that deviance definitions are created to protect the prestige of a society's dominant groups. The passage of laws serves to symbolize the moral superiority and political dominance of the established groups. In *Wayward Puritans* (1966), Kai Erikson provides us with another way to understand how and why deviance definitions are created. Drawing on the initial insights of Emile Durkheim, Erikson argues that deviance in society serves certain positive functions. One of these important functions is to maintain the boundary line between acceptable and intolerable conduct. When certain undesirable behaviors become prevalent, but there is no law to forbid them, society will literally manufacture a law thereby making the behaviors in question deviance. A society will create deviance (by making laws the violation of which is deviance) in order to define the moral boundaries of society. With this basic idea in mind, let us turn to Erikson's intriguing analysis of Puritanism in colonial New England.

In *Wayward Puritans*, Erikson skillfully shows how deviance is created by societies when individuals or groups begin to challenge the boundaries of conformity. In Salem Village, a Massachusetts Bay Colony of colonial New England in 1630, the Puritan ministers had almost total authority in decisions regarding deviance and morality. Most importantly, they had the exclusive right to translate the meaning of the Bible. During that period, Anne Hutchinson began to argue that the Boston ministers did not have sole authority when it came to interpreting the Bible. While the ministers claimed that she was attempting to undermine the authority of the church, it was difficult to deal with her.

After all, Anne Hutchinson was a righteous, good, and law-abiding citizen of the Salem community. Since the church and government were really the same thing in Salem, she was challenging the authority of the ruling elite. Something had to be done. If she were allowed to continue, the clear rules prohibiting this kind of behavior might begin to erode and the absolute power of the state would be diminished. Since there were no existing laws prohibiting her behavior, *the ministers literally created a category of deviance by writing a law forbidding her conduct.* They tried Anne Hutchinson, found her guilty, and ran her out of Salem Village.

During her trial, Anne Hutchinson asked of then Governor Winthrop why she was being thrown out of the colony. "Say no more," Governor Winthrop responded. "The court knows wherefore and is satisfied" (Erikson, 1966:100). The fact is that Governor Winthrop could not provide a satisfactory answer. There was no traditional category of deviance to place her in. As Erikson wrote:

> *The court did know why Mrs. Hutchinson had to be banished, but it did not know how to express that feeling in any language then known in New England. The settlers were experiencing a shift in ideological focus, a change in community boundaries, but they had no vocabulary to explain to themselves or anyone else what the nature of these changes were. The purpose of the trial was to invent that language, to find a name for the nameless offense which Mrs. Hutchinson had committed (Erikson, 1966:100–101).*

Societies "manufacture" deviance to clarify the boundaries between conformity and nonconformity. It is in this light that Erikson interprets his historical analysis of Salem village. But it also seems plausible that his historical data have strong implications for an interest group theory of deviance creation. Rather than creating deviance for the maintenance of the moral boundaries for society as a whole, the actions of Anne Hutchinson and her followers may have been designated as deviance because they threatened the interests of a small but powerful segment of the Salem community. As Erikson pointed out:

> [T]he use of the Bible as a source of law was [troublesome in that] many thoughtful people in the colony soon became apprehensive because so many discretionary powers were held by the leading clique . . . "the people" themselves . . . were anxious to obtain an official code of law; and so a constitutional battle opened which had a deep impact on the political life of the Bay. On one side stood the people . . . who felt that the Bible would supply a clearer and safer guide to law if the elders would declare at the outset how they intended to interpret its more ambiguous passages. On the other side stood the ruling cadre of the community, the ministers and magistrates, who felt that the whole enterprise would be jeopardized if they were no longer able to interpret the Word as they saw fit (Erikson, 1966:59).

Therefore the lines were drawn between what Erikson calls the "people" and the "ruling cadre." When Anne Hutchinson began gathering large numbers of people at her home, where she rendered interpretations of the Bible that were at odds with the interests of the "ruling cadre," her actions were defined as deviance and she as a deviant. If viewed from this vantage point, Erikson's historical analysis of "crime" in the Salem community lends support for an interest group theory of the creation of deviance definitions as well as the idea that deviance may serve to clarify the boundaries between deviance and conformity.

Evaluating Interest Group Theories.   The interest group theories we have been discussing focus on how deviance definitions (including formal laws) are created. Neo-Marxist theories focus on how the creation and enforcement of deviance definitions serve the material interests of the capitalist class. Gusfield's analysis shows how the passage of laws serves to maintain the status of dominant groups. Erikson's analysis in *Way-* *ward Puritans* demonstrates how behaviors may be defined as criminal to clarify the boundaries between acceptable and unacceptable conduct. His theory also has important implications for interest group politics because his historical analysis shows that the ruling elite was the group whose interests would be most served by the banishment of Anne Hutchinson.

The interest group orientation guides us to look for how the creation of criminal definitions (and deviance definitions generally) serve a *variety* of interests of the powerful. While the interest group approach has served to enlighten us about how deviance definitions are created, the approach does not stand without criticism. In neo-Marxist theory, there is a tendency to emphasize conflict to the exclusion of consensus in the process by which deviance definitions are created. While there may be considerable conflict between groups (or classes) as to what acts constitute deviance, there nonetheless appears to be a good deal of consensus across class boundaries regarding certain serious criminal offenses such as murder, rape, robbery, and assault. The conflict theorist argues that acts defined as criminal are those acts that threaten only the capitalist class. But do laws prohibiting serious crimes such as murder and rape merely reflect ruling-class interests? This question appears particularly troublesome for the non-Marxist because the laboring class is disproportionately victimized by serious crimes. It is as much in the interest of the laboring class as the capitalist class to define serious acts such as murder, rape, and robbery as crime.

Additional criticism of interest group theories is more methodological in nature. For example, it may be argued that the historical analyses undertaken by scholars such as Gusfield and Erikson are too subjective; other researchers may not be able to draw the same conclusions even if they examined the same historical documents. Even so, the historical approach appears necessary if we are to examine how laws change through time. Moreover, interest group theorists have not been clear in specifying what constitutes an interest group. Are interest groups social classes, religious groups, segments of society divided along race or gender lines? Most likely, all of these are interest groups to one interest group theorist or another. Thus, what critics are calling for is a more precise specification of what interest groups are and how they may be located in the real world.

Organizational Theories of Deviance Definitions

Organizational theories turn our attention to the deviance-producing activities of agencies of social control. Included here are social control agencies, for example, the police, mental institutions, and rehabilitation and treatment programs, such as those designed for helping the blind. Each social control agency, whatever its specific mission, is a social organization with formal norms (rules) as to how things should get done. But within every formal organization, there is an informal organization with its own cultural norms stipulating how things get done in practical, everyday, routine situations. Organizational theories of deviance concentrate on the role informal organizational relations play in shaping the experiences of individuals undergoing formal processing by social control agencies. One of the most important of these experiences is that of being defined as some kind of deviant. Social control organizations are in the business of defining individuals as deviant. An understanding of the informal operating rules of organizations of control is necessary if we're to grasp how deviance categories are created and how individuals are placed in them.

The Social Organization of Police Arrest. Donald Black's (1971) central concerns in his analysis of the social organization of police arrests are reflected in the form of a series of questions: (1) "Are there operating rules that flow from the informal organization of police work that shape the likelihood that an offender will be arrested?" (2) "Do these rules tend to determine the arrest of a person independently of whether the person actually violated a law?" (3) "Do these rules lead to a failure to arrest even though a suspect may have actually engaged in an illegal act?" If there are such informal operating rules, then police organizations are literally *producing deviance* apart from the actual incidence of deviance in the population. This may occur either by not arresting suspects when arrest is legally warranted or by arresting when arrest is unwarranted. The implications of Black's thesis suggest that police work involves a definitional process that is guided by informal organizational rules of thumb. These rules of thumb operate independently of what the law requires or what the actual rules of the formal organization of social control are.

According to Black, there are a number of operating rules that guide the likelihood of arrest as police conduct their work. Each informal rule prescribes a set of general guidelines for how police will conduct themselves as they deal with various aspects of the arrest situation. Here, we examine five aspects of the arrest situation Black identified that, against the backdrop of the informal rules of the police culture, either increase or decrease arrest probability.

The first may be called *mobilization*. It stipulates that "most arrest situations arise through citizen rather than police initiative" (Black, 1971:1101). In this sense, criminal law is similar to civil law. Civil law involves a legal complaint of one person against another when no criminal law has been violated. For example, persons may sue their neighbor for allowing a pet to damage their lawn. There is no criminal law regulating this kind of incident. Therefore, the party who feels damaged must initiate punishment through private action in civil court. Black is suggesting that much of criminal law actually is enforced in this way. Citizens must initiate a complaint against an offender. They must call police attention to it. If the complaint is not lodged, then the offense (however serious) may not become part of the official record of criminal statistics. For crime to be a social reality, it must be known to those in power who can do something about it.

A second organizational rule relates to the *complainants*. Black's analysis indicates that arrest practices reflect the preferences of citizen complainants. This is the case when the desire is for leniency and also, though less frequently, when the complainants demand arrest (Black, 1971:1095). In this sense, the police are an instrument of the complainant in two ways. First, the police tend to handle (respond to) offenses the citizens want them to handle. Secondly, police tend to handle the complaint in the way the complainant prefers and prescribes (Black, 1971:1095). For example, a complaint may or may not be lodged against a spouse in an instance of domestic violence. If a complaint is lodged, the police will tend to follow the wishes of the complainant even if it is clear that a criminal law has been violated. Often, the complainant will drop the charges following the arrival of the police. Conversely, if the complainant prefers arrest, the police are likely to abide by those wishes. Here again, it is an operating principle (rule) that pervades the culture of police work that guides the likelihood of arrest. Thus, according to Black, it is not so much acts on the part of offenders that produce crime rates but the reactions of the police, guided by organizational rules of thumb, that create the social reality of crime.

A third aspect of the arrest situation for which there is an organizational rule prescribing how the situation will be handled is the degree of *intimacy* between the offender and victim. "The greater the relational distance between complainant and a suspect, the greater is the likelihood of arrest" (Black, 1971:1107). If the victim of an offense demands that the police arrest a suspect, the likelihood of arrest increases if the victim and suspect are strangers. Conversely, if the suspect and complainant are not strangers (for example, if they are neighbors, acquaintances, or even friends), arrest is less likely. Arrest is least probable if the complainant and suspect are family members.

A fourth aspect of the arrest situation relates to the level of *disrespect* the suspect shows toward the arresting officer. "The probability of arrest increases when a suspect is disrespectful toward the police" (Black, 1972:1108). Interestingly, even disrespectful complainants are punished in a way because their complaints are less likely to be recognized by the police—that is, the police are less likely to arrest the suspect.

A fifth aspect of the arrest situation is *discrimination*. According to Black (1972:1109), police are no more likely to arrest African Americans than whites. Indeed, Black argues that the higher arrest rate for African Americans does not relate to race discrimination but to the fact that African Americans are more likely to be disrespectful to the arresting officer. Since disrespect is a fundamental breach of the working culture of the police, then the higher arrest rate for African Americans may be understood in these terms:

> The evidence . . . simply indicates that blacks are treated differently not because they are black, but because they manifest other behavioral patterns, such as disrespect for the police, more frequently than whites. The question of why blacks disproportionately show disrespect for the police cannot be addressed with the observational data. We could speculate, for example, that in anticipation of harsh treatment blacks often behave disrespectfully toward the police, thereby setting in motion a pattern that confirms their expectations (Black, 1972:1109).

Black's theory is concerned with how operating rules and guidelines developed within the social and cultural organization of police work serve to shape the responses of police to aspects of arrest situations. Once socialized into the police organization, individual officers develop a set of perceptual lenses through which they see the world. They come to share a common perspective and gauge their conduct accordingly. Peculiar to this perspective are operating rules—how situations should be handled. And, as Black has shown, these rules heavily influence how police officers will respond to different aspects of the arrest situation and, ultimately, who will and who will not become defined as deviant.

The Moral Career of the Mental Patient. Donald Black was concerned with how the informal social organization of police work influences the production of criminal definitions. The informal organizational processes whereby individuals are channeled into official categories defined as deviant is also a central concern for Erving Goffman (1961). Goffman refers to this theory as a theory of moral careers. He uses the term *moral* to refer to an individual's self-concept and, more specifically, to a person's judgment of his or her self-worth. Goffman's writings on total institutions, such as mental hospitals, focus on how institutionalization affects a person's self-image. While this is the most commonly recognized contribution of Goffman's book *Asylums*, his work also makes explicit the sociological forces at work through which individuals come to be publicly defined as persons who have mental illness. We focus on this aspect of his theorizing here. To begin, let us turn to Goffman's usage of the term *career*.

Goffman uses a *career model* to help understand how some individuals wind up being hospitalized for mental illness. He does not use the term *career* in reference to success or failure as it is typically used in, for example,

industry. Rather, he uses the term to denote the "changes over time as are basic and common to the members of a social category, although occurring independently of each other" (Goffman, 1961:126). As applied to his analysis of psychiatric hospitalization, the term suggests that all psychiatric patients go through some very similar stages as they move through the process of becoming institutionalized as mental patients.

For Goffman, the similarities that mark the career of the person who is to eventually become institutionalized clearly cannot be accounted for by similarities in personality or psychiatric condition. Patients who are presented for hospitalization display a wide range of personalities and problems. As Goffman observes:

> Persons who become mental hospital patients vary widely in the kind and degree of illness that a psychiatrist would impute to them, and in the attributes by which laymen would describe them. But once started on the way, they are confronted by some importantly similar circumstances and respond to these in some importantly similar ways. Hence these similarities do not come from mental illness, they would seem to occur in spite of it. It is thus a tribute to the power of social forces that the uniform status of mental patient can not only assure an aggregate of persons a common fate and eventually, because of this, a common character, but that this social reworking can be done upon what is perhaps the most obstinate diversity of human materials that can be brought together by society (Goffman, 1961:129).

Since an important part of this common fate—hospitalization for mental illness—cannot be easily explained by such a *diversity* of human conditions, Goffman attempts to identify the formal and informal organizational forces that may account for similar career patterns among individuals who are eventually hospitalized. From his research as participant observer at a major psychiatric institution, Goffman believes he has identified the crucial phases in the career of the psychiatric patient. Further, he suggests that each stage is characterized by critical interactions between the patient, his or her family, and the psychiatric community (specifically, the hospital ward psychiatrists) that affect the process by which the patient will ultimately be accorded the diagnosis (definition) of mental illness. Goffman's central thesis may be put in the form of a question: "What are the informal and formal organizational forces operating that cause selected persons to be admitted to a psychiatric hospital and accorded the status of mental illness?"

In making this career understandable, Goffman divides the career of the mental patient into three distinct phases: the prepatient phase, the inpatient phase, and the expatient phase. Because we are interested here in how individuals get officially defined as deviant, our presentation of Goffman's work will be confined to the first, or prepatient, phase. During this critical phase, a person is perceived as being ill by informal social audiences, is brought to the attention of formal agencies of social control, becomes the target of a collaborative effort between audiences and agencies to commit the person to an institution, and is finally involuntarily committed.

The most significant event in the prepatient phase occurs when some complainant, takes action against the prepatient. "Here is the social beginning of the patient's career, regardless of where one might locate the psychological beginning of his mental illness" (Goffman, 1961:134). Many so-called "offenses," for instance, talking to oneself, emotional outbursts such as crying spells or violence, extreme social withdrawal, and even attempts at suicide, may result in an effective complaint. But whether a complaint will be effective seems to depend less on the symptoms being manifested and more on the social circumstances surrounding the complaint. Goffman refers to these circumstances as "career contingencies." The notion that

mental patients have career contingencies is quite similar to the idea that all careers have contingencies that determine career outcomes often independently of the skills and general "qualifications" of the employee. In like fashion, whether a prepatient will ultimately "make it" in terms of being hospitalized may hinge less on his or her "qualifications" (his or her psychiatric symptoms) and more on the social circumstances (contingencies) that surround a complaint. For example, factors such as the social class background of the prepatient, the visibility of the illness, and the number of treatment facilities in the area where the complaint is made figure heavily into determining whether the complaint will result in hospitalization—whether it will be "effective."

In addition to the complainant, there are other important role players in the prepatient phase of the psychiatric patient. One such role player, according to Goffman, is the *next-of-relation*. This is "the person whom the prepatient sees as the most available of those upon whom he should be able to most depend in times of trouble; in this instance the last to doubt his sanity and the first to have done everything to save him from the fate which, it transpires, he has been approaching" (Goffman, 1961:136). The next-of-relation may be the original complainant, but this is not always the case. Typically, however, the next-of-relation role is played by a relative of the prepatient. For adolescents, it is usually the parents. For the elderly, it is typically their adult children.

Still another important set of role players are the *mediators*—the sequence of agents and agencies to which the prepatient is referred and through which he is relayed and processed on his way to the hospital" (Goffman, 1961:129). Included among these mediators are the police, clergy, family doctors, social workers, and the psychiatric staff at the hospital. One of the mediators (often a judge) will have the legal power to involuntarily commit the prepatient to an institution. Once this has taken place, the institutional psychiatrist or hospital administrator becomes the sole mediator, and all others retire from the scene.

The roles of the complainant, next-of-relation, and mediator fit together as the prepatient moves from the status of civilian to that of mental patient. As the next-of-relation (most often a family member) works with the mediator (ultimately the institutional psychiatrist), the prepatient begins to feel a sense of betrayal. After all, the next-of-kin are those in whom the prepatient has placed unquestionable trust. Now, the prepatient finds that they are conspiring with the institutional psychiatrist to have the patient committed. The patient senses what Goffman has termed an *alienative coalition*. In Goffman's words:

> *Upon arrival at the office the prepatient suddenly finds that he and his next-of-relation have not been accorded the same roles, and apparently that a prior understanding between the professional and the next-of-relation has been put in operation against him. In the extreme but common case the professional first sees the prepatient alone, in the role of examiner and diagnostician, and then sees the next-of-relation alone, in the role of advisor, while carefully avoiding talking things over seriously with them both together . . . And even in those nonconsultative cases where public officials must forcibly extract a person from a family that wants to tolerate him, the next-of-relation is likely to be induced to "go along" with the official action, so that even here the prepatient may feel that an alienative coalition has been formed against him (Goffman, 1961:138).*

As we have described above, Goffman views the process whereby individuals come to be accorded the status of mental patient (and therefore defined as mentally ill) as a natural history with predictable phases. Whether an individual is ultimately accorded the status of mental patient, whether he or she is officially defined as deviant, depends on a host of sociological forces operating at various stages. If any of the social contingencies operating to channel a prepatient into an institution are absent, the prepatient is not as likely to be institutionalized *irrespective of the kind and degree of his or her illness*. From this perspective, mental illness is not discovered as an objective condition but manufactured by a collaborative effort between informal social audiences and formal agencies of social control.

The Making of Blind Men. Robert Scott (1969) applies organizational theory to understand the ways in which organizations for the blind actually create blindness! And since blindness is a personal attribute that violates norms regarding "ideal" conditions of being, the blindness organizations are also creating deviants. They do so by creating conceptions and misconceptions about blindness that are ultimately accepted by the general public. These conceptions and misconceptions are not only accepted by the general public. They are also accepted by persons with vision problems who find themselves caught up in the formal and informal social organization of the "blindness system." Scott underscores the point dramatically:

> *When those who have been screened into blindness agencies enter them, they may not be able to see at all or they may have serious difficulties with their vision. When they have been rehabilitated, they are all blind men. They have learned the attitudes and behavior patterns that professional blindness workers believe blind people should have. In the intensive face-to-face relationships between blindness workers and clients that make up the rehabilitation process, the blind person is rewarded for adopting a view of himself that is consistent with his rehabilitators' view of him and punished for clinging to other self-conceptions . . . Indeed, passage through the blindness system is determined in part by his willingness to adopt the experts' views about self (Scott, 1969:119) [emphasis added].*

Intense socialization is the fundamental process by which blindness organizations fashion the self-images, attitudes, and behavioral patterns of the blind. According to Scott, blindness is learned. "Blind men are not born, they are made" (1969:120). What he means is that blindness is as much a social role as it is a physical condition. The role behaviors and accompanying attitudes are learned in the context of organizations for the blind. As Scott suggests, the process is compelling:

> My analysis suggests that such organizations create *for blind people the experiences of being blind. Such organizations are not, as some have suggested, merely helpers of the blind that facilitate or change processes already occurring; rather they are active socializing agents that create and mold the fundamental attitudes and patterns of behavior that are at the core of the experience of being a blind man (Scott, 1969:121).*

Through time, the beliefs, attitudes, and behaviors of the blind come to correspond with the assumptions and commonsense theories that workers with the blind hold about blindness (Scott, 1969:121). These beliefs correspond to either of two alternative approaches or philosophies of treatment for the blind. The first, or *restorative approach,* assumes that blind people can resume lives of relative independence if they confront the fact of their blindness. As the approach suggests, the aim of organizations guided by this conception is to restore the blind person to meaningful participation in the sighted world. The second, or *accommodative approach,* assumes that the blind person will have to remain dependent on the agencies and organizations designed to help them. The goal of a life of independence in the sighted world is unrealistic from this perspective. The blind must accommodate themselves to the protective environments provided by blindness agencies and organizations.

As it turns out, most blindness organizations embrace the accommodative philosophy. There are some very practical reasons for this. That is, there are *organizational imperatives*—things an organization must accom

plish to remain a viable concern—that push a blindness agency in the direction of an accommodative philosophy. First, blindness organizations must respond to outside pressures if they are to survive as going concerns. One such pressure stems from the "unconscious desire of many persons in the sighted community to avoid blind people by hiding them" (Scott, 1969:120). Agencies that provide this function for the community are more likely to receive healthy donations. Generous donations are vital for the survival of blindness organizations. Second, blindness agencies must compete for clients. "Competition . . . arises between blindness agencies in the same community for the comparatively small number of blind people in it who can benefit from the services they offer" (Scott, 1969:120). Given that competition is often fierce, the accommodative approach ensures a stable and relatively constant supply of clients. Third, the blindness workers need to protect their jobs. Most have received little or no professional training. They are quick to learn that their jobs are more secure in an agency that is financially sound. They cannot "ignore the fact that the agency's fiscal integrity is more secure when an accommodative approach is adopted" (Scott, 1969:120).

The above organizational imperatives make adequate socialization into the blindness agency even more important. Adequate socialization creates blindness as a fundamental self-conception and as a public identity. Moreover, the blind must come to accept the accommodative philosophy to ensure that the organizational imperatives of the blindness agency will be met. If socialization is effective, if the person with vision problems is transformed into a "blind man" or "blind woman," then the blindness organization will survive as a going concern.

Evaluating Organizational Theories. Organizational theorists seek to uncover the informal rules of agencies of social control.

These rules guide the creation of deviance categories and placement of people within them. The theoretical interest, almost of necessity, requires a participant observation methodology. The intention is to get inside the experience of the agency worker (law enforcement officer, social worker, blindness worker, and so on) in order to capture the world as they see it. Only from the standpoint of the agency worker may one ever hope to understand the informal rules and working assumptions that guide deviance creating activities.

Some critics have argued that, since participant observation methodologies involve the subjective perceptions of the observer, conclusions based on such an approach may be less than reliable—less than scientific. The criticism comes, of course, from sociologists of deviance who adhere to the more "objective" approach usually associated with rigorous quantitative techniques. But is that approach really more objective? Scott and Douglas (1972) believe it is not. They argue that sociologists who think that they are being objective by not getting in touch with the subjective experiences of the people they study are really substituting their own biased conceptions of reality for those of the common person. Here, Scott and Douglas are drawing from the philosophy of science known as phenomenology. From the phenomenological perspective, there are the experiences of those being studied and then there are the experiences of those who are studying them (the sociologists). The experiences of those being studied are called "constructs of the first order" (Schutz, 1962:5). The constructs (conceptions) of the "objective" scientist are really constructs of the constructs of the everyday person. Hence, they are "constructs of the second order" (Schutz, 1962:6). They are one step removed from reality as it is experienced by the person being studied. Good phenomenological inquiry is always a study of first-order constructs. As it pertains

to the current discussion, organizational theorists who study the personal experiences of the agency worker are doing what they should do: investigating the true reality as it is revealed in the everyday experiences of agency personnel.

MICRO-SUBJECTIVIST THEORIES

Macro-subjectivist theories aim at identifying large-scale social, economic, and political forces that influence the creation of deviance definitions. Micro-subjectivist theories center attention on the social interaction processes through which audiences interpret, define, and label acts as deviance or persons as deviants.

Those who are interested in how deviance definitions are created and applied at the micro level, study two related sets of phenomena. First, as we shall see from the work of Kitsuse (1962), they attempt to capture the social-psychological processes that operate in constructing deviance definitions. What goes on in the psychological world of the labelers that leads them to the conclusion that someone is essentially deviant? Called by some the "phenomenological approach," this method aims to make explicit the inner world of meanings social audiences use to draw conclusions about the deviant status of an alleged offender.

The other phenomenon studied by those interested in the creation of deviance definitions at the micro level are the social conditions under which individuals are more or less likely to be labeled deviant. Such variables as age, sex, race, and physical appearance are examined with the claim that such social factors are important in predicting whose acts will be defined as deviance and who will be branded as deviant even if behavior is held constant! That is, whether individuals receive the deviant label may depend less on what they do and more on who they are!

Definitional Theories

Retrospective Interpretation and Sexual Deviance.
John Kitsuse (1962) may be considered one of the foremost proponents of the micro-subjectivist approach. Conceptualizing deviance in subjectivist terms, he suggests that the focus of theory and research on deviance should turn away from deviant behavior toward the reactions of others to it:

> *I propose to shift the focus of theory and research from the forms of deviant behavior to the* processes by which persons come to be defined as deviant by others. *Such a shift requires that the sociologist view as problematic what he generally assumes as given—namely, that certain forms of behavior are per se* deviant *and are so defined by the "conventional or conforming members of a group." This assumption is frequently called into question on empirical grounds when the societal reaction to behaviors defined as deviant by the sociologist is nonexistent, indifferent, or at most mildly disapproving* (Kitsuse, 1962:248).

If it is not norm-violating behavior but the reaction of others that distinguishes deviance from conformity and deviants from conformists, then what are the essential elements of these societal reactions? Kitsuse proposes the following three elements as central to the interactional sequence that results in deviance designation:

> *[D]eviance may be conceived as a process by which the members of a group, community, or society (1) interpret behavior as deviant, (2) define persons who so behave as a certain kind of deviant, and (3) accord them the treatment considered appropriate to such deviants (Kitsuse, 1962:248).*

It is clear that, in seeking understanding of how deviance definitions are created, Kitsuse is interested in the social-psychological processes that operate in the minds of the labelers. His sequential model of deviance designation is presented in Table 3–1. Interpretation involves the process by which a social audience gathers various kinds of evidence that the behaviors (real or rumored) signify that deviance has occurred. Defining individuals (labeling) as being the kinds of people the labelers believe them to be involves reinterpreting their past in light of an initial interpretation. Finally, whether a person will be disapproved of (sanctioned) will depend on the results of the definitional processes of interpretation and labeling.

To test his model, Kitsuse interviewed 700 undergraduates about various types of deviance. Of the 700, 75 said they had known a homosexual—the type of sexual deviance Kitsuse was interested in studying. Kitsuse asked the respondents three questions, each one eliciting information about the definitional processes in his model. For example, the question, "When was the first time you noticed (found out) that this person was homosexual?" provided answers indicating that the kinds of behaviors people use as evidence of homosexuality vary a considerable degree. Contrary to the objectivist conception of deviance, the norms stipulating sex-appropriate (or sex-inappropriate) behaviors are not as clear or widely shared as the objectivist would appear to suggest. "[T]he concepts of persons in everyday life concerning 'sex-appropriate' or 'sex-inappropriate' behavior may lead them to interpret a variety of behavioral forms as indications of the same deviation, and the 'same' behavioral forms as indications of a variety of deviant as well as 'normal' behavior" (Kitsuse, 1962:255).

The second question, "What did you make of that?" yielded information on "the inferential process by which the subject linked his information about the individual to the deviant category 'homosexual'" (Kitsuse, 1962:253). The critical issue is the process whereby kinds of behaviors are taken as evidence of kinds of people. In this connection, the respondents often used *retrospective inter-*

TABLE 3.1	Kitsuse's Sequential Model of Deviance Designation.				
Behavior	→	Interpretation	→	Labeling	→	Sanctions

pretation to document their initial imputation of homosexuality.

> A general pattern revealed by the subjects' responses to this section of the interview schedule is that when an individual's sexual "normality" is called into question, by whatever form of evidence, the imputation of homosexuality is documented by retrospective interpretations *of the deviant's behavior*, a process by which the subject re-interprets the individual's past behavior in the light of the new information concerning his sexual deviance *(Kitsuse, 1962:253) [emphasis added].*

The third question posed by Kitsuse was "What did you do then?" This question was aimed at documenting societal reactions (sanctions) to the imputed deviance. The responses to this question showed that the reactions ranged from "explicit disapproval and immediate withdrawal" to "no disapproval and relationship sustained" (Kitsuse, 1962:254). To the extent that sanctions by social audiences serve to distinguish deviants from non-deviants, the variation in reaction found by Kitsuse suggests that sanctions are important *independent* variables in the process whereby deviance is socially constructed.

Deviance and Respectability. Kitsuse's theory centered on the social-psychological processes employed by social audiences in creating and applying deviance definitions. Another approach taken by micro-subjectivists, as they seek to understand the definitional process, is to study various social status characteristics such as age, race, sex, and appearance of the alleged offender. The micro-subjectivist would predict that being branded deviant depends as much on *who you are* as it does on *what you do* in terms of norm-violating behaviors.

Guided by the subjectivist's emphasis on societal reactions in defining deviance, Darrell Steffensmeier and Robert Terry (1973) conducted a field experiment to test the basic idea that shoplifters are more likely to be reported by an observer if the shoplifter is male rather than female and is dressed like a "hippie" rather than a "straight" person. The reason for their hypotheses stems from the notion that an "actor's social identity is a crucial determinant of reactions to deviant behavior" (Steffensmeier and Terry, 1973: 418). Certain social identities are more likely to be stigmatized and used as a basis upon which others infer deviant characteristics beyond the particular social identity at hand. As Steffensmeier and Terry observe:

> Much of the literature in the [labeling] perspective has argued that differential treatment is accorded persons with poor social backgrounds, less than perfect social identities, or "bad" reputations. Many analyses of deviant categories are founded on the assumption that particular classes of people are more likely to perform deviant acts and to be particular types of deviant persons . . . Such studies are highly consistent in arguing that respectability decreases the likelihood of deviant imputation, whereas "unrespectability" has the opposite effect (Steffensmeier and Terry, 1973:418).

Their research involved getting the cooperation of the management at various department stores. Then the researchers had one of their research assistants (either a male "hippie," a female "hippie," a male "straight" person, or a female "straight" person) shoplift in the presence and clear vision of a regular store customer. Confident that the customer had seen the shoplifting event, another research assistant dressed in clothing worn by other store personnel, approached the customer and asked if they had observed anything suspicious. If the customer was unwilling to report the shoplifter, then another research assistant approached the customer a second time to attempt to prod the customer into reporting what they had seen.

Of special interest for the subjectivist orientation that guided the research was whether the sex of the shoplifter, sex of the customer, or appearance of the shoplifter ("hippie" versus "straight") influenced customers' willingness to report the shoplifting event. While sex of either shoplifter or customer did not appear to influence reporting, the *appearance* of the shoplifter had a strong impact:

> *The evidence presented clearly indicates that a hippie appearance constituted a highly salient basis for social differentiation. From the perspective of "middle class" America, hippies and other beatnik types are viewed as basically unstable, as lacking in ambition and ability, and as marginal contributors to the social system. By the mere fact of being a hippie the person has demonstrated his lack of moral worth, his unrespectability, from the dominant cultural perspective (Steffensmeier and Terry, 1973:424).*

The research by Steffensmeier and Terry provides support for the hypothesis that the attribution of a deviant label is often determined by actors' social identity rather than their norm-violating behavior. The point is particularly convincing because the experiment was rigged so that *all* "shoplifters" were seen taking merchandise without intent to pay. Since all "shoplifters" were equally guilty, the only way to account for the customers' willingness to report the crime was to consider the customers' attributions about the kinds of people "hippies" really are.

Evaluating Definitional Theories. How do social audiences construct deviance definitions? This question is at the heart of definitional theories, the most notable example being Kitsuse's sequential theory of deviance. Since deviance is conceptualized as a defini-

tion, the theories tend to ignore norms in trying to understand how deviance definitions are created. If one were to suggest that acts or persons are defined as deviance or deviants because norms have been violated, the statement would be automatically suspect, because norms do not define deviance or deviants; only audience reactions do that. Therefore, we have to study the social-psychological processes of the social audience to grasp how deviance definitions are created. But what determines when and if an audience will react? Does behavior have anything to do with it? Are norms completely irrelevant? If the answers to these questions are in the affirmative, then what determines the kind and intensity of reactions in the absence of normative considerations?

The above questions reflect standard criticism of the micro-subjectivist orientation, and particularly Kitsuse's expression of it. While the criticisms should be taken seriously (and they have), they appear less forceful when considering behaviors over which there is little normative agreement. What else will define cheating on a college exam as deviance except the reactions of some social audience? Clearly, there is not widespread agreement about whether students who cheat on such exams are engaging in deviance. Cheating is not deviance because it violates generally agreed-upon norms; such norms are ambiguous at best. Therefore, while the standard criticisms of the micro-subjectivist appear most forceful when considering behaviors about which there are clear and unambiguous norms, the criticisms are less lethal when considering acts that are normatively ambiguous. It is in these cases that audience reactions become most salient in defining deviance (acts) or deviants (persons).

Labeling Theories

In our discussion of micro-subjectivist theories thus far, we have seen that the principal focus was on definitional processes. This involved both how deviance definitions are created and how and to whom they are applied. In this section, we include labeling theories that attempt to account for the processes by which audience reactions, in the form of sanctions and stigmatizing labels, serve to increase the very behaviors complained of. Here, the link between societal reactions and deviant careers becomes a central theme.

The Dramatization of Evil.   Frank Tannenbaum, in a brief but penetrating statement from his book *Crime and Community* (1938), describes the subtle process by which a definition of an act committed by an individual as evil is transformed into a definition of the individual as evil. Defining the person (rather than his or her behavior) as deviant, takes its toll on the person's self-concept. A changed self-image as deviant has a tendency to influence future deviance in the labeled individual. For Tannenbaum, defining a person as deviant is a crucial step in creating the very behaviors complained of. Let us examine his thesis in greater detail.

First, a person is likely to be defined as deviant when his or her acts violate the conventional standards of the larger community. The definition arises out of conflict between what the "delinquent" defines as "play, adventure, excitement, interest, mischief . . . or fun" (Tannenbaum, 1938:8). For example, such acts as stealing fruit from pushcarts, skipping school, running through other people's porches, smashing windows, and annoying people in general, are defined as normal from the point of view of the juvenile (Tannenbaum, 1938:8). To the community, however, "these activities may and often do take on the form of a nuisance, evil, delinquency, with the demand for control, admonition, chastisement, punishment, police court, truant school" (Tannenbaum, 1938:8). Slowly, the definition of the situation is redefined such that the juvenile is seen in a completely different light:

There is a gradual shift from the definition of the specific acts as evil to a definition of the individual as evil, so that all his acts come to be looked upon with suspicion. In the process of identification his companions, hang-outs, play, speech, income, all his conduct, the personality itself, become subject to scrutiny and question. From the community's point of view, the individual who used to do bad and mischievous things has now become a bad and unredeemable human being (Tannenbaum, 1938:17).

This "dramatization of evil" not only has a public aspect. That is, an individual is not only perceived and defined as evil from the perspective of the larger community. The person begins to think of himself or herself as evil as well. The one who is singled out and labeled begins to recognize that he or she is looked upon as being different from the rest of the other youth in the school, street, neighborhood, or community. "This recognition on his part becomes a process of self-identification. . . . [t]he young delinquent becomes bad because he is defined as bad *and* because he is not believed if he is good" (Tannenbaum, 1938:18). It appears that the harder the conventional community attempts to correct, the greater the likelihood of a deviant self-identification on the part of the person labeled. Further, the tendency of the labeled individual to continue in a deviance career is increased. The conflict between the juvenile and the conventional community becomes a clash of wills.

It is the dramatization of evil, then, that serves more than any other factor to make the deviant. The labeled person now lives in a different world. It is not only the person's acts that are regarded as evil, but the very person himself or herself. Tannenbaum summarizes the process:

This process of making the criminal, therefore, is a process of tagging, defining, identifying, segregating, describing, emphasizing, making conscious and self-conscious; it becomes a way of stimulating, suggesting, emphasizing, and evoking the very traits that are complained of. If the theory of relation of response to stimulus has any meaning, the entire process of dealing with the young delinquent is mischievous in so far as it identifies him to himself or to the environment as a delinquent person (Tannenbaum, 1938:19).

In Tannenbaum's statement of the "dramatization of evil," once public labeling has occurred, the juvenile begins to engage in the self-same behaviors that the community has complained of—a special case of what Merton has called the self-fulfilling prophecy.

The Theory of Secondary Deviation. In 1951, Edwin Lemert published his now influential book entitled *Social Pathology*. In a way, the title of his book is misleading because he was rejecting the idea that deviants were somehow "pathological" at the level of personality. Rather, his thesis was to show that deviance was the product of the *interaction* between social actors and the reactions of society to them. A central concept in Lemert's theory is *societal reaction*, which he defined as the "over-all responses of persons and groups of a society to deviation" (Lemert, 1951:49). Though Lemert appeared to suggest that there was a fairly high correspondence between the seriousness of norm-violation and the intensity of societal reaction, he still contended that "cases are easily discovered in which a somewhat minor violation of legal rules has provoked surprisingly stringent penalties" (1951:55). In pointing to the discrepancy (rather than correspondence) between act and label, Lemert is acknowledging the importance of the subjectivist conception of deviance.

The most lasting contribution of Lemert's theorizing lies in his distinction between primary and secondary deviance. *Primary deviation* refers to instances of norm-violation without the actor viewing himself or herself as engaging in a deviant role. As Lemert pointed out, "deviations remain primary deviations . . . as long as they are rationalized or otherwise dealt with as functions of a so-

cially acceptable role" (Lemert, 1951:75). Cheating on a classroom exam, for example, may be perceived by the cheater as normal behavior for a college student. After all, "everybody does it!" Or, getting drunk every Friday night at the local campus hangout may not be viewed as deviant by drinkers because their behavior has remained somewhat invisible to their heavy drinking peers.

But what if the heavy drinking continues to the point at which there is a societal reaction? Friends, and maybe even the police, call attention to the behavior and react negatively. If the individual continues to engage in heavy alcohol use, perhaps as a show of resentment and hostility toward those who are condemning, then one possible outcome of such an interactional sequence is secondary deviation. *Secondary deviation* is when "a person begins to employ his deviant behavior or a role based upon it as a means of defense, attack, or adjustment to the . . . problems created by the consequent societal reaction to him" (Lemert, 1951:76).

At this point, a reorganization of self-concept occurs so that the self becomes consistent with the deviant role. Societal reactions may not have caused the initial (primary) deviance, but once it is publicly labeled, a self-fulfilling prophecy creates the very behavior complained of. Lemert presents an example of how primary deviation may culminate in secondary deviation, which is the result of negative societal labels:

> *As an illustration of this sequence the behavior of an errant schoolboy can be cited. For one reason or another, let us say excessive energy, the schoolboy engages in a class-room prank. He is penalized for it by the teacher. Later, due to clumsiness, he creates another disturbance and, again he is reprimanded. Then, as sometimes happens, the boy is blamed for something he did not do. When the teacher uses the tag "bad boy" or "mischief maker" or other invidious terms, hostility and resentment are excited in the boy, and he may feel that he is blocked in playing the role expected of him. Thereafter, there*

may be a strong temptation to assume his role in the class as defined by the teacher, particularly when he discovers that there are rewards as well as penalties deriving from such a role (Lemert, 1951:77).

It is critical to note here that there must be a spreading corroboration of a deviant self-conception and social reinforcement at each stage in the process of becoming a secondary deviant (Lemert, 1951:77). Deviant self-conceptions are reinforced by others' negative labels, which are, in turn, perpetuated by the deviant's norm-violating actions.

The Theory of Career Deviance. Howard Becker's *Outsiders* (1963) did more to popularize labeling theory than any other single work. Indeed, the very term itself appears to come from Becker's subjectivist conception of deviance:

> *[D]eviance is not a quality of the act the person commits, but rather a consequence of the application by others of rules and sanctions to an "offender." The deviant is one to whom that label has successfully been applied; deviant behavior is behavior that people so label (Becker, 1963:9).*

But Becker's contribution to the sociology of deviance goes beyond his insistence upon conceptualizing deviance in terms of societal reactions. Like Lemert, he was interested in the process by which deviant labels influence secondary deviance or, for Becker, "deviant careers." Even so, norm-violation or, for Becker, "rule breaking," should not be interpreted as behavior that violates the normative consensus of society. For Becker, deviance is always a label affixed to acts and persons by social audiences. With this in mind, let us turn to the essential ingredients of Becker's theory of how societal reactions produce career deviance.

You may recall from our discussion of Becker's typology of deviance in Chapter 1 that many people engage in rule breaking but go undetected. They are, for Becker, engaging in "secret deviance." For the most part, those

who commit secret deviance are likely to be perceived as living predominantly conventional lives. They are not embarked on a criminal career. A little cheating here, a little shoplifting there, but no deep commitment to a life of crime.

But what if their deviance is detected? What if they get caught? For Becker, one of the most important steps in the process of becoming involved in a deviant career is "the experience of being caught and publicly labeled as deviant" (Becker, 1963:31). And, "being caught and branded has important consequences for one's further social participation and one's self-image" (Becker, 1963:31). Others tend to act as though the labeled person is generally rather than specifically deviant. In other words, the labeled person is cast into a master status of deviant. The *master status of deviant* causes an individual to be identified as a deviant prior to any other social identifications:

> *Treating a person as though he were generally rather than specifically deviant produces a self-fulfilling prophecy. It sets in motion several mechanisms which conspire to shape the person in the image people have of him (Becker, 1963:34).*

Moreover, being cast into a master status of deviant, such as "ex-con," "fag," or "drunk," operates so that "one tends to be cut off . . . from participation in more conventional groups" (Becker, 1963:34). As labeled individuals are denied active participation in conventional groups, they become increasingly involved in organized deviant groups whose members have been similarly labeled. Over time, the group members begin to share a common *deviant subculture*, "a set of perspectives and understandings about what the world is like and how to deal with it (Becker, 1963:38). Being a member of a deviant subculture helps reinforce the labeled person's identity as the kind of deviant he or she has been defined as. With a new identity as deviant, and a deviant subculture to provide justifications and rationalizations for further deviance, the deviant "is more likely than ever before to continue in his ways" (Becker, 1963:39).

On Being Mentally Ill.   In his theory of mental illness, Scheff (1966) continues the labeling tradition that Tannenbaum originated in 1938. Scheff begins his role theory of mental illness by rejecting the view that the symptoms of mental illness reflect deep underlying personality disorders or genetic influence. Rather, he argues that what are traditionally thought of as symptoms of mental illness are really behaviors that don't quite fit into the categories of deviance or conformity generally recognized by members of society. Since society has not developed clear labels for these behaviors (symptoms), we tend to think of them as strange, weird, or bizarre and as evidence of deep psychological disturbance. Table 3–2 contains all of Scheff's propositions of becoming mentally ill. We may capture the essential points of his propositions by way of an example.

Suppose that every time you had a conversation with a fellow student he talked with his back toward you. He might carry on a perfectly reasonable conversation. Nothing else is odd except that he talks with his back toward you. Scheff uses this as an example of what he calls *residual deviance*. The word

residual means "what's left over." Scheff uses it to refer to social behaviors that don't quite fit into our ideas of acceptable or unacceptable behavior. They are behaviors that are odd but are not generally regarded as full blown deviance:

> *The culture of the group provides a vocabulary of terms for categorizing many norm violations: crime, perversion, drunkenness, and bad manners are familiar examples. Each of these terms is derived from the type of norm broken, and ultimately, from the type of behavior involved. After exhausting these categories, however, there is always a residue of the most diverse kinds of violations, for which the culture provides no explicit label . . . For convenience of the society on constructing those instances of unnamable deviance which are called to its attention, these violations may be lumped together into a residual category: witchcraft, spirit possession, or in our society, mental illness (Scheff, 1966:33–34).*

According to Scheff, persons who engage in these types of behaviors are most likely to be labeled "mentally ill" thereby triggering a sequence of events that culminate in the labeled individual adopting the role of mental illness. What is the nature of this sequence of events? What happens when a person who engages in residual deviance is labeled "mentally ill"? According to Scheff, the labeled person has learned during childhood how mentally ill people behave. Through cartoons in childhood and the mass media and normal

---

TABLE 3.2   Propositions in Scheff's Theory of Mental Illness.

1. Residual deviance arises from fundamentally diverse sources.
2. Relative to the rate of treated mental illness, the rate of unrecorded residual deviance is extremely high.
3. Most residual deviance is "denied" and is transitory.
4. Stereotyped imagery of mental illness is learned in early childhood.
5. The stereotypes of insanity are continually reaffirmed, inadvertently, in ordinary social interaction.
6. Labeled deviants may be rewarded for playing the stereotyped deviant role.
7. Labeled deviants are punished when they attempt the return to conventional roles.
8. In the crisis occurring when a primary deviant is publicly labeled, the deviant is highly suggestible, and may accept the proffered role of the insane as the only alternative.
9. Among residual deviants, labeling is the single most important cause of careers of residual deviance.

social interaction in adulthood, individuals learn the stereotyped imagery of the "kook," the "nut," and the "insane." In other words, through the mass media and other sources, stereotyped images of the mentally ill role have become institutionalized in our society, what Scheff refers to as the "institution of insanity." Once labeled "mentally ill," a person becomes "suggestible." This implies that people become psychologically insecure when confronted by official and unofficial charges of mental illness. Because of this insecurity, they are rendered more likely to accept the definition others have of them and the mentally ill role into which they are being cast. As Scheff suggests:

> *The rule-breaker is sensitive to the cues provided by these others and begins to think of himself in terms of the stereotyped role of insanity, which is part of his own role vocabulary also, since he, like those reacting to him, follow[s] the pattern suggested by his own stereotypes and the reactions of others. That is, when a primary deviant organizes his behavior within the framework of mental disorder, and when his organization is validated by others, particularly prestigious others such as physicians, he is "hooked" and will proceed on a career of chronic deviance (Scheff, 1966:88).*

From Scheff's role theory of mental illness, it is clear that labeling is the single most important cause in the development of the mentally ill role and, more generally, in the development of deviant careers.

Evaluating Labeling Theories. The idea that societal reactions may have adverse consequences for the person who is their target is an important contribution to the sociology of deviance. Prior to the development of labeling theories, societal or audience reactions were considered only as dependent variables. That is, the reactions of social audiences, such as the police and courts, were in response to norm-violating behaviors. Response was always thought to follow deviance. With the advent of labeling theory, societal reactions

were reconceptualized as important independent variables. From this point of view, societal reactions could lead to the development of further deviance. One may state a central hypothesis that emphasizes this point: Official or unofficial labels will increase the probability of future deviance.

This is a theoretical statement amenable to empirical testing. While some studies have reported favorable evidence for this hypothesis, a comprehensive evaluation by Gove (1975) and his collaborators suggests that the hypothesis enjoys far less support than labeling theorists would claim. Especially important was the review of the evidence by Tittle (1975). He examined studies for which there were sufficient data to permit a comparison between labeling theory and the deterrence doctrine. Of course, deterrence theory predicts exactly the opposite of the labeling approach. For deterrence theory, the greater the official or unofficial sanctioning, the less the likelihood of deviance. According to Tittle's analysis, the majority of the studies supported the deterrence doctrine.

In spite of these negative findings regarding the labeling hypothesis, the theory is not dead! Additional research is needed to determine under what conditions labeling will either increase or decrease future deviance. As a possibility, labeling theory suggests that negative labels influence self-concepts, which, in turn, influence deviance. If Tittle's review had factored in self-concepts among those who were labeled, he might have found that labeling does serve to increase deviance among those whose self-concepts were altered by the labeling experience. Indeed, a recent study by Ward and Tittle (1993) showed that informal peer sanctions increased stigmatizing labels and that these labels influenced the self-concepts of those labeled. Self-concepts, in turn, increase the likelihood of future deviance, in this case cheating on classroom exams. Ward and Tittle conclude that labeling theory may better predict the impact of sanctions on behavior when minor forms of deviance are concerned, whereas deterrence theory may better predict the relationship between sanctions and behavior when more serious forms of deviance are at issue. The validity of their conclusion will have to be determined by future research.

SUMMARY

Macro-subjectivist theories center attention on the social, economic, and political factors involved in the creation of deviance definitions, including formal laws. Though there are important differences between theories, we have suggested that all macro-subjectivist theories may be subsumed under the category of *interest group theories*. Neo-Marxist theories contend that deviance definitions (particularly, formal laws) are created by the state to protect the material interests of the capitalist class. Gusfield's theory of status politics suggests that laws are enacted by the powerful to symbolize their status in society and to reaffirm their cultural superiority. Erikson emphasized that deviance definitions are created to define the boundaries between deviance and conformity. Also, according to Erikson's analysis, deviance definitions are created to protect the interests of the powerful.

Another category of macro-subjectivist theories are organizational theories. *Organizational theories* focus on how the needs and culture of organizations of social control, such as law enforcement officers, psychiatric institutions, and agencies for the blind, produce deviance by selecting individuals from the total population of suspected rule breakers to be included in the categories defined as deviant. The deviance categories for each organization or agency reflect its particular *organizational imperatives*—the things that must get done for the organization to remain a viable concern.

Black's analysis of the social organization of police arrests shows that the practical rules of police work guide the officer in responding to certain aspects of the arrest situation. Goffman's work on involuntary commitment to mental institutions points to the importance of both informal and formal social organization in channeling the prepatient into the status of the mentally ill. Finally, Scott's penetrating analysis, *The Making of Blind Men*, underscores the organizational dynamics involved in creating the publicly regarded status of blindness.

Micro-subjectivist theories may be divided into two categories: definitional theories and labeling theories. *Definitional theories* seek to understand the social interaction processes through which informal social audiences create and apply deviance definitions. Interpreting, defining, labeling, and sanctioning are all parts of this definitional process. Other definitional theorists attempt to discover the social conditions that increase the likelihood that an offender will be labeled deviant. For example, Steffensmeier and Terry were able to show that an offender's personal appearance predicted whether witnesses to a crime would report the crime.

Labeling theory focuses on the social interaction processes whereby audience reactions (labels) create the very behaviors labeled deviance. These theories go beyond the definitional process to explore the way social interaction between labelers and labeled results in secondary deviation or "career deviance." Early on, Tannenbaum suggested that "tagging" may create the very behaviors complained of through a self-fulfilling prophecy. Later, Lemert, by distinguishing between primary and secondary deviance, underscored the importance of audience reactions in creating deviance. *Primary deviance* refers to norm-violating acts that do not result in a stigmatizing label. *Secondary devi-*

ance refers to norm-violating acts that result from the self-fulfilling nature of the labeling process. Becker was interested in how the labeling process pushes labeled individuals in the direction of participation in deviant subcultures. The concept of master status is central to Becker's formulation of the negative consequences of stigmatizing labels. A *master status* is a social status that carries more weight than any other status a person holds in shaping others' reactions toward that person. To be labeled "deviant" casts an individual into a master status; others tend to react toward the individual almost exclusively in terms of his or her deviant social identity. According to Becker, being cast into the master status of deviant cuts a person off from participation in more conventional social relationships and, by consequence, pushes the person further in the direction of a deviant subculture. Scheff's role theory of mental illness centers around the concept of residual deviance. *Residual deviance* refers to behaviors that may be regarded as odd but for which society has not created a deviance category within which such behaviors may be readily placed. According to Scheff, those persons who engage in residual deviance have a high probability of being labeled "mentally ill."

GLOSSARY

Alienative coalition In Goffman's portrayal of the moral career of the mental patient, a situation in which the patient is being conspired against by close relatives and friends on the one hand and the institutional psychiatrist on the other. The coalition is particularly critical when the case involves involuntary commitment to a psychiatric hospital.

Definitional theories Micro-subjectivist theories that seek to understand the social interaction processes through which social audiences create deviance definitions.

Dramatization of evil For Tannenbaum, the process whereby acts defined as deviance are transformed into persons defined as deviants.

Institution of insanity Stereotyped images of the mentally ill role that have become institutionalized in a society through their portrayal in the mass media.

Interest group theories Theories that point to social, economic, and political factors in the creation of deviance definitions. While there are differences between interest group theories, they have a common thread: Deviance definitions are the product of battles between competing interest groups. The group that gains political power is able to translate its value and material interests into laws.

Labeling theories Micro-subjectivist theories that focus on the social interaction processes whereby audience reactions (labels) create the very behavior labeled "deviance."

Macro-subjectivist theories Deviance theories that center attention on the social, economic, and political factors involved in the creation of deviance definitions, including formal laws.

Master status A social status that carries more weight than any other status a person may hold in shaping others' reactions to that person. To be labeled as a kind of "deviant" casts an individual into a master status causing others to respond to that person almost exclusively in terms of the deviant social identity.

Moral career Goffman's term suggesting that mental patients go through quite similar stages in the process by which social control agencies shape the patient's privately held self-concept and publicly acknowledged social identity.

Organizational theories Macro-subjectivist theories that emphasize the importance

of informal norms of organizations of social control in the process by which individuals come to be defined as deviant.

Primary deviance   According to Lemert, rule-
breaking acts that do not result in a stigmatizing label.

Residual deviance   Behaviors that may be regarded as odd but for which society has
not created a deviance category. According to Scheff, those who engage in
residual deviance are prime candidates
for the label "mental illness."

Retrospective interpretation   The process by
which social audiences reinterpret the
history of a person who has been labeled
"deviant" to legitimize a stigmatizing
label.

Secondary deviance   According to Lemert,
norm-violating acts that result from the
self-fulfilling nature of the labeling process.

SUGGESTED READINGS

Erikson, Kai. *Wayward Puritans.* New York: Wiley,
1966. In this engaging analysis, Erikson uses
historical data of the great crime waves of
Puritan New England to show how societies
create deviance definitions to maintain the
moral boundaries of society.

Goffman, Erving. *Asylums.* Garden City, N.Y.: Anchor Books, 1961. In this penetrating study,
one of the most insightful students of human
interaction examines the many sociological
forces at work in total institutions—complex
organizations such as prisons and mental institutions—to show how they transform the
identities of individuals in order to manage
them.

Gusfield, Joseph R. *Symbolic Crusade.* Urbana, Ill.:
University of Illinois Press, 1963. This is one of
the most graphic presentations of the interest
group perspective in the creation of deviance
definitions. Gusfield traces the social, political, and historical forces at work in outlawing
the production, sale, and consumption of alcohol in American society during Prohibition.

Scott, Robert. *The Making of Blind Men.* New York:

Sage, 1969. In this illuminating work, Scott
shows that the social organization of blindness foundations is structured to transform
clients into believing they need the blindness
organization for their personal survival—a
classic case of the "helpers need the helped!"

REFERENCES

Axthelm, Pete and David L. Gonzalez, "A 'Death
Wish' Vigilante" *Newsweek* January, 1985: p.
34.

Becker, Howard S. *Outsiders.* New York: Free Press,
1963.

Black, Donald J. "The Social Organization of Arrest." *Stanford Law Review* 23 (1971): pp.
1087–1111.

Carter, Timothy and Donald Clelland, "A Neo-
Marxian Critique, Formulation and Test of Ju-
venile Dispositions as a Function of Social
Class," *Social Problems* 27, 1979: pp. 96–108.

Erikson, Kai. *Wayward Puritans.* New York: Wiley,
1966.

Goffman, Erving. *Asylums.* Garden City, New
York: Anchor Books, 1961.

Gove, Walter R. ed. *The Labeling of Deviance.* New
York: Wiley, 1975.

Gusfield, Joseph R. *Symbolic Crusade.* Urbana, Ill.:
University of Illinois Press, 1963.

Kitsuse, John I. "Societal Reaction to Deviant Behavior: Problems of Theory and Method." *Social Problems.* 9 (1962): pp. 247–256.

Lemert, Edwin M. *Social Pathology.* New York:
McGraw-Hill, 1951.

New York Times, Saturday, January 1, 1989: p. 30.
Sullivan, Ronald, "Goetz Is Given One-Year
Term on Gun Charge."

Quinney, Richard. *Class, State and Crime.* New York:
David McKay, 1977.

Scheff, Thomas, J. *Being Mentally Ill.* Chicago: Aldine, 1966.

Schutz, Alfred. *Collected Papers I: The Problem of
Social Reality.* Maurice Natanson (ed.) The
Hague: Martinus Nijhoff, 1962.

Scott, Robert. *The Making of Blind Men.* New York:
Russell Sage Foundation, 1969.

Scott, Robert, and Jack Douglas. *Theoretical Perspectives on Deviance.* New York: Basic Books, 1972.

Spitzer, Steven. "Toward a Marxian Theory of Deviance." *Social Problems* (22) 1975: pp. 638–651.

Steffensmeier, Darrell J., and Robert M. Terry, "Deviance and Respectability: An Observational Study of Reactions to Shoplifting." *Social Forces* 51 (1973): pp. 417–426.

Tannenbaum, Frank. *Crime and the Community.* New York: Ginn, 1938.

Ward, David A., and Charles, R. Tittle. "Deterrence or Labeling?: The Effects of Informal Sanctions." *Deviant Behavior* (16) 1993.

Chapter 4

Alcohol Use as Deviance

"KEEPING SECRETS"

Blond, sexy and funny, Suzanne Somers vaulted to national prominence in the late 1970s as Chrissy on the popular television comedy, "Three's Company." She left the show in 1981 to become one of the most dazzling performers of song and dance ever witnessed on the night club strip of Las Vegas. Her performances were so successful that she was named Female Entertainer of the Year in 1986 following a six-month engagement before standing-room-only crowds.

Despite her beauty and success, there was a secret side of Suzanne Somers very few people knew about. She was an adult child of an alcoholic family. "The public knew she was blond, sexy, funny. They didn't know the rest—that she was battling to recover from the effects of family alcoholism" (Meacham, 1988:18).

As a child, Suzanne lived in a family atmosphere riddled with fear and uncertainty. She never really knew what to expect upon returning from school. "Would people be hitting each other, would Dad be passed out on the floor, would furniture be broken—or would he be in one of his 'good moods'?" She did not dare bring friends home with her for fear of what they might learn. Instead, she spent hours fantasizing in her bedroom closet and struggled with chronic bed-wetting well into her adolescence (Meacham, 1988:18).

During her performances at Las Vegas' Ceasar's Palace, she would return to her hotel suite only to stay awake until the wee hours of the morning writing about her dark secrets. Her writing became her therapy and later she published her thoughts in a now widely read autobiography entitled *Keeping Secrets*. From this process, Suzanne Somers found an inner peace and her story has become an inspiration to literally thousands of adult children of alcoholics as they seek to overcome the scars of their childhood.

As the story of Suzanne Somers clearly shows, alcoholism not only adversely affects the alcoholic but the non-alcoholic family members as well. In this chapter, we explore some of the potential causes of alcoholic drinking and examine ways of overcoming its harmful effects.

DRINKING IN SOCIAL AND CULTURAL PERSPECTIVE

A common belief about the effects of alcohol on behavior is that alcohol automatically reduces inhibitions. Those who are intoxicated are believed to be more likely to commit physical violence and engage in promiscuous sexual adventures. Could it be, however, that we may feel less inhibited not because of the direct effects of alcohol but because we have learned that we should feel less inhibited? Put simply, is our drinking behavior more affected by the alcohol we drink or by how we think we are expected to act when we drink?

While the direct physical effects of alcohol may define the broad outlines of intoxicated behavior, social and cultural conditioning can play a critical role as well. This is dramatically illustrated in cross-cultural studies. For example, the Reichel-Dolmatoffs provide data showing that alcohol consumption per se has anything but a "disinhibiting" effect. In their description of the youth of Aritama, a small village in northern Colombia, they note:

> Boys of fifteen or sixteen years will occasionally spend a night singing, drinking, and playing music in the company of older men who invite them on such sprees. However, the youth rarely seems to enjoy drinking and takes part in such nightly adventures mainly to demonstrate his new manliness. But as soon as the new status is achieved, i.e., when the boy has left his home, such sprees become rare and are marked by increased seriousness. A man might drink and drum all night long without once losing his composure, without becoming aggressive, sentimental, verbose, or amorous (Reichel-Dolmatoff and Reichel-Dolmatoff, 1961: 25) [emphasis added].

After reviewing the wealth of cross-sectional evidence regarding the effects of alcohol on behavior, MacAndrew and Edgerton were led to a clear sociological conclusion about the alleged "disinhibiting" effects of alcohol:

> [I]n and of itself, the presence of alcohol in the body does not necessarily even conduce to disinhibition,

*much less inevitably produce such an effect . . .
We must conclude that drunken comportment is an
essentially learned affair . . .*

*Over the course of socialization, people learn about
drunkenness what their society "knows" about
drunkenness, and, accepting and acting upon the
misunderstandings thus imparted to them, they become the living confirmation of their society's teachings (MacAndrew and Edgerton, 1969: 87–88).*

As the abundance of cross-cultural evidence shows, social and cultural forces
strongly influence whether people will drink
and how they will feel and act while under
the influence of alcohol. The evidence also
shows that whether drunken behavior will
be considered deviance depends on how it is
defined within a given cultural system
(Glassner and Berg, 1980).

WHAT IS ALCOHOLISM?

Given the tremendous diversity among cultures as to whether drunkenness will occur
and, if it occurs, whether it will be regarded
as deviance, will it ever be possible to adequately answer the question, "What is Alcoholism?" While it may not be possible to
provide an answer with which everyone will
be comfortable, sociologists can offer a
unique way of approaching the issue. Soon,
we shall see how sociologists answer the
question, "What is alcoholism?" For now, let
us begin our examination of the question by
considering the most influential definition
currently available, namely, the disease concept of alcoholism.

It is fair to say that the most popular definition of alcoholism is that it is a disease.
From this perspective, the defining characteristic of alcoholism is loss of control over one's
drinking. While loss of control can be a slip-
pery notion, it suggests that a person cannot
quit drinking once he or she has started. It is
assumed that a person manifesting such a
symptom has alcoholism. Those who sub-

scribe to the theory that alcoholism is a disease believe that loss of control is the result
of an inherited biochemical susceptibility
(Ward, 1990).

From a sociological perspective, this physical view of alcoholism is limited in at least two
respects. First, a strictly biological theory does
not adequately explain cultural differences in
rates of alcoholism, for example, the vast difference in alcoholism rates between the Irish
and Jewish cultures (Glassner and Berg, 1980).
Some who subscribe to such a biological theory argue that cultural differences may be attributed to biological evolution. In one version
of this position, Milam and Ketcham (1983)
maintain that it is a cultural group's duration
of exposure to alcohol that determines its alcoholism rate. This is so, they contend, because
evolutionary selection will eliminate individuals vulnerable to alcoholism (Peele, 1986).
While it is true that cultural differences in sensitivity to alcohol and variations in alcohol
metabolism have been found, these differences are not good predictors of alcoholism
rates. Peele underscores the weakness of the
strictly biological argument:

*[W]hile metabolic differences and variations in sen-
sitivity to alcohol have been found among ethnic
and cultural groups . . . these group differences
have not been found to predict alcohol misuse . . .
The most striking case of divergent cultural patterns
of drinking in the face of prominent racial reactions
to alcohol is the pattern established by the Chinese
and Japanese Americans on the one hand, and the
Eskimo and American Indian groups on the other.
Drinking in these groups is marked by a distinctive
facial reddening and accelerated heart beat, blood
pressure and other circulatory system measures, as
well as by acetaldehyde and other alcohol metabolism abnormalities. However, the Chinese and Japanese Americans have the lowest alcoholism rates of
all American cultural groups and the Eskimos and
American Indians have the highest such rates
(Peele, 1986:66).*

The second limitation of a strictly biological view of alcoholism is related to the impor-

tance of cultural definitions in the making of deviance. Whether any form of drinking (however excessive) will be considered deviance depends upon how it is defined within the cultural group under consideration. There is nothing inherent in the drinking behavior itself that will inform us about whether it will be considered deviance. Any excessive drinking is considered deviance among Orthodox Jews, whereas heavy drinking is normative among Irish Americans (Glassner and Berg, 1980). The second limitation suggests that even if alcoholism were the result of genetic factors, the drinking behavior itself would remain neutral until evaluated in relationship to particular cultural definitions of what constitutes deviant drinking. This is to acknowledge that the notion of "disease" (like the idea of deviance in general) is as much a social construction as it is a medical condition (Conrad and Schneider, 1980).

Despite the observed limitations of biological theories of alcoholism, the disease concept has some benefits. Indeed, increasing acceptance of the disease conception of alcoholism has led to a shift away from viewing the alcoholic as weak-willed or criminal to viewing the problem drinker in more humanistic terms. Moreover, the idea that the alcoholic is a sick person may serve to reduce self-blame and relieve guilt, thereby making recovery that much more likely. Even so, these benefits do not establish the claim that alcoholism is, in fact, an inherited disorder. Rather, the benefits point to some of the advantages associated with making the *assumption* that alcoholism is a genetically determined disease.

The disease concept of alcoholism is so widely accepted today, in large measure, because of the hard work, dedication, and political influence of Alcoholics Anonymous (AA). With the help of the seminal scientific writings of E. M. Jellinek (1960), AA was instrumental in bringing about the decriminal-

ization of public drunkenness and took the lead in shaping public opinion toward accepting alcoholism as a treatable disorder (Nusbaumer, 1990). And, while there are large-scale governmental programs based on the assumption that alcoholism is a disease, the assumption is more the result of interest politics than the outcome of scientific research. "The disease concept owes its life to these variously interested parties, rather than to substantive scientific findings. As such, the disease concept of alcoholism is primarily a social rather than a scientific or medical accomplishment" (Schneider, 1978:371).

Sociological Conceptions of Alcoholism

If the disease concept is more an outgrowth of power politics than of scientific research, and if cultural and societal variations in use and abuse of alcohol seriously challenge the assertion that alcoholism is an inherited trait, then "What is alcoholism?" As it turns out, one's definition often reflects a perspective or special angle of vision through which a particular subject matter, such as alcoholism, may be examined. While not necessarily intent upon disputing biological theories, sociologists emphasize social and cultural forces in their approach to drinking behaviors. Accordingly, as with the other forms of deviance examined in this text, we shall define alcoholism as sociologists see it. Our definition may not embrace every aspect of the phenomenon, but the perspective is unique. It places the search for the causes of alcoholism, and indeed the very definition of alcoholism, within a social context.

The Objectivist Conception. Among sociologists who adopt an objectivist conception of deviance, the term *alcoholism* is scarcely used. The reason is quite simple. The term *alcoholism* has been too long associated with the disease conception of alcohol abuse. Since sociologists tend not to think of excessive alcohol use as having an inherited basis, they avoid using the word *alcoholism*. Rather, sociologists who adopt an objectivist conception are more inclined to refer to excessive alcohol use as *deviant drinking*. Certainly, this inclination is perfectly consistent with the view that drinking (however excessive) can only be deviance in relation to some system of norms. Accordingly, *deviant drinking* may be defined as "drinking behavior that violates the norms of acceptable alcohol consumption for a group, community, or society."

The Subjectivist Conception. Sociologists who adopt a subjectivist conception often utilize the term *alcoholism* in their writings. However, the word is not used because the subjectivist believes that alcoholism is an inherited disease. The subjectivist is interested in the label "alcoholism" as a definition that has been socially constructed and applied to specific behaviors by social audiences. Those who adopt a subjectivist viewpoint are interested in how it is that only certain individuals (or categories of individuals) are chosen from the total population of heavy drinkers to be included in the category called "alcoholic." Thus, from the subjectivist viewpoint, *alcoholism* is a label imputed to drinking behaviors (real or imagined) by social audiences, and *alcoholic* is a label affixed to persons who are believed by others to have the condition alcoholism.

WHO ARE THE DEVIANT DRINKERS?

Based on national surveys, such as the U.S. Department of Health and Human Services report (DHHS, 1990), approximately ten percent of the adult drinking population in the United States experience adverse consequences because of heavy alcohol consumption. Those who manifest problems with alcohol are not located in a single social category but are widely dispersed across differ-

ent social locations according to social class, age and sex, rural-urban residence, region of the country, and race, ethnicity, and religion.

For some time, the stereotype persisted that problem drinkers were mostly on "skid row" or lived primarily in the lower rungs of society. This mistaken impression was fostered, in part, because more statistics on problem drinking were provided by treatment agencies. Of course, those from the lower classes were the only ones who ever wound up in such treatment facilities. The well-to-do either remained hidden from public view or were treated in private settings.

With the advent of national surveys, evidence began to accumulate that problem drinking touched almost every social and economic group in society. This is not to suggest that drinking problems are evenly distributed throughout society. Indeed, this is far from the case. Problem drinking is disproportionately high in some groups and almost nonexistent in others. Data gathered through large national surveys of the U.S. population provide information concerning just where problem drinking is most prevalent. Let us turn now to some of the important findings that relate selected social and demographic variables with the presence or absence of problem-drinking behavior.

Social Class

One of the most consistent findings from national surveys is the link between social class and alcohol use (DHHS, 1990). As it turns out, a disproportionate number of people in the upper social classes drink. However, the lower social classes are overrepresented among serious, problem drinkers (Dunham, 1990). Drinking, then, is directly related to social class, whereas problem drinking is inversely related to social class standing. Unlike the upper classes who drink for interpersonal reasons, members of the lower classes are more likely to drink to escape socially and economically induced stress (DHHS, 1990).

Gender

One can predict more about an individual's drinking behavior by knowing her or his gender than by any other social or personal characteristic (Dunham, 1990). Men are more likely to drink than women. Among drinkers, men show a greater likelihood to be heavy drinkers and are more likely than women to have problems associated with their drinking.

Recent evidence indicates that the majority of younger women drink (DHHS, 1990). This is in sharp contrast to the pattern of abstention so dominant among older women. This higher rate of alcohol consumption is thought to increase the risk of alcohol abuse. Concern over this possibility has led researchers to identify the social factors that contribute to alcoholism among women.

One theory relates problem drinking to the changing roles of women (Dunham, 1990). Researchers hypothesize that, as women's roles become more similar to the roles of men, their drinking and problem-drinking rates will more closely approximate those of men. Accordingly, we would expect a further narrowing of the differences in rates between male and female drinking and problem drinking as women's roles continue to change and converge with those of men. Indeed, research by Wilsnack and Cheloha (1987) at least partially supports this thesis. To determine the connection between women's drinking patterns and gender roles, women were studied with respect to traditional versus modern sex-role orientations. Women with the most nontraditional role configurations—women who had never married or were separated or divorced, had no children, had an advanced degree, and were employed in male-dominated occupations— were more likely to be heavy or problem

drinkers (DHHS, 1990:39–40). Put differently, the data showed that rates of excessive drinking and drinking problems were significantly higher among women who characterized themselves as being more similar to men in their sex-role orientations. Despite such supportive evidence, the validity of the sex-role convergence hypothesis will have to await additional research. Particularly, it must be shown that problem-drinking rates among women are in fact converging with those of men. This would seem to require data gathered over a longer time span than is now available.

Marital Status

Men and women who are separated or divorced or who have never married are most likely to be heavy and problem drinkers. By comparison, widows and widowers are for the most part abstainers and light drinkers, perhaps because of their advanced ages. The national survey by Wilsnack, Wilsnack, and Klassen (1984) confirms these relationships. Divorced and never-married men and women, as compared to those who are married, are more likely to be heavy drinkers and less likely to be abstainers.

Even so, the relationship between marital status and problem-drinking behavior appears to be more complex than the above comparisons. Marital status seems to interact with gender and age in the extent to which it influences problem drinking. Research shows that women drinkers in the 21-to-34 age group are least likely to report alcohol-related problems if they are married and have a stable work role. Young women without children at home are more likely than women with children to manifest alcohol-related problems. Yet young, single mothers, with full-time paid employment, are consistently less likely to exhibit alcohol-related problems than are young single mothers without full-time jobs. Thus, the best evidence indicates that marital status interacts with work roles and age in influencing problem drinking behaviors (DHHS, 1990:39).

Race and Ethnicity

Among the most consistent findings of early research on drinking and problem drinking are the number of cultural and subcultural variations. These variations include attitudes toward alcohol, drinking patterns, and drinking problems.

Among all special population groups in the United States, the highest frequency of problems associated with drinking has been attributed to American Indians (Dunham, 1990). There are about 1.5 million American Indians and Alaskan Natives in the United States (DHHS, 1987). American Indians have rates of alcohol abuse and alcoholism many times higher than rates in the general population. Even so, drinking behaviors and consequent problem levels vary widely across tribal groups (DHHS, 1990).

African Americans are the largest minority group in the United States. Research findings from national surveys show that African-American and white men have similar drinking patterns, although African-American men have somewhat higher abstention rates than whites (29 percent as compared to 23 percent) and white men are more likely to be heavier drinkers. While consumption levels are quite similar for African-American and white men, African-American men experience considerably higher rates of a variety of social and health complications from alcohol consumption than white men, and these higher rates of alcohol-related problems are concentrated among African Americans who are among the economically disadvantaged segment of the population (DHH, 1990:52).

A quite similar pattern is found among African-American women, but the differences are more pronounced. Nearly half of African-American women are found to be ab-

stainers (46 percent), compared with one-third (34 percent) of white women. A larger proportion of white women are heavy drinkers, although when abstainers are excluded from statistical analyses, a somewhat higher proportion of African-American women drinkers are found to drink heavily (DHHS, 1990:51). Thus, whether male or female, African Americans are at greater risk for problem drinking than whites (DHHS, 1990:52).

The Hispanic population of the United States is characterized by great cultural diversity. Although debate continues over an acceptable definition of Hispanic ethnicity, Hispanics in the United States generally have origins in Mexico, Puerto Rico, Cuba, and other Latin American countries (DHHS, 1990:52).

The first nationwide survey of drinking patterns and alcohol problems among Hispanics was conducted by Caetano (1989). The survey revealed dramatic differences in alcohol consumption between Hispanic men and women. More than 70 percent of Hispanic women drank either less than once a month or not at all. In contrast, almost 70 percent of men were drinkers. Rates of heavier drinking increased sharply among Hispanic men in their thirties but declined thereafter. Among women, rates of heavier drinking were very low except for a significant increase among women in their forties and fifties, but the rate dropped to zero among women aged 60 or over. Mexican-American men and women have much higher rates of both abstention and heavier drinking than men and women of Puerto Rican or Cuban origin (DHHS, 1990:53).

SOCIOLOGICAL THEORIES OF DEVIANT DRINKING

Sociologists view excessive alcohol use as a form of deviance. Though they don't dismiss physical dependency as a possible cause, sociologists who adopt an objectivist view of deviance emphasize that excessive alcohol use is a norm-violating behavior to be explained by examining social and cultural forces. Excessive alcohol use varies widely between social categories within societies and between different societies. This tremendous variation in misuse strongly suggests that social forces are critical factors in accounting for the variation.

Sociologists not only seek to understand how social forces affect alcohol use that violates social norms. They also try to understand why excessive alcohol use is socially regarded as deviance in the first place. Societies differ as to whether drunkenness is publicly regarded as bad or deviance; therefore, it is important to understand the social, economic, and political forces that operate to cause a particular form of alcohol use to be designated as deviance. Those who adopt a subjectivist conception of deviance focus on how excessive drinking comes to be defined as deviance.

Macro-Objectivist Theories

Macro-objectivist theories seek to explain differences in rates of problem drinking between social categories within society. Most research at the macro level falls within two research traditions: the anomie tradition and the neo-Marxist tradition.

Anomie and Problem Drinking. As we noted in Chapter 2, Merton (1967) is the most widely acknowledged proponent of anomie theory among contemporary deviance theorists. In brief, Merton argues that anomie is a social condition that arises when there is a disjuncture between culturally defined success goals and the objective opportunities to obtain them. Because of artificial barriers such as race and ethnic discrimination inherent in a stratified society, members of the lower classes are systematically denied access to legitimate opportunities to obtain cultural goals such as material success. Thus, Merton predicts higher rates of deviance among the lower socioeconomic classes as a result of opportunity blockage.

When applied to problem drinking, anomie theory would predict an inverse relationship between social class and problem-drinking behavior. As we noted earlier in this chapter, the most consistent finding from studies of the epidemiology of alcoholism is that there is a higher rate of alcohol misuse among the lower classes. Thus, evidence from epidemiologic studies supports a fundamental claim of anomie theory.

In addition to epidemiological research, investigators have attempted to assess the relevance of anomie theory to the development of alcoholism at the individual level. For example, Hughes and Dodder (1985) sought to determine if anomie was a significant correlate of self-reported drinking behavior. They studied three culturally diverse samples: 534 U.S. students from a university in the Southwest; 120 international students from the same southwestern university, and; 178 students from a university in Western Australia (Hughes and Dodder, 1985:265).

To measure differences in anomie among the students, the researchers took a social-psychological approach. That is, instead of constructing a measure of anomie as a disjuncture (imbalance) between individual aspirations and objective opportunities to achieve them, they sought to determine the degree to which each student felt a sense of hopelessness and helplessness in their lives. To accomplish this, they had each student respond to questions contained in an "anomia" scale developed by Srole (1956). In addition, the researchers gathered information on the students' drinking behavior using two indexes: (1) a quantity (how much)/frequency (how often) index of drinking behavior and (2) a social consequences index designed to determine the number of adverse social experiences each student had encountered as a direct result of her or his alcohol misuse.

The results showed that, in general, anomie was not significantly correlated with the quantity and frequency of drinking. However, when the researchers computed the correlations between anomie and problem drinking, significant results emerged. For both the U.S. and international samples, anomie was a weak but significant correlate of problem drinking. For the Australians, however, the relationship was not significant (Hughes and Dodder, 1985:266). Thus, with the exception of the Australian students, the researchers find a significant correlation between anomie and problem drinking.

Though the study by Hughes and Dodder (1985) found a correlation between anomie and problem drinking, we are not able to conclude that anomie causes problem drinking, because correlational studies do not permit us to separate cause from effect. To accomplish this, longitudinal studies are required—studies that gather data at a number of points in time. If problem drinking is measured at two distinct time periods, then it is reasonable to conclude that anomie "causes" problem drinking if a correlation is found between anomie measured during the first wave of data collection and problem drinking measured during the second wave of data collection, after statistically controlling for scores on the problem-drinking measure during the first wave of data collection plus any other variable (or variables) that might cause anomie and problem drinking to correlate.

This logic for establishing a cause-effect relationship between anomie and alcoholism was employed in a study by Lee, DeFrank, and Rose (1990). Their research design consisted of five waves of data collection in which they measured anomie and problem drinking among 302 air-traffic controllers. Upon completion of data collection, they correlated scores on an anomie measure during an early wave of data collection with scores on measures of problem drinking during a later wave of data collection. They found no significant correlation between the two after statistically controlling for prior drinking behavior, marital status, education, and age.

These negative findings from a relatively strong research design cast doubt on earlier correlational studies that link anomie and alcoholism. Even so, it would be premature to rule out anomie as a determinant of problem drinking based solely on the study by Lee, DeFrank, and Rose (1990). As the researchers acknowledge:

> [T]he lack of an association may in part be due to the characteristics of our sample. The link between anomie and alcohol may be strongest among groups experiencing the most alienation and hopelessness and weakest in well-educated adults with good jobs, among whom other reasons to drink may predominate. . . . A prudent course for future research would be to examine a wider range of occupations, age and education among both men and women so that the existence of such a gradient might be established (Lee, DeFrank, and Rose, 1990:420).

What the researchers are acknowledging is that all of the air-traffic controllers in their study were relatively well-educated, most were married and, by definition, all were employed. Thus, the degree of variation in anomie scores was probably quite low. In all likelihood, all of the 302 respondents scored relatively low on the anomie measure. If this is true, then anomie for the sample is a virtual constant, which makes a correlation between anomie and problem drinking almost impossible to detect. Only future research, with a sample of respondents who vary on both anomie and problem drinking measures, would allow one to fully determine the extent to which a lack of variation in scores in the Lee, DeFrank, and Rose study may have masked an otherwise significant relationship between anomie and problem drinking.

Marxist Theory and Deviant Drinking. In Chapter 2, we learned that neo-Marxist theories point to the oppressive and alienating nature of a capitalist economic system as the fundamental cause of crime and deviance in modern, industrial society. Karl Marx did not write specifically about the impact of capitalism on the development of alcoholism. But, his long-time intellectual collaborator, Fredrick Engels (1969), did formulate fragments of a political economy of alcoholism. Here, we concentrate on two aspects of Engels's theory about the link between alcoholism and the development of industrial capitalism: (1) his observation that alcohol use is a primary means by which an alienated labor force might cope with the oppressive nature of capitalist economic relations and (2) his observation that the state facilitates the growth of the alcohol industry to control the labor force and to assure capital accumulation for the alcohol industry itself.

Engels wrote about the way in which alcohol use helps the working class cope with the alienating nature of a capitalist system.

> *Liquor is almost their only source of pleasure, and all things conspire to make it more accessible to them . . . [Drunkenness provides] the certainty of forgetting for an hour or two the wretchedness and burden of life and a hundred other circumstances so mighty that the worker can, in truth, hardly be blamed for yielding to such overwhelming pressure. Drunkenness has here ceased to be a vice . . . They who have degraded the working man to a mere object have the responsibility to bear (Engels, 1969:133–134).*

Engels also drew attention to the ways that working-class drinking maintains social solidarity among an otherwise alienated work force (Singer, 1986:117). He observed that for the worker "his social need can be gratified only in the public-house [tavern], he has absolutely no other place where he can meet his friends" (Engels, 1969:137). Though not explicitly Marxist in orientation, research by Seeman, Seeman, and Budros partially supports Engels's theorizing. In a study of some 500 working-class males, the researchers did not find a direct effect of alienated work on problem drinking. However, they did find a highly significant relationship between alienated work, friendship integration, and problem drinking. Workers who experience less latitude in

terms of decision making on the job (high levels of work alienation), and who are integrated into a network of drinking friends, have the highest rates of problem drinking (Seeman, Seeman and Budros, 1988:193).

A second aspect of Engels's theorizing is that the state aids in the production and sale of alcohol. According to Singer (1986:119), historical research documents that the involvement of the state in the production, distribution, and control of alcohol consumption has undergone three identifiable stages. During preindustrial times, the state viewed the production and consumption of alcohol as a way of increasing tax revenues. With the advent of industrialization and the rise of the proletariat as a distinct social class, the posture of the state toward alcohol consumption shifted. Supporting Singer's thesis is the claim of Makela et al. (1981) that the posture of the state shifted toward temperance and "a strong concern about the effects of drinking on industrial efficiency and discipline of the working class" (Makela et al. 1981:67). As Johnson has noted:

> *Temperance propaganda promised masters social peace, a disciplined and docile labor force and an opportunity to assert moral authority over their men. The movement enjoyed widespread success among the merchants and masters who considered themselves respectable . . . Temperance men talked loudest in 1828 and 1829, years in which the autonomy of working-class neighborhoods grew at a dizzying rate . . . Wage earners . . . now . . . drank only in their own neighborhoods and only with each other, and in direct defiance of their employers (Johnson, 1978:81–82).*

The third stage of state involvement in the distribution and sale of alcohol followed the Second World War. During this stage, the posture of the state changed from a policy of temperance to one of support for the capital accumulation of an emerging alcohol industry. In a systematic analysis of the California wine industry, Bunce (1979) documented this pro-industry bias of the state in California and found that the state played a critical role in helping to secure the capital interests of the largest California grape growers (Singer, 1986:120). The California wine industry has become highly centralized and is primarily dominated by the Gallo family, who have received political favors in exchange for large campaign contributions to Senator Alan Cranston and former Governor and presidential candidate Jerry Brown (Singer, 1986:120). Thus, "a very strong lobby of big distillers was established which constantly tried to shape the tax laws according to their own interests, and with much success since the second half of the 19th century" (Bunce, 1979:54).

Our analysis of neo-Marxist theory as applied to alcoholism suggests that state policy regulating the production, distribution, and control of alcohol consumption is heavily influenced by the material interests of the capitalist class. The production and distribution of alcohol in an industrial society generates profits for a lucrative distillery industry and, at the same time, dulls the sense of despair that accompanies alienated labor in a capitalist economic system. From this Marxist perspective, alcohol intoxication (as long as it is not in the workplace) may be regarded as a way of dulling the revolutionary potential of a large class of oppressed workers.

Micro-Objectivist Theories

Micro-objectivist theories are designed to account for the acquisition and maintenance of deviant behavioral patterns at the individual level of analysis. Among micro-objectivist theories, two have been most often applied in an attempt to understand problem drinking behavior: social learning theory and social control theory.

Alcohol Misuse and Social Learning.   More empirical research about the development of problem drinking has been conducted from a social learning perspective than any other

theoretical approach. Here, we review three relatively recent studies that, in large part, are typical of studies conducted within the social learning tradition. Each study draws attention to all, or some, of the following social learning concepts examined in Chapter 2: differential associations, deviance definitions (including beliefs and attitudes), reinforcers and punishers, and alcohol use/abuse.

Johnson (1988) analyzed two waves of data from a three-year longitudinal study about adolescent drug use and abuse. While her analysis considered both alcohol and marijuana use, we focus our attention on her analysis and conclusions regarding alcohol abuse.

From an initial sample of 882 adolescents from New Jersey, Johnson selected youth who met the criterion of being alcohol users during the first interview (wave 1). Using this criterion for selection, 396 adolescents were eligible for inclusion in the study.

The concept of differential associations was measured by the proportion of a respondent's friends who used alcohol and whether these friends approved or disapproved of the respondent's alcohol use. The concept of deviance definitions was measured by the respondents' attitudes toward alcohol. Alcohol use was measured by both the quantity and frequency of alcohol consumption. Analysis of Johnson's data revealed findings consistent with social learning theory. The quantity and frequency of use was influenced by whether a respondent's friends used alcohol and the extent to which these friends approved of the respondent's alcohol use. Moreover, the influence of differential associations (friends' use) on respondents' use was, to some extent, mediated by deviance definitions (respondents' attitudes toward alcohol). We may depict this process as follows: Friend's use → Respondent's attitudes → Respondent's alcohol use. Since Johnson found a direct effect of friends' use on alcohol use of her respondents, her data suggest that other learning processes such as direct modeling may better account for her findings than Sutherland's differential association theory. Even so, her data show at least partial support for Sutherland's theory and some support for differential-reinforcement theory since positive reinforcements were found to influence continued adolescent alcohol use once initial use was instigated by differential associations.

Most research designed to test a social learning theory of problem drinking has been conducted on samples of adolescents. Akers et al. (1989) carried out a study to determine if a learning theory of alcohol use and abuse may be applied to the elderly. Data were gathered through face-to-face interviews of 1,410 people at least 60 years of age who resided in New Jersey and Florida.

Three social learning concepts were central to their study: differential associations, deviance definitions (attitudes), and differential reinforcements. The concept of differential associations was measured by interview questions that ascertained whether respondents' friends, spouses, adult children, and other family members drank and, if so, how often and how much. Deviance definitions were measured by asking questions about respondents' attitudes toward drinking and whether they felt drinking was justified under certain circumstances. Differential reinforcement, as a social learning concept, was measured with questions about others' reactions to the respondents' drinking. These "others" included spouses, family members, and friends. Additionally, respondents were questioned about the reinforcing effects of alcohol itself as, for example, whether alcohol results in "good things" such as "it helps me relax" (Akers et al., 1989:629).

Each of these three social learning variables was correlated with two measures of alcohol use. One measure was a simple frequency measure: It asked how often the respondent drank alcohol during the past 12 months. The second measure was a quantity/frequency index created by determining both how much (quantity) and how often (frequency) a respondent drank. Respondents were categorized on the quantity/frequency index according to whether they were abstainers, light drinkers, moderate drinkers, heavy drinkers, or excessive drinkers (12 or more drinks once or twice a week to 7 or more drinks daily). Analysis of the data showed that each of the social learning variables was a significant predictor of drinking behavior. The differential-reinforcement variable was the strongest predictor, while differential associations and deviance definitions were relatively less powerful but, nonetheless, significant predictors themselves.

We can compare the Akers et al. (1989) findings with Johnson's (1988) results. First, it is reasonable to conclude that social learning processes are important in explaining both youthful and adult drinking patterns. Second, despite the presence of social learning for both youthful and adult drinking patterns, youthful drinking appears to be more influenced by differential associations (how much and how often friends drink) whereas adults, and particularly older adults, are more influenced by the reinforcing effects of alcohol itself (Akers et al, 1989:634). While this is an important difference, it is still reasonable to conclude from these separate studies that differential associations and differential reinforcements are important mechanisms in learning to drink. And, this appears to be the case despite one's stage in life.

In yet another, and more recent study, Sellers and Winfree (1990) followed a sample of junior and senior high school students over a six-month period to examine the degree to which changes in differential associations (drinking friends) affected changes in definition (attitudes about drinking) and, ultimately, changes in drinking behavior. In terms of the source of deviance definitions, the researchers asked that students distinguish between definitions, favorable and unfavorable to drinking, learned from peers as opposed to definitions learned from adults. Their analysis led to two interesting conclusions. First, definitions learned from peers were more important than definitions learned from adults in determining youthful drinking. Second, among junior high school students, differential associations (what friends do in terms of drinking) were a better predictor of drinking frequency than definitions (attitudes) about drinking; among high school youth, definitions (internalized attitudes) were better predictors of drinking frequency than differential associations (how frequently friends drank). This finding reveals that social learning is a *process* in which imitation might be more dominant in initial learning while internalization of attitudes (deviance definitions) might be more dominant in influencing drinking behavior during later stages of the learning process.

To summarize the available literature on social learning and drinking behavior, each of the variables outlined in Chapter 2 under social learning theory is implicated in one way or another in the process whereby drinking and problem drinking is acquired. And, it appears that the process by which drinking behavior is learned is, despite some variations, generally applicable across the various stages of the life cycle.

Deterrence Theory and Deviant Drinking. The most visible example of the application of control theory to deviant drinking is the attempt of the criminal justice system to deter the drunk driver. The emphasis, here, is on formal legal controls.

Drinking-and-driving laws are believed to be effective deterrents if they provide for certain, severe, and swift punishment (Ross, 1984). Law enforcement agencies attempt to increase the public's perception of the certainty of apprehension for drunk driving by implementing programs such as sobriety checkpoints. Significant decreases in alcohol-related crashes and traffic deaths have been reported for periods when checkpoints have been in effect (Ross, 1985). Statistical comparisons of public perceptions in areas where checkpoints were and were not in use indicated that the likelihood of arrest for alcohol-impaired driving is perceived as being greater in checkpoint areas. Despite differences in estimates of the risk of punishment, however, there appear to be no differences in reported drinking-and-driving behavior between residents of checkpoint and comparison areas (Ross, 1985). While the chances of arrest for drinking and driving were perceived to be higher in the checkpoint areas, they may have still been too low to deter drivers from drinking.

Hingson et al. (1987) have examined the effects on automobile crashes of Maine's 1981 drunk-driving law, considered one of the toughest in the nation. The law introduced a civil charge for driving while impaired (DWI). This meant that the state needed to prove only preponderance of evidence rather than guilt beyond a reasonable doubt in order to obtain a conviction. A blood alcohol level of .10 became evidence per se of driving under the influence of alcohol. Alcohol-impaired drivers with prior convictions were no longer allowed second jury trials, and minimum mandatory penalties were established (DHHS, 1986).

During the first year following the passage of the law, there were increases in DWI arrests, an 85 percent increase in the conviction rate, and increased perceptions by the driving public that alcohol-impaired drivers would be stopped, arrested, convicted, and given automatic fines, license suspension, and jail sentences. During the first two years after the law was implemented, significantly more Maine drivers decided not to drive after drinking when compared with drivers from other New England states. Fatal crashes and single-vehicle nighttime crashes decreased by 35 percent. This decrease was significantly greater than in other New England states during the same period (DHHS, 1986).

Three years after the passage of the law, however, drivers chose more frequently to drive after drinking. Also, fatal crashes returned to the pre-1981 level. Moreover, by the third year, the public no longer regarded the penalties as severe. While alcohol-impaired drivers who were arrested were more likely to be convicted in Maine, so few were stopped and arrested that the perceived likelihood of being punished for alcohol-impaired driving appeared to decline to ineffective levels (DHHS, 1986).

Other strategies focus more on the severity of punishment. License revocation may have a deterrent effect because there is evidence that it is perceived by the public as a relatively severe sanction. However, increasing the severity of other types of penalties for DWI offenses appears to have little long-term deterrent effect. Mandatory jail sentences for DWI are on the books in at least 25 states, in many instances even for first-time offenders. The evaluations of these programs indicate that delays and postponements of trials, failure of defendants to appear, a decreasing number of convictions in response to pleas of innocence, and case dismissals tend to reduce the deterrent effects of the law (DHHS, 1986).

Macro-Subjectivist Theories

Here we consider two macro-subjectivist theories. Both are interest group theories. They focus on the social, political, and historical forces involved in the creation of deviance definitions.

Interest Group Theory: From Drunkenness to Disease. The disease concept has emerged as the most influential model of alcoholism among both policymakers and the general public. But how could this be possible given its less than convincing scientific foundation?

For an answer to this puzzling contradiction, we must trace the socio-historical process whereby the *social control of drunkenness* was claimed and, in large measure, won by those who support the theory that alcoholism is an inherited disease. It will become clear that "how drunkenness became a disease" can only be understood if we understand the social and political history of the battle. The interest group theoretical approach examined in Chapter 3 will serve as our guiding perspective.

During the seventeenth and eighteenth century in the U.S., drinking was not considered deviant and drunkenness was certainly not a rare event (Lender, 1973; Keller, 1976).

> *If anything was "bad" about drinking it was not drink itself, which even prominent clergy called a "good creature of God." Churches and drinking houses, as social centers of the community, were often close together. Concern about public drunkenness was expressed by a small few scholarly, aristocratic church leaders who warned against the sin of drunken excess, sometimes attributed to the work of the Devil (Schneider, 1978:362).*

Chronic drunkenness or in contemporary language, alcoholism, was viewed as a sign of moral decay. In a word, alcoholism was a sin.

Chronic drunkenness was believed to be the result of a rational, willful attempt to seek pleasure and self-indulgence. Given the religious heritage of the colonies, the notion that drunkenness may be the result of uncontrollable addiction or disease simply did not fit into the colonists' world view (Conrad and Schneider, 1980). According to this world view, all stood before God and either chose to live the righteous life or a life of moral degeneration. Thus, the church was charged with the responsibility for controlling chronic drunkenness. "Punishment was initially a clerical admonition, followed by the extreme sanction of suspension, and finally by excommunication as the ultimate, although probably infrequently used, religious control" (Schneider, 1978:362).

Toward the end of the eighteenth century, a new conception of alcoholism was being advanced. In his *An Inquiry into the Effects of Ardent Spirits upon the Human Body and Mind* (1785), Benjamin Rush was the first to suggest that chronic drunkenness was an "addiction." He referred to the addiction as a "disease of the will." Unlike the moral tradition that preceded him, he did not believe that a "diseased will" was the result of the sinful nature of human beings. Rather, he argued that chemical addiction to alcohol weakens one's capacity to willfully control drinking. In a word, loss of control over alcohol was a result of a diseased will, weakened by chemical addiction (Conrad and Schneider, 1980).

Rush's idea that alcoholism was a disease of the will had an important impact on the medical community of his day. "They avoided the traditional description of the drinker's 'love' of drink and supplied new terms such as 'craving,' and 'insatiable desire' to describe the link between the individual and alcohol" (Schneider, 1978:363). These new terms reflected the contention that alcoholism was not a willful sin as the moralist of the earlier era maintained, but a disease beyond the willful control of the alcoholic. Moreover, the view advanced by Rush and his followers served to replace the punitive approach taken by the church with a control strategy based on the more humanitarian measures of medical treatment. The final impact of the influential work of Benjamin Rush, was twofold: (1) he influenced a basic change in thinking about "what alcoholism is" from the idea that it was a sin to the idea that it was a disease, and (2) he influenced a change in what social institution would have jurisdiction over its control. The institution of medicine replaced to a great extent the church and civil authorities.

As the nineteenth century got underway, a new approach to combating the problem of drunkenness was gaining momentum: the American Temperance Movement. As Gusfield (see Chapter 3) has forcefully shown, temperance, or abstinence from alcohol, was symbolic of one's commitment to middle-class values. Indeed, the Prohibition Era, which lasted from 1920–1933 in the United States, was a symbolic victory for those who embraced the traditional values of hard work, abstinence, and social and personal reserve. This period in U.S. history is important insofar as it underscores the social and political processes whereby behaviors like drinking can be transformed into behaviors publicly regarded as deviance; however, it tells us less about the social history of the disease concept of alcoholism. Only after Prohibition had been repealed did the notion of alcoholism as a disease reemerge as a dominant theme among organizations aimed at the prevention and treatment of alcoholism.

Within a decade following the repeal of Prohibition, a number of scientific and lay organizations were formed with the goal of combating alcohol addiction. The most influential of such organizations was Alcoholics Anonymous (AA). This self-help approach to alcoholism was founded by two men, both of whom were alcoholics. They came to believe that alcoholic drinking was an "allergy of the body." The idea suggested to them that alcoholics were physiologically different from average social drinkers. Their "physiological sensitivity" made them susceptible to addiction and loss of control. Not since the influential writings of Benjamin Rush had the idea that alcoholism was a physical disease been so forcefully set forth. The alcoholic, under the AA philosophy, was not morally inferior to the social drinker. Rather, the alcoholic was victimized by an illness over which he or she had no control. "Although medical opinion was generally skeptical of this questionable formulation . . ., the concept of alcoholism as a mark of physiological sensitivity rather than moral decay was appealing and the allergy concept came to occupy a central although implicit place in AA ideology" (Schneider, 1978:366).

It took almost 40 years, however, before the disease ideology would become part of the official policy of the U.S. government. In 1969, under the leadership of Senator Harold Hughes, a recovering alcoholic and one committed to the philosophy of AA, the U.S. Senate established a Special Subcommittee on Alcoholism and Narcotics. Based on the hearings of this senate subcommittee and the support of important interest groups such as AA, the National Institute on Alcohol Abuse and Alcoholism (NIAAA) was established with the passage of the Comprehensive Alcohol Abuse and Alcoholism Prevention, Treatment, and Rehabilitation Act of 1970. The National Institute became the official agency of the federal government responsible for the establishment of governmental policy regarding prevention, research, and treatment of alcoholism. With the passage of the Comprehensive Prevention, Treatment, and Rehabilitation Act, public drunkenness was decriminalized and alcoholism was legally transformed into a disease. Thus, 1970 may be regarded as the historical landmark for the medicalization of deviant drinking and "the federal government recognized, accepted, and supported the disease model of deviant drinking (commonly referred to as the disease of alcoholism) over competing theoretical models . . . (Nusbaumer, 1990:160).

Interest Group Theory: Drinking Drivers as Deviants. Social problems, and specifically problems associated with alcohol consumption, have careers that come and go independently of the "objective" incidence of the behaviors that are thought to comprise them (Reinarman, 1988:91). This observation underscores the subjectivist contention that deviance is a social construction, created by groups that have the power to transform a

particular kind of behavior into a socially regarded, and publicly recognized, form of deviance (Langton, 1991). Perhaps there is no better contemporary example of this than the efforts of Mothers Against Drunk Drivers (MADD), a social movement that succeeded in redefining the drinking driver as deviant.

In the summer of 1980, Candy Lightner's 13-year-old daughter Cari was struck down and killed by a hit-and-run driver while she was walking along a bicycle path in a suburb of Sacramento, California. When finally apprehended, it came to light that the driver who had killed Cari was intoxicated at the time he hit her. Even more, he was on probation for several prior DWI convictions and was out on bail for another hit-and-run drinking-and-driving offense committed just days before he took the life of Candy Lightner's daughter.

Candy Lightner was grief-stricken, rendered almost immobile by the tragic and untimely death of her daughter. But she didn't remain immobilized for long. After closely monitoring the routine way in which the criminal justice system handled the case of the man who killed her daughter, Candy was changed forever. Her grief and pain turned to anger and outrage as she came to the full realization that DWI offenders were treated with extreme leniency within our justice system. She began to lobby elected representatives in the California legislature for tougher DWI laws. Because Candy was no pro at politics, things moved slowly at first. Then, with the help of a handful of lawmakers who were sympathetic to her cause, and mounting numbers of mothers who had been similarly victimized by drunk drivers, Candy's efforts began to pay off. She held emotional press conferences and gave dramatic testimony before legislative committees while at the same time successfully launching a nationwide organization that would ultimately bear the name MADD (Mothers Against Drunk Drivers) (Reinarman, 1988:96–100).

The impact of MADD on local, state, and national drinking-and-driving legislation was nothing less than dramatic. MADD's influence went beyond persuading former President Ronald Reagan to sign into law legislation that raised the drinking age to 21. As Reinarman notes:

Less noticed but equally striking was the passage of more than 230 new anti-drunk driving laws at the local level. In virtually every state and city, MADD was acknowledged as the leading force behind the new statutes. All fifty states toughened their laws against drinking and driving between 1981 and 1985, and the number of states requiring mandatory jail sentences for first offenders convicted of DUI doubled in the same period. Other states sharply raised fines, began to suspend licenses, curtailed judicial discretion with minimum sentence requirements, or enacted "per se" standards that make driving with certain blood-alcohol content (BAC) levels criminal offenses in and of themselves. More broadly, under the momentum of the MADD movement, an additional one hundred alcohol control statutes were passed between 1981 and 1984, including severe liability laws and bans on happy hours (Reinarman, 1988:100).

What accounted for the success of MADD? Clearly, others had tried to dramatize the fact that alcohol-related traffic fatalities had been occurring at alarming rates year in and year out for over two decades. But though the objective condition existed, an acknowledged social problem did not exist in the collective consciousness of the people in the U.S. or in the legislative priorities of politicians. From an interest group perspective, the question becomes: "How did an undesirable objective condition (drinking and driving) get transformed into a publicly acknowledged social problem?"

According to Reinarman, "the viability of a claim that a problem exists depends upon the *interaction* of at least two factors—the credibility of the claim-makers and the historical context in which such claims become utterable and resonate with the dominant

discourse" (Reinarman, 1988:92). In terms of MADD, no one would challenge the credibility of the claims of literally thousands of mothers whose children had been victimized by drunk drivers. But, as Reinarman observes, though the claim-makers may be credible, their credibility is not sufficient to effect a change in public policy. A second factor must be present: The claim-makers (those who are claiming that a "real" social problem exits) must make their claims during a time when the political climate of the nation is receptive to the claims being made. As we noted earlier, others had tried to effect changes in public policy regarding the drunk driver with little success. Were their claims any less credible? Clearly, the answer is no. If Reinarman is correct, they were simply making their claims during a time when the dominant political climate of the country was not receptive to their pleas.

Unlike the claim-makers who preceded MADD but staked their claims in an unreceptive political climate, Candy Lightner and MADD found the national political climate ripe to hear their pleas. The time was the 1980s. Ronald Reagan had been elected president, and the nation seemed virtually intoxicated by the wave of ultra-conservatism ushered in by Reagan's election and, four years later, his reelection. As Reinarman observes:

I shall refer to the political culture of Reaganism and suggest that MADD's claims were ideologically harmonious with the policy rhetoric of the Right . . . MADD's origins . . . lie in victims' rights movements, which seek retribution from criminals. MADD's Lightner chose an organization name that ends with "drunk drivers" rather than "driving" and yields an acronym symbolizing moral anger; MADD members repeatedly rail against the "Killer Drunk" . . . MADD's organizing strategy is explicitly one of personal vilification, and it assiduously avoids attention to corporate interests and structural sources of alcohol problems in favor of a rhetoric of individual responsibility, the private moral choice *of drinkers, and solutions based upon self-regulation . . . (Reinarman, 1988:104–105).*

None of this is to suggest that the founders and followers of MADD intentionally designed MADD to fit with the social, moral, and political conservatism of the New Right that so dominated public policy during the 1980s. Still, it is highly doubtful that MADD would have been able to influence a redefinition of the drinking driver as deviant if the movement had emerged at another, less conservative, period in U.S. history.

Micro-Subjectivist Theories

Here, we consider two types of micro-subjectivist theory. First, we examine what we refer to as definitional theories. These theories focus on the everyday interactions between actors and social audiences, how this interaction results in the creation of the label "alcoholic," and how this label is applied to selected persons suspected of problem-drinking behavior. Second, we examine labeling theories. Labeling theories are interested in how the application of the label "alcoholic" results in a self-fulfilling prophecy, first by causing the labeled individual to accept the label "alcoholic" as a fundamental conception of self and, second, how this altered self-concept may lead to more serious drinking behavior. In a word, labeling theory is interested in whether there might be "disease consequences of a disease label."

Definitional Theories. A basic process by which social audiences come to define a person as deviant is stereotyping. Stereotypes are beliefs people have about what entire categories of people are like and how they may be expected to act. Stereotypes serve an important purpose; they help us "typify," or categorize, people so that we can predict what they are likely to do. If we think we are able to predict others' actions, it gives us a sense of control. This is not to suggest that stereotypes (the beliefs we hold that help us "type" people) are accurate. In fact, they are often quite inaccurate. Still, stereotyping is a basic process of all social interaction. And, stereotyping is central to understanding how deviance definitions are created and sustained at the micro-level of analysis.

We hold stereotypes about a wide variety of persons considered deviant. For example, most people hold stereotypes about the blind, midgets, drug addicts, people with AIDS, and alcoholics. When a person is labeled "deviant," the stereotypes held toward entire categories of people thought to be "that kind of deviant" will be applied to the labeled person. At this point, the person has been stigmatized. He or she has come to possess a devalued, spoiled social identity. All of the stereotypical beliefs about deviants of his or her "kind" are now assumed to exist *within* the stigmatized person.

A study by Cash et al. (1984) shows how a deviant label causes social audiences to devalue the labeled person. The researchers chose the label "alcoholic" for the focus of their study. Many who subscribe to the disease concept of alcoholism believe that it is necessary for the excessive drinker to admit that he or she is an alcoholic for recovery to be successful. This is the fundamental belief of AA. But, while the label "alcoholic" may aid in the recovery process as long as the excessive drinker remains within the supportive environment of AA, it may have an opposite and stigmatizing effect outside the interpersonal network of those who show support and concern. For Cash et al., the research question became: "Does the label 'alcoholic' cause social audiences to be accepting or rejecting of an excessive drinker?"

To explore this question, they asked a random half of a sample of university students to listen to an audiotape of an interview between a psychologist and someone who the researchers labeled as an "alcoholic." The other half listened to an identical recording, but this time the person being interviewed (the interviewee) was not labeled an "alcoholic." After controlling for the "interviewees'" drinking status, the researchers found that students tended to attribute devalued traits and characteristics to the person labeled "alcoholic." The students tended to define the "alcoholic" as being maladjusted, ineffective, and they tended to blame his alcoholism on his own personal failings. The students were less likely to want the "alcoholic" as a friend or a coworker and were less likely to invite him to a party. As the researchers concluded, "The present findings corroborate and extend prior evidence . . . of the social stigma of 'the alcoholic' " (Cash et al., 1984:274).

The theory guiding this interesting study suggests that an important process by which deviance definitions are created involves the attribution of devaluing traits and characteristics. Stereotypes shape the kinds of stigmatizing attributions that will be made and the kind of deviant social identity that will be assigned to a person.

Another provocative study of the way in which stereotypes are central to how social audiences construct deviance definitions was completed by Burk and Sher (1990). They studied how peers and professionals react to persons labeled as "children of alcoholics" (COAs). While programs for COAs are, perhaps, beneficial for those under distress, the potentially negative consequences of being labeled "a child of an alcoholic" have not been systematically investigated. The research by Burk and Sher was designed to fill this gap in the research literature.

Their study comprised two separate but related parts. First, they had 570 male and female high school students complete a questionnaire in which students were asked to rate the roles of "COAs," "Average Students," and "Mentally Ill Students" on a variety of bipolar adjectives such as "good-vs-

bad." Their analysis showed that students rated "Mentally Ill Students" and "COAs" less positively than "Average Students," and they tended to lump the "COAs" with the "Mentally Ill Students" in their evaluations.

In the second part of the study, Burk and Sher asked 80 mental health workers to watch videotapes of a teenager who was described as having either a positive or negative family history of alcoholism and who was either a "school leader" or "one who was having problems" in school. Actually, the teenagers shown on the videotape rehearsed a script designed by one of the experimenters. The interviewer in the videotapes was a doctoral student and the interviews were scripted to be ambiguous about parental psychopathology and the current psychological and behavioral functioning of the adolescent actors (Burk and Sher, 1990:159). By virtue of the research design, if the mental health workers diagnosed problems in the adolescents (the actors), the diagnoses would have to be a result of the labels attached to the actors by the experimenters—in this case, the labels of "COA" or "one who was having problems" in school.

The results of the study supported the labeling hypothesis that negative labels influence the way in which social audiences (in this case, mental health workers) evaluate those who are labeled. In terms of their assessment of the adolescents current functioning, the mental health workers saw those who were labeled "COAs" as isolated from friends and family, generally unhappy with their lives, pessimistic about their future, and manifesting higher levels of psychological dysfunction. Those labeled "COAs" were also perceived by the mental health workers to be more likely to be currently abusing alcohol and drugs, to have a number of school-related problems, and to be unpopular among their peers. Burk and Sher summarize the results from both parts of their study in this way:

COAs may feel the harmful effects of labeling both within their peer group and in any interactions they may have with mental health professionals. Within their peer group, the stigma surrounding COAs could lead to their being rejected by their classmates. Acceptance by one's peers is a crucial part of adolescence, and exclusion often increases feelings of frustration and sadness. Speculating about the COA, then, the feeling of rejection resulting from being equated with mentally ill teenagers may culminate in depression and decreased self-esteem for the identified COA. Furthermore, COAs might attempt to fulfill their need for acceptance with members of a deviant peer group. In either case, one could argue that the act of labeling has created a self-fulfilling prophecy of deviance (Burk and Sher, 1990:162).

The studies we have just examined sought to determine how the "alcoholic" label shapes evaluative judgments made by social audiences. Tottle (1987) extended this line of research into the workplace. Consistent with the emphasis of definitional theories, Tottle's research question may be put this way: "Do work supervisors treat potential employees who have been labeled 'recovering alcoholics' in the same way that they would treat anyone else, or does the label 'alcoholic' cause supervisors to act on the basis of stereotypes associated with the label 'alcoholic'?"

To provide answers to these questions, Tottle interviewed over 2,000 randomly selected supervisors from a sample of 100 federal installations in the Atlanta and Dallas areas. To determine if a person labeled "a recovering alcoholic" would be regarded as an acceptable employee, Tottle developed a social acceptance scale. She asked each supervisor to respond yes or no to the following four items:

1. Assuming his technical skills were appropriate, would you be willing to have this man work in this installation?
2. Would you be willing to have this man as your subordinate?
3. Would you be willing to give this man access to confidential information which

could damage this agency if it becomes public?
4. Would you be willing to have this man take over for you while you are on vacation?

If you assign a "1" to "yes" answers and a "0" to "no" answers, you may calculate the degree of social acceptance a given supervisor holds toward a person labeled "alcoholic." Thus, "yes" to all four questions yields a total score of 4 showing a high degree of social acceptance. By contrast, "no" to all questions shows a very low level of social acceptance.

Tottle's analysis of the data showed that over 43 percent of the supervisors were willing to have the person labeled "alcoholic" in their installations, to have him as a subordinate, to give him access to confidential information about the organization, and to have him take over for the supervisor while he was on vacation (Tottle, 1987:277). Thirty percent of the supervisors agreed to all items except providing the alcoholic with confidential information, while 19 percent were also reluctant to allow the recovering alcoholic to assume their supervisory responsibilities while on vacation (Tottle, 1987:277). According to Tottle, "This demonstrates that social acceptance of the labeled deviants (in this case one who is clearly attempting rehabilitation) may be considerably less than believed, confirming the impact of stigma" (Tottle, 1987:277).

Labeling Theories.   A central focus of labeling theory centers on the process by which persons get classified as deviant and what impact that label has on their self-concepts and future behaviors. In the previous section, we examined how stereotypes shape the reactions of social audiences to persons who have been labeled "alcoholic." Now, our attention is aimed at understanding how the label "alcoholic" may influence the self-image and actions of those so labeled.

Roman and Trice (1968) have suggested that assigning the label "alcoholic" to an alcohol abuser may lead to negative consequences. There may be "disease consequences of the disease label." In Chapter 3, we learned, in connection with Lemert's concept of secondary deviation, how deviant labels may affect a person's self-image and subsequent behaviors. Roman and Trice argue that a similar process operates when persons are tagged with the label "alcoholic." They note that the label "alcoholic" carries with it the idea that the individual has an illness or disease. Persons who are labeled in this way are assigned a sick role (Parsons, 1951). Sick-role assignment implies that a person is no longer responsible for his or her behavior. Specifically, the label "alcoholic" suggests that a person cannot moderate his or her drinking because of a disease process over which he or she has no control. The "alcoholic" label implies that the problem drinker has inherited a physical weakness that makes that person susceptible to alcoholism. Therefore, one outcome of the "alcoholic" label and sick-role assignment is the self-fulfilling prophecy. When problem drinkers are confronted with a drinking situation, they may believe they cannot drink responsibly. Once the first drink is taken, there is no attempt to control their drinking because of the belief that it is impossible. This self-fulfilling prophecy results in loss of control. This view suggests that loss of control over one's drinking is not due to an inherited tendency. Rather, the inability to drink responsibly is a result of the disease label, sick-role assignment, and the self-fulfilling prophecy.

In a recent application of labeling theory to the development of alcoholism, Combs-Orme, Helzer, and Miller (1988), studied a sample of 1,289 treated alcoholics who varied in the number of alcoholic labels imputed to

them by family and nonfamily members. For the labeling thesis to be confirmed, others' alcoholic labels must lead to self-acceptance of those labels, which, in turn, leads to serious problem drinking. While the researchers did find some evidence of differential labeling (problem-drinking males were more likely to be labeled "alcoholic" by family members than females were), their analysis showed no connection between others' labels and the acceptance of those labels by the subjects. In fact, the best predictors of future problem drinking were past problems with alcohol and gender. Women, and respondents with less severe drinking problems in the past, were most likely to be drinking moderately at follow-up, whereas males with a history of drinking problems were more likely to manifest drinking problems five to eight years after treatment (Combs-Orme, Helzer, and Miller, 1988:87).

While the authors conclude that the evidence does not favor a labeling theory of the development of alcoholism, measurement problems may be the reason why the investigators found no connection between others' labels and self-labels. Their measure of self-labels consisted of the question: "How would you describe your own drinking at the time you were drinking the most—would you describe yourself as: (1) a non-drinker or almost one? (2) a normal drinker? (3) someone who drank too much, but had no real problem? (4) a problem drinker? (5) an alcoholic?" Their measure of labels by nonfamily members was: "Have any friends, an employer, or anyone outside your family ever said you were drinking too much for your own good?" The problem is that this measure of others' labels does not provide a very good indication of whether others' thought the subject was an alcoholic. If this measure had asked: "Do others feel you are an *alcoholic*," perhaps a significant correlation between others' labels and self-labels would have been found. This would have provided evidence favoring labeling theory since self-labels in the data were correlated with alcoholic drinking. In other words, if the alternative measure of others' labels were used, the researchers might have found that others' labels influence self-labels and that self-labels, in turn, influence alcoholic drinking. Thus, given this measurement issue, one cannot conclude that a labeling theory of alcoholism has been invalidated.

Most tests of a labeling theory of alcoholism are based on the hypothesis that negative labeling increases the probability of more serious future drinking. Dunham (1983) departed from this traditional focus to determine whether there may be conditions under which labeling may actually *decrease* future problem drinking. Is it possible that stigmatizing labels may actually serve to conventionalize a person's deviant behavior? Under what conditions might this conventionalizing influence occur?

To address these questions, Dunham studied approximately 1,000 individuals who had been admitted to an alcoholism treatment center in Spokane, Washington. Dunham selected two separate groups for comparison: (1) clients who had been referred to the treatment center by the courts for an alcohol-related criminal offense, and, thus, had been legally stigmatized as problem drinkers and (2) clients who came to the center voluntarily, primarily through self-referral. After controlling for a number of socio-demographic variables and prior drinking status, Dunham found that clients who had been legally stigmatized (publicly labeled "problem drinkers") showed *greater* improvement in drinking status during treatment than those who sought treatment voluntarily. "In summary then, the overall proposition—that stigmatizing labels can result in conventionalizing behavior—was supported by this research (Dunham, 1983:264).

While Dunham's conclusions suggest that legal stigma *decreases* problem drinking dur-

ing treatment (a conclusion opposite to the prediction of labeling theory), there is an alternative explanation of his findings. Clients who were legally mandated to treatment may have shown greater improvement because of the threat of imprisonment if they did not actively participate in the treatment program. Thus, it is possible that when the legal threat of a jail sentence was no longer in force, the stigmatized clients may have shown *poorer* drinking status than the control group, a prediction consistent with the labeling assertion that there may be "disease consequences of a disease label." While Dunham's data do not provide an assessment of this possibility, it remains a viable alternative to his conclusion. Despite Dunham's provocative study, it cannot be concluded with confidence that legal stigma actually leads to more *improved* treatment outcome.

Our review of recent literature on a labeling theory of alcoholism leaves us with necessarily inconclusive results. The research neither supports nor refutes all of the claims of the labeling approach. Future research, with more rigorous research designs and better measurement of the relevant concepts central to the labeling approach, will hopefully provide the necessary evidence regarding the viability of labeling theory as a theory of the development of alcoholism.

SOCIAL POLICY AND TREATING THE DEVIANT DRINKER

Guided by a macro-subjectivist orientation of "how drunkenness became a disease," our application of interest group theory revealed how social and political forces operating throughout U.S. history caused the disease ideology to become woven into the fabric of governmental policy on alcoholism (Nusbaumer, 1990). The transformation of the deviant drinker from one who is either weak-willed or criminal to one who has a disease led to a change in who has social control jurisdiction over the alcoholic. The authority for the control of drunkenness began to move toward the community of medical professionals and lay practitioners with a rehabilitative orientation and away from the traditional criminal justice system with its more punitive orientation. To this extent, deviant drinking had been "medicalized" (Conrad and Schneider, 1980).

Social Policy

The disease conception of alcoholism remained the centerpiece of governmental policy on alcoholism prevention, research, and treatment during the early part of the 1970s. Beginning in the mid-1970s until the present, however, a shift away from a purely disease model for alcohol problems and toward a "New-Temperance" ideology may be discerned (Langton, 1991; Beauchamp, 1988). This New-Temperance ideology is based on a *public health model* of alcohol problems. The public health model contends that only a minute fraction of the full scope of a society's alcohol problem can be explained by the small percentage of drinkers who may have inherited a biochemical susceptibility to alcoholism. Indeed, a society's alcohol problem spans well beyond the "alcoholic" to include alcohol-related problems involving nonalcoholic social drinkers. Some of these problems include alcohol-related traffic fatalities, spouse and child abuse involving alcohol, and recreational accidents where alcohol is involved. From the public health perspective, these alcohol problems result from institutional arrangements within society rather than from within the individual, as the disease conception would contend. Among the institutional arrangements that either facilitate or curb a society's alcohol problem are the following: whether a society exercises control over the age at which people are allowed to consume alcohol; whether a society reduces the sup-

ply of alcohol by imposing excise taxes on alcoholic beverages or; whether a society imposes restrictions on the strategies used by the distillery industry in marketing beverage alcohol.

In summing up the current state of affairs regarding alcohol policy, Langton writes:

> The current directions of alcohol policy seem to be shifting toward restricting the availability of alcohol and toward placing limits on the advertising of alcoholic beverages. There are at least two new temperance groups which support this policy: the public health advocates who emphasize alcohol and other drug use as public health problems, and the moralists who emphasize alcohol use as an example of moral evil. The actions of each of these groups to mobilize their resources to influence the direction of future alcohol policy will be the focus of continued research (Langton, 1991:248).

Treating the Deviant Drinker

In the sections that follow, we examine two opposing treatment approaches to alcoholism. The Alcoholics anonymous approach has as its foundation the disease conception of alcoholism. Thus, it is more wedded to the public policy that prevailed during the early 1970s. Other approahces to treatment are at variance with the disease ideology, and are more consistent with a public health model.

alcoholics anonymous. No single organization has worked harder for the success of the disease concept of alcoholism than Alcoholics Anonymous. And, probably no single organization has benefited more from that success. AA stands as the most popular treatment approach for alcoholism today. While AA does not endorse any political party or program, it nonetheless has tremendous political influence.

Believing that alcoholism is an inherited disease, AA argues that the only acceptable goal in the treatment of alcoholism is total abstinence. Clearly, if alcoholism is inherited, the only reasonable way to treat it is to stop drinking. If the alcoholic should drink, he or she will lose control. "One Drink, One Drunk!" Moreover, since alcoholism is inherited, there is no ultimate cure. Therefore, according to AA, there are no "recovered" alcoholics only "recovering" alcoholics.

From the beginning, the founders of AA were interested in helping other alcoholics get sober. Together, they set forth a plan of recovery involving 12 steps. Taking these "steps" is felt to embody the critical ingredients for recovery:

Step One: We admitted we were powerless over alcohol—that our lives had become unmanageable.

Step Two: Came to believe that a Power greater than ourselves could restore us to sanity.

Step Three: Made a decision to turn our will and our lives over to the care of God *as we understood Him.*

Step Four: Made a searching and fearless moral inventory of ourselves.

Step Five: Admitted to God, to ourselves, and to another human being the exact nature of our wrongs.

Step Six: Were entirely ready to have God remove all these defects of character.

Step Seven: Humbly asked Him to remove our shortcomings.

Step Eight: Made a list of all persons we had harmed, and became willing to make amends to them all.

Step Nine: Made direct amends to such people wherever possible, except when to do so would injure them or others.

Step Ten: Continued to take personal inventory and when we were wrong promptly admitted it.

Step Eleven: Sought through prayer and meditation to improve our conscious contact with God *as we understood Him,* praying only for knowledge of His will for us and the power to carry that out.

Step Twelve: Having had a spiritual awakening as the result of these Steps, we tried to carry this message to alcoholics, and to practice these principles in all our affairs.

The above 12 steps are learned and adhered to by all AA members. There appears to be therapeutic value in the steps themselves. But alcoholics often achieve sobriety through the mere process of *affiliating* with other recovering alcoholics. Since the AA view of alcoholism is often seen as being at odds with sociological conceptions of the problem, many of the important sociological aspects of AA are often overlooked. For example, the idea of a strong affiliation is similar to the concept of social integration that Durkheim emphasized in his research on suicide. Recall that Durkheim theorized that suicide would be greatest when social integration was low. To generalize Durkheim's theory, the greater the social integration the less the likelihood of personal pathology, including alcoholism. Therefore, AA is doing good Durkheimian sociology!

There are other important sociological principles in AA's recovery program. The recovering alcoholic is reinforced for continuing sobriety. As we saw in connection with social learning theory, social reinforcers are powerful motivators of human behavior. Moreover, the affiliation of AA serves as an important reference group replacing the old group of "drinking buddies." Also, the recovering alcoholic is exposed to sober and responsible role models through an AA sponsor (an AA member who guides a new member in the Alcoholics Anonymous philosophy). Again, it appears that those involved in the AA program are applying sound sociological principles in their program for recovery.

In spite of the many positive features of the AA program, as with any other treatment approach, the AA philosophy has some weaknesses. First, as Roman and Trice (1968) have pointed out, a "disease label may have disease consequences." It appears true that alcoholism is a merry-go-round of denial, making it necessary for the alcoholic to admit his or her problem before recovery may be achieved. However, to accept the "alcoholic" label is to accept sick-role assignment. To be "sick" implies that alcoholics are not responsible for their disease and, therefore, cannot control its course. Since one cannot control the course of the disease, loss of control becomes inevitable. They become the very thing they are said to be. This would not be a problem if all recovering alcoholics refrained from ever drinking again. However, as is often the case, many labeled "alcoholics" slip. If this occurs, loss of control may follow, not necessarily because of any inherited tendency, but because the persons have come to believe they have a disease over which they have no control.

The second weakness of the AA philosophy (and for other treatment approaches that embrace the disease theory of alcoholism) are the legal complications stemming from the assumption that alcoholism is a disease. To assume that alcoholism is a disease is to deny that the alcoholic bears responsibility for his or her alcoholism. After all, we do not hold persons who have diseases such as sugar diabetes or breast cancer blameworthy. We consider them ill but not accountable since their illness is not of their own choosing. It has "invaded" them against their will so to speak. Clearly, this has important implications for those who commit alcohol-related criminal offenses. Can a society hold people legally responsible for their behavior if that behavior is a result of the alcoholic condition? This dilemma has created much heated controversy, particularly, in cases of crimes that have resulted in the death of the victim.

Behavioral Therapy.   Behavioral therapy is based on the principles of social learning. To

this extent, behavioral therapy is more consistent with a sociological perspective on alcoholism. Social learning theorists contend that problem drinking is learned like any other behavior. Just as alcoholic drinking can be learned, it can be unlearned. Drinking problems arise because excessive drinking is being reinforced. According to behavioral therapy, excessive drinking can be terminated through the application of punishers. In order for a punisher to work, it must occur with or immediately following a drinking occasion. The typical hangover that occurs the day after does not terminate excessive drinking because there is too long a delay between the drinking episode and the hangover. But, if an awful headache occurred simultaneously with every drinking occasion, this may be sufficient punishment to decrease the likelihood that drinking would continue. Drinking alcohol would become less and less pleasurable and more and more painful. The general procedure whereby drinkers can learn to hate that which they now love is called *aversion conditioning*.

There are two popular aversion conditioning procedures used in the treatment of alcoholism. One is chemical aversion, and the other is electrical aversion. In the case of chemical aversion, extreme nausea is induced in the alcoholic patient by an injection of some nausea-producing substance like Emitine. At about the same time, the patient is required to drink the alcoholic beverage of choice. Additionally, there is an attempt to surround the patient with as much visual stimuli associated with alcohol as possible. In short, the sight, smell, and taste of alcohol are paired with extreme nausea. After a few days of this treatment, it is not surprising that the alcoholic will report no desire to drink! The constant craving is broken and the alcoholic is given the chance to contemplate an alternative way of life. In a sense, the patient has regained his or her will. As is often observed, we cannot make it impossible for you to drink, but we can make it possible for you not to drink.

Chemical aversion could be dangerous if esophageal varices (swollen veins in the esophagus) are present in the alcoholic, because the procedure entails a good deal of vomiting. In this case, electrical aversion may be used. Typically, the patient is wired to an electrical apparatus that allows the therapist to administer shocks. Then the alcoholic is required to drink the beverage of choice. Whenever an approach response is made, the therapist will administer a shock. After a number of these sessions, the alcoholic is repulsed by the sight, smell, and taste of alcohol. The same aversion to alcohol that was created by the chemical approach is established with this method, but there is no threat of hemorrhage of the esophagus because no vomiting is involved.

Some behavioral therapists have modified the aversion-conditioning procedure in an attempt to determine if true alcoholics may be able to regain control over their drinking. Sometimes referred to as "controlled drinking" experiments, these kinds of research and treatment have resulted in the greatest controversy in the field of alcoholism treatment. The basis of the controversy centers on the concept of loss of control and the disease theory of alcoholism. Recall that according to the disease conception of alcoholism, loss of control results from an inherited biochemical abnormality. Since it is genetic, there is only one way to treat alcoholism and that's through total abstinence. As we have noted, if it could be shown that true alcoholics could regain control over their drinking, the disease concept would be invalidated.

Those who conduct controlled drinking experiments combine the aversion-conditioning procedure described above with what is called Blood-Alcohol-Level (BAL) discrimination training. BAL discrimination training involves teaching alcoholics to accurately estimate their blood alcohol levels at any given point during a drinking occasion. Once the alcoholic achieves this ability, the researchers allow the alcoholic to drink freely with only one stipulation: If the alcoholic exceeds a pre-designated BAL (for example, .10), then electrical shocks will be administered. Also, shocks may be administered if the alcoholic "gulps" drinks instead of sipping and if the alcoholic orders drinks too fast.

In the most widely publicized of the controlled drinking studies, Sobell and Sobell (1973) reported that many "loss of control" alcoholics were, indeed, able to learn to drink without losing control. The findings reported by Sobell and Sobell created heated debate in the field of alcoholism treatment. Defenders of AA and the disease view of alcoholism were among the sharpest critics. Clearly, the disease ideology had been brought into question.

Approximately ten years after the publication of the original findings by Sobell and Sobell, Pendery and her collaborators (1982) attempted to locate the 20 alcoholics who participated in the original Sobell and Sobell study. Pendery, Maltzman, and West (1982) suggested that the outcomes reported by Sobell and Sobell were incomplete and, that upon a ten-year follow-up, 4 of the original 20 alcoholics had died of what appeared to be alcohol-related problems. Furthermore, the "successes" reported by Sobell and Sobell were far less dramatic than the researchers implied.

The Pendery, Maltzman, and West report appeared to establish forever the assertion that true alcoholics cannot control their drinking and, by inference, that the disease concept is, after all, valid. However, further analysis of the Pendery, Maltzman, and West study indicated a clear bias in favor of the disease concept. For example, the control subjects in the original Sobell and Sobell study were alcoholics who underwent traditional AA therapy. Pendery and her collaborators elected not to provide data from the ten-year follow-up on these subjects. When those data were gathered by the Sobells, 6 of the 20 alcoholics who were treated by the abstinence-oriented AA therapy had died by the time of the ten-year follow-up (Sobell and Sobell, 1984). This, of course, is a higher mortality rate than the alcoholics who were treated by the controlled drinking approach.

Whether alcoholics may be able to regain control over their drinking remains a question for scientific research. Given the political fallout from the Pendery, Maltzman, and West follow-up of the Sobells' original study, it is unlikely that research into this question will be financially supported by the National Institute of Alcohol Abuse and Alcoholism (NIAAA). Scientifically justified or not, the disease concept is "in" and remains the cornerstone of NIAAA policy regarding both research and treatment of alcoholism.

SUMMARY

Whether one drinks, how much one drinks, and how alcohol affects behavior are strongly influenced by social and cultural forces. This is dramatically shown when the disinhibition hypothesis is subjected to cross-cultural evidence. According to the *disinhibition hypothesis*, the physical effects of alcohol automatically cause people to release emotional and behavioral tendencies that are otherwise held in check. For example, it is commonly believed, at least in U.S. society, that alcohol increases sexual arousal and causes people to become more aggressive in interpersonal situations. But, cross-cultural evidence shows that alcohol consumption leads to a variety of behaviors, suggesting that the way people act when they are intoxicated is the way they have learned to act within their particular cultural environment.

The most popular definition of alcoholism is that it is a disease. The *disease concept* suggests that alcoholism is inherited. From a sociological perspective, there are two important limitations to this biologically based view. First, it does not easily explain social and cultural variations in alcoholism rates. Second, a strictly biological theory does not tell us why a particular form of drinking behavior is socially regarded as a disease. As we ultimately learned, the belief that alcoholism is a disease is as much a social and political accomplishment as it is a medical discovery.

Some sociologists employ the objectivist conception of alcoholism while others adopt the subjectivist conception. Objectivists do not use the term *alcoholism* because it has been associated far too long with the disease conception. Rather, they are inclined to refer to excessive alcohol use as deviant drinking. *Deviant drinking* is defined as drinking behavior that violates the norms of acceptable alcohol consumption for a group, community, or society. Sociologists who conceptualize alcoholism in subjectivist terms use the term *alcoholism*, not because they accept a biological theory of alcoholism, but because they are interested in using the very terms social audiences employ when they label an act as "alcoholism" or a person as "alcoholic." Thus, the subjectivist defines *alcoholism* as a label imputed to drinking behaviors (real or imagined) by social audiences. The subjectivist defines *alcoholic* as a label affixed to persons who are believed by others to have the condition alcoholism.

National surveys of problem drinking show wide variation in drinking and problem drinking depending on socio-demographic variables such as social class, gender, marital status, race, and ethnicity. In general, drinking is directly related to social class, but problem drinking is inversely related to social class. A greater percentage of men as compared to women are problem drinkers. Whether this difference will diminish due to sex-role convergence within U.S. society cannot be fully determined based upon available data. In terms of marital status, those who are divorced, separated, single, or widowed have a higher probability of becoming problem drinkers than those who are married. The highest rate of problem drinking has been attributed to Native Americans. Still, the rate of problem drinking varies greatly among different tribes. African-American and white men have similar rates of problem drinking but African-American men have a higher incidence of medical complications associated with their excessive alcohol use. A high percentage of Hispanic men drink as compared to only a small percentage of Hispanic women. The highest incidence of problem drinking among Hispanic men occurs in their thirties but tends to decline thereafter. Among women, the highest incidence of problem drinking occurs in their forties and fifties, but the rate drops to near zero among women aged 60 or over.

We considered two macro-objectivist theories of deviant drinking. *Anomie theory* suggests that higher rates of problem drinking will occur among those who experience a greater discrepancy between aspirations and objective opportunities to achieve them. Most tests of an anomie theory of problem drinking have measured anomie as a social-psychological variable—that is, whether individuals experience a sense of alienation, two aspects of which are hopelessness and social isolation. In general, anomie is not related to the quantity and frequency of drinking but tends to be related to negative social consequences associated from excessive alcohol use.

Neo-Marxist theory suggests that problem drinking derives from the oppressive nature of work in a capitalist economic system. Thus, workers who do not feel a sense of control in the workplace should show higher rates of escapist alcohol use. While research studies are sparse, some evidence exists to support this assertion. An additional hypothesis stemming from neo-Marxist theory is that the state supports the production and sale of alcohol as a means of dulling the despair associated with alienated labor. While this notion is provocative, empirical tests are virtually nonexistent.

Two micro-objectivist theories were considered. *Social learning theory* suggests that definitions (attitudes) favorable to excessive alcohol use are learned in association with heavy-drinking peers and that these definitions, along with reinforcers, will lead to problem drinking among those who have internalized them. In general, research leads to the conclusion that similar learning processes operate in accounting for the acquisition and maintenance of problem drinking despite a person's specific stage in life. Still, youthful drinkers appear to be more influenced by differential associations (what their peers do), while older drinkers are more influenced by the reinforcing properties of alcohol itself.

Deterrence theory is at the center of the attempt on the part of the criminal justice system to combat drunk driving. Deterrence theory proposes that drunk driving will be reduced if punishments are certain, severe, and swift. Systematic research indicates that a variety of countermeasures designed to deter the drunk driver have short-term effects but the effects tend to decline with the passage of time.

When considering macro-subjective theory, we saw how *interest group theory* provides valuable insights into how drinking comes to be defined as deviance and how drinkers come to be defined as deviants. Gusfield's social-historical analysis laid the theoretical groundwork for us to understand how "drunkenness became a disease." Our examination of *MADD* (Mothers Against Drunk Drivers) showed how an interest group can shape social policy if (1) the *claim-makers* are perceived to be legitimate, and (2) the claims are made during a time when the national political climate is receptive to a change in social policy.

Our consideration of micro-subjectivist theories led to an examination of two bodies of research. First, *definitional theories* focus on how a stigmatizing label such as "alcoholic" may cause social audiences to respond negatively to those so labeled. The research is quite consistent in showing that being labeled "alcoholic" causes social audiences to devalue the labeled individual. Moreover, even being labeled a child of an alcoholic, or *COA*, may lead both peers and professionals to make negative attributions to the labeled child. It appears that while the label "alcoholic" may have positive consequences within the somewhat protective environment of AA, the same label apparently serves as a stigma in non-AA settings.

Second, *labeling theory* asserts that there may be "disease consequences of a disease label." This means that, when people are labeled "alcoholic," they are cast into a sick role. *Sick-role assignment* absolves individuals of the responsibility for controlling their drinking. If the labeled person should drink, loss of control may occur because of a self-fulfilling prophecy. In the context of our discussion, a *self-fulfilling prophecy* refers to the fact that drinkers lose control over their alcohol consumption because they have come to believe they cannot do otherwise. The empirical evaluations of this labeling hypothesis suffer from certain methodological shortcomings that make definitive conclusions difficult to draw. The weight of the evidence, however, provides only partial support for the labeling thesis.

Current social policy regarding the causes, prevention, and treatment of alcoholism is in a state of transition. In the early to mid-1970s the disease concept served as the very centerpiece of governmental policy on alcoholism. Recently, the *public health model* has gained acceptance among a number of professionals in the field. The disease model locates a society's alcohol problem within the individual. The emphasis is on treatment. By contrast, the public health model locates a society's alcohol problem within institutional arrange-

ments and, thus, emphasizes measures, such as taxation and laws regulating the drinking age, in hopes of reducing the incidence of problem-drinking behavior within society. The emphasis is on prevention.

Alcoholics Anonymous is perhaps the most popular treatment program for alcoholics. Though based on a disease conception of alcoholism, we noted that AA incorporates a number of sociological principles in its recovery program. For example, the fact that AA is an intense affiliation suggests that AA is cognizant of the importance of social integration in the recovery process. Thus, we felt that AA is doing good Durkheimian sociology. Behavioral therapy is often considered antagonistic to the AA treatment program. Clearly, the most hotly contested issue in the treatment of alcoholism is whether true alcoholics can regain control over their drinking. The AA view is that they cannot. By contrast, those who subscribe to the behavioral approach feel that regaining control is at least theoretically possible because behaviorists believe that all behaviors, including problem drinking, are acquired through the same learning principles.

GLOSSARY

Alcoholic.   From the subjectivist conception, a label affixed to persons who are believed by others to have the condition alcoholism.

Alcoholism.   From the subjectivist conception, a label imputed to drinking behaviors (real or imagined) by social audiences.

Anomie theory.   As an explanation of problem-drinking behavior, the theory that problem drinking arises from an imbalance between culturally induced aspirations and the objective opportunities to achieve them.

Claim-makers.   Members of interest groups or social movements who attempt to define an objective condition perceived to be undesirable as a publicly acknowledged social problem.

COAs. An acronym for *Children of Alcoholics.* It can refer to either nonadult or adult children of alcoholic parents.

Definitional therapy. A micro-subjectivist theory that focuses on how a stigmatizing label such as "alcoholic" may cause social audiences to respond negatively to those so labeled.

Deterrence theory. As applied to problem drinking, deterrence theory proposes that problem drinking will be reduced if punishments are certain, severe, and swift. Deterrence theory is at the center of the attempt on the part of the criminal justice system to combat drunk driving.

Deviant drinking. From the objectivist conception, drinking behavior that violates the norms of acceptable alcohol consumption for a group, community or society.

Disinhibition hypothesis. The claim that the physical effects of alcohol automatically cause people to release emotional and behavioral tendencies that are otherwise held in check.

Disease concept. The view that alcoholism is inherited. The disease concept is the central idea in Alcoholics Anonymous as a philosophy for recovery.

Interest group theory. A macro-subjectivist theory that focuses on the social, political, and historical forces involved in defining different forms of drinking as deviance or different kinds of drinkers as deviants.

Labeling theory. A micro-subjectivist theory that asserts that there may be "disease consequences of a disease label." The critical concepts in labeling theory are an imputed label by a social audience, sick-role assignment, altered self-concepts, and the self-fulfilling prophecy.

MADD (Mothers Against Drunk Drivers). An interest group that has been successful in influencing anti-drunk driving legislation because the members (claim-makers) were perceived as legitimate and because their claims were made during a time when the national political climate was receptive to a change in policy regarding the drinking driver.

Neo-Marxist theory. As an explanation of problem drinking, the theory that problem drinking derives from the oppressive nature of work in a capitalist economic system.

Public health model. The public health model locates a society's alcohol problem within institutional arrangements and, thus, emphasizes measures, such as taxation and laws regulating the drinking age, in hopes of reducing the incidence of problem-drinking behavior within society. The emphasis is on prevention, as opposed to treatment.

Self-fulfilling prophecy. In the context of a discussion of a labeling theory of alcoholism, the fact that drinkers lose control over their alcohol consumption because they have come to believe they cannot do otherwise.

Sick-role assignment. An assignment of a label, and by implication a role, by a social audience that absolves those labeled of the responsibility for controlling their drinking.

Social learning theory. A theory suggesting that definitions (attitudes) favorable to excessive alcohol use are learned in association with heavy-drinking peers and that these definitions, along with reinforcers, will lead to more severe problem drinking among those who have internalized them.

SUGGESTED READINGS

Beauchamp, Dan E. *The Health of the Republic: Epidemics, Medicine, and Moralism as Challenges to Democracy.* Philadelphia: Temple University

Press, 1988. In this provocative volume, Beauchamp presents the public health approach as an alternative to conceptualizing alcoholism as a disease. The social policy implications of the public health approach are explored.

Conrad, Peter, and Joseph Schneider. *Deviance and Medicalization: From Badness to Sickness.* St. Louis, Mo.: Mosby, 1980. In addition to alcoholism and drug addiction, Conrad and Schneider explore the social, political, and historical forces that led to the transformation of a variety of behaviors from being evil to being ill. The approach reflects an interest group, power politics approach to the construction of deviance definitions.

Langton, Phyllis A. *Drug Use and the Alcohol Dilemma.* Boston: Allyn and Bacon, 1991. In this readable text, Langton approaches the issue of alcoholism and drug abuse from an institutional perspective showing how the alcohol and drug problem reflects larger institutional arrangements and social movements within society.

Ward, David A. *Alcoholism: Introduction to Theory and Treatment.* 3rd ed. Dubuque: Kendall/Hunt, 1990. This is a comprehensive overview of theory and treatment regarding problem drinking behavior. The text takes an issues, controversies, and debates approach, which presents competing sides of many hotly contested issues in the field.

REFERENCES

Akers, Ronald, Anthony LaGreca, John Cochran, Christine Sellers. "Social Learning Theory and Alcohol Behavior Among the Elderly." *The Sociological Quarterly* 30 (1989): pp. 625–638.

Beauchamp, Dan E. *The Health of the Republic: Epidemics, Medicine, and Moralism as Challenges to Democracy.* Philadelphia: Temple University Press, 1988.

Bunce, R. "The Political Economy of California's Wine Industry." Toronto: Addiction Research Foundation, 1979.

Burk, Jeffery, and Kenneth Sher. "Labeling the Child of an Alcoholic: Negative Stereotyping by Mental Health Professionals and Peers." *Journal of Studies on Alcohol* 51 (1990): pp. 156–163.

Caetano, R. "Drinking Patterns and Alcohol Problems in a National Sample of U.S. Hispanics." NIAAA Monograph 18. DHHS Publication No. (ADM) 89–1435. Washington, D.C.: Superintendent of Documents. U.S. Government Printing Office (1989): pp. 147–162.

Cash, Thomas, Dan Briddell, Barry Gillen, and Carol MacKinnon. "When Alcoholics Are not Anonymous: Socioperceptual Effects of Labeling and Drinking Patterns." *Journal of Studies on Alcohol* 45 (1984): pp. 272–275.

Combs-Orme, Terri, John E. Helzer, and Richard M. Miller. "The Application of Labeling Theory to Alcoholism." *Journal of Social Service Research* 11 (1988): pp. 73–91.

Conrad, Peter, and Joseph Schneider. *Deviance and Medicalization: From Badness to Sickness.* St. Louis, MO: Mosby, 1980.

Dunham, Roger G. "The Role of Legal Stigmatization in the Enhancement of Treatment Goals for Problem Drinkers." *Deviant Behavior* 4 (1983): pp. 257–266.

———. "The Social Distribution of Drinking and Problem Drinking." *Alcoholism: Introduction to Theory and Treatment.* David A. Ward. 3rd ed. Dubuque: Kendall/Hunt, 1990: pp. 92–117.

Engels, Frederick. *The Condition of the Working Class in England.* London: Grenada, 1969. Originally published in 1845.

Glassner, B., and B. Berg. "How Jews Avoid Alcohol Problems." *American Sociological Review* 45 (1980): pp. 647–664.

Hingson, Ralph, Tim Heeren, David Kouenock, Thomas Mangione, Allan Meyers, Suzette Morelock, Ruth Lenderman, and Norman Scotch. "Effects of Maine's 1981 and Massachusetts' 1982 Driving-Under-the-Influence Legislation." *American Journal of Public Health* 77 (1987): pp. 593–597.

Hughes, Stella and Richard A. Dodder. "Anomie as a Correlate of Self-Reported Drinking Behavior." *The Journal of Social Psychology* 125 (1985): pp. 265–266.

Jellinek, E. M. *The Disease Concept of Alcoholism.* Highland Park, N.J.: Hillhouse Press, 1960.

Johnson, P. E. *A Shopkeeper's Millennium.* New York: Hill and Wang, 1978.

Johnson, Valerie. "Adolescent Alcohol and Marijuana Use: A Longitudinal Assessment of a Social Learning Perspective." *American Journal of Drug and Alcohol Abuse* 14 (1988): pp. 419–439.

Keller, Mark. "The Disease Concept of Alcoholism Revisited." *Journal of Studies of Alcohol* 37 (1976): pp. 1694–1717.

Langton, Phyllis A. *Drug Use and the Alcohol Dilemma.* Boston: Allyn and Bacon, 1991.

Lee, David J, Richard S. DeFrank, and Robert Rose. "Anomie, Alcohol Abuse and Alcohol Consumption: A Prospective Analysis." *Journal of Studies on Alcohol* 51 (1990): pp. 415–421.

Lender, M. "Drunkenness as an Offense in Early New England: A Study of Puritan Attitudes." *Quarterly Journal of Studies on Alcohol* 34 (1973): pp. 353–366.

MacAndrew, Graig, and Robert Edgerton. *Drunken Comportment: A Social Explanation.* Chicago: Aldine, 1969.

Makeła, K, Robin Room, E. Single, P. Sulkunen, and B. Walsh. *Alcohol, Society and State.* Vol 1. Toronto: Addiction Research Foundation, 1981.

Meacham, Andrew. "The Re-emergence of Suzanne Somers." *Changes* 1988: pp. 18, 50–54.

Merton, Robert K. *Social Theory and Social Structure.* Free Press, 1967.

Milam, J. R. and K. Ketcham. *Under The Influence: A Guide to the Myths and Realities of Alcoholism.* New York: Bantam Books, 1983.

Nusbaumer, Michael R. "Alcoholism and the State: Deviance Management and the Creation of Social Capital." *Research in Social Policy* 2 (1990): pp. 157–175.

Parsons, Talcott. *The Social System.* New York: Free Press, 1951.

Peele, Stanton. "The Implications and Limitations of Genetic Models of Alcoholism and Other Addictions." *Journal of Studies on Alcohol* 47 (1986): pp. 63–73.

Pendery, Mary, L., Irving M. Maltzman, and Jolyon L. West. "Controlled Drinking by Alcoholics?" *Science* 217 (1982): pp. 169–175.

Reichel-Dolmatoff, G., and A. Reichel-Dolmatoff. *The People of Aritama.* London: Routledge and Kegan Paul, 1961.

Reinarman, Graig. "The Social Construction of an Alcohol Problem: The Case of Mothers Against Drunk Drivers and Social Control in the 1980s." *Theory and Society* 17 (1988): pp. 91–120.

Roman, Paul, and Harrison Trice. "The Sick Role,, Labelling Theory, and the Deviant Drinker." *International Journal of Social Psychology* 14 (1968): pp. 245–251.

Ross, Lawrence H. "Deterring Drunken Driving: An Analysis of Current Efforts." *Journal of Studies on Alcohol* Supplement No. 10 (1985): pp. 122–128.

———. "Social Control Through Deterrence: Drinking-and-Driving Laws." *Annual Review of Sociology* 10 (1984): pp. 21–35.

Rush, Benjamin. "An Inquiry into the Effects of Ardent Spirits upon the Body." *Quarterly Journal of Studies on Alcohol* 4 (1943): pp. 321–341. Originally published in 1785.

Schneider, Joseph, W. "Deviant Drinking as Disease: Alcoholism as a Social Accomplishment." *Social Problems* 25 (1978): pp. 361–372.

Seeman, Melvin, Alice Seeman, and Art Budros. "Powerlessness, Work, and Community: A Longitudinal Study of Alienation and Alcohol Use." *Journal of Health and Social Behavior* 29 (1988): pp. 185–198.

Sellers, Christine S., and Thomas L. Winfree. "Differential Associations and Definitions: A Panel Study of Youthful Drinking Behavior." *The International Journal of the Addictions* 25 (1990): pp. 755–771.

Singer, Merril. "Toward a Political-Economy of Alcoholism: The Missing Link in the Anthropology of Drinking." *Social Science and Medicine* 23 (1986): pp. 113–130.

Sobell, Mark, and Linda Sobell. "The Aftermath of Heresy." *Behavior Research and Therapy.* 22 (1984): pp. 413–440.

———. "Alcoholics Treated by Individualized Behavior Therapy." *Behavior Research and Therapy.* 11 (1973): pp. 599–618.

Srole, Leo. "Social Integration and Certain Corollaries: An Exploratory Study." *American Sociological Review* 21 (1956): pp. 709–716.

Tottle, Deborah, M. "Social Acceptance of the Recovering Alcoholic in the Workplace: A Research Note." *Journal of Drug Issues* 17 (1987): pp. 273–279.

U.S. Department of Health and Human Services (DHHS). Seventh Special Report to the U.S.

Congress on Alcohol and Health. Rockville, MD: National Institute on Alcohol Abuse and Alcoholism, 1990.

Ward, David A. *Alcoholism: Introduction to Theory and Treatment* (3rd ed.) Dubuque, Iowa: Kendall/Hunt, 1990.

U.S. Department of Health and Human Services (DHHS). *Sixth Special Report to the U.S. Congress on Alcohol and Health.* Rockville, MD: National Institute on Alcohol Abuse and Alcoholism, 1987.

Wilsnack, R. W., and R. Cheloha. "Women's Roles and Problem Drinking Across the Lifespan." *Social Problems* 34 (1987): pp. 231–248.

Wilsnack, R. W., S. C. Wilsnack, and A. Klassen. "Women's Drinking and Drinking Problems: Patterns from a 1981 National Survey." *American Journal of Public Health* 74 (1984): pp. 1231–1238.

Chapter 5

Drug Use as Deviance

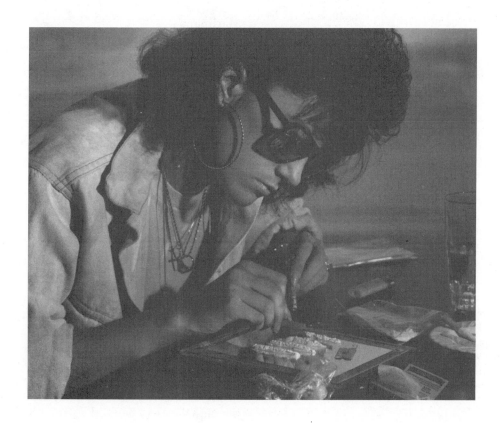

"PRINCE OF THE BARRIO"

While there are a variety of forms of deviance, perhaps none has captured the attention of the U.S. public more than the recent gang wars among youth of the inner cities. Lying, cheating, torture, robbery, sexual assault, and murder are everyday occurrences among youth and their families who live out their uncertain lives in the nation's major cities. Consider the case of a young boy of the inner city of Los Angeles:

The home boys call him Frog. But as he swaggers through the Rancho San Pedro Housing Project in East Los Angeles, Frog is a cocky prince of the barrio. His mane of lustrous jeri curls, his freckled nose, and innocent brown eyes belie his prodigious street smarts. Frog is happy to tell you that he rakes in $200 a week selling crack, known as rock in Los Angeles. He proudly advertises his fledgling membership in an ultra-violent street gang, the Crips. And he brags that he has used his drug money to rent a Nissan Z on weekends. He has not yet learned how to use a stick shift, however, and at 4 ft. 10 in., he sometimes has trouble seeing over the dashboard. Frog is 13 years old (Time, 1988:20).

Frog, and literally thousands of youth like him, have become major figures in the sale of illicit drugs, the most popular being crack cocaine. Why are substantial numbers of an entire generation of youth being propelled into such a hazardous and clearly lethal way of life? In this chapter, we explore some possible answers. Then, we will examine governmental efforts to deal with the problem as well as alternative drug control strategies that many regard as superior to existing governmental policy.

DRUG USE IN A CROSS-CULTURAL PERSPECTIVE

It is a common misconception that any use of a mind-altering substance not prescribed by a medical doctor is automatically a form of deviance. Yet, as our examination of cross-

cultural evidence will show, almost every society has used some type of mind-altering substance at some point in its historical development. And, as we examine drug use cross-culturally, we gain the clear understanding that whether drug use is regarded as deviance depends, in large measure, on the cultural context within which that use takes place. Thus, a cross-cultural perspective on drug use would seem an appropriate starting point for gaining understanding into how drug use comes to be regarded as deviance.

Marijuana

Marijuana is the popular name of the drug prepared from the dried leaves and flowering tops of the hemp plant, a plant also known as *Cannabis Sativa*. *Hashish* is the drug prepared by drying the resin produced by the marijuana plant. Typically, hashish (or, in street jargon, "hash") is more potent than marijuana.

The oldest archaeological evidence, dating from the Chou dynasty (1124–249 B.C.), indicates that ancient China may have been the first culture to use marijuana, primarily as a source of fiber. It was also used for medical purposes but does not seem to have been an extremely important part of the Chinese pharmacopeia (Abel, 1980).

India, with its many cultures, seems to have been one of the first societies where marijuana was used for purposes other than a fiber source. Its use on some occasions, and in some forms, had religious significance. The Vedas, a collection of Hindu holy books, tell of how Shiva brought the cannabis plant from the Himalayas to be used by the peoples of India merely for the purpose of enjoyment. Bhang, a mild liquid preparation containing leaves of the cannabis plant, has played a similar role in Indian society as has alcohol in Western cultures (Abel, 1980).

Africa also has a history of cannabis use.

Since the hemp plant is not native to Africa, it was obviously introduced from elsewhere. Most likely the plant was first brought to Africa by Arab traders. In Africa, marijuana use varies from tribe to tribe. Some tribes use marijuana for ceremonial purposes, some for recreational purposes, and some for a combination of purposes. Still other tribes do not have any history of cannabis use (Abel, 1980).

It is interesting to note that while hemp has been grown in the United States since colonial times, it was not considered deviance until the 1930s. At that time, Harry Anslinger, the director of the Federal Bureau of Narcotics, was looking for a new "killer drug" to justify increased funding for the bureau. This, combined with a growing sentiment against Mexican immigrants in the border states, made the drug a convenient scapegoat for social problems (Musto, 1987; Seigel, 1989; Stafford, 1983).

Cocaine

Cocaine is the drug found in the leaves of the coca plant (*Erythroxylon coca*). The coca plant is a very plain looking shrub native to Latin America. The leaves of the coca shrub have been chewed by the Indians of certain areas of Latin America as a mild stimulant and a dietary supplement, since before the time of the Spanish conquest. Despite disapproval by the Spanish authorities following the conquest, there is no evidence that chewing coca led to any serious social problems. This may have been, in part, a result of the belief that coca was a gift from the gods and, as such, should not be used recklessly.

In the late 1800s, coca became a popular ingredient in tonics and patented medicines. While no great problems seem to have developed from this use of the coca leaf, problems with addiction and compulsive use were seen to develop when cocaine was extracted from the coca leaf. Cocaine was, and still is, valu-able as a local anesthetic. In its early days, it was often overprescribed by doctors who embraced it as the new miracle drug and were not aware of its potentially addictive properties (Seigel, 1989; Weil and Rosen, 1983).

Hallucinogens

Hallucinogens is the common name for a variety of psychoactive drugs; the name is derived from the tendency of the drugs to cause hallucinations. In most cultures, religious ceremonies and magical practices are the most common uses of hallucinogans. For example, hallucinogens like peyote are important as tools for shamans among some Indian tribes in Mexico, such as the Yaqui (Castaneda, 1969). Tribes in other parts of Latin America also use various hallucinogens including, but not limited to, peyote and similar cacti, and various hallucinogenic mushrooms (De Rios, 1984; Stafford, 1983). In some cultures, hallucinogens play an important role in ceremonies marking an adolescent's transition into adulthood (De Rios, 1984; De Rios and Grob, 1992).

In Siberia, types of *Amanita* mushrooms, which contain anticholinergic compounds, are used for a variety of purposes including recreation, shamanistic trance, and capturing reindeer (Stafford, 1983).

In some parts of Africa, Ibogaine is used as a hallucinogen. Ibogaine, a compound extracted from the *Iboga* plant, is similar in action to LSD (Weil and Rosen, 1983). LSD is a powerful hallucinogenic chemical synthesized from ergot in 1938 and is probably the best known hallucinogen in the United States.

Hallucinogens are used in many cultures without reports of major abuse problems. This may be, in part, because the effects of the drug seem to have low physical addition properties. Also, in many cultures, the use of hallucinogenic drugs is often associated with ceremonies and rituals, factors which may reduce abuse potential.

WHEN IS DRUG USE DEVIANCE?

Given the considerable variation in drug use between and within cultures, will we ever be able to answer the question, "When is drug use deviance?" The answer, of course, depends on your conception of deviance.

In general terms, the objectivist conception defines deviance as acts that violate norms. Thus, for the objectivist, drug use becomes deviance when it violates group or societal norms regarding appropriate drug-using behavior. In some cultural contexts, the norm regarding drug use may stipulate that any use of drugs whatsoever is deviance. Still, in other cultures, norms about appropriate drug use may not require total abstinence, as our cross-cultural examples at the outset of this chapter have shown. And, this appears to be true irrespective of the particular drug in question.

As we learned in Chapter 1, the subjectivist conception defines deviance as a label created by social audiences. When this more general definition is applied to drug use, it suggests that drug use becomes deviance when it is labeled as such by others. Thus, deviant drug use is drug use so labeled. The subjectivist will not withdraw from this position even when drug use involves physical dependency, however severe. The reason is that not all physical dependence to drugs is regarded as deviance. Consider, for example, the difference in the way an elderly person who is addicted to barbituates is publicly regarded (defined by social audiences) as compared to an equally addicted adolescent. Both people are chemically dependent, but the elderly person's addition is less likely to be defined as a form of deviance than the addictive behavior of the teenager. In the example, the label of "deviance" is not a result of the addictive behavior *per se*, but to differen-

tial responses by social audiences. Therefore, the subjectivists maintain their position that drug use is deviance only when it is labeled as such, irrespective of the severity of the drug-using behavior.

PATTERNS OF DRUG USE

Much of the scientific information on patterns of drug use in the United States comes from national surveys sponsored by the National Institute on Drug Abuse (NIDA). Two such NIDA sponsored national surveys are the *National Household Survey on Drug Abuse* (NHSDA) and the *Monitoring the Future* project carried out by NIDA and the University of Michigan (Johnston et al., 1991b). Our examination of patterns of drug use in the United States draws heavily on these two national surveys.

Marijuana Use

Marijuana has traditionally been the drug of choice among those who use drugs in the United States. As shown in Figure 5–1, approximately one-third of those responding to the 1990 NHSDA reported use of marijuana at sometime in their lives. Approximately 10 percent of respondents reported use in the last year, and about 5 percent reported use in the past 30 days. This translates into approximately 66 million people having used marijuana at sometime in their lives, about 20 million reporting use in the past year, and approximately 10 million reporting use in the past 30 days.

Demographic Profile of Pot Users. As shown in Figure 5–2, of those reporting marijuana use in the past month, approximately 60 percent (6.1 million) are male and about 40 percent (4.1 million) are female. Rates of use in the last month based on ethnicity show that African Americans were more likely to have used in the past month than were

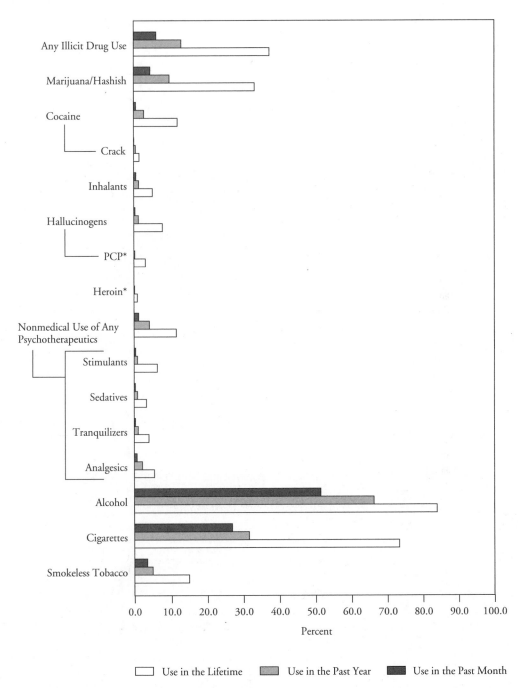

FIGURE 5–1. Percentage of the U.S. Household Population Aged 12 and Older Reporting Use of Illicit Drugs, Alcohol, and Tobacco in the Lifetime, Past Year, and Past Month: 1990

*Note: Low precision; no estimate reported for past month.
Source: NIDA, National Household Survey on Drug Abuse, 1990.

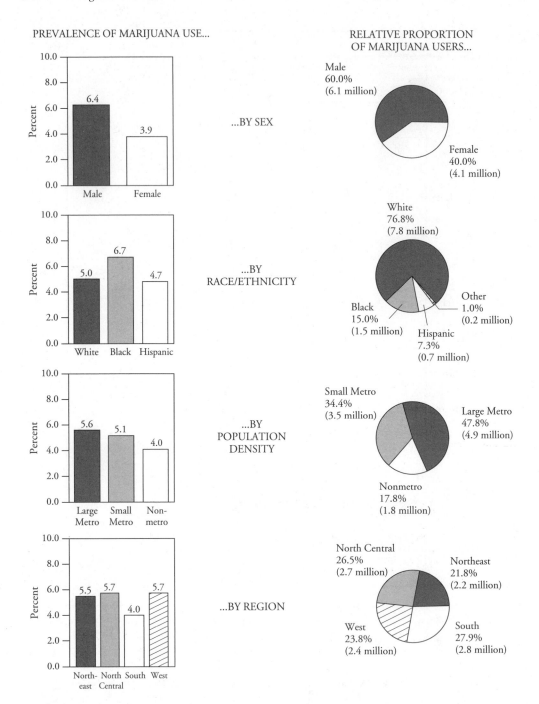

FIGURE 5–2. Prevalence and Relative Proportion of Marijuana Use in the Past Month, by Demographic Characteristics: 1990

Source: NIDA, National Household Survey on Drug Abuse, 1990.

whites; however, the difference is not statistically significant. People residing in large and small metropolitan areas are more likely to report use of marijuana in the past month than respondents living in nonmetropolitan areas. Similarly there are differences in use between regions of the country. Those in the West are significantly more likely to have used marijuana in the past month. However, other differences between regions of the country are not significant (NIDA, 1991a).

Trends in Pot Use. Since NHSDA began conducting national surveys in 1972, long-term trends show a decrease in marijuana use in all age groups, with the exception of those 26 and older. The 12-to-17 age group has undergone a steady decline in use since a high point in 1979. The 18-to-25 age group has shown a similar pattern of decline in use since a peak in 1979. The 26 and older age group has shown either an increase or has remained constant in most levels of use. This is believed to be due, in part, to the aging of this cohort which began using marijuana during the high-use period of the 1970s.

Cocaine Use

Returning to Figure 5–1, we find that approximately 11 percent of the U.S. population has used cocaine (excluding crack) at least once. Three percent report having used cocaine in the past year, while about 1 percent report using in the last month (NIDA, 1991a).

Demographic Profile of Coke Users. Figure 5–4 shows that males are almost twice as likely as females to report having used cocaine in the past month, 1.1 percent for males as compared to 0.5 percent for females. Race and ethnicity also influence levels of use. African Americans and Hispanics report significantly higher rates of use over the past month than do whites. However, African-American and Hispanic rates of cocaine use do not significantly differ from one another. Rates of reported cocaine use over the past month differ among respondents living in large metropolitan areas as opposed to smaller metropolitan areas and rural communities. Among the four regions of the country studied by NHSDA (Northcentral, Northeast, South, and West) there were no statistically significant differences in reported rates of cocaine use (NIDA, 1991a).

Trends in Coke Use. As shown in Figure 5–5, cocaine use has declined for all of the stages of the life cycle. This includes 12-to-17-year-old adolescents, 18-to-25-year-old young adults, and those in various stages beyond young adulthood.

Trends for Adolescents. Among the 12-to-17 age group, the percentage of those reporting cocaine use at sometime in their lives has decreased from a high point of approximately 7 percent in 1982 to a 1990 level of about 2.5 percent. A similar decrease can be seen among those reporting use during the past year, with use declining from a high point of approximately 3.75 percent during the period 1979 to 1985 to about 2.5 in the 1990 survey. A similar pattern is found for those reporting use in the past month. In 1982, approximately 2.25 percent reported use as compared to a 1990 level of about 0.625 percent (NIDA, 1991a).

Trends for Young Adults. The patterns for young adults are similar to those for teens, though the extent of use has been higher. The percentage reporting cocaine use at sometime in their life has decreased from a 1982 high of about 28.75 percent to a 1990 level of approximately 19 percent. Similarly, the levels of those reporting use in the past year has declined from a high of approximately 19 percent in 1979 to a level of about 7.5 percent in 1990. Data on cocaine use in the past month show a similar decline from a 1979 level of 9 percent to a 1990 level of approximately 2.5 percent, with the exception of a brief rise of approximately 1 percent between the 1982 and 1985 surveys (NIDA, 1991a).

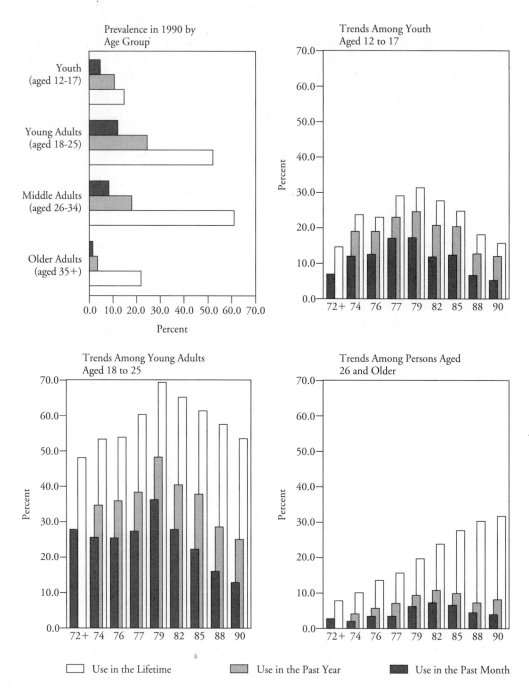

FIGURE 5-3. Trends in the Percentage Reporting Marijuana Use, by Age Group: 1972–1990

+Note: Data not available for past year use estimates for 1972.

Source: NIDA, National Household Survey on Drug Abuse, 1972–1990.

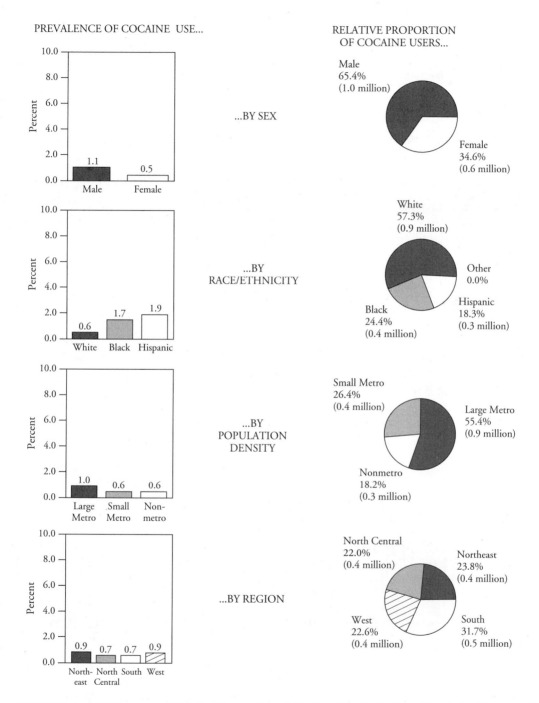

FIGURE 5–4. Prevalence and Relative Proportion of Cocaine Use in the Past Month, by Demographic Characteristics: 1990

Source: NIDA, National Household Survey on Drug Abuse, 1990.

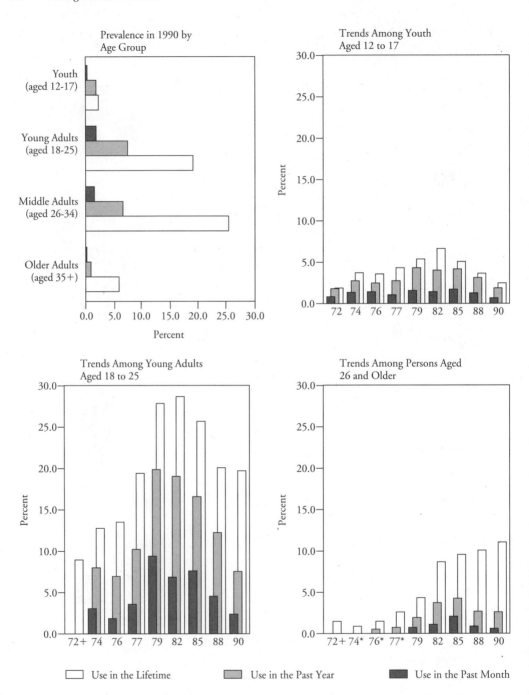

FIGURE 5–5. Trends in the Percentage Reporting Cocaine Use, by Age Group: 1972–1990

⁺Note: Data not available for past year and past month estimates.

*Note: Low precision; no estimate reported for older adults in the past year and/or the past month.

Source: NIDA, National Household Survey on Drug Abuse, 1972–1990.

Trends Beyond Young Adulthood. Data for respondents age 26 and over who report cocaine use during sometime in their life does not follow the same pattern as the other age categories. Rather than showing a steady decline from the 1979–1982 time period, respondents report an increase from 1974, when the level was approximately 2.5 percent, to a 1990 level of about 11 percent. This is most likely due to the fact that this age group was originally exposed to drug use during the 1970s. The data for those reporting cocaine use in the past year shows a similar pattern to data for other age groups. A clear decline may be discerned from a 1985 high of 4 percent to approximately 2.5 percent in the 1990 survey. Among those reporting cocaine use in the past month, a similar pattern of decline is found from a high of 2 percent in 1985 to a level of about 1 percent in 1990 (NIDA, 1991a).

Crack Use

Crack is the name given to the crystals that precipitate from heating a water solution containing baking soda and cocaine. With the increasing attention given to crack cocaine and its apparently potent addictive potential, it is important to consider crack use separately from the use of cocaine hydrochloride (HCL).

Based on the 1990 NHSDA, 1 percent of those in the 12-to-17 age group reported using crack at sometime in their lives and approximately 0.75 percent reported having used crack in the past year. In the 18-to-25 age group, approximately 2.75 percent used crack at some point in their lives, 1.4 percent reported using in the past year, and approximately 0.70 percent indicated using crack in the past month (NIDA, 1991a). Among respondents in the 26-to-34 age group, about 3 percent reported use at sometime in their lives, 1 percent self-reported use in the past

year, and about 0.60 percent indicated use of crack in the past month.

Demographic Profile of Crack Users. Based on the NHSDA survey, people age 18 to 34 are more likely to report crack use at sometime in their lives than any other age grouping. A higher percentage of crack use is also found among African Americans, those who reside in a large metropolitan area, respondents who are from the western region of the country, those who have less than a college degree, and respondents who are currently unemployed (NIDA, 1991b).

Trends in Crack Use. Based on findings from the *Monitoring the Future* survey, crack use appears to be decreasing. Though the survey only began gathering information on crack use in 1987, comparisons between 1987 and 1990 provide at least short-term data from which we may speculate about a trend of longer duration.

Among high-school students, the highest percentage of respondents reporting crack use at sometime in their lives was the class of 1987, the first year the survey gathered information on crack use. Among those in the 1987 class, 5.4 percent reported using crack at sometime in their lives as compared to 3.5 percent for the class of 1990. Among those in the 1987 class, 4.1 percent reported using crack during the past year as compared to 1.9 percent for the 1990 class (Johnston, O'Malley, and Bachman, 1991a:53). Among those reporting use in the past month, 1.3 percent of the 1987 class reported use as compared to only 0.7 percent among the 1990 class.

Among college students one to four years beyond high school, similar trends may be discerned. In 1987, 3.3 percent of the respondents indicated crack use at sometime during their lives as compared to 1.4 percent in 1990 (Johnston, O'Malley, and Bachman, 1991b: 140). In 1986, 1.3 percent of all respondents indicated having used crack in the past year,

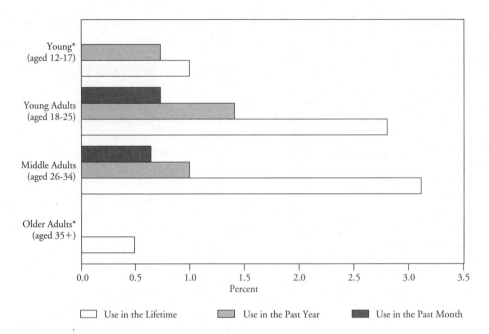

FIGURE 5–6.   Prevalence of Crack Use, by Age Group: 1990

*Note: Low precision; no estimate reported for youth in the past month or older adults in the past year or the past month.

Source: NIDA, National Household Survey on Drug Abuse, 1990.

whereas by 1990 that figure had fallen to 0.6 percent. Even so, during the intervening years, the percentage of users has fluctuated, indicating that more time will have to elapse before we can determine if the downward trend is meaningful. Among those reporting crack use during the last month, 0.4 percent of the 1987 survey reported use. Then, in 1988, the percentage rose to 0.5 only to decrease between 1988 and 1990 to a level of 0.1 percent (Johnston, O'Malley, and Bachman, 1991b: 142).

Among the 19-to-28 age group, the survey shows that 6.3 percent of those in the 1987 survey reported crack use at sometime in their lives. This figure rose to 6.9 percent in 1988 but has declined since then to 5.1 percent in 1990 (Johnston, O'Malley, and Bachman, 1991b:88). In 1986, 3.2 percent of respondents reported use of crack in the past year. This 1986 figure has either decreased or remained

relatively constant in all later years, having decreased to 1.6 percent in 1990 (Johnston, O'Malley, and Bachman, 1991b:69). In terms of crack use during the past month, 1 percent of the 1987 survey indicated use, 1.2 percent in the 1988 survey reported use, but only 0.4 percent reported use in the 1990 survey (Johnston, O'Malley, and Bachman, 1991b:70).

SOCIOLOGICAL THEORIES OF DRUG USE AS DEVIANCE

Macro-Objectivist Theories

Macro-objectivist theories explain drug misuse by locating the motivation for drug use in the social and cultural structure of society. Much of the empirical work has centered on an application of the concept of anomie as found in Merton's theory which was reviewed in Chapter 2.

Anomie Theory. Do individuals who experience a greater sense of normlessness and powerlessness tend to engage in more drug use? This was the focus of a study by Akers and Cochran (1985). Drawing on the concept of anomie first introduced by Durkheim in his works *Suicide* (1897) and the *Division of Labor* (1895) and later extended by Merton (1938) to apply to deviance more generally, Akers and Cochran sought to determine if anomie was associated with marijuana use. While Akers and Cochran provide a comparative test between social bonding, social learning, and anomie theories, here we present only the analysis and findings pertaining to anomie theory.

Respondents were a random sample chosen from junior and senior high schools located in communities considered representative of communities in three midwestern states (Akers and Cochran, 1985:327). Data on relevant variables were obtained through self-report questionnaires.

The dependent variable, marijuana use, was a six-point frequency-of-use scale with response categories ranging from "everyday" to "never." Anomie was measured in three different ways. First, *perceived anomie* was measured in two areas: (1) the discrepancy between educational aspirations and the expectations of achieving them, and (2) the discrepancy between occupational aspirations and the expectations of achieving them. The hypothesis from anomie theory is that as the discrepancy between aspirations and expectations widens, the greater the likelihood of marijuana use. Second, was a measure of *alienation*, which refers to the degree to which respondents feel a sense of powerlessness in their lives. Third, Akers and Cochran included a measure of *locus on control*, which is the degree to which individuals feel a sense of control over events in their lives as opposed to believing that life events are determined by fate, chance, or luck.

Each of the three indicators of anomie (perceived anomie, alienation, and locus of control) were correlated with the frequency of marijuana use. Of the three indicators, only alienation was significantly correlated with the frequency of marijuana use. Thus, the researchers concluded that "[a]lmost no support is found for anomie or strain theory as an explanation of adolescent marijuana use in this sample" (Akers and Cochran, 1985:336).

Most studies of drug use/misuse have surveyed samples of adolescent populations, which makes generalizations to adult populations questionable. Dull (1983) departed from this by studying a sample of 1,449 Texas residents who participated in the 1981 *Texas Crime Poll*, conducted by the Survey Research Program at Sam Houston State.

Dull measured anomie at the social-psychological level with Srole's (1956) anomia scale. The scale consists of five items including statements such as, "Nowadays a person has to live pretty much for today and let tomorrow take care of itself," and "These days a person doesn't really know who he can count on." In addition, each respondent was asked whether he or she used any of five types of drugs: alcohol, marijuana, tobacco, amphetamines, and barbituates. For each type of drug use, the respondent was placed into one of three categories: never users, past users, and, present users. Present users were those who indicated that they had used one or more of the drugs in the past year.

Dull's analysis showed that, while anomie is weakly correlated with alcohol and tobacco use, it is not significantly correlated with use of the more "serious" drugs, such as marijuana, barbituates, and amphetamines. Since few significant relationships were found for the total sample, Dull decided to see if anomie and drug use were related for various subgroups within the larger sample. Accordingly, he calculated the anomie/drug use relationship within different categories of variables such as age, race, and educational level. Still, he found few significant relationships. Thus, Dull's overall analysis does not provide support for a theory of anomie and drug use.

Despite the negative findings of the research by Akers and Cochran (1985) and Dull (1983), caution should be used in interpreting these results as a wholesale indictment of anomie theory as a theory of drug use/misuse. In the case of Dull's research, his measurement of the drug-use variables may have made it difficult to detect a relationship between anomie and drug use even if one were present. The reason is that his measure only distinguished between use and nonuse, not the quantity and frequency of use. If respondents were measured on the amount and frequency of use, Dull might have found more significant correlations than he did. While Akers and Cochran (1985) did measure drug use by obtaining information on both quantity and frequency of use, their study was confined only to marijuana use. Perhaps, if their study had examined other drugs such as amphetamines, barbituates, or cocaine, support for anomie theory might have been found.

Micro-Objectivist Theories

Micro-objectivist theories focus on the processes whereby single individuals acquire and maintain deviant behavioral patterns. The most dominant theories in this category are deterrence theory, social bonding theory, and social learning theory.

Deterrence Theory. Erickson and Murray (1989) conducted a study to determine if the severity of perceived legal sanctions deters active cocaine users from future use. In addition to perceived legal sanctions, the researchers hypothesized that intentions to continue or quit cocaine use would be predicted by perceived health risks associated with use, the extent of disapproval from peers if use continued, and the extent to which re-

spondents have easy access to purchasing cocaine—what the researchers call the "availability" of cocaine.

The sample consisted of 111 active cocaine users. Examination of socio-demographic characteristics such as age and sex indicated that the respondents were similar to cocaine users identified in a general survey conducted by Smart and Adlaf in Ontario, Canada (1984).

Since deterrence theory assumes that individuals rationally weigh the costs and benefits of engaging in deviance, it is questionable whether cocaine use is even deterrable, given the somewhat widespread conception that cocaine has a high dependence liability. In this connection, Erickson and Murray observe:

> [A] number of nonclinical studies of cocaine users have questioned the extreme dependence-producing power of cocaine. . . . It seems clear that as with most illicit drugs, far more people try cocaine, use it only a few times, or use it infrequently, than progress to regular, heavy use. . . . The respondents in the present study, moreover, were not addicted to or heavy users of cocaine. Thus, there is no reason to assume that cocaine use is less suitable for deterrence research than other forms of criminal activity (1989:143).

Results showed that perceived severity of legal sanctions was related to a respondent's intention to continue cocaine use; when a respondent thought he or she would receive a jail sentence if caught, then he or she was more inclined to quit using. Still, other variables were more important predictors of intentions to continue use. For example, perceived health risks—whether respondents thought they might become addicted—were more important in shaping intentions about future use than was fear of legal sanctions. Moreover, concern over peer disapproval and whether cocaine was thought to be easily available were also more powerful predictors of intentions to continue use or quit than were perceived legal sanctions.

Based on their findings, the researchers suggest that social policy should be oriented more toward dramatizing the health risks of cocaine than focusing on deterring users through formal, legal sanctions. While their policy recommendations are reasonable, they tend to undervalue the importance of legal deterrence because they only considered perceived severity of legal punishment in their analysis. They restricted their analysis to perceived severity since the far majority of respondents did not perceive it to be at all likely that they would be caught using cocaine (perceived certainty of punishment). But for punishment severity to have a deterrent effect, respondents must perceive at least a minimal probability of being caught. This may have been the reason for the small effect of the perceived severity variable in their study and, thus, the researchers tendency to undervalue the importance of legal deterrence.

Still, perceived health risks and peer disapproval are important extra-legal deterrents to drug use. Indeed, a recent study by Bachman, Johnston, and O'Malley (1990) sought to explain the long-term decline in both marijuana and cocaine use noted at the outset of this chapter. Noting that availability of pot and coke has not decreased substantially over the last decade, the researchers turned to other explanations for the decline. In accordance with Erickson and Murry (1989), Bachman, Johnston, and O'Malley found that the two most important factors accounting for the decline were perceived health risks from pot and coke use and the extent to which respondents developed a disapproving attitude toward drug use. The researchers concluded:

> Reported availability of either drug has not been reduced. Instead, increases in perceived risks and disapproval appear to have contributed substantially to the recent declines in use of marijuana and cocaine. The findings provide strong support for the use of realistic information about risks and consequences as an important ingredient in efforts to prevent drug use. Coupled with the findings of availability, the results emphasize the importance of efforts to reduce demand (as opposed to supply) (Bachman, Johnston, and O'Malley, 1990:173).

In, perhaps, the most recent study of the effects of legal sanctions on drug use, Burkett and Ward (1993) sought to determine whether individuals who morally condemn drug use are more or less deterred by legal punishments than those who do not condemn drug use on moral grounds. The idea is that perceived legal sanctions may deter some types of individuals, whereas they are largely irrelevant for others. The researchers hypothesized that among those who morally condemn pot use, legal sanctions will have less of a deterrent effect than among those who do not condemn the use of marijuana. Among those who do not regard pot use as morally wrong, legal sanctions may be the only barrier to use.

Respondents were 704 youth attending two public high schools in a medium-size city (estimated population 46,000) in the Pacific Northwest. Although one of the schools was located near the center of the city and the other in a suburban area, the social class makeup of each was similar (38 percent white-collar, 62 percent blue-collar). Because no differences by sex, social class, or school could be detected, all respondents were treated as a single study population.

Two items were used to measure perceived certainty of punishment. Respondents were asked to indicate the extent to which they agreed or disagreed with the following statements: "If I were to use marijuana I would probably get caught;" "If I used marijuana and were caught, I'm sure I'd be swiftly punished by the authorities." The measure of moral condemnation was based on responses to the statement, "Smoking marijuana is a sin." Respondents were asked to indicate whether they "strongly agreed," "agreed," "disagreed," or "strongly disagreed." Data on self-reported marijuana use were obtained through a question about frequency of marijuana use during the last year. Response alternatives were "never," "a few times," "once a month," "two to three times a month," and "once a week or more."

Findings indicated that whether perceived certainty of punishment deterred pot use depended on the level of moral condemnation. Sanction threats appear to stand alone in reducing marijuana use among those who are morally uncommitted—that is, among those who do not believe pot use is a sin. Indeed, among those who show no moral commitment, fear of apprehension and punishment may be the only barrier to deviance. Thus, based on the Burkett and Ward results, legal sanctions should not be totally dismissed as a potential deterrent to drug use/abuse. Perhaps, a policy that addresses both the supply and demand side of the drug equation better reflects the actual state of empirical findings than a policy that would emphasize one side to the total exclusion of the other.

Social Bonding Theory. In our earlier review of empirical tests of anomie theory, we presented the work of Akers and Cochran (1985). We noted at that point that, while their research was a comparative study of the relative explanatory power of three competing theories—anomie, social learning, and social bonding—we had limited our examination of their work only to the findings directly pertinent to an anomie theory of drug use. Here, we present their findings relating to social bonding theory.

The primary independent variables in their test of social bonding theory were the elements of the bond proposed by Hirschi: attachment, commitment, involvement, and belief. They argue, however, that the element of involvement in conventional activities is really the time dimension of commitment to conventional goals. Thus, Akers and Cochran

exclude involvement and measure only three elements of the social bond.

The dependent variable is marijuana use, measured by a frequency-of-use scale during the past 12 months. Response categories for the pot-use scale ranged from "everyday" to "never." After measuring each element of the social bond and the extent of marijuana use among a sample of 3,065 junior and senior high school students from three mid-western communities, Akers and Cochran calculated correlations to determine if there was empirical support for social bonding theory. Their findings showed moderate support for the theory. Each of the three elements of the social bond were significantly related to marijuana use. The element of commitment and belief showed the strongest influence on the frequency of marijuana use, with attachment showed only a weak relationship. In a word, the stronger the commitment and belief, the less frequently a respondent will use marijuana.

In another test, Taub and Skinner (1990) combined social bonding theory with what has come to be known as the drug-progression model of drug abuse (Kandel and Adler, 1982). The drug-progression model suggests that drug misuse manifests itself as a sequence of stages: The use of minor drugs may eventually lead to the use of more dangerous drugs through the use of less dangerous drugs in the middle stages. Drugs used in the middle stages are regarded as stepping stones to hard drug use occurring later in the abuse sequence. In this connection, marijuana is often regarded as the stepping stone drug that links use of less serious drugs, such as tobacco and alcohol, with use of more serious drugs, such as amphetamines and cocaine.

Taub and Skinner suggest that a shortcoming of social bonding theory is its inability to predict more serious forms of drug use. By the same token, a shortcoming of the drug-progression model is that it does not provide an explanation of why some individuals come to use drugs in the first place. Thus, a combination of social bonding theory and the drug-progression model may overcome the shortcomings of each by providing a model capable of accounting for both drug initiation and the process whereby individuals come to engage in more dangerous drug use. Thus, Taub and Skinner propose the following social control drug-progression model: Weak Social Bonds → Alcohol/Tobacco → Marijuana → Amphetamines. The model suggests that weak bonds lead to the use of amphetamines only indirectly through their influence on the use of less serious drugs.

To test their model, Taub and Skinner used questionnaire data from 1,624 senior high school women who were part of the *Monitoring the Future* National Survey of High School Seniors mentioned earlier in this chapter. Three of the elements of Hirschi's social bond were measured: attachment to parents and peers; commitment to conventional activities and goals; and beliefs in the moral validity of conventional norms and values (Taub and Skinner, 1990:83).

The dependent variable was use of prescription amphetamines in the past 12 months without a physician's orders. Response categories ranged from 1 to 40 or more amphetamine pills during the 12-month period. Since the theoretical model suggests that the influence of the social bond on amphetamine use is indirect and, thus, mediated by less serious drugs, the researchers also obtained data on the mediating variables of cigarette smoking, alcohol use, and marijuana use.

Analysis of the findings showed general support for the social bonding drug-progression model proposed by Taub and Skinner. The social bonding variables influenced less serious drug use such as alcohol, tobacco, and marijuana, but exerted only an indirect

influence on amphetamine use supporting the model: Weak bonds influence → less serious drug use which is a stepping stone to → use of more serious drugs, such as amphetamines.

Social Learning Theory. Our examination of social learning theory in Chapter 2 revealed at least three different versions of the theory: Sutherland's differential association theory; Akers's differential association-reinforcement theory; and Glaser's differential identification theory. We noted then that Sutherland's theory could be depicted as follows: Differential associations → Deviance definitions → Deviant behavior. For Sutherland, the concept of differential associations reflects the extent to which individuals are exposed to deviant role models, deviance definitions are attitudes favoring deviance, and deviant behavior indicates whether individuals engage in the deviance in question.

In a recent study of the influence of deviant peer associations on drug use, Pruitt et al. (1991) questioned 1,004 eighth- and tenth-grade students in 23 randomly selected small Central/East Texas communities to determine whether self-reported drug use among the respondents was related to the respondents' perceptions of drug use among their friends. To accomplish this, the researchers gathered information on seven forms of illegal drug use by ascertaining whether the respondents had used any of the drugs in their lifetime. Answers to each type of drug used were added to create an overall index of drug-using behavior. In addition, a measure of perceived drug use among the respondents' friends was constructed based on the respondents' perceptions of the frequency with which friends used the same illegal drugs that had been used to create the index of drug use for the respondents. By correlating friends' drug use with drug use among the respondents, the researchers were able to assess a major hypothesis of differential association theory. The correlations indicated a strong connection between the frequency with which friends used various drugs and the level of drug use among respondents.

While the study by Pruitt et al. (1991) provides at least supportive data for the social learning thesis, by not measuring respondents' "deviance definitions" (attitudes toward illegal drug use), their conclusions favoring Sutherland's version of social learning theory must be regarded only as tentative. This is because Sutherland's original formulation posited that deviant peers influence deviance in the respondent only indirectly through the shaping of attitudes favorable to deviance on the part of the respondent. To correct for this, Warr and Stafford (1991) designed a study to determine if the mediating variable of deviance definitions actually intervenes between peers' deviance and respondents' deviance, or whether respondents acquire deviant behavioral patterns more directly through such learning processes as imitation. To this end, Warr and Stafford analyzed data from the National Youth Survey, a national probability sample of 1,726 persons age 11 to 17. While the researchers examined three forms of delinquency (cheating, marijuana use, and larceny), we focus on their marijuana-use findings here.

Three variables central to a social learning theory of drug use were measured. First, friends' marijuana use was measured by asking respondents how often their friends used marijuana. Second, respondents' attitudes toward pot use were measured by questions such as, "How wrong is it for someone your age to [smoke marijuana]?" with response categories ranging from "not wrong at all" to "very wrong." Finally, respondents' own marijuana use was measured by responses to the question, "How many times in the last year have you [smoked marijuana]?"

Analysis of the data showed that, in the case of marijuana use, friends' marijuana use

influenced respondents' attitudes toward use. Respondents' attitudes, in turn, had a causal influence on respondents' frequency of marijuana use. These findings provide general support for differential association theory. Even so, Warr and Stafford offer the following reservation:

> Still, the single most striking feature . . . is the strong direct *effect of peers' behavior on respondents' behavior. No other variable . . . exerts a stronger influence on adolescents' behavior than the behavior of their friends, and the effect of friends' behavior is both direct and substantially greater than that of respondents' attitudes . . . (Warr and Stafford, 1991:857).*

Thus, while the findings of Warr and Stafford are generally supportive of Sutherland's theory, their data point to the fact that mechanisms other than attitude transmission may be responsible for the process by which drug-using peers influence drug use among those under study.

Macro-Subjectivist Theories

Macro-subjectivist theories focus on the social, political, economic, and historical forces that go into defining drug use as deviance. In this section, we consider two macro-subjectivist theories. First, we will examine historical evidence that supports an interest group explanation of how drug use comes to be defined as deviance. For interest group theorists, the creation of deviance definitions by the more powerful groups in society serves to protect their value and material interests. In addition to certain economic rewards, defining the life-style of less powerful groups as deviance confers social status on the victors while, at the same time, lowering the status of groups who are the targets of the deviance defining process. As Gusfield (1963) showed in connection with the passage of the Eighteenth Amendment to the Constitution, which made unlawful the production, sale, and consumption of alcohol, the law was a symbolic victory of the moral superiority of the rural, white establishment over the heavy-drinking European immigrants.

In addition to interest group theory, we will consider neo-Marxist theory as an explanation of the process whereby drug use comes to be defined as deviance. For neo-Marxists, the deviance defining process arises out of a struggle between those who seek to protect their economic interests and those who would threaten them. Class conflict within a capitalistic economic system is the underlying mechanism that accounts for deviance definitions.

Interest Group Theory. Until the mid- to late-nineteenth century, there were no illegal drugs in the United States. All drugs were as legal and accessible as aspirin (Brecher, 1986). But, in 1875, San Francisco passed a city ordinance banning the smoking of opium. Though opium smoking was relatively non-problematic (at least when there was low morphine content), its use was still banned. The ordinance was passed, not out of concern for public health or crime reduction, but primarily as a tool against the Chinese laborers who had been "imported" earlier in the century to work on the railroad but were now competing with U.S. workers for increasingly scarce jobs. As well as providing an additional means to discriminate against the Chinese and, thus, restrict them from competition for scarce jobs, the new anti-opium regulations permitted the white establishment to reaffirm, at least to itself, its moral superiority over the nonwhite segments of society by outlawing a behavior that was part of the cultural tradition of a foreign people.

Cocaine use was initially outlawed because of its association with groups that threatened the values and life-style of the controlling elite. In this case, cocaine prohibition was connected with attempts to disenfranchise and resubordinate African Americans whose marginal gains in civil rights following the civil war were regarded as a threat to the white establishment (Musto, 1983). Support for the movement to outlaw cocaine use was bolstered by lurid tales of how cocaine use would induce African-American men to attack white women and by reports of how some southern law-enforcement officers had found it necessary to switch from .32 to .38 caliber handguns because the less lethal pistols were supposedly ineffective against cocaine-crazed African-American males.

As suggested in the discussion above, drug laws have frequently served the same function as alcohol legislation served in the days of the Prohibition (Gusfield, 1963). Laws that have made drug use deviance serve to symbolize the moral superiority of the white middle class over groups whose life-styles are perceived to threaten the values and norms of the dominant culture.

Neo-Marxist Theory. The neo-Marxist theories of Quinney (1977) and Spitzer (1985) contend that the legal institutions of society, and specifically the criminal justice system, are nothing more than instruments of the capitalist class as it seeks to protect its material interests and to perpetuate the capitalist economic system. From this perspective, drug use will be transformed into deviance when it threatens capital accumulation, for instance, when drug use reduces motivation to participate in the competitive environment of a capitalist mode of economic production. Ironically, the impetus for renewed marijuana control during the 1960s was not the fear that pot use would make the working classes violent or more prone to crime, but just the opposite. The capitalist class feared that the popularity of pot smoking, particularly among the youthful segments of society, would undermine their motivation to participate in the capitalist economic system (Abel,

1980; Brecher, 1986; Musto, 1987; Reinarman and Levine, 1989).

From a neo-Marxist perspective, the transformation of drug use into deviance serves to legitimize surveillance of the working class in the workplace. In this case, the instrument of social control is the drug test. Drug testing in the workplace has been upheld in the courts. This has essentially allowed management to extend its control over workers beyond the shop floor and office into employees' leisure time, and into other areas of employees' private lives; thus, it greatly increases the power of the bourgeoisie over working-class employees (Gerber et al., 1990; O'Malley and Mugford, 1991).

Micro-Subjectivist Theories

Labeling Theory.   Our assessment of labeling theory in Chapter 3 suggested that a reasonable depiction of Lemert's theory of secondary deviation is as follows: Primary deviance → Stigmatizing labels → Altered identities → Secondary deviation. Primary deviance is norm-violation in the absence of labeling. Secondary deviance is norm-violation resulting from labeling. Between primary and secondary deviance fall two concepts central to labeling theory. The two concepts suggest that if one is caught engaging in primary deviance, the person may be negatively labeled. This negative labeling may result in an alteration in the person's fundamental conception of self. Finally, if one comes to define oneself as a deviant, this may lead to additional norm-violating behavior.

Little in the way of empirical tests of labeling theory exists in the area of drug use/misuse. There is one noteworthy exception. Burkett and Hickman (1982) conducted a study to determine if formal legal sanctions deter adolescents from further deviance or, as labeling theory would propose, lead to additional deviance through altered self-concepts and a self-fulfilling prophecy. As part

of an ongoing study of adolescent drug use, the researchers gathered questionnaire data from students attending two high schools. Items in the questionnaire measured self-concepts (whether one perceived of self as a "deviant"), quantity and frequency of marijuana use, and perceptions of the probability of being caught and punished by the authorities for marijuana use.

In addition to the questionnaire data, the researchers searched the records of the county juvenile courts to determine who among the students at the two high schools had been officially labeled "delinquent." Their search of the records revealed that 33 males and 27 females had official records. Thus, they computed correlations between the labeling and deterrence variables mentioned earlier to see if support could be found for the labeling approach.

The analysis revealed that official labeling by the courts had a different effect for males than for females. For females, official court labeling influenced the extent to which women held deviant identifies, but deviant identities did not increase the frequency of subsequent marijuana use. For males, there was no influence of official court labeling on deviant identifies and subsequent pot use. The researchers concluded that "we find only marginal support for the hypothesis derived from labeling theory that those who have been labeled delinquent will become more deeply involved with marijuana using peers, develop negative attitudes toward the law and themselves, and lessen their fears of future sanctions as a direct or indirect consequence of the experience in juvenile court" (Burkett and Hickman, 1982:85).

SOCIAL POLICY: THE WAR ON DRUGS

Despite the investment of literally billions of dollars, it is highly questionable whether the United States is winning the "War on Drugs."

Over the last decade, a number of questions have been raised about the basic assumptions that underlie current U.S. drug policy. At present, U.S. drug policy is being debated among some of the most highly respected intellectuals in the world.

A central feature of U.S. anti-drug policy is deterrence. Increased law enforcement is designed to reduce the supply of drugs. This is supposed to force the price of drugs up, making them less attractive and less available to users (Nadelman, 1989; Office of National Drug Control Policy, 1992; Trebach, 1987). In reality, however, the market for illegal drugs had not responded as predicted. The price of cocaine, for example, has either remained steady or actually decreased from its level in the early 1980s. And, the retail purity of cocaine has increased (from 12 percent in the early 1980s to a current level of approximately 60 percent) even as the wholesale price has gone down, and as the retail price has remained steady (Inciardi, 1991; Nadelmann, 1991; Trebach, 1990).

Similar trends in other drugs appear to indicate that the drug-related law-enforcement efforts are not only failing but may be backfiring as both consumers and producers are driven away from lower potency drugs, such as marijuana, and switching to more compact and potent substances such as cocaine (HCL), or crack cocaine (Nadelmann, 1991). And, despite the claims for the effectiveness of sanctions targeted at users, we are left with one intractable fact: There has been no evidence to show that the declines in drug use noted earlier in this chapter are related to government-supported legal sanctions targeted at users. Indeed, some critics such as Gostin (1990:387) contend that there is no empirical evidence that user-directed punishments have been effective according to any reasonable measure of success. In fact, Gostin (1990) and Peele (1990), as well as Rouse and Johnson (1991), all raise the question of whether current governmental drug policy is really aimed at increasing public safety and health or merely based on a desire to punish what is subjectively viewed by influential interest groups as immoral self-gratification.

Another concern expressed over U.S. drug policy surrounds the potential threat of the policy for the civil liberties of U.S. citizens. Although some feel that the expansion of police powers is a necessary part of the drug war (Inciardi and McBride, 1989), others fear that the Bill of Rights is being eroded as police are given broader search-and-seizure powers and courts grant more latitude to prosecutors to use illegally seized evidence. In addition, many observers see as a troubling aspect of present policy the weakening of the Posse Comitatus Act, which bars military personnel from becoming involved in civilian law-enforcement activities (Inciardi, 1991). These concerns serve to raise the spector of an Orwellian Big Brother monitoring every action of U.S. citizens, all for "their own good."

In addition to the issues noted above, current drug policy raises important foreign policy issues with serious ethical implications. For example, while the U.S. government has freely admitted that for its supply suppression programs to have any hope of success, governments in source and transshipment countries must follow the demands set for them by the U.S. government (Office of National Drug Control Policy, 1992). For many, this raises the moral issue of whether the U.S. government is justified in interfering with the political sovereignty of other countries by ordering them to cease an activity that may be traditional for some segments of their respective societies (Henman, 1990) or that may be an important source of income for their, often poor, labor force (Morales, 1990; Nadelmann, Kleiman, and Earls, 1990). Further, the war on drugs leads to continued erosion of human rights in many foreign countries, destroying what is left of civil liberties by excusing continued or increased repression of ordinary civilians (Jonas, 1991; van Mastright, 1990).

In part, U.S. anti-drug policy has been relatively unsuccessful in its attack on the supply side of the drug equation because of its failure to consider economic factors that drive continued cocaine production. As Wisotsky notes, "drug law yields to a higher law, the law of the marketplace, the law of supply and demand" (1991:107). The U.S. government faces the strong economic forces that serve to continue coca production and processing, and it must confront the failure of its attempts at air, sea, and land interdiction. The agencies responsible for the interdiction efforts admit that they are unable to stop more than a small quantity of illegal drugs from entering the country (Nadelmann, 1991). In this connection, interdiction efforts appear to have reached their maximum level of effectiveness and probably cannot be expected to increase greatly in effectiveness. This is because of logistical considerations and the fact that smugglers can, and do, adapt to deal with interdiction efforts (Benjamin and Miller, 1991; Reuter, Crawford, and Cave, 1988).

Legalization as an Alternative to Current Policy

In response to critics of the current "War on Drugs," supporters of current policy attempt to paint a grim picture of what awaits us if we consider any of the various alternative proposals to liberalize drug policy. The two most common arguments are as follows: (1) the current policy is working and all alternative plans are flawed and will lead to disaster (Inciardi and McBride, 1991), and (2) public opinion supports the current policy, which relies heavily on the application of legal sanctions (Erickson, 1990). Despite these counterarguments by those who would defend current policy, given the current state of affairs, we should consider the implications of alternative positions.

The first alternative is legalization. *Legalization* is the political and legal process whereby unlawful drug activities are made legal. *Full legalization* is the political and legal process of making all drug activities legal. Arguments for full legalization have been advanced from both ends of the political spectrum including, perhaps surprisingly, the conservative economist Milton Friedman and noted conservative political commentator and author William F. Buckley, Jr.

Proponents of full legalization contend that by eliminating the majority of legal sanctions on drugs, and with them the pressure that pushes drug users into criminal subcultures, the government would be eliminating the *defacto* subsidy it currently provides to drug traffickers by reducing the incentive of suppliers to market drugs. In other words, adhering to current policy only raises the price of drugs. This pumps an estimated $100 billion a year into the underground economy, thereby fueling much of the drug-related violence and corruption that is a major problem with the illegal market (Aldrich, 1990; Nadelmann, 1991; Wisotsky, 1991).

Another argument is that legalization will permit more suppliers to enter the drug market, which should act to reduce much of the harm caused by contamination and uncertain dosages of street drugs. In addition, more suppliers will have the effect of lowering prices of formerly illegal drugs, thereby reducing the number of crimes carried out by those who need excessive amounts of money to meet inflated drug costs. Further, there will probably be a decline in the number of frauds carried out in drug transactions, and a corresponding reduction in violence stemming from price and quality disputes.

Moreover, more suppliers will allow buyers to purchase from those who offer the best price and product. Thus, the self-interest of consumers will motivate them to distribute information regarding suppliers, not only through word of mouth but also through such means as the publication and distribution of lists of good and bad suppliers. This will provide a strong incentive for suppliers to keep both their products and their businesses clean, since those who distribute bad products, or attempt to defraud their customers, would find themselves quickly losing business as word spreads (Stevenson, 1990).

Added to the arguments above, legalization will also make available enforcement assets currently committed to enforcing drug prohibition. This would improve deterrence efforts targeted at serious crimes that are not connected to the drug trade. The many billions of dollars currently budgeted for the support of prohibition policies could be used to reduce the national debt, or to fund social programs such as improving education and reducing unemployment, two factors that are known to be related to drug use in the first place. Finally, legalized drug sales and use could reduce the massive budget deficit by increasing tax revenues from the drug industry. By some estimates, this lost revenue may be as much as $10 billion per year (Nadelmann, 1991; Stevenson, 1990).

The Partial Legalization Alternative

Despite the benefits involved in legalization as an alternative to the present policy of prohibition, concerns are raised about the efficacy of full legalization as the preferred alternative. These concerns run the gamut from the dire warnings of the defenders of current policy noted earlier to those who point out the possible need for some fine-tuning if a policy of legalization were to replace the current prohibition policy (Benjamin and Miller, 1991; Gostin, 1990; Karel, 1991; Trebach, 1990).

Many drug policy reformers espouse some form of partial legalization. *Partial legalization* is the political and legal process whereby only those drugs considered to have little or no adverse personal and social consequences are legalized. Proponents of partial legalization make distinctions between various types of drugs. They concede that while several currently illegal drugs can probably be legalized in a controlled manner, there are some drugs that probably cannot be successfully legalized for use, either because of an unacceptably high addictive liability (for example, crack) or because of the unpredictability of their effect on the user (for example, PCP).

A chief advocate of the partial legalization position is Karel (1991). He proposes to establish a system that makes distinctions between various forms of drugs that are currently lumped together by existing policy. Specifically, his proposal would make a distinction between the different forms of cocaine: coca, cocaine (HCL), and crack cocaine. Coca leaves, or simple extracts from the leaves, have more in common with coffee than with cocaine HCL or crack. In fact, there is a long history of the use of coca leaves and coca-containing beverages in many cultures without causing serious social problems. The cross-cultural examples at the beginning of this chapter illustrate this point. Even daily use of coca leaves by some societies does not seem to be correlated with social dysfunction or health problems (Karel, 1991).

Karel's proposal implies that by legalizing and allowing access to coca, and to some degree cocaine HCL, the plan will remove the drug, at least partially, from the criminal subculture. His plan also provides for the controlled dispensing of cocaine through an ATM-like system. The dispenser would provide the consumer with a gum containing a small dose of cocaine. An additional feature of the dispensing system is that it entails a time-control aspect, allowing access to the vending system only once every 48 to 72 hours. This method of drug delivery should also reduce the addictive liability of cocaine HCL, since chewing, and subsequent oral absorption of the drug, provides a much more moderate dosage than the intranasal method commonly used.

Karel's proposal allows for sales of some coca-containing products as over-the-counter stimulants, similar to coffee, tea, and cola, and more limited sales of cocaine HCL preparation through either the vending machine system or, in some cases, through dispensation by a pharmacist; but the proposal recognizes that crack is a drug that is, by current standards, too much of an addictive liability to consider legalizing. Karel hopes that by making less harmful forms of cocaine available through legalization, individuals will choose to use these forms rather than the more dangerous, and still illegal, crack.

Marijuana in its various forms is also at the center of the debate over legalization strategies. Many drug experts (Trebach, 1987) reject the prohibitionist's contention that marijuana is a "gateway drug," meaning that its use will frequently lead to use of more dangerous substances. In fact, Trebach feels that marijuana plays just the opposite role. By providing a means of fulfilling a need for consciousness alteration, Trebach claims that marijuana actually diverts many individuals away from use of "harder" drugs.

Many of the various partial legalization proposals also include treatment plans. However, they differ from the current policy in that they do not follow a coercive strategy to recruit persons into treatment. Rather, these proposals recommend a system of allowing drug-dependent individuals who are otherwise functioning well in society to decide when, and if, they wish to enter treatment. Also, many legalization programs propose that maintenance doses be given to those users who are functioning well in other aspects of life (Trebach, 1990; Wong, 1990). Trebach (1987) points out that, by providing maintenance for these individuals, users are

more likely to remain as contributing members of society. And, of equal importance, maintenance may help keep users from being drawn into a criminal subculture. Also, by allowing a functioning individual to choose when he or she would enter treatment (rather than being forced into treatment by coercive methods), there is a greater chance of successfully overcoming drug addiction in the long term. Trebach's assertion is based on the belief within the treatment community that therapy is more likely to be successful when undertaken voluntarily (Bandura, 1977; Peele, 1988; Trebach, 1990).

Supporters of current drug policy such as Inciardi and McBride (1989, 1991) claim that legalization of illicit drugs would provide an escape from personal problems and, thus, reinforce the user's failure to face problems and develop important coping skills. However, these same supporters overlook the fact that a significant segment of the U.S. population already uses licit drugs as a way of coping with anxiety and stress. Thus, critics of current policy argue that, rather than eliminating so-called dangerous drugs, the more reasonable approach is to reduce the dangerous use of drugs of any kind (Aldrich, 1990; Nadelmann, 1989; van de Winjgaart, 1990; van Mastright, 1990). This position means that we must acknowledge the existence of illicit drug use and licit drug abuse! It demands that we realize illicit drug use cannot be easily legislated or punished out of existence and current governmental policy may actually be creating harm by forcing the illicit drug user into a criminal subculture.

Among these harm reduction models, the most widely accepted is the public health approach (Erickson, 1990; Jonas, 1991). The *public health approach* considers the most important priority to be that of reducing the harm associated with drug use, not eliminating the use of drugs. This approach is unpopular with prohibition supporters because it does not equate harm reduction with drug prohibition and in some cases finds that prohibition policies may actually create as much harm as the drugs themselves (Aldrich, 1990; Gostin, 1990; van Mastright, 1990). An example of this may be seen in the way current policy deals with the connection between intravenous (IV) drug use and risk of HIV infection. The most effective reduction of risk and harm caused by needle-borne infections has come, not from the federally supported punitive programs, but from needle exchange and outreach programs. The programs, which have focused not on the drugs but on the dangerous circumstances of their use, have been relatively successful despite attempts on the part of the federal government to interfere with them (Beckman, 1990; Hagen et al., 1991; Aldrich, 1990).

There is also antagonism between current drug policy and the public health approach in the area of drug education. Current policy requires that we teach no tolerance for drugs and espouse the idea that any use is likely to have both legal and serious health-related consequences (National Commission on Drug Free Schools, 1990; Office of National Drug Control Policy, 1992). Critics point out that this approach has been tried in the past with dubious results as, for example, the debacle surrounding the film *Reefer Madness* earlier in this century, or the failure of the alcohol prohibition movement in the United States (Peele, 1990).

Most critics of current policy feel that drug use should be an informed choice, and some suggest that factual information should be accurately and objectively provided about both the pleasures and dangers of the use of various mind-altering substances. Critics of prohibition policy further agree that accurate information is the key to harm reduction not only by providing information on the relative dangers of various drugs and their means of consumption, but also by promoting what has been referred to as a health culture in which individuals may be less likely to resort to chemical solutions to problems when viable nondrug alternatives exist. The idea of a health culture would also likely extend to other issues of public health, which tend to be ignored in the current "War on Drugs" (Aldrich, 1990; Jonas, 1991).

Prevention and Treatment of Drug Misuse

Throughout our nation's history, there have been many different forms of prevention education for alcohol and drug abuse. They have ranged from the moral preachings of the early temperance movement to teaching students about responsible alcohol and drug use by imparting factual, unbiased information about psychoactive substances (Musto, 1987; Weisheit, 1990).

Drug Education and Prevention Programs. Current school-based drug education and prevention programs have as an underlying premise the notion that any use of an illegal drug is abuse. The position regarding legal and moderate use of alcohol varies from program to program. Some programs support moderate licit use of alcohol, while others encourage lifelong abstinence (Roger, Howerd-Pitney, and Bruce, 1989). While there are a large array of school-based education and prevention programs, space will allow us to examine only a few representative programs.

One of the best-known substance abuse prevention programs is the Drug Abuse Resistance Education program (DARE). In this program, uniformed police officers act as classroom instructors, partially on the theory that a police officer will be considered a credible authority figure among children (Dejong, 1986; Marx and Dejong, 1988). The goals of this program, as described by Marx and Dejong, are to (1) equip students with the skills to recognize and resist the social pressure to use licit or illicit psychoactive substances, (2) develop self-esteem, (3) instruct students in positive alternatives to substance use, (4) develop students' decision-making abilities, and (5) build interpersonal and communication skills. Also, the police departments sponsoring the DARE programs hope that the programs will improve the image of police officers in the eyes of students, and in the broader community.

The structure of the DARE program consists of 17 sessions each taught by an officer who has been assigned to a given school. The program was originally designed for fifth and sixth graders, but additional programs have been designed for grades K–4 and for junior high school students (Dejong, 1986).

There have been criticisms directed towards the DARE program. For example, some question the assumption that police officers will necessarily be viewed as credible sources of information. Also, as in many anti-drug programs, all drugs tend to be lumped together as dangerous and highly addictive. However, when children find out either through experimentation or word of mouth that this is not the case, the anti-drug message tends to be discredited (Rosenbaum, 1989).

Another drug education and prevention program that is now popular, is the "Here's Looking At You 2000" (HLAY-2000) program designed with a K–12 curriculum. This program is the third in a series that represents the evolution of a drug education curriculum that had as its antecedents, "Here's Looking At You" (HLAY) and "Here's Looking At You 2" (HLAY2).

Similar to its antecedents, the HLAY-2000 program is somewhat representative of the majority of school-based drug education and prevention programs (Mauss, et al. 1988). The goals are to provide information on alcohol and other drugs and to address other issues influencing adolescent substance use. More specifically, the aims are to impart information about drugs as pharmacological agents and to develop attitudes supporting either abstinence or moderate and licit use of alcohol and total abstinence from illicit drugs. Students are also expected to gain in their sense of self-esteem and to develop the assertiveness and refusal skills necessary to withstand social and peer pressure to experiment with alcohol or other drugs. Moreover, students are expected to learn the skills to deal with life's problems and stresses without resorting to drugs for the purpose of escaping personal and societal responsibilities (Hopkins et al., 1988; Roger, Howard-Pitney, and Bruce, 1989).

HLAY-2000 has received favorable evaluation by Roger, Howard-Pitney, and Bruce (1989) for the content of its curriculum. Because the program is the third in a series of drug prevention curricula, its designers have had ample opportunity to benefit from the criticisms of researchers who have evaluated its earlier versions (Hopkins et al., 1988).

In analyzing any school-based prevention program, it is important to recognize that many of the factors that influence substance use are found in the broader society. Indeed research indicates that some social and psychological factors that can have a strong influence on drug and alcohol use choices are not highly amenable to change within the context of a school-based prevention program (Mauss et al., 1988). This underscores the usefulness of making a school-based prevention program part of a multifaceted prevention program that includes segments focusing on community and family issues as well as other social and environmental influences (Kumpfer, 1988; Rhodes and Jason, 1988).

The Treatment of Drug Misuse. Current U.S. drug policy seeks to control drug use and abuse through two general strategies: (1) reducing the supply of drugs, and (2) reducing the demand for drugs. The supply-side strategies attempt to control the availability of drugs through interdiction programs, tactics designed to reduce the production of drugs in other countries, and through the application of formal legal sanctions for individuals who engage in drug production or sales. The demand-side strategies focus on the users of controlled substances and seek to control drug use either through legal sanctions for use or through prevention and treatment programs (Office of National Drug Control Policy, 1992; Roman, 1992).

Whether the drug user is more or less likely to be the subject of punishment as opposed to treatment depends upon the prevailing political climate. When drug misuse is considered a disease (often because of the efforts of interest groups), there tends to be stronger support for treatment. By contrast, when the predominant social and political view is that drug use is a willful and immoral activity, then the reaction of the public is more likely to call for punitive sanctions (Musto, 1987; Peele, 1990; Roman, 1992).

Drug Treatment Contexts. There are three basic treatment contexts within which drug therapy takes place: residential settings, outpatient settings, and aftercare treatment (Roman, 1992).

Residential Treatment. *Residential treatment* involves treatment in a confined setting, often with other addicted patients and therapists who are, themselves, recovering addicts. Residential treatment takes many forms. Perhaps the most common is the therapeutic community model such as the Synanon program (Cook, 1988; Roman, 1992; Westermeyer, 1991).

The *therapeutic community model* draws on self-help strategies in which therapists are often recovering addicts who emphasize the 12 steps and other recovery precepts of Alcoholics Anonymous (AA) and Narcotics Anonymous (NA) (AA, 1976; Cook, 1988; NA, 1988; Westermeyer, 1991). Therapeutic community programs are usually multistage programs requiring a lengthy stay, often 15

months or more. These programs have distinct residential and reentry (preparation for return to living in the community) phases.

Other programs follow a multidisciplinary model, which frequently involves at least some of the AA and NA principles and precepts such as the 12 steps during the residential phase and a transition stage during which the patient resides in a halfway house environment in preparation for returning to full participation in the community. The *multidisciplinary model* differs from the traditional therapeutic community in that it is a professionally based therapeutic community requiring a less lengthy period of treatment, usually between 21 and 90 days (Roman, 1992).

Outpatient Treatment. *Outpatient treatment* is therapy similar to that provided in traditional residential programs but without the inpatient phase. Outpatient programs are often based on the 12 steps and provide one-to-one counseling, as well as counseling within groups (Roman, 1992).

Aftercare. *Aftercare* consists of continued counseling contact with the patient after he or she has completed treatment. As well as maintaining contact with patients to help them monitor their progress, and to help them deal with situations that might present a stumbling block to recovery, aftercare frequently includes helping the client to establish necessary employment contacts and to find new interests to replace substance-using activities and friends (O'Connell, 1985; Sisson and Azrin, 1989). Another important part of aftercare is participation in support groups. Support groups are a valuable resource for recovery. Still, care must be taken in fitting the patient to a particular support group because a mismatch between patient and support group could be a source of stress that would endanger recovery and sobriety.

Treatment Approaches and Techniques.
Within the three treatment contexts, there are
various treatment approaches and techniques
used. Among these are detoxification, maintenance therapy, antagonist therapy, behavioral approaches, and psychotherapy.

Detoxification.   Most treatment providers do
not consider detoxification to be a complete
treatment but think of it as an important ad-
junct to therapy. *Detoxification* brings the patient to a drug-free state, which many
therapists feel is necessary for any further
treatment to be effective. Detoxification involves allowing the patient's system to
achieve a drug-free state. The detoxification
process varies depending on a number of factors including the following: the patient's
level of dependency; the drug or drugs being
used; and whether the patient has any preex-
isting or accompanying medical or psychological abnormalities. Detoxification may
merely require allowing the patient to metab-
olize the substances out of his or her system.
Or, it may involve medical monitoring of the
patient and the medical use of drugs to control withdrawal effects (Alterman, O'Brien
and McLellan, 1991; Roman, 1992).

Maintenance.   Maintenance is used most frequently in the treatment of opioid addiction.
Maintenance involves supplying addicts with
controlled doses of either their drug of choice
or a substitute chemical that may have a more
stable effect. The current goal of maintenance
therapy is to keep addicts in a stable condition until such time as they can be weaned
of the substance and placed into a treatment
program.

The most common form of maintenance
therapy used in the United States is methadone maintenance. Any of the opioids, or
their synthetic analogs, can theoretically be
used in maintenance therapy. However, some
drugs are better suited than others because
of such factors as intensity of effect and

length of action. For example, levo-alpha ace-
tyl methadol (LAAM) is viewed as an especially promising alternative to methadone
maintenance therapy because it has a longer
action. One only needs to administer LAAM
three times a week as compared to methadone, which is typically administered daily
(Alterman, O'Brien, and McLellan, 1991;
Thomason and Dilts, 1991; Trebach, 1987).

Although the ultimate goal of maintenance therapy is to prevent withdrawal until
the patient can be placed in a treatment program, some point out that there is a positive
feature to maintenance itself, it allows the
addict to be retained as a contributing member to society as a short-term goal while re-
taining the long-term goal of eventually
weaning the patient off drugs entirely. Some
contend that by providing the patient with a
grace period to make his or her own choice
about whether to undergo treatment improves the chances of successful treatment
outcome by enhancing the patient's sense of
self-efficacy (Bandura, 1977; Peele, 1988; Trebach, 1987).

Antagonist Therapy.   *Antagonist therapy* involves using drugs that block the effects of
abused drugs. Examples are naloxone and
naltrexone. These drugs act by blocking the
receptor sites that the narcotic drugs act on
to produce their effects (Alterman, O'Brien,
and McLellan, 1991; Thomason and Dilts,
1991). This form of treatment is usually found
as part of an aftercare program as a means
of relapse prevention, especially as a guard
against impulsive substance use (Alterman,
O'Brien, and McLellan, 1991).

Behavioral Approaches.   Behavioral approaches are based on the idea that drug misuse comes about because the user has been
reinforced for misuse. The behavioral approach to treatment has a distinct parallel to
social learning theories, which we previously

discussed in connection with sociological theories of the causes of drug misuse.

Perhaps, the most common form of behavioral therapy is based on the approach of extinction of conditioned responses. This involves helping the patient to recognize some of the stimuli that can trigger drug craving, and to avoid these dangerous stimuli. Moreover, the technique involves helping the patient to defuse these trigger stimuli. This is best achieved through a gradual, progressive exposure to the stimuli that trigger craving in combination with nondrug relaxation techniques (Mackay, Donovan, and Marlatt, 1991; O'Connell, 1985). *Aversion therapy* is a form of behavioral treatment that involves pairing the patient's drug of choice with an unpleasant physical stimulus. The unpleasant stimulus can be either nausea or an uncomfortable, but harmless, shock. The goal is to condition the patient so that their previous drug of choice is no longer a desirable substance (Frawley and Smith, 1990; Ward, 1990). *Relaxation therapy* is used to teach a patient to deal with situations that provoke anxiety and other feelings that, in the past, have led to substance use. Relaxation and meditation techniques are also taught to provide patients with a nondrug means of achieving an altered state of consciousness (Marlatt, 1985; Ray and Ksir, 1990; Roman, 1992).

Psychotherapy. Psychotherapy is a therapeutic approach designed to treat drug misuse by resolving underlying psychological and emotional conflicts. In some patients, there may be underlying factors that not only instigate drug misuse but aggravate misuse because of the self-medicating aspects of drug consumption (Roman, 1992). In attempting to locate underlying causes, psychotherapists use techniques such as hypnosis, free association, and dream analysis. Once the underlying psychological causes for drug misuse are discovered, the therapist seeks to help the patient resolve them through developing self-awareness. If this is successful, the need for escapist drug use is expected to disappear.

SUMMARY

Cross-cultural studies show that drug use is found in all cultures. Use of the same drug may be deviance in one culture but conformity in another. Thus, examining drug use cross-culturally underscores the importance of norms and audience reactions in determining whether drug use will or will not be regarded as deviance. Moreover, such an examination dramatizes the fact that there is nothing inherent in a drug, or its use, that makes it deviance.

Whether drug use is deviance depends on one's conception. The objectivist conception defines deviant drug use as drug use that violates the norms of the group or community. The subjectivist conception contends that drug use is deviance only when defined as such by social audiences.

Patterns of drug use vary widely across social categories such as age, sex, race, and ethnicity. Over the last decade, there has been a steady decline in drug use. This appears to be true for both *marijuana* and *cocaine*.

Among the macro-objectivist theories that seek to account for drug use as deviance, anomie theory has received the greatest empirical attention. Available research does not provide much support for anomie theory as a theory of drug use/abuse. Among micro-objectivist theories, social learning theory has been widely supported. There is also support for both deterrence theory and social bonding theory.

Among macro-subjectivist theories, historical evidence supports the claim that interest groups are important in the making of drug laws and in shaping drug policy. Drug testing in the workplace, while threatening individual liberties, has been upheld by the courts. Neo-Marxists view this as a flagrant act by the courts to protect the capitalist economic system. There is little evidence to evaluate the viability of labeling theory. The available evidence provides only weak support at best.

Current U.S. anti-drug policy is based on deterrence. The hope is that increased legal sanctions will reduce supply and increase price thereby making drugs less attractive to the potential buyer. By most standards, the current drug policy has not been successful. Thus, alternatives have been proposed ranging from full legalization to partial legalization.

Drug education and prevention efforts seek to increase knowledge about the harmful effects of drugs, alter attitudes, and improve decision-making skills. Popular drug prevention programs are DARE and HLAY-2000.

Treatment of drug misuse occurs in three settings: inpatient settings, outpatient settings, and *aftercare*. Within each of these settings, a number of treatment approaches and techniques are practiced, ranging from *detoxification, maintenance, antagonist therapy,* behavioral therapy (including *aversion* conditioning and *relaxation therapy*), and psychotherapy.

GLOSSARY

Aftercare   Continued counseling contact with a patient after he or she has completed treatment.

Antagonist therapy   Therapy that involves using drugs to block the effects of abused drugs.

Aversion therapy   A form of behavioral treatment that involves pairing the patient's drug of choice with an unpleasant physical stimulus.

Cocaine   The drug found in the leaves of the coca plant.

Crack   The name given to the crystals that precipitate from heating a water solution containing baking soda and cocaine.

Detoxification   A procedure that involves allowing the patient's system to achieve a drug-free state.

Full legalization   The political and legal process of making all drug activities legal.

Gateway drug   A less dangerous drug that is believed to lead to more dangerous drug use.

Hallucinogens   The common name for a variety of psychoactive drugs that tend to cause hallucinations.

Hashish   The drug prepared by drying the resin produced by the marijuana plant. Typically, hashish (or, in street terms, "hash") is more potent than marijuana.

Legalization   The political and legal process whereby unlawful drug activities are made legal.

Maintenance   Supplying addicts with controlled doses of either their drug of choice or a chemical substitute that may have a more stable effect.

Marijuana   The popular name of the drug prepared from the dried leaves and flowering tops of the hemp plant, also known as *Cannabis Sativa*.

Outpatient treatment   Therapy similar to that provided in traditional residential programs but without the inpatient phase.

Partial legalization   The political and legal process whereby only those drugs considered to have little or no adverse personal or social consequences are legalized.

Posse Comitatus Act   The act that bars military personnel from becoming involved in civilian law enforcement.

Public health approach   An approach to the drug problem that considers the most important priority to be one of reducing the harm associated with drug use rather than eliminating the use of drugs.

Relaxation therapy   A therapy used to teach a patient to deal with situations that provoke anxiety and other feelings that, in the past, have led to substance use.

Residential treatment   Treatment in a confined setting, often with other addicted patients and therapists who are, themselves, recovering addicts.

Therapeutic community model   A residential treatment model that draws on self-help strategies in which therapists are often recovering addicts who emphasize the 12 steps and other recovery precepts of Alcoholics Anonymous (AA) and Narcotics Anonymous (NA).

SUGGESTED READINGS

Inciardi, James. Ed. *The Drug Legalization Debate.* Newbury Park, Calif.: Sage, 1991. This is the most recent analysis of the legalization debate with views expressed by a number of scholars in the field.

Mieczkowski, Thomas. *Drugs, Crime and Social Policy.* Allyn and Bacon, Boston, Mass., 1992. This is an excellent book analyzing the drug problem from a sociological perspective. Highly recommended.

Peele, Stanton. *The Diseasing of America.* Lexington, Mass.: Lexington Books, 1988. Peele is perhaps the most provocative thinker about substance abuse in our time. In this controversial book, he suggests that rather than approach drug misuse and alcoholism as diseases, we should view them as behaviors over which individuals have control and, thus, should exercise responsibility in their use.

Trebach, Arnold S. *The Great Drug War.* New York: Macmillan, 1987. Here, Trebach presents an analysis of current drug policy and examines the advantages and disadvantages of a full legalization policy.

REFERENCES

Abel, E. L. *Marijuana: The First Twelve Thousand Years.* New York: Plenum Press, 1980.

Akers, Ronald, and John K. Cochran. "Adolescent Marijuana Use: A Test of Three Theories of Deviant Behavior." *Deviant Behavior* 6 (1985): pp. 323–346.

Alcoholics Anonymous: The Story of How Many Thousands of Men and Women Have Recovered from Alcoholism. 3rd ed. New York: Alcoholics Anonymous, 1976.

Aldrich, M. R. "Legalize the Lesser to Minimize the Greater: Modern Applications of Ancient Wisdom." *The Journal of Drug Issues* 20 (1990): pp. 543–553.

Alterman, A. I., C. P. O'Brien, and A. T. McLellan. "Differential Therapeutics for Substance Abuse." *Clinical Textbook of Addictive Disorders.* R. J. Frances and S. I. Miller eds. New York: Builford Press, 1991: pp. 369–390.

Bachman, J. G., L. D. Johnston, and P. M. O'Malley. "Explaining the Recent Decline in Cocaine Use Among Young Adults: Further Evidence that Perceived Risks and Disapproval Lead to Reduced Drug Use." *Journal of Health and Social Behavior* 31 (1990): pp. 173–184.

Bandura, A. "Self Efficacy: Toward a Unifying Theory of Behavioral Change." *Psychological Review* 84 (1977): pp. 191–215.

Beckman, S. "Court Finds Needle Possession Justified to Limit Spread of AIDS." *The Drug Policy Letter* 2 (1990): pp. 1–3.

Benjamin, D. K., and R. L. Miller. *Undoing Drugs: Beyond Legalization.* New York: Basic Books, 1991.

Brecher, E. M., "Drug Laws and Drug Law Enforcement: A Review and Evaluation Based on 111 Years of Experience." *Drugs and Society* 1 (1986): pp. 1–27.

Burkett, Steven, and David A. Ward. "A Note of Perceptual Deterrence, Moral Condemnation, and Social Control." *Criminology* February 1993. pp. 119–134.

Burkett, Steven and Carol A. Hickman. "An Examination of the Impact of Legal Sanctions on Adolescent Marijuana Use: A Panel Study." *Journal of Drug Issues* Winter (1982): pp. 73–87.

Burkett, Steven, and Bruce Warren. "Religiosity, Peer Associations, and Adolescent Marijuana Use: A Panel Study of Underlying Causal Structures." *Criminology* 25 (1987): pp. 109–131.

Castaneda, C. *The Teachings of Don Juan: A Yaqui Way of Knowledge.* New York: Ballantine Books, 1969.

Cook, C. H. "The Minnesota Model in the Management of Drug and Alcohol Dependency: Miracle, Method, or Myth? Part 1. The Philosophy and the Programme." *British Journal of Addiction* 83 (1988): pp. 625–634.

Dejong, W. "Project DARE: Teaching Kids to Say No to Drugs and Alcohol." *NIJ Reports* 196 (1986): pp. 2–5.

De Rios, M. D. *Hallucinogens: Cross-Cultural Perspectives*. Albuquerque: University of New Mexico Press, 1984.

De Rios, M. D., and C. Grob. "Adolescent Drug Use in Cross-Cultural Perspective." *Journal of Drug Issues* 22 (1992): pp. 121–128.

Dishion, Thomas J., and Rolf Loeber. "Adolescent Marijuana and Alcohol Use: The Role of Parents and Peers Revisited," *American Journal of Drug and Alcohol Abuse* 11 (1985): pp. 11–25.

Dull, Thomas. "An Empirical Examination of Anomie Theory and Drug Use." *Journal of Drug Education* 13 (1983): pp. 49–62.

Erickson, P. G. "A Public Health Approach to Demand Reduction." *The Journal of Drug Issues* 20 (1990): pp. 563–575.

Erickson, P. G. and Glenn F. Murry. "The Undeterred Cocaine User: Intention to Quit and its Relationship to Perceived Legal and Health Threats." *Contemporary Drug Problems* Summer (1989): pp. 141–156.

Frawley, P. J., and J. W. Smith. "Chemical Aversion Therapy in the Treatment of Cocaine Dependence as a Part of a Multimodal Treatment Program: Treatment Outcome." *Journal of Substance Abuse Treatment* 7 (1990): pp. 21–29.

Gerber, J., E. L. Jensen, M. Schreck, and G. M. Babcock. "Drug Testing and Social Control: Implications for State Theory." *Contemporary Crises* 14 (1990): pp. 243–258.

Goplerund, E. N. Editor's Introduction. *Preventing Adolescent Drug Use: From Theory to Practice*. Ed. E. N. Goplerund. (OSAP Monograph 8) Rockville, Md.: Office of Substance Abuse Prevention, 1991: pp. 1–12.

Gostin, L. "Waging A War on Drug Users: An Alternative View." *Law, Medicine and Health Care* 18 (1990): pp. 385–394.

Gusfield, J. R. *Symbolic Crusade*. Urbana: University of Illinois Press, 1963.

Hagan, H., D. C. Des Jarlais, D. Purchase, T. Reid, and S. R. Friedman. "The Tacoma Syringe Exchange." *Journal of Addictive Diseases* 10 (1991): pp. 81–88.

Henman, A. R. "Coca and Cocaine: Their Role in Traditional Cultures in South America." *The Journal of Drug Issues* 20 (1990): pp. 577–588.

Hopkins, R. L., A. L. Mauss, K. A. Kearney, and R. A. Weisheit. "Comprehensive Evaluation of a Model Alcohol Education Program." *Journal of Studies on Alcohol* 49 (1988): pp. 38–50.

Inciardi, J. A. "American Drug Policy and Legalization Debate." in Inciardi, J. A. Ed. *The Drug Legalization Debate*. Newbury Park, Calif.: Sage, 1991, pp. 7–15.

Inciardi, J. A., and D. C. McBride. "Legalization: A High Risk Alternative in the War on Drugs." *American Behavioral Scientist* 32 (1989): pp. 259–289.

Johnston, L.D., P. M. O'Malley, and J. G. Bachman. *Monitoring the Future: Drug Use Among American High School Seniors, College Students and Young Adults, 1975–1990: Vol. 1, High School Seniors*. (DHHS Publication No. ADM 91–1813) Washington D.C.: U.S. Government Printing Office. 1991a.

Johnston, L. D., P. M. O'Malley, and J. G. Bachman. *Monitoring the Future: Drug Use Among American High School Seniors, College Students and Young Adults, 1975–1990: Volume 2, College Students and Young Adults* (DHHS Publication No. 91–1835) Washington D.C.: U.S. Government Printing Office. 1991b.

Jonas, S. "The U.S. Drug Problem and the U.S. Drug Culture: A Public Health Solution." In Inciardi 1991: pp. 161–182.

Kandel, Denise B., and Israel Adler. "Socialization into Marijuana Use Among French Adolescents: A Cross-Cultural Comparison with the United States." *Journal of Health and Social Behavior* 23 (1982): pp. 295–309.

Karel, R. B. "A Model Legalization Proposal." In Inciardi pp. 183–194.

Kumpfer, K. L. "Environmental and Family Focused Prevention: The Cinderellas of Prevention Want to go to the Ball, Too." *Prevention Research Findings: 1988*. Eds. K. H. Rey, C. L. Faegre, and P. Lowery. (OSAP Monograph 3) Rockville Md: Office of Substance Abuse Prevention, 1988: pp. 194–220.

Mackay, P. W., D. M. Donovan, and G. A. Marlatt. "Cognitive and Behavioral Approaches to Alcohol Abuse." *Clinical Textbook of Addictive*

Disorders. R. J. Frances and S. I. Miller. Eds. New York: Builford Press, 1991: pp. 452–481.

Marlatt, G. A. "Lifestyle Modification." *Relapse Prevention: Maintenance Strategies in the Treatment of Addictive Behaviors.* Eds. G. A. Marlatt and J. R. Gordon. New York: Guilford Press, 1985: pp. 280–348.

Marx, E., and W. Dejong. *An Invitation to Project DARE: Drug Abuse Resistance Education. Program Brief.* Washington D.C.: Bureau of Justice Assistance, 1988.

Mauss, A. L., R. L. Hopkins, R. A. Weisheit, and K. A. Kearny. "The Problematic Prospects for Prevention in the Classroom: Should Alcohol Education be Expected to Reduce Drinking by Youth? *Journal of Studies on Alcohol* 49 (1988): pp. 51–61.

Merton, Robert K. "Social Structure and Anomie." *American Sociological Review* 3 (1938): pp. 672–682.

Morales, E. "Comprehensive Economic Development: An Alternative Measure to Reduce Cocaine Supply." *The Journal of Drug Issues* 20 (1990): pp. 629–637.

Musto, D. F. *The American Disease: Origins of Narcotics Control.* expanded ed. New York: Oxford University Press, 1987.

Nadelmann, E. A. "The Case for Legalization." In Inciardi pp. 17–44.

Nadelmann, E. A. "Drug Prohibition in the United States: Costs, Consequences, and Alternatives." *Science* 245 (1989): pp. 939–947.

Nadelmann, E. A., M. A. R. Kleiman, and F. J. Earls. "Should Some Drugs be Legalized?" *Issues in Science and Technology* 6 (1990): pp. 43–49.

Narcotics Anonymous. 5th ed. Van Nuys, Calif: Narcotics Anonymous, 1988.

National Commission on Drug Free Schools. *Toward A Drug Free Generation: A Nation's Responsibility.* Washington D.C.: U.S. Government Printing Office, 1990.

National Institute on Drug Abuse. *National Household Survey on Drug Abuse: Highlights 1990* (DHHS Publication No. ADM 91–1789). Washington D.C.: U.S. Government Printing Office, 1991a.

National Institute on Drug Abuse. *National Household Survey on Drug Abuse: Main Findings 1990* (DHHS Publication No. ADM 91–1788).

Washington D.C.: U.S. Government Printing Office, 1991b.

National Institute on Drug Abuse. *National Household Survey on Drug Abuse: Population Estimates 1990* (DHHS Publication No. ADM 91–1732). Washington D.C.: Government Printing Office, 1991c.

O'Connell, K. R. *End of the Line: Quitting Cocaine.* Philadelphia: Westminster Press, 1985.

Office of National Drug Control Policy. *National Drug Control Strategy.* Washington D.C.: Government Printing Office, 1989.

Office of National Drug Control Policy. *National Drug Control Strategy: A Nation Responds to Drug Use.* Washington, D. C.: Government Printing Office, 1992.

O'Malley, P., and S. Mugford. "Moral Technology: The Political Agenda of Random Drug Testing." *Social Justice* 18 (1991): pp. 122–254.

Peele, S. *The Diseasing of America: Addiction Treatment Out of Control.* Lexington, Mass.: Lexington Books, 1988.

Peele, S. "A Values Approach to Addiction: Drug Policy that is Moral Rather than Moralistic." *Journal of Drug Issues* 20 (1990): pp. 639–646.

Pruitt, B. E., Paul M. Kingery, Elaheh Marzaee, Greg Heubberger, and Robert Hurley. "Peer Influence and Drug Use Among Adolescents in Rural Areas." *Journal of Drug Education* 21 (1991): pp. 1–10.

Quinney, Richard. *Class, State and Crime.* New York: McKay, 1977.

Ray, O., and C. Dsir. *Drugs, Society, and Human Behavior.* Boston: Times Mirror/Mosby, 1990.

Reinarman, C., D. Waldorf, and S. B. Murphy. "Scapegoating and Social Control in the Construction of a Social Problem: Empirical and Critical Findings on Cocaine and Work" *Research in Law, Deviance and Social Control* 9 (1988): pp. 638–651.

Reinarman, C. and H. G. Levine. "Crack in Context: Politics and Media in the Making of a Drug Scare." *Contemporary Drug Problems* 16 (1989): pp. 535–577.

Reuter, P., G. Crawford, and J. Cave. *Sealing the Borders: The Effect of Increased Military Participation in Drug Interdiction.* (Report No. R–3594–USDP) Santa Monica, Calif.: Rand Corporation, 1988.

Rhodes, J. E., and L. A. Jason. "The Social Stress

Model of Alcohol and Other Drug Abuse: A Basis for Comprehensive, Community-based Prevention." *Prevention Research Findings 1988.* K. H. Rey, C. L. Faegre, and P. Lowery. Eds. (OSAP Monograph 3) Rockville Md.: Office of Substance Abuse Prevention, 1988: pp. 155–171.

Roger, T., B. Howard-Pitney, and B. L. Bruce. *What Works? A Guide to School-based Alcohol and Drug Abuse Prevention Curricula.* Palo Alto: Health Promotion Resource Center, 1989.

Roman, S. "The Treatment of Drug Abuse: An Overview." In *Drugs, Crime, and Social Policy.* Ed. T. Mieczkowski Boston: Allyn and Bacon, 1992: pp. 222–249.

Rosenbaum, M. *Just Say What? An Alternative View on Solving America's Drug Problem.* San Francisco: National Council on *Crime and Delinquency,* 1989.

Rosenbaum, M., and R. Doblin. "Why MDMA Should not Have Been Made Illegal." In Inciardi pp. 135–146.

Rouse, J. J., and B. D. Johnson. "Hidden Paradigms of Morality in Debates about Drugs: Historical and Policy Shifts in British and American Drug Policies." In Inciardi (1991) pp. 183–214.

Seigel, R. K. *Intoxication: Life in Pursuit of Artificial Paradise.* New York: Dutton, 1989.

Sisson, R., and N. Azrin. "The Community Reinforcement Approach." Eds. R. K. Hester and W. R. Miller. *The Handbook of Alcoholism Treatment Approaches.* New York: Pergamon Press, 1989: pp. 242–258.

Smart, R. G. and E. M. Adlaf. *Alcohol and Drug Use Among Ontario Adults in 1984 and Changes Since 1982.* Toronto: Addiction Research Foundation, 1984.

Spitzer, S. "Toward a Marxian Theory of Deviance." *Theories of Deviance.* Eds. S. H. Traub and C. B. Little. 3rd ed. Itasca, Ill.: Peacock Publishers, 1985: pp. 406–422.

Srole, L. "Social Integration and Certain Corollaries: An Exploratory Study." *American Sociological Review* 21 (1956): pp. 709–716.

Stafford, P. *Psychedelics Encyclopedia.* (rev. ed.) Los Angeles: J. P. Tarcher, 1983.

Stevenson, R. "Can Markets Cope with Drugs?" *Journal of Drug Issues* 20 (1990): pp. 659–666.

Taub, D. E. and W. F. Skinner. "A Social Bonding-Drug Progression Model of Amphetamine Use Among Young Women" 16 (1990): pp. 77–95.

Thomason, H. H., Jr., and S. L. Dilts. "Opioids." Eds. R. J. Rances and S. I. Miller. *Clinical Textbook of Addictive Disorders.* New York: Builford Press, 1991: pp. 103–120.

Time (May 9, 1988). Lamar, Jacob V. "Kids Who Sell Crack." pp. 20–33.

Trebach, A. A. *The Great Drug War.* New York: Macmillan, 1987.

Trebach, A. S. "Tough Choices: The Practical Politics of Drug Policy Reform." *American Behavioral Scientist* 32 (1989): pp. 249–258.

Trebach, A. S. "A Bundle of Peaceful Compromises." *The Journal of Drug Issues* 20 (1990): pp. 515–531.

van de Wijngaart, G. F. "The Dutch Approach: Normalization of Drug Problems." *The Journal of Drug Issues* 20 (1990): pp. 667–678.

van Mastright, J. E. "The Abolition of Drug Policy: Toward Strategic Alternatives." *The Journal of Drug Issues* 20 (1990): pp. 647–657.

Ward, David A. *Alcoholism: Introduction to Theory and Treatment.* 3rd (Ed.) Dubuque, Iowa: Kendall/Hunt, 1990.

Warr, Mark, and Mark Stafford. "The Influence of Delinquent Peers: What They Say or What They Do?" *Criminology* 29 (1991): pp. 851–866.

Weil, A., and W. Rosen. *Chocolate to Morphine: Understanding Mind Active Drugs* Boston: Houghton Mifflin, 1983.

Weisheit, R. A. "Contemporary Issues in the Prevention of Adolescent Alcohol Abuse." *Alcoholism: Introduction to Theory and Treatment.* David A. Ward. 3rd ed. Dubuque: Kendall/Hunt, 1990: pp. 199–207.

Westermeyer, J. "Historical and Social Context of Psychoactive Substance Disorders." *Clinical Textbook of Addictive Disorders.* Eds. R. J. Frances and S. I. Miller. New York: Guilford Press, 1991: pp. 23–40.

White, Helene Raskin. "Marijuana Use and Delinquency: A Test of the 'Independent Cause' Hypothesis." *Journal of Drug Issues* 21 (1991): pp. 231–256.

Wisotsky, S. "Beyond the War on Drugs." In Inciardi (1991), pp. 103–129.

Wong, L. S. "Critical Analysis of Drug War Alternatives: The Need for a Shift in Personal and Social Values." *The Journal of Drug Issues* 20 (1990): pp. 679–688.

Chapter 6

Mental Disorder

"THE HILLSIDE STRANGLERS"

Between October of 1977 and February of 1978, Los Angeles's infamous "Hillside Strangler" raped, tortured, and strangled to death several young women. As it turned out, there were actually two Hillside Stranglers—Kenneth Bianchi, 26, and his 46-year-old cousin, Angelo Buono. After stumping Los Angeles police for over two years, the case finally broke in January of 1979 when Bianchi, who had moved to Bellingham, Washington, killed two young women on his own and was arrested. After police checked his California driver's license, Bianchi was linked to the Los Angeles murders as well. As the evidence unfolded, authorities in California were led to Angelo Buono. The Hillside Stranglers had been caught (O'Brien, 1985).

Our interest in this case centers around the prosecution of Bianchi. Bianchi, an intelligent and articulate young man, hardly seemed the "mass murderer type." Assuming he was guilty, and prosecutors were sure he was, why had he done it? Bianchi told his court-appointed lawyer, Dean Brett, that he could not remember anything about January 11, 1979 (the night the two Washington women were murdered), and that he was so distressed about this amnesia—about what could have happened that night—that he was considering suicide. Fearing that his threats were real, the court called in a psychiatrist to counsel Bianchi. Because Bianchi claimed to be experiencing amnesia, the psychiatrist wondered if he was suffering from a multiple-personality disorder. The psychiatrist told Bianchi's lawyer of his suspicion and hinted at it to Bianchi (O'Brien, 1985).

While having no formal education in psychology, Bianchi had read a considerable amount of it and fancied himself a quasi-psychologist. In fact, he had from time to time masqueraded as a psychologist in Los Angeles in hopes of attracting unsuspecting victims. He had read about multiple personalities and figured that faking the disorder might be his only way to escape the electric chair. As luck would have it, two nights before he was scheduled to meet with a forensic psychiatrist, Bianchi was turning through the channels on the TV in his jail cell when he happened on the movie *Sybil*, a story of a multiple personality starring Joanne Woodward and Sally Field. Bianchi took

in all he could about Sybil, actually taking notes on how she had been abused as a child, how she frequently had nightmares, and, perhaps most importantly, how she referred to her various personalities—their voices, their actions, and so on (O'Brien, 1985).

As it turned out, the forensic psychiatrist that interviewed Bianchi two days later did not pursue the question of a multiple personality. He did, however, feel that such a possibility should be examined by a multiple-personality expert. The defense found their expert in Dr. John G. Watkins, a psychologist from the University of Montana and a well-known author on multiple personalities. When Bianchi was finally interviewed by Dr. Watkins, he was ready to put on the show of his life. Under hypnosis (which Bianchi faked), he told Dr. Watkins that it was "Steve," not Ken (Bianchi), who had been the murderer. Steve hated women. Steve hated his mother. Steve hated Ken. Steve was the killer. Bianchi was convincing, at least to Dr. Watkins, who suggested to Bianchi's lawyer that they enter a plea of not guilty by reason of insanity (O'Brien, 1985).

Since the trial now hinged on Bianchi's insanity plea, the court called in another expert, Dr. Ralph B. Allison, a psychiatrist from Davis, California. With some more reading and a successful performance under his belt, Bianchi was even more convincing in his performance for Dr. Allison. To provide further support, Dr. Watson administered a Rorschach test to Ken and to "Steve." The Rorschach is a personality test in which subjects are shown a series of ink blots and asked to describe what they see. Where Ken saw people dancing or a butterfly, Steve saw "two elephants f_____," "two women getting it on," an abortion, and so on. The Rorschach was sent to another psychologist, one who knew nothing of the case. "Mr. K" was evaluated as being "near normal." Of "Mr. S", however, the psychiatrist wrote, "this is one of the sickest Rorschachs I have ever seen in working with this test for more than 40 years. . .I would expect him to be a rapist and a killer" (O'Brien, 1985:259). Dr. Allison and Dr. Watson were now even more convinced; Ken Bianchi was a multiple personality and should not be held responsible for the killings.

Fearing that the case was slipping from their grip, the prosecution brought in their own "big gun," Dr. Martin Orne, head of the unit for Experimental Psychiatry at the Institute of Pennsylvania Hospital in Philadelphia. Dr. Orne was (and still is) considered the world's expert on hypnosis and had developed several techniques to determine if someone was faking hypnosis. The logic of these techniques was to lead Bianchi into a behavior known to be inconsistent with actual hypnosis. For example, Dr. Orne asked Bianchi to imagine that another person was in the room with them. At one point, Bianchi tried to shake the hand of the other person. No hypnotized person had ever tried to shake the hand of a hallucination. Inconsistencies such as these confirmed to Dr. Orne that Bianchi had been faking the hypnosis. Such confirmation by itself, however, did not prove that Bianchi was faking the multiple personality. In an attempt to see whether Bianchi was faking the multiple personality Dr. Orne hinted to Bianchi that he questioned the multiple personality diagnosis because in most such cases there were more than two personalities involved. Sure enough, during the next session with Dr. Orne, Bianchi introduced "Billy," a shy childlike figure (O'Brien, 1985).

In the end, Bianchi, admitted it was all a hoax. Realizing that the cards were stacked against him, he accepted a plea bargain whereby he would plead guilty to several of the murders and become a state's witness against Angelo Buono. In return, the prosecution would not seek the death penalty. Based in part on the testimony of Bianchi, Buono was convicted. The Hillside Strangler murders were solved.

WHAT IS A MENTAL DISORDER?

What is a mental disorder? How are such labels determined? How utterly bizarre must a person's behavior be before it may be considered an instance of mental disorder? If a woman claims to actually have conversations with God, does she have a mental disorder? If a woman claims she is God, does she have a mental disorder? If a man chooses not to wear clothes in public, does he have a mental disorder? If a man chooses to wear clothes in a nudist colony, does he have a mental

disorder? As we shall seen in this chapter, the answer to these questions depends, at least in part, on how one conceptualizes mental disorder. Answers depend on whether mental disorder is conceptualized as a disease (the medical model), as a nonnormative behavior (the objectivist conception), or as a label (the subjectivist conception).

The Medical Model[1]

As with the objectivist conception (discussed below) the medical conception places considerable emphasis on norms. Norms dictate what is and is not acceptable behavior. Of course people violate behavioral norms all the time. Most men part their hair on the right, but some part it on the left. Most women get their ears pierced, but some get their noses pierced. Most men and women do not pick their noses in public, but some do. Different strokes for different folks, as they say.

The psychiatrists, psychologists, and other mental health professionals who comprise the medical perspective recognize that not everyone will act in exactly the same way. Furthermore, they recognize that there is not necessarily anything wrong with individualism. From the medical perspective, however, there exists a point at which norms *do not* matter; at some point, nonnormative, or independent behavior, becomes "dysfunctional" or "unhealthy" or "sick" behavior. Importantly, from the medical perspective this "sick" behavior exists "out there." That is, the abnormal behavior exists independent of cultural norms which determines the rightness or wrongness of the behavior.

The medical model assumes that bizarre behaviors can be grouped into specific diagnostic categories. This, for a mental health perspective, is what a mental disorder is. It is a diagnostic category of bizarre behavior. The diagnostic procedures associated with specific behavioral problems are standardized in the *Diagnostic and Statistical Manual of Mental Disorders*, first published by the American Psychiatric Association in 1952, and due to be released in its fourth edition (*DSM-IV*) in early 1994.

The medical model is not a sociological conceptualization of mental disorder. However, there are several important reasons why we need to consider it here. First, the medical model is the most commonly accepted perspective on mental disorder. Indeed, the word *sickness* has become so commonly used to describe bizarre behavior that it is hardly questioned.

A second and related reason to consider the medical model is that sociologists are, in general, critical of the medical model. It stands to reason that if we are to understand the challenge sociology poses to the medicalization trend, we must understand the medical model.

Sociologists also remind us that the medical model does not inform us as to why the disorders are regarded as deviance in the first place. From a sociological point of view, behaviors are deviance if either they violate norms (objectivist conception) or are labeled deviance by social audiences (subjectivist conception). From either of these sociological conceptions, deviance is always understood in relation to society—its norms or its reactions.

The Objectivist Conception

The objectivist conception defines deviance as norm-violating behavior. Norms serve as objective standards by which deviant behavior is discovered. In the absence of norms, there is no deviance. In response to the medical conception of mental disorders, therefore, the objectivist is likely to ask, "but what about norms?" Medical theorists do not point to norm violation as a basis of mental disorder. Objectivists often criticize this aspect of medical thinking and point to cross-cultural differ-

ences in defining mental disorder to make their point. If in fact certain non-normative behaviors are "diseases" in one culture, how can the same behavior be "health" in another culture? Since those subscribing to the medical model argue that some bizarre behaviors are indications of an underlying disease process, they are implying that mental disorder exists in the absence of norms.

From an objectivist perspective, bizarre behavior can be clearly defined because it represents a violation of normative standards. To call such behavior "illness," however, is to ignore the role norms play in defining the behavior.

The Subjectivist Conception

The subjectivist conception defines deviance as a label. In the absence of societal reactions, there is no deviance. Strongly rejecting medical conceptions, the subjectivist is interested in how the label "mental disorder" is itself a social creation.

Clearly, those subscribing to the subjectivist conception are not concerned with providing an explanation of bizarre behavior per se. Indeed, from a subjectivist point of view, the quality of the act is not what defines mental disorder. Rather, it is a "consequence of the application by others of rules and sanctions to an 'offender' " (Becker, 1963:9). From this perspective, "mental disorder" is a label affixed to acts or persons by social audiences. If no label is affixed, no mental disorder exists!

How do subjectivist and objectivist conceptions of mental disorder differ from one another? For the objectivist, since bizarre behavior violates normative standards, it is real and problematic and, most importantly, in need of an explanation. Therefore, objectivist theories (discussed later) are etiological in focus. That is, they attempt to explain bizarre behavior. In contrast, those subscribing to the subjectivist conception are less concerned with providing an explanation for bizarre behavior. Instead they are interested in explaining the creation and application of deviant labels. In other words, their interest is in studying the rule makers as opposed to the rule breakers. The subjectivist is interested in the process by which society labels some behaviors as deviance and some individuals as deviants.

THE SOCIAL DISTRIBUTION OF MENTAL DISORDER

Many scholars have decided to leave the definitional issues to others and have instead concentrated on questions of epidemiology. Epidemiology is the study of differing rates of diseases within and between various groups in a population. Epidemiological studies of mental disorder, therefore, estimate variation in rates of mental disorder across particular groups within the general population. Epidemiologists tend to de-emphasize definitional problems and assume that mental disorder is sufficiently defined and diagnosed so as to justify population estimates.

The Forms of Mental Disorder

In order to discuss epidemiological estimates, we must first consider diagnostic schemes used by psychiatrists and psychologists to classify bizarre behavior. A review of this diagnostic scheme is necessary, as epidemiological estimates are themselves based on this scheme. At the same time, however, we must recognize that it is this very classification scheme sociologists often criticize.

Historically, mental disorders have been divided into two broad categories; *organic* and *functional*. "Organic" disorders are believed to result from some organic or physical problems. Such disorders can be present at birth (for example, Down's syndrome) or can result from problems later in life (for example, Alzheimer's disease). Also included are those disorders that are the direct result of

drug and alcohol use (for example, amnesia and dementia resulting from drug use). "Functional" disorders, which are a much broader and less clearly defined category of mental problems, are generally thought to be a result of psychological rather than organic or physiological causes.[2] They can be divided into three subcategories: "psychosis," "neurosis," and "personality disorders." These terms are not used as diagnostic categories in the two most recent editions of the *Diagnostic and Statistical Manual of Mental Disorders* (American Psychiatric Association 1980 & 1981). However, much epidemiological research has relied on these diagnostic entities and, therefore, these terms continue to be important categories for referring to different types of disorders.

Psychosis refers to a serious and incapacitating set of disorders, including schizophrenia and various mood disorders (e.g., unipolar and bipolar depression). *Neurosis*, on the other hand, refers to a broad range of less severe disorders that do not entail a loss of contact with reality. Such disorders include various anxiety disorders (e.g., specific phobias, obsessive-compulsive disorder, post-traumatic stress disorder), somatoform disorders (symptoms of physical illness that have psychological causes), and sexual disorders (e.g., paraphilia and sexual dysfunctions) (Cockerham, 1989). *Personality disorders* are often used as a catchall category for behaviors that cannot be diagnosed as either psychoses or neuroses. This category is used for a broad range of behavior, including anything from criminal activity and vagrancy (e.g., antisocial personality disorder), to exaggerated expressions of emotion (e.g., histrionic personality disorder) (Cockerham, 1989).

The Prevalence of Mental Disorder

Several factors make epidemiological research problematic. First, estimates of mental disorder vary depending on whether they are reported as incidence or prevalence. *Prevalence* refers to the total number of people who have or have had the disorder at a particular point in time (e.g., people who have ever been diagnosed as schizophrenic). *Incidence* is the rate at which cases are being reported for a particular period of time (e.g., people who have been diagnosed as schizophrenic in the past year). Incidence rates are especially relevant in macro-level attempts to estimate the effects of societal changes on rates of mental disorder. In an attempt to narrow our focus somewhat, our discussion will focus specifically on the prevalence of mental disorder.

A second difficulty in epidemiological research concerns the nature of estimates of mental disorder. Such estimates vary depending on whether they are based on self-report surveys or official (treatment) statistics. Official statistics include only those people who are undergoing treatment at mental hospitals, outpatient clinics, or are receiving treatment through private psychiatrists. Self-report surveys, on the other hand, estimate the number of "psychologically impaired" people in a given population. Since only a fraction of those who are "psychologically impaired" are actually in treatment, these two methods will obviously yield very different estimates of prevalence. Surveys provide better estimates of what epidemiologists sometimes refer to as "true" prevalence rates.

Third, as long as definition and diagnosis remain problematic, reliable and valid data on prevalence rates will remain elusive. To the degree that diagnoses continue to reflect differing training and cultural biases of psychiatrists, estimates will remain somewhat crude (Dunham, 1964). In addition, each new version of the *DSM* offers a slightly different diagnostic scheme, making comparisons across time especially difficult.

Because of these obstacles, estimates of the rates of mental disorder often vary dramatically. For example, in a sample of the general population in Manhattan, Strole et al. (1968) estimated the prevalence rate of serious psychiatric impairment at 23 percent. This figure seems high, especially in light of research conducted in Baltimore that estimated the rate of serious mental disorder to be between 5 and 10 percent (Pasmanic et al., 1964). Other research estimates prevalence rates for functional disorders to be between 16 and 25 percent (Dohrenwend et al.,1980). The discrepancies in these reported rates, of course, are more likely a result of differing definitions than actual fluctuation in the rate of mental disorder. Quite obviously, any estimate of a national rate of mental disorder is very rough, thus limiting the usefulness of such estimates.

Despite the problems associated with epidemiological estimates, several social factors have been shown to be related to mental disorder. In some ways, these relationships are impressive precisely because they survive the definitional and methodological problems associated with epidemiological studies (Dohrenwend, 1975).

Social Class. By far the most frequently studied and consistently demonstrated correlate of mental disorder is social class. The lower classes have the greatest prevalence of mental disorder, especially schizophrenia and personality disorders. In a classic early epidemiological study, Faris and Dunham (1939) examined the records of 35,000 Chicago-area patients admitted to mental hospitals between 1922 and 1934. The highest rates of mental disorder were found in the poorest areas of the inner city. In a later study, Hollingshead and Redlich (1958) similarly examined the records of treated patients in New Haven, Connecticut, and found the prevalence of psychoses to be almost ten times higher in the lower classes than in the upper classes.

Both of these early studies relied upon samples of treated cases; thus, they do not measure true prevalence rates of mental disorder in the general public. Surveys of the general public also demonstrate that the relationship exists even in non-treated populations. For example, Strole and his colleagues (1968) interviewed 1,660 persons, obtaining information about their personal background, past history of psychopathology, and current mental state. The information was reviewed by psychiatrists who assessed the mental state of the respondents. Once again, the rate of mental disorder was much higher in the lower class.

Urban Versus Rural Setting. One of the themes that has historically dominated sociological theory is that the modern, industrial, impersonal world creates problems in living. Following such logic, sociologists have generally assumed that the rates of social "ills" (including mental disorder) would be much higher in urban areas. The research distinguishing rates of mental disorder in urban and rural settings, however, is somewhat inconclusive. In general, the findings depend on the specific mental disorder considered and the type of data examined (treatment data vs. survey data). For example, research consistently demonstrates that rates of treatment for schizophrenia are considerably higher in urban areas than in rural areas. However, there is no significant rural/urban difference in survey samples (Eaton, 1986). This discrepancy appears to be largely a result of greater access to mental health facilities in urban areas (Dohrenwend, 1975). For some mood disorders (especially depression), prevalence rates are actually higher in rural areas (Eaton, 1986; Dohrenwend, 1975).

Surveys do demonstrate consistently higher rates in urban areas for various anxiety and personality disorders (Eaton, 1986; Dohrenwend, 1975; Dohrenwend et al., 1980; Cockerham, 1989). While the reasons are not clear, these data seem to support the conclusion that urban residents have higher rates of relatively minor neuroses and personality disorders and slightly lower rates of more severe disorders, especially mood disorders (Dohrenwend and Dohrenwend, 1974).

Gender. The relationship between gender and mental disorder also depends, at least in part, on the type of disorder one considers. With regard to general estimates of true prevalence, there appear to be no significant differences between men and women (Dohrenwend and Dohrenwend, 1974; 1976). When considering specific disorders, however, several patterns do emerge. Research has consistently shown that women are more likely to suffer from mood disorders (i.e., unipolar and bipolar depression), various anxiety and phobic disorders (Lin, Dean, and Ensel, 1986; Eaton, 1986; Gove and Tudor, 1973), and other kinds of neuroses (Dohrenwend et al., 1980). Men, on the other hand, have higher rates of personality disorders (Dohrenwend, et al., 1980) and substance-induced and substance abuse disorders (Cockerham, 1989).

Table 6–1 shows the distribution of admissions to state and county mental hospitals by gender and diagnosis. Among men admitted to state and county hospitals in 1980, 35.2 percent entered the hospital for alcohol and drug-related disorders, whereas the rate among women was considerably lower (12.2 percent). Notice as well that the percentage of admissions with mood disorders is about twice as high among women (19.8 percent) as it is among men (10.0 percent).

Marital Status. The data on marital status indicate that single people (those who are divorced, or never married) have the highest rates of mental disorder (Gove, 1972; Lin, Dean, and Ensel, 1986). The data for admissions to state and county mental hospitals in 1980, presented in Table 6–2, illustrate this point. What is perhaps most interesting about these data is that the consequences of being

TABLE 6.1   Admission to State and County Mental Hospitals by Primary Diagnosis and Sex: United States, 1980

PRIMARY DIAGNOSIS	MALE	FEMALE
Schizophrenia and other psychotic disorders	35.3%	42.9%
Alcohol/Drug related	34.2%	12.2%
Mood Disorders	10.0%	19.8%
Organic Disorders	4.0%	4.5%
All Other	16.5%	20.5%

Source: National Institute of Mental Health. "Characteristics of Admission to the Inpatient Services of State and County Hospitals, United States, 1980." Mental Health Statistical Note No. 177. Washington, D.C.: U.S. Department of Health and Human Services, 1986.

TABLE 6.2   Percentage of Admissions to State and County Mental Hospitals by Marital Status and Gender: United States, 1980

MARITAL STATUS	MALE	FEMALE
Married	18.2%	25.7%
Never Married	51.5%	34.2%
Divorced/Separated	27.9%	29.7%
Widowed	2.3%	10.4%

Source: National Institute of Mental Health. "Characteristics of Admission to the Inpatient Services of State and County Hospitals, United States, 1980." Mental Health Statistical Note No. 177. Washington, D.C.: U.S. Department of Health and Human Services, 1986.

single appear to be less problematic for women than for men.

Race. There are studies that demonstrate that rates of mental disorder are higher among African Americans. However, African Americans are also more likely to be from lower socioeconomic groups and, as we know from the previous discussion, mental disorder is overrepresented in lower socioeconomic groups. Once the relationship between race and social class is controlled, race does not appear to be related to mental disorder in any significant way (Cockerham, 1989).

WHAT CAUSES MENTAL DISORDER?

From a medical perspective, bizarre and inappropriate behavior is merely a visible symptom of an underlying disease. Conceptualized in this way, inappropriate behavior might be determined to be an indication of a specific mental disease just as chest pain and shortness of breath might be interpreted to be an indication of a physical disease. If one can treat and cure the underlying disease, the observed symptoms will disappear. If a woman bites her nails, for example, she could be diagnosed with an anxiety disorder. From a medical perspective, if we treat her behavior without treating her illness the illness will merely manifest itself in another behavior (e.g., if you get the woman to stop biting her nails, she may merely start pulling her hair out).

Medical Theories

According to Cockerham (1989), there are two separate categories of medical theories.

The first and purest category, the *biogenetic* model, "attributes mental abnormalities to physiological, biochemical, or genetic causes and attempts to treat these abnormalities by way of medically grounded procedures. . ." (Cockerham, 1989:70). While for the most part the link between bizarre behavior and disease is assumed rather than demonstrated, increasingly there is research that suggests physiological and genetic links to mental disorder. Twin and adoption studies, for example, consistently demonstrate a genetic link to schizophrenia and some mood disorders. Children of schizophrenics raised by foster parents are approximately ten times more likely to have schizophrenia than are children without a family history of schizophrenia (Cockerham, 1989). While environmental factors also clearly play a role, it seems reasonable to assume that some people "are genetically 'primed' for certain mental disorders as a result of heredity" (Cockerham, 1989:75).

Another factor that has provided some indirect support for a biogenetic model of mental disorder is the efficacy of drugs in treating mental disorder. Drug therapy is the most effective short-term treatment available to psychiatrists (Conrad and Schneider, 1980). While the reasons for the success of drugs are not fully understood, the very fact that they are so successful lends some support to the conclusion that there is some kind of a biochemical component to mental disorder.

The second category of medical theories is based on the *psychoanalytic* model, which can be traced to the Viennese physician Sigmund Freud. According to Cockerham, the psychoanalytic model is "analogous to the medical model in that it also focuses attention on internal factors that affect the mental health of the human being" (1989:78). From this perspective, an individual might be physically healthy but psychologically ill. Since the mind is disordered, the individual is unable to control his or her behavior.

Sociological Theories of Mental Disorder

Our purpose in this chapter is not to "disprove" medical theories. To the contrary, as scholars attempting to understand mental disorder, we must be open to the possibility that some mental disorders are genetically based. At the same time, however, even if we fully accept medical explanations of bizarre behavior (which in many cases we will not), this does not eliminate the need for a sociology of mental disorder. Sociological theories provide insight into several issues that medical theories either cannot or do not address.

First, as we have already mentioned, to conceptualize mental disorder as a pathological condition is to challenge sociological understandings of the relative nature of norms. Indeed, a medical conception of mental illness ignores the question of why the behavior is deviance in the first place. Genes may cause certain forms of behavior, but since genes cannot predict what the social norms will be, or what reaction to the behavior the social audiences will take, a genetic or even psychological approach to why mental disorders are deviance is uninformative.

Second, sociologists, especially subjectivists, question the commonly accepted view that the medical community is in charge of bizarre behavior because it is a medical problem. From a sociological point of view, it may be more accurate to conclude the opposite: that bizarre behavior is considered a medical problem because the medical community is in charge.

Finally, even if we accept the medical argument that some people are "genetically primed" for some types of mental disorder, this does not mean that sociological and social-psychological factors are causally unimportant. Medical theories clearly do not fully explain mental disorder (Cockerham, 1989). If one assumes that behavioral patterns are genetically preprogrammed (a biogenetic model), or form early in life (a psychoanalytic model), then it is easy to forget that our behavior and our self-perceptions are formed in interaction with others. Environmental factors are clearly important as we attempt to understand the etiology of bizarre behavior.

Objectivist Theories. To illustrate the tension between medical and sociological explanations of mental disorder, consider how the two perspectives might explain social distribution patterns of mental disorder. Recall that we discovered that the mentally disordered are disproportionately lower class, single, and, for various kinds anxiety and personality disorders, urban residents. Medical theorists generally adopt a *social selection* perspective, which suggests that the social condition of the individual is a *result* of his or her mental state. The social selection model is interested in how the mental disorder affects the status attainment of the individual (Eaton, 1986). The assumption is that the more mental problems the individual has, the less likely he or she is to get married, find a good job, and so forth (Turner and Gartrell, 1978). It is certainly reasonable to assume, for example, that a person who acts "strange" is less likely to be able to find a spouse.

From a social scientific standpoint, the *social causation* perspective is more useful. From this perspective, there is something about sociocultural factors like social class and marital status that cause mental disorders. Perhaps the pressures and stress of being poor creates mental disorders; or, perhaps single people lack the social supports to lean on in times of crisis. Hypotheses such as these have led researchers to a more general interest in stress and life events as causes of mental disorder and social support as a buffer from mental disorder. While the specific explanations may differ, the assumption is that social factors have considerable influence over the mental health of the individual. Research in the area is somewhat mixed, with some studies supporting a social selection interpretation (e.g., Turner and Gartrell, 1978) and some sug-

gesting a social causation interpretation (Dohrenwend, 1975; Wheaton, 1978). Despite the tendency to address the causation versus selection issue in an either/or manner, the most feasible conclusion is that both processes are valid to some degree.

In this section, we are primarily interested in environmental causes of bizarre behavior, so our discussion will focus on social causation issues.

Macro-Objectivist Theories
Anomie Theory. In his now classic study on suicide, Emile Durkheim (1951) argued that people are more likely to kill themselves when they become separated from social attachments (egoistic suicide) and when there is a breakdown in the normative system regulating individualistic behavior (anomic suicide). In both cases, he was referring to structural conditions that produce feelings of detachment—either detachment from others or detachment from society's norms.

American sociologist Robert Merton (1957) borrowed Durkheim's term *anomie* and argued that normlessness is especially likely when there is a disjunction between cultural goals (the American Dream) and structural means (opportunities) for achieving those goals.

Neither theorist focused specifically on mental disorder. Durkheim was primarily interested in suicide, and Merton was primarily interested in crime.[3] At the same time, however, in focusing on structural preconditions to strain and normlessness, Durkheim and Merton remind us that large-scale societal conditions may contribute to rates of social ills (including crime, suicide, and mental disorder).

Drawing upon the considerable sociological literature on poverty and urbanization, many early studies of mental disorder focused on anomie and structural stain as causes of mental disorder. For example, Faris and Dunham (1939) found that mental disorder is more pronounced in the slums of Chicago. The reason, they maintained, is that the inner city is socially disorganized:

> *In these most disorganized sections of the city and, for that matter, of our whole civilization, many persons are unable to achieve a satisfactory conventional organization of their world. The result may be lack of any organization at all, resulting in a confused, frustrated, and chaotic personality (Faris and Dunham, 1939:159).*

More recent research has similarly shown that hopelessness and helplessness are related to rates of mental illness. In her study of a small agricultural village in western Ireland, anthropologist Nancy Scheper-Hughes (1979) found rates of schizophrenia to be especially high among middle-aged, single, male farmers. Deteriorating economic conditions and government pressure to turn small low-production farms into large agricultural corporations had a devastating effect on the morale of the community (Cockerham, 1989). Conditions worsened as many of the young women of the community left in search of more favorable economic and social conditions. Demoralized and alone, a disproportionately high number of the men became schizophrenic (Cockerham, 1989).

There is also anomie and strain research that focuses on the effect of societal economic changes on the rate of mental disorder (Cockerham, 1989). Brenner (1973), for example, found that admissions to mental hospitals increased during recessions and depressions. Consistent with anomie theory, furthermore, the increase occurred primarily among the lower classes (Cockerham, 1989).

A Neo-Marxist Perspective on Bizarre Behavior. The neo-Marxists have offered few explanations of bizarre behavior. The theoretical expectations of neo-Marxism are nonetheless predictable. From the neo-Marxist perspective, mental disorder is a result of the exploitation and alienation inherent in

capitalism. Workers know that they will always be workers. They know that their value depends only on their ability to produce. They work long, inflexible, monotonous hours. The capitalist culture, furthermore, is said to "isolate people because it depicts self-consciousness as the essence of being an individual" (Cockerham, 1989:34). Self-consciousness produces isolation, which produces alienation. From the neo-Marxist perspective, therefore, mental disorder results from a "sense of alienation from the general social environment. This alienation is based on feelings of despair associated with the exploitation of one's labor and disadvantaged position in life" (Cockerham, 1989:35).

Micro-Objectivist Theories

Stress and Mental Disorder. While little research has drawn an explicit connection between mental disorder and Merton's anomie theory, there has been considerable research that, in the tradition of Merton, has focused on the effects of environmentally induced "stress" and "strain" (Dohrenwend, 1975). Most of this research, however, has been less structural than that initiated by Merton. That is, while Merton was primarily interested in how social structure produces categories of "strained" people, the mental disorder literature focuses on the accumulation of stress in the lives of *individuals*. In this literature, stress is thought to occur "when individuals are faced with a situation for which their usual modes of behavior are inadequate and the consequences of not adapting to the situation are perceived as serious" (Cockerham, 1989:95). This research has focused on the mental health consequences of stress and stressful life events, such as loss of a job, financial hardship, divorce, death in the family, and physical illness. (For a review, see Kessler et al., 1985).

Much of the research on stress has been directed at people in extreme situations, for example, victims of natural disasters, victims of prisoner of war camps, and survivors of war. (See Cockerham, 1989 for a review.) This research convincingly demonstrates that extreme situations "will produce a wide variety of psychiatric signs and symptoms in all or most previously normal persons" (Dohrenwend, 1975:383).

While such extreme events are relatively rare, the fact that these events have such a profound effect on mental health has encouraged research on more common stressors. For example, a common assumption is that the poor are exposed to greater stress. Not only is someone from the lower class more likely to experience stress associated with financial difficulties, but the poor person is also likely to experience the stress of other social ills more common in the lower class (e.g., high morbidity and mortality rates, crime, urban living, and illness). The greater exposure of the lower class to stress is illustrated in the following excerpt from a study on Puerto Rican schizophrenics:

A complicated pregnancy was followed by the death of a baby under provocative circumstances; unemployment decimated the family's meager store of economic resources, and Mrs. Padilla's children suffered; when Mr. Padilla did find work he shared his earnings with a 'concubine'; the interpersonal relations of the Padillas underwent a series of stress-provoking incidents; as Mrs. Padilla became more disturbed over her husband's behavior she began to quarrel with the neighbors. Her dream of a legal marriage to him has never been realized—she goads him; he retaliates with infidelity.

The breaking point was reached when Mrs. Padilla returned from the hospital and found her "lazy sister" sitting in the middle of the floor reading with the house "torn to pieces," the 17-day-old twin of the sick infant screaming in the basket, and food and dishes scattered over the floor by the older children. The last link connecting Mrs. Padilla with reality broke when the baby died (Rogler and Hollingshead, 1965:196–197).

Of course the lower classes are not alone in their exposure to stressful life events. The wealthy become ill, experience the death of loved ones, fall victim to rape, and get divorced. To what extent do stressful life events such as these accumulate to cause mental disorder? Interest in answers to questions such as this has led to the development of several stress scales, the most influential being the Social Readjustment Rating Scale (SRRS), developed by Holmes and Rahe (1967).

The SRRS, which is shown in Table 6–3, is designed to estimate the level of stressful life events in the lives of individuals. This scale is based on the assumption that any change, whether it be positive or negative, can produce stress and thereby influence a person's mental health. There is considerable evidence supporting this assumption (Dohrenwend, 1973; Thoits and Hannan, 1979), especially for schizophrenia (Brown and Birley, 1968). However, most authors contend that undesirable events are better predictors of disorder than are desirable events (Lin, Dean, and Ensel, 1986).

The SRRS is based on data collected from hundreds of people who were asked to prioritize life events in terms of the amount of readjustment a particular event required. In general, the events that are rated as requiring the most amount of adjustment are undesirable (e.g., death of spouse, divorce, and marital separation), although several less negative changes are also high on the stress scale (e.g., marriage and marital reconciliation). Holmes and Rahe (1967) argue that the accumulation of over 200 points in a one-year period puts a person at risk for a mental disorder (Cockerham, 1989).

The SRRS has been used extensively and, for the most part, has been found to estimate stress about as well as any other scale. Critics, however, argue that some of the life events in the SRRS are as likely to be consequences of mental disorder as they are to be causes of mental disorder (Cockerham, 1989; Dohrenwend, 1975).

Another problem associated with research

TABLE 6.3   Social Readjustment Rating Scale

STRESSFUL LIFE EVENT	STRESS VALUE
Death of spouse	100
Divorce	73
Marital separation	65
Jail term	63
Death of close family member	63
Personal injury or illness	53
Marriage	50
Fired at work	47
Marriage reconciliation	45
Retirement	45
Change in health of family member	44
Pregnancy	40
Sex difficulties	39
Gain of new family member	39
Business readjustment	39
Change in financial state	38
Death of close friend	37
Change to different line of work	36
Change in number of arguments with spouse	35
Foreclosure of mortgage or loan	30
Change in responsibilities at work	29
Son or daughter leaving home	29
Trouble with in-laws	29
Outstanding personal achievement	28
Wife begin or stop work	26
Begin or end school	26
Change in living conditions	25
Revision of personal habits	24
Trouble with boss	23
Change in work hours or conditions	20
Change in residence	20
Change in schools	20
Change in recreation	19
Change in church activities	19
Change in social activities	18
Change in sleeping habits	16
Change in number of family get-togethers	15
Change in eating habits	15
Vacation	13
Christmas	12
Minor violations of the law	11

Source: T. H. Holmes and R. H. Rahe. "The Social Readjustment Rating Scale." *Journal of Psychosomatic Research* 11, Table 3–1 (1967): 213. Reprinted with permission.

on stressful life events is that stress has not proved to be a particularly powerful predictor of mental disorder. Most research indicates that the correlation between life events and various symptoms of mental disorder is only .15–.20 (Kessler and McRae, 1981). This means that the overwhelming majority of people who are exposed to stressful life events do not develop a mental disorder (Kessler et al., 1985). These findings certainly suggest that there are factors other than stress that are important in understanding the onset of mental disorder. One possible explanation is that the actual occurrence of a stressful life event is less important than the perception of stress (Kessler and McRae, 1981). That is, the people who are *experiencing* stress (as measured by the Holmes and Rahe scale) are not necessarily the same people who are *feeling* stressed. It is also possible that the impact of stress may be modified by social supports (discussed in the following section). Whatever the case, other factors are obviously at work.

Control Theory. A related research area considers the importance of *social support* in protecting individuals from the effects of various stressful life events. As is mentioned above, interest in the influence of social supports has emerged, in part, as a result of findings indicating that social stress is an incomplete explanation of mental disorder. Social support research reflects the interests of early sociologists like Durkheim, who argued that the greater the social integration of a particular category of people, the lower the rates of suicide. Contemporary research on mental disorder has taken a similar approach, borrowing from Durkheim an interest in the buffering effects of social support. In the mental disorder research, however, the approach is much more on the micro level than that employed by Durkheim, thus reflecting more closely Hirschi's (1969) version of control theory.

It is theoretically informative to note that strain theory also traces its roots to Durkheim's work on suicide. Indeed, strain theory and control theory have similar theoretical roots, one suggesting that social disintegration provides a motivation—a strain—toward deviance (strain theory), and the other suggesting that social disintegration results in a breakdown of support and control systems that serve to prevent deviance (control theory). The similarity between these two theoretical traditions is evident in the mental disorder literature. Increasingly, researchers are simultaneously considering stress as an impetus toward mental disorder and social support as a protection against mental disorder (e.g., Gore, 1978; Kessler et al, 1985; Lin, Dean, and Ensel, 1986). In fact, these terms have become so interconnected that models of stress that fail to consider the potential modifying effects of social support (e.g., Holmes and Rahe, 1967) have been criticized.

The study of social support has proven fruitful in adding to the explanatory usefulness of social stress models. For example, Susan Gore (1978) studied the buffering effects of social support for 100 blue-collar male workers who were laid off after the closure of two plants. In this study, social support was measured by asking the individual to rate his wife, friends, and relatives as supportive or unsupportive. Gore found that the unsupported blue-collar workers felt greater self-blame and had more psychological symptoms and health problems than supported blue-collar workers. In a sample of women experiencing significant life stress, Brown and Harris (1978) have similarly demonstrated that the presence of a husband or boyfriend served to protect women from depression. More recently, Lin and his colleagues (1986) report that intimate and confiding partners (especially opposite sex partners) can mediate the effects of stressful life events.

These data can be used to explain many of

the epidemiological patterns we previously discussed. For example, Lin, Dean, and Ensel (1986) contend that the reason women have more depressive symptoms is because they are less likely to have opposite sex confidants. Importantly, when research includes only married men and women, the relationship between gender and depressive symptoms all but disappears. Another pattern that can be explained with these data is the relationship between marital disruption (i.e., divorce, separation, and death of spouse) and mental disorder. Not only is marital disruption an extremely stressful life event, but often it also results in the disintegration of one's previous social supports. Not only does the individual lose a spouse, but he or she may also lose friends and family associated with the marriage.

Learning Theory. Learning theorists are especially critical of the medical assumption that an underlying psychic or biological disease causes problematic behavior. What learning theorists attempt to explain is the troublesome behavior, the *symptoms,* rather than the *disease* that is presumably causing the symptoms. From a learning perspective, whether the person adopts the role of the mentally ill is "determined more by the nature of interpersonal relationships and the changing environment than on the unfolding imperatives of an underlying dynamic illness" (Akers, 1985:331). Learning theorists, therefore, emphasize environmental and interactional factors rather than intrapersonal psychic factors. They attempt to "shift the spotlight" away from individualistic notions of bizarre behavior as a "disease" or a "condition" or a "syndrome of symptoms," and focus instead on relationship and process (Lemert, 1967:3).

In its original formulation, Sutherland's theory of differential association assumed that deviance is learned in interaction with deviant others. In discussing drug use or ju-

venile delinquency, it is easy to see how deviant behavior could be learned. With mental disorder, however, the learning process is not always so obvious. Through modeling or socialization "sick" behavior may sometimes be learned directly from other "sick" people, but it seems likely that the learning process is generally less overt. Contemporary learning theorists assume that troublesome behavior develops as a conditioned response to the environment. Therefore, to the extent that bizarre behavior is conditioned, however inadvertent or unintended rewards and punishments are, the behavior will persist.

Empirical support for the learning approach has come from observational studies in the community and in mental hospitals (Akers, 1985). Lemert (1967), for example, observed the interaction patterns of family members who had initiated commitment proceedings against a family member believed to be paranoid. He demonstrates that the imagined conspiracy the paranoid person feels is not merely imagined. Whatever the initial source of their paranoid behavior, the paranoid subjects in Lemert's study were accurate in their belief that were being isolated, excluded, and turned upon.

Observational studies of mental institutions reveal that often it is the "sick" behavior rather than the "healthy" behavior that is reinforced (Akers, 1985). Those with the most direct contact with patients—ward attendants or aides—are often concerned less with treatment than with getting through each day with as few hassles as possible. A good patient is one who is passive and cooperative. Patients learn that the few rewards that exist in institutions—free time, desirable job assignments, extra attention, and the like—are handed out by aides. Patients soon learn as well that independence, opinion, and trouble-making behavior are not rewarded. "Faced with this, many patients become extremely apathetic, develop vegetative and childlike behavior patterns. . . , and other responses which are taken by the staff as further confirmation of sickness" (Akers, 1985:335).

The success of therapies based on learning principles also provides some support for the learning perspective. Even for severe disorders like schizophrenia, when coherent responses are rewarded through attention and social response, behavior becomes more normal (Akers, 1985). Sometimes the treatment involves actually receiving points when certain goals associated with mental health are achieved (e.g., doing well at school or on the job, taking care of oneself, keeping one's room clean). These points can then be exchanged for privileges (e.g., time off the ward, a radio in the room, room preference) which are designed to further encourage healthy behavior (Akers, 1985). According to Akers, the success of social learning programs of this nature "provide emphatic demonstration that behavior labeled mental illness of the most serious kind is affected by individuals' relationships to their social environments" (1985:337).

Subjectivist Theories.   Subjectivist theories attempt to explain the origins and application of deviance definitions and explanations (interest group theories), the social process by which individual labelers define deviants (definitional theories), and the effect of these societal reactions on the behavior of individual "deviants" (labeling theories). Since the medical model, which dominates the study of mental disorder, so directly challenges these subjectivist interests, mental disorder has been a favorite topic of subjectivist theorists.

Macro-Subjectivist Theories.   Much of the macro-subjectivist criticism of the medical model has been directed at the mental health profession's self-professed ability to identify the difference between healthy and unhealthy behavior. This criticism is more often directed at the less extreme forms of mental disorder (e.g., personality disorders like dependent personality) than at more extreme and more debilitating mental disorders (e.g., psychotic disorders like schizophrenia). Macro-subjectivist theorists argue that mental disorder categories are not based on objectively defined criteria. Contrary to medical claims, they do not exist "out there." They are socially constructed. It is impossible to prove, for example, whether homosexuality is a normal or abnormal variation in sexual expression. Science cannot tell us whether the behavior is "sick" or not. The labels "normal" or "abnormal" are just that, labels.

To understand where these labels come from, we must consider the interest groups involved in the debate of definitions and explanations of mental disorder.

Interest Group Theory.   Interest group theories focus on the social, political, and economic forces involved in the creation of deviant labels. For interest group theorists, all deviance is a social construction and is to be understood only in a socio-historical context. Since subjectivist theorists assume that deviance categories are socially constructed, the medical assumption that a mental "disease" exists "out there" is severely criticized. If we accept, for example, Erikson's (1966) argument that deviance is created in order to maintain and reinforce the normative standards of the established order, then deviance may be nothing more than behavior that threatens the status quo (Gove, 1982b).

Interest group theorists remind us further that psychiatrists and others in the mental health profession are important agents of social control and have a vested interest in defining mental illness and other forms of deviance (e.g., alcoholism, drug abuse) as disease. These observations set the stage for a very interesting interest group debate.

Conrad and Schneider (1980:38–72) provide an interest group theory for how bizarre behavior came to be viewed as a medical problem. They maintain that bizarre behavior represents the original case of medicalized deviance. The "madness-as-illness concept" is a product of 200 years of changing conceptions of reality. Consistent with the political dimensions of interest group theory, they begin with the following assumption:

> The greatest social control power comes from having the authority to define certain behaviors, persons, and things. This right to define may reside in an abstract authority such as 'the law' or God but is implemented commonly through some institutional force such as the state or church. Such institutions, then (or, perhaps better, the people who represent them), have the mandate to define the problem (e.g., as deviance), designate what type of problem it is, and indicate what should be done about it (Conrad and Schneider, 1980:8).

Conrad and Schneider argue that in the Old Testament, individuals who exhibited uncontrolled and unreasonable behavior were viewed in various ways—sometimes as prophets and sometimes as sinners. During the Middle Ages, the dominant conception of madness was theological—resulting either from God's punishment or demonic possession. It was during the fifteenth century that those acting in nonnormative ways began to be defined as witches who had made a pact with the Devil (Conrad and Schneider, 1980). During the famous witch-hunts of this period, perhaps as many as half a million people were burned, hung, or drowned (Conrad and Schneider, 1980).

In time, of course, bizarre behavior was seen less and less in religious terms. But if individuals who acted bizarrely were not the responsibility of the religious leaders, whose responsibility were they? What should be done with them? For the most part, those who were of no danger to themselves or others were allowed to roam the streets freely.

By the middle of the seventeenth century, however, cities began to take steps to rid themselves of these "socially useless" people (e.g., the insane, unemployed, poor). Institutions were created and, while they were called "hospitals," their function was social control rather than medical service (Conrad and Schneider, 1980).

By the late eighteenth century, the "mad" were separated from other groups of "socially useless" people. With the increasing labor needs associated with the rise of industrialization, able-bodied deviants proved to be an important reserve labor pool. Since the prevailing wisdom was that madness was contagious, able-bodied deviants needed protection. It is important to remember, therefore, that from a sociological viewpoint, "the separation and segregation of the mad from other deviants was accomplished largely for social and economic reasons, not for medical reasons" (Conrad and Schneider, 1980:45).

There remained the problem, however, of who should assume responsibility for the insane. By the end of the eighteenth century, insanity had come to be defined as a medical problem and medical certification was required for institutional confinement. Importantly, therefore, as the label "witchcraft" began to disappear, modern psychiatry was born (Conrad and Schneider, 1980; Szasz, 1970). Psychiatrists, of course, view this as a triumph of modern medical advances. Indeed, they would look to an earlier time and conclude that since "witches" were actually "mentally ill," "instead of being persecuted for heresy they should have been treated for insanity" (Szasz, 1970:xix).

Not everyone, however, feels this definitional change should be viewed as a victory for medical advances. There are those who argue that "mental disorder" is no less a societally created label than "witchcraft" was before it. Conrad and Schneider (1980) argue that there was seemingly no empirical reason why physicians should become authorities on madness. They had no theories—no "cures":

> Certainly, if physicians could provide useful curative and rehabilitative treatments, then it would be clear why medicine came to dominate the realm of madness. But this does not seem to be the case. Most of the therapies used by 18th-century physicians were ancient ones: bloodletting, dunking and purgation were popular treatments (Conrad and Schneider, 1980:45).

If the physicians were themselves unsuccessful in explaining and treating madness, why were they successful in claiming authority over bizarre behavior? Conrad and Schneider (1980) suggest that with success in the control of diseases like leprosy, smallpox and malaria, there grew an optimism that medicine could cure all of society's ills. Society "gave" the medical community bizarre behavior because it did not know what else to do with it.

Among the more outspoken scholars who share this view with Conrad and Schneider is Thomas Szasz (1961, 1970). Szasz's criticisms have received considerable attention within the social scientific and psychiatric communities because, interestingly, he is a psychiatrist. When compared to most in the mental health profession, he offers a very different interpretation of the process by which witchcraft became mental "illness":

> I say it happened (the redefinition of witchcraft as mental illness) because of the transformation of a religious ideology into a scientific one: medicine replaced theology; the alienist, the inquisitor; and the insane, the witch. The result was the substitution of a medical mass-movement for a religious one, the persecution of mental patients replacing the persecution of heretics.
>
> In the past, men created witches; now they create mental patients. . . .The point is that these mental patients do not choose the role of mental patient; they are defined and treated as mental patients against their will; in short, the role is ascribed to them. As far as the accused mental patients are

concerned—they would elect, were they given the choice, to be left alone by the holders of Medical and State power (Szasz, 1970:xx–xxi).

From this perspective, mental disorder represents nothing more than a label created by a society that is far too intolerant of behavior it views as "strange" and "weird." For these scholars, treatment is nothing more than a mechanism by which society controls its undesirable. Therefore, the issue is partly a matter of civil liberties—the freedom to be different and the freedom to avoid the judgmental condemnation of "mean ole society."

The interest group perspective has been further articulated by Stuart Kirk and Herb Kutchins, who in their recent book, *The Selling of DSM: The Rhetoric of Science in Psychiatry* (1992) offer a scathing critique of the role of the American Psychiatric Association in medicalizing bizarre behavior. Although Kirk and Kutchins are not sociologists (both are social workers), they draw directly from macro-subjectivists in studying the "claims making activities" of the psychiatric community. Their critique focuses specifically on the making and selling of the *DSM-III* (APA, 1980), which, when it was first released in 1980, was heralded as a triumph of the science of psychiatry. In the words of Robert Spitzer, the primary architect of the *DSM-III*:

> The adoption of DSM-III by the American Psychiatric Association has been viewed as making a signal achievement for psychiatry. Not only did the new diagnostic manual represent an advance toward fulfillment of the scientific aspirations of the profession, but it indicated an emergent professional consensus over the procedures that would eliminate the disarray that characterized psychiatric diagnosis (Bayer and Spitzer, 1985:187).

Kirk and Kutchins maintain, however, that research and empirical data played a very limited role in resolving conflicts that arose in the making of the *DSM-III*. Such conflicts were resolved politically, not empirically. And the *DSM-III* was a triumph of modern psychiatry, not modern science. The rhetoric of science, however, proved useful to psychiatry as it attempted in the *DSM-III* to further exert its dominance over the "mental health enterprise" (Kirk and Kutchins, 1992:8).

Kirk and Kutchins (1992) make explicit what should by now be obvious: The mental health profession has a vested interest in how bizarre behavior is defined. Clearly, the mental health profession is based on the assumption that mental illness exists. The more mental disease that is discovered and diagnosed, the greater the need for psychiatrists and psychologists. The greater the empirical justification for the discoveries, the greater the societal clout such discoveries will command. And perhaps most importantly, the people who are placed in charge of "discovering" the mental disease are the same people who stand to gain the most from its discovery. The Hillside Strangler case provides a classic example of this. Both psychotherapists brought in by the prosecution were "experts" in multiple personalities. They had written books and articles arguing that multiple personalities were more common than most mental health professionals believed them to be. One of the experts, Dr. Allison, even went so far as to brag of his credentials to Ken Bianchi:

> *"I have collected up to now fifty cases I've seen,"* he told Bianchi, *"which is not a world's record, but it's close to it. I know another psychiatrist who's had about sixty-five back in Philadelphia and one that had about that in Honolulu. The three of us have the largest numbers. . .I've got three in therapy right now in my clinic"* (O'Brien, 1985:275).

Interest group theory reminds us that although Dr. Allison was brought in as an objective "expert," he clearly had a vested interest in the "discovery" of multiple personality disorder. The more multiple personality disorders he discovered, the more significant his view on multiple-personality disorder would become. Under these condi-

tions, perhaps it should not surprise us that he was so quick to diagnose Bianchi as a multiple-personality disorder.

Of course the medical authority over bizarre behavior is not always unchallenged. Other interests are constantly vying for the right to define and explain nonnormative behavior. A contemporary example concerns the treatment of, and societal response to, homosexual behavior. With increasing acceptance during the 1960s, homosexuality, like witchcraft before it, came to be defined as mental disorder. Psychiatrists and psychologists became "the natural custodians, defenders, and ultimate authority of the mental disorder perspective on homosexuality (Spector, 1977:52). When the American Psychiatric Association (APA) first published the *Diagnostic and Statistical Manual of Mental Disorders (DSM-I)* in 1952, homosexuality was included under the category "Sociopathic Personality Disturbance." In 1968, the *DSM-II* included homosexuality under the category "Sexual Deviance" (APA 1968). By 1973, after several years of pressure from gay groups angered by the classification of homosexuality as a mental disorder, the APA once again changed its position, this time classifying homosexuality as "Sexual Orientation Disturbance," defined as a disorder only if the individual desires a change in sexual orientation. Consider this description offered by the APA:

> This category is for individuals whose sexual interests are directed primarily toward people of the same sex and who are either disturbed by, in conflict with, or wish to change their sexual orientation. The diagnostic category is distinguished from homosexuality which by itself does not necessarily constitute a psychiatric disorder. Homosexuality per se is one form of sexual behavior and, like other forms of sexual behavior which are not by themselves psychiatric disorders, is not listed in this nomenclature of mental disorders. . . (quoted in Spector, 1977:53).

In other words, homosexuality is a disorder only if the person involved does not want to be a homosexual. In *DSM-III*, the APA (1980) further modified its stance on homosexuality, introducing the category "Ego-dystonic Homosexuality." Once again it is obvious how the APA, very conscious of criticism from gay interest groups, has chosen its words carefully:

> This category is reserved for homosexuals for whom changing sexual orientation is a persistent concern, and should be avoided in cases where the desire to change sexual orientations may be a brief, temporary manifestation of an individual's difficulty in adjusting to a new awareness of his or her homosexual impulses (APA, 1980:281).

In the *DSM III-Revised*, even the category "Ego-dystonic homosexuality" has been dropped because "it suggests to some that the homosexuality itself was considered a disorder" (APA, 1987:426). Homosexuality, wanted or not, is no longer a mental disorder.

While many defend the "empirical basis" upon which the definitional changes were based (e.g., see Gonsiorek, 1991), it seems clear that the demise of homosexuality as a mental disorder is tied more to interest group pressures than to a scientific understanding of homosexuality. The conflict over homosexuality was, in the words of Kirk and Kutchins, a political struggle, where "questions of reliability and other more-or-less data-related issues were overshadowed by the politics of diagnosis" (1992:77). It is, after all, impossible to "prove" whether homosexuality is a healthy or unhealthy behavior. Such definitions—such labels—are not dependent on scientific understandings.

In recent years, many other interest groups have joined in on the battle for the right to define and explain mental disorder. In addition to the sociologists, psychologists, and psychiatrists who often differ in their interpretation of the problem, there are organizations committed to protecting the rights of mental patients (e.g., the Network Against Psychiatric Assault and Mental Patients' Liberation Front) as well as organizations promoting an increasing emphasis on the treatment of mental disorders (e.g., American Schizophrenic Association) (Grusky and Pollner, 1981).

Neo-Marxist Theory. For a minority of interest group theorists, mental disorder categories are created by capitalists in an effort to protect their economic interests. These neo-Marxists maintain that there are only two interest groups in capitalist societies: the haves (the capitalist class) and the have-nots (the working class). The "haves" make the rules in order to ensure that their interests will be protected. Unlike more mainstream interest group theorists who maintain that mental health professionals are a powerful interest group in and of themselves, the neo-Marxists maintain that the mental health community merely reflects and protects the interests of society's elites.

Scull's (1988) neo-Marxist interpretation of the rise of the insane asylum is not unlike Conrad and Schneider's (1980) interpretation of the creation of mental disorder more generally. The difference is that Scull (1988) views medicalization as an explicit attempt by capitalists to protect their economic interests. Scull argues that the economic domination and exploitation that emerged as a result of capitalism severed "the reciprocal notions of paternalism, deference, and dependence" that had characterized rich-poor relations in earlier times (1988:104). Capitalism produced an upper class that felt little responsibility for the problems of the lower class. These factors, in combination with the increasing size of the working class, led to the need to find a place to "store" socially useless people.

Just as vagrancy laws arose as an attempt to "discipline" a population of people who presented problems for the capitalist class (Chambliss, 1964), mental institutions arose as an attempt to "discipline" those who were not pulling their economic weight:

> *The quasi-military authority structure of the total institution seemed ideally suited to the inculcation of 'proper' work habits among those marginal elements of the workforce most resistant to the monotony, routine, and regularity of industrialized labor. . .And, undoubtedly, one of the attractions of the asylum as a method of dealing with the insane was its promise of instilling the virtues of bourgeois rationality into that segment of the population least amenable to them" (Scull, 1988:105).*

There were those, however, whose bizarre behavior meant that there was little hope that they would ever prove useful to the capitalist class. Capitalists were also concerned that bizarre behavior could actually be caught like the flu (Conrad and Schneider, 1980). The ruling class was therefore faced with a dilemma: how to "care" for those who were useless without "contaminating" those who might eventually prove to be a useful resource.

The involvement of the medical profession provided legitimacy to capitalist-class claims that such groups had to be separated and "treated." Even more significantly, it demonstrated the "humanitarian," "altruistic" interests of the capitalist class. According to Scull (1988), however, the true function of the asylums was (and is) control and management of a problem population.

Micro-Subjectivist Theories. Many defenders of the medical model agree with the macro-subjectivists to a point, admitting that mental disorder is exceedingly difficult to define absolutely (Gorenstein, 1984) and that an individual is not mentally ill until a psychiatrist or psychologist defines him or her as such (Gove, 1982b). Many of these same defenders of the medical model further admit that these facts do lend credibility to the micro-subjectivist argument that "psychiatrists create mental illness by labeling someone mentally disordered and treating them accordingly"

(Gove, 1982b:294). For the most part, however, defenders of the medical model take exception to the micro-subjectivist claims that mental disorder diagnoses are arbitrary (the concern of the definitional theorists) and that societal reactions actually create bizarre behavior (the concern of the labeling theorists).

Definitional Theories. What is interesting to *definitional* theorists is how definitions of deviance, which are themselves subjectively defined, are used as objectively defined standards by which individuals are diagnosed. In other words, the definitional problems with which macro-subjectivists concern themselves (i.e., What is mental disorder?) naturally lead to diagnosis problems with which micro-subjectivists concern themselves (Who are the mentally disordered?).

Given such concerns, it may be fruitful to wonder, as psychologist David Rosenhan has wondered, "If sanity and insanity exist, how shall we know them?" (1973:250). Rosenhan's response to his own question is as follows:

> *The question is neither capricious nor itself insane. However much we may be personally convinced that we can tell the normal from the abnormal, the evidence is simply not compelling. It is commonplace, for example, to read about murder trials wherein eminent psychiatrists for the defense are contradicted by equally eminent psychiatrists for the prosecution on the matter of the defendant's sanity. (Rosenhan, 1973:250)*

Rosenhan, and other definitional theorists like him, do not deny the existence of mental disorder or the problems that are often associated with mental disorder. Anxiety, depression, and psychological suffering do exist. What micro-subjectivsts question is the assumption that abnormality can be clearly and reliably distinguished from normality.

To demonstrate the problems with diagnosis, Rosenhan organized a group of eight colleagues who feigned mental disorder and voluntarily admitted themselves to mental hospitals. Each "pseudopatient" complained of hearing voices and, based upon these "symptoms," all but one was admitted with the diagnosis of schizophrenia. Once admitted to the hospital, the pseudopatients stopped faking any symptoms of abnormality. Despite the absence of symptoms, however, the pseudopatients were never detected as fakes. The success of Rosenhan's colleagues in gaining admission to the mental hospital leads Rosenhan to question diagnostic procedures. He writes:

> *Whenever the ratio of what is known to what needs to be known approaches zero, we tend to invent "knowledge" and assume that we understand more than we actually do. We seem unable to acknowledge that we simply don't know. . .The facts of the matter are that we have known for a long time that diagnoses are often not useful or reliable, but we have nevertheless continued to use them. We now know that we cannot distinguish insanity from sanity (Rosenhan, 1973:257).*

Concerns such as these have led to considerable research on the process by which diagnostic decisions are made. (For a review, see Link and Cullen, 1990.) In experimental research, for example, Temerlin (1968) has demonstrated that mental health professionals who are told by "prestigious colleagues" to expect psychotic behavior in a particular patient are, when compared to those who do not receive similar input, more likely to label bizarre behavior "psychotic." Simon and Zusman (1983) similarly wonder how it is that, in civil suits in which victims are claiming psychological damage, psychiatrists hired by the plaintiffs and psychiatrists hired by the defense can offer such contradictory psychological assessments. Once again we are reminded of the Bianchi case where two experts hired by the defense discovered multiple personality and the one expert hired by the prosecution discovered that Bianchi had been misdiagnosed.

Many definitional theorists maintain that being labeled deviant depends as much on who you are as it does on what you do. In his now famous micro-subjectivist statement on mental illness, Thomas Scheff (1966) argued that it is the less powerful who are most likely to be labeled "mentally ill." Scheff assumed that a white, rich man who does "weird" things might be labeled "eccentric," while a poor, Hispanic man might be labeled "crazy." Research on the role of social status, however, is somewhat mixed. Contrary to Scheff's (1966) argument, Strole and his colleagues (1968) maintain that the rich are actually more likely to be treated (i.e., officially labeled) for mental disorder. They found that only 21 percent of lower-class respondents who were judged by a team of psychiatrists to be psychologically impaired had received treatment for their impairment. This compared to 23 percent of the middle-class respondents and 53 percent of the upper-class respondents. Based upon evidence such as this, defenders of the mental health profession like Walter Gove (1982b) agree with Scheff that the poor are disadvantaged but maintain that they are disadvantaged because they lack the resources to obtain needed treatment. According to Gove (1982b), the process is working in the exact opposite direction predicted by the definitional theorists.

There is, however, some evidence that lends support to Scheff's (1966) argument. Mental patients with low status are less likely to receive the preferred treatment (Link and Cullen, 1990). In addition, low-status people are more likely than high-status people to be involuntarily committed to a mental institution (Goldstein, 1979; Rosenfield, 1984).

While considerable debate remains as to whether it is the powerless who are more likely to be labeled, there is considerable evidence that, in general, social factors do influence diagnostic decisions (Krohn and Akers, 1977; Link and Cullen, 1990). For example, in an observational study on the relationship between gender and recommendations for psychiatric hospitalization, Rosenfield (1982) found that men diagnosed with "female" disorders (e.g., mood disorders like depression) are more likely to be hospitalized than women diagnosed with the same disorder. Similarly, women with "male" disorders (e.g., personality disorders and substance abuse) are more likely to be hospitalized than men with the same disorder. Because they violate gender-role norms they are perceived as being more troubled than those whose psychiatric symptoms are consistent with gender-role expectations (Link and Cullen, 1990). This and other research has led Krohn and Akers (1977), and more recently, Link and Cullen (1990) to conclude that social factors do influence admission and discharge decisions. Few agree with Scheff (1966), however, that such factors are the *most* important determinants of societal reactions. With increasing evidence of a genetic link to disorders such as schizophrenia (Gove, 1982a) and evidence that those diagnosed have more psychiatric symptoms than those who are not diagnosed (Gove, 1982a, 1982b; Link and Cullen, 1990), the suggestion that the behavior of those diagnosed is no different from the behavior of those who are not diagnosed seems misguided.

The interest of definitional theorists in the mental health profession does not stop with criticism of diagnostic procedures. Rosenhan (1973), for example, shares Kitsuse's (1962) concern about how diagnostic labels affect the perceptions of others. Rosenhan argues that the psychiatric label applied to the pseudopatients so dominated hospital staff conceptions that "normal" behavior was either unnoticed or was interpreted as an indication of sickness. For example, the pseudopatients took extensive notes in the hospital. They also asked many questions of the hospital staff. Neither behavior is especially "crazy." In fact, the behavior of the pseudopatients was so "normal" that many of the real patients suspected that the pseudopatients were faking it. The hospital staff, on the other hand, was more likely to see the constant note-taking or the barrage of questions as confirmation of the disorder.

In light of these observations, Rosenhan poses several important questions:

> *How many people, one wonders, are sane but not recognized as such by our psychiatric institutions? How many have been needlessly stripped of their privileges of citizenship, from the right to vote and drive to that of handling their own accounts. . .How many are stigmatized by well-intentioned, but nevertheless erroneous, diagnoses? (Rosenhan, 1973:257)*

Labeling Theory. The unique contribution of *labeling theory* is that it sensitizes us to the potentially harmful effects of the "deviant" label. Indeed, this is Lemert's (1967) interest when he distinguishes between primary and secondary deviance. *Primary deviance* is uninteresting to the labeling theorist except to the degree that others react to it. Upon the reaction of others, one possible outcome is *secondary deviance*, which is "deviant behavior or social roles based upon it, which becomes a means of defense, attack or adaptation to the overt and covert problems created by the societal reaction to primary deviation" (Lemert, 1967:17). Labeling theorists argue that mental disorder is especially illustrative of the usefulness of labeling theory because the label "mentally ill" is thought to be highly stigmatizing. Certainly it is intriguing to wonder what becomes of the woman who struggles to maintain a self-conception of normality in the face of others' deviant definitions. Should everyone think her crazy, what "choice" has she but to think herself crazy?

Before considering the empirical evidence pertaining to the effects of deviant labels, it would be helpful to reintroduce the history of labeling explanations of mental disorder. The most original and thorough labeling theory of mental disorder is provided by Scheff

(1966), whose theoretical framework is introduced in Chapter 3. Scheff introduces the term *residual deviance* as a category of unacceptable behavior that does not fit into other deviance categories. Most residual deviance is common and insignificant and, for the most part, does not produce any official societal reaction. However, when society does react, a stereotypical label is imposed on the individual thereby triggering a sequence of events that culminate in the labeled individual adopting the role of the "mentally ill."

In his original formulation, Scheff listed nine propositions (see Chapter 3, Table 3–2) that provide a general explanation of how an individual adopts the role of the mentally disordered. There is considerable support for many of the propositions (Eaton, 1986). Most residual deviance does indeed go unnoticed (proposition 2) and/or is transitory (proposition 3). Most scholars would agree that a cultural stereotype of mental disorder exists (propositions 4 and 5) and that these stereotypes lead to the devaluation and discrimination of the mentally ill (Link et al., 1989). There is also reason to believe that labeling involves rewards for appropriate playing of the deviant role and punishment for attempts to return to conventional roles (propositions 6 and 7 (Akers, 1985)). The real debate concerns the final two propositions. Proposition 8 involves the issue of secondary deviance: the extent to which the labeled individual assumes the role of the mentally ill and that role acts as a master status. Proposition 9 has also proved controversial; in it, Scheff poses a direct challenge to medical and psychoanalytic theories by suggesting that labeling offers the best theory of mental disorder. Scheff would no doubt agree with Szasz (1961) that mental "illness" is a myth. Understandably, many psychiatrists and psychoanalysts have been angered by the suggestion that they have devoted their careers to the study and perpetuation of a myth (Gorenstein, 1984).

Among sociologists, the most outspoken critic of the labeling perspective has been Walter Gove (1970; 1975; 1982a; 1982b). In an early critique of the labeling argument, Gove (1970) summarizes the studies cited by Scheff (1966), questioning the data and methods, and, perhaps most importantly, Scheff's interpretation of these data. In his response to Gove's criticisms, Scheff (1974) has defended his interpretation and the support it provides for labeling theory. Later exchanges (Gove, 1975; Scheff, 1975) have been repetitive, with both researchers being somewhat blind to the weaknesses of their own perspective and arguing in an all-or-nothing style (that their own perspective is "right" and the other "wrong"). As a result, the debate has served to obscure the important issue of whether mental disorder exists apart from (or prior to) societal reactions (Goldstein, 1979).

Summarizing the data pertaining to the labeling perspective is a cumbersome task. First, there is a tremendous amount of data that addresses one or more aspects of labeling theory. Second, the process by which the labeled person assumes the role of the mentally disordered is not clearly specified, prompting some to argue that labeling theory is essentially useless. At the very least, the fact that labeling theory is not clearly specified has made tests exceedingly difficult.

When labeling theorists talk about the consequences of being labeled, they seem to be interested primarily in hospitalization. To what extent is the stigma associated with hospitalization severe enough to produce career deviants? Even labeling theory's most outspoken critic, Walter Gove (1982a), admits that in years past there was some truth to the notion that hospitalization actually produced mental disorder. "From past experience," Gove argues (1982b:288), "it is clear that mental hospitals can be debilitating places where some patients come to accept the preferred role of the insane and, over time, develop skills and a world view adapted to the institutional setting." In other words, Gove is arguing that during the 1950s and 1960s, when Scheff (1966), Szasz (1970), and Goffman (1961) were raising questions about the violation of human rights and the dehumanizing effects of hospitalization, labeling theorists pointed to some very real processes. However, Gove argues that "in the past 25 years there have been so many developments in psychiatry that the issues raised by labeling theory have been largely resolved, and that from a pragmatic perspective a general labeling explanation of mental illness is no longer tenable" (Gove, 1982a:307). Gove describes several changes (1982a:308–318): (1) Since 1955 there has been a dramatic decrease in the length of hospitalization and a shift toward outpatient treatment. "Given the short period and location of treatment, it is difficult to imagine that the stigma of treatment acts as a master status that persists in shaping patients' lives by placing them in the role of the (permanently) mentally ill" (1982a:310). (2) Treatment has become increasingly effective. (3) Attitudes toward the mentally ill are changing to such an extent that the stigma is not what it was 25 years ago. While in Gove's estimation "most mental patients experience some stigma,. . .the stigma appears to be transitory and does not appear to pose a severe problem" (1982b:290). (4) The violation of civil rights associated with involuntary commitment, an important consideration for both Scheff (1966) and Szasz (1961), has become increasingly rare as a result of legal reforms. (5) With recent revisions of the *DSM*, diagnosis has reached a "satisfactory" level of reliability.

Such changes lead Gove to conclude:

The labeling theory of mental illness points to some real processes, but these processes were more important in the past than they are in the present. In fact, a careful review of the evidence demonstrates that the labeling theory of mental illness is substantially invalid, especially as a general theory of mental illness (Gove, 1982b:295).

In other words, contrary to the argument of labeling theory, the most common outcome of being labeled "mentally ill" is not more severe mental illness. Patients react much less negatively to hospitalization than labeling theorists suggest (Weinstein, 1983), and they are less likely to adopt a mental illness role than labeling theorists suggest (Gove, 1975).

Gove assumes that because labeling seemingly does not produce full-blown mental illness, labeling theory is disproved. Many labeling theorists, including most recently Bruce Link (1987; Link et al., 1989; Link and Cullen, 1990), however, criticize this assumption, noting that detrimental effects can be more subtle. Link (1987), in fact, argues that the debate over labeling has been hampered by the assumption that the only consequences that would support a labeling perspective are full-blown mental disorders. There are psychological consequences that may be only indirectly related to "mental illness."

In surveys of treated patients and untreated community residents, Link and his colleagues (1987; Link et al., 1989; Link and Cullen, 1990) demonstrate that, in general, respondents "have internalized a generally negative view about what it means to be a mental patient" (Link et al., 1989:419). Importantly, these conceptions of psychiatric patients being devalued and discriminated against become personally applicable for those who are labeled. This expectation of rejection can have negative effects on the psychological and social functioning of mental patients. Link (1987) demonstrates empirically that those who fear rejection and are publicly labeled "mentally ill" have lower self-esteem, feel hopeless and demoralized, have less income, and have higher rates of unemployment. In a more recent study, Link and his colleagues (1989) demonstrate further that mental patients tend to cope with their diagnosis with withdraw and secrecy. Withdrawal and isolation contribute further to the negative effects of labeling. Link and his colleagues summarize the process as follows:

With time, their [the patients'] beliefs about the implications of the label they carry and their way of dealing with it shape the nature of their social connectedness. Those patients who are most concerned with stigma are likely to have insular support networks consisting of safe and trusted persons on whom they rely extensively. At the same time, such patients have considerably less support available from individuals outside their immediate household (Link et al., 1989:419).

In short, Link and his colleagues strongly challenge the "notion that labeling and stigma are inconsequential in the lives of psychiatric patients" (1989:420–421).

While these data clearly support the labeling argument, Link admits that the question of whether the negative consequences of labeling causes and stabilizes mental disorders remains unexplored (Link and Cullen, 1990: 97). In other words, we still do not have data that either confirms or refutes a connection between societal reactions and secondary deviance. At the same time, the negative consequences Link and his colleagues point to (e.g., self-esteem, employment status, and social networks) are themselves often discussed as causal factors in the etiology of mental disorders. Therefore, while these symptoms "are not full-blown manifestations of mental disorder specified in Scheff's (1966) formulation of the consequences of labeling, they are considered widely in psychiatric evaluations. The linking of a modified labeling perspective to the emergence of these symptoms is a direct empirical challenge to critics of labeling theory on this issue" (Link, 1987:110–111).

In conclusion, Gove (1970) is justified in his frustration over the implicit claim of labeling theory that problematic behavior exists only as a result of the arbitrary reactions of others. Clearly, labeling does not by itself create mental disorder. As Link and his colleagues have reminded us (Link, 1987; Link et al., 1989; Link & Cullen, 1990), however, this does not mean that labeling is not a real and detrimental process. Societal reactions do

have a powerful effect on self-conceptions. Scheff (1974) has himself recognized that the value of labeling theory may be that it is a sensitizing approach. As a sensitizing approach, it has been successful and, for this reason, will likely remain important in the sociological study of mental disorder.

SOCIAL POLICY AND SOCIAL CONTROL

The implications of the medical model for the social control of and social policy toward mental disorder should not be underestimated. First, as has already been discussed in Chapter 3, the disease label may have disease consequences. To the extent that the mental patient must accept the label "mentally ill," and along with it the notion that he or she has no control over the "disease," what prospects are there for recovery? In addition, to the extent that the patient truly believes he or she has a disease, the disease can become a rationale for bizarre behavior.

Mental Disorder and the Law

Because the disease presumably controls behavior, blame and moral condemnation are removed from the individual. How do we punish (or should we even punish) people whose deviant behavior is a result of a mental disorder? This question received some attention during 1989 when former baseball great Pete Rose was accused of betting on baseball, an offense that carries a lifetime ban from involvement in professional baseball. Gambling is another form of deviance that has been medicalized in recent years (Rosecrance, 1985), and there were those in gambling support organizations like Gamblers Anonymous who argued that Rose, who is known to have a "problem" with gambling, had a disease. If in fact he had a disease, some argued, how could baseball justify punishing him for behavior he presumably could not control?

Even more significantly, what are the implications of the medical model for the treatment of more serious criminals who are mentally disordered? For example, if serial murderer Ted Bundy was mentally disordered, should he have been held responsible for his crimes? In the end, of course, he was held responsible for his crimes and died in Florida's electric chair in 1989. Or what about Minnesota "mad man" Jeffrey Dahmer, who killed and cut up several victims in 1991? Was Dahmer "crazy"? The defense argued that he was, but the courts found otherwise.

The insanity defense has historically been based on the "Durham rule," which states simply that the "accused is not criminally responsible if his unlawful act was the product of mental disease or mental defect" (Conrad and Schneider, 1980:60). One problem with the insanity defense is that not everyone agrees with the assumption that mental disorder is a disease. In addition, the insanity defense assumes that psychiatrists can reliably diagnose mental disorder. As we have already discussed, psychiatric diagnosis has often been criticized as being unreliable (Rosenhan, 1973). The insanity defense also removes blame from the individual (Kittrie, 1971). "Thus the defendant attempts to shift responsibility away from himself or herself to the presence of mental disorder. The culprit then becomes the "mental disorder" in that *it* kept the person from doing whatever a normal person would have done in those circumstances" (Cockerham, 1989:315).

Underlying the debate is a basic philosophical dispute between those who view the primary role of the criminal justice system as rehabilitative and those who view it as punitive. Should criminal behavior be regarded as "sickness" in need of treatment or "badness" in need of punishment (Mechanic, 1969)? As a society, we seem truly confused. On the one hand, our society has become increasingly fascinated with the medical model of deviant behavior. If we are to believe what the "experts" are telling us, then one can today be "addicted" to everything from gambling, to shopping, to religion, to sex, to chocolate, to. . . .; the list goes on and on. It seems any "compulsive" behavior that the person "can't stop" is defined as addictive. At the same time, as a society we seem increasingly unwilling to excuse criminal behavior that results from a mental or physiological disorder. We are, for example, increasingly intolerant of drunk drivers, although many would argue that most drunk drivers have a disease.

Labels and Social Control

Another implication of the medical model concerns the power it provides the state in matters of social control. For example, Conrad and Schneider (1980) point to the former Soviet Union's history of abusing the term "mental illness" for political purposes. Conrad and Schneider argue that some Soviet political dissidents, who are perfectly sane by Western standards, have been committed to mental institutions. Medicalization, therefore, provides a swift, nonpolitical solution to dissent. While this blatant disregard for human rights may be rare in Western cultures, as long as the state defines bizarre behavior as disease and assumes authority over controlling the disease, the potential for abuse remains. This point is perhaps most clearly summarized by Irving Zola, who writes:

C.S. Lewis warned us more than a quarter of a century ago that "man's power over Nature is really the power of some men over other men, with Nature as their instrument." The same could be said regarding man's power over health and illness, for the labels health and illness are remarkable "depoliticizers" of an issue. By locating the source and the treatment of problems in an individual, other levels of intervention are effectively closed. By the very acceptance of a specific behavior as an "illness" and the definition of illness as an undesirable state, the issue becomes not whether to deal with a particular problem, but how and when. Thus the debate over homosexuality, or drugs or abortion becomes focused on the degree of sickness attached to the phenomenon in question or the extent of the health risk involved. And the more principled, more perplexing, or even moral issue, of what freedom should an individual have over his or her own body is shunted aside (Zola, 1972:500).

Recall that for labeling theorists, mental disorder is not a disease; it is a label imposed by an intolerant society. The concern over involuntary commitment, therefore, is that important civil rights are sometimes violated. Gove (1982a, 1982b) argues that during the 1950s and 1960s violations of human rights were not uncommon. However, as a result of legal and procedural changes, such violations have become increasingly rare. In most states, Gove (1982b) argues, people can only be committed to mental institutions if they pose a clear danger to themselves or others. With rather stringent standards of dangerousness, this means that in many states, people whom most psychiatrists would think of as severely disordered and in need of help cannot be committed and are allowed to roam the streets.

The Treatment of Mental Disorder

Since there is little agreement on what mental disorder is and even less agreement on what causes mental disorder, it should come as no surprise that there is no agreed upon treatment program for its cure. In contrast, consider the state of knowledge for certain physical diseases. When the arteries of the heart become clogged, for example, the treatment alternatives are clear and, for the most part, agreed upon. A detailed description of the multiple treatment programs available is obviously beyond the scope of this chapter.

However, in the remaining sections, two widely debated treatment issues will be discussed.

The Mental Hospital. According to Goldstein, "studies about mental hospitals comprise the single largest topic of investigation by sociologists regarding society's response to mental illness" (1979:399). For the labeling theorists, of course, the mental hospital represented the epitome of the *"total institution,"* and surely represented the ideal setting in which to investigate the stigmatizing effects of being labeled. Within the confines of the mental hospital, many sociologists would argue, "a world develops that is usually antithetical to the stated rehabilitative goals of the institution. Indeed, the negative effects of incarceration on the inmate's self-concept may not be remediable" (Goldstein, 1979:399).

During the late 1950s and early 1960s, several studies of mental hospitals were conducted (e.g., Stanton and Schwartz, 1954; Barton, 1959; Dunham and Weinberg, 1960; Goffman, 1961). Essentially, these scholars argued that once the mentally disordered are placed in institutions, their chances for recovery are minimal. Institutionalization merely increases their dependency on the institution and exacerbates the very behavioral problem it is trying to alleviate (Eaton, 1986). Among the more influential of these studies is Erving Goffman's *Asylums*. Goffman, who spent a year as a participant observer in a large public mental hospital in Washington D.C., describes in vivid detail the dramatic effects of institutionalization on the self-concept.

Drug Treatments and the Trend Toward Deinstitutionalization. Beginning in the mid-1950s, the population of hospital patients reached an all-time high and began a steady decline. The decline in institutionalization was accompanied by an increase in outpatient and community programs. There were at least two reasons for this "deinstitutionalization movement." First, the considerable labeling research on institutionalization raised consciousness levels about the potentially harmful effects of institutionalization. This research also created concern for the legal rights of patients. Secondly, and perhaps more importantly, the development of drugs to treat severe mental disorders like schizophrenia, unipolar and bipolar depression, panic disorder (Link and Cullen, 1990) allowed patients to function more normally.

Despite the general success of drug treatments, the psychiatric community is often criticized for turning to such treatments too quickly. Besides the potential physiological and social side effects of drug use, drugs generally do not offer a "cure" of mental disorders. For example, learning theorist Albert Bandura argues that, along with the emphasis on drugs, there has been a de-emphasis on the search for a solution to bizarre behavior. Indeed, he argues that the overemphasis on drugs has led "to heavy reliance upon physical and chemical intervention, unremitting search for drugs as quick remedies for interpersonal problems, and long-term neglect of social variables as influential determinants of deviant response patterns" (Bandura, 1969:16).

The deinstitutionalization movement has itself produced a number of problems. Many would argue, in fact, that the civil rights pendulum has swung too far. That is, in our attempt to protect the civil rights of the mentally disordered, we have ignored and neglected a great many people who do in fact need psychiatric help. Many people who might have been in mental hospitals during the 1950s wander the streets today. They may be dangerous, they may be easily victimized, or they may be homeless. At any rate, critics of the deinstitutionalization movement maintain that we have failed to help a group of people who badly need our help (Isaac and Armat, 1990).

SUMMARY

Students sometimes wonder why it is that sociologists study mental disorder. Of all the forms of deviance discussed in this book, mental disorder seems to fall most squarely under the purview of psychology and psychiatry. However, when psychologist David L. Rosenhan (1973:250) asks the question, "If sanity and insanity exist, how shall we known them?" he raises a theoretically important and controversial question, and one that requires sociological insights. At what point does "strange," "weird," or even individualistic behavior become mental "illness"? Certainly, the vast majority of those within the *mental health profession* contend that mental disorder can be sufficiently defined, diagnosed, and treated. However, others argue that definitions of mental "illness" are hopelessly dependent on social and cultural standards of normality, that diagnosis is unreliable, and that treatment does more harm than good.

The most dominant conception of mental disorder in contemporary society is based on a *medical model*. According to the medical model, bizarre behavior is an abnormal, unhealthy manifestation of an invisible disease. To eliminate the bizarre behavior, one must treat and cure the disease. Medical theories most often attribute bizarre behavior to *biogenetic* factors, although *psychoanalytic* theories, which assume the disorder is psychological rather than physiological, also suggest that bizarre behavior is a result of an underlying disease.

Sociologists who challenge the medical model generally conceptualize mental disorder in one of two ways. First, from the objectivist point of view, medical conceptions are of limited usefulness because they fail to consider norm-violations as a basis of deviant definitions. Subjectivists, on the other hand, strongly reject medical conceptions, contending that mental disorder is nothing more than a societal label. In the absence of a societal reaction, there is no mental disorder.

Considerable attention has been directed toward the *epidemiology* of mental disorder. These studies suggest that mental disorder is more prevalent among the lower class, the unmarried and divorced, and for more serious disorders, urban residents. There is, however, considerable debate concerning how these patterns should be interpreted. From a *social selection perspective,* these patterns emerge as a result of mental disorders. From a *social causation perspective,* these factors cause mental disorder. In general, social scientists adopt a social causation perspective and argue that stress and stressful life events exert pressure toward mental disorder, and social supports provide protection from mental disorder. Another line of social causation research has looked at mental disorder as learned behavior.

Those who contend that mental disorder is a societal reaction obviously have little interest in questions of *etiology.* Macro-subjectivist theories focus on the social construction of mental disorder. Interest group theorists trace the historical changes in definitions of bizarre behavior. According to interest group theory, the state, the churches, the medical community, and the social science community have all competed for the right to define and explain bizarre behavior. The currently accepted belief that bizarre behavior is a medical problem emerged not as a result of medical understandings of bizarre behavior, but emerged out of a more general optimism that medicine could cure all of society's ills.

Micro-subjectivist theories focus on the social process by which individual labelers define deviants (definitional theories), and the effects of these societal reactions on the behavior of individual "deviants" (labeling theories). Concerning variation in the application of deviant labels, the data would seem to suggest that social factors (e.g., race, class, and gender) do influence admission and discharge decisions. However, to suggest that social factors are the most significant determinants of who gets labeled is clearly overstating the case.

So too have labeling theorists overstated the idea that the stigma associated with being labeled "mentally disordered" is so severe that it leads to a self-fulfilling prophecy in which the deviant identity is adopted. Those who are labeled do have lower self-esteem, feel hopeless and demoralized, have less income, have higher rates of unemployment, and have few social supports. However, there is no evidence that these factors produce full-blown mental disorders.

Because the medical model assumes that bizarre behavior is caused by a mental or physical disease, blame and moral condemnation are removed from the person. From this perspective, the medical model provides a justification for bizarre and even criminal behavior. It also raises the question, "How do we punish someone whose criminal behavior is an outgrowth of a disease?"

Finally, in the treatment of mental disorder, concern over the rights of mental patients, evidence of the potentially damaging effects of institutionalization, and the increased effectiveness of drugs have led in recent years to a trend toward deinstitutionalization.

GLOSSARY

Biogenetic model   A subcategory of the medical model, which attributes mental disorders to "physiological, biochemical, or genetic causes and attempts to treat these abnormalities by way of medically grounded procedures. . ." (Cockerham, 1989:70).

Diagnostic and Statistical Model (DSM) A classification manual, first published in 1952, and due to be released in its fourth edition in 1994, which includes specific diagnostic criteria for mental and developmental disorders. It is the "bible" of the mental health profession.

Epidemiology The study of differing rates of diseases within and between various groups in a population.

Etiology The study of the causes, in this discussion, of deviant behavior.

Medical model At a definitional level, a model involving the belief that some behavior is healthy and some behavior is "unhealthy." Importantly, this abnormal behavior exists independent of cultural norms regarding the rightness or wrongness of the behavior. At a theoretical level, the medical model involves the belief that bizarre behavior is merely a visible symptom of an underlying disease.

Mental health profession Psychologists, psychiatrists, and other professionals who are in the business of defining and treating "unhealthy" behavior.

Neurosis Referring to a broad range disorders that do not entail a loss of contact with reality. Specific disorders include various anxiety disorders (e.g., specific phobias, obsessive-compulsive disorder, and posttraumatic stress disorder), somatoform disorders (symptoms of physical illness that have psychological causes), and sexual disorders (e.g., paraphilia and sexual dysfunctions).

Organic disorders Disorders, such as Down's syndrome and Alzheimer's disease, that result from specific organic and physical abnormalities.

Personality disorders A category used for a broad range of behavior, including anything from criminal activity and va-grancy (e.g., antisocial personality disorder), to exaggerated expressions of emotion (e.g., histrionic personality disorder).

Psychosis Referring to a serious and incapacitating set of disorders, including schizophrenia and various mood disorders (unipolar and bipolar depression).

Psychoanalytic model A subcategory of the medical model, which focuses on internal psychological factors that affect the mental health of the human being. Since the mind is disordered, the individual is unable to control his or her behavior.

Social causation perspective A perspective more consistent with a social scientific view of mental disorder, which suggests that there is something about sociocultural factors (e.g., social class and marital status) that *causes* mental disorders. In other words, it focuses on the environmental causes of mental disorders.

Social selection perspective A perspective more consistent with the medical model, which suggests that the status attainment of the individual is a *result* of his or her mental disorder.

SUGGESTED READINGS

Cockerham, William. *Sociology of Mental Disorder.* Englewood Cliffs, N.J.: Prentice-Hall, 1989. This book is a very complete summary of the sociological approach to mental disorder. Cockerham is balanced in his presentation, giving the medical model its due credit while at the same time reaffirming the need for a sociology of mental disorder.

Kirk, Stuart and Herb Kutchins. *The Selling of DSM: The Rhetoric of Science in Psychiatry.* New York: Aldine de Gruyter, 1992. This book examines the politics of the making and selling of the DSM-III. It poses a direct challenge to the claims of the American Psychiatric Association that the DSM-III represents a triumph of modern science.

Link, Bruce G., and Francis T. Cullen. "The Labeling Theory of Mental Disorder: A Review of Evidence." *Research in Community and Mental Health.* 6(1990):75–105. This article examines the current research on the labeling approach to mental disorder. Link and Cullen conclude that, while the extreme labeling approach cannot be empirically supported, specific aspects of the labeling approach remain informative.

Scheff, Thomas. *Being Mentally Ill: A Sociological Theory.* Chicago: Aldine, 1966. Despite its age, this book remains significant because it represents the beginning of a labeling approach to mental disorder.

REFERENCES

Akers, Ronald. *Deviant Behavior.* Belmont, Calif.: Wadsworth, 1985.

American Psychiatric Association *Diagnostic and Statistical Manual of Mental Disorders (DSM-I)* Washington, D.C.: APA, 1952.

———*(DSM-II)*, 1968

———*(DSM-III)*, 1980

———*(DSM-III-R)*, 1987

Bandura, Albert. *Principles of Behavioral Modification.* Holt, Rinehart and Winston: New York, 1969.

Barton, Russell. *Institutional Neurosis.* Bristol, U.K.: John Wright and Sons, 1959.

Bayer, R & R.L. Spitzer "Neurosis, Psychodynamics, and DSM-III: A History of the Controversy." *Archives of General Psychiatry,* 42(1985):187–195.

Becker, Howard. *Outsiders: Studies in the Sociology of Deviance.* New York: Free Press, 1963.

Brenner, Harvey M. *Mental Illness and the Economy.* Cambridge, Mass.: Harvard University Press, 1973.

Brown, George W., and J. L. T. Birley. "Crisis and Life Changes and the Onset of Schizophrenia." *Journal of Health and Social Behavior* 9(1968):203–214.

Brown, George W., and Tirril Harris. *Social Origins of Depression: A Study of Psychiatric Disorder in Women.* New York: Free Press, 1978.

Burgess, Robert L., and Ronald L. Akers. "A Differential Association-Reinforcement Theory of Criminal Behavior." *Social Problems* 14(1966):128–147.

Chambliss, William. "A Sociological Analysis of the Law of Vagrancy." *Social Problems* 12(1964):67–77.

Cockerham, William. *Sociology of Mental Disorder.* Englewood Cliffs, N.J.: Prentice-Hall, 1989.

Conrad, Peter, and Joseph W. Schneider. *Deviance and Medicalization.* St. Louis: Mosby, 1980.

Dohrenwend, Barbara S. "Life Events as Stressors: A Methodological Inquiry." *Journal of Health and Social Behavior* 14(1973):167–175.

Dohrenwend, Bruce P. "Sociocultural and Social-Psychological Factors in the Genesis of Mental Disorders." *Journal of Health and Social Behavior* 16 (December 1975):365–392.

Dohrenwend, Bruce P., and Barbara S. Dohrenwend. *Social Status and Psychological Disorder: A Causal Inquiry.* New York: Wiley, 1969.

———. "Social and Cultural Influences on Psychopathology." *Annual Review of Psychology.* 25(1974):417-452.

———. "Sex Differences and Psychiatric Disorder." *American Journal of Sociology* 81(1976):1447–1454.

Dohrenwend, Bruce P., Barbara. S. Dohrenwend, M. A. Gould, B. S. Link, R. Neuberger, and R. Wunsch-Hitzig. *Mental Illness in the United States: Epidemiological Estimates.* New York: Praeger, 1980.

Dunham, H. Warren. "Anomie and Mental Disorder." *Anomie and Deviant Behavior: A Discussion and Critique.* Ed. Marshall Clinard. Free Press: Toronto, 1964. 128–157.

Dunham, H. Warren, and S. K. Weinberg. *The Culture of the State Mental Hospital.* Detroit: Wayne State University Press, 1960.

Durkheim, Emile. 1951 *Suicide.* New York: Free Press.

Eaton, William W. *The Sociology of Mental Disorders.* New York: Praeger, 1986

Erikson, Kai R. *Wayward Puritans.* New York: Wiley, 1966.

Faris, Robert E. L., and Warren H. Dunham. *Mental Disorders in Urban Areas.* Chicago: University of Chicago Press, 1939.

Gallagher, Bernard J. *The Sociology of Mental Illness.* Englewood Cliffs, N.J.: Prentice-Hall, 1980.

Goffman, Erving. *Asylums.* Garden City, N.Y: Anchor Press, 1961.

Goldstein, Michael S. "The Sociology of Mental Illness." *Annual Review of Sociology* 5(1979): 381-409.

Gonsiorek, John. "The Empirical Basis of the Demise of the Illness Model of Homosexuality."*Homosexuality: Research Implications for Public Policy.* Eds. J. Gonsiorek and J. Weinrich. Beverly Hills: Sage, 1991, 115–136.

Gore, Susan. "The Effect of Social Support in Moderating the Health Consequences of Unemployment." *Journal of Health and Social Behavior* 19(1978):157—165.

Gorenstein, Ethan E. "Debating Mental Illness: Implications for Science, Medicine, and Social Policy." *American Psychologist* 39(1984):50-56.

Gove, Walter. "Societal Reaction as an Explanation of Mental Illness: an Evaluation." *American Sociological Review* 35:(1970)873-884.

———. "The Relationship Between Sex Roles, Marital Status and Mental Illness." *Social Forces* 51(1972):34–44.

———. "Labeling and Mental Illness: A Critique." *The Labeling of Deviance: Evaluating a Perspective.* Ed. Walter Gove. New York: Halsted Press, 1975. 35–81.

———. "Labeling Theory's Explanation of Mental Illness: An Update of Recent Evidence." *Deviant Behavior* 3(1982a):307-327.

———. "The Current Status of the Labeling Theory of Mental Illness." *Deviance and Mental Illness.* Walter Gove Ed. Beverly Hills, Calif.:Sage, 1982b. 273–300

Gove, Walter, and J. F. Tudor. "Adult Sex Roles and Mental Illness." *American Journal of Sociology* 78(1973):812–835.

Grusky, Oscar, and Melvin Pollner, eds. *The Sociology of Mental Illness: Basic Studies.* New York: Holt Rinehart and Winston, 1981.

Hirschi, Travis. *Causes of Delinquency.* Berkeley: University of California Press, 1969.

Hollingshead, August B., and Frederick Redlich. *Social Class and Mental Illness.* New York: Wiley, 1958.

Holmes, T. H., and R. H. Rahe. "The Social Read-justment Rating Scale." *Journal of Psychosomatic Research* 11(1967):213–225.

Isaac, Rael J., and Virginia Armat. *Madness in the Streets: How Psychiatry and the Law Abandoned the Mentally Ill.* New York: Free Press, 1990.

Kessler, Ronald C., and James A. McRae. "Trends in the Relationship Between Sex and Psychological Distress: 1957—1976." *American Sociological Review* 46(1981):443–452.

Kessler, Ronald C., Richard H. Price, and Cammile B. Wortman. "Social Factors in Psychopathology: Stress, Social Support, and Coping Processes." *Annual Review of Psychology* 36(1985):531-572.

Kirk, Stuart and Herb Kutchins *The Selling of DSM: The Rhetoric of Science in Psychiatry.* New York: Aldine de Gruyter, 1992.

Kitsuse, John "Societal Reaction to Deviant Behavior: Problems of Theory and Method." *Social Problems* 9 (1962):247–256

Kittrie, Nicholas N. *The Right to be Different.* Boston: The Johns Hopkins Press, 1971.

Krohn, Marvin D. and Ron Akers. "An Alternative View of the Labeling Versus Psychiatric Perspectives on Societal Reaction of Mental Illness." *Social Forces* 56(1977):341–361.

Lemert, Edwin M. *Human Deviance, Social Problems, and Social Control.* Englewood Cliffs, N.J.: Prentice-Hall, 1967.

———. "Paranoia and the Dynamics of Exclusion," *Sociometry* 25 (March, 1962):2–20

Lichtman, Richard. *The Production of Desire: The Integration of Psychoanalysis into Marxist Theory.* New York: Free Press, 1982.

Lin, Nan, Alfred Dean, and Walter Ensel. *Social Support, Life Events, and Depression.* Orlando, Florida: Academic Press, Inc, 1986.

Link, Bruce G. "Understanding Labeling Effects in the Area of Mental Disorders: an Assessment of the Effects of Expectations of Rejection." *American Sociological Review* 52 (1987):96–112.

Link, Bruce G., and Francis T. Cullen. "The Labeling Theory of Mental Disorder: A Review of Evidence." *Research in Community and Mental Health.* 6(1990):75–105.

Link, Bruce, Francis Cullen, Elmer Struening, Patrick Shrout, and Bruce Dohrenwend. "A Modified Labeling Theory Approach in the Area of Mental Disorders: An Empirical Assessment." *American Sociological Review* 54(1989): 400–423.

Loring, Marti, and Brian Powell. "Gender, Race, and DSM-III: A Study of the Objectivity of Psychiatric Behavior." *Journal of Health and Social Behavior* 29(1988):1–22.

Mechanic, David. *Mental Health and Social Policy.* Englewood Cliffs, N.J.: Prentice-Hall, 1969.

Merton, Robert. *Social Theory and Social Sturcture.* Revised and enlarged edition. New York: Free Press, 1957.

O'Brien, Darcy. *Two of a Kind: The Hillside Stranglers.* New York: New American Library, 1985.

Pasmanic, Benjamin, Dean Roberts, Paul Lemkau, and Dean Krueger. "A Survey of Mental Disease in an Urban Population: Prevalence by Race and Income." *Mental Health of the Poor.* Eds. Frank Riessman et al. 1964. 39–48

Rogler, Lloyd H., and August B. Hollingshead. *Trapped: Families and Schizophrenia.* New York: John Wiley, 1965.

Roman, P. M., and H. M. Trice eds. *Sociological Perspectives on Community Mental Health.* Philadelphia: F. A. Davis, 1974.

Rosecrance, John. "Compulsive Gambling and the Medicalization of Deviance." *Social Problems* 32(1985):275–284.

Rosenfield, Sarah. "Sex Roles and Societal Reactions to Mental Illness: The Labeling of 'Deviant' Deviance." *Journal of Health and Social Behavior* 23(1982):18–24.

———. "Race Differences in Involuntary Hospitalization: Psychiatric vs. Labeling Perspectives." *Journal of Health and Social Behavior* 25(1984):14–23.

Rosenhan, David L. "On Being Sane in Insane Places." *Science* 179(1973):250–258.

Scheff, Thomas. *Being Mentally Ill: A Sociological Theory.* Chicago: Aldine, 1966.

———. "The Labeling Theory of Mental Illness." *American Sociological Review* 39(1974):444–452.

———. "Reply to Chauncey and Gove." *American Sociological Review* 40(1975):252–257.

Scheper-Hughes, Nancy. *Saints, Scholars, and Schizophrenics: Mental Illness in Rural Ireland.* Berkeley: University of California Press, 1979.

Scull, Andrew T. "Madness and Segregative Control: The Rise of the Insane Asylum." in *Social Deviance,* Ronald A Farrell and Victoria L. Swigert (eds.) Belmont, California: Wadsworth, 1988:104–109.

Simon, Rita J., and J. Zusman. "The Effect of Contextual Factors on Psychiatrists' Perception of Illness: A Case Study." *Journal of Health and Social Behavior* 24(1983):186–198.

Spector, M. "Legitimizing homosexuality." *Society* 14(1977):52-56.

Stanton, A. A., and M. S. Schwartz. *The Mental Hospital.* New York: Basic Books, Inc, 1954.

Strole, Leo, T. Langner, S Michael, M. Opler, and T. Rennie. *Mental Health in the Metropolis: The Midtown Manhattan Study.* Eds. L. Strole and A. Fischer. rev. and enl. ed. L New York: Harper and Row, 1968.

Szasz, Thomas. *The Myth of Mental Illness.* New York: Hoeber-Harper, 1961.

———. *The Manufacture of Madness.* New York: Harper and Row, 1970.

Temerlin, M. "Suggestion Effects in Psychiatric Diagnosis." *Journal of Nervous and Mental Disease* 147(1968):349-353.

Thoits, Peggy, and Michael Hannan. "Income and Psychological Distress: The Impact of an Income-Maintenance Experiment." *Journal of Health and Social Behavior* 20(1979):120–138.

Turner, R. Jay, and John W. Gartrell. "Social Factors in Psychiatric Outcome: Toward the Resolution of Interpretive Controversies." *American Sociological Review* 43(1978):368–382.

Wheaton, Blair. "The Sociogenesis of Psychological Disorder: Reexamining the Causal Issues with Longitudinal Data." *American Sociological Review* 43(1978):338–403.

Weinstein, Raymond. "Labeling Theory and the Attitudes of Mental Patients: A Review." *Journal of Health and Social Behavior* 24(1983): 237–258.

Zola, Irving Kenneth. "Medicine as an Institution of Social Control." *Sociological Review.* 20(1972):487–504.

ENDNOTES

1. We are including in the medical camp psychiatrists, clinical psychologists, and other mental health professionals who are in the business of defining and treating "unhealthy" behavior.

2. Although increasingly psychoses like schizophrenia and mood disorders (unipolar and bipolar depression) are being linked to biological/physiological factors (Cockerham, 1989).

3. Merton (1957) *retreatists* are the individuals most likely to become alcoholics, drug addicts, and mentally disordered. According to Merton, retreatism results when individuals, in light of continued failure at achieving success, give up on their culturally defined goals of success.

Chapter 7

Suicide

"DR. DEATH"

In June 1990, Janet Adkins, a 54-year-old grandmother with Alzheimer's disease, ended her life by lethal injection from Dr. Jack Kevorkian's suicide machine. Alzheimer's is a progressive and, at present, incurable disease. As reported in *Newsweek* (1990:46–49), Janet was vital in mind and body at the time of her death. She had tried experimental medical treatment; she consulted with her minister; she participated in family counseling; and she had grieved with her husband and sons before she chose her time, place, and method of death. Janet Adkins and her husband flew 2,000 miles to consult with Dr. Kevorkian about his suicide machine. They agreed that she would be the first to die by his invention. All that was left was for Janet to decide when to die.

During the week prior to her death, Janet had beaten her adult grandson at tennis. At week's end, she had a romantic weekend with her husband. On the following Monday, in Dr. Kevorkian's Volkswagen van, Dr. Kevorkian inserted a needle into Janet's arm and began a saline solution. It was Janet who pushed the button that first released a sedative, and then the lethal potassium chloride (*Newsweek*, 1990:46).

In June 1990, Dr. Kevorkian was charged with the murder of Janet Adkins. In October of that year, his case came to trial. The judge ruled that Janet's death was suicide, not murder (Caplan, 1991:19). Furthermore, there was no law in Michigan against assisting in a suicide. Therefore, there was no legal basis for the prosecution of Dr. Kevorkian. Freed of legal wrongdoing, Dr. Kevorkian was free to use his suicide device again. Not, however, in Oakland County, Michigan, where a restraining order prohibiting its use was issued (Caplan, 1991:19).

On October 23, 1991, two more women died by Dr. Kevorkian's killing machine. On February 5, 1992, Dr. Kevorkian was once again charged with murder (*Weekly World News Digest*, 1992:133). And, once again the charge was dismissed. Since then, Dr. Kevorkian has assisted in twelve more suicides. On February 25, 1993, the Michigan legislature banned assisted suicides statewide effective immediately.

Should patients have the right to die? If so, what kinds of patients—only the elderly, only those who are terminally ill, or all who suffer from progressive and incurable diseases? Should doctors help their patients die? Dr. Jack Kevorkian argues that he invented his three-part suicide machine to "benefit humanity" (*U.S. News and World Report*, 1990:27).

The questions above are a few among many complex medical, legal, and moral right-to-die questions. However, 66 percent of Americans surveyed by Gallup believe that a person with "no hope of improvement" has the moral right to die, and 64 percent of Americans surveyed by Roper favor medically assisted suicide for the terminally ill (*Newsweek*, 1991:41; *U.S. News and World Report*, 1990:27).

Are death counseling and obituary medical specialties in our immediate future? Is Dr. Kevorkian's vision of suicide clinics a part of a "Brave New World" for the 1990s. In December 1990, the Patient Self-Determination Act went into effect. It requires hospitals participating in Medicaid or Medicare to ask patients if they have "advance directives," for example, a living will, health-care proxy, or durable power of attorney for health care. In November 1991, Washington State residents voted against an assisted-suicide law. In November 1992, California residents voted by a narrow margin against doctor-assisted suicide. These laws would have permitted doctors to help the terminally ill die.

Similar legislative reforms are certain to follow. These legislative efforts reflect changing reactions to suicide by law makers, medical practitioners, and the public. Reactions to suicide and the nature and extent of suicide within and across societies are central to the sociological study of suicide. In this chapter, we will examine competing definitions of suicide, the extent and patterns of suicide, the social characteristics of those who commit suicide, the causes of suicide, and policies designed to prevent suicide.

WHAT IS SUICIDE?

The Objectivist Conception

According to the objectivist conception of deviance, deviant behavior is behavior that violates social norms. Suicide, the intentional taking of one's own life, is an act that violates a fundamental, widely shared belief that life is sacred and should be preserved. As straightforward as this definition appears, determining what behaviors constitute suicide is problematic. For example, is chronic alcohol or drug use, heaving smoking, or highly risky behavior suicidal behavior? Are these behaviors distinct from a more immediate self-inflicted wound, ingestion or inhalation; or are they long-term methods of self-destruction? To answer this question correctly one must know what an actor intended by his or her behavior.

Attempted suicides are also problematic for an objectivist definition of suicide. Are attemptred suicides simply failed efforts at self-destruction? Is luck or from the victim's point of view, bad luck the only factor that separates suicide from attempted suicide? Certainly, some genuine attempts at self-destruction fail. And, some of those who only intended a suicide attempt, but did not want to die, may have died.

For the objectivist, suicide requires an appropriate interface between the actual intent of one's behavior and the outcome (death) of one's behavior. The interface between intention and outcome is depicted in Figure 7–1.

In cell I, the person intends to take his or her life and is successful. This is a "true" suicide. In cell II, the person makes a genuine attempt to commit suicide, but for some unforeseen reason is unsuccessful. The behaviors included in cells I and II are "suicidal behaviors." At a conceptual level, objectivists are able to distinguish these "suicidal behaviors" from the "suicidal gestures" that make up cells III and IV. In cell III, a person intends a suicidal gesture, but not to kill himself or herself; contrary to intent, he or she dies. For example, a person may have carefully planned and rehearsed a suicide gesture to be coupled with rescue, but for one reason or another the rescue did not occur. That is to say, the attempt at a true attempted suicide failed. For objectivists, cell IV describes the "true" attempted suicide. Here, a person does not intend to die and survives the suicide gesture (Stephenson, 1985:240–241).

The objectivist conception of suicidal behaviors and suicidal gestures is logical, but not plausible. The outcome, death or survival, may mask the actor's intended behavior. If one is dead, how does another know for certain the deceased's intent? If one survives, how does another know beyond the survivor's own account what his or her intention was? For example, a person may portray an accident or foolish act as an attempted suicide in order to gain attention or to place guilt on another. Or a survivor of a genuine attempt at suicide might wish to cover up his or her intention in order to avoid detection or to protect another. In some states, attempting suicide is an unlawful offense, and in about

---

FIGURE 7.1   Suicide: Interface between Actual Intent and Behavior

	Dies	Lives
To Die	I	II
INTENTION		
To Live	III	IV

Adapted from Maurice Faber, Theory of Suicide, 1968:7 (In *Death, Grief & Mourning,* John S. Stephenson, Glencoe, Ill.: The Free Press, 1985:241).

half of the states, aiding or assisting another to commit suicide is a crime (Gardner, 1985:278). In real-life situations, suicidal behavior and suicidal gestures are difficult to distinguish accurately. Confusion, ambiguity, and inconsistency characterize both official and unofficial definitions of suicide.

How, then, do objectivists define suicide for the purposes of research? Most often, they accept as suicide only those deaths that have been officially designated as suicide by appropriate authorities—coroners or medical examiners. This operational definition of suicide has a constant error factor that is acknowledged by social scientists and medical examiners alike. Research demonstrates that coroners vary considerably in their background, training, available resources, and investigatory and classification procedures (Nelson, Farberow, and MacKinnon, 1978). In addition, medical examiners admit to a significant undercounting of actual suicides (Jobes, Berman, and Josselsen, 1986). So, objectivists are cautious in their generalizations about suicide, but they prefer the standardization of an official definition to the ambiguity resulting from their own competing definitions and classifications of suicide.

The Subjectivist Conception

For the subjectivist, suicide is not a behavior; it is how a death is defined by audiences including the victim, intimates of the victim, officials, and the public. This means that suicide is a judgment and, therefore, subjective. According to subjectivists, the confusion and ambiguity that objectivists encounter in attempting to define suicidal behavior is evidence that suicide is, in reality, a matter of judgment. Furthermore, the official designation of suicide by a coroner or medical examiner is an evaluation of death, not the recognition of an objective cause of death.

Suicide is defined by subjectivists as a label that is applied to one's death by social audiences. The central research question for subjectivists is, "How do various social audiences come to define a given instance of death as suicide?" In the case of Dr. Jack Kevorkian, one important audience, the Michigan legislature, has now defined Kevorkian's behavior of assisting suicide as an act of criminal homicide.

THE PREVALENCE OF SUICIDE

The actual number of people who commit suicide each year is unknown. Most often, then, we rely on official estimates of suicide in examining its prevalence. As previously mentioned, the coroner or medical examiner is responsible for the official designation of suicide. These suicidal deaths are then reported to the National Center for Health Statistics. Information about these suicides such as time, location, method of death, and characteristics of suicide victims (e.g., age, sex, race, and marital status) are published annually in the *Vital Statistics of the United States* (Seiden, 1983). Researchers using these data accept that there is a constant error of undercounting in official suicide statistics. Seiden (1983), for example, estimates this error to range somewhere between 25 and 50 percent. Many medical examiners, too, believe that official suicide statistics significantly underestimate the actual number of suicides. In a study of 200 medical examiners, more than half believed that the actual number of suicides each year is more than twice the official number (Jobes, Berman, and Josselsen, 1986).

The Extent of Official Suicide

The suicide rate in the United States has remained about the same for more than two decades, ranging from a low of 11.6 per 100,000 in 1970 to a high of 12.4 per 100,000 in 1988. In the United States, the rate of suicide is higher than the rate of homicide. For this same period, homicide rates ranged from a low of 8.3 per 100,000 in 1970 to a high of 9.0 per 100,000 in 1988 (U.S. National Center for Health Statistics, 1991:81).

Suicide rates vary considerably from country to country. How does the U.S. rate of suicide compare to that of other nations? Table 7–1 presents suicide rates from a sampling of countries in North America, South America, Asia, and Europe.

Table 7–1 shows that, for the most part, industrialized nations have higher rates of suicide than nonindustrialized nations. For example, in North America, suicide rates are highest in Canada and the United States and lowest in the relatively nonindustrial countries of Latin America. Also, suicide rates are highest in Europe, which was industrial long before North America. However, Asian countries have relatively high rates of suicide whether they are heavily industrialized, as in Japan, or not, as in China. This suggests that cultural factors may influence suicide as well as economic factors. Cultural, economic, and other factors also contribute to significant differences in suicide rates for regions and

groups within a society. Let us review the rate of suicide for various socio-demographic groups in the United States.

Regional Variations in U.S. Suicide Rates

Few countries have such a large proportion of their population living in urban places as in the United States. Beginning as a nation of farmers, we have become a nation of industrial and commercial workers who live in urban places. Throughout the nineteenth century and well into the twentieth century, the United States rapidly urbanized. Sociologists have long attributed increases in many social ills such as crime, mental illness, and suicide to urbanization. However, contemporary studies do not consistently report a positive association between urbanization and suicide (Stack, 1982; Lester and Frank, 1990). Perhaps, we are more accustomed to urban life, therefore, this familiarity lowers the disruption of life in a new environment; or, perhaps, important changes have occurred in rural life. For example, the spread of urban culture

---

TABLE 7.1   Suicide Rates per 100,000 for Select Countries from Four Continents

NORTH AMERICA		SOUTH AMERICA		ASIA		EUROPE	
1989 Canada	13.3	1986 Brazil	3.1	1987 China	17.6	1989 Austria	24.9
1988 Costa Rica	5.0	1987 Chile	5.5	1987 Hong Kong	11.0	1986 Belgium	22.3
1986 Mexico	2.2	1988 Ecuador	4.6	1989 Japan	17.2	1989 Bulgaria	16.2
1987 Panama	3.8	1986 Paraguay	1.5	1989 Korea	7.1	1989 Czechoslovakia	17.7
1989 Puerto Rico	9.2	1987 Uruguay	8.5	1987 Singapore	11.6	1988 Finland	28.3
1988 United States	12.4	1988 Bahrian	3.0			1989 France	20.9
						1989 Hungary	41.6
						1988 Italy	7.6
						1989 Netherlands	10.2
						1988 Norway	16.8
						1989 Poland	11.4
						1988 Sweden	18.8
						1989 United Kingdom	7.4
						1989 Yugoslavia	16.5
						1988 USSR	19.5

Source: 1990 Demographic Yearbook, United Nations, New York, 1992: 454–473.

through mass media, closer proximity to urban places, and centralized school districts may lead to higher suicide rates in rural areas. Another explanation for the decline in urban and rural differences in suicide rates may be the changing community migration patterns. Stack (1982) has suggested that increased community migration is related to an increased rate of suicide. The 1970 U.S. Census showed the first increase in the rural population as a proportion of the total population in this century. In part, this increase reflects a movement by some urban people to rural locations. Therefore, migration from rural to urban places has slowed, while migration from urban to rural places has increased. During this process, rural areas may have become more disintegrated. Many of these new rural residents are urbanites who work and shop in urban areas, and who enjoy the cultural activities and entertainment of urban places. Their rural homes are largely domiciles. These changing migration patterns may affect the degree of community integration in both urban and rural places, resulting in a decrease in urban and rural suicide rate differences. The relationship between social integration and suicide is central to some established sociological theories of suicide. For now, however, the suggested relationship between community migration, integration, and urban-rural suicide rates is an empirical question that awaits more thorough and systematic study.

Suicide rates also vary between geographic regions in the United States. The highest suicide rate, 15.8 per 100,000 population, is in the Western region. The suicide rate is second highest in the South, 13.6; followed by the Midwest, 12.2; and lowest in the Northeast, 9.3. In the West, the Mountain states (Montana, Idaho, Wyoming, Colorado, New Mexico, Arizona, Utah, and Nevada) have the highest suicide rate, 19.0. Nevada, 26.0, and New Mexico, 22.8, have the highest suicide rates in the nation. The other sections of the western region also have relatively high suicide rates: 13.9, in the Pacific states and, 13.2, in the southwestern states (U.S. National Center for Health Statistics, 1991:87–88).

Why does the western region have the highest rate of suicide, and why do the Mountain states, Nevada and Montana in particular, have such high rates of suicide? Is it the socio-demographic composition of their population? Or, could it be something about life in the West? To date, researchers have been unable to provide satisfactory answers to these questions.

Temporal Patterns

Over the years, numerous studies have found suicide rates to be affected by temporal variables such as the season of the year, holidays, the month, day of the month, and day of the week. Howard Gabennesch reviewed this extensive body of research and presents six established temporal patterns of suicide.

1. Suicide is most frequent in the spring months and least frequent during the winter.
2. A secondary peak occurs in the fall, but primarily among women.
3. Suicide peaks on Monday, then declines to a trough on the weekend.
4. The suicide rate is typically lower than normal on major holidays, but it tends to be higher than normal on New Year's Day.
5. Suicide is most common near the beginning of the month and least common near the end of the month.
6. It is not unusual for a despondent individual to commit suicide just when he or she had recently seemed to display noticeable improvement in mood (Gabennesch, 1988:129).

Despite the frequency with which these findings have been reported by a variety of researchers, there is, to date, no theory that connects these temporal patterns. Gabennesch (1988), however, suggests a precipitating factor that connects these temporal correlates of suicide: "the broken-promise effect." The broken-promise effect is the discrepancy between how one feels relative to how one expects to feel. Spring, weekends, and holidays heighten one's expectations for feeling better because they imply new beginnings. If and when the heightened expectation of a new beginning is not realized, the individual is left feeling even worse than before. The discrepancy between expected feelings and actual feelings is widened. Therefore, times associated with anticipations of improvement produce a suicide trough before they arrive and a suicide peak after they occur. For example, the hope of spring produces a winter trough, whereas failed hope in spring produces a peak. Similarly, the hope of a weekend produces a mid- to late-weekday trough, and the failed weekend produces an increase in suicide by Sunday and a peak on Monday. In the case of holidays, the peak that would be predicted to follow Thanksgiving and Christmas is delayed by New Year's promise of a new beginning, and it is on New Year's Day, then, that suicide is higher than normal.

The broken-promise effect is interesting and plausible. However, as Gabennesch (1988) himself recognizes, it is only one among other precipitators of suicide, and it most likely varies across demographic groups such as age, gender, race, and ethnicity. The usefulness of the broken-promise effect awaits a broader sociological theory that incorporates suicide precipitators and connects the broken promises of temporal events with the cultural norms, social attachments, and group memberships that shape human life and death.

Socio-Demographic Variations in Suicide

Age. Table 7–2 presents suicide rates for the various age groups ranging from 10 to 65 years of age and older for the years 1970, 1980, and 1988.

In the United States, suicide rates generally increase as age increases. A few exceptions to this pattern can be noted for various time periods. For example, in 1970 suicide rates increased steadily among 55 to 64 year olds, then declined slightly for those 65 years and older. In 1980, the four age categories that ranged from 25 to 64 had slightly lower rates of suicide than those 20 to 24, then increased to the highest rate for those 65 years and older. Similarly, in 1988 the two age categories for those 35 to 54 had slightly lower suicide rates than 25 to 34 years olds, then increased steadily to the highest rate for those 65 years and over.

During the past decade three age related patterns are discernible. First, the suicide rate for teenagers is increasing. Second, suicide rates for young adults and people in early middle age, 20 to 44, have declined slightly. Third, the rate of suicide for those 65 years and older remains the highest, and is increasing the most.

What do these age-related patterns for suicide rates mean? Any interpretation made on the basis of data for a short duration of time, such as the temporal variation in Table 7–2, must be made with extreme caution. A very different picture could emerge if data for a longer period of time were available. And, a very different picture of teenage suicide does, in fact, emerge when temporal variation is increased. The major increase in teenage suicide occurred between 1954 and 1977—a rise of 240 percent compared with a 32 percent increase for non-teenagers. During the 1980s, teenage suicide rates actually leveled off (Stack, 1986). Stack attributes the pre1980 increase to increases in divorce of teenagers' parents, higher teenage unemployment, and decreases in church attendance. During the 1980s, divorce rates stabilized, teenage unemployment decreased, and church attendance increased. Other factors attributed to the pre1980 surge in teen suicide are increased

TABLE 7.2   Suicide Rates by Age Group: Per 100,000 1970–1988

	1970	1980	1988
Ages	11.6	11.9	12.8
10–14 years old	.6	.8	1.4
15–19 years old	5.9	8.5	11.3
20–24 years old	12.2	16.1	15.0
25–34 years old	14.1	16.0	15.4
35–44 years old	16.9	15.4	14.8
45–54 years old	20.0	15.9	14.6
55–64 years old	21.4	15.9	15.6
65 years and over	20.8	17.8	21.6

Source: U. S. National Center for Health Statistics, Vital Statistics of the United States, Annual. Washington, D.C., U.S. Government Printing Office, 1991:36, 37, 50, 51.

drug use and the increased use of combinations of drugs (Downey, 1990–91). Surveys by the National Institute on Drug Abuse show real declines in drug use among teenagers during the 1980s.

Rather than speculate here on the age-related patterns from Table 7–2, suffice it to say that, presently, there are no firm explanations for these patterns. And, eventual explanations demand longitudinal research on suicide rates. Let us conclude our discussion of age and suicide with a review of research on suicide among the young adults, middle-aged adults, and the elderly.

Youth suicide, 15–24, more than doubled from 1960 to 1980 (Maris, 1985). The increase was greater for males, although female suicides have also increased (Kastenbaum, 1986). Suicide by a firearm is more frequent for young adult males, but firearms have become the most common method of suicide for both sexes (Kastenbaum, 1986). Suicide rates are higher for college students than their noncollege peers (Kastenbaum, 1986). Some researchers have attributed this finding to stress. Seiden (1969, in Kastenbaum, 1986:194), for example, found that college suicide victims had higher grade point averages than other undergraduates, but they were not meeting their own expectations. Also, college students who attend more prestigious universities are more likely to commit suicide

(Peck and Schrut, 1971). Once again, however, we must be cautious in relating suicide to stress. Keep in mind, college students are older than the average young adult population between 15 and 24. Suicide rates are higher in the general population among 20 to 24 year olds than in the teenage years (see Table 7–2). Also, college students are less likely to be living near or among their immediate family, less likely to be employed, married, or with children than noncollege 20 to 24 years olds. That is to say, they lack many of the social ties of their noncollege peers.

Middle-aged adults, ages 40 through 59, are in a life stage that has been described as a time of crisis (mid-life crisis) or a time of transition. That is, mid-life is either stressful or a time of opportunity and well-being. Humphrey and Palmer (1990–91) examine these competing models of mid-life in relation to suicide victimization. Their findings do not clearly support either model. However, they do find that mid-life may trigger suicide in low-risk groups, women, and married persons.

The elderly are more likely to commit suicide than any other age group, and their rate of suicide is increasing. The vast majority of elderly persons do not contemplate suicide. However, the ratio of suicide attempts to completed suicides is smaller for the elderly than it is for other age groups. The elderly who do commit suicide are less integrated than the elderly who do not. That is, those among the elderly who are not married and who do not remain close to their children or relatives are more likely to commit suicide (Kastenbaum, 1986).

Ethnicity and Race. In the United States, Native Americans have the highest rate of suicide. Asian Americans have higher rates of suicide than whites, and suicide rates are lowest for African Americans.

The rate of suicide among Native Americans is genuinely higher than it is for other racial groups; however, researchers argue that this may be a result of overreporting of suicides among Native Americans (McIntosh, 1983–84). Overreporting of Native-American suicides is likely because much suicide research is designed to document the need for suicide prevention programs or to evaluate existing programs (Backer, Hannon, and Russell, 1982:207). Therefore, generalizations about the character and circumstances of Native-American suicides are difficult. However, a review of the literature suggests the following facts about Native-American suicides:

1. The rate of suicide for Native Americans varies tremendously between tribes and reservations (Kastenbaum, 1986:196). Some tribes have rates similar to the general population, whereas other tribes have rates 5 to 10 times higher (Backer, Hannon, and Russell, 1982:206).
2. Suicide rates are highest for young Native Americans and lowest among the elderly. This is the opposite of the trend among the general population (Kastenbaum, 1986:197).
3. Although alcohol and alcoholism are associated with suicide in the general population, this is more often the case for Native Americans (Kastenbaum, 1986:196).

Asian Americans have higher rates of suicide than white or African Americans. In part, their higher rate of suicide has been attributed to a traditional acceptance of suicide in their country of origin. As we have seen, Table 7–1, the Asian countries of Japan and China have higher rates of suicide than the United States. However, in many ways Asian-American suicides are actually parallel, to the suicide patterns and trends of white Americans. Kastenbaum and Aisenberg (1972) attribute this finding to the relative ease with which Asian Americans assimilate into U.S. society and to their intact families and class position.

White and African Americans are the two racial groups most frequently compared, and for which data are more easily obtained. Table 7–3 presents U.S. suicide rates among whites and African Americans for select years from 1970 to 1988.

Table 7–3 shows that suicide rates for both whites and African Americans have remained relatively stable over time. Also, the suicide rate for whites is almost twice as high as it is for African Americans. However, a significant increase in suicide among young African Americans has been reported. According to Stack (1986), young African Americans are as likely to commit suicide as young whites. Suicide rates for African Americans above age 40 remain much lower than the suicide rates for whites at a similar age. Stack (1986) attributes the increased suicide rates for young African Americans to their political and economic progress, which has made them more likely to blame themselves rather than others for their failures.

African-American suicide rates also vary according to the proportion of African Americans in a state's population. In states where the proportion is low, their suicide rate is higher than it is in states with large African American populations. Lester (1990) attributes this finding to the fact that, where African Americans are few, they more resemble whites in terms of education, income, and

TABLE 7.3   Suicide Rates for White's and African Americans: per 100,000 1970 to 1988

	White	*African American*
1970	12.4	6.1
1980	12.1	6.4
1985	12.3	6.4
1988	13.4	6.7

Source: U.S. National Center for Health Statistics, Vital Statistics of the United States, 1991:81.

intact families than they do in states with large African-American populations.

Gender. Men commit suicide more often than women. This is true across cultures, through time, and among demographic and social groups—age, race, social class, and marital status. In the United States, men are about three times more likely to kill themselves than women are. This is the case in all age groups and for both whites and African Americans (U.S. National Center for Health Statistics, 1991:81). These differences are commonly associated with traditional sex-role expectations. Males are less regulated by family than women, and their successes and failures are more clearly defined by their job roles. This leads some researchers to predict an increase in female suicide as women's participation in the labor force increases (Davis, 1981). However, Stack (1985) reports that increased female participation in the labor force has a greater impact on male suicide than female suicide. Does increased female participation in the labor force increase married men's sense of failure because they are no longer the sole "breadwinners"? According to Stafford and Weisheit (1988), this is not likely because suicide rates for young white males show similar increases for all marital groups—single, married, and widowed.

Changing age patterns for male and female suicide rates in the United States have been noted. Stafford and Weisheit (1988) found that prior to 1970 suicide rates increased with age for both white males and white females. By 1980, however, suicide rates for white females increased with age, peaking at ages 50 to 54, then decreased with advancing age. For white males, suicide rates increased until age 29, decreased between 30 and 49, and then increased with advancing age. The age patterns for white males and females have become less concordant. Contrary to the age pattern for whites, nonwhite male and female suicide rates have become more concordant. Prior to 1960, nonwhite male and female suicide rates peaked at quite different ages; but by 1960, nonwhite male and female suicide rates peaked at age 64. By 1970, non-white male and female suicide rates peaked between ages 25 and 29 and then declined. This pattern has held from 1970 to 1983. Stafford and Weisheit (1988) found all existing sociological theories of suicide inadequate for explaining these changing age patterns in male and female suicide rates. They argue that existing theories only relate two or more factors, such as age and suicide, at one point in time, rather than, for example, age differences in suicide rates by gender, race, marital status over time. In the future, sociological theories must attempt to explain changes in the relation between variables over time (Stafford and Weisheit, 1988).

Social Status. In this section, we will review the literature on the relation between social class and suicide; marital status and suicide; and religious affiliation and suicide.

In his classic study of suicide, Emile Durkheim (1896) found higher rates of suicide for persons in higher occupational status positions; unmarried persons; and for Protestants, followed by Catholics and Jews.

Since Durkheim, research on social class and suicide has been contradictory. Some researchers duplicate Durkheim's finding (Lester, 1983). Other researchers find higher suicide rates in the lower class (Stack, 1982). Still other researchers find no relation between class and suicide rates (Marks, 1980). To some extend, these contradictory findings can be attributed to the different ways that researchers use to measure class; for example, some use income, while others use occupational status.

On the other hand, research on the relation between marital status and suicide has consistently reported a lower suicide rate for married persons, especially those with children (Stack, 1982). This is true regardless of age, race, or gender. However, the relation between suicide and marital status is stronger for whites than African Americans (Davis, 1979).

Research findings on religious affiliation and suicide rates have also been consistent, and they support Durkheim's original findings. Suicide rates are highest among Protestant groups, lower for Catholics, and lowest for Jews (Stack, 1982). However, Jacobs (1967) analysis of suicide notes found that strong religious beliefs are often used by suicide victims to justify their behavior.

EXPLANATIONS OF SUICIDE

Class, marital status, and religious affiliation are commonly used by researchers as measures of concepts central to established sociological theories of suicide; as are age, race, and gender. Therefore, let us now turn to objective and subjective theories of suicide.

Macro-Objectivist Theories

Suicide varies from one society to another, and between groups within a society. Macro-objectivist theories attempt to explain these variations in suicide by examining the impact of societal arrangements (i.e. economy, family, religion, and education) and the social positions of groups (i.e. occupations, marital status, age, gender, and race) on rates of suicide.

Durkheim's Classic Theory of Suicide. Durkheim's (1963) monumental study of suicide remains the most influential theory of suicide. Although complex and rich in detail, Durkheim's theory of suicide can be narrowed down to two major causes of suicide, and a four-type classification of suicide.

Why do people commit suicide? According to Durkheim, the probability of suicide depends on the degree to which an individual is integrated into the broader society and the degree of regulation a society has on its individual members. Society's force is that of a double-edged sword. On the one side, society attracts the "sentiments and activities of individuals," on the other side, it is "a power controlling them" (Durkheim, 1963:241). The two causes of suicide, then are social integration and social regulation.

Social integration refers to the attachment of the individual to his or her culture. All individuals are socialized to the norms of their culture, but they may be weakly or strongly integrated into a culture. Their degree of integration depends on their position relative to others in the broader society. For example, married persons, especially those with children, are more strongly integrated into the broader society than single persons because of their position in one of society's core social institutions—the family. *Social regulation* refers to the degree of social solidarity of society as a whole. Society's regulation of an individual's social life depends on the cohesiveness of society: stable and regulated or unstable and disrupted. For example, when society is disrupted by crises, such as economic depression or prosperity, the collective order of society is disturbed and, hence, incapable of regulating the "insatiable desires" of individuals (Durkheim, 1963:247).

In total, the risk of suicide depends on the relation between the individual and society: Individuals are more or less integrated into a society that has more or less solidarity. The complex relation between the individual and society relative to suicidal behavior is best illustrated by Durkheim's four types of suicide: egoistic, altruistic, anomic, and fatalistic.

Egoistic and altruistic suicides are opposites that result from the same cause—social integration. *Egoistic* suicide is committed by persons who are less integrated into society. Individuals who are in positions relatively removed from society's constraints on social life and participation are less integrated and more likely to commit suicide. That is to say, people who are in positions to go their own way, for example recluses or people who live or work in isolation, are less integrated and, thereby, freer to commit suicide. Durkheim related marital status and religious affiliation to egoistic suicide. Single people are freer to go their own way than married people. Single people are less constrained by the social obligations and reciprocity of marital and family relations. Similarly, Protestants have a higher degree of religious individualism than Catholics and Jews. The higher the religious individualism the lower the integration into the church and the lesser the constraints of church. *Altruistic* suicide, on the other hand, is committed by persons who are extremely integrated into their culture or group. Such extreme integration may result in a person taking his or her own life for the benefit of others. Soldiers who kill themselves for the

ultimate victory, individuals who kill themselves because they have brought shame or dishonor to their people or ruler, and persons who commit suicide because they have violated cultural taboos are examples of altruistic suicide. Durkheim (1963) noted a type of altruistic suicide resulting from military spirit. He found suicide to increase with time in the service; there were higher suicide rates for volunteers and reenlistments and higher suicide rates for officers and noncommissioned officers than for privates.

Anomic and fatalistic suicides are also opposites that result from a single cause—social regulation. *Anomic* suicide occurs when an individual feels no longer regulated by society's norms because a crisis has disrupted the normative constraints of the society, community, or group. Disruption sets the individual adrift, so to speak. Durkheim (1963) found that suicide rates increase with the economic crises of depression and prosperity. In addition to economic anomie, Durkheim (1963:259) noted "domestic anomie" which follows the death of a spouse, divorce, and separation. *Fatalistic* suicide results from excessive regulation. This occurs among "persons with futures pitilessly blocked and passions violently choked by oppressive discipline" (Durkheim, 1963:276). For Durkheim, the suicides among slaves are of the fatalistic type. To live by inflexible rules aggravates fatalistic suicides, whereas the breakdown of rules aggravates anomic suicides.

For the most part, Durkheim's classic theory of suicide has withstood the test of time. There are many separate and partial tests that support most but not all of Durkheim's generalizations and original findings. For example, Lester's (1990–91) regional analysis of suicide rates shows that much suicide in the United States is egoistic in nature. However, social disintegration variables were strongly related to suicides among whites, but not suicides among African Americans. There are also two important modifications of Durkheim's theory of suicide. These are in basic agreement with Durkheim, but they replace social integration with related concepts such as external restraint (Henry and Short, 1954) and status integration (Gibbs and Martin, 1964). Henry and Short attempt to link homicide and suicide in a more general theory of violence. Gibbs and Martin reformulate Durkheim's egoistic suicide in what they believe to be a more measurable format. Let us now review these two post-Durkheimian theories of suicide.

External Restraint Theory. According to Henry and Short (1954), frustrated persons are prone to violent aggression. The direction of violent aggression, outward (homicide) or inward (suicide), is explained by one's degree of external restraint. *External restraint* refers to the degree to which one needs to conform to the expectations and demands of others. Where the need to conform is high, external restraint is strong. Where external restraint is strong, an individual attributes frustration to external sources and violent aggression is expressed outward (homicide). On the other hand, where external restraint is weak, individual frustration is attributed to personal inadequacy. Here, then, one's aggression is directed inward (suicide). According to Henry and Short (1954), aggression is structured by one's social status. High-status persons, such as males, whites, and those with high incomes, are less influenced by the demands and expectations of others. Therefore, frustrations for high-status individuals lead to feelings of personal failure and aggression is directed inward. As previously noted, suicide rates are higher for males and whites. However, research findings on social class and suicide are mixed. Some find higher rates of suicide within the upper classes. Some find suicide rates higher in lower class, while others find no relation between suicide and social class.

Henry and Short elaborate on the relationship between personal frustration and social status by examining the relationship between societal economic trends and suicide rates. They show that suicide rates increase in times of economic depression and decrease in times of prosperity. Henry and Short acknowledge that the frustration induced by economic hard times increases suicides for all social classes, but more so in the higher classes. Simply put, higher-class individuals experience greater frustration because their losses are greater.

In support of external restraint theory, suicide rates are higher for males and whites. However, we discussed earlier in this chapter, research findings on the relationship between social class and suicide are mixed. Furthermore, external restraint theory predicts that females, who are more regulated by the demands and expectations of others than males, will have higher rates of homicide. Clearly, that is not the case.

According to Henry and Short, suicide and homicide are both results of external restraints and will demonstrate opposite relationships on a variety of social variables. Lester (1990–91) did not find the opposite associations with social variables and homicide and suicide rates as predicted by external restraint theory. In sum, support for Henry and Short's external restraint theory as applied to suicide rates is limited to the social variables of gender and race. The relationship between gender and race and suicide, however, can be accounted for by alternative explanations, for example, social integration.

Status Integration Theory. Gibbs and Martin's (1964) theory of status integration was inspired by Durkheim's sociological theory of suicide. These researchers, however, conclude that, in its present form, Durkheim's theory is untestable because key concepts, such as social integration, are difficult to measure; thus, they are not amenable to empirical verification. Status integration theory is a testable reformulation of Durkheim's more general theory of suicide.

Through a series of five postulates, Gibbs and Martin deduce: "The suicide rate of a population varies inversely with the degree of status integration in the population" (1964:27). Status integration is measured as one's pattern of status occupancy. Persons who occupy conflicting statuses have low status integration and higher rates of suicide. Persons who occupy concordant statuses have higher status integration and lower rates of suicide. For example, a 22-year-old senior executive occupies conflicting statuses—young age and high occupational position. This status inconsistency makes it difficult to establish and maintain social relationships. This young person, then, will experience low status integration and be more prone to suicide. High status integration exists when knowledge of one's status leads to an accurate prediction of other occupied statuses. For example, young age, and the occupational status of junior executive. Other examples of maximum status integration might include middle-aged and married; college-educated and white-collar occupation; or male and auto mechanic. These are relatively common (predictable) combinations of statuses. They are, then, more conducive to durable social relationships, and suicide rates will be low.

Gibbs and Martin's (1981) tests of status integration theory yielded strong empirical support. However, Gibbs (1982) found limited empirical support of status integration and suicide among white females. Stafford and Gibbs (1985) provided the most extensive test of status integration theory, and they found little support. Stafford and Gibbs (1985) also pointed out that status integration theory is very difficult to test, because an adequate test requires simultaneous measures of status integration. Stafford and Gibbs note, for example, that "black males ages 30–34 are never simply married; they are also carpenters, insurance agents, mail carriers, physicians, etc" (1985:647). Therefore, cross-classification of the combinations of statuses, such as age, sex, race, employment, household, marital, and residential, is required. This, then, requires large samples and detailed information on status characteristics that are seldom available. Furthermore, Stafford and Gibbs (1985) argued that the theory's assumption that all statuses are of the same importance is erroneous; the relative importance of statuses may vary through time. For example, occupational status may be more important for white males than African-American males; but it has now become as important for young African-American males, under 40, as it is for white males as a whole. In sum, despite their claim of testability, Gibbs and Martin's status integration theory is extremely difficult to test completely because the importance of statuses for various demographic groups through time is required.

Micro-Objectivist Theories

Micro-objectivist theories focus on the social conditions of one's life situation that give rise to suicidal behavior. Micro-objectivists ask: "What social factors motivate an individual to commit suicide or work to lessen the social prohibitions on suicide and, thereby, make suicide a legitimate option for certain individuals?"

Social Learning Theory. Ronald Akers suggests that there are "two learning paths to suicide":

1. Learning to behave suicidally, but not fatally, and ultimately reaching the point of suicide
2. Learning about and developing a readi-

ness of suicide and completing it without prior practice in specifically suicidal behavior (Akers, 1985:229).

In the first path to suicide, suicide is reinforced by acting suicidal in the past. Some anecdotal information can be cited to illustrate instances of reinforced suicidal behavior. For example, in a suicide note, the victim may reveal a history or progression of suicidal thoughts, gestures, and attempts prior to his or her completed suicide. Also, persons who have made one attempt are likely to make further attempts and have a slightly higher risk of eventually completing a sui-cide. The majority, 90 percent, of attempters, however, do not commit suicide (Seiden, 1983). These data are merely suggestive of reinforced suicidal behavior for some persons. A systematic test of reinforced suicide requires an examination of persons' motivations that compares non-attempters, attempters, and completers of suicide.

In the second path to suicide, learning a "readiness of suicide . . . without prior practice" suggests that one had acquired attitudes accepting the appropriateness of suicide, for at least some circumstances, or attitudes of tolerance toward others who attempt and complete suicide. Again, systematic research on the relationship between attitudes and suicidal behavior over time, for demographic groups, and by geographic location, is required. Presently, attitudinal studies of suicide lack the scientific rigor to make confident generalizations about the relationship between attitudes toward suicide and suicidal behavior. Furthermore, attitudes are not necessarily good predictors of behavior. However, some attitudinal research does suggest that sympathetic attitudes toward those who attempt and complete suicides may affect suicide outcome differences for men and women.

Sex differences in suicide have been historically documented. From Durkheim's (1896)

study of suicide to today's reported suicide rates, men are significantly more likely to commit suicide than women. For attempted suicides, however, the reverse is true. Women are more likely to attempt suicide than men (Seiden, 1983). Some estimate that women attempt suicide ten times more often than men (Hendin, 1982). Some studies suggest that men have acquired sex-role attitudes that increase their likelihood of completing suicide without prior practice. For example, Linehan (1973:33) found that men and women viewed those who completed suicide as "more masculine" and "more potent" than those who attempted suicide. This is, of course, consistent with sex-role stereotypes of men as independent, strong, and decisive. Perhaps, then, men approach a suicide in a manner that increases the probability of success. A failed attempt would be perceived by the perpetrator and others as "unmanly."

White and Stillion (1988) provided a more systematic examination of male and female attitudes toward suicide targets (attempters and completers). Unlike previous studies, these researchers included a nonsuicidal comparison group. That is to say, attitudes towards three adolescent groups were compared: nonsuicidal troubled adolescents, troubled adolescents who attempted suicide, and troubled adolescents who completed suicide. The results of this study did not support the notion that females often attempt suicide for attention or sympathy. Females were as sympathetic toward nonsuicidal adolescents as they were toward suicidal adolescents, both attempters and completers. On the other hand, men were less sympathetic toward all troubled adolescents than females, but men were more sympathetic toward nonsuicidal adolescents. Men's low level of sympathy for suicidal behavior may affect men's high completion rate. White and Stillion conclude: "Troubled males considering suicide may arrange the contingencies in such a way as to guarantee completing the act rather than face the stigma which they and other males attach to suicidal behavior" (1988:364).

The studies presented here do not provide direct evidence that suicidal behavior is reinforced or that a readiness of suicide is learned. They merely suggest that learned sex-role attitudes may, in part, affect suicide outcomes. It seems reasonable, then, that learning plays a role in the suicidal behavior of various demographic groups. The effects of learning may also vary by time and place. Clearly, more research is necessary.

Another aspect of learning, for which systematic research is available, is the effect of imitation on suicide. Human beings learn through imitation as well as reinforcement. Durkheim (1963) acknowledged that imitation may precipitate some suicides, but he believed that imitation was not the original cause of suicide. In Durkheim's words: "Except in the very rare instances of a more or less complete 'fixed idea,' the thought of an act is not sufficient to produce a similar act itself in an adult, unless he is a person himself specifically so inclined" (1963:141).

Convincing evidence contrary to Durkheim's assertion that imitation was not an original factor for suicide was first presented by David P. Phillips in 1974. He conducted a large-scale study of the imitation effect by examining fluctuation in U.S. suicide rates before and after highly publicized suicide stories. He reported a significant increase in suicides after publicized suicide stories. The more the publicity, the greater the increase in suicides. Also, the major increases in suicides were in the geographic locations where the suicide story was publicized. However, was the imitation effect noted by Phillips a precipitating factor or an original factor of suicide? To answer this question, Phillips reasoned that, if suicide stories precipitate suicides, the rise in suicides after publicity would be followed by a decline in suicides to below the normal rate. This is because people would have "moved up" the date of their suicide

creating a temporary dearth in the number suicides that would have occurred later if not precipitated by the publicity. Phillips (1974) found no such decline and, therefore, concluded that publicized suicide stories triggered suicides that would not have otherwise happened.

One researcher (Wasserman, 1984) suggested that the suicide stories were imitated only if the suicides were of celebrities (e.g., Marilyn Monroe's highly publicized suicide). However, Stack (1987) reinvestigated the effect of celebrity suicide stories on imitation suicides. Stack (1987) included celebrity stories omitted in Wasserman's study, controlled for the amount of publicity, and found no significant difference for celebrity and noncelebrity suicide stories.

Not all suicides are recorded as such, some may be misclassified as auto accidents, especially those involving a single car and one driver. Therefore, Phillips (1979) investigated the imitation effect further by examining the relationship between suicide stories and rates of auto accidents. His findings were striking. Phillips found that there was a 31 percent increase in auto accidents on the third day following suicide stories and that the increase was much larger for single-vehicle crashes. Also, the increase was higher following highly publicized suicide stories and higher in the locations where the suicide stories were more publicized. Phillips's (1979) data was limited to California motor vehicle fatalities. A replication study in Detroit supported all of Phillips's earlier findings, and found a 35 percent increase in motor vehicle fatalities following suicide stories (Bollen and Phillips, 1981).

There is an important follow-up question to the research on imitated suicides: "Does the imitation effect vary for demographic groups?" Phillips and Carstensen (1988) examined the effects of suicide stories on various demographic groups. These researchers found that suicide stories affected all demographic groups (e.g., age, race, and sex), but the affect is most evident for teenagers.

The research discussed thus far has examined the effect of "real-life" suicide stories on subsequent suicides. Let us now review the research on the effect of fictional television suicides on subsequent suicides. Gould and Shaffer (1986) found increases in adolescent suicides following the broadcast of suicidal behavior by fictional television characters. A replication study, however, did not find a significant relationship between fictional television suicides and increases in adolescent suicides (Berman, 1988). Similarly, Gould, Shaffer, and Kleinman conclude from their replication study: "The impact of the television broadcasts of fictional stories featuring suicidal behavior appears less widespread than we had originally proposed" (1988:95). However, Gould, Shaffer, and Kleinman (1988) found that the impact of fictional television depictions of suicidal behavior varied significantly by geographic location. Television broadcasts had a significant effect on adolescent suicides in New York and Cleveland, but not in Dallas or Los Angeles.

Control Theory.   According to Jacobs (1967), the social meanings of suicide by and large define suicide as immoral. The social meanings of suicide, then, are social prohibitions against suicide. These social prohibitions are internalized by individuals who themselves view suicide as immoral. Thus, the central question asked by Jacobs is: How does an individual overcome the social prohibitions of suicide and come to take his or her own life? Jacobs identifies a ten-stage suicidal process.

1. Individuals find themselves faced with unexpected, intolerable, and unsolvable problems.
2. They view these problems not as isolated incidents, but as part of a long-standing history of problems. At the same time, they expect more problems in the future.
3. They believe that death is the only way to solve these problems.
4. Their belief in the efficacy of death intensifies through increasing social isolation, because they cannot share their problems with others.
5. They now work hard to overcome the social prohibition against suicide, which they have so internalized that they view suicide as immoral.
6. They succeed in overcoming the social prohibition because they already feel isolated from others and therefore feel freer to act on their own.
7. They succeed in overcoming the social prohibition by rationalizing their intended suicide in such ways as, "Killing myself doesn't necessarily mean I don't hold life sacred. In fact, I still hold life sacred despite my suicide."
8. They are convinced by their rationalizations because they define the problem as not of their own making, as unsolvable despite their great personal effort to find a less painful solution, as solvable only through suicide.
9. Defining suicide as the necessary solution, they feel that they do not have the choice not to kill themselves; they thereby free themselves from a sense of responsibility for their impending suicide and from the feeling of guilt.
10. Finally, just to make sure that they will not be punished in the afterlife, they pray to God for forgiveness or leave a suicide note requesting the survivors to pray for their souls. Then they decisively kill themselves (Jacobs, 1967:67).

These stages are self-explanatory. Together they constitute the social process by which an individual neutralizes the negative meanings of suicide. Through evermore convincing rationalization, a person overcomes his or her internalized social prohibitions against suicide and is freed to take his or her own life. Jacob's suicidal process is both logical and plausible. However, how do we obtain data on the social process of suicide? Victims can not be questioned, and they are seldom observed by anyone other than affected parties, such as friends or family. This leaves us with suicide notes, which are often not written and are sometimes written by others or destroyed by others. When notes have been written by the victim, they vary in detail and intent; they may ask for forgiveness, instruct survivors, blame someone else, and so on. Therefore, Schneidman (1976) does not believe that suicide notes should be used to test theories of suicide.

> That special state of mind necessary to perform a suicidal act is one which is essentially incompatible with an insightful recitation of what was going on in one's mind that led to the act itself (Schneidman, 1976:266).

Macro-Subjectivist Theories

Macro-subjectivist explanations focus on the social processes by which behaviors come to be defined as deviance. There are two types of macro-subjectivist explanations: interest group explanations and organizational explanations. For the former, emphasis is on various interest groups that compete to create official definitions of deviance, such as laws. For the latter, focus is on the organizational forces of a particular work setting that influence workers' definitions of deviance. Official agents (e.g., police, prosecutors, social workers, and mental health workers) produce official deviants and official rates of deviance.

Interest Group Explanations. Interest group explanations seek to discover the economic, political, social, and moral considerations that prompt interest groups to create definitions of behavior as deviant, immoral, or illegal. In the case of suicide, Hoffman and Webbs's (1981) historical inquiry reveals the economic and class interests that shaped the law-making and law-enforcing policies surrounding suicide. What follows is largely a summary of Hoffman and Webbs's (1981: 372–384) investigation of the origin of suicide as murder.

By common law, suicide was self-murder. For a suicide to be a self-murder, the person must have been of sound mind. The punishment was forfeiture of property and burial at a crossroads. Also, a common English practice was to bury the self-murder at night with a stake through the heart and a stone over the face.

Prior to English common law, the forfeitured property of those who committed self-murder was possessed by feudal lords. By the fourteenth century, English common law defined self-murder as a crime against the state, which designated itself as the recipient of all forfeitured property. The common-law transfer of forfeitured property from feudal lords benefited the state in two ways. First, the legal prohibition of suicide increased the authority of the state over the traditional authorities of community and church. Second, forfeitured property increased revenues for the state. Hoffman and Webb (1981:376) suggest that the common law of suicide is best understood as a part of the political-economic transition from the "lord-vassal relations" of feudal society to the "merchant-state relations" of a system of commerce.

There is, however, sufficient evidence that the common law of suicide was not popular among English citizens; therefore, it was not often enforced. Forfeiture of property was required only for those suicides that had been officially designated as self-murder. An official designation of self-murder was the responsibility of the state-appointed coroner and a jury of the offender's peers. The jury was comprised of 12 or more men from nearby communities. If the official inquest found the offender to have been "sane" at the time of killing, religious burial was denied and property forfeitured. If the inquiry yielded a finding of "insane," the offender was entitled to a religious burial and property remained with the family. "Insane" was the most frequent finding, and this finding increased steadily through the centuries. By the late eighteenth century, a finding of "sane" was very rare. Hoffman and Webb (1981:379) interpret this trend as evidence of "widespread popular opposition" to suicide as murder. This widespread opposition contributed, in part, to major reforms in suicide law. These reforms include the abolition of forfeiture and the right to religious burial. However, reforms in the suicide law paralleled changes in the inheritance laws. According to Hoffman and Webb (1981), these legal changes were linked to the expansion of a capitalist economy, which gave rise to the need for the private accumulation of capital. The depenalization of suicide served the interests of the wealthiest property holders in capitalist society, the bourgeoisie, by moving in line with the laws guaranteeing the hereditary transfer of wealth.

To conclude, Hoffman and Webb (1981) suggest that the law of suicide as murder and its eventual depenalization was shaped by economic forces that gave rise to the dominant interest groups who controlled wealth: feudal lords, the state, and the bourgeoisie.

Organizational Explanations. According to organization explanations, official agents produce suicide rates. In the case of suicide, the official agents are coroners and medical examiners. They are ultimately responsible for designating the cause of death. The organizational features of the coroner's or medical examiner's office affect the agent's classification of deaths as suicides. Such organizational features include caseloads, available resources, and external pressures from victim's family, law-enforcement officials, and insurance investigators.

The social organization view of suicide suggests two important points about suicide rates. First, organizational pressures lead to systematic underreporting of suicides by official agents whose task it is to classify suspicious deaths. Second, suicide rates are social artifacts, themselves to be explained, rather than "objective" recordings of suicide behaviors. Suicide rates, then, cannot be used, the way objectivists have used them, to discover the social correlates of suicide or to test causation theories of suicide. Pescosolido and Mendelsohn (1986) put the social organization view of suicide to the test. These researchers, first, test the effect of organizational features on classification of suspicious deaths as suicide. Second, they test the effect of misreporting on the relation between some social correlates (age and gender) suggested by causation theories of suicide and suicide rates.

To test the effect of organizational factors on classifying suspicious deaths, Pescosolido and Mendelsohn (1986) identify three legal and organizational variables that increase or decrease the discretion of coroners and medical examiners. First, coroners or medical examiners are elected in some areas and appointed in others. Pescosolido and Mendelsohn suggest that officials who are elected are more attuned to "community interests," whereas appointed officials are more "removed from partisan politics" (1986:83). Second, in some areas authority to call an inquest is granted to attorneys rather than coroners. Denying that authority to coroners "decreases discretion and the likelihood of a reporting error" (Pescosolido and Mendelsohn, 1986:83). Third, the availability of toxicology and pathology facilities varies. If they are available, the premise for classification of death shifts to "more scientific criteria" (Pescosolido and Mendelsohn, 1986:83). Therefore, coroner systems, elected status, and the authority to call an inquest increase discretion and decrease reported suicides. On the other hand, medical examiner systems, appointed status, and the availability of toxicology and pathology facilities decrease discretion and increase reported suicides (Pescosolido and Mendelsohn, 1986:84). The relation between these factors and suicide rates was examined for eight categories of age and gender combinations (18–24, 25–44, 45–64, 65+ and males and females).

Pescosolido and Mendelsohn (1986) found that organizational factors do lead to consistent underreporting of suicides, but not necessarily in the way that they had predicted. Elected status only lowered the suicide rate for one of the eight age and gender categories. The medical examiner's system lowered suicide rates for two of the eight categories. The availability of toxicology and pathology facilities lowered suicide rates for three of the eight categories. Pescosolido and Mendelsohn suggest that the organizational factor of caseloads may cancel the effect of other factors. That is to say, high caseloads demand that officials "produce a consistent performance" (Pescosolido and Mendelsohn, 1986: 95) which may cancel out elected or appointed status and the ability to call an inquest in both coroner and medical examiner systems. Also, coroners may actually have more discretion in classifying a death as suicide because they are less bound by scientific medical evidence. Clearly, more research on these suggested organizational features is needed.

Although organizational factors contribute to consistent underreporting of suicides, consistent underreporting does not significantly affect the relationship between social correlates of suicide and suicide rates. Pescosolido and Mendelsohn conclude: "Despite the fact that suicides may be unilaterally underreported, we find that this makes very little difference in unraveling the fundamental causes of suicide in the United States." (1986:94). This is, of course, good news for objectivists who use official suicide reports to test causation theories of suicide.

Micro-Subjectivist Theories

Micro-subjectivists examine how various audiences, including witnesses, intimates of the victim, and officials, come to define a particular death as a suicide. They do not deny that some persons intend to take their own lives and succeed. They argue that what comes to be officially classified as a "suicide" is largely a matter of definition. Subjectivists view official suicides and suicide rates as the end products of a wide spectrum in interpretations and judgments by various audiences. Suicide rates, then, cannot be used to test causal theories of suicidal behavior because predictor variables (e.g., age, gender, race, class, religion, and marital status) are more strongly associated with individuals' differences in perceptions and cognitions of death and suicide than they are with actual suicidal behavior. For example, Douglas suggests that there are "strong class differences in both ability and willingness of individuals to manipulate information-giving phenomena in such a way as to produce desired choices (of, for example, categorizations of the cause of death) by other individuals" (1967:210). This means that upper-class persons have the status to impose their will (interpretations and judgments) on the will of others, including officials. In the case of suicide, upper-class persons may have more to lose because of the stigma attached to suicide, which increases their willingness to persuade officials of a cause of death other than suicide. Upper-class persons are also better able to succeed in concealing a suicide because of their power in the community.

Indeed, the official classification of a suicide is, in part, a matter of definition. In determining the cause of death, coroners make subtle judgments that are probably influenced by both the coroner's own perceptions and cognitions of death as well as those of others. Together, coroners and various others construct an official cause of death. The social characteristics of various audiences are also likely to be related to the particular perceptions and cognitions of death that different individuals use in their interpretations of a given death. However, systematic study of the subtle decision-making process involved in official classifications of death or of the effect social characteristics have on various perceptions and cognitions of death has not been done. Rather, the subjective elements of the suicide phenomena have been largely assumed; and the evidence provided has been anecdotal information (e.g., Douglas, 1967:190–229).

There is, however, a sizable body of literature on misclassifications of suicides, which results in serious underreporting. A review of this literature suggests that suicide rates underestimate the extent of suicide by as much as 25 to 50 percent (Seiden, 1983; Kleck, 1988). Phillips and his colleagues performed the most convincing studies of misclassifications of suicides as auto accidents (Phillips, 1974; 1979; Bollen and Phillips, 1981). As previously discussed, Phillips (1979) found a 31 percent rise in motor vehicle fatalities after media publicized suicides in California. Similarly, Bollen and Phillips (1981) found a 35 percent rise in motor vehicle fatalities following publicized suicides in Detroit. Many suicides may be misclassified as accidents other than motor vehicular, or, even as death from natural causes. It has been suggested, for example, that drowning deaths may represent a large number of suicides misclassified as accidents (Douglas, 1967; Kleck, 1988). And, the suicides by persons with terminal illnesses may often be seen as a death resulting from natural causes (Kleck, 1988). These are a few among other types of misclassified suicides that could contribute to a serious under-

counting of suicides. From a review of studies on miscounting suicides, however, Kleck (1988) argued that claims of seriously underreported suicides in the United States have been exaggerated. Let's review Kleck's findings.

Gary Kleck (1988) examined deaths occurring in the United States in 1980 that were certified as "suicidal," "accidental," and "undetermined." Kleck (1988) found that even when he included as suicides all accidents and undetermineds with a physical cause of death (e.g., suffocation due to hanging?, gunshot wound, and drowning), the increase in the official count of suicide was modest. He calculated ratios comparing the total deaths by physical means, regardless of their classifications, to the number of certified suicides. For the most common methods of suicide, such as gunshots and suffocation by hanging, the ratios were small, indicating little undercounting due to misclassification as accidental or undetermined death. The ratio was largest for analgesic poisoning and drowning (Kleck, 1988:225). Kleck's (1988:232–33) calculations for potential undercounts of suicides are as follows:

drowning suicides misclassified (972/13.6%)
other common method suicides misclassified as accidents (4,209/59.0%)
other common method suicides misclassified as undetermined (1,232/17.3%)
rare method suicides misclassified as accidents or undetermined (426/6.0%)
poisoning suicides misclassified as natural deaths (291/4.1%)
total potential undercounted suicides (7,130/100%)

Compared to the total number of certified suicides, the total number of potential misclassified suicides represents 26.5 percent. This percentage of error is on the lowest end of most previous estimates of the percentage of undercounted suicides. However, Kleck (1988) further notes that a certain percentage of accidental or natural deaths may be misclassified as suicides. That is to say, there is also the likelihood of overcounting of suicides. To adjust for overcounting, Kleck (1988:233–34) reviewed previous research that examined certified suicides that an autopsy later revealed to have been accidental or natural deaths. From these studies, Kleck (1988:234) figured that, for every 11 suicides misclassified as accidental or natural deaths, there are 8 accidental or natural deaths that are misclassified as suicides. Therefore, for every 11 deaths added to the total number of suicides, there are 8 deaths that need to be subtracted. Applying this formula to the 1980 U.S. death totals, Kleck estimated that the total number of suicides was undercounted by only 7.2 percent. Kleck's (1988) estimate of undercounting is surprisingly low when compared with the long-accepted estimate of 25 to 50 percent. Kleck's (1988) assertion that previous research has overestimated "hidden" suicides and underestimated the accidental and natural deaths that were misclassified as suicides is supported by other research. Pescosolido and Mendelsohn's (1986) study of the effects of organizational features on misclassifications of suicide revealed significant overcounting and undercounting of suicides. Pescosolido and Mendelsohn (1986) further found no systematic error in misclassifying suicides. Therefore, the research on miscounting suicides fails to support subjectivists' claim that official suicide rates cannot be used to examine the social correlates of suicide or to test causal theories of suicide. These studies do not disclaim that certified suicides are, in part, a matter of definition. Rather, they underscore the need for rigorous and systematic research on where, when, and how predictor variables (e.g., age, sex, race, marital status) affect the suicide classification process.

SOCIAL POLICY

Objectivist theories of suicide try to identify the causes of suicide. Logically, then, programs could be designed to alter these causal factors and reduce instances of suicide. To date, however, suicide prevention programs are not guided by sociological theory. This may be true, in part, because there are several rival theories instead of a predominant theory of suicide. Also, the implementation of some sociological theories of suicide would require social change at the community or societal level. Social change is typically seen by policymakers as impractical, especially when compared to treatment programs that focus on problem individuals. Finally, many of the temporal and demographic factors that are strongly associated with rates of suicide are of little practical value for reducing suicides. For example, it is not possible to eliminate Mondays or springtime; the elderly cannot be made younger nor whites made black. So, suicide prevention strategies are based more on commonsense than theory. According to Seiden (1983), present suicide prevention strategies can be placed under one of two model: the clinical model or the environmental risk-reduction model.

The Clinical Model

The clinical model includes individual and group therapy approaches that are aimed largely at suicidal persons and attempt to prevent their eventual suicide. The suicide prevention center and suicide therapy groups are popular prevention approaches of the clinical type.

The Los Angeles Suicide Prevention Center was established in 1958. A major component of the center was the "suicide hot line" and other types of telephone counseling (Seiden, 1983). Similar centers were established in many states throughout the United

States during the 1960s and 1970s. These centers typically depend on a large number of volunteer workers who keep the center's services going 24 hours a day, seven days a week (Seiden, 1983). These centers handle a large number of calls each year, but their success in preventing suicide is not known. A study by Miller, Coombs, Leeper, and Barton (1984) found suicide prevention centers to have little effect on suicide rates. Prevention center advocates could, however, counter with the argument that, if only one suicide is prevented, the center is a success.

Some communities also have therapy groups for suicidal persons. Their effectiveness is also difficult to determine. However, because many suicidal persons express loneliness, the social nature of the group is seen as appropriate. Group support may alleviate feelings of loneliness and provide interactions and relationships that continue outside the group (Seiden, 1983).

The Environmental Risk-Reduction Model

Environmental risk-reduction strategies attempt to control the physical means commonly used to commit suicide or to physically alter places that provide opportunities for suicide. Gun control and substance control are two proposed strategies that attempt to reduce suicides by regulating means often used to commit suicide.

Firearms are the preferred means of successful suicides, and the use of firearms in completed suicides is increasing. In 1970, 58.4 percent of male suicides and 30.2 percent of female suicides were committed with a firearm. By 1980, the percentages were, respectively, 63.1 and 38.6. In 1986, 64.1 percent of male suicides and 39.5 percent of female suicides were committed with a firearm (U.S. National Center for Health Statistics, 1991:85). High rates of gun ownership are related to high rates of gun-related violence in accidents, homicides and suicides (Seiden,

1983). In the United States, however, legislation to regulate or control gun manufacturing, sales and ownership has been met by opposition from powerful lobby groups, especially the National Rifle Association, and political resistance—former Presidents Reagan and Bush have opposed gun control. Also, there are already many gun-control laws in the United States, and their effectiveness for reducing gun-related violence has not been demonstrated.

Substance control, especially of barbiturates, has also been proposed to reduce suicides. Proposals have ranged from forbidding barbiturates, except for hospitalized patients and seizure control, to simply dispensing them in blister packs to make it more difficult to take many of them quickly (Seiden, 1983). Proponents of regulating barbiturates may point out that there are a wide variety of alternative, less dangerous drugs that can be prescribed for the same problems that barbiturates are used for. On the other hand, opponents of barbiturate control could argue that there are too many other lethal substances available for persons who wish to commit suicide. It also seems likely that any large-scale effort to control a legal drug would meet with strong resistance from present users, some physicians, and drug companies.

Another environmental risk-reduction strategy is to physically alter places that provide opportunities for suicide, such as high buildings and bridges. Seiden (1983), for example, points out that more suicides take place at San Francisco's Golden Gate Bridge than any place else in the world. The railings could be extended to provide less of an opportunity to jump. Similar physical structures have been placed on the Empire State Building, the Eiffel Tower, and the Arroyo Seco Bridge in Pasadena (Seiden, 1983:1525). Opponents could argue that such physical modification are futile because there are too many other places to go and too many methods of suicide to choose from. Proponents, on the other hand, could argue that notable suicide monuments, such as the Golden Gate Bridge, may suggest suicide to one who is there at a particularly vulnerable time.

Preventing Adolescent Suicide

Concern about the increasing rate of suicide among teenagers has led to the proliferation of adolescent suicide prevention programs. The majority of these prevention programs are school based. The number of U.S. schools using a suicide prevention program more than doubled from 787 in 1984 to 1,709 in 1986 (Garland, Shaffer, and Whittle, 1989:932). The majority of school-based programs target high school students. They are brief in duration, two hours or less. They present the facts of suicide and identify the warning signs of potential suicides. The typical program is presented by mental health professionals in conjunction with teachers and counselors (Garland, Shaffer, and Whittle, 1989:932).

Like suicide prevention strategies in general, school-based adolescent suicide prevention programs are not theoretically informed. Rather, the majority of programs are based on a "stress model" of suicide. That is, "suicide is seen as a response to extreme stress, to which everyone is vulnerable" (Garland, Shaffer, and Whittle, 1989:932). Garland and her colleagues (1989) have serious doubts about the "stress model." These researchers point out that targeting all teenagers rather than just those who are at risk is ineffective and dangerous. School-based suicide prevention programs are ineffective because few teenagers commit suicide, and these programs reach only about 1 percent of the 15- to 19-year-old population. Using 1985 suicide rates, Garland and her colleagues found that these programs would have reached only 18 of the 1,849 teenagers who committed suicide that year (1989:933). Further, Garland and her col-

leagues suggests that the "stress model" is dangerous because it increases teenager's awareness of suicide which, in turn, might increase the possibility of youth imitating suicide (1989:934). As pointed out earlier in this chapter, the imitation effect on suicide is particularly evident among teenagers. (See, for example, Phillips and Carstensen, 1988.)

Given the diversity of people most at risk for suicide (i.e., the elderly, whites, males, singles, and divorced and separated people), one prevention strategy probably won't effectively reduce national rates of suicide. However, rigorous evaluations of existing prevention strategies need to be connected to the process of theory construction. Theoreticians, too, need to extrapolate from their theories and research on the implications of suicide policy. Presently, theories of suicide remain in the academic community, often as end products. And, suicide prevention programs are often the end products of policymakers who are responding to public outcry and political pressure for something, anything, to be done.

SUMMARY

What is suicide? According to the objectivist conception of deviance, *suicide* is the intentional taking of one's own life. This definition requires an appropriate interface between an actor's intended behavior and the outcome (death or survival) of his or her behavior. The interface between intent and outcome yields two distinct types of behavior: suicidal behaviors and suicidal gestures. *Suicidal behaviors* include genuine intents to take one's own life that either succeed or fail. *Suicidal gestures* include the deaths and survivals of those who did not actually intend to die. Suicidal behaviors are the subject matter of objectivists' suicide theories and research. However, in real-life situations, suicidal behaviors and suicidal gestures are difficult to distinguish accurately.

According to the subjectivist conception of deviance, "suicide" is a label that is applied to one's death by social audiences. Subjectivists are not concerned with suicidal behaviors, rather they attempt to explain how various audiences come to define a death as suicide.

The actual number of suicides each year is unknown. Official rates of suicide, however, are highest in Asian countries. Within Europe and North America, suicide rates are highest in industrialized countries. In European countries and the United States, suicide rates vary by the season of the year, holidays, the month, day of the month, and day of the week. Temporal variations in suicide rates, perhaps, can be explained by "the broken-promise effect." *The broken-promise effect* is the discrepancy between how one feels in relation to how one expects to feel. Spring, weekends, and holidays, for example, heighten one's expectations for feeling better because they promise new beginnings. The anticipation of new beginnings produces a trough in suicides during the winter, weekdays, and on the holidays. As new beginnings often fail to improve one's feelings, new beginnings are followed by increased suicides in the spring, on Mondays, and following holidays.

In the United States, suicide rates are highest among the elderly, Native Americans, men, Protestants, and single persons. Research findings on social class and suicide rates are inconsistent. Macro-objectivist theories of suicide attempt to explain these correlates of suicide in relation to the impact of societal arrangements (economy, family, religion, and education) on various social groups (age, gender, race, marital status, and social class). The best-known macro-objectivist theory is Durkheim's classic theory of suicide. According to Durkheim, there are two causes of suicide: social integration and social regulation. *Social integration* refers to the attachment of the individual to his or her culture.

Social regulation refers to the degree of social solidarity of society as a whole. Social integration is the source of egoistic and altruistic suicides. *Egoistic* suicide is committed by persons who are less integrated into society. For example, marital and family relations increase the degree of social integration; therefore, married persons are less likely to commit suicide than single persons. *Altruistic* suicide is committed by persons who are extremely integrated into their culture: for example, persons who kill themselves for their country's ultimate victory. Social regulation is the source of anomic and fatalistic suicides. *Anomic suicides* occur when people no longer feel regulated by societal, communal, or group norms. Suicides during rapid economic downswings or upswings are examples. *Fatalistic suicide* results from extreme social regulation. The suicides of captives and slaves are examples of fatalistic suicide.

Two contemporary modifications of Durkheim's theory of suicide are external restraint theory by Henry and Short (1954) and status integration theory by Gibbs and Martin (1964). *External restraint* refers to the degree to which one needs to conform to the expectations and demands of others. When external restraint is low, individual frustrations are directed inward, resulting in higher suicide rates. Empirical support for the association between external restraint and suicide is weak. *Status integration* refers to the pattern of statuses that one occupies. Where statuses conflict (e.g., young age and high occupational prestige), status integration is low and suicides are high. Status integration is difficult to measure and empirical support is weak.

Micro-objectivist theories focus on the social conditions of one's life situation that give rise to suicidal behavior. There is no direct evidence that persons are predisposed to suicide by socialization. However, there is strong evidence that many suicides are imitated. The *imitation effect* refers to the rise in suicide rates following publicized "real-life" suicide stories.

Macro-subjectivist interest group theories seek to discover the social, economic, and political considerations that prompt interest groups to create definitions of suicide as deviant or criminal. By English common law, suicide constituted the crime of self-murder. The penalty was forfeiture of property. The rise of capitalism led to the depenalization of suicide. The abolition of forfeitures served the *bourgeoisie*, the wealthiest property owners in capitalist society, by guaranteeing the hereditary transfer of wealth.

Macro-subjectivist organizational theories focus on the organizational features of work settings that influence official agents' construction of official suicide rates. There is evidence that the organizational demand to produce a consistent performance is related to a consistent underreporting of suicides by coroners and medical examiners alike.

Micro-subjectivists seek to understand the social interaction processes through which social audiences create a definition of a given death as a suicide. Micro-subjectivists suggest that social characteristics (age, race, gender, class, religion) of various audiences (witnesses, friends, family members, police, and coroners) affect their interpretation of a death as suicide. However, the systematic study of the effect social characteristics have on audience perceptions and cognitions of death and suicide has not been done. There is only evidence that misclassifications of death produce both overcounting and undercounting of suicides.

Suicide prevention programs are not generally based on sociological theories of suicide. They are driven by the practical demand to do something, anything. Presently, there are two predominant suicide prevention models: the clinical model and the environmental risk-reduction model. *The clinical model* includes individual and group therapy treatment of suicide-prone individuals. *The environmental risk-reduction model* attempts to reduce opportunities for suicide. The physical alteration of bridges and towers where suicides often occur is one strategy. Other strategies include gun control and drug control. There is little empirical evidence that either model effectively reduces suicides.

In addition to these prevention models, many schools across the United States have introduced adolescent suicide prevention programs. These school-based programs are largely based on a stress model of suicide. The *stress model* assumes that suicide is a response to individual stress to which all adolescents are vulnerable. Stress models are ineffective; and they are potentially dangerous because they increase teenagers' awareness of suicide, which might trigger imitation suicides.

GLOSSARY

Altruistic suicide   The type of suicide committed by persons who are extremely integrated into society. Suicides by martyrs who take their lives for the glorification or honor of their society are altruistic suicides.

Anomic suicide   The type of suicide committed by persons who no longer feel regulated by society's norms. The social disruption caused by economic depression weakens society's normative constraints on individuals, resulting in increased suicides.

Bourgeoisie   The ruling class in capitalist society, who own and control the predominant mode of production, wealth, and property.

The broken-promise effect   A proposed explanation for temporal variations in suicide rates. Spring, weekends, and holidays heighten one's expectations for feeling better, which results in low suicide rates during winter, early weekends, and on the holidays. When heightened expectations are not realized, the discrepancy between how one feels in relation to how one expects to feel is widened resulting in higher suicide rates in the spring, late weekend, or early week, and after holidays.

The clinical model   A theory approach that treats suicide-prone individuals in order to reduce their suicidal tendencies.

Egoistic suicide   The type of suicide committed by persons who are less integrated into society. According to Durkheim, being single and religious individualism lower social integration and increase egoistic suicides.

The environmental risk model   Strategies to control the physical means commonly used to commit suicide, such as gun and drug control, or to make physical alterations to places, such as bridges and towers, that provide opportunities for suicide.

External restraint   The degree to which one needs to conform to the expectations of others. Henry and Short (1954) suggest that, when external restraint is high, homicide is high; when external restraint is low, suicide is high.

Fatalistic suicide   The type of suicide that results from excessive regulation. According to Durkheim, many suicides by captives and slaves are fatalistic suicides.

The imitation effect   Suicide rates that increase following the publicity of "real life" suicide stories. The effect is especially pronounced among young people.

Social integration   The attachment of the individual to his or her culture. According to Durkheim, as the degree of social integration increases, suicide decreases.

Social regulation   The solidarity or cohesiveness that characterizes a society as a whole. As social solidarity decreases, suicide rates increase.

Status integration   Conflicting statuses (e.g., when person is young but holds a position of power and authority), which lower the degree of status integration and increases the probability of suicide.

The stress model   Broad-based education and counseling programs that target high-risk groups, for example, teenagers. The stress model assumes that all teenagers are vulnerable to extreme stress and, therefore, prone to suicide.

Suicidal behaviors   Genuine intents to take one's own life that either succeed or fail.

Suicidal gestures   Deaths and survivals of those who did not intend to take their own life.

Suicide   According to the objectivists, the intentional taking of one's own life. According to the subjectivists, a label applied to one's death by social audiences.

SUGGESTED READINGS

Hoffman, Dennis E., and Vincent J. Webb. "Suicide as Murder at Common Law: Another Chapter in the Falsification of Consensus Theory." *Criminology* 19(1981):372–384. Here is a historical inquiry into the law-making and law-enforcing processes of criminal laws prohibiting suicide. Historical data are used to demonstrate that economic forces shaped suicide laws in ways favorable to powerful interest groups that controlled production and wealth.

Kleck, Gary. "Miscounting Suicides." *Suicide and Life-Threatening Behavior* 18(1988):219–236. Kleck reviews research on misclassifications of suicide, and analysis of cause of death mortality data in the United States. Misclassifications include both overcounting and undercounting of suspicious deaths as suicide. The maximum net undercount of suicides is estimated to be about ten percent.

Pescosolido, Bernice A., and Robert Mendelsohn. "The Social Organization of Suicide Rates." *American Sociological Review* 51(1986):80–100. This quantitative and qualitative analysis explores the impact social organization has on the recording of official suicide rates and the effect misreporting has on testing sociological theories of the causes of suicide.

Phillips, David P., and Lundie L. Carstensen. "The Effect of Suicide Stories on Various Demographic Groups, 1968–1985." *Suicide and Life-Threatening Behavior* 18(1988):100–113. This review presents research on the imitation effect on suicide rates, including an analysis of the effect of television news stories of suicides on various demographic groups over an extended period of time.

Seiden, Richard H. "Suicide." *Encyclopedia of Crime and Justice.* ed. Sanford H. Kadish. New York: Free Press, 1983, 1521–1526. Here is a brief but comprehensive review of the suicide literature that includes definitions of suicide, methods of suicide, social correlates of suicide, theories of suicide, and suicide prevention strategies.

Stack, Steven. "Suicide: A Decade Review of the Sociological Literature." *Deviant Behavior* 4(1982):41–66. The author provides a systematic review of sociological research findings on suicide and an evaluation of explanations of suicide.

REFERENCES

Akers, Ronald L. *Deviant Behavior: A Social Learning Approach.* 3rd ed. Belmont, Calif.: Wadsworth, 1985.

Backer, Barbara A., Natalie Hannon, and Noreen A. Russell. *Death and Dying: Individuals and Institutions.* New York: Wiley, 1982.

Berman, Alan L. "Fictional Depiction of Suicide in Television Films and Imitation Effects." *American Journal of Psychiatry* 145(1988): 982–986.

Bollen, Kenneth A., and David P. Phillips. "Suicide Motor Vehicle Fatalities in Detroit: A Replication." *American Journal of Sociology* 87(1981): 404–412.

Caplan, Arthur L. "Bioethics on Trial." *Hastings Center Report.* March–April (1991):19–20.

Davis, Robert A. "Black Suicide in the Seventies: Current Trends." *Suicide and Life-Threatening Behavior* 9(1979):131–140.

Davis, Robert A. "Female Labor Force Participation, Status Integration and Suicide, 1950–1969." *Suicide and Life-Threatening Behavior* 11(1981):111–123.

Department of International Economic and Social Affairs, Statistical Office. *1990 Demographic Yearbook.* 42nd ed. United Nations, 1992.

Douglas, Jack. *The Social Meanings of Suicide.* Princeton: Princeton University Press, 1967.

Downey, Ann M. "The Impact of Drug Abuse Upon Adolescent Suicide." *Omega* 11(1990–1991):261–275.

Durkheim, Emile. *Suicide.* Glencoe, Ill.: Free Press, 1963. Originally published in 1897.

Gabennesch, Howard. "When Promises Fail: A Theory of Temporal Fluctuations in Suicide." *Social Forces* 67(9188):129–145.

Gardner, Thomas J. *Criminal Law: Principles and Cases.* 3rd ed. New York: West, 1985.

Garland, Ann, David Shaffer, and Barry Whittle. "A National Survey of School-Based, Adolescent Suicide Prevention Programs." *Journal of the American Academy of Child and Adolescent Psychiatry* 28(1989):931–934.

Gibbs, Jack P. "Testing the Theory of Status Integration and Suicide Rates." *American Sociological Review* 47(1982):227–237.

Gibbs, Jack P., and Walter T. Martin. *Status Integration and Suicide: A Sociological Study.* Eugene, Or.: University of Oregon Press, 1964.

———"Still Another Look at Status Integration and Suicide." *Social Forces* 59(1981): 815–823.

Gould, Madelyn, and David Shaffer. "The Impact of Suicide in Television Movies: Evidence of Imitation." *New England Journal of Medicine* 315(1986):690–694.

Gould, Madelyn, David Shaffer, and Marjorie Kleinman. "The Impact of Suicide in Television Movies: Replication and Commentary." *Suicide and Life-Threatening Behavior* 18(1988): 90–99.

Hendin, Herbert. *Suicide in America.* New York: Norton, 1982.

Henry, Andrew F., and James Short, Jr. *Suicide and Homicide*. New York: Free Press, 1954.

Hoffman, Dennis E., and Vincent J. Webb. "Suicide as Murder at Common Law: Another Chapter in the Falsification of Consensus Theory." *Criminology* 19(1981):372–384.

Humphrey, John A., and Stuart Palmer. "The Effects of Race, Gender, and Marital Status on Suicides Among Young Adults, Middle-Aged Adults, and Older Adults." *Omega* 22 (1990–91):277–285.

Jacobs, Jerry. "A Phenomenological Study of Suicide Notes." *Social Problems* 15(1967):60–72.

Jobes, David A., Alan L. Berman, and Arnold R. Josselsen. "The Impact of Psychological Autopsies on Medical Examiners' Determination of Manner of Death." *Journal of Forensic Science* 31(1986):177–189.

Kastenbaum, Robert J., and Ruth B. Aisenberg. *The Psychology of Death*. New York: Springer, 1972.

———*Death, Society, and Human Experiences*. Columbus: Charles E. Merrill, 1986.

Kleck, Gary. "Miscounting Suicides." *Suicide and Life-Threatening Behavior* 18(1988):219–236.

Lester, David. *Why People Kill Themselves*. Springfield, Ill.: Charles C. Thomas, 1983.

———"Demographic Attributions Related to Black Suicide." *The Journal of Social Psychology* 128(1990):407–409.

———"Mortality From Suicide and Homicide for African Americans in the USA: A Regional Analysis." *Omega* 22(1990–91):219–226.

Lester, David, and Michael L. Frank. "Suicide and Homicide in Rural Areas: A Study of Arkansas." *Psychological Reports* 66(1990):426.

Linehan, Michael M. "Suicide and Attempted Suicide: Study of Perceived Sex Differences." *Perceptual and Motor Skills* 37(1973):31–34.

Maris, Ronald W. "The Adolescent Suicide Problem." *Suicide and Life-Threatening Behavior* 15(1985):91–109.

Marks, Alan. "Socioeconomic Status and Suicide in the State of Washington: 1950–1971." *Psychological Reports* 46(1980):924–926.

Miller, H.L., D.W. Coombs, J.D. Leeper, and S.N. Barton. "An Analysis of the Effects of Suicide Prevention Facilities on Suicide Rates in the United States." *American Journal of Public Health* 74(1984):340–343.

Nelson, Franklin L., Norman Farberow, and Douglas MacKinnon. "The Certification of Suicide in Eleven Western States: An Inquiry into the Validity of Reported Suicide Rates." *Suicide and Life-Threatening Behavior* 8(1978):75–88.

Newsweek. "The Doctor's Suicide Van." June 18, 1990: 46–49.

———"Last Rights." Aug. 16, 1991:41–46.

Peck, M., and A. Schrut. "Suicidal Behavior Among College Students." *HSMHA Health Report* 86(1971):149–156.

Pescosolido, Bernice A., and Robert Mendelsohn. "The Social Organization of Suicide Rates." *American Sociological Review* 51(1986):80–100.

Phillips, David P. "The Influence of Suggestion on Suicide: Substantive and Theoretical Implications of the Werther Effect." *American Sociological Review* 39(1974):340–354.

———"Suicide, Motor Vehicle Fatalities, and the Mass Media: Evidence Toward a Theory of Suggestion." *American Journal of Sociology* 84(1979):1150–1174.

Phillips, David P. and Lundie L. Carstensen. "The Effects of Suicide Stories on Various Demographic Groups, 1968–1985." *Suicide and Life-Threatening Behavior* 18(1988):100–114.

Schneidman, Edwin S. *Suicidology: Contemporary Developments*. New York: Grune and Stratton, 1976.

Seiden, Richard H. "Suicide." *Encyclopedia of Crime and Justice*. Ed. Sanford H. Kadish. New York: Free Press, 1983, 1521–1526.

Stack, Steven. "Suicide: A Decade Review of the Sociological Literature." *Deviant Behavior* 4(1982):41–66.

———"The Effect of Domestic/Religious Individualism on Suicide, 1954–1978." *Journal of Marriage and the Family* 47(1985):431–447.

———"A Leveling Off in Young Suicide." *Wall Street Journal*, May 28, 1986: 30.

———"Celebrities and Suicides: A Taxonomy and Analysis." *American Sociological Review* 52(1987):427–436.

Stafford, Mark C., and Jack P. Gibbs. "A Major Problem with the Theory of Status Integration and Suicide." *Social Forces* 63(1985):643–660.

Stafford, Mark C., and Ralph A. Weisheit. "Changing Age Patterns of U.S. Male and Female

Suicide Rates, 1934–1983." *Suicide and Life-Threatening Behavior* 18(1988):149–163.

Stephenson, John S. *Death, Grief, and Mourning.* Glencoe, Ill.: Free Press, 1985:239–255.

U.S. National Center for Health Statistics. "Vital Statistics of the United States, Annual." Washington, D.C.: U.S. Government Printing Office, 1991.

U.S. News and World Report. "The Odd Odyssey of 'Dr. Death'." Aug. 27/Sept. 3, 1990:27–28.

Wasserman, Ira M. "Imitation and Suicide: A Reexamination of the Werther Effect." *American Sociological Review* 49(1984):427–436.

Weekly World News Digest. "U.S. News Brief." Feb. 27, 1992:133.

White, Hedy, and Judith M. Stillion. "Sex Differences in Attitudes Toward Suicide." *Psychology of Women Quarterly* 12(1988):357–366.

Chapter *8*

Homosexuality

"SEXUAL BEHAVIOR IN CULTURAL CONTEXT"

The Sambia, of Papua, New Guinea (Herdt, 1987) are, in many ways, not unlike people in Western cultures. Like most Americans, they believe that men must be masculine and desirable as husbands and lovers. However, unlike Americans, the Sambia believe that boys must acquire semen orally from older boys and men if they are to grow into manhood. A boy only becomes a "man"—masculine, strong, and sexually attractive to women—if he performs fellatio. Sambia boys generally do not enjoy fellatio, but they do it because they believe the more semen they ingest, the stronger and more masculine they will become. To encourage this masculine development, Sambia males are separated from their mothers between the ages of seven and ten to live in an all-male society.

After the onset of puberty, Sambia boys become the providers rather than recipients of semen. While being fellated is clearly more enjoyable for the Sambia than being the fellator, Sambia sexual fascination apparently remains primarily with women. Women are, to the Sambia boys, an erotic, yet forbidden fruit (Baldwin and Baldwin, 1989).

Once manhood is achieved (in the late teens or early twenties), the male marries. After marriage, all homosexual activity ceases. The Sambia believe that a child can only be conceived as a result of multiple ejaculations. Therefore, all of the semen must be saved for the woman (Baldwin and Baldwin, 1989).

The Etoro of Papua, New Guinea, similarly believe that in order for boys to grow into men they must ingest the semen of older men. Because of the culturally essential relationship between boys (age ten to adulthood) and older men, there are no sexual taboos attached to their behavior. They can have sex any time they want and anywhere they want. Sexual relations between adolescents, however, is discouraged because it is believed that adolescents who provide semen will not properly develop into men. Heterosexuality is similarly discouraged because it is believed that heterosexuality is needed only for reproduction (Kottak, 1991).

The Sambia and Etoro represent two of the many examples of how sexual behavior varies across culture and time. Indeed, such variation is well documented (e.g., Carrier, 1980; Karlen, 1980;

Herdt, 1987; Greenberg, 1988). Among the ancient Greeks, for example, same-sex sexual encounters were commonplace. In his famous dialogue *Symposium*, Plato writes of dinner guests who, when asked to talk about love, openly discussed their sexual relations with other men (Weinrich and Williams, 1991).

Clearly, what is or is not an acceptable sexual practice is bound by social norms and by societal reactions. Activities we might consider "gross" or "indecent" may not be gross or indecent to the Sambia. This is perhaps the most basic observation made by sociologists and anthropologists studying sexuality and other cultures.

WHAT IS HOMOSEXUALITY?

Given the tremendous diversity of cultural norms pertaining to sexual contact between members of the same sex, defining homosexuality is more difficult than it might first appear. At the *behavior* level, the definition of homosexuality seems easy enough: Homosexuality is sexual contact between two people of the same sex. Certainly this is an obvious starting point. However, as we discuss above, sexual contact between same-sex partners is not always defined as deviance. If our intent is to study homosexuality as a form of deviance, are we to include those people who engage in same-sex sexual behaviors that are not considered deviance? Even in this country, where homosexuality is generally not condoned, behavioral definitions are problematic. We often dismiss adolescent experimentation, for example, as "natural" or "normal" experimentation. Same-sex experimentation between adolescents may or may not be considered homosexuality. Similarly, one can be primarily attracted to the opposite sex but may find same-sex experience less lonely than masturbation (Humphreys, 1970; Diamant, 1987). Is this person "a homosexual"? The problem is obvious. As long as we focus on behavior, we have a problem identifying who it is we are trying to study.

Perhaps homosexuality is better defined

as an *erotic orientation*. If so, the simplest definition may be, "A homosexual is any individual whose sexual object choice is someone of the same sex" (Gould, 1979:36). Erotic attraction and behavior are clearly not the same thing. People can be attracted to members of their own sex without ever acting on those attractions. From this perspective, a person who has homosexual feelings is "a homosexual," even if he or she has had no experience.

Homosexuality can also be defined as an *identity*. Regardless of behaviors or physical attractions, a homosexual may be one who accepts and internalizes the master status, homosexual. Although a homosexual identity is most likely to develop as a response to same-sex experiences and erotic sensations, it need not necessarily include either factor. A man can have same-sex experiences or even feel same-sex attractions without thinking of himself as a homosexual. In a similar way, given certain kinds of societal labels (e.g., "faggot" and "gay boy") an adolescent could conceivably see himself as a "fag" without necessarily having homosexual feelings or experiences.

Of course, we will not settle the definitional debate here. What we will do instead is consider how one's definition of homosexuality depends, in part, on the conception of deviance from which one is working; that is, it depends on whether one adopts an objectivist conception or a subjectivist conception.

The Objectivist Conception

Objectivists conceptualize deviance as a behavior that violates a norm. Since the norms of appropriate sexual behavior are easily identifiable—that is, sexual behavior should be limited to consenting adults who are not members of the same family and are not members of the same sex—homosexuality is easy to identify.

The problem here, as with the objectivist

conception more generally, is that the objectivists can tell us more about what deviance is than about who the deviants are. The objectivists may be able to define the behavior for us (*doing* deviance), but they tell us little about the conditions under which a person is likely to be defined as deviant (*being* deviant). If we assume, as objectivists seem to assume, that deviants are those who engage in deviance, then is everyone who has had a homosexual experience a homosexual?

Because objectivists focus exclusively on behavior, they cannot really tell us who the "real" homosexuals are. Indeed, this is something objectivists fully admit. As the well-known sex researcher Alfred C. Kinsey argued over 40 years ago, it is impossible to know who the "real" homosexuals or "real" heterosexuals are because:

The world is not to be divided into sheep and goats. Not all things are black nor all things white. It is a fundamental of taxonomy that nature rarely deals with discrete categories. Only the human mind invents categories and tries to force facts into separate pigeon holes. The living world is a continuum in each and every one of its aspects. The sooner we learn this concerning human sexual behavior the sooner we shall reach a sound understanding of the realities of sex (Kinsey, Pomeroy, and Martin, 1948:639).

At the same time, however, implicit in the objectivist conception is the assumption that the more one *does* homosexuality, the more likely one is to *be* homosexual. In this sense, doing and being are, from an objectivist perspective, closely related.

The most well-known behavior indicator of homosexuality was developed by Kinsey and his colleagues in 1948. As shown in Table 8–1, Kinsey created a seven-point continuum of homosexuality in which "0" represents exclusive homosexual experiences and "6" exclusive heterosexual experiences. The midpoint on the continuum is bisexuality. This scale represents a ratio of homosexual/het-

---

TABLE 8.1 Kinsey's Heterosexual/Homosexual Rating Scale. The ratings represent the ratio same-sex to opposite-sex experiences for an age period in a person's life.

Heterosexual-0 .... 1 .... 2 .... 3 .... 4 .... 5 .... 6-Homosexual

0, all heterosexual; 1, largely heterosexual, some homosexual history, 2, largely heterosexual, distinct homosexual history; 3, equally heterosexual and homosexual; 4, largely homosexual, distinct heterosexual history; 5, largely homosexual, some heterosexual history; 6, all homosexual.

Source: Kinsey, Alfred C., Wardell B. Pomeroy, and Clyde E. Martin, *Sexual Behavior in the Human Male.* Philadelphia: W.B. Saunders, 1948.

erosexual experiences during a person's life. Anyone scoring 1 or more has had at least one orgasm with a same-sex partner. Anyone scoring 4 or more has had more same-sex orgasms than opposite-sex orgasms.

Kinsey's conceptualization is objectivist because it focuses on behavior. Whether one is considered primarily homosexual or primarily heterosexual depends upon the ratio of homosexual to heterosexual behaviors.

The Subjectivist Conception

Subjectivists argue that deviance cannot be fully understood by focusing on the behaviors of the deviant person. Rather, "one always has to consider the 'deviant' in relationship to those groups and individuals who define him so" (Plummer, 1975:21). It is true that the violation of norms may greatly influence society's reaction, but the behavior does not by itself determine what is and is not considered homosexuality or who is or is not considered a homosexual. What becomes interesting to the subjectivist, therefore, is the social process by which people or behaviors come to be considered deviant. In focusing on societal reactions, the subjectivists make three important contributions to the study of homosexuality.

First, the subjectivist conception offers us considerably more than the objectivist conception in explaining the problematic relationship between *being* and *doing*. Kinsey, in assuming that homosexuality is defined solely on the basis of behavior, attaches more significance to sexual acts than to the *meanings* those acts have to self and others (Greenberg, 1988). The subjectivists, in focusing on meanings other people attach to thoughts and behaviors, come closer to explaining how one develops a deviant identity. From a subjectivist point of view, adolescent same-sex experimentation is only homosexuality if others define it as such. In prison, same-sex behavior is common because it is the only form of sex available. Interestingly, however, within the prison community, such behavior is typically defined as homosexuality for the passive partner (the insertee) but not for the aggressive partner (the inserter) (Diamant, 1987). Clearly, the behavior has little to do with the label. Despite the fact that the passive partner may have been physically coerced, he or she is the one who is more likely to be defined as homosexual.

Second, the subjectivist conception tells us about why homosexual identities occur in some societies and not others (McIntosh, 1968; Goode, 1981) and about why they have different meanings and social sanctions attached to them (Warren, 1980; Greenberg, 1988; Diamant, 1987). Homosexual *identities* "occur only in societies where it is stigmatized" (Diamant, 1987:248). Since the social disgrace characteristic of stigma is dependent on the reactions of others, subjectivist insights become important (Plummer, 1975).

Third, the subjectivist conception explains how one can be defined as a homosexual without actually having performed a homosexual act. Since "homosexuality" is a label, it need not have anything to do with sexual behavior. In our society, for example, two men who have developed a strong emotional bond and express their emotions physically are likely to be perceived as being homosexuals, whether they have had sex or not. Or what about the man who has feminine characteristics and a lispy voice? Is he gay? While knowing nothing of his sexual experiences, society might well define his as gay. As we shall see in sections to come, people often use stereotypes about homosexuals to help them decide who is and is not a homosexual. In such cases, societal reactions have nothing to do with sexual behavior.

A Note on Homosexuality as Deviant Behavior

Because of the social sensitivity of our topic, before pressing onward it might be useful to review the sociological conception of deviant behavior. Throughout this book, we have conceptualized deviance as either a norm violation (objectivist conception) or a societal reaction (subjectivist conception). Using either conceptualization, homosexuality *is* deviance. It violates a norm (objectivist conception) and others define it as wrong (subjectivist conception). In neither case are we suggesting, however, that homosexuality, or any form of deviance for that matter, is necessarily immoral, sick, or even wrong. As sociologists we may study the social process by which a society defines a behavior as wrong without passing moral judgment ourselves.

With homosexuality, we walk an especially fine line because, regardless of how we approach this discussion, we are likely to offend someone. On the one hand, our discussion may offend those absolutists who

believe homosexuality does not "fit" relativistic sociological conceptions of deviant behavior. Homosexuality, they contend, is dependent on neither norms nor societal reactions. It is wrong, plain and simple. On the other hand, those who contend that homosexuality is a perfectly natural alternative lifestyle may resent our inclusion of homosexuality in a deviance book (alongside other forms of deviance, such as corporate crime, mental illness, drug use, and so on), assuming incorrectly that *deviance* and *pathology* are synonyms.

Undoubtedly, some will also resent the fact that, in this chapter, we examine some of the etiological aspects of homosexuality. This resentment may, in part, be justified given a history of theorizing about the causes of homosexuality so that a "cure" can be discovered. Many homosexuals, who feel as if they were born homosexual and are completely satisfied with their sexual orientation, resent any suggestion, however subtle it might be, that they can or should be cured of their "ailment."

One final note: The overwhelming majority of research on homosexuality focuses on gay men. Lesbians are all but ignored.[1] As a result, our discussion will also primarily be focused on gay men.

THE SOCIAL DISTRIBUTION OF HOMOSEXUALITY

The most significant research on the distribution of homosexuality was conducted by Alfred C. Kinsey during the 1940s. His work culminated in the publication of *Sexual Behavior in the Human Male* in 1948 (co-authored with Wardell B. Pomeroy and Clyde E. Martin) and *Sexual Behavior in the Human Female* in 1953 (co-authored with Pomeroy, Martin, and Paul Gebhard). Despite the age of the Kinsey reports, the sheer size of the sample (5,300 men and 5,900 women) and the quality and content of the interviews make these books relevant even today.

Prevalence of Homosexuality

When the results of Kinsey's conclusion about homosexuality were first published in 1948, they shocked the country. Kinsey reported that, out of the total number of orgasms reported, 6 percent had come from homosexual contacts. Even more surprisingly, 37 percent of the men in the sample had, between the adolescent and age 55, reached at least one orgasm in a homosexual encounter. While only 4 percent were exclusively homosexual (scoring 6 on the Kinsey scale), 13 percent had been more homosexual than heterosexual (scoring 4, 5, or 6 on the Kinsey scale) for at least three years.

The prevalence of homosexual experiences reported by women in the United States was considerably less. Whereas Kinsey reported that 37 percent of men had experienced a homosexual orgasm, only 13 percent of women had done so. Only 5 percent were, for any three-year period, more homosexual than heterosexual (4, 5, or 6 on the Kinsey scale) and only 2 percent were exclusively homosexual (6 on the Kinsey scale).

A more recent reanalysis of Kinsey's research, which includes data collected through 1963, reports similar findings (Gebhard and Johnson, 1979). There is, however, one major problem with Kinsey's research: the estimates are based on a non-representative sample—what sociologists call a "convenience" sample. Kinsey was offered entrée to certain institutional groups through friends and contacts. The resulting sample was overloaded with people from Midwestern colleges and thus overrepresented young, educated, urban whites. Given that Kinsey's own research demonstrated that sexual practices vary depending on factors such as these, we must interpret these data with a degree of caution (Fay, Turner, Klassen, and Gagnon, 1989).

More recent studies with more representative samples have suggested that Kinsey's figures are probably too high. Hunt (1974), for example, conducted telephone interviews of a representative nationwide sample, and estimated that 17 percent of men had at least one homosexual experience, and 1 percent were exclusively homosexual (recall that Kinsey reported 37 percent and 4 percent, respectively). For women, 13 percent reported at least one experience (the same percentage reported by Kinsey) and .5 percent reported exclusive homosexuality (compared to Kinsey's 2 percent).

Robert Fay and his colleagues (Fay, Gagnon, Klassen, and Turner, 1989) re-examined data from a 1970 Kinsey Institute of Sex Research (of Indiana University) survey of 1450 adult men. After incorporating adjustments for possible biases resulting from the non-representative data, they estimate that 20 percent of all adult men in the United States in 1970 had, at some point in their life, had sexual contact to the point of orgasm with another man. Only 7 percent had homosexual contact after the age of 19 and just less than 2 percent had homosexual contact in the previous year. They also estimated that "3 percent of adult men had, at some time during adulthood, same-sex sexual contacts at least 'fairly often' or 'occasional' " (Fay, Gagnon, Klassen, and Turner, 1989).

In an analysis of the General Social Survey collected annually by the National Opinion Research Center, Smith (1991) found that only 2 percent of sexually active men 18 years or older reported homosexual activity during the previous 12 months (the same figure reported by Fay and his colleagues). Among both men and women respondents, 5 to 6 percent reported some homosexual activity since turning 18 (compared to 7 percent of men reported by Fay and his colleagues).

Only 1 percent of men and women reported exclusively homosexual activity.

Even more recently, Billy and his colleagues (Billy; Tanfer, Grady, and Klepinger, 1993) at the Battelle Human Affairs Research Center in Seattle, Washington, estimate that only 1 percent of a representative national sample of 3,321 20–39 year old men had engaged in "exclusively homosexual" sexual activity in the previous ten years. Perhaps even more surprisingly, only 2 percent had engaged in any homosexual activity in the previous ten years. Despite the fact that these estimates were not dramatically different from those reported earlier by Fay and his colleagues (1989), and by Smith (1991), the Battelle study attracted national headlines when it was released in April of 1993 (e.g., *New York Times,* 1993). Much was made of the fact that these estimates were dramatically lower than those reported by Kinsey 45 years earlier. The press seemed especially intrigued by these findings since Bill Clinton had actively courted the presumably significant homosexual vote, and had actively fought to have the military ban on homosexuality lifted. If homosexuality is so uncommon, they wondered aloud, why all the fuss?

But are these estimates accurate? Because of the sensitivity of homosexuality questions, even the more current and methodologically sophisticated estimates are probably low. Indeed, it seems reasonable to conclude, as Fay and his colleagues have (1989:346), "that more men will falsely report the absence of same-gender sexual experiences than will report experiences that never occurred." This seems especially true in face-to-face surveys, which is the method used by Fay and his colleagues, 1989, Smith, 1991, and Billy and his colleagues, 1993. In face-to-face interviews respondents may feel less anonymous than they would in a written survey or a phone survey.

Given the various problems with these studies, what are we to conclude about the prevalence homosexuality? The most obvious conclusion is that we simply do not know how prevalent homosexual behavior is. Indeed, all estimates must be interpreted with caution. If we are to take findings of the more current studies to be conservative, then we might conclude that at least 5 to 7 percent of men and women have had at least one homosexual orgasm since they have been adults (after the age of 18 or 19). Significantly fewer people have engaged in homosexual behavior in the previous year (perhaps 2 to 4 percent of men), and even fewer (perhaps 1 to 2 percent of men) have been exclusively homosexual for a significant period of time.

We might also conclude from these data that there are at least three important demographic correlates of homosexuality. The first is gender. While many of the more recent studies have focused exclusively on male homosexuality, most research suggests that homosexuality is much less common in women than it is in men (e.g., Kinsey, Pomeroy, Martin, and Gebhard, 1953; Hunt, 1974). The second is age. Notice that while Fay and his colleagues (1989) estimate that almost 20 percent of men have had a homosexual experience some time in their life, slightly less than 7 percent have had an experience after turning 20 years old. The third important demographic factor is education. Fay and his colleagues (1989) report much higher levels of homosexual experiences among the educated, with 32 percent of college graduates and 17 percent of those with less than a high school education reporting at least one homosexual experience.

Forms of Homosexuality

Another way to consider social distribution issues is to isolate various forms of homosexuality. There are any of a number of ways researchers may do this. Some researchers, especially those who define homosexuality as a behavior, have found it fruitful to make distinctions between different kinds of homo-sexuals (i.e., people who participate in differ-ent kinds of homosexual behavior). Laud Humphreys, for example, talks about the "trade" (Humphreys, 1970—a married, het-erosexual man who, unsatisfied with his sex life at home, might occasionally seek a sexual outlet (in the role of insertee) in a public re-stroom or park. David Luckenbill (1985) talks about adolescents and young men who enter into homosexuality as prostitutes. Using the justification that they are only doing it for money, and putting limits on the kinds of acts in which they will engage (usually they assume the role of insertee), they can main-tain a heterosexual identity (Luckenbill, 1985). There are, of course, also prostitutes who view themselves as homosexual and will do just about anything for their clients (Pitt-man, 1971). The prison homosexual has also received a good deal of attention (Gagnon and Simon, 1968b; Wooden and Parker, 1982). Like the "trade," he views himself as a hetero-sexual who, because he has few heterosexual outlets, seeks sexual satisfaction from other men.

For those who define homosexuality as an "erotic orientation," it makes little sense to talk about different kinds of homosexuals be-cause there is only one kind of "true" homo-sexual. The "true" homosexuals are those who are sexually attracted to members of their own sex. But even their experiences and adjustments will be different. Bell and Wein-berg (1978) argue that homosexuals can be distinguished along empirical indicators of "coupling" (i.e., whether the person is in a stable relationship), sexual problems, adjust-ment problems, promiscuity, and amount of "cruising" (i.e., actively searching for homo-sexual partners). The *closed-couple* category is for homosexuals in a stable relationship who score low on number of sexual problems, number of sexual partners, regret about their homosexuality, and amount of cruising. The *open-coupled* are those in a stable relationship

who are active sexually, do considerable cruising, engaged in a wide variety of sexual techniques, and tend to regret their homosex-uality. The *functionals* are not coupled, score high on sexual activity and number of part-ners, and score low on regret over their homosexuality and sexual problems. The *dys-functionals* are not coupled, are very active sexually, but regret their homosexuality and have many sexual problems. Finally, the *asex-uals* are not coupled, are sexually inactive, have a number of sexual problems, and regret their homosexuality.

For those who define homosexuality as an "identity," the only kind of typology that is useful is one that focuses on the process by which one adopts a homosexual identity. The most significant typology of this kind has been introduced by Richard Troiden (1988; 1989), who draws upon the work of other subjectivist sociologists like Kenneth Plum-mer (1975) and Barbara Ponse (1978) as well as his own research (1979). Troiden contends that one becomes a homosexual in four stages. The *sensitization* stage occurs before puberty. During this stage, lesbians and gay men do not see themselves as homosexual but they begin to have social experiences that will be interpreted later life as indications that they were somewhat unlike same-sex peers. They may not feel the same attractions or enjoy the same games and activities as their same-sex peers (Troiden, 1988). Lesbians describe being more "masculine," enjoying "male activities" more than "female activi-ties," and gay men report not liking sports the way other boys do. While there is consid-erable debate as to whether this difference is real or merely perceived in retrospection (Kitsuse, 1962; Green, 1987), for the subjectiv-ist it really does not matter. In the social con-struction of the self, perceived differences *are* real differences, at least in their functional consequences.

The *identity confusion* stage occurs as ado-lescents who have largely taken their heterosexuality as a given begin to question their sexual identity. This identity confusion may result from increased awareness that one enjoys different activities from same-sex peers, is physically attracted to same-sex peers, or it may come from actual sexual experiences. Homosexual adults report that same-sex attractions began to occur at the average age of 13 for men and 15 for women. Adolescents, however, do not begin to think they "might" be homosexual until the average age of 17 (men) and 18 (women) (Troiden, 1988).

In the *identity assumption* stage, most often occurring in late adolescence or young adulthood, the individual begins to accept and, at least to other homosexuals, present a homosexual identity. This homosexual self-definition is most likely to occur in women as a result of a prolonged attachment to another woman. For men, it more likely occurs after social and sexual contacts at a gay bar or some other homosexual gathering. It occurs slightly earlier for men (between 19 and 21) than for women (between 21 and 23). During the identity assumption stage, homosexuals may tolerate their new definition of self, but they are not likely to be entirely pleased with it (Troiden, 1988).

During the *commitment* stage, the individual becomes more comfortable with a homosexual identity. There is increased happiness associated with what is now seen as a valid identity. Homosexuals are also more likely to accept homosexuality as a way of life rather than merely a sexual identity. Externally, commitment manifests itself in same-sex romantic relationships and disclosure to nonhomosexual friends and family (Troiden, 1988).

Homosexual Experiences

Other descriptive research has focused on the experiences of those who perceive themselves to be homosexuals. The most important research of this kind comes from interviews of 929 self-identified homosexuals (651 men and 278 women) conducted by Alan Bell and Martin Weinberg (1978) of the Alfred C. Kinsey Institute of Sex Research. Of course, the very fact that the respondents identified themselves as homosexual and were willing to talk to researchers means that the sample is very unique. Therefore, we should be careful not to overgeneralize these findings.

Concerning sexual promiscuity, Bell and Weinberg (1978) found that homosexual women are, in comparison to men, less interested in impersonal sexual encounters, are more likely to emphasize monogamy in their relationships, and have fewer sexual partners. Men are also much more likely to look for sex in public places. At the same time, however, sex in public restrooms, theaters, and parks is, even for men, relatively uncommon. More common among homosexual men is cruising gay bars (Bell and Weinberg, 1978). Bell and Weinberg (1978) maintain that promiscuity in the male homosexual community should not come as a surprise because males are, in general, more likely to separate sex from affection. Gay men do tend to be more promiscuous than heterosexual men. This should not be surprising either, given that society "provides them with little or no opportunity to meet on anything more than a sexual basis. Driven underground, segregated in what have been termed 'sexual marketplaces,' threatened but perhaps also stimulated by the danger of their enterprise, homosexual men would be expected to have an enormous number of fleeting sexual encounters" (Bell and Weinberg, 1978:101). The promiscuity of the male homosexual community should not be taken to suggest that gay men are uninterested in long-lasting monogamous relationships (Peplau, 1991). Many homosexual women *and* men desire lasting relationships but, with considerable societal forces stacked against them—few of the legal rights of heterosexual married couples, family pressures and rejections, increased job tensions because of sexual orientation—long-term relationships are difficult (Bell and Weinberg, 1978).

Only about one-fourth of the homosexual sample regretted or had seriously considered stopping their homosexual activity, and over 85 percent would not take a "heterosexual pill," even if one existed.

Somewhat surprisingly, homosexual men reported no more work dissatisfaction or mistreatment than is typical among heterosexual men. While the picture was somewhat less clear for homosexual women, in general they did not report dramatically less satisfaction than heterosexual women.

Concerning religion, homosexual men were somewhat alienated from formal religious organizations. These patterns were even more pronounced for women who, in addition to feeling rejected because of the deviant sexual identity, likely reject the "femininity" of the female role in many churches.

Only about one-fifth of the gay men had been married, while slightly more than one-third of the lesbians Bell and Weinberg interviewed had been married. Bell and Weinberg suggest that the higher incidence of marriage among women might, in part, be attributed to the fact that women can have a sexual relationship without being aroused. For men, this is impossible. It is also possible that, because women are likely to accept their homosexual identity somewhat later in life, they have a higher incidence of marriage.

Bell and Weinberg report that homosexuals tend to be less psychologically well-djusted and not as happy as heterosexuals. However, these differences are largely a result of the psychological problems of "dysfunctionals" and "asexuals" (discussed earlier). Those homosexuals who have "come to terms with their homosexuality, who do not regret their sexual orientation, and who can function effectively sexually and socially, are no more distressed psychologically than are heterosexual men and women" (Bell and Weinberg, 1978:216).

THEORIES OF HOMOSEXUALITY

In this section, we will introduce both medical and sociological theories of homosexuality. These different theoretical traditions vary widely not only in how they explain deviance but, perhaps more importantly, in what they are trying to explain. From a medical perspective, homosexuality is generally assumed to be a *sexual orientation* that either exists at birth or develops early in life (Troiden, 1988). Medical theories, furthermore, tend to look for the roots of sexual orientation in the biological or psychiatric makeup of the individual. From a sociological standpoint, homosexuality is generally defined as a *behavior* (objectivist conception) or an *identity* (subjectivist conception). Sociological theories, especially subjectivist theories, are much less concerned with questions of etiology. Sociologists generally focus on explanations and consequences of norms and societal reactions. Instead of asking questions such as, "Why do they do it?" sociologists are more inclined to ask, "Why do we care that they do it?" In fact, many sociologists, again primarily subjectivists, are outspoken in their criticism of the medical preoccupation with etiology (e.g., Simon and Gagnon, 1967; Plummer, 1975; Goode, 1981). When sociological theories are etiological in focus (primarily objectivist theories), the search for explanations generally begins with environmental rather than biological factors.

Medical Theories of Homosexuality

There are at least two important reasons for reviewing medical theories of homosexuality. First, the medical theories dominate current explanations of homosexuality; indeed, given their predominance, we would be remiss not to mention them. Second, in order to demonstrate the limitations of such theories (and thus the need for a sociology of homosexuality), we must be willing to educate ourselves as to what the theories are.

Medical theorists are, for the most part, *essentialist* in perspective. (For a detailed description of the essentialist perspective, see Goode, 1981; Plummer, 1984; Harry, 1985; Risman and Schwartz, 1988.) Essentialists assume that homosexuality is a relatively distinct category of *sexual orientation* that exists independent of time and space. Unlike other forms of deviance that are culturally defined, homosexuality just is. It is immutable, appearing in all societies at about the same rate, and being characterized by similar elements in all societies (Whitam and Mathy, 1986:182). It exists a priori to any cultural definitions as to its "rightness" or "wrongness." Since homosexuality exists independent of culture, it stands to reason that essentialists assume culture to be largely irrelevant as an etiological factor. The causes of homosexual erotic desires are the same in the United States as they are in New Guinea because homosexuality in the United States is the same as homosexuality in New Guinea.

There are two perspectives within this medical tradition, each varying widely in its political and social implications. The first, the *sickness model*, has been dominated by psychiatrists and other medical theorists intent on explaining the "abnormality" homosexuality. Homosexuality is, from this perspective, a pathological divergence from a natural heterosexual identity. Homosexuality is something someone *has*.

The second, and currently more popular medical perspective, is that one is born homosexual, or is at least born with a homosexual predisposition. From this *biological predisposition* perspective, homosexuality is not seen as something someone *has* or even *chooses*. Rather, it is something someone *is*.

The sickness model begins with Sigmund Freud (1905). Freud believed that it was healthy for men and women to pass through a homoerotic stage on their way to heterosexuality. However, a male who had an abnor-

mally close relationship with his mother might develop a feminine or passive nature. If he also had a distant and strained relationship with his father (resulting in an unsatisfactory masculine identification), he could become "fixated" in homosexuality during the phallic stage of psychosexual development (Gould, 1979; Marmor, 1980; Diamant, 1987).

The Freudian influence has resulted in numerous studies on the relationship between parents and children in the etiology of homosexuality. These studies have shown that homosexual men, in comparison to heterosexual men, tend to come from dysfunctional homes and often have overprotective, seductive mothers and absent or hostile fathers (e.g., Bieber, 1962; Saghir and Robins, 1973; Bell, Weinberg, and Hammersmith, 1981). Compared to heterosexual men, gay men are also more likely to have been physically abused as children (Harry, 1989). Critics argue, however, that homosexuals can and do come from perfectly "healthy" families. They come from families with distant mothers and dominant fathers (Marmor, 1980). Similarly, dominant mothers and distant fathers are not uncommon among heterosexuals (Marmor, 1980).

The Freudian (or psychoanalytic) model played a significant role in the controversial stance taken toward homosexuality by the American Psychiatric Association (APA) during the 1950s, 1960s, and 1970s (discussed in Chapter 6). Because the APA has generally accepted psychoanalytic theories of sexual "perversion," homosexuality has fit nicely alongside other psychological disorders listed in the APA's *Diagnostic and Statistical Manual of Mental Disorders (DSM)*. As we discussed in Chapter 6, however, the APA no longer lists homosexuality as a mental disorder. Many would argue, however, that the APA dropped homosexuality as a disorder not because scientific evidence has proved it to be something other than perversion, but because it became politically damaging to categorize homosexuality as a sickness.

If homosexuality is not an illness, then what is it? For a time, it was popular to conceptualize it as a sexual *preference*. From this perspective one simply chooses, *and should have every right to choose,* a homosexual lifestyle. Interestingly, however, for some gay rights advocates this is only slightly more palatable than conceptualizing homosexuality as sickness. Such a conception is not only empirically inaccurate, they argue, but such assumptions make it easier to discriminate against those who make "immoral" choices. Medical theorist John Money, an advocate of homosexual rights, sees it this way:

> *In the human species, a person does not prefer to be homosexual instead of heterosexual, nor to be bisexual instead of monosexual.* Sexual preference *is a moral and political term. Conceptually it implies voluntary choice, that is, that one chooses, or prefers, to be homosexual instead of heterosexual or bisexual, and visa versa. Politically,* sexual preference *is a dangerous term, for it implies that if homosexuals choose their preference, then they can be legally forced, under threat of punishment, to choose to be heterosexual (Money, 1987:385).*

Medical theorists like Money are in an interesting position. Like those who believe that one should have the right to "choose" homosexuality, they want to distance themselves from the psychiatric assumption that one sexual orientation is normal and the other abnormal. But for Money and others like him, one's "right" to be a homosexual comes because one *is* homosexual—because one has no choice but to be homosexual. Homosexuality is not a sexual preference, it is a sexual *orientation*. From this perspective, homosexuals and heterosexuals are just different. No better, no worse. Like left-handers and right-handers they are just different.

Is there any evidence that people are born

homosexual? In an important early twin study, Kallman (1952) studied 85 twin pairs where at least one of the twins was overtly homosexual. Of the 45 dizygotic (fraternal) twin pairs, the concordance rate (10 percent) was not unlike the proportion of male homosexuals found in the general population. Of the 40 monozygotic (identical) pairs, however, the concordance rate was 100 percent. That is, for 40 identical twin pairs, homosexuality in one twin always meant homosexuality in the other. Attempts to replicate these findings have produced either much lower concordance rates, or no concordance at all, leading many to question the usefulness of genetic theories (Diamant, 1987). However, in a recent twin study, psychologist Michael Bailey and psychiatrist Richard Pillard have rekindled the interest in genetics, demonstrating that the concordance rate among identical twins is three times higher than among fraternal twins (*Newsweek*, 1992). While many social scientists remain somewhat skeptical (after all, identical twins not only share identical genes, but they also tend to share identical environments), this evidence creates the very real possibility that genetics play a part in determining homosexuality.

Research on the source of the genetic link has often focused on prenatal hormones, which supposedly influence fetal development along masculine or feminine paths (e.g., Money, 1987; 1988). The basic argument is that high levels of androgen predispose one to be attracted to women and low levels of androgen predispose one to be attracted to men. Why hormonal levels vary is a matter of some debate, but most of the research has focused on the hypothalamus, a part of the brain that determines the production of sex hormones (Troiden, 1988). Simon LeVay, a neurobiologist at the Sauk Institute for Biological Studies in La Jolla, California, examined 41 brains (19 gay men who had died of AIDS; 16 presumably heterosexual men, 6 of whom had died of AIDS; and 6 women), and found the hypothalamus to be smaller in gay men than heterosexual men, more like that found in women (*Time,* 1991). When the news broke in the popular media in September of 1991, the hypothalamus became famous overnight. Finally, many people quickly assumed, we have found the key to homosexual orientation. Like other "too good to be true" explanations, however, this study has its flaws. Since AIDS affects the brain, perhaps the disease causes the size difference. Or, perhaps the size difference is the result of homosexuality rather than the cause. Whatever the case, the point is that this study has in no way settled the etiological debate.

Other evidence for a biological predisposition has come from studies suggesting that homosexuals perceived themselves as being "different" from their same-sex peers at a very early age. Saghir and Robins (1973), for example, examined the childhood histories of 90 homosexual men. Two-thirds reported being girllike during childhood, and 77 percent remembered avoiding male games and playing primarily with girls. Approximately 3 percent of the heterosexual controls reported similar experiences. More recent researchers (Harry, 1985; Bell, Weinberg, and Hammersmith, 1981; Whitam, 1983; Green, 1987) have reported similar patterns.

But there is a problem. This research is retrospective. That is, homosexual adults are asked to recount their childhood experiences and feelings. As we will discuss in more detail shortly, there are problems with retrospective research of this type. Not only can one forget childhood experiences, but past experiences can sometimes be reinterpreted in light of a redefinition of self as a homosexual.

To avoid the problems inherent in retrospective studies, psychiatrist Richard Green conducted a longitudinal cohort study of 60 "feminine," or "sissy," boys between the ages of 4 and 12. Sissy boys wanted to be girls, preferring dresses to pants, dolls to trucks, girl playmates to boy playmates, and little girl games to rough sports. A matched control sample of "normal" boys was also studied. Importantly, the sissy boys were not picked because they had identified themselves as gay. Most, in fact, were too young to perceive of themselves in sexual terms. They were picked because they had extremely "feminine" qualities.

Fifteen years later, three-fourths of the "sissy" boys and only one of the "normal" boys reported being homosexual or bisexual. Other measures of sexual orientation (e.g., sexual fantasies and erotic images during masturbation) similarly suggested much greater rates of homosexuality among the "sissy" boys.

Again, at face value, these findings are convincing, but what do they mean? Are cross-gender behavior tendencies the cause of homosexuality or the result of an innate homosexuality orientation? It all depends on the theoretical framework out of which one works. Psychoanalysts, for example, cite findings such as these to support their contention that an overly possessive mother leads to a female identification of the male child and impedes normal psychosexual development toward heterosexuality. It is also possible that feminine boys are labeled "fags," and their subsequent homosexuality is merely the fulfillment of that societally imposed label. These two interpretations are seemingly as feasible as the more commonly accepted biological perspective, which views cross-gender behavior as an outward manifestation of a biological predisposition.

There are social scientists doing cross-gender behavior research such as this (e.g., Whitam and Mathy, 1986), but they also tend to be biological predispositionalists, assuming cross-gender behavior is evidence of a sexual orientation that exists at birth (Troiden, 1988).

Even though biological predisposition theorists are generally outspoken in their support of homosexual rights, their very suggestion that homosexuals are biologically different from heterosexuals promotes:

> . . . *the very intolerance of homosexuality they hope to alleviate through their research. The prejudice against homosexuality does not stem fundamentally from the simple rejection of homosexual acts and emotional reactions. This prejudice springs from the belief that homosexuals are not quite the men or women they ought to be and, in fact, are the females and males they ought not to be (De Cecco, 1987:111).*

Sociological Theories of Homosexuality

Before we begin our discussion of sociological perspectives on homosexuality, one point should be clarified. It is not necessarily our intention to "disprove" medical theories and "prove" sociological theories. We fully accept the feasibility of predispositional factors. This is an important admonition because sociological and medical theorists are often seen as offering conflicting or contradictory explanations. However, we would argue that medical and sociological theories do not necessarily contradict one another. The two perspectives merely explain different things. It is not a matter of one being right and the other wrong. Each ignores or dismisses as unimportant the very aspects of homosexuality that the other finds most intriguing.

What is it that sociologists find most intriguing about homosexuality? First, even if biological theories can account for a behavioral tendency, they cannot tell us why this behavior is deviance in the first place. In order to do this, we need to consider either norms (objectivist conception) or labels (subjectivist conception).

Second, even if biological theories can account for a behavioral tendency, they have to this point been unsuccessful at explaining the entire etiological story. Most studies of identical twins indicate that when one twin

is gay the other is not always gay; this suggests that something other than biology is going on.

Third, even if biological theories can account for a behavioral tendency, we need a sociology of homosexuality to explain the origin of homosexual self-perceptions. Medical theorists might tell us where homosexual orientations come from but they can tell us nothing of the social meaning of being "a homosexual." In this sense, homosexuality is, as sociologist Richard Troiden reminds us, a social construction:

> *Before they can identify themselves in terms of a social condition or category, they must learn that a social category representing the activity or feelings exists (e.g., homosexual preferences or homosexual behavior); discover that other people occupy the social category (e.g., homosexuals exist as a group); and perceive that their own socially constructed needs and interests are more similar to those of persons who occupy that social category than they are different. In addition, they must begin to identify with those included in the social category; decide that they qualify for membership in the social category on the basis of activities and feelings in various settings; elect to label themselves in terms of the social category on the basis of activities and feelings in various settings; elect to label themselves in terms of the social category (i.e., define themselves as "being" the social category in contexts where category membership is relevant); and incorporate and absorb these situationally linked identities into their self-concepts over time (Troiden, 1988:1–2).*

Finally, even if biological theories can account for a behavioral tendency, this empirical fact cannot be itself explain the current popularity of biological theories. Sociologists, especially subjectivists, have looked with fascination upon homosexuality as it has been defined as "sin," redefined as "sickness," redefined as "preference," and redefined again as "a biological predisposition." From a sociological standpoint, these shifts have not necessarily occurred because of an increased scientific understanding of the roots of homosexuality. We might hypothesize that the shift has, at least in part, occurred as the gay rights movement, and others sensitive to gay causes, have demanded that a shift occur. As sociologists, then, we will argue that "accepted" conceptions and explanations have changed as societal reactions have changed. Changes in explanations of homosexuality may appear to be supported by empirical evidence, and it is certainly true that proponents of the various viewpoints have "attempted to cloak themselves in the respectability of science" (Gonsiorek and Weinrich, 1991a:xii), but these changes have not occurred only because of empirical findings.

This represents but a few of the issues important in the sociology of homosexuality. How the sociologist addresses these issues depends in part on whether he or she sees the world through the eyes of an objectivist or a subjectivist.

Objectivist Theories. Objectivists are interested in why people break the rules. Like medical theorists, they focus on the rule breakers. There are, however, important differences between medical and objectivist theories. First, medical theorists generally define homosexuality as a sexual orientation, while objectivists generally define it as a behavior. Also, medical theorists are essentialists, arguing that homosexual orientations exist independent of cultural norms. Since they assume that homosexuality transcends time and space, their theories must be able to explain homosexual orientations in the United States and New Guinea equally well. Since, from an objectivist perspective, there is no deviance apart from norms, explanations of deviance must begin with a consideration of important social and cultural forces (structural strains, a breakdown of social bonds, and social learning) outside the individual. Objectivists argue that it is misguided to explain deviance with internal theories if the

very behavior one is trying to explain is only considered deviance because it violates cultural norms. How do the genes know what the norms are?

There are very few objectivist theories of homosexuality. This neglect by objectivists is indeed unfortunate because there are a few *social* facts about homosexuality that the biological predisposition theories seem to be inadequate in explaining. How does the biological predisposition theorist explain, for example, the tendency to grow out of homosexuality? Can he or she explain the higher rates of homosexuality among men than women? What about the greater homosexual experiences of the educated? How does the biological predisposition theorist explain the tendency for individuals to move in to and out of homosexuality at various times in their life? Biological predispositions do not come and go so easily, do they?

Micro-Objectivist. We may get some of the answers with a consideration of micro-objectivist theories. Micro-objectivist theories are not designed to explain variation in rates of norm-violating behavior. However, because they focus on social factors in individual norm-violations, they may provide some insights into rates and patterns.

Although there are no *control* theories that focus explicitly on homosexuality, we can speculate as to how a control theorist might explain homosexual behavior. As a behavior with considerable social disapproval, we could hypothesize that homosexuality would increase as stakes in conformity decrease (Hirschi, 1969). That is to say, the stronger one feels attached to family and friends (Hirschi's attachment), the greater one's commitment to and investment in conventional activities (Hirschi's involvement), and the more one believes homosexuality is wrong (Hirschi's belief), the less likely he or she is to violate sexual norms.

There is, however, a problem. Hirschi all but ignores the question of motivation, assuming that we are all born with an inclination toward aggression and selfishness. His is not theory of deviance, but of conformity. We would all be deviants if we thought we could get away with it without hurting family, our chances for a comfortable life, and so on. The equivalent assumption in the study of homosexuality would be that we are all born with an inclination toward homosexuality but that cultural controls "force" heterosexuality on us. This seems unlikely. Even if we assume sexual preference to be neutral at birth, we cannot explain how a breakdown of social bonds could, by itself, explain homosexuality. Given these problems, it may be useful to consider how biological predispositions and social bonds work together to explain behavior. Perhaps some are predisposed toward homosexuality, but whether they engage in homosexual behavior depends on their stake in conformity.

There is another way in which control theory might be used. We might focus on one's ability to *neutralize* the norms against homosexuality. Thus, for example, a man who engages in impersonal bathroom sex (Humphreys, 1970) may believe strongly in the norm against homosexuality. He justifies his act, however, by claiming that he is not sexually satisfied at home. In a similar way, prison inmates may engage in homosexuality while maintaining heterosexual self-perceptions. Their justification is that there are no other options for sex. Even those who have accepted the identity of homosexual may only be able to do so after coming to believe that they were born homosexual. In believing homosexuality to be something that was forced upon them, they are able to justify a behavior that they themselves may believe to be wrong.

Social Learning theories are micro-objectivist theories that focus on the social process by which one learns that a particular kind of behavior is rewarding. Refusing to get caught up in the debate over who the "real" homosexuals are, learning theorists focus their attention on explaining homosexual behavior.

We only need to look to other cultures to realize that homosexual behavior is to a large extent learned. In cultures where same-sex behaviors are encouraged, same-sex behaviors are commonly practiced. Thus, among the Sambia of New Guinea, who we introduced at the beginning of this chapter, prepubertal boys are required to ingest semen, which, they are told, will make them grow strong and live long lives (Baldwin and Baldwin, 1989).

In cultures where homosexuality is not condoned, we must look harder for a connection to learning theory. One explanation that is commonly accepted by the general public is that homosexuality can be "taught" by those who condone homosexual behavior. However, there is no empirical evidence that supports this position (Slovenko, 1980). If homosexuals are not teaching other homosexuals, how is homosexuality learned? Social learning might occur through *differential reinforcement* (Burgess and Akers, 1966) of homosexual thoughts and experiences. As Kinsey and his colleagues have reminded us (1948), homosexual experiences are relatively common, especially among adolescents. For example, adolescents will sometimes masturbate together (Akers, 1985). The more pleasurable these experiences are, the more likely they are to be repeated. The more they are repeated, the more likely that sexual pleasure will be associated with other males. The more that sexual pleasure is associated with other males, the more likely that fantasy during masturbation will involve other males. Taken together, these pleasurable experiences will further condition males to be sexually attracted to other males and increase the probability that homosexual experiences will be repeated (Akers, 1985). If reinforcing homosexual thoughts and experiences are combined with negative heterosexual experiences, the reinforcement values of homosexual contact will be exaggerated.

Differential reinforcement could also include parental reinforcement of gender-inappropriate thoughts and behaviors. Previous research on cross-gender behavior has demonstrated that homosexual men were "girllike" during childhood and homosexual women "boylike" during childhood (see Bell, Weinberg, and Hammersmith, 1981; Green, 1987). Many of the effeminate boys in Green's study (1987) were actually encouraged in their cross-gender behavior. From a social learning perspective, a boy who is encouraged to act and feel like a girl is probably more likely to engage in future gender-inappropriate behavior, including homosexuality. As he comes to identify with the interests, needs, and desires of women, he sees himself as a woman and seeks to satisfy his erotic desires as a woman would (Green, 1987). This is not to say that, if a mother lets her girl play with trucks or her boy with dolls, her child is likely to grow up to be a homosexual. A more reasonable conclusion is that a son who is encouraged to act like a daughter is more likely to experience feelings of confusion and inadequacy (Bjorklund and Bjorklund, 1988).

Learning also takes place within the context of the homosexual subculture through the process of *differential identification*. Surrounded by others who think and feel the same way, the homosexual is no longer abnormal. Within the subculture, homosexuals learn that there is nothing wrong with being homosexual. They learn a "vocabulary of motives" (Troiden, 1988)—a set of explanations for why they are the way they are. The subculture provides the knowledge and skills needed to function as a full-fledged member of the group (Humphreys and Miller, 1980). Contrary to popular belief, the values and norms of the homosexual subculture do not always differ from those of the dominant culture. That is, "they" may not be all that different than "we" are. At the same time, however, homosexuals who are fully integrated into the homosexual subculture may look and act more like homosexuals, according to popular stereotypes, are "supposed" to look and act.

Subjectivist Theories.

Given the importance of 'reaction' in shaping the nature of homosexual experiences, it is surprising that most studies of homosexuality perform what would have appeared to be the impossible: they divorce homosexuality from the societal context, take for granted the existence of "reactions," and study homosexuality as an individualistic phenomenon. But I am arguing that the homosexual experience is very much a social product, variable between cultures and historical periods, and that it simply cannot be comprehended apart from the broader societal context in which it is enmeshed (Plummer, 1975:102).

Subjectivist theories attempt to explain the origins and application of deviance definitions and explanations (interest group theories), the social process by which individual labelers interpret and define deviants (definitional theories), and the effect of these societal reactions on the behavior of individual "deviants" (labeling theories). The primary focus is on the consequences—both for society and individual—of societal reactions. Since societal reactions are *the* key to understanding deviance, subjectivists are, as we can see in the preceding quote, somewhat critical of those who have failed to recognize their importance.

Given that societal reactions are often ignored by those who study homosexuality, it is not surprising that subjectivist theories take as problematic the very "facts" others unquestioningly accept about homosexuality. As an example, consider how the subjectivists challenge the commonly accepted essentialist assumption that humans have a single, stable, "true" sexual orientation (see McIntosh, 1968; Plummer, 1975; Risman and Schwartz, 1988). Even if people can be placed on a sexuality continuum based on their sexual behaviors (Kinsey, Pomeroy, and Martin, 1948), essentialists assume that, in terms of their "true" sexual orientations, there are primarily two types of people: homosexuals and heterosexuals (McIntosh, 1968). Those scientists who assume homosexuality to be an "orientation" and hope to discover the "cause" of this orientation by studying a group of homosexuals are, from a subjectivist perspective, missing the point. Subjectivist theories assume instead that conceptualizing homosexuality as a stable orientation is, in itself, a possible object of study (McIntosh, 1968:183). From a subjectivist point of view, such distinctions only exist because people believe they exist; that is, they exist *because of* societal reactions. Society both creates and enforces this distinction.

This point is perhaps most clearly articulated by Mary McIntosh who, in an early subjectivist statement, criticized the tendency to dichotomize homosexual orientations:

> One might expect social categorizations of this sort to be to some extent self-fulfilling prophecies: if the culture defines people as falling into distinct types— black and white, criminal and non-criminal, homosexual and normal—then these types will tend to become polarized, highly differentiated from each other (McIntosh, 1968:184).

The currently popular tendency to dichotomize homosexual orientations effectively demonstrates the usefulness of subjectivist theories. Focusing on important interest groups involved in creating popular understandings, macro-subjectivist theories explain how society has come to accept the empirically questionable belief that two discrete sexual orientation categories exist. Micro-subjectivist theories, on the other hand, consider how this categorization impacts the experiences and perceptions of individual labelers and those who are labeled.

Macro-Subjectivist Theories.   Given the variability of the "deviance" label across cultures, it seems reasonable to wonder, as Kenneth Plummer (1981b:61) has wondered, "what makes people respond as they do to homosexuality?" Why have we bothered "to invent a concern for homosexuality at all?" Even beyond definitional questions such as these, macro-subjectivist theories focus on the social construction of commonly accepted conceptions of homosexuality (e.g., that humans have a single, stable, "true" sexual orientation) and the social construction of explanations of deviance (e.g., that prenatal hormones cause homosexuality).

Interest group theories assume that deviance is a product of the power struggle among competing interests in society. As Conrad and Schneider (1980) and, more recently, Greenberg (1988) remind us, definitions of homosexuality as deviance—or perhaps more accurately, sin—go back many centuries to early biblical accounts of homosexuality. One of the most influential biblical stories is found in Genesis 19:1–11; it describes God's destruction of the town of Sodom (where we get the word sodomy) because of the assumed homosexual "wickedness" of its residents. The biblical account tells how the men of Sodom demanded that two male guests be turned over to them so that they might "know them." The meaning of the Hebrew verb *to know* has generally been interpreted to mean "sexual intercourse." Similarly condemning in the Old Testament is the Leviticus 21:13 reference to "men lieing with men." In the New Testament, Paul condemns women who "exchanged natural relations with unnatural ones" and men who, abandoning "natural relations with women," were "inflamed with lust for one another" (Romans 1:26–27, New International Version).

The exact meanings of these passages, which continue to be debated by biblical scholars, are of less interest to us here than the fact that these passages have generally been interpreted by contemporary Jews and Christians to mean that homosexuality is an immoral "sin against nature." This has caused, and continues to cause (e.g., Hiltner, 1980; Clark, Brown, and Hochstein, 1990), considerable tension between homosexuals and the churches.

Given the historical connection between church and state, biblically based beliefs about the "immoral" nature of homosexuality have often been translated into legal statutes against homosexuality. According to Conrad and Schneider (1980:178), throughout much of history the churches welcomed the opportunity to turn punitive responsibilities over to the state. The state served as a kind of "henchman" for the church.

Beginning in the 1700s, there was increasing speculation that homosexuality could be more appropriately conceptualized as "sickness" rather than "sin." This medicalization trend resulted, during the late 1800s, in the first genetic theories of homosexuality. Interestingly, during the same time period, there was also an increasing trend toward stiff criminal penalties. The simultaneous occurrence of these two trends seems puzzling. After all, how do you punish a genetic illness? Conrad and Schneider (1980), however, maintain that the criminalization trend may actually have stimulated medicalization. This is where the interest group theory becomes fascinating. The churches and the medical community have historically offered, and continue to offer, competing explanations of homosexuality. The churches say it is choice (i.e., sin), and the medical community, while divided on specific explanations, generally focuses on forces (either psychological or psychological) outside the control of individuals. The churches and the medical community are, in effect, competitors. We might hypothesize that during the 1700s, the churches, feeling challenged by medical explanations, used the strong arm of the state to further solidify their domain over homo-

sexuality. Yet, as faith in medical theories increased, their attempt to stake an exclusive claim over homosexuality was unsuccessful. In fact, the trend toward increased prosecution merely made medical definitions and interventions more viable and more urgent (Conrad and Schneider, 1980).

The interest group struggles are, of course, far more complicated than this because, as we discussed earlier in the chapter, the medical community is itself divided on conceptualizations and explanations of homosexuality. For the earliest medical theorists, homosexuality was a communicable disease—something one "caught." For the physicians of the early 1800s, on the other hand, homosexuality remained a sexual deviation, a "disease," but it was congenital rather than acquired. By the late 1800s, increasing numbers of physicians challenged assumptions of abnormality, arguing that homosexuality could be most accurately and compassionately understood as a sexual *variation* rather than a sexual *deviation*. Finally, during the early 1900s, Austrian physician Sigmund Freud repopularized the sexual deviation perspective, arguing that "normal" psychological development always resulted in heterosexuality. Homosexuality was, from this perspective, a "mental illness" (Conrad and Schneider, 1980).

Given the supposed progression of scientific knowledge, it might come as some surprise to learn that most of these explanations, with the exception of the "homosexuality as contagion explanation," remain viable today. That is, despite years of research, the scientific community remains divided on the "real" causes of homosexuality.

As medical and religious leaders continued to fight with each other and among themselves for the right to define and explain homosexuality, there emerged during the 1950s and 1960s another important interest; homosexuals themselves. As a stigmatized, persecuted, and even hated minority, homosexuals had long had reason to be angry and frustrated. However, throughout most of history, homosexuals had no vehicle through which to recognize and express their frustration and demand their rights. It is within this context that the first gay rights movement, the Mettachine Society, emerged with "the heroic objective of liberating one of our largest minorities from . . . social persecution."[2] Given the conservative political climate of the 1950s, the gay rights movement kept a low profile in its first decade, protecting the anonymity of its participants and discouraging direct challenges to the status quo (D'Emilio, 1983). The 1960s, however, brought with it an idealistic president, a new emphasis on civil rights, and a "new breed" of radical gay activists (D'Emilio, 1983). This "new breed" unapologetically pronounced the validity of the homosexual life-style and argued that constitutional rights for homosexuals would come only as a result of political action.

With the advantage of hindsight, we would suggest that the gay rights movement has impacted, and continues to impact, the homosexual community (and, ultimately, society more generally) in at least three important ways. First, the gay rights movement, especially in its early years, was important as a consciousness-raising movement. Homosexuals have historically been ashamed and embarrassed by their "ailment." Rather than seeing themselves as disadvantaged and exploited, they have more commonly seen themselves as the heterosexual community has seen them; as troubled, sick, sexual perverts. The gay rights movement encouraged homosexual men and women to believe that "gay is good" and to see themselves as members of an oppressed minority deserving of full rights and privileges (Voeller, 1980; D'Emilio, 1983).

Second, the gay rights movement has been outspoken in its claims that homosexuality is not a sin, an illness, a weakness, or a disorder. It is not something someone "has," and

it does not need to be "fixed." It is something someone "is." Such claims have been important to homosexuals as they attempt to gain equal rights. Indeed, empirical evidence demonstrates that people who believe that homosexuals are "born that way" hold more positive attitudes toward homosexuals than do people who believe homosexuals "choose to be that way" or "learn to be that way" (Innala and Whitam, 1989).

Finally, with the confidence that, indeed, "gay is good," the gay rights movement has emerged as a political force to be reckoned with (Adam, 1987). With increasing activism, radical organizations like ACT UP and Queer National have used a variety of means (e.g., pickets, visits to public officials, press conferences, and court cases) to bring their causes before the public. ACT UP (the AIDS Coalition To Unleash Power) was formed in 1987 by a small group of New Yorkers who felt that the government was not responding quickly enough to the AIDS crisis (*Newsweek*, 1990). Tired of ACT UP's focus on AIDS, Queer Nation[3] formed in 1990 to employ similar tactics on a number of other issues important to the gay community. Queer Nation will sometimes stage "nights out" or "kiss-ins" in which several groups of gay couples will go into straight bars and begin openly kissing. It is their intent to force the heterosexual world to recognize the realities of the homosexual world (*Newsweek*, August 12, 1991; *Maclean's*, 1990).

Understanding the history of struggles between religious, legal, medical, and homosexual interests is important because it sets the stage for what is today a very emotional battle over homosexuality. Remember that from an interest group perspective, contemporary understandings of homosexuality depend, in large part, on who wins these battles. Is homosexuality an illness, a preference, an orientation, a sin, a crime? Clearly, the answer depends on who one asks.

As a concluding example, consider the

current debate over the morality of homosexuality. The primary players in the debate are the churches, the scientific and medical community, and the homosexual community. Each interest group uses (and sometimes misuses) whatever "facts" it can to support its position. Each is also prone to recognize the biases of another's perspective without recognizing the biases of its own. This is what interest group struggles are all about.

In a recent attempt to answer the question, "Is homosexuality natural?" zoologist John Kirsch and psychobiologist James Weinrich responded to the biblical assertions in Romans 1:26–27 that homosexuality is "against nature," "vile," or "unseemly" with the statement: "Frankly, we believe that many arguments against homosexuality are mere opinion, like this one" (1991:30). Kirsch and Weinrich are, of course, correct. Such assertions are "opinion." But are assertions that homosexuality is *not* "against nature," "vile," or "unseemly" based any less on opinion?

Suppose, for example, that research "proves" homosexuality to be biologically predetermined at birth. This does not mean that religious leaders, even if they fully accept the scientific findings, will finally conclude that homosexuality is moral behavior. It may change how religious leaders respond to the homosexuals (after all, it is no longer their "fault"), but it will not necessarily affect moral judgment of homosexual behavior (Jones and Workman, 1989). To illustrate, consider how society might respond to the "proof" that alcoholics are biologically predetermined to be alcoholics. Acceptance of this "proof" will not necessarily change society's belief that alcohol and alcoholism are "bad." Regardless of what causes someone to be an alcoholic, powerful elements in society are still likely to condemn the *behavior* as unhealthy or immoral.

Do not misunderstand the purpose of our comparison. We are only trying to show that, regardless of the scientific understanding of the causes of a behavior, interest group "opinions" concerning rightness or wrongness are likely to continue. To many religious leaders, homosexuality is sinful like alcohol abuse. They believe that it is wrong. Despite its claims, the scientific community cannot prove otherwise (see Jones and Workman, 1989 for a Christian perspective on homosexuality).

Micro-Subjectivist Theories.   Definitional theories focus on what goes on inside the mind of an individual labeler as he or she reaches the conclusion that someone is deviant. This is an especially interesting issue with respect to homosexuality because, as we have already discussed, popular perception holds that sexual orientations are discrete. The general assumption is that people have a single, "true," sexual orientation. In this section, we want to find out how people determine that someone is "a homosexual" and how they treat that person accordingly.

To address this issue we must look to John Kitsuse (1962), who we introduced in Chapter 3. Challenging the popular view that one is deviant because of his or her behavior (the objectivist view), Kitsuse proposes that we focus on societal definitions of people as deviants (1962).

In interviews with 75 college students who "had known a homosexual," Kitsuse found that suspicions that a person might be sexually "different" often result from behaviors that " 'everyone knows' are indications of homosexuality" or that deviate "from the behaviors-held-in-common among members of the group" (Kitsuse, 1962:249–250). The suspicion may also result from hearsay, indirect evidence, or rumor. In short, we rely on incomplete evidence when making judgments about people.

In part, our judgments depend on stereotypes. Stereotyping involves the categorization of people on the basis of traits that are "unrelated to the criteria for group membership" (Herek, 1991:67). It is one of the strategies we use for "judging the importance of information and for integrating it with our past experiences" (Herek, 1991:67). Stereotypes about homosexuality often involve assumptions of male "femininity" and female "masculinity." As we have already discussed, there is evidence that gay men perceived themselves to be more feminine while growing up (Bell, Weinberg, and Hammersmith, 1981), and that feminine boys are more likely to grow up to be homosexual (Green, 1987). But it is important to recognize that, while this evidence no doubt reinforces popular stereotypes, it does not necessarily make them true. Because stereotypes are traits that are attributed to *all* members of a group, they are, in almost all cases, false. Of course, there is the occasional "swishy faggot" that clearly stands out, but not *all* gay men are feminine and limp-wristed. Similarly, not *all* lesbian women are masculine "butches." Therefore, despite macho heterosexual claims that a "homo" or a "dyke" can be spotted from a mile away, homosexuals do not *necessarily* look and act differently from heterosexuals.

Even more damaging, perhaps, are stereotypes pertaining to the internal motivations of homosexuals. For example, homosexuals are perceived to be hypersexual, heretical, and conspiratorial[4] (Herek, 1991). Such stereotypes have no doubt contributed to the belief that homosexuals are more likely than heterosexuals to seduce and molest children. While there is no evidence to support this belief, the stereotype nonetheless persists (Herek, 1991).

Empirical evidence has also challenged popular stereotypes that homosexual couples, especially gay couples, are interested only in short-term sexual relationships. Homosexual relationships can be, and often are, stable, happy, and functional (Peplau, 1991). In addition, not all gay and lesbian couples model traditional heterosexual relationships, with one assuming the masculine role (bread-

winner and sexual aggressor) and the other the feminine role. The most recent research demonstrates that most homosexual couples actively reject the masculine/feminine model (Peplau, 1991).

Micro-subjectivist theorists remind us that people use stereotypes such as these to interpret, define, label, and judge acts as deviance or people as deviant. Stereotypes are the cognitive maps we use to tell us who is and is not "a homosexual" (if he or she looks like one, acts like one, talks like one . . .). They also lead us to make assumptions about other aspects of a homosexual's life-style (since he or she is a homosexual, and homosexuals are . . . he or she must be . . .).

Stereotypes can also influence our perceptions. If we hold a stereotypical image of homosexuals, we tend to see only those traits that are consistent with our stereotypes (Herek, 1991). Kitsuse (1962) claims, for example, that once the subjects in his study had decided that they had indeed found "a homosexual," they set out to "prove" their evaluation (to themselves and others) through a process of "retrospective interpretation":

> The subjects . . . reviewed their past interactions with the individuals in question, searching for subtle cues and nuances of behavior which might give further evidence of the alleged deviance. This retrospective reading generally provided the subjects with just such evidence to support the conclusion that "this is what was going on all the time" (Kitsuse, 1962:251).

In another study of retrospective interpretation, Snyder and Uranowitz (1978) asked college students to read the life history of a woman named "Betty K." Afterwards, some students were told that Betty went on to live a happy and successful life as a doctor, wife, and mother. Others were told she was lesbian and went on to live a happy and successful life as a doctor living with her female lover. Upon being questioned about Betty, students who were told that she was a lesbian remembered different facts about Betty's life (e.g., she never had a steady boyfriend in high school) than did students who were told that she was heterosexual (e.g., that she enjoyed dating in high school). The point is that, once subjects had been told how Betty's life turned out, they remembered back to facts that seemed to explain Betty's life circumstances (Herek, 1991).

Given that we often think in stereotypical ways, it is easy to imagine how this might happen. Once we are told a person is "a homosexual," we remember back to past interactions with the person—we remember that he did like modern dance, she did wear men's jeans a lot, his voice was a little lispy, he didn't seem all that interested in girls, or she did have some masculine features. It all makes sense! She was a lesbian all the time! What is important, of course, is that past behaviors that, at the time, seemed reasonably "normal" are actually reinterpreted as evidence that the person is "abnormal." The behaviors have not changed, but the meanings that the labels hold for us have changed.

Interestingly, the concerns of the *labeling* theorists were expressed in the early writings of Alfred Kinsey who, although certainly no labeling theorist (or sociologist for that matter), nevertheless sounded very much like one when he wrote the following:

> One of the factors that materially contributes to the development of exclusively homosexual histories, is the ostracism which society imposes upon one who is discovered to have had perhaps no more than a lone experience. The high school boy is likely to be expelled from school and, if it is a small town, he is almost certain to be driven from the community. His chances of making heterosexual contacts are tremendously reduced after the public disclosure, and he is forced into the company of other homosexual individuals among whom he finally develops an exclusively homosexual pattern for himself (Kinsey, Pomeroy, and Martin, 1948:617, quoted in Plummer, 1981a:18).

Few question the fact that homosexuals are often ostracized, excluded, and hated be-

cause of their sexual practices. There is a stigma associated with homosexuality (Warren, 1980). This exclusion, furthermore, is no doubt influential in the creation and maintenance of the deviant subculture (Becker, 1963). Having been rejected by the "straight" world, homosexuals may look to others like themselves for encouragement and acceptance. In this sense, society might actually "force" some people into deviant identities.

But do societal reactions actually cause homosexual behavior? Labeling theorists argue that, to some degree, they might. From the labeling perspective, the stigmatizing effects of the "deviant" label can be so powerful that the individual is actually "forced" into a deviant self-definition. Having adopted the deviant identity, he or she then engages in behavior that is consistent with that self-definition.

One of the most important assumptions labeling theorists make is that a homosexual orientation is not fixed. It is not something that we have at birth. It is not something that is written in stone. Rather, it is something that we, as we examine our feelings and our interactions with others, actively construct. In this sense, homosexuality is a socially constructed identity. According to Plummer (1981a; 1981b), those who assume this *identity construct model* focus on the

> . . . cognitive process by which members of a society interpret their sexual selves by scanning their past lives (their bodies, group involvements, feelings and behaviors) and connecting these to "accounts" available to their contemporary worlds (through friends, family, psychiatrists, media). The focus here is not upon childhood determinations and permanent "real" orientations; rather it is upon the process of building identities throughout life through significant encounters. . . .The constructionist approach suggests that perhaps initially our experiences are much more random, unstructured and uncrystallized than we choose to believe, and that it is through the definitional process that this randomness becomes channelled into stable sexual identities (Plummer, 1981b:69).

Notice how this differs from the *essentialist*, or *sexual orientation* model (Plummer, 1981b; Harry, 1985). Essentialists believe that sexual orientation is fixed and firmly established by early childhood. The homosexual identify, therefore, results when, as a result of homoerotic attractions, individuals come to recognize their "true" homosexual orientation (Bell, Weinberg, and Hammersmith, 1981).

Labeling theorists remind us that many people make essentialist assumptions about homosexuality. Given our assumptions that there are only two kinds of people, homosexuals and heterosexuals, what are we likely to think of ourselves if we begin to have homosexual feelings? We may begin to assume that we are "a homosexual." Since homosexual feelings are, in general, more likely to be felt than expressed, this process of self-labeling may be especially important to our understanding of homosexuality. Plummer describes the process as follows:

> *A person who experiences a homosexual feeling does not have to be hounded out of town, sent to prison, or treated by a psychiatrist to come to see himself as a homosexual—he may quite simply "indicate" to himself, through the "interpretation" of the given feeling and the accompanying awareness of the societal hostility, that he is a homosexual (Plummer, 1975:21).*

To illustrate another way that self-labeling could occur, consider the story of Doug Barnett. Doug's quest to discover his "true" sexual identity is summarized in *Newsweek* (1992:46):

> *Until the age of 28, Doug Barnett was a practicing heterosexual. He was vaguely attracted to men, but with nurturing parents, a lively interest in sports and appropriate relations with women, he had little reason to question his proclivities. Then an astounding thing happened: his identical brother "came out" to him, revealing that he was gay. Barnett, who believed sexual orientation is genetic, was bewildered. He recalls thinking, "If this is inherited and we're identical twins—what's going on*

here?" To find out, he thought he should try sex with men. When he did, he says, "The bells went off, for the first time. Those homosexual encounters were more fulfilling" (1992:46).

Of course, we have no way of knowing whether Doug was a "real" homosexual or not. What we do know is that Doug "believed sexual orientation is genetic." Given this belief, what was he to think of himself when he found out his brother was gay? He either needed to change his belief or his sexual identity. From a micro-subjectivist point of view, it is interesting that he only began questioning his sexual identity when he learned his twin brother was gay.

Another way that societal reactions might influence self-perception is through the labeling of behaviors that "everyone knows" are indicators of homosexuality. In our society "boy things" and activities are clearly differentiated from "girl things" and activities. It is "unnatural" for boys to act like girls and for girls to act like boys. It is also commonly assumed, both among scholars and in the general public, that cross-sex behavior is an early indication of homosexuality (Saghir and Robins, 1973; Bell, Weinberg, and Hammersmith, 1981; Green, 1987). From a labeling perspective, an artistic boy who does not like sports and is labeled "sissy," "fag," or "homo," or a mathematical girl who likes sports and is labeled "masculine," "lesbian," or "dyke," may actually get "pushed" into opposite gender roles by the actions from people around them (Marmor, 1980). Considering the variability and frequency of homosexual thoughts and experiences (Kinsey, Pomeroy, and Martin, 1948), we might further hypothesize that being labeled "sissy," "fag," or "homo" might have an especially dramatic effect on adolescents who are questioning their sexual identity. Perhaps this "push" occasionally ends in full-blown homosexuality.

Notice what we have done. With this labeling interpretation, we have now offered three different explanations (one from an essentialist/sexual orientation perspective, one from learning perspective, and one from a labeling perspective) for the same empirical generalization, namely, that cross-gender behavior in children (boys preferring "feminine" activities, girls preferring "masculine" activities) is positively related to homosexuality in adults.

Which one is "right"? The answer, of course, depends on whether one asks an essentialist, a learning theorist, or a labeling theorist. As we have already stated, the most common explanation is the essentialist explanation, which suggests that cross-gender behavior is merely an indication of a person's "true" sexual orientation. But how does one "prove" that this the correct interpretation of the data? Kinsey Institute researchers Bell, Weinberg, and Hammersmith (1981) attempt to offer proof, but their proof is unlikely to convince those who question the essentialist model. Bell and his colleagues, who are essentialists, admit that the homosexual men and women in their sample say that they were labeled "homosexual" or sexually "different." However, after considering empirically a number of factors theoretically related to homosexuality, they conclude that labeling is a *"result* of an emerging homosexual orientation rather than a cause or even a secondary contributor to it" (Bell, Weinberg, and Hammersmith, 1981:185).

Labeling theorists, while offering no convincing data of their own, remain unconvinced. They merely dismiss these and other studies as being methodologically inadequate, beside the point, and "naive and oversimple" (Plummer, 1981a; 1981b). In the absence of convincing experimental evidence, causal explanations must be accepted on faith.

SOCIAL POLICY AND SOCIAL CONTROL

Survey data remind us that homosexuality is a volatile subject (Herek, 1991).[5] Less than

half (47 percent) believe that homosexual relations should be legal (Gallup, 1990), and over half (52 percent) would prefer not to work around people who are homosexual (the Roper Organization). As of the early 1990s, a majority of Americans (54 percent) also believe that homosexual behavior is morally wrong. Interestingly, approximately the same percentage of Americans (53 percent) believed homosexuality was wrong in 1978 (*Time,* June, 1992).

Despite the continued disapproval of homosexual behavior, however, there is some evidence that, in the last 20 years, increasing numbers of Americans support the civil rights of homosexuals (Gallup, 1990; Herek, 1991). For example, the proportion of Americans who believe that homosexuals should have equal rights in jobs has increased from 56 percent in 1977 to 71 percent in 1989 (Gallup, 1990). The National Opinion Research Center reports that the proportion of Americans who believe that a person who "admits he is a homosexual" should be allowed to teach in a college or university has increased from 47 percent in 1973 to 57 percent in 1988 (Herek, 1991). According to Gallup (1990), from 1977 to 1989, acceptance has similarly increased for homosexual doctors (44 to 56 percent), members of the armed forces (51 to 60 percent), clergy (36 to 44 percent), and elementary school teachers (27 to 42 percent).

These trends, which point to a pattern of "increasing willingness to extend basic civil liberties to gay men and lesbians" (Herek, 1991:62) obscure what in many ways is the more interesting pattern of increasing *intolerance* of homosexuality during the mid-1980s. The 1987 Gallup poll, for example, found that only 33 percent of adults in the U.S. felt that homosexual relations between consenting adults should be legal; that is *down* ten percentage points from 1977. Why the increased intolerance of homosexuality during the mid-1980s? AIDS! According to Gallup (1990), intolerance of homosexuality increased at a time when the fear of AIDS was at an all-time high: "As the backlash toward homosexuals that grew out of the AIDS epidemic subsides, support for the civil rights of gays has increased dramatically . . . " (Gallup, 1990:217).

These survey results remind us that homosexuality continues to be a controversial social policy issue, especially given the fact that AIDS is perceived to be a homosexual disease.

Homosexuality and the Law

In Iran, homosexual men can be put to death. For homosexual men in Saudi Arabia, a first offense brings only a prison sentence or lashings, but repeat offenses can result in death by decapitation (West, 1988). The United States, while far more tolerant, remains one of the few Western countries to restrict consensual adult sexual practices (West, 1988; Law, 1988).

Prior to the early 1960s, laws against "unnatural" sex were common. In fact, with so many "unnatural" sexual acts criminalized, the overwhelming majority of Americans violated sexual conduct laws (Rivera, 1991). By the mid-1970s, many states had adopted the Model Penal Code, which decriminalized all consensual sex between adults. Despite the trend toward decriminalization, through the 1980s and up until the early 1990s, 25 states and the District of Columbia continue to regulate sex between consenting adults.[6] The laws in most of these states generally pertain to "unnatural" sodomy (which generally includes oral or anal sexual relations) rather than explicit homosexuality; but there are some states that, despite adopting the Model Penal Code, have recriminalized homosexual conduct (Rivera, 1991).[7]

Because anti-sodomy laws are not typically enforced, they have little impact on the actual practices of homosexuals. At the same time, many people resent the fact that private practices are criminalized. Criminalization alienates, discriminates, and exploits (West,

1988). Besides, many legal experts agree that anti-sodomy laws are unconstitutional. However, because anti-sodomy laws are rarely enforced, gay legal advocates have had few opportunities to challenge the constitutionality of such laws. In the 1986 Supreme Court case, *Bowers v. Hardwick,* gay rights groups felt that they finally had the case that would force states to decriminalize anti-sodomy laws. In this particular case, Michael Hardwick was arrested in his own bedroom for having consensual sex with another man. The local prosecutor chose not to press charges, but Hardwick decided to contest the constitutionality of Georgia's anti-sodomy law. The Supreme Court, citing a very long history of Judaic and Christian moral teachings against homosexuality, shocked the legal and social scientific world when it held five-to-four that "homosexual sodomy" is not protected under the constitutional right to privacy (Melton, 1989).

More significant for the average homosexual American are laws that limit the rights of homosexuals, especially in employment and family issues. The U.S. military, for example, has prohibited homosexuals from service since World War II, generally arguing that "they hurt recruiting, create disciplinary problems, lower morale, and raise security issues" (Slovenko, 1980:209). The military was especially aggressive in investigating suspected homosexuals and discharging confirmed homosexuals in the 1980s. Between 1982 and 1992, 13,000 homosexual men and women were discharged. While most of the dismissals were honorable, the discharge papers left little doubt as to the reason for the dismissal (*Newsweek,* 1993).

The 1990s, however, brought with it renewed hope in the homosexuality community that the ban might soon be lifted. In June of 1991, for example, the U.S. Army released an internal memorandum stating that the Army should accept "persons whose sexual orientations deviate from the customary" given that they "exercise appropriate restraint and discretion . . ." (Healy, 1991). Even more importantly, in January of 1993 Bill Clinton was elected president of the United States. During the 1992 presidential campaign, Clinton had made his stance on the military ban quite clear. He felt it was wrong, plain and simple. It was no less wrong than discriminatory practices against blacks in the military in the 1940s. Within days of his inauguration, Clinton set out to make good on his pledge to eliminate the ban. Yet, with many top pentagon and congressional leaders outspoken in their support of the ban, and with the American people also generally in favor of the ban,[8] Clinton was faced with a problem. In the end, Clinton and the pentagon reached a compromise: the military would no longer ask recruits about their sexual orientation, nor would they actively investigate suspected homosexuals. This compromise would give Clinton and his aides time to research a more permanent solution (*Newsweek*, 1993; Duffy, 1993; Smolowe, 1993).[9]

Even outside the military, homosexuals are not offered full employment protection. According to Rivera (1991), most state employment laws are dictated by the legal principle, "employment at will." This means that the employer can terminate the employee "at will." While there are certain limitations to the "at will" doctrine, especially for government employees, homosexuals are still left to wonder about the professional ramifications of a public disclosure of their sexual orientations (Rivera, 1991).

Another important area of legal debate concerns homosexual families. To date, no states allow same-sex marriages. At the same time, however, many homosexual couples are choosing to proclaim their relationship publicly in "bonding ceremonies, holy unions, ceremonies of commitment or covenanting ceremonies " (*Seattle Post-Intelligencer*, 1991). Because homosexual couples are not legally recognized as married, employers will gener-

ally not offer benefits accorded the spouses of employees.[10] Another important issue for many homosexual couples is the desire to have children. In their attempts to adopt children, homosexual couples are not only challenging traditional conceptions of family but also stereotypical fears that homosexuals are mentally ill, sexually promiscuous, likely to "teach" their children homosexuality, and incapable of leading a life-style conducive to the healthy development of a child (Melton, 1989).

The AIDS Issue

AIDS—Acquired Immune Deficiency Syndrome—has become the most pressing public health issue of our time. The disease first came to the attention of the U.S. public in 1981, when the Federal Center for Disease Control reported that five gay men in Los Angeles had been diagnosed with a rare form of pneumonia. On the same day, five gay men in San Francisco reportedly had the disease as well. Shortly thereafter, gay men in New York were diagnosed with an extremely rare type of skin cancer. In each of these cases, the disease spread quickly, seemingly unchecked by immune systems.

In 1984, medical researchers in France discovered the problem. They linked AIDS to a virus, the Human Immunodeficiency Virus, or HIV (Perlman, 1991). The HIV virus can live in the body for years before any symptoms of AIDS develop.[11] Once AIDS develops, the virus destroys the immune system. Incapable of combating disease, the infected person is vulnerable to 70 or more deadly conditions. There is no cure. AIDS is always fatal.

AIDS is not a homosexual disease. Intravenous drug users get AIDS, hemophiliacs get AIDS, heterosexuals get AIDS, children get AIDS. Certainly it is true, as ex-professional basketball player Magic Johnson stated many times after admitting that he had contracted the HIV virus: "anyone can get AIDS." However, because AIDS has, at least in this country, largely been contracted through homosexual contact, it "has been and remains a crisis of unmitigated proportions for the gay male community" (Gonsiorek and Shernoff, 1991). There are two reasons why AIDS remains an especially important issue for gay men. First, despite the fact that the percentage of HIV-infected people who are homosexual or bisexual has decreased by 20 percent in recent years, AIDS remains a disease that disproportionately affects gay men. Approximately two-thirds of AIDS victims are homosexual males, and experts estimate that between 20 and 60 percent of gay men who are not in monogamous relationships are infected with HIV (Gonsiorek and Shernoff, 1991). Second, because in this country AIDS disproportionately affects gay men, gay rights advocates fear that, in an effort to control the spread of AIDS, the civil rights of homosexuals will be violated. These fears are not unjustified. For a vocal minority of Americans, AIDS is the "gay plague." Some people have even suggested that AIDS is God's punishment for homosexual behavior. From this perspective, homosexuals are no longer just sexual deviants, they are disease-carrying sexual deviants. They should be locked up and left to die. This attitude has no doubt contributed to increasing physical violence directed at homosexuals—sometimes called "gay bashing." In November of 1991, *Newsweek* reported that crimes against homosexuals in six cities had increased by 42 percent between 1989 and 1990.

Civil rights issues are further complicated by the fact that the general public remains somewhat uninformed about AIDS. Fearing that they can contract the disease through casual contact, many Americans reject AIDS victims and people suspected of having the HIV virus. This rejection sometimes takes the form of "housing and job discrimination and the denial of health insurance at a time they

need it most" (Dejowski et al., 1991:220). The fact is, however, that AIDS is a very difficult disease to contract. Magic Johnson is right to say, "anyone can get AIDS." But you can only get it doing certain kinds of things. AIDS is almost always contracted through a contaminated blood transfusion, sexual contact (primarily intercourse, and especially anal intercourse), or a contaminated needle. Despite these facts, Gallup (1990) reports that a significant minority of Americans surveyed in 1989 mistakenly believe that AIDS can be contracted from a blood donation (44 percent), from a drinking glass (16 percent), from being coughed or sneezed upon (14 percent), or from a toilet seat (11 percent). These misperceptions about AIDS probably fuel unrealistic fears of the disease and of homosexuals.

Among the more pressing social control issues currently facing gay rights activists is the possibility that AIDS prevention policy will soon require "contact tracing" (Dejowski et al., 1991). For example, the so-called "Dannemeyer Initiative" (California Proposition 102), which California voters rejected in 1988, would have required health officials to investigate the sources and possible transmittal, including notification of the patient's spouse, sexual partners, and others who might have been exposed (Dejowski et al., 1991). Representative Dannemeyer has introduced similar bills at the federal level, arguing that such bills would legally force AIDS victims to disclose their contacts: "Under the law, if you choose not to reveal your sexual contacts, we will come and arrest you and take you into custody until the message gets through . . ." (Dejowski et al., 1991:221).

A related proposal, introduced by North Carolina Senator Jesse Helms, would impose prison sentences on health care workers who fail to disclose that they are HIV positive (*Seattle Post-Intelligencer*, 1991). The concern over health care workers can be traced, at least in part, to Kimberly Bergalis, a Florida woman who reportedly contracted AIDS from her dentist. Before dying in December, 1991, Bergalis made national headlines when she testified before Congress on the need for health care restrictions.

For gay rights activists, the problem with the Helms measure, as with "contact tracing" measures more generally, is their tone. Coercive threats, they contend, are unneeded and ineffective. Drawing lines in the sand will only serve to further ostracize a group of people who already perceive themselves to be outsiders (Becker, 1963). For Dejowski and his colleagues, a more positive, cooperative tone will convey "understanding and support" and will "help infected persons do what is in the final analysis best for themselves and for the rest of society" (1991:228). They suggest a much less offensive "partner notification" program, whereby sexual partners of HIV-positive people would be encouraged to get tested, would receive an education message on the risks of HIV infection, and would be counseled on how to reduce the risk.

These are but a few of the AIDS-related issues that are likely to dominate social policy debates in the years to come. With the number of AIDS cases expected to increase by 500,000 in the next ten years (Schwartz, 1991), we can anticipate that AIDS will be the most significant public health issue in our lives.

THE TREATMENT OF HOMOSEXUALITY

Given the current trend toward greater tolerance of homosexuality as an alternative lifestyle, it should come as no surprise that treatment is a very controversial topic. In the third edition of the *Diagnostic and Statistical Manual of Mental Disorders* the American Psychiatric Association removed all general references to homosexuality as a mental disorder (APA, 1980). Yet until 1987 when the APA removed the controversial "ego-dystonic homosexual-ity" (APA, 1987) diagnosis (defined as an unwanted homosexual orientation), treatment was still a viable option for homosexuals who were unhappy with their erotic orientation. Now that the APA has removed all references to homosexuality in the *DSM*[12] many gay rights activists believe that " 'change-of-orientation' programs are ethically improper and should be eliminated" (Davison, 1991:148). However, some mental health professionals and paraprofessionals continue to "treat" homosexuality. Many of these therapists are Christians who maintain that, while homosexuality may no longer be a disorder in the eyes of the APA, it remains unnatural and immoral in the eyes of God.

Some Christian therapies, in hopes of succeeding where others have failed, incorporate a psychological therapy into a "supernatural framework." Critics complain that Christian therapies such as these are unethical; they violate the APA's affirmative-action policies on homosexuality, and perhaps most importantly, they do not work (Haldeman, 1991; Davison, 1991). Because they do not work, they do more harm than good for an already confused homosexual (Haldeman, 1991). Efforts could more effectively be spent focusing on the "life problems of some homosexuals" (Davison, 1991:148) and on "healing and educating an intolerant social context" (Haldeman, 1991:159–160). Some critics of homosexual therapy even go so far as to question a homosexual's "right to choose" a homosexuality treatment, arguing that such a choice is "almost always based on the internalized effects of a hostile family and an intolerant society" (Haldeman, 1991:160).

The battle over the right to treat homosexuality once again points to the importance of interest group struggles in the homosexuality debate. Psychiatrists and other mental health professionals who believe homosexuality is a natural and immutable sexual orientation complain that Christian therapists are unethical for attempting to change homosexual behavior. From their perspective, science has "proved" that homosexuality is not a disorder. But how does one "prove" that a particular behavior is a "normal" variation rather than an "abnormal" variation? As far as we can tell, you can't. Indeed, it is interesting that the mental health professionals would criticize the "intolerance" of Christian therapists when the mental health profession has itself been severely criticized over the years for its "intolerance." As we discussed in Chapter 6, macro-subjectivist theorists have long criticized psychiatrists as being little more than formal agents of social control forcing their notions of mental "health" on powerless people who may simply be different. At least in the case homosexual therapies, patients want to change. Many maintain, furthermore, that they should have every right to obtain therapy if they want therapy (Jones and Workman, 1989).

Christian therapists, of course, are not without their own biases. As they firmly hold on to the belief that, "homosexuality is wrong!", they may naively and irresponsibly create treatment programs without considering the potentially damaging consequences (to the individual) of failure. They may also be quick to sing the praises of therapies that have not been thoroughly evaluated.

SUMMARY

Homosexuality is a very sensitive topic. Given the sensitive nature of the topic, it is likely that in this chapter we have offended someone. Those who believe homosexuality is "wrong" will think we have been too soft on homosexuality. Those who think homosexuality is "right" will resent the fact that we have defined homosexuality as deviance (perhaps assuming that we are using the words *deviance* and *pathology* as synonyms). Importantly, however, from a sociological

point of view, homosexuality is deviance. From an objectivist perspective, homosexuality is deviance because it is a behavior that violates the norms of heterosexuality. From a subjectivist perspective, homosexuality is deviance because others define it as deviance.

Each conceptualization has its strengths and weaknesses. The objectivist conception effectively defines what homosexual behavior is, but it cannot tell us so easily how one becomes a homosexual. To understand the relationship between doing and being, we must examine homosexuality from a subjectivist point of view. Because the subjectivist conception focuses on societal reactions, it can more effectively explain how one adopts a deviant identity.

Research on the prevalence of homosexuality has demonstrated that homosexual behavior is much more common than is generally assumed. Of the 5,300 men and 5,900 women studied by Alfred Kinsey and his colleagues (1948; 1953), 37 percent of the men and 13 percent of the women had reached orgasm in the context of homosexual contact. In addition, 13 percent of the men and 5 percent of the women had, during a three-year period, been more homosexual than heterosexual. More recent research, however, has suggested that Kinsey's estimates may have been too high. Fay and his colleagues (1989), for example, estimate that about 20 percent of adult men have had at least one homosexual experience to the point of orgasm. Only 7 percent had homosexual contact after the age of 19 and just less than 2 percent had homosexual contact in the previous year. Like Fay and his colleagues, Smith (1991) found that only 2 percent of men reported a homosexual experience in the previous year, and 5 to 6 percent of men and women indicated that they had a homosexual experience since turning 18. Billy and his colleagues (1993) found the rates to be even lower, with 2 percent of men reporting a homosexual experience in the past 10 years. Because of the sensitivity of homosexuality questions, these more recent studies probably underestimate the level of homosexuality in society.

There is considerable disagreement among social scientists and the medical community as to what causes homosexuality. The disagreement begins with the basic assumptions medical theorists and social scientists make. In general, medical theorists make "essentialist" assumptions about homosexuality. *Essentialists* assume that homosexuality is a relatively distinct and immutable category of *sexual orientation* (as opposed to a *sexual preference*) that either exists at birth or is formed very early in life. While norms concerning homosexual behavior may vary from one culture to the next, homosexual orientations do not.

How, from a medical point of view, is this sexual orientation formed? According to the *sickness model*, which traces its roots to Sigmund Freud, homosexuality is a psychological abnormality. Now mostly discredited (politically, if not empirically), most sickness theories of homosexuality have today given way to various *biological predisposition* theories, which most often focus on prenatal hormones and their influence on fetal development along masculine or feminine paths. Whatever their exact content, most biological predisposition theories suggest that homosexual orientation exists at birth and often shows itself early in life in the form of *cross-gender behavior.*

The most feasible social scientific explanation of homosexual behavior (i.e., objectivist theory) is social learning theory, which suggests that cross-gender behaviors may sometimes be reinforced, thus causing the person to identify with the needs and desires of the opposite sex. Homosexual behavior may also be reinforced when positive homosexual experiences are combined with negative heterosexual experiences.

Apart from social learning theory, most

sociological theory has ignored questions of *etiology.* More interesting to sociologists has been the source and impact of societal reactions. Macro-subjectivist theories (primarily interest group theories) suggest that if we are to understand the contemporary debate over homosexuality as deviance, we must understand the history of interest struggles between the churches, legal authorities, the scientific community, and homosexuals themselves. From this perspective, if we are to understand currently accepted "knowledge" about homosexuality (e.g., that homosexuality is not a mental disorder and that homosexual orientations are discrete and fixed) then we must understand this interest struggle.

Micro-subjectivist definitional theories focus on how labelers use stereotypes and *retrospective interpretation* to define and interpret the behavior of deviants. Labeling theorist assume an *identity construct model* and argue that a homosexual identity is formed in interaction with others. Once these labels (e.g., "sissy," "homo," "fag," "dyke,") are affixed, labeling theorists remind us that they can have a powerful impact on the identity and the subsequent behavior of the individual.

In terms of social policy and social control, homosexuality remains a volatile subject. *Sodomy,* for example, is still a crime in 25 states and the District of Columbia. Homosexuals suffer from other forms of discrimination and from violence as well. Despite an overall trend toward increasing acceptance of homosexuality, Americans became somewhat more intolerant during the mid-1980s. The reason may, in part, be linked to concerns about *AIDS* (and the *HIV* virus more generally). While AIDS is not a homosexual disease, it has disproportionately affected gay men. As a result, any attempt to control the spread of AIDS will influence the homosexual community. Especially worrisome to the homosexual community are *contact tracing* laws, which would require health officials to investigate all sexual contacts of victims of AIDS.

GLOSSARY

AIDS (Acquired Immune Deficiency Syndrome) A deadly disease that destroys the immune system, making the infected person vulnerable to 70 or more deadly conditions. It is most often contracted from a contaminated blood transfusion, sexual contact (primarily intercourse, and especially anal intercourse), or a contaminated needle.

Biological Predisposition A perspective based on the idea that one is born with a biological predisposition toward homosexuality.

Cross-Gender Behavior Gender-inappropriate behavior (i.e, boys who act like girls, and girls who act like boys). Many researchers maintain that cross-gender behavior is an early indication of homosexuality.

Essentialist Perspective A perspective based on the idea that homosexuality is a relatively distinct category of sexual orientation that is immutable, appears in all societies, and is characterized by similar elements in all societies. People who hold this view assume that everyone has a single "true" sexual orientation.

Etiology The study of causes. Etiological theories of homosexuality focus on the causes of homosexual behavior and orientation.

HIV (Human Immunodeficiency Virus) The virus that causes AIDS. It can live in the body for years before any symptoms of AIDS develop.

Homosexuality Variously defined as sexual contact between two people of the same sex (a behavior perspective), a person who is sexually attracted to someone of the same sex (an erotic orientation perspective), or someone who sees himself or herself as a homosexual (a self-identification perspective).

Identity Construct Model Suggests that people interpret their sexual selves and construct their sexual identities by scanning their past experiences and feelings.

Retrospective Interpretation The process of reinterpreting past behaviors in light of new definitions of self or others.

Sexual Orientation Referring in general to one of two erotic orientations: homoerotic or heteroerotic. Sexual orientation either exists at birth, or is formed early in life. In either case, it is generally fixed.

Sexual Preference A perspective based on the idea that one simply chooses, and should have every right to choose, to have sex with whomever one pleases. Many critics maintain, however, that one does not choose to be homosexual; one is homosexual.

Sickness Model A model based on the notion that homosexuality is a psychological abnormality or a pathology.

Sodomy "Unnatural" sex—most often, oral or anal sexual relations.

SUGGESTED READINGS

Bell, Alan P., and Martin S. Weinberg. *Homosexualities: A Study of Diversity Among Men and Women.* New York: Simon and Schuster, 1978. This book is based upon detailed interviews of 929 self-identified homosexuals (651 men and 278 women). Bell and Weinberg provide an excellent summary of the experiences and backgrounds of homosexuals.

D'Emilio, John. *Sexual Politics, Sexual Communities: The Making of a Homosexual Minority in the United States, 1940–1970.* Chicago: University of Chicago Press, 1983. Here is a well-written and historically accurate history of the homosexual struggle to achieve equality.

Gonsiorek, John C., and James D. Weinrich, eds. *Homosexuality: Research Implications for Public Policy.* Newbury Park, Calif.: Sage, 1991. This anthology includes the most up-to-date research on homosexuality (largely from a medical perspective) along with the implications for public policy stemming from this research.

Greenberg, David F. *The Construction of Homosexuality.* Chicago: University of Chicago Press, 1988. This is a very detailed work on the history of societal reactions toward homosexuality.

Troiden, Richard. *Gay and Lesbian Identity: A Sociological Analysis.* Dix Hills, N.Y.: General Hall, 1988. Focusing primarily on societal reactions, this book develops an ideal-typical model of homosexual identity transformation.

REFERENCES

Adam, Barry D. *The Rise of a Gay and Lesbian Movement.* Boston: Twayne, (1987).

Akers, Ronald L. *Deviant Behavior: A Social Learning Approach.* 3rd ed. Belmont, Calif.: Wadsworth, 1985.

American Psychiatric Association. *Diagnostic and Statistical Manual of Mental Disorders (DSM-III).* (3rd ed.) Washington, D.S.: APA, 1980

———. *Diagnostic and Statistical Manual of Mental Disorders (DSM-III-R).* (3rd ed., revised). Washington, D.C.: APA, 1980.

Baldwin, John D., and Janice I. Baldwin. "The Socialization of Homosexuality and Heterosexuality in a Non-Western Society." *Archives of Sexual Behavior* 18 (1989):13–29.

Becker, Howard S. *Outsiders: Studies in the Sociology of Deviance.* New York: Free Press, 1963.

Bell, Alan P., and Martin S. Weinberg. *Homosexualities: A Study of Diversity Among Men and Women.* New York: Simon and Schuster, 1978.

Bell, Alan, Martin Weinberg, and S. Hammersmith. *Sexual Preference: Its Development in Men and Women.* Bloomington: Indiana University Press, 1981.

Bieber, Irving, Harvey Dain, Paul Dince, Marvin Drellich, Henry Grand, Ralph Gundlach, Malvina Kremer, Alfred Rifkin, Cornelia Wilbur, and Toby Bieber. *Homosexuality: A Psychoanalytic Study of Male Homosexuals.* New York: Vintage Books, 1962.

Billy, John O., Koray Tanfer, William Grady, and Daniel Klepinger. "The Sexual Behavior of Men in the United States." *Family Planning Perspectives* 25(1993):52–60.

Bjorklund, David, and Barbara Bjorkland.

"Straight or Gay? Researchers are Unraveling the Origins of Homosexuality." *Parents Magazine* 63 Oct. 1988:93–98.

Burgess, Robert L., and Ronald L. Akers. "A Differential Association Reinforcement Theory of Criminal Behavior." *Social Problems* 14 (Fall 1966):128–147.

Carrier, J.M. "Homosexual Behavior in Cross-Cultural Perspective," in Marmor, pp. 101–121.

Clark, J. Michael, Joanne Carlson Brown, and Lorna M. Hochstein. "Institutional Religion and Gay/Lesbian Oppression." *Marriage and Family Review* 14.3–4. The Haworth Press, 1990:265–284.

Conrad, Peter, and Joseph W. Schneider. *Deviance and Medicalization: From Badness to Sickness.* St. Louis: Mosby, 1980.

Davison, Gerald C. "Constructionism and Morality in Therapy for Homosexuality" Gonsiorek and Weinrich 230–243.

De Cecco, J.P. Homosexuality's Brief Recovery: From Sickness to Health and Back Again. *Journal of Sex Research* 23 (1978):106–114.

Dejowski, Edmund F., Lidia Dengelegi, Stephen Crystal, and Pearl Beck. "Partner Notification as an Instrument for HIV Control" Gonsiorek and Weinrich (1991a), pp. 215–229.

D'Emilio, John. *Sexual Politics, Sexual Communities: The Making of a Homosexual Minority in the United States, 1940-1970.* Chicago: University of Chicago Press, 1983.

Diamant, Louis, ed. *Male and Female Homosexuality: Psychological Approaches.* Washington D.C.: Hemisphere Publishing, 1987.

Duffy, Michael. "Obstacle Course." *Time* (Feb. 8, 1993):27–28.

Fay, Robert E., John H. Gagnon, Albert D. Klassen, and Charles F. Turner. "Prevalence and Patterns of Same-Gender Sexual Contact Among Men." *Science* 243 (January 20, 1989):338–348.

Freud, Sigmund. "Three Essays on Sexuality and other Works." *The Standard Edition of the Complete Psychological Works of Sigmund Freud.* Ed. J. Strachey. Vol. 3. London: Hogarth, 1953. Originally published in 1905.

Gagnon, John H. and William Simon. "Sexual Deviance in Contemporary America." *Annals of the American Academy of Political and Social Science* 376 (1968a):107–122.

———. "The Social Meaning of Prison Homosexuality." *Federal Probation* 32 (1968b):23–29.

Gallup, George, Jr. *The Gallup Poll*. Wilmington, Del.: Scholarly Resources, 1990.

Gebhard, Paul, and A.B. Johnson. *The Kinsey Data: Marginal Tabulations of the 1938-1963 Interviews Conducted by the Institute for Sex Research*. Philadelphia: W.B. Saunders, 1979.

Gonsiorek, John C., and James D. Weinrich. "Introduction." *Homosexuality: Research Implications for Public Policy*. Eds. J. Gonsiorek and J. Weinrichs. Newbury Park, Calif.: Sage, 1991, pp. xi–xv.

———. "The Definition and Scope of Sexual Orientation." Ibid., pp. 1–12.

Gonsiorek, John C., and Michael Shernoff. "AIDS Prevention and Public Policy: The Experience of Gay Males." Gonsiorek and Weinrich (1991), pp. 230–243.

Goode, Erich. "Comments on the Homosexual Role." *Journal of Sex Research* (Feb. 17, 1981): 54–65.

Gould, Robert E. "What We Don't Know About Homosexuality." *Gay Men: The Sociology of Male Homosexuality*. Ed. Martin P. Levine. New York: Harper and Row, 1979, 36–50.

Green, Richard. *The "Sissy Boy Syndrome" and the Development of Homosexuality*. New Haven, Conn.: Yale University Press, 1987.

Greenberg, David F. *The Construction of Homosexuality*. Chicago: University of Chicago Press, 1988.

Haldeman, Douglas C. "Sexual Orientation Conversion Therapy for Gay Men and Lesbians: A Scientific Examination." Gonsiorek and Weinrich (1991), pp. 149–160.

Harry, Joseph. "Sexual Orientation as Destiny." *Journal of Homosexuality* 10 (1985):111–124.

———. "Parental Physical Abuse and Sexual Orientation in Males." *Archives of Sexual Behavior* 18 (1989):251–261.

Hatfield, L. "Method of Polling." *San Francisco Examiner* (June 5, 1989):120.

Healy, Melissa. "Gays May Get OK to Join the Army." *Seattle Times* (June 25, 1991):A1.

Herdt, Gilbert. *The Sambia: Ritual and Gender in New Gunia*. New York: Holt, Rinehart and Winston, 1987.

Herek, Gregory M. "Stigma, Prejudice, and Violence Against Lesbians and Gay Men." Gonsiorek and Weinrich (1991), pp. 60–79.

Hiltner, Seward. "Homosexuality and the Churches." Marmor, 219–231.

Hirschi, Travis. *Causes of Delinquency*. Berkeley: University of California Press, 1969.

Humphreys, Laud. "Tearoom Trade: Impersonal Sex in Public Places." *Transaction* (Jan. 7, 1970):17–18.

Humphreys, Laud, and Brian Miller. "Identities in the Emerging Gay Culture." Marmor (1980), pp. 142–155.

Hunt, Morgon. *Sexual Behavior in the 1970s*. Chicago: Playboy, 1974.

Innala, Sune M., and Frederick L. Whitam. "Biological Explanation, Psychological Explanation, and Tolerance of Homosexuals: A Cross-National Analysis of Beliefs and Attitudes." *Psychological Reports* 65 (1989):1003–1010.

Jones, Stanton L., and Don E. Workman. "Homosexuality: The Behavioral Sciences and the Church." *Journal of Psychology and Theology* 17 (1989):213–225.

Kallman, Franz J. "Comparative Twin Study on the Genetic Aspects of Male Homosexuality." *Journal of Nervous and Mental Disease* 115 (1952):283–298.

Karlen, Arno. "Homosexuality in History." Marmor (1980), pp. 75–99.

Katz, Jonathan, ed. *Gay American History: Lesbians and Gay Men in the U.S.A.* New York: Cromwell, 1976.

Kinsey, Alfred C., Wardell B. Pomeroy, and Clyde E. Martin. *Sexual Behavior in the Human Male*. Philadelphia: W.B. Saunders, 1948.

Kinsey, Alfred C., Wardell B. Pomeroy, Clyde E. Martin, and Paul Gebhard. *Sexual Behavior in the Human Female*. Philadelphia: W.B. Saunders, 1953.

Kirsch, John A.W., and James D. Weinrich. "Homosexuality, Nature, and Biology: Is Homosexuality Natural? Does it Matter?" Gonsiorek and Weinrich (1991), pp. 13–31.

Kitsuse, John I. "Societal Reactions to Deviant Behavior: Problems of Theory and Method." *Social Problems* 9 (Winter 1962):247–257.

Kottak, Conrad P. *Cultural Anthropology*. 5th ed. New York: McGraw-Hill, 1991.

Law, Silvia A. "Homosexuality and the Social Meaning of Gender." *Wisconsin Law Review* (1988):187–235.

Luckenbill, David F. "Entering Male Prostitution." *Urban Life* 14 (July 1985):138.

Maclean's. "A Gay Backlash: Queer Nation is Waging War on Homophobia." (Sept. 10, 1990):48.

Marmor, Judd. "Overview: The Multiple Roots of Homosexual Behavior." Ed. J. Marmor. *Homosexual Behavior.* New York: Basic Books, 1980, 8.

McIntosh, Mary. "The Homosexual Role." *Social Problems* (Fall 1968):182–192.

Melton, Gary B. "Public Policy and Private Prejudice: Psychology and Law on Gay Rights." *The American Psychologist* 44 (June 1989):933–941.

Money, John. "Sin, Sickness, or Status?: Homosexual Gender Identity and Psychoneuroendocrinology." *American Psychologist* 42 (9187): 384–399.

———. *Gay, Straight, and in Between: The Sexology of Erotic Orientation.* New York: Oxford University Press, 1988.

Newsweek. "A Government in the Bedroom." July 14, 1986:36–38.

Newsweek. "The Future of Gay America." March 12, 1990:20–26.

Newsweek. "What is Queer Nation?" Aug. 12, 1991:24–25.

Newsweek. "Battling the Bias." Nov. 25, 1991:25.

Newsweek. "Born or Bred?" Nov. 24, 1992:25.

Newsweek. "Gays and the Military." Feb. 1, 1993: 52–55.

Peplau, Letitia Anne. "Lesbian and Gay Relationships." Gonsiorek and Weinrich (1991), pp. 177–195.

Perlman, David. "AIDS: Today There is More Hope." *Seattle Post-Intelligencer* (June 6, 1991): C1, C9.

Pittman, David J. "The Male House of Prostitution." *Transaction* 8 (March/April 1971): 21–28.

Plummer, Kenneth. "Building a Sociology of Homosexuality." *The Making of the Modern Homosexual.* Ed. K. Plummer. Totowa, N.J.: Barnes and Noble, 1981a, 17–29.

———. *Sexual Stigma: An Interactionist Account.* London: Routledge and Kegan Paul, 1975.

———. "Homosexual Categories: Some Research Problems in the Labeling Perspective of Homosexuality." *The Making of the Modern Homosexual.* Ed. K. Plummer. Totowa, N.J.: Barnes and Noble, 1981a, 53–75.

———. "Sexual Diversity: A Sociological Perspective." *The Psychology of Sexual Diversity.* Ed. Kevin Howells. New York: Basil Blackwell, 1984, 219–253.

Ponse, Barbara. *Identities in the Lesbian World: The Social Construction of Self.* Westport, Conn.: Greenwood Press, 1978.

Risman, B., and P. Schwartz. "Sociological Research on Male and Female Homosexuality." *Annual Review of Sociology* 14 (1988): 125–147.

Rivera, Rhonda R. "Sexual Orientation and the Law." Gonsiorek and Weinrich (1991), pp. 81–99.

Ross, Michael W. "Married Homosexual Men: Prevalence and Background." *Marriage and Family Review* 14. The Haworth Press, 1990:35–57.

Saghir, Marcel T., and Eli Robins. *Male and Female Homosexuality: A Comprehensive Investigation.* Baltimore: Williams and Wilkins, 1973.

Schofield, Michael. *Sociological Aspects of Homosexuality: A Comparative Study of Three Types of Homosexuals.* Boston: Little, Brown, 1965.

Schwartz, Jerry. "Grim Predictions: A Half-Million More Cases of AIDS." *Seattle Post-Intelligencer* June 6, 1991:C9.

Seattle Post-Intelligencer. "Aids Jail Threat to Health Workers." (July 19, 1991):A1, A6.

Sell, R.L., J.A. Wells, A.J. Valleron, A. Will, M. Cohen, and K. Umbel. "Homosexual and Bisexual Behavior in the United States, the United Kingdom, and France." Paper presented at the Sixth International Conference on AIDs, San Francisco, Calif. June 1990.

Shilts, Randy. "What's Fair in Love and War." *Newsweek* (Feb. 1, 1993):58–59.

Simon, William, and John Gagnon. "Homosexuality: The Formation of a Sociological Perspective." *Journal of Health and Social Behavior* 8 (1967):177–185.

Slovenko, Ralph. "Homosexuality and the Law: From Condemnation to Celebration." Judd Marmor (1980), pp. 194–217.

Smith, W. T. "Adult Sexual Behavior in 1989: Number of Partners, Frequency of Intercourse and Risk of AIDS." *Family Planning Perspectives* 23(1991):102–107.

Smolowe, Jill. "Sex, Lies and the Military." *Time* (Feb. 8, 1993):29–30.

Snyder, M., and S.W. Uranowitz. "Reconstructing the Past: Some Cognitive Consequences of Person Perception." *Journal of Personality and Social Psychology* 36 (1978):941–950.

Time. "Are Gay Men Born That Way?" Sept. 9, 1991:60–61.

Troiden, Richard R. "Becoming Homosexual: A Model of Gay Identity Acquisition." *Psychiatry* 42 (Nov. 1979):362–373.

———. *Gay and Lesbian Identity: A Sociological Analysis.* Dix Hills, N.Y.: General Hall, 1988.

———."The Formation of Homosexual Identities." *Journal of Homosexuality* 17 (1989): 43–73.

Voeller, Bruce. "Society and the Gay Movement." Marmor (1980), pp. 232–252.

Warren, Carol. "Homosexuality and Stigma." Marmor (1980), pp. 123–141.

Weinrich, James D., and Walter L. Williams. "Strange Customs, Familiar Lives: Homosexualities in Other Cultures." Gonsiorek and Weinrich (1991), pp. 44–60.

West, D.J. "Homosexuality and Social Policy: The Case for a More Informed Approach" in *Law and Contemporary Problems* 51 (Winter, 1988): 181–199.

Whitam, Frederick L. "Culturally Invariable Properties of Male Homosexuality: Tentative Conclusions From Cross-Cultural Research." *Archives of Sexual Behavior* 12 (June, 1983): 207–226.

Whitam, Frederick L., and Robin M. Mathy. *Male Homosexuality in Four Societies: Brazil, Guatemala, the Philippines, and the United States.* New York: Praeger, 1986.

Wooden, Wayne S., and Jay Parker. *Men Behind Bars: Sexual Exploitation in Prison.* New York: Plenum Press, 1982.

Young, Thomas J. "Regional Differences in Sodomy Laws." *Psychological Reports* 68 (February, 1991):228–230.

ENDNOTES

1. Many lesbians, angered that research has ignored them, believe that the neglect is merely another indicator of society's sexism (*Newsweek*, 1992).

2. The remarks of Harry Hay, founding leader of the Mattachine Society, as he addressed the initial gathering of the organization. (As quoted in D'Emillio, 1983:9)

3. It is interesting that the homosexuals in Queer Nation refer to themselves "queers." They believe that by calling themselves what heterosexuals have often used to insult them, they will "disarm" homophobics (people who have an irrational fear of homosexuals) of some of their ammunition (*Newsweek,* Aug. 12, 1991).

4. This cultural image has historically been a characteristic attributed not only to homosexuals, but to other minority groups such as African Americans and Jews (Herek, 1991).

5. This section summarizes information provided by Herek (1991), who reviews survey results from *The Los Angeles Times,* Yankelovich, Gallup, Roper, and the National Opinion Research Center.

6. The 25 states in which sodomy remains illegal are Alabama, Arizona, Arkansas, Delaware, Florida, Georgia, Idaho, Kansas, Kentucky, Louisiana, Maryland, Michigan, Minnesota, Mississippi, Missouri, Montana, Nevada, North Carolina, Oklahoma, Rhode Island, South Carolina, Tennessee, Texas, Utah, Virginia. In five of these states (Arkansas, Kansas, Montana, Nevada, Texas) only homosexual sodomy is illegal (Young, 1991).

7. In 1989, for example, Tennessee replaced "crimes against nature" with "homosexual acts."

8. When *Time* (Duffy, 1993) asked a random sample of Americans, "Do you favor Clinton's plan to allow gays and lesbians to serve in the military?" 43 percent answered yes and 48 percent answered no.

9. One apparent inconsistency in the military policy has not escaped the scrutiny of some homosexual advocates. Shilts (1993) argues that the homosexual ban has been relaxed during times of war. He demonstrates that during Vietnam and the Korean war, discharges were approximately one-half what they were prior to and after the wars.

10. There are notable exceptions to this pattern. The city of Seattle, for example, has a "Domestic Partnership" plan, whereby city employees who are in a committed relationship can receive the health benefits of a spouse.

11. The difference between the HIV virus and full-blown AIDS was likely clarified for many Americans in November 1991, when a very healthy looking Magic Johnson announced that he had contracted the HIV virus and would be retiring from the NBA. It was further

clarified when Magic actually played in the 1992 Olympics and even planned to return to the Lakers for the 1992–1993 season. The controversy surrounding Magic's return eventually led to Magic's second retirement from the NBA, in November of 1992.

12. In the 1987 version of the *DSM* (DSM III rev. ed.) the "Ego-Dystonic Homosexuality" category was removed. But the DSM-III-R added the category "Sexual Disorder Not Otherwise Specified," defined as the presence of "persistent and marked distress about one's sexual orientation" (Davison, 1991:138). Therefore, while homosexuality is no longer a disorder, distress about homosexuality is a disorder.

Chapter 9

Prostitution

PROSTITUTION: Sweet, Sweet Connie

*"Sweet, sweet Connie, doin' her act
she had the whole show and that's a fact"*

These are lyrics from Grand Funk's 1973 hit song "We're an American Band." Who is "Sweet, sweet Connie"? She is, perhaps, the best known rock'n'roll groupie in the country. Having sex with rock'n'roll musicians and singers, Connie boasts, "is my life" (Hamzy and Wells, 1992:68).

In "Confessions of a Rock'n'Roll Groupie" (Hamzy and Wells, 1992), Connie describes herself as having been an ordinary student in high school who was physically attractive and popular with the boys. Connie began to express her sexuality before high school. Connie states, "I was also one mean kisser, having mastered the art of tonguing by the time I was in seventh grade" (Hamzy and Wells, 1992:68). She had sex with her first rock musician by the age of 15, and she hasn't stopped. She has had all kinds of sex, from kinky to straight intercourse, with "hundreds" of rock musicians, singers, and their crews. As many as "24 guys in one night," Connie boasts (Hamzy and Wells, 1992:152). Connie claims that what separates her from other groupies is that she knows what she's there for, and she delivers. She is satisfied with her life, and she has no plans on retiring.

Sweet Connie is a career groupie who provides a variety of sexual services, for a variety of men, pretty much on demand.

She is often rewarded for her services with travel, lodging, meals, gifts, and drugs—to say nothing of the cash value of her notoriety.

WHAT IS PROSTITUTION?

Is Connie a prostitute? The answer depends on one's definition of prostitution. Let us, therefore, turn to a review of objectivist and subjectivist definitions of prostitution.

The Objectivist Conception

For the objectivist, deviant behaviors are behaviors that violate social norms. In the case of prostitution, however, a precise definition of norm-violating behaviors is problematic. This may appear curious. Isn't prostitution simply "sex for pay"?

One familiar objectivist definition, the law, accepts that prostitution is strictly "sex for pay." According to law, prostitution is any one of three nonmarital acts involving "sex for pay." The three acts are the following:

1. engaging in sexual relations with another person for a fee or something of value
2. offering (or soliciting) to engage in sexual relations with another person for a fee or something of value
3. requests (or agrees) to pay a fee or something of value to another person for sexual services and acts (Gardner, 1985:366).

Legally, prostitution applies to men and women. The person offering to pay for sex may also be convicted of a crime. This is typical of most state prostitution statutes (Gardner, 1985).

Does "sex for pay" adequately distinguish prostitution from other human sexual relations? The law excludes marital sexual relations from prostitution. But, what about the person who marries for money? Also, in courtship and in marriage, persons often exchange their sexuality for nonsexual favors, advantages, or gains. Is this prostitution? According to one objectivist, Jennifer James, prostitution is "any sexual exchange in which the reward is neither sexual nor affectional" (1983:1305). Although this definition is closer to the social meaning than the legal definition of prostitution, it is not very useful. How can one distinguish between a sexually active woman who receives gifts from lovers and a female prostitute? According to Heyl (1979), a distinction between legitimate and illegitimate sexual encounters on a "sex for reward" basis is erroneous. This is because Heyl (1979) believes that some commoditization is at the core of human sexuality in general. In our society, for example, extreme emphasis is placed on a woman's physical attractiveness. Therefore, women commonly perceive themselves and present themselves as sexual objects. By presenting themselves as sex objects, women are expressing their sexuality to themselves and others; and female sexuality is highly valued. In marriage a woman's sexuality is exchanged for respectability, social status, and long-term economic support. Other women may exchange their sexuality for a "fast life," independence, power over men, or cash gifts.

If commoditization is at the core of human sexuality, as Heyl (1979) suggests, the difference between conventional sex exchanges and prostitution is one of degree, rather than one of kind. How, then, does Heyl define prostitution? According to Heyl (1979:2) prostitution is nonmarital sex engaged in and viewed by the service provider as a vocation. Simply stated, a female prostitute is a woman who defines herself as a prostitute.

For a moment, let's return to "Sweet Connie." Are her sexual activities acts of prostitution? According to the law and James's definition of prostitution, some of Connie's behaviors probably constitute prostitution. For example, Connie admits that she gives sex to gofers or stagehands who offer her cocaine, backstage passes, or access to the band (Hamzy and Wells, 1992:160). According to Heyl's definition of prostitution, however, Connie is what she says she is—a rock'n'roll groupie, not a prostitute.

In sum, objectivists who use a legal definition of prostitution overlook the similarities between conventional sexuality and sexuality regulated by criminal law. Rather, they assume that the law rests on some clear behavioral distinction, "sex for pay," which separates prostitution from other sexual relations. For other objectivists, the commoditization of sex, which is more or less evident in most sexuality, seriously questions the behavioral distinction assumed by the law. These objectivists offer their own definitions of prostitution, but objectivists have not

reached a consensus on what specifically and precisely constitutes prostitution. Therefore, it is fair to say that objectivist research on prostitution is unsystematic, and often limited to studies with small local samples of persons who either define themselves or are defined by the criminal justice system as prostitutes. Ironically, these samples more accurately reflect a subjectivist definition of prostitution.

The Subjectivist Conception

From the subjectivist point of view, a sexual exchange constitutes prostitution only if social audiences define it as such. The prostitute is one to whom that label has been applied. This perspective leads sociologists away from questions concerning causes of prostitution. Instead, subjectivists focus on the conditions by which prostitutes are created by public and official definitions of sexuality. According to subjectivists, "Sweet Connie" is not a prostitute.

THE PREVALENCE OF PROSTITUTION

Prostitution, often termed "the oldest profession," has existed throughout the world from antiquity to the present. It is surprising, then, how limited scientific inquiry on prostitution has been. Most empirical studies of prostitution were published during the past three decades, the 1960s through the 1980s. Earlier publications focused primarily on the morality of prostitution (James, 1983). In the 1990s, scholarly discourse on prostitution is increasingly oriented toward the "sexual politics" of feminism, civil liberties, and the AIDS epidemic (Jenness, 1990). Despite changes in prostitution discourse, female prostitutes have been the primary target of moral condemnation, scientific investigation, and political change. Therefore, our review of the prostitute's life and subculture, theories of prostitution, and social policy toward prostitution is limited largely to female prostitution. To begin, however, let us examine the extent of prostitution in the United States and then briefly describe the male prostitute.

The Extent of Prostitution in the United States

The actual number of working prostitutes in the United States is unknown. Estimates range from a low of 84,000 (Potterat et al., 1990) to a high of 2,000,000 (Gibson-Ainyette et al., 1988). The estimate most often given is somewhere between 250,000 and 500,000 (Decker, 1979; Rathus, 1983). Several researchers believe that female prostitution is declining. Studies of the frequency of male patronization of prostitutes demonstrate a marked decline since World War II (Kinsey et al., 1948; 1953; Hunt, 1974). These studies attribute the decline in male patrons to the liberalization of sexual mores. Simply stated, men use prostitutes less because other females are sexually available than before.

In recent years, the fear of AIDS has, perhaps, also contributed to a decline in prostitution. Berk (1990:608), for example, suggests that because prostitution is a high-risk activity, prostitutes may seek other sources of income, and potential customers may avoid sex with prostitutes. This, however, is difficult to determine. A decline in female prostitution, for example, may have more to do with improved economic opportunities for women or, as has already been suggested, the greater sexual availability of other women. Also, it is entirely possible that the fear of AIDS does not influence the supply or demand of prostitutes. For example, the number of male homosexual prostitutes is increasing (Earls and David, 1989). The fear of AIDS, however, may change prostitutes' sexual practices, for example, the use of condoms and abstinence from particular sex acts (Earls and David

1989:411). Similarly, customers may be requesting what they perceive to be lower-risk acts. As one male prostitute states, "Aids hasn't been such a bad thing for us—there's a lot more demand for kinky things, which are more pleasant to do than f_____" (Robinson, 1990:12).

Ironically, if the fear of AIDS increases the demand for sex acts other than intercourse (anal and vaginal), the result might be an increased demand for the services of prostitutes. Although prostitutes have not been found to be instrumental in the transmission of AIDS (Acheson, 1986; Leishman, 1987; Rosenberg, 1988), prostitutes are being blamed by officials and some scientists, too, because of their potential to spread the deadly disease (Pheterson, 1990).

Regardless of whether the actual number of prostitutes is up or down from previous decades, arrests for prostitution in the United States increased during the past decade. The dramatic increase in arrests of male prostitutes accounts for the overall rise in prostitution arrests. According to the *Uniform Crime Reports* (FBI, 1992:218), from 1982 to 1991, the arrests of male prostitutes increased 6.5 percent. For female prostitutes arrests declined 22.7 percent. Interpretations of these arrest trends must proceed with caution. Although, as previously noted, some researchers believe that female prostitution is declining and male prostitution is increasing, arrest trends often reflect changing enforcement patterns rather than actual changes in law violations. Arrests of prostitutes have been described as highly discretionary, arbitrary, and capricious (Carmen and Moody, 1985). Remember that most male prostitutes engage in homosexual activities, and the only people that police dislike more than homosexuals are cop-fighters (Lindquist et al., 1989:279). Perhaps, then, the dramatic rise in arrests of male prostitutes reflects a police response to the increased openness of homosexuality. Also, increased public concern about AIDS may be contributing to a police crackdown on prostitution, especially homosexual prostitution.

In the United States, the highest arrest rates for prostitution are in the West (57.8 per 100,000 population) and in the Northeast (53.3), followed by the Midwest (32.8) and South (30.3). Also, arrests for prostitution are highest in our largest cities, those with populations of 250,000 and more (148.6 per 100,000). Arrests descend in relation to city size to a low of 2.6 per 100,000 population in cities under 10,000 population (FBI, 1992: 215). According to the *Uniform Crime Reports* (FBI, 1992:218), the majority of persons arrested for prostitution are females between the ages of 25 and 29 (28 percent), and whites (60 percent). However, African Americans are overrepresented in prostitution arrests (38 percent), given their percentage of the overall population, which is about 12 percent (FBI, 1992:223–224). The social characteristics of arrested prostitutes are similar to descriptions from self-report studies of prostitutes. Let us, then, turn to the literature for a more detailed description of the prostitute, his or her activities and life.

Male Prostitutes

Little is known about male prostitution. Research on male prostitution is sparse and sketchy. It appears, however, that the majority of male prostitutes are young, ranging in age from 16 to 29 years, white, homosexual or bisexual, and from diverse socioeconomic backgrounds (Earls and David, 1989). Presently, the majority of male prostitutes identify themselves as homosexual or bisexual (Allen, 1980; Weisberg, 1985; Earls and David, 1989; Boyer, 1989). This, however, has not always been true. In studies prior to the last two decades, male prostitutes predominantly identified themselves as heterosexual (Earls and David, 1989), although many of them

provided homosexual sex services. Earls and David (1989:416) offer two possible explanations for the discrepancy in sexual orientation reported by male prostitutes in earlier and later studies. First, more males are willing to admit their homosexuality because homosexuality is now more socially acceptable. Second, there is an actual increase in male homosexual prostitution. That is, with changes in sexual morality, male homosexuals more actively and openly seek sexual partners. This, in turn, increases both the supply of and demand for homosexual prostitutes.

Like female prostitution, male prostitution is stratified. Luckenbill (1986:284) identifies three levels of male prostitutes: "street hustlers," "bar hustlers," and "escort prostitutes." Male prostitutes rank these modes of prostitution according to income and safety from arrest. Street hustlers earn between $10 and $25 per trick, bar hustlers between $50 and $75, and escort prostitutes receive 60 percent of each trick which ranges between $150 and $200. Also, street hustlers are arrested more often than bar hustlers. Escort prostitutes are the least likely to be arrested (Luckenbill, 1986:286). Furthermore, Luckenbill (1986:286–287) discovered three career mobility patterns for male prostitutes: "stability," "minimum ascent," and "maximum ascent." The most common mobility pattern was the minimum ascent from street hustler to bar hustler. The most infrequent mobility pattern was maximum ascent from street hustler to bar hustler to escort prostitute.

Why do men become prostitutes? Who are the men who become prostitutes? Research suggests that men from diverse backgrounds choose to become prostitutes largely for the money (Earls and David, 1989; Robinson, 1990). Entry into male prostitution is related to monetary gain, sexual orientation (homosexuality), and early childhood sexual experiences (Earls and David, 1989). Almost all research on prostitution finds monetary gain to be an important determinant for entry into prostitution. In addition, research finds that having a homosexual identity and early childhood sexual experiences are important for entry into male prostitution (Boyer, 1989; Robinson, 1990). However, there is disagreement among researchers as to the nature of these early childhood sexual experiences. On the one hand, Boyer (1989:171–172) characterizes male prostitutes' early sexual experiences as "sexual victimization"; 42 percent had been raped, and 36.3 percent had been molested prior to their involvement in prostitution. On the other hand, Robinson (1990:10) found that fewer than a quarter of his sample reported child sexual abuse. Also, many male prostitutes spoke positively of their early sexual experiences with older men, especially if they had been paid. These different findings may not be as contradictory as they appear. Boyer's (1989) sample of prostitutes comprised street hustlers, whereas, Robinson's (1990) sample primarily comprised sexual masseurs and escort prostitutes. Perhaps, both early sexual experiences and modes of prostitution are related to factors in social background, such as family stability, social class, and race. This, however, remains an empirical question.

No doubt, heterosexual and homosexual male prostitution exist, but until the past decade, they have received little attention from the law. Social scientists, too, have historically and overwhelmingly focused on female prostitution. Let us now begin our examination of female prostitution with a description of who these prostitutes are and how they live.

Female Prostitutes

Female prostitutes are, for the most part, young. In a study of 1,013 female prostitutes from 1970 to 1983 in Colorado Springs, Potterat and his colleagues (1990:236) found that about 75 percent of these women were under 25 years old. Only 1.3 percent were over 34 years old. The majority of Colorado Springs prostitutes were white (54.9 percent). African American women made up 35.6 percent of the sample; 6 percent were Hispanic; and the remaining 3.5 percent were predominantly East Asians (Potterat et al., 1990:236). The age and ethnic distributions of Colorado Springs prostitutes are similar to those reported by national arrest data. According to the *Uniform Crime Reports* (FBI, 1992:231), the number of arrests of female prostitutes increases steadily among women from ages 18 to 24; then, the number peaks for women at 25 to 29 and steadily declines thereafter.

Many female prostitutes begin prostitution as adolescents. Although several studies report child sexual abuse as a characteristic of adolescent prostitutes, Seng (1989) reports that the running away, not sexual abuse, leads to prostitution. That is to say, sexual abuse is related to running away, and runaways are the ones who are likely to engage in prostitution. Adolescent female prostitutes are generally in their upper teens, white, and from both lower- and middle-class backgrounds (Weisberg, 1985; Seng, 1989).

Females begin prostitution in their early years, and they leave prostitution when they are still young. Potterat and his colleagues (1990) found that women remain in prostitution a short time, four or five years. Similarly, James (1983) reports that many women leave prostitution in their twenties. According to James (1983:1310), prostitution is a "temporary adaptation" to "needs of survival" more than it is a career. During their short careers, many female prostitutes travel from one location to another. For example, Potterat and his colleagues (1990) found that more than half of their sample were circuit prostitutes who worked in any one location only for a few weeks a year. Prostitutes also often move from one type of prostitution to another during their careers (James, 1983; Potterat et al., 1990). Therefore, the status of one type of prostitution in relation to another is unclear.

However, by all accounts, "streetwalkers" make up the bottom level and "call girls" the top level of the prostitution hierarchy. Let us identify the various prostitution styles.

Styles of Female Prostitution. Styles of prostitution differ according to work setting, income, safety from arrest, and, to some extent, status. Prostitution styles include streetwalkers, bar girls, massage parlor prostitutes, hotel prostitutes, house prostitutes, and call girls. It is estimated that streetwalkers make up about 20 percent of all female prostitutes; 15 percent are bar girls; 25 percent are massage parlor prostitutes; 10 percent are hotel prostitutes; 15 percent are house prostitutes; and 15 percent are call girls (Simon and Witt, 1982:253).

Streetwalkers solicit customers "on the block," or "on the stroll." Generally, they stand on street corners or in doorways, and subtly ask, "Do you want a date?" "Lonesome?" "Where are you headed?" "Are you from out of town?" or something similar (Winick and Kinsie, 1971; James, 1983). If the man is interested, the streetwalker is quick to state her price and services to be rendered. Once an agreement is made she may take him to a hotel, apartment or "trick house" where cheap rooms are available to prostitutes (James, 1983). She may also perform her service in a doorway, hallway, or backseat (Winick and Kinsie, 1971).

The streetwalker's business is the "hustle," not customer satisfaction. The "hustle" entails getting money from the client. This may take the form of talking him into more expensive types of sex, or selling drugs, or robbing him. Streetwalkers are often part of a "deviant street network," which is involved in a variety of other illegalities including drug selling, larceny, fraud, and robbery (Miller, 1986). However, because the streetwalker works in a public setting, she herself is vulnerable to customer violence, police harassment, and arrest. This vulnerability has pushed many streetwalkers toward suburban shopping centers and airports (James, 1983). To put it mildly, the life of a streetwalker is one of high risks and, contrary to conventional wisdom, limited monetary reward. Many streetwalkers work for the "man" (a pimp). His take of her labor is 100 percent. We will discuss the pimp shortly. For now, let us continue with our review of the styles of prostitution.

Bar girls, as the term suggests, hustle bar customers for drinks and sex. They may subtly approach a prospect, but most often they wait for a customer's approach. Their "hustle" is to build up a customer's bar tab and to solicit pay for sex. Like the streetwalker, the bar girl often takes the customer to a hotel, apartment, or "trick house." The bar setting, however, protects her from the violence of the streets and constant police scrutiny. Her clientele and income depend on the quality of the bar (James, 1983). The bar manager takes from 40 to 50 percent of her earnings (Simon and Witt, 1982).

Massage parlor prostitutes are most often licensed masseuses who provide sexual services for a fee. Many services have a set fee. Some masseuse prostitutes limit themselves to particular sex services, for example, masturbation or oral sex. Others provide whatever the customer is willing to pay for, if the price is right. The owner of the massage parlor does not let on to customers that he or she is aware that sex services are being provided (James 1983). The establishment owner pays the masseuse a commission of 40 to 50 percent of the total fee for each customer. Their commission plus tips may amount to as much as $40,000 a year (Velarde and Warlick, 1973). Most likely, this figure is much higher today. Their clients are predominantly business men who most often request masturbation. Today, many but not all massage parlors are fronts for sex services. The growth in massage parlor prostitution occurred primarily between 1975 and 1979 (Potterat et al., 1990).

Hotel prostitutes are sometimes given hotel rooms to live in so that they will be available to customers. These are generally second-rate hotels just off the beaten path. The most common working arrangement, however, is for the prostitute to be referred to a customer by a bellboy or manager, rather than to be provided with a room (James, 1983). Like managers of bars and massage parlors, hotel managers generally pay the prostitute a commission of 40 to 50 percent (Simon and Witte, 1982).

House prostitutes work in a house often called a "brothel," "bordello," "parlor house," or, less eloquently stated, a "whorehouse." Nevada is the only state in which houses of prostitution are legal in all counties except the urban counties where Reno, Las Vegas, and Lake Tahoe are located (James, 1983). In the rural counties of Nevada, where prostitution is legal, house trailers most often serve as bordellos, not the homes with a plush parlors or receiving room and upstairs bedrooms where the girls lived and worked in the late nineteenth and early twentieth centuries. Nevada prostitutes carry identification cards. They are fingerprinted by the police and routinely checked by the local health officials (James, 1983). Where prostitution is controlled, as in Nevada, the prices for sex services are lower than in places where it is illegal. House managers take from 50 to 60 percent of a prostitute's earnings (James, 1983).

Call girls are the "elites" among prostitutes. They are in the "call business." That is, prostitution by telephone (James, 1983). A call girl may work in her own apartment or home, or she may be received at her client's residence. Call girls often begin their careers as apprentices to another call girl. The apprentice learns some sexual techniques and how to "hustle," but most important she builds a clientele (Bryan, 1965). The call girl's high-priced services, $100 or more per job and annual earnings up to $50,000 or more, reflect her "higher-

class" clients (Rosenblum, 1975; James, 1983). These figures are, most likely, higher at the present. The call girl does not cheat or exploit her customer. She does her best to satisfy the customer. This is because her new business is most often referred by previous customers. Other working girls are another common source of referral. Some call girls have managers, "the man" or "madam," who act as referral agents for several call girls (James, 1983). Finally, her mode of operation, telephone referrals, protects the call girl from police scrutiny and public ostracism.

Thus far, we have examined only the "supply side" of prostitution. However, our discussion of styles of prostitution reveals that agents or managers play a central role in prostitution. Also, "it takes two to tango." Who, then, are the prostitutes' customers (or "johns")? Why do they solicit her services? We will first examine the role of the "pimp." Second, we will examine the john.

The Pimp

The pimp or "the man," as he is often called, is a central player in the life of prostitution. Although most female prostitutes are individual entrepreneurs, they often work with a pimp (James, 1983). This is especially true for streetwalkers. Our discussion of the pimp is largely based on Carmen and Moody's (1985:99–132) view of him in terms of the values and culture of prostitute society. According to Carmen and Moody, by media and middle-class standards, the pimp is stereotyped as the ultimate "badass":

> *The pimp is always Mr. Mean, who preys on unhappy girls who've run away from home, or is a sadistic woman beater who claims his woman to the life from which there is no escape. He is a conning dope dealer whom the prostitute clings to out of fear for her life (Carman and Moody, 1985:100).*

In prostitute society, however, the pimp is not a "procurer for prostitutes" or "protector of the women." He does not "turn out" women into a life of prostitution, or choose the women who comprise "his stable" (Carmen and Moody, 1985:100–104). The pimp does not actively "seek out" clients. However, he may refer clients to prostitutes he suspects are considering leaving the life or that he suspects are holding back money. The pimp is seldom with his prostitute and, therefore, does not protect her from street violence and police harassment. The prostitute's ability to avoid these dangers improves her standing with "her man." Pimps seldom "turn out" prostitutes. Prostitutes generally train themselves by trial and error on the streets or with the assistance of other women. The pimp, however, sometimes refers his woman to a call girl or madam for training (Bryan, 1965; Heyl, 1977). Finally, the prostitute chooses "her man," rather than the other way around. Prostitutes sometimes move from one pimp to another. Her relationship with a "high-class" pimp can improve her standing in the prostitution subculture (James, 1983).

What, then, does the pimp do? First and foremost, the pimp takes 100 percent of the prostitute's earnings. He also manages the money, provides her clothing, jewelry, food, an allowance; and he often keeps her children and gives her a home. His relationship with his women involves a complex of roles. He is her "businessman," her "father," her "brother," her "therapist," and her "lover" (Carmen and Moody 1985:108). Singly, he is all of the men in her life, except for the john who is strictly a client. His women are his "stable," and his women are known as "wives-in-law" to one another.

Why is the pimp so important in a prostitute's life? Away from the life of "tricks," the pimp is the "centrifugal force" in the subculture's vision of "home and hearth" and "nuclear family" (Carmen and Moody 1985:99–100). The patriarchal structure of prostitute society is a reproduction of conventional culture in a deviant subculture. In the words of Jennifer James:

It is clear that women in American society are socialized to believe that they need a man to take care of them, to "take care of business," to "complete" them, to love them, and to make a home for them. Prostitutes are no exception (James, 1983:1307).

The John

In the subculture of prostitution, the prostitute's customer is known as the john. Although prostitution is clearly a supply and demand business, the john has been largely ignored. Like the prostitute, the john is engaging in an illegal activity. Unlike the prostitute, however, he is seldom arrested. Sociologists, too, have shown little research interest in the john. This sex bias in the study of prostitution may, in part, reflect cultural differences in sex-role expectation. According to our cultural ideal, sex norms largely reserve sexual freedom for men, while imposing chastity and fidelity on women. Therefore, the female prostitute is perceived as deviant, whereas her male patron is perceived as normal (James, 1983:308). A few studies of male customers, their background characteristics, and motivations, however, are available. These studies provide some insights on prostitute-customer transactions.

Who are the men who solicit prostitutes? An early study by Kinsey and his colleagues (1948:600) found that prostitute customers were largely from the lower class. Seventy-four percent had only a grade school education. This may no longer be true. Jennifer James and Jane Meyerding, for example, found that the majority of customers of 136 Seattle, Washington, prostitutes were businessmen and professionals. These men were predominantly white, middle-aged (41.4 mean age), married, and from the suburbs (Symanski, 1981:73). Politicians and power brokers are also reported to frequent female prostitutes (Janus, Bess and Saltus, 1977). Janus, Bess, and Saltus (1977:67) further examined the sexual preferences of politicians and power brokers who frequented female prostitutes. The most frequently requested services included fellatio, exhibitionism, voyeurism, cross-dressing, fetishism, threesomes, flagellation, verbal and physical humiliation, bondage, and power games. Straight intercourse was an uncommon request. Many of the most frequently requested services are considered perverted by a majority of persons. These "special services," however, are commonly requested by customers regardless of their social class background (James, 1983:1308). In addition to "special services," customers' motivations include variety in women, variety in services, therapy for sexual dysfunctions, companionship, sexual release, and temporary relief while away from home (James, 1983:1308).

EXPLANATIONS OF PROSTITUTION

Macro-Objectivist Theories

Macro-objectivists attempt to explain the origin and persistence of prostitution. Their focus is on the structure of prostitution. These theories suggest that forces derived from legitimate social institutions give rise to prostitution. In this regard, they emphasize the social and economic organization of society that frames human relations, including sexual relations. There are two predominant macro-objectivist explanations of prostitution: exploitation explanations and functional explanations.

Exploitation Explanations.   In much of the world, male economic and social dominance is a fact of life. Not surprisingly, then, exploitation is viewed by many commentators and scholars, alike, as the cause of female prostitution. Emma Goldman, an early twentieth-century feminist, who was deported from the United States in 1919, argued that social and economic exploitation forced women into prostitution (Symanski, 1981:59). Another prominent woman of that era, Jane Addams, reported that many of the small-town girls who came to Chicago in search of jobs were preyed upon by men who lured and coerced them into prostitution (Symanski, 1981:59). It appears that their view was shared by policymakers of the time who shaped international treaty and domestic legislation prohibiting trafficking in women. In 1904, 13 nations signed the International Agreement for the Suppression of the White Slave Traffic. By 1910, these nations agreed to punish any person who procured another by force or fraud or who assisted a girl under 20 years old in becoming a prostitute (Winick and Kinsie, 1971). In the United States, the Bennet Act prohibits international traffic in persons and the Mann Act prohibits interstate traffic in persons (Winick and Kinsie, 1971).

Poverty and the social inequality of women persists in the late twentieth century. Perhaps, nowhere is the combination of poverty and social inequality of women more severe than in the third world. There, today, women remain vulnerable to procurement and prostitution (Barry, 1984). From a study of child prostitution in Brazil, Symanski (1981) reports that as many as 2,000 prostitutes, aged 11 to 17, work the district outside Rio de Janeiro. Here, in one month "a girl of 12 can earn ten times as much as her factory-working father" (Symanski, 1981:61). Similarly, in Thailand young girls are sold into prostitution. Often, they are sold by their families (Kunstel and Albright, 1987). In the third world, sexual slavery is reinforced by governmental indifference. Barry (1984:67) notes, "At levels of government and international authority where action could be taken against the slave trade, one finds at best suppression of evidence and at worst complicity in it."

Shifting our focus back to the United States, there is poverty, especially for the uneducated and unskilled. And, women generally lack economic and social parity with men. Do poverty and social inequality combine to force women into prostitution in the United States? At first glance, it may seem so. In the United States, prostitution is by far heterosexual—female sex workers and male patrons. Historically, prostitutes have predominantly come from lower socioeconomic backgrounds, and economic depressions have been associated with increasing numbers of prostitutes in several U.S. cities (Symanski, 1981).

No doubt, economic and social inequality play a role in female prostitution, but there is no hard evidence that poverty or social inequality forces women into prostitution (Gebhard, 1969; James, 1977; Carmen and Moody, 1985). Several scholars suggest that it is economic incentive that motivates women to become prostitutes, not economic hardship (Davis, 1937; Pomeroy, 1965; Gebhard, 1969; James, 1977; Carmen and Moody, 1985). In point of fact, all types of prostitutes (call girls, in-house prostitutes, streetwalkers, housewife operators, and drug addicts) make more money than other women of comparable age, marital status, education, and socioeconomic background (Exner et al., 1977).

Perhaps, women in more recent times do not face the economic predicament of their early twentieth-century counterparts. Even early studies suggested that economic incentive was as much a motivation for women entering prostitution as was economic hardship. For example, a 1915 New York City commissioned study of department store saleswomen discovered that higher paid saleswomen were more likely to become prostitutes (Symanski, 1981:62). Why this apparent irony? According to Symanski's (1981:62) summary of the study's findings, higher paid saleswomen were led into the brothels by "an environment of spending and

accumulation that caused rising expectation." Similarly, in a more recent study, Jennifer James (1977) reported that 64 percent of 137 Seattle, Washington, prostitutes described their family backgrounds as middle to upper class. Furthermore, James (1977) found that only 8 percent of these prostitutes claimed to have entered prostitution because of economic necessity, whereas 57 percent were motivated by the desire for money and spending.

Whether motivated by need or by greed, Schur (1983) argues that prostitution is intrinsically exploitive and oppressive to women. Schur (1983:168) believes that few women would choose prostitution if they were rewarded equally for other work. Schur assumes that women are deprived of adequate or wanted income, and, therefore, turn to prostitution for compensation. If women were guaranteed adequate work and pay, female prostitution would vanish. For Schur (1983), then, prostitution is caused by economic exploitation. Years ago, however, Davis (1937) argued that economics fails to recognize that prostitution meets important needs other than material needs. We will examine Davis's explanation of prostitution later. Here, we present Davis's argument that increased economic rewards for women will not eliminate prostitution. In Davis's words:

> In a competitive system as soon as the salaries of working girls are increased, the supply of prostitutes diminishes. The resulting scarcity increases the effective demand, in the form of price, which rises as supply diminishes. . . With the rise in price, working girls even with good salaries will be tempted into the profession. Moreover, it will be possible for more women to live on the proceeds of prostitution alone. . . The net result will be as much prostitution as before, and in terms of actual money invested and changing hands, there may be more (Davis, 1937:751).

If Davis is correct, one might argue that prostitution is not inherently exploitive. Rather, capitalist society exploits all workers including prostitutes. But, Symanski asks, "If prostitution is simply another form of exploited labor, why is there so little female demand for male prostitutes?" (1981:68). It would seem, in capitalist society, the female demand for male prostitution would be quickly met—if it were there. Despite the so-called sexual revolution and increased job alternatives and increased pay for women, there remains little female demand for male prostitutes (Symanski, 1981:68).

Perhaps, there is limited female demand because where men dominate women, men simply will not allow the sale of sexual favors to women. For example, some scholars argue that female prostitution exists and persists because it preserves the sexual double standard (Adler, 1975; Bullough and Bullough, 1978). In Freda Adler's (1975:57) words:

> Given the sexual freedom men have reserved for themselves and the code of premarital chastity and post-marital fidelity they have imposed on women, prostitution is the only mechanism which would permit the coexistence of these two mutually exclusive and contradictory ideals (Adler, 1975:57).

Where capitalism and patriarchy are combined, a system of male economic and social dominance prevails. Here, female prostitution flourishes and, thereby, reinforces male domination. This logic is difficult to falsify because female prostitution and male social and economic dominance are so widespread. If women have more control over society, will they be less likely to sell their sexual favors to men?

Anthropologist Dennis Werner (1984) provides some valuable insights into this question. Werner studied the Mekranoti Indians of Central Brazil. In Mekranoti society, there is little economic differentiation or gender inequality. Mekranoti women hold positions of high status, including that of chief. Yet, among the Mekranoti are "kupry" women. The kupry are unmarried women with children who provide sex to men in exchange for

food, beads, and other items. Kupry women are held in lower esteem than other women, but the Mekranoti recognize kupry status as a woman's choice (Werner 1984:397).

Why do some Mekranoti women choose to become kupries? Is there an economic incentive? Do kupry women work less? Kupry women have no more or no less possessions than Mekranoti married women. There is no material gain. Similarly, kupry women spend as much time in the same sorts of work as do Mekranoti married women (Werner, 1984:397–98). Contrary to the suggested link of women's oppression to prostitution, the kupry illustrate that something like prostitution exists even in an egalitarian society.

Werner's research on kupry women contributes to the sociological study of prostitution in two important ways. First, his research suggests that it may be misleading to attribute prostitution solely to the social and economic gender inequality observed in much of the modern world. Second, Werner contends that kupry status is created by social pressures that derive from established social institutions, such as the monogamous family, and that kupry status preserves social order. Werner's explanation of prostitution parallels in many ways Kingsley Davis's (1937) functional analysis of prostitution. Let us review Davis's functional explanation of prostitution.

Functional Explanations.   The best known sociological explanation of prostitution is Kingsley Davis's (1937) classic analysis of the functions of prostitution. Davis identifies the core element of prostitution as "the employment of sex for non-sexual ends within a competitive-authoritative system" (1937:746). However, Davis notes that this does not distinguish prostitution from sexual expressions in society's approved relationships, for example, engagement and marriage. Instead, the use of sex for nonsexual gains, such as favors, gifts or money, varies in degree along a continuum of relations from courtship and marriage to prostitution. Prostitution, then, resembles behavior expressed in morally and socially approved relationships. What distinguishes prostitution from approved patterns of sexuality is its functional relationship to the broader society. Engagement and marriage link sexuality to society's most vital needs, reproduction and socialization of future generations. Erotic expressions, even for nonsexual ends, are legitimate if subsumed under cultural arrangements that are linked to reproduction or to patterns that are intended to lead to such an arrangement. Outside of courtship and marriage, sex for nonsexual ends is purely commercial, and, therefore, morally and legally condemned. Why, then, does purely commercial sex (i.e., prostitution) exist? How does it survive in the face of moral and legal condemnation?

The answer, according to Davis (1937), rests on the functional relation between commercial prostitution and the monogamous family. Society's attempt to control sex, to make it exclusive, to tie it to love, to restrict it to institutions of reproduction and child rearing, creates the opportunity for prostitution. Therefore, the family "limits the variety, amount, and nature of a person's satisfactions" (Davis, 1937:753). On the other hand, pure commercial prostitution is the "most malleable," "most uninvolved" outlet for sexual "variety," "perverse gratification," "mysterious and provocative" surroundings, and "intercourse free from entangling cares and civilized pretense. . ." (Davis, 1937:753). Prostitution, then, satisfies desires that, if otherwise not met, could threaten the durability of the monogamous family. From this point of view, prostitution preserves social order in two important ways. First, prostitution involves sex free from reproduction and emotional, social, or long-term economical obligations. As such, prostitution does not threaten or compete with the family's tasks, status, or ability to endure. By contrast, premarital and extramarital affairs often require personal involvements that are more likely to compete with family functions, and, thereby, threaten family stability. Second, prostitution provides an outlet for those who, as a consequence of personal, social, physical, or mental defect, seek sexual expression outside society's approved and restricted patterns of sexuality. In this way, prostitutes satisfy cravings that might otherwise be imposed on those who prefer sexual limits, exclusivity, and commitment.

To Davis's credit, others have attributed the origin and persistence of prostitution to its functional relation to the broader society, in particular, the monogamous family structure. For example, anthropologist Dennis Werner (1984) explains prostitution, "kupry status," as a function of the monogamous family structure of the Mekranoti Indians of Central Brazil. Werner (1984) further concludes that "kupry status" functions to preserve social order. Among the Mekranoti, the monogamous family survives, in part, because kupry women provide a sexual service that might otherwise be met by an alternative family structure—polygyny (one man with two or more wives). Furthermore, the availability of kupry women to all men prevents internal fighting over women, thereby, preserving social order (Werner, 1984:403). To some extent, then, Davis's theory of prostitution can be extended to "primitive" and unstratified societies.

It is also to Davis's credit that several features of prostitution in the contemporary United States fit with his theory of prostitution. As noted earlier, men go to female prostitutes for variety in sexual activities and in sexual partners and for perverse sexual gratification. These reasons are among the functional advantages of prostitution recognized by Davis. Also, the majority of men who frequent prostitutes are married men. This fact, perhaps, speaks to the limitations of sexual expression that Davis attributed to the monogomous family. Finally, Davis argued that a decline in family stability and a decline in female prostitution result from a single cause—sexual freedom. In the United States, as a result of the sexual revolution and the present feminist movement, many freedoms for women have increased. Women are freer to seek gratifications (sexual, social, and economic) outside of the family. Currently, divorce is at record levels. So, too, is the number of single-parent families. Also, as previously mentioned, contemporary scholars believe that female prostitution is declining. Is it true as Davis (1937:755) suggested, ". . .unrestricted indulgence in sex for the fun of it by both sexes is the greatest enemy, not only of the family, but also of prostitution"?

Criticism of Davis focuses on his suggestion that prostitution in some form is inevitable and that it has desirable social effects. For example, Lowery notes that prostitution has all but vanished in China and Cuba (1974:203). Yet, these are societies with a system of social dominance, social restrictions on sexual freedom, and monogamous family structures. Similarly, although Werner's analysis of prostitution among the Mekranoti Indians parallels Davis's observations in many ways, Werner's discovery of prostitution in a cooperative, egalitarian society raises questions about the basic element of prostitution identified by Davis—the use of sex for nonsexual ends in a competitive, authoritarian system. Also, concerning the desirable effects of prostitution, there is no hard evidence that prostitution saves marriages or reduces rape (Rio, 1991).

A final criticism of Davis's theory is that he emphasizes the social effects of prostitution rather than its causes. The functional relation between the family and prostitution is not necessarily a causal relation. The question, "Why do women enter prostitution?" remains unanswered. At best, one might conclude from Davis's theory that male

dominance generates both the male appetite for sex and the motive for women to employ sex for nonsexual ends. Davis (1937) assumes that a system of dominance is inevitable, and, therefore, prostitution in some form is also inevitable. What this means, then, is that Davis uses one universal, a system of dominance, to explain another universal, prostitution. Given that one universal can always be used to explain another universal, Davis's theory is unfalsifiable. Davis's theory is only testable if it can be demonstrated that dominance and prostitution are not universals. However, attempts to demonstrate this would undoubtedly lead to unsolvable questions about how to define both dominance and prostitution (Werner, 1984:402).

Micro-Objectivist Theories

Micro-objectivists attempt to explain why certain individuals become prostitutes. Their explanations emphasize the social structures and processes that motivate one to become a prostitute. This is different from macro-objectivists who focus on the origin and persistence of prostitution. As you have seen, for macro-objectivists, prostitution is itself an institution that exists and persists because of its relation to the social and economic organization of the broader society. On the other hand, micro-objectivists focus on background and situational factors that motivate women to prostitute themselves. There are two major micro-objectivists explanations of why a woman becomes a prostitute: tri-factor theory and social learning theory.

Tri-factor Theory. According to Benjamin and Masters (1964:90–91), three categories of factors combine to explain why a particular woman becomes a prostitute. These three categories are "predisposing," "attracting," and "precipitating" factors. Predisposing factors include background features, such as a broken home and parental promiscuity. Attracting factors include advantages one perceives in choosing to become a prostitute, such as lots of money, easy money, easy work, and adventure. Finally, precipitating factors include economic hardship, no prospect of a good marriage, or persuasion by those in the trade (pimps and known prostitutes).

Furthermore, Benjamin and Masters distinguish between voluntary prostitutes and compulsive prostitutes (1964:89–91). Voluntary prostitutes choose the "life" freely and rationally. Compulsive prostitutes are driven into the "life" by some psychological reason, need, or desire. Benjamin and Masters (1964) believe that the majority of prostitutes are of the voluntary type. For voluntary prostitutes, "attracting" factors are most important. As we noted earlier, the importance of attracting factors, in particular the money, has been purported by several researchers as being the primary incentive for becoming a prostitute. The money factor has been empirically established; but other attracting factors noted by Benjamin and Masters have not been, for example, that prostitution is "easy" work or that some prostitutes sexually "enjoy" their work. In fact, there is sufficient literature suggesting that easy work and sexual satisfaction are myths. Prostitutes often give a large percentage of their income to pimps; parlor, hotel, and brothel managers; bellboys; cab drivers; police; physicians; and other support persons. Also, prostitutes receive no job security or benefits. Furthermore, prostitutes, streetwalkers in particular, are the recipients of violence, police harassment, arrest, fines, and prison sentences. Frequent arrests and convictions contribute to the prostitute's financial debt and isolation from more respectable associates, friends, and family, making it ever more difficult to get out of the life or find other work (Schur, 1983:170). Finally, there is much evidence that prostitutes avoid sexual self-indulgence. Refraining from an orgasm while giving one is a part of the prostitute's hustle. The hustle is the essence of

the profession, which all prostitutes must learn. Let us, then, turn to learning theories of prostitution.

Learning Theories.　The notion that prostitutes are made not born is well supported by studies of prostitutes. Professional prostitutes, house prostitutes, call girls, and streetwalkers can generally identify one person (a pimp, a prostitute, or a madam) who taught her the techniques, skills, and rules of the profession (Bryan, 1965; Winick and Kinsie, 1971; Heyl, 1977; Carmen and Moody, 1985). There are important differences and similarities in the learning process for various types of prostitutes. For example, direct instruction characterizes the training of house prostitutes (Heyl, 1977); whereas observation is the primary mode of learning for the call girl (Bryan 1965); and trial and error is the predominant mode of learning for streetwalkers (Winick and Kinsie, 1971). Let us, then, begin with the house prostitute, because her training is the most intense and extended. Then we will examine the training of call girls and streetwalkers to locate similarities and differences in their training.

House Prostitutes.　The most comprehensive study of the training of house prostitutes is provided by Barbara Heyl (1977). She examines the role of madam as teacher. As noted earlier, the high-class whorehouse is a thing of the past in the United States The house prostitute of today works out of trailers, motels, and luxury apartments (Heyl, 1977).

According to Heyl (1977), the training of house prostitutes is more formal than that of other prostitutes because establishment madams or managers will not hire a novice. The requisite of experience gives rise to a "house" devoted strictly to training novice prostitutes. One such establishment, Ann's house, was the focus of Heyl's study of the madam as teacher. Ann's house "turns out" about 20 prostitutes a year. Most girls are referred by pimps. Prices are relatively low to ensure a limited but loyal and known clientele (Heyl 1977:546). The content of training involves three components: "physical skills and strategies," "client management," and teaching the "racket" (Heyl, 1977:547–551). Our discussion of these components is taken exclusively from Heyl's (1977) observations.

Physical skills and strategies involve teaching the physical and psychological techniques of fellatio, combinations of fellatio and intercourse, straight intercourse, and self-defense. Fellatio, called "french tricks," involves male orgasm during oral sex. The combination of fellatio and intercourse is termed a "half and half." Techniques for "french tricks" and a "half and half" involve strategies for maximizing sexual stimulation for the client while providing self-protection for the prostitute. The combination of stimulation and self-protection is also evident in the techniques of straight intercourse. For example, "during coitus, the woman is to move her hips 'like a go-go dancer's' while keeping her feet on the bed and tightening her inner thigh muscles to protect herself from the customer's thrust and full penetration. . .and the woman is taught to keep one of her arms across her chest as a measure of self-defense in this vulnerable position" (Heyl 1977:547). Beyond these techniques, the madam teaches the house rules. The rules include learning the fees for specific sex acts and examining a man for genital sores or symptoms of venereal disease (VD).

Client management is "hustling." The essence of hustling is learning how to get the most money from a client in the shortest period of time. Hustling involves verbal skills and bedside manner. Heyl (1977:549) notes that hustling is difficult for women to learn because they are not used to being the aggressor or discussing specific sex acts. If the prostitute is too aggressive (e.g., if she gets to the type of trick or fee quickly and abruptly), she risks turning off the client. If she is not aggressive enough, she will probably spend too much time with one client on low-fee sex acts such as straight intercourse. The "half and half" brings a higher fee and often a quicker male orgasm than straight intercourse.

The "racket" is the professional ideology of prostitution. The ideology of prostitution involves loyalty to one's kind and a personal identity with the "life." Novices learn to value "fairness" in working with other prostitutes and "fidelity" to their manager, pimp, or madam (Heyl 1977:550–551). Fairness prohibits strategies to undercut other prostitutes, that is, "dirty-hustling." "Dirty hustling" strategies include "appearing in the line-up partially unclothed; performing certain disapproved sexual position, such as anal intercourse; and allowing approved sexual extras without charging additional fees" (Heyl, 1977:551). "Dirty-hustling" may also involve a prostitute's "act," especially if it is seen as intending to take clients away from other girls (Tabor, 1971).

Another element of a professional ideology is the prostitute's belief that her work is honest work that serves important social functions for society. Bryan (1966) discovered that prostitutes often indicate that they save marriages, protect other women from sex crimes, and serve as psychotherapeutic agents. Prostitutes also view themselves as morally superior to the "squares" who are hypocritical and resentful of prostitutes. Immersion in the new values and life-style of prostitution further isolates the prostitute from her previous life and acquaintances in "square society," and promotes in-group solidarity (Heyl, 1977:551-552).

Call Girl and Streetwalkers. How does the learning process for the house prostitute compare with that of the call girl and street-walker? To begin with, the call girl and the streetwalker receive less formal training. Their apprenticeships are much shorter in duration than that of the house prostitute. Like the house prostitute, some call girls and streetwalkers work for pimps or managers. However, the majority of call girls and street-walkers are "outlaws." That is to say, they live and work without a pimp or manager. Now let us examine the content of their learning.

Physical skills and strategies for the call girl, primarily evolve around the art of giving oral sex and information on physical and sexual hygiene. Call girls are also encouraged not to have orgasms and not to turn a trick while on alcohol or drugs (Bryan 1965:293).

Streetwalkers may learn some sexual strategies from other working girls, but mostly they learn on the job by trial and error. Often, they learn from the instructions and special requests of their clients (Gray 1973:413).

Client management, the hustle, is the principle part of the call girl and streetwalker's learning. The art of hustling is learning to exploit the exploiters (clients). Hustling requires good interpersonal skills and to a lesser extent, sexual techniques. Interpersonal skills are required in making "pitches." For the call girl, telephone conversations are where she must separate the wheat from the chaff. Bryan notes that this is difficult for women because initiating sexual encounters and discussing sex specifically is unfamiliar and distressing to women (1965:293). The use of an answering service or tape-recorded message may reduce the prostitute's distress somewhat. However, this technology may lose customers who are hesitant or who decide later that they are not in the mood (Rosenblum, 1975).

The streetwalker, too, must use interpersonal skills, verbal and observational, to know who is a serious customer or big spender. The streetwalker often works "quickies" in doorways and alleys, so she also learns exploitive sexual techniques. For example, Winick and Kinsie (1971:165) note, "Many a prostitute has found that if she keeps her legs together the customer does not penetrate her but is unaware that he has not done so."

The racket, or the "life," is a worldview shared by all prostitutes. The immediate world of the house prostitute, call girl, and street walker is very different, and there is little interaction between prostitutes at different levels. However, they all share the view that their life is an honest life. However, the exploitation of customers is honest work only for the streetwalker. Unlike the house prostitute and the call girl, the streetwalker does not depend on return customers or referrals. Also, part of the streetwalker's underworld life is a network with other prostitutes and companions in a variety of other hustles and crimes including gambling, drug trafficking, robbery, burglary, and larceny.

Learning is a salient feature of prostitution. Through normal gender-role socialization, women come to see themselves and present themselves as sex objects. Female sexuality is valued and rewarded. Prostitution, then, is an extreme form of commercialized sex that reinforces the value of female sexuality. Once a woman engages in prostitution, the value of sex for pay is reinforced by a subterranean subculture of prostitutes who view their work as honest and view themselves as morally superior to other women. In addition, to these rationalizations for prostitution, novice prostitutes learn skills and techniques from other prostitutes. These data fit well with differential association theory (which was discussed under "Learning Theories" in Chapter 2). That is, a woman becomes a prostitute because she has acquired more definitions favorable to commercial sex than definitions unfavorable to commercial sex.

Macro-Subjectivist Theories

Macro-subjectivist explanations focus on the social structures and processes that cause people to define acts as deviance. There are two macro-subjectivist explanations: interest group theories and organizational theories. Interest group theories examine the social-historical context within which certain groups emerge and compete to create official definitions of deviance. Organizational theories examine the organizational context within which official agents come to define instances of deviance.

Interest Group Theories.   Interest group theories seek to discover the economic, political, social, and moral forces that prompt various interest groups to create definitions of deviance. U. S. public and legal reactions leading to laws against prostitution historically demonstrate that "sexual politics makes strange bedfellows" (Walkowitz, 1983:419). We will first review the nineteenth-century abolitionist movement that culminated in the legal prohibition of prostitution. Second, we will discuss contemporary movements that seek to legalize prostitution and the groups that oppose legalization.

Defining Prostitution as Crime: The Abolitionist Movement.   In the early colonial United States, female prostitution was morally condemned, but it was not a crime. There is little evidence of commercial prostitution during early colonial times. Instead, early colonialists referred to a variety of disapproved sexual relations as prostitution. For example, sex between an African-American man and a white woman, or between a Native-American woman and a white man was termed prostitution. The exchange of sexual favors for food or goods was also termed prostitution (Rosen, 1982:1). Early colonialists viewed any of these sexual behaviors as a personal

vice, a "temporary state of sin," rather than as a commercial occupation (Rosen, 1982:2).

Commercial prostitution emerged with the growth of colonial cities in the late seventeenth and early eighteenth centuries. "Bawdy" or brothel houses came to exist in all seaport cities. However, commercial prostitution remained in colonial cities where bawdy houses were often connected with local taverns (Pivar, 1973:21–23). Urban colonialists' opposition to commercial prostitution was sporadic and localized but steady throughout the eighteenth century. Local opposition efforts included vigilance committee attacks on bawdy houses; the development of charities to assist the victims of vice; economic programs for unemployed women; and municipal laws prohibiting bawdy houses and "nightwalkers" (Rosen, 1982:2). By the late eighteenth and early nineteenth centuries, "whorehouse riots" had become common in U.S. cities.

By the mid-nineteenth century, the newly formed urban police took charge of controlling prostitution. At their discretion, police arrested prostitutes for "lewdness," "vagrancy," and keeping a "disorderly house" (Rosen, 1982:4). Prostitution became a source of revenue for police, politicians, and doctors, among others. Police and doctors eventually became the core of a "regulationists" campaign to register prostitutes, and, thereby, place prostitutes under their control. Regulationists' efforts were opposed by a coalition of feminists and "social purity" advocates who formed an "antireglementarian" movement. Although social purity reformers opposed feminists on important issues, such as women's suffrage, employment, and education, both sought to abolish prostitution.

Social purity reformers sought to purify Americans by reforming the sexual mores of U.S. society. In addition to abolishing prostitution, purity reformers sought to censor pornography and establish a woman's right to deny marital sex (Rosen, 1982:11). Feminists sought to eliminate the exploitation of women. For feminists, prostitution epitomized the social, economic, and sexual exploitation of women.

Together, feminist and social purity groups succeeded in ending prostitute licensing plans that had been proposed by regulationists in several U.S. cities. With regulationists defeated, abolitionists actively sought municipal and state legislation to repress prostitution. The criminalization of prostitution in the United States culminated in the Mann Act of 1910, which prohibits the transportation of women for "immoral purposes." Abolitionist reformers also sought judicial and penal reform for the prevention of prostitution. States responded by creating special morals courts to separate prostitutes from other criminals and by placing prostitutes on probation or in women's reformatories for the purpose of "rehabilitation." (Rosen, 1982:19). These judicial and penal reforms made the criminalization of prostitution complete. In Rosen's words:

> By creating a separate, highly elaborate penal and judicial system to deal with female sexual deviance, reformers provided the ultimate classification of prostitution as a crime. The creation of special moral courts, moreover, gave extra impetus to special morals, or vice, squads to entrap and imprison prostitutes (Rosen, 1982:19).

The feminist, social purity coalition movement of the late nineteenth and early twentieth centuries, did not decrease the sexual exploitation of women, as early feminists had hoped. Rather, it created a new class of female criminals (Messerschmidt, 1987). Similarly, Snider (1990) argues that early feminists' dependence on state intervention to promote feminist concerns by abolishing prostitution actually promoted control over women, especially lower- and working-class women.

The history of prostitution reform does not end here. Prostitutes' rights organizations, such as COYOTE (an acronym for "Call Off

Your Old Tired Ethics"), have emerged in the last two decades. Once again, feminists are an important party in a coalition movement to redefine prostitution. Let's briefly examine this contemporary movement that attempts to redefine prostitution as "work," rather than as "crime."

Defining Prostitution as Work: The Prostitutes' Rights Movement. Valerie Jenness (1990) describes the foundation, organization, and goals of the contemporary crusade to transform prostitution from "Sex As Sin to Sex As Work." According to Jenness, COYOTE, founded in 1973 in San Francisco by ex-prostitute Margo St. James, began as "a coalition of housewives, lawyers, feminists, and prostitutes" who sought "to expose laws and law enforcement procedures that make prostitution problematic" (1990:403). COYOTE now leads a prostitutes' rights movement in the United States and abroad. COYOTE's objectives are threefold: (1) to repeal all prostitution laws; (2) to elevate prostitution to the status of legitimate service work; and (3) to protect prostitutes' right to work (Jenness, 1990:405). While these goals remain, the political organization of COYOTE has changed because of the women's movement and the AIDS epidemic.

COYOTE's early discourse concentrated on law-enforcement abuses of prostitutes. COYOTE's concern with the official abuse of prostitutes fit well with the women's movement's discourse on violence against women in general. By relating prostitution to the status of women, COYOTE established ties with the women's movement, developed coalitions, and emerged as a national civil rights organization (Jenness 1990:411).

However, prostitution is a dilemma for feminists. After all, is prostitution the ultimate right of a woman to control her own sexuality, or, is prostitution the ultimate degradation of a woman's sexuality? Although the National Organization of Women (NOW)

has resolved to repeal prostitution laws, other feminists have resolved to abolish prostitution. In the 1980s, WHISPER (an acronym for "Women Hurt in Systems of Prostitution Engaged in Revolt") emerged in New York City. Like their nineteenth-century feminist sisters, the women in WHISPER view prostitution as slavery, claiming that "no woman chooses prostitution, and that all prostitutes are victims." (Jenness 1990:412-413). According to Jenness (1990:414), the emergence of WHISPER is evidence that COYOTE's point of view has been taken seriously "both within the women's movement and before a wide public audience." As yet, WHISPER's counterclaim that prostitution is slavery, not work, has not circumvented COYOTE's goal of decriminalization. However, the AIDS epidemic may.

The aids epidemic has altered the politics of COYOTE in two important ways. First, COYOTE has been put on the defensive. Prostitutes have been "scapegoated" for the spread of AIDS (Pheterson 1989:28). Therefore, COYOTE is working to counter such claims with an education campaign on AIDS through public announcements, conferences, media releases, and public protests to oppose mandatory testing for AIDS among prostitutes (Jenness 1990:415). Second, the AIDS epidemic, ironically, has put COYOTE in a position to work within the system to eventually further prostitutes' rights. As Jenness notes, "Prostitutes' organizations such as COYOTE are in a position to provide access to prostitutes who may need AIDS education, and knowledge about how to effectively educate prostitutes" (1990:415). Already, key government organizations such as centers for disease control in Atlanta and the State of California Department of Health have solicited the cooperation of prostitutes' rights organization to investigate the role of prostitution in the spread of AIDS (Jenness, 1990:415).

To date, the prostitutes' rights movement has not attained its major goals. According to Weitzer (1991), the prostitutes' rights movement has failed because its organizations have failed to mobilize the material and human resources necessary to succeed. Weitzer (1991) argues that "deviance liberation movements," such as prostitutes' rights, gay rights, and abortion rights, can prevail even against a high level of perceived immorality if they mobilize sufficient material and human resources. If Weitzer's (1991) resource mobilization theory of deviance liberation movements is correct, the AIDS epidemic may provide the opportunity for the prostitutes' rights campaign to legitimate its claims and accomplish its goals. Will prostitutes' rights organizations build coalitions with large, influential, and well-financed groups or organizations that are mobilizing to educate the public about and stop the spread of AIDS? This remains to be seen. However, today, as in the past, the politics of sex may make for strange bedfellows.

Organizational Theories. Organizational theories examine the activities of official agents, such as police, prosecutors, defense attorneys, and judges, who produce definitions of deviance within an organizational setting. An organizational theory of prostitution explains prostitution as a definition of sexuality that is applied by officials to certain sexual exchanges. Official rates of prostitution, then, are products of official reactions to supposed "violators." We will first focus on the organization of policing prostitutes. Second, we will examine the organization of adjudicating and sentencing prostitutes. Our discussion of the policing of prostitutes is based largely on Carmen and Moody's (1985) observations of "working women." We, however, have put these observations together to construct the organizational context within which officials come to define prostitutes and produce official rates of prostitution.

Policing Prostitutes.   The police are as central to the "life" of a prostitute as are pimps and johns. However, unlike pimps and johns, the police are the enemy. Or, are they? In one regard, they are surely enemies. Prostitutes are the "disreputable offenders" of public morality. The police are the crusaders who are sworn to protect and defend public morality. Constant police surveillance is bad for a prostitute's business. On the other hand, lack of police surveillance would likely be followed by public accusations of police incompetence. Yet, police and prostitutes have resolved this inherent conflict of interests in a way that allows police to meet their organizational demands and prostitutes to continue business as usual. Police and prostitutes have developed a symbiotic relation (Carmen and Moody, 1985). The nature of the relation differs according to the type of police, anti-crime cops or vice-cops (Carmen and Moody, 1985:139–141). Anti-crime cops work in high-crime-rate areas to prevent and intercept serious street crimes, such as murder, rape, assault, and robbery. These serious offenders often victimize prostitutes and drive away potential clients. Therefore, although they are criminals in the eyes of the law, prostitutes often work as police informants. This assists the police in apprehending "dangerous" criminals, protects the prostitute from theft or physical harm, and ensures a steady flow of customers.

Vice-cops also have, for the most part, developed a cooperative working relationship with prostitutes. Carmen and Moody refer to the informal rules that guide vice-cop-prostitute interaction as the "game" (1985:138). Carmen and Moody describe the mutually accepted game as follows:

The prostitute knows that if the cop catches her fair and square while she is soliciting him, and she hasn't been to jail for a while, then she won't resent the arrest. . .the policeman believes that when he tells a woman to get out of his precinct because the pressure's on to clean up the street, or when he has his nightly quota to meet and picks a woman for arrest at an appointed time and place and tells her

to be there, compliance is in order (Carmen and Moody, 1985:1389).

Of course, there are breakdowns in the "game" between particular cops and prostitutes; but they are episodes rather than the norm. These episodes most often occur when the "fairness doctrine" of the game is somehow violated. For example, the "sassy prostitute" who shows disrespect for the police officer's competence or authority. So too, a police officer, perhaps for personal reasons, may take unfair advantage of his or her authority. One angry prostitute describes such an incident.

You know that fuzz got some gall. He saw me down at 100 Centre. I just got out of court after forty-eight hours in the pit, and he says come on, I want to show you something. He takes me to some kind of policeman's room and says he wants a blow job. I can't believe that man. He's one who is always picking on us. He says to me, "You owe me one. I let you go one night when I should a hauled your ass in." I didn't want no trouble, so I gave him a blow job right there on top of the desk. I bet that motha didn't write that one up. Can you believe that? (Carmen and Moody, 1985:137).

Again such instances are frequent, but they are personalized conflicts that are contained in the context of an overall cooperative venture. So cooperative is the policing of prostitutes in some areas, for instance, in the Times Square area of New York City, that the police keep books containing the names of prostitutes who are scheduled for their next arrest. Here, police often notify a prostitute of the pending arrest a few days in advance so that she can turn the extra tricks to pay her fine (Carmen and Moody, 1985:144–145).

Adjudicating and Sentencing Prostitutes. The organizational demand of the criminal court is efficiency in terms of time and expense. Efficiency is maximized by processing cases in a routine manner. In most criminal cases, the central figure in the routinization of court cases is the prosecutor. In the official processing of prostitutes, however, routinization is initiated at the police level. For example, in the Manhattan district courts, prostitutes are "prearraigned" before going to court (Carmen and Moody 1985:149). *Prearraignment* means that the arresting officer swears to the circumstances of arrest and custody that make up the deposition order. The deposition order is, then, sworn to in court by another police officer. This maximizes efficiency because it allows beat cops to return to the streets while one designated cop swears to the depositions of several prostitutes who appear before the court in bunches. Prearraignment, then, is an organizational feature that fits the presumption of guilt ideology of our modern-day efficient, bureaucratic criminal court.

Indeed, the majority of prostitutes plead guilty. In return, their sentences seldom disrupt, other than for a short duration, their return to business as usual. A common sentence is "time served" and a fine. "Time served" means that custody prior to sentencing is satisfactory punishment. When there is a fine, judges often delay payment, allowing the prostitute time to raise the money. Everyone, the police, lawyers, judges, and the prostitute herself, knows that being given the time to pay the fine means she has time to turn the tricks necessary to raise the money (Carmen and Moody, 1985:152–155). Again, all players know the game, and they are willing to play it because of the mutual benefits. The prostitute stays in business, the police efficiently make a high number of arrests, and the court efficiently processes a large number of convictions. In turn, the high number of arrests and convictions demonstrate active official enforcement in defense of public decency and moral order.

Micro-Subjectivist Theories

According to micro-subjectivists, the prostitute is one who has been so labeled. There-

fore, "prostitute" is a product of the interpretations and responses of others rather than a person who has engaged in a specific sexual act. Micro-subjectivist researchers ask two important questions. First, who gets labeled "prostitute," and why? Second, does the label "prostitute" produce subsequent acts of prostitution on the part of those so labeled? The first question concerns differential labeling. Here, researchers examine the various individual and audience characteristics, such as gender, race, and class, that produce deviant labels. The second question is central to a labeling theory of prostitution. Researchers, here, examine the effect of deviant labels on one's self-identity and subsequent behavior.

Differential Labeling of Prostitutes. Few studies have systematically examined prostitution in terms of differential labeling. However, gender bias has been suggested. For example, Schur (1983) suggests that negative deviant labels associated with sexuality are reserved for women. A woman may be said to "look like a prostitute" or "act like a prostitute" whether she sells her sexuality or not. Conversely, men who express their sexuality in appearance, attitude, or behavior are more likely to be labeled "hunk" or "stud." "Prostitute," then, is one deviant label among others, such as "slut" and "whore," that works to control women's sexuality and keep women in their "place" (Schur, 1983:53). Few would argue with Schur, but his observation reveals nothing in particular about when, where, or, by whom women are labeled prostitutes. To some extent, these particulars have been examined for the officials who process prostitutes.

Do processing agents (police, prosecutors, and judges) reflect cultural prejudices about social groups in the enforcement and adjudication of prostitution? Does one's gender, race, or sexual preference (homosexual or heterosexual), for example, relate to agents' charging and sentencing of prostitutes? Let us see. Bowker (1978) argues that many men are charged with prostitution and that sentencing of male and female prostitutes is similar. However, racial bias has been reported. Cohen's (1980:76) study of prostitutes in New York City found that African Americans and Hispanics made up about 50 percent of the "visible street prostitutes," but represented over 68 percent of those arrested for prostitution.

Lindquist and his colleagues (1989) provide the most systematic study of the effects of gender, race, and sexual preference (heterosexual or homosexual) on the official processing of prostitutes. These researchers examined the judicial processing of persons charged with prostitution. Their research is particularly important because it overcomes many limitations found in previous research. For example, previous research has been limited to small samples of prostitutes taken at one point in time and has seldom controlled for the effect of legal factors or examined all stages of judicial processing. Lindquist and his colleagues (1989) sampled 2,859 men and women charged with prostitution from 1973 to 1985 in a south central Texas metropolitan area to determine how legal and extralegal (gender and race) variables were related to three judicial outcomes: adjudication (guilt or innocence), sentence (probation or jail), and length of sentence. Lindquist and his colleagues (1989:288) found some evidence of different adjudications for men and women. Females were more likely to be found not guilty, but sentencing was similar for the men and women who were found guilty of prostitution. Racial bias, however, was evident at the point of sentencing. Minority offenders were more likely to be sent to jail and given stiffer sentences (Lindquist et al., 1989: 287–288). Finally, the effect of the sexual offense (homosexual or heterosexual) with which the offender was charged was evident at the initial stage of sentencing (probation or jail). Heterosexual offenders were more likely to be sent to jail. First-time homosexual offenders were least likely to be sent to jail (Lindquist et al., 1989:289). Perhaps, this is true because putting young homosexuals in jail is, as one judge said to Lindquist and his colleagues "like throwing meat to lions" (1989:289).

A Labeling Theory of Prostitution. From a study of 30 female prostitutes in three correctional facilities, Nanette Davis (1971) puts forth a labeling theory of prostitution. Davis (1971) identifies three stages to becoming a prostitute: drift, transition, and professionalization.

In the first stage, the young girl drifts from promiscuous sex to her initial act of prostitution (sex for money). The drift to prostitution is a vague and extended period of time in which a sexually active girl is labeled as "loose," a "slut," a "whore," and so on; she is increasingly seen by others as "one of those" who are similarly labeled. Vitaliano, Bowker, and James (1981) found that having been called a "whore" by classmates, friends, parents, and others, is important in explaining a girl's eventual involvement in prostitution. Labeling and stigmatizing sexually active girls is also a consequence of our juvenile justice system. For example, Schaffer and De-Blassie (1984) note that female juvenile offenders are given a physical examination, whereas, most male juveniles are not. Further, doctors note on examination reports whether the girl is a virgin or not. These reports follow these girls to the institutions or foster homes in which they are placed. Schaffer and De-Blassie (1984:694) report that in one Pennsylvania home for girls offenders are classified as virgins and nonvirgins. The virgins and nonvirgins wear dresses of different colors. Schur (1983) believes that females are particularly vulnerable to the negative impact of labeling. This is because females lack relevant social, economic, and psychological supports and resources to effectively resist stigmatization.

In the second stage, transition, the girl begins to redefine herself as one who is in it for business rather than for fun or adventure. During this stage, a girl may turn an occasional trick, but more as an opportunistic arrangement than as a contract. Perhaps, she was paid, but did not solicit money from a date. Or, perhaps, she agreed to accept money for having sex with a friend of a friend because she needed the money. In the transitional stage, a girl's view of herself vacillates between a conventional and a deviant identity. She vacillates between self-condemnation and self-acceptance in terms of sex as a vocation. The more she comes to deny the appropriateness of convential views of sexuality and comes to accept the legitimacy of sex for money, the closer she moves to a deviant identity. Her development of a deviant identity is facilitated by engaging in acts of prostitution that likely lead to acquaintanceship and friendship with clients, prostitutes, and pimps who seek out and identify with the unconventional life of hustling. Furthermore, her acts of prostitution and association with johns, prostitutes, and pimps increases her likelihood of arrest and conviction as a prostitute. Once officially labeled "a prostitute," her return to conventional associations and activities is less likely, and her official deviant status is more likely to become her conception of self.

The final stage, professionalization, occurs once she defines herself as a prostitute. Now, her vacillation and experimentation are over. She is oriented to sex as business. Having internalized a set of beliefs about the "life" and become skilled as a "hustler," she enters a career of prostitution.

No doubt, many women follow the pattern just described. The importance of labeling in becoming a prostitute is well established in the literature. However, not all who engage in the business of prostitution develop a deviant identity, or value the "life." In fact, James suggests that for an increasing number of young men and women, prostitution is "less a career" and more a "temporary adaptation" to social and economic needs (1983:1310). Housewives may work in massage parlors to supplement family income, co-eds may work as call girls to pay college expenses, and for some adolescents prostitution may be a way to seek out excitement or raise spending money.

SOCIAL POLICY

Social policy on prostitution is linked to patterns of legal treatment of prostitution. Three legal treatment approaches can be distinguished: the prohibitionist approach, the regulationist approach, and the abolitionist approach (Richards, 1983). These legal treatment approaches suggest three different policy strategies for prostitution.

The Prohibitionist Approach

As you have learned, nineteenth-century feminists and social purity groups formed "purity leagues" to abolish prostitution in the United States. The nineteenth-century purity movement led to the criminalization of prostitution. This remains today as our nation's official policy on prostitution, except in Nevada, where prostitution is legal in certain counties.

Why criminalize prostitution? At least four reasons are given for continuing the policy of legal prohibition. First, the majority of Americans support legal sanctions to punish, deter, and rehabilitate prostitutes. Second, prohibition of prostitution will prevent the spread of sexually transmitted diseases. Third, legal prohibition of prostitution will prevent many other crimes that are associated with prostitution, especially drug-related crimes. Fourth, prohibition of prostitution will protect female victims of abuse, psychological deficiencies, and male predators from being forced into prostitution.

Linda Rio (1991) reviews these arguments in relation to existing research on prostitution. She concludes that the prohibitionists' approach is a failed policy and prostitution research does not support arguments for its continence. First, a variety of opinion surveys over an extended period of time demonstrates that a majority of Americans do not view prostitution as immoral. Some surveys even show that a majority of Americans favor legalization of prostitution (Rio, 1991: 206–207). Furthermore, there is no evidence that criminal sanctions punish, deter, or rehabilitate prostitutes. As we noted earlier, criminal sanctions meet the organizational demands of officials and allow prostitutes to continue with business as usual. Second, few facts are better established in research on prostitution than that prostitution is not associated with the spread of sexually transmitted diseases, including AIDS. When drug use is taken into consideration prostitutes do not test higher for the AIDS virus than other women (Acheson, 1986; Jenness, 1990). Third, some studies suggest that drug addiction among prostitutes has been exaggerated. Perhaps, as few as 4 percent of prostitutes are addicted to drugs (Gebhard, 1969), and only about 15 percent of prostitutes sell sex to support drug habits (Datesman and Inciardi, 1979). Also, criminal activities by prostitutes are largely limited to streetwalkers. Fourth, research evidence consistently finds that women are not forced into prostitution (James, 1983). Also, studies that compare prostitutes with nonprostitute control groups do not find pathology characteristics (social, psychological, or sexual) among prostitutes.

The Regulationist Approach

The most common regulationist approach involves the licensing of prostitutes. Licensing of prostitutes was a practice in ancient Greece and Rome. Even today, licensing is common on the European continent (Richards, 1983). As we mentioned earlier, police and doctors in the nineteenth-century United States favored licensing. Their regulation efforts, however, were defeated by the social purity movement. In the United States today, only Nevada regulates prostitution by the legal registration of prostitutes. Proponents of legal regulation argue that regulation provides revenue through taxation, reduces VD through regular medical examinations, and reduces the public nuisance aspects of prostitution. No doubt, legally regulated prostitution raises revenue that is otherwise lost in an underground economy in which prostitution is illegal. The disease argument is logical, but currently prostitutes account for only five percent of the VD in the United States (Rio, 1991:207). In regard to the public nuisance aspect of prostitution, regulations on the place, time, and method of prostitution would probably protect citizens from unwanted exposure. For example, in Reno, Nevada, there is an "almost total absence of streetwalkers) (Rio, 1991:213).

Contemporary feminists are divided on their views of the best policy on prostitution. However, feminists agree in their opposition to regulation. WHISPER, constituted, in part, by modern feminists, favors the elimination of prostitution. On the other hand, COYOTE, also constituted, in part, by modern feminists, favors total decriminalization of prostitution. Modern prohibition feminists argue that licensing of female prostitutes legally embraces a double standard, that is, sexual freedom for men and chastity for women. Moreover, they argue that even regulation degrades women and labels prostitutes, making it more difficult for women to leave the profession. This second argument is shared by feminists who favor decriminalization of prostitution (Richards, 1983). Let us, then, turn to the third policy approach to prostitution: the abolitionist approach.

The Abolitionist Approach

The abolitionist approach calls for the abolishment of all laws of prostitution, both those that prohibit it and those that regulate it. Some feminists (e.g., COYOTE affiliates) argue that the decriminalization is necessary to transform prostitution from sin to work. COYOTE links prostitution to women's rights to work and choose, and to women's civil liberties (Jenness, 1990). Linda Rio (1991) makes a persuasive argument for decriminalization. She argues that decriminalization would protect prostitutes from violence by customers and police. Decriminalization would also eliminate a major source of police corruption. Furthermore, third-party exploitation by pimps and, perhaps, even organized crime would be reduced. Finally, decriminalization is sound economics. Rio (1991:213) points out that legal workers pay taxes, and the present cost of legal prohibition is wasteful. Rio (1991:214) reports on two studies that estimate the cost of prohibition to be about $1 million a year in Seattle, Washington, and in California it costs over $1 thousand to arrest and convict a prostitute. In addition to this direct cost, prohibition efforts cost the public wasted dollars and human resources on ineffective law enforcement. However, Rio's (1991) arguments in favor of decriminalization would probably be met by regulation. Therefore, the strongest argument for decriminalized, unregulated prostitution is that it would eliminate an unjust control of a woman's sexuality.

SUMMARY

What is prostitution? This is a troublesome question for objectivists. Objectivists have not reached a consensus on what behaviors specifically constitute prostitution. However, they generally define prostitution as indiscriminate sex in exchange for money. For subjectivists, prostitution is limited to those acts that social audiences define as such.

Surprisingly, empirical studies of prostitution are relatively limited in number. Most research has focused on female prostitutes. However, some researchers believe that male prostitution is increasing and female prosti-

tution decreasing in the United States. This is reflected in national prostitution arrest rates. Most male prostitutes engage in homosexuality and are, themselves, homosexual or bisexual. Male prostitutes are generally young (16–19 years old) and white, but they are from diverse social class backgrounds. There are three tiers of male prostitutes: "street hustlers," "bar hustlers," and "escort prostitutes" (Luckenbill, 1986). *Street hustlers* solicit customers on streets. They often work a known territory, referred to as a *stroll*. *Bar hustlers* work in drinking establishments, where they most often work in collusion with the bar owner or manager. *Escort prostitutes* are the elites among male prostitutes. They give up to 60 percent of client fees to the owners of dating or escort services.

Female prostitutes are also young (15–25 years old), predominantly white, and from diverse social class backgrounds. Many females entered prostitution as adolescent runaways. Their careers are short, four to five years. During their careers, they often move from one type of prostitution to another. The relation between one type of prostitution and another is not clear, but "streetwalkers" occupy the bottom level and "call girls" the top level of the prostitution hierarchy. *Streetwalkers* solicit clients, *johns*, or *tricks* on their "stroll." Streetwalkers often work for a *pimp*. Female prostitutes living with a pimp are known to one another as a *wife-in-law*. Prostitutes who work without a pimp are known as *outlaws*. *Call girls* are high-class prostitutes who work by telephone or private referral. They make the most money, and they are relatively safe from customer abuse and arrest. The middle echelon of female prostitution comprises "bar girls," "massage parlor prostitutes," "hotel prostitutes," and "house prostitutes." *Bar girls* hustle bar customers for drinks and sex. They work with bar managers who receive a percentage of prostitutes' fees. *Massage parlor prostitutes* are licensed masseuses who provide sex for a fee. Each type of sex generally has a set fee, and the parlor owner takes a percentage of the total fee. *Hotel prostitutes* generally work in second-rate hotels where customers are referred to them by bellboys and hotel managers. *House prostitutes* work in a *brothel* or *bordello* where customers come to exchange money for sex. House prostitutes are common in Nevada counties where prostitution is legal. They are generally paid a commission by the house manager.

Studies of the male patrons of prostitutes are rare. However, some researchers report that the typical male customer is white, middle-aged, married, and works in business or a profession. These men most frequently request oral sex, *fellatio. Special services* are also a common request. These services include a variety of sex acts that most persons consider perverted.

Macro-objectivists seek to explain why prostitution exists and persists. Two macro-objectivist explanations are exploitation theories and functional theories. Exploitation theories suggest there is a system of male social and economic dominance that gives rise to female prostitution. Therefore, male dominance forces women into prostitution. There is little empirical support for the notion that women are forced into prostitution. Also, there is evidence of female prostitution in societies in which there is little male domination or economic inequality. Functional theories suggests that legitimate sexual institutions, such as the monogamous family, create a need for prostitution and that prostitution provides positive functions for society. However, in some societies with monogamous family structures, prostitution is rare. Furthermore, there is no hard evidence of the positive effects of prostitution.

Micro-objectivist theories attempt to explain why women enter prostitution. There is evidence that learning is a salient feature of prostitution. Learning theories suggest that through normal gender-role socialization,

women come to see themselves and present themselves as sex objects. Female sexuality is valued and rewarded. Prostitution, then, is an extreme form of commercialized sex that reinforces the value of female sexuality. Once a woman engages in prostitution, the value of sex for pay is reinforced by a subterranean subculture of prostitutes who have developed a view of their work as honest and a view of themselves as morally superior to women in the *square world*—middle-class culture. In addition, *turn-outs* or novice prostitutes, often learn sexual techniques and client management skills from other prostitutes. However, Jennifer James (1983) points out that many prostitutes are part-timers who value the money, not the work, and who have little contact with the subculture of prostitution.

Macro-subjectivists explain definitions of prostitution. Interest group theories trace the definition of prostitution as a crime to the nineteenth-century coalition of feminists and social purity advocates who formed *purity leagues* to legally prohibit prostitution. Organizational theories, on the other hand, focus on the organizational features of law enforcement and adjudication that affect official agents' definitions of women as prostitutes. Efficiency in terms of time and expense is the organizational demand that determines police and court agents' definitions of prostitution. Official processing of prostitutes is a cooperative venture that maximizes arrests and convictions while allowing prostitutes to continue business as usual.

Micro-subjectivists seek to discover who gets labeled a prostitute and whether the official label leads to further prostitution by those so labeled. Who gets labeled? One important study found that males are more likely to be found guilty of prostitution than females. At the point of sentencing, minority and heterosexual offenders were more likely to be jailed. As to the effect of labeling, there is evidence that labeling is a salient feature in the transition from promiscuous sex to acts of prostitution. Informal and official labeling contributes to the development of a deviant identity and subsequent self-identification with prostitution as a profession. However, many women who engage in prostitution have not been labeled "prostitute" and do not identify with the profession (James, 1983).

There are three policy approaches to prostitution: the prohibition approach, the regulation approach, and the decriminalization approach. *The prohibitionist approach* seeks to abolish all forms of prostitution. Historically, prohibitionists have sought legal prohibition of prostitution. *The regulationist approach* calls for the legalization of a government-regulated form of prostitution. The licensing of prostitutes is the typical strategy. *The abolitionist approach* calls for the repeal of all laws and government regulations on prostitution. The ultimate goal is to transform prostitution from sin to work.

GLOSSARY

The abolitionist approach   The complete repeal of all laws and public agency regulation of prostitution. Also known as *decriminalization.*

Bar girls   Female prostitutes who hustle men in bars for drinks and sex.

Bar hustlers   Male prostitutes who solicit clients in public and private bars.

Brothel   A whorehouse where people exchange money for sex services. Also known as a *bordello.*

Call girls   High-class female prostitutes who receive clients by telephone service or private referral.

Escort prostitutes   Elite male prostitutes whose clients, dates, are provided by an escort or dating service.

Fellatio   Oral sex provided by a woman for a man.

Hotel prostitutes   Female prostitutes who work in hotels, providing sex to custom-

ers who are referred to them by bellboys and hotel managers.

House prostitutes   Female prostitutes who work out of a managed house that is established for the sex business.

Johns   The clients of female prostitutes. Also known as *tricks.*

Massage parlor prostitutes   Female prostitute masseuses who provide sex for a fee in the parlor setting.

Outlaws   Prostitutes working and living without a pimp.

Pimp   A man who provides shelter, food, clothing, an allowance, companionship, or love to female prostitutes in exchange for 100 percent of their fees.

The prohibitionist approach   The elimination of all forms of prostitution.

Purity leagues   The coalition of nineteenth-century feminists and social purity advocates that led to the criminalization of prostitution.

The regulationist approach   The legal regulation of the business of prostitution by licensing prostitutes.

Special services   A variety of sex acts likely to be considered perverted, such as physical beatings, bondage, and voyeuristic acts.

Street hustlers   The lowest strata of male prostitutes who solicit clients on the streets.

Stroll   The street territory on which male street hustlers and female streetwalkers solicit clients.

Streetwalkers   Low-status female prostitutes who work the streets for clients.

Turn-out   A woman who recently became a prostitute.

Wife-in-law   A term used to describe the relationship between several female prostitutes who share a pimp.

SUGGESTED READINGS

Carmen, Arlene, and Howard Moody. *Working Women.* New York: Harper and Row, 1985.

This well-written case study of prostitutes in New York City is a partisan and empathic account of "working women" that is based on existential involvement with the life of street prostitutes.

Earls, Christopher M. and Helene David. "A Psychosocial Study of Male Prostitution." *Archives of Sexual Behavior* 18(1989):401–419. In this study, 50 male prostitutes and 50 non-prostitutes were matched in age, sex, and socioeconomic status. The research focuses on the family, sexual, and criminal history; current life situation; sexual practices; and substance abuse among both groups. Findings are compared with a good review of previous literature.

James, Jennifer. "Prostitution and Commercial Vice: Social and Organizational Aspects." *Encyclopedia of Crime and Justice.* Sanford H. Kadish. New York: Free Press, 1983, 1305-1310. Here is a brief and informed review of the prostitution literature. Topics covered include types of prostitution, organization of prostitution, customers, and the prostitute subculture.

Jenness, Valerie. "From Sex as Sin to Sex as Work: COYOTE and the Reorganization of Prostitution as a Social Problem." *Social Problems* 37(1990):403–420. This work focuses on COYOTE's crusade to transform prostitution from its historical association with sin and crime to a social problem of women's work, choice, and civil rights. This crusade is followed through three events that have changed its nature of discourse: the early debate with law enforcement, the feminist movement, and the public health agencies' concern with the AIDS epidemic.

Rio, Linda M. "Psychological and Sociological Research and the Decriminalization or Legalization of Prostitution." *Archives of Sexual Behavior* 20(1991):205–218. This is an excellent review of research pertinent to three policy approaches to prostitution: the prohibitionist approach, the regulationist approach, and the decriminalization approach. The author positions herself with regulationist and decriminalization efforts.

Rosen, Ruth. *The Lost Sisterhood: Prostitution in America, 1900–1918.* Baltimore: John Hopkins University Press, 1982. This book offers a historical inquiry into the "purity league" coalition groups during the American progressive era from 1900 to 1918. This movement led to the criminalization of prostitution, culminating in the Mann Act of 1910.

Schuv, Edwin. *Labeling Women Deviant: Gender, Stigma, and Social Control.* Philadelphia: Temple University Press, 1983. This book contains a good discussion of how women are labeled as prostitutes, as well as the place of stigma and social control in prostitutes' lives and for deviant women as a whole.

Weisberg, D. Kelly. *Children of the Night.* Lexington, Mass.: D.C. Heath, 1985. A comprehensive review of the literature on male and female adolescent prostitution, this book focuses on the causes, life-styles, and juvenile-justice reactions to adolescent prostitution. Special attention is given to the relationship between adolescent prostitution and child abuse and runaway behavior.

Werner, Dennis. "Paid Sex Specialists Among the Mekronoti." *Journal of Anthropological Research* 40(1984):394–405. This analysis of preliterate society's prostitutes (i.e., unmarried mothers who provide sexual services in exchange for gifts) provides an excellent functional analysis of prostitution and demonstrates the similarity of these women to prostitutes in modern societies.

REFERENCES

Acheson, E.D. "AIDS: A Challenge for the Public Health." *Lancet* Mar. 1986:662–666.

Adler, Freda. *Sisters in Crime: The Rise of the New Female Criminal.* New York: McGraw-Hill, 1975.

Allen, Donald M. "Young Male Prostitutes: A Psychological Study." *Archives of Sexual Behavior* 9(1980):399–426.

Barry, Kathleen. *Female Sexual Slavery.* New York: New York University Press, 1984.

Benjamin, Harry, and R.E.L. Masters. *Prostitution and Morality.* New York: Julian, 1964.

Berk, Richard A. "Drug Use, Prostitution and the Prevalence of AIDS: An Analysis Using Census Tracts." *The Journal of Sex Research* 27 (1990):607–621.

Bowker, L.H. *Women, Crime, and the Criminal Justice System*. Lexington, Mass.: D.C. Heath, 1978.

Boyer, Debra. "Male Prostitution and Homosexual Identity." *Journal of Homosexuality* 17(1989): 151–184.

Bryan, James H. "Apprenticeships in Prostitution." *Social Problems* 12(1965):287–297.

———. "Occupational Ideologies and Individual Attitudes of Call Girls." *Social Problems* 13(1966):441–450.

Bullough, Vern L., and Bonnie Bullough. *Prostitution: An Illustrated History*. New York: Crown, 1978.

Carmen, Arlene, and Howard Moody. *Working Women*. New York: Harper and Row, 1985.

Cohen, Bernard. *Deviant Street Networks: Prostitutes in New York City*. Lexington, Mass.: D.C. Heath, 1980.

Datesman, Susan K., and James A. Inciardi. "Female Heroin Use, Criminality, and Prostitution." *Contemporary Drug Problems* 8(1979): 455–473.

Davis, Kingsley. "The Sociology of Prostitution." *American Sociological Review* 2(1937):744–755.

Davis, Nannette J. "The Prostitute: Developing a Deviant Identity." *Studies in the Sociology of Sex*. Ed. James M. Henslin. New York: Appleton-Century-Crofts, 1971, 297–322.

Decker, John F. *Prostitution: Regulation and Control*. Littleton, Col.: Fred B. Rothman, 1979.

Earls, Christopher, and Helene David. "A Psychosocial Study of Male Prostitution." *Archives of Sexual Behavior* 18(1989):401–419.

Exner, John E., Joyce Wylie, Antonia Leura, and Tracey Parrill. "Some Psychological Characteristics of Prostitutes." *Journal of Personality Assessment* 41(1977):474–485.

Federal Bureau of Investigation. *Uniform Crime Reports*. Washington, D.C. Government Printing Office.

Gagnon, John H., and William Simon. *Sexual Conduct: The Social Sources of Human Sexuality*. Chicago: Aldine, 1973.

Gardner, Thomas J. *Criminal Law: Principles and Cases*. 3rd ed. New York: West, 1985.

Gebhard, Paul H. "Misconceptions About Female Prostitutes." *Medical Aspects of Human Sexuality* 3(1969):455–473.

Gibson-Ainyette, I., D.I. Templar, R. Brown, and L. Veaco. "Adolescent Female Prostitutes." *Archives of Sexual Behavior* 17(1988):431–438.

Gray, Diana. "Turning-Out: A Study of Teenage Prostitutes." *Urban Life and Culture* 1 (1973):401–425.

Hamzy, Connie, with Melanie Wells. "Confessions of a Rock'n'Roll Groupie." *Penthouse* Jan. 1992:67 + .

Heyl, Barbara S. "The Madam as Teacher: The Training of House Prostitutes." *Social Problems* 24(1977):545–555.

———.The Madam as Entrepreneur: Career Management in House Prostitution. New Brunswick, N.J.: Transaction, 1979.

Hunt, Morton M. *Sexual Behavior in the 1970's*. New York: Dell Books, 1974.

James, Jennifer. "Prostitutes and Prostitution." *Deviants: Voluntary Action in a Hostile World*. Eds. Edward Sagarin and Fred Montanino. Morristown, N.J. General Learning Press, 1977 368–428.

———. "Prostitution and Commercial Vice: Social and Organizational Aspects." *Encyclopedia of Crime and Justice*. Ed. by Sanford H. Kadish, New York: Free Press, 1983, 1305–1310.

Janus, Sam, Barbara Bess, and Carol Saltus. *A Sex Profile of Men in Power*. Englewood Cliffs: Prentice-Hall, 1977.

Jenness, Valerie. "From Sex as Sin to Sex as Work: COYOTE and the Reorganization of Prostitution as a Social Problem." *Social Problems* 37(1990):403–420.

Kinsey, Alfred C., Wardell B. Pomeroy, and Clyde E. Martin. *Sexual Behavior in the Human Male*. Philadelphia: Saunders, 1948.

Kinsey, Alfred C., Wardell B. Pomeroy, Clyde E. , Martin, and Paul H. Gebhard. *Sexual Behavior in the Human Female*. Philadelphia: Saunders, 1953.

Kunstel, Marcia, and Joseph Albright. "Prostitution Thrives on Young Girls." *C.J. International* 3(1987):9–11.

Leishman, Kenneth. "Heterosexuals and AIDS: The Second Stage of the Epidemic." *Atlantic Monthly* Feb. 1987:39–58.

Lindquist, John N., Terrence Tutchings, O.Z. White, and Carl D.Chambers. "Judicial Processing of Males and Females Charged with Prostitution." *Journal of Criminal Justice* 17(1989):277–291.

Lowery, Ritchie P. *Social Problems: A Critical Analysis of Theories and Public Policy*. Lexington, Mass.: D.C. Heath, 1974.

Luckenbill, David F. "Deviant Career Mobility: The Case of Male Prostitutes." *Social Problems* 33(1986):283–296.

Messerschmidt, James. "Feminism, Criminology and the Rise of the Female Sex 'Delinquent', 1880–1930." *Contemporary Crisis* 11(1987):243-263.

Miller, Eleanor. *Street Women*. Philadelphia: Temple University Press, 1986.

Pheterson, Gail. (Ed.). A *Vindication of the Rights of Whores*. Seattle, WA: The Seal Press, 1989.

———. "The Category "Prostitute" in Scientific Inquiry." *The Journal of Sex Research* 27(1990):397–407.

Pivar, David J. "Purity Crusade Sexual Morality and Social Control, 1868–1900." Westport, Conn.: Greenwood, 1973.

Pomeroy, Wardell B. "Some Aspects of Prostitution." *Journal of Sex Research* 1(1965):177–187.

Potterat, John J., Donald E. Woodhouse, John B. Muth, and Stephen Q. Muth. "Estimating the Prevalence and Career Longevity of Prostitute Women." *The Journal of Sex Research* 27(1990):233-243.

Rathus, Spencer. *Human Sexuality*. New York: Holt, Rinehart and Winston, 1983.

Richards, David A.J. "Prostitution and Commercial Vice: Legal Aspects." *Encyclopedia of Crime and Justice*. Ed. Sanford H. Kadish. New York: Free Press, 1983, 1310–1314.

Rio, Linda M. "Psychological and Sociological Research and the Decriminalization or Legalization of Prostitution." *Archives of Sexual Behavior* 20(1991):205–218.

Robinson, Tim. "Boys' Own Stories." *New Statesman and Society* 3(1990):10–12.

Rosen, Ruth. *The Lost Sisterhood: Prostitution in America, 1900–1918*. Baltimore: John Hopkins University Press, 1982.

Rosenberg, Michael J. "Prostitutes and AIDS: A Health Department Priority?" *American Journal of Public Health* 78(1988):418–423.

Rosenblum, Karen. "Female Deviance and the Female Sex Role: A Preliminary Investigation." *British Journal of Sociology* 25(1975):169–185.

Schaffer, Bernie, and Richard R. DeBlassie. "Adolescent Prostitution." *Adolescence* 19(1984): 689–696.

Schur, Edwin. *Labeling Women Deviant: Gender, Stigma, and Social Control*. Philadelphia: Temple University Press, 1983.

Seng, Magnus J. "Child Sexual Abuse and Adolescent Prostitution: A comparative Analysis." *Adolescence* 24(1989):665–675.

Simon, Carl P., and Ann Witte. *Beating the System: The Underground Economy*. Boston: Auburn House, 1982.

Snider, Laureen. "The Potential of the Criminal Justice System to Promote Feminist Concerns." *Studies in Law, Politics, and Society* 10(1990):143–172.

Symanski, Richard. *The Immoral Landscape: Female Prostitution in Western Societies*. Toronto: Butterworths, 1981.

Tabor, Pauline. *Memoirs of the Madam on Clay Street*. Louisville, Ky.: Touchstone, 1971.

Velarde, Albert J., and Mark Warlick. "Massage Parlors: The Sensuality Business." *Society* 11(1973):63–74.

Vitaliano, Peter, Debra Boyer, and Jennifer James. "Perceptions of Juvenile Experiences: Females Involved in Prostitution versus Property Offenders." *Criminal Justice Behavior* 8 (1981):325–342.

Walkowitz, Judith R. "Male Vice and Female Virtue: Feminism and the Politics of Prostitution in Nineteenth-Century Britain." *Powers of Desire: The Politics of Sexuality*. Eds. Ann Snitow, Christine Stansell, and Sharon Thompson. New York: Monthly Review Press, 1983, 419-438.

Weisberg, D. Kelly. *Children of the Night*. Lexington, Mass.: D.C. Heath, 1985.

Weitzer, Ronald. "Prostitutes' Rights in the United States: The Failure of a Movement." *The Sociological Quarterly* 32(1991):23–41.

Werner, Dennis. "Paid Sex Specialists Among the Mekronoti." *Journal do Anthropological Research* 40(1984):394–405.

Winick, Charles, and Paul M. Kinsie. *The Lively Commerce*. Chicago: Quadrangle, 1971.

Chapter 10

Family Violence

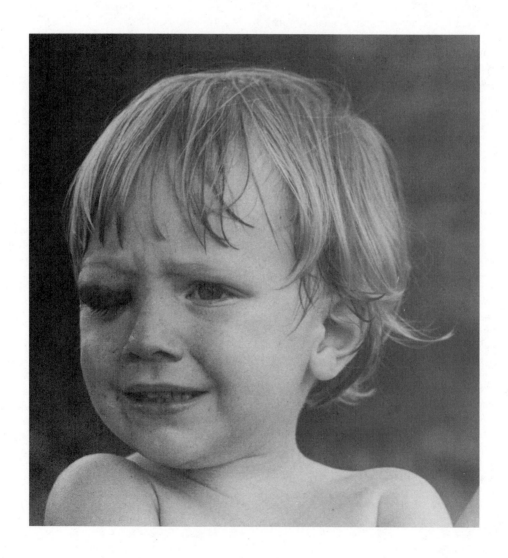

"THE BURNING BED"

Probably the most publicized case of family violence involved Francine Hughes, of Dansville, Michigan. On March 9, 1977, Francine doused her bedroom, her bed, and her sleeping husband with gasoline, dropped a match, and drove herself and her children to the Ingham County Sheriff's Office. As the facts in the case emerged, it became obvious that this was more than a simple case of murder. Francine was a battered wife. In attempting to justify Francine's actions, defense attorney Aryon Greydanus was faced with a problem. He felt that he could not win a case based on self-defense. Mickey Hughes had been asleep and had posed no immediate threat to Francine. Greydanus eventually chose to enter a plea of innocent by reason of insanity. In the end, after hours of evidence about her brutal existence came out in court, Francine was acquitted (Gelles and Straus, 1988).

Because of the unusual method of defense[1] and the timing of the case (wife battering was just being recognized as a major social problem), the plight of Francine Hughes attracted considerable attention. Francine appeared twice on "Donahue," and her story was eventually recreated in a book and a television movie called *The Burning Bed* (Gelles and Straus, 1988). Yet, importantly, the case of Francine Hughes is not an isolated incident. There are any of a number of other stories we could tell, not only about battered women but about battered children as well.

Family violence seemingly makes no sense—a mother beating her own child to death, a husband relentlessly tormenting the women he has vowed to love and cherish. How do we explain the unexplainable? In part, that is what we will try to do in this chapter. We will try to explain the unexplainable. It is important to recognize at the outset, that, while the case of Francine Hughes is in no way an isolated incident, it is somewhat atypical of family violence. Indeed, if we focus our explanations on the Francine Hugheses of the world, we are likely to paint a very unrealistic picture of family violence in the United States. As we broaden our scope to include less extreme cases of family violence, we will undoubtedly uncover many questions to which sociologists might help us find answers.

FAMILY VIOLENCE: "THE" PROBLEM OF THE 1980S?

There is a dizzying amount of literature on family violence. To appreciate the size of the research literature, consider this: There are several professional journals that are either devoted exclusively to family violence or publish a disproportionate number of family violence articles (e.g., *Journal of Family Violence, International Journal of Child Abuse and Neglect, Journal of Interpersonal Violence, Violence and Victims, Protecting Children, Journal of Elder Abuse and Neglect, Journal of Child Sexual Abuse*). Four times a year, the Family Violence Research and Treatment Program at the University of Texas at Tyler publishes the *Family Violence Bulletin*. The *Family Violence Bulletin* includes, among other things, a list of over 300 references to articles (both published and presented at professional conferences) and books on family violence. In other words, there are over 1,200 books and articles about family violence every year.

The volume of literature is even more amazing when one realizes that family violence is a relatively new area of research. Prior to the early 1970s, there was so little research that it could, according to well-known family violence researchers Richard Gelles and Murray Straus, "be read in one sitting" (1988:11).

One of the reasons for the volume of family violence research is that so many different kinds of behaviors—child physical, sexual, and emotional abuse; sibling violence; adolescent violence directed towards parents; spouse abuse (often referred to as domestic violence); and elder violence—fall under the family-violence umbrella. Another reason, one that is especially appealing to objectivist scholars, is that family violence offends the collective morality—the norms—of society. A father beats his own child to death—his own flesh and blood—and we are truly offended. The volume of research, it could be argued, merely reflects the degree to which we are offended by the behavior.

But surely, those who come from more of subjectivist perspective remind us, there is more to it than that. After all, child abuse is not new. Fathers beat their children in the 1950s, and the 1940s, and the 1930s. Were we not offended then? In asking these questions, the subjectivists remind us that the current popularity of family violence research may have less to do with the morally offensive nature of the act than with the social and political process by which family violence has become the problem it is perceived to be today.

WHAT IS FAMILY VIOLENCE?

The Objectivist Conception

We begin with the word *violence*. What is violence? For those who approach family violence from an objectivist perspective, including the "big names" in family violence research (e.g., Murray Straus, Richard Gelles, and Suzanne Steinmetz), the working definition of violence is "an act carried out with the intention of, or an act perceived as having the intention of, physically hurting another person" (Steinmetz, 1987:729). This definition is broad enough to include non-normative behavior (e.g., a wife killing a husband) as well as normative behaviors (a father slapping the hand of a child who continues to reach for the stereo). If we are interested in family violence *as deviance*, where does this leave us?

To help clarify the matter, Gelles and Straus (1979) suggest that family violence can be conceptualized along two separate continuums. The legitimate/illegitimate continuum represents the degree to which social norms legitimize violence. The instrumental/expressive continuum represents the degree to which violence is used as a means to an end—"to induce another person to carry out or refrain from an act" (Gelles and Straus, 1979: 557), or as an end in itself (e.g., hitting

someone out of anger). These two continuums result in a four-cell taxonomy of family violence as shown in Table 10–1.

These four types of violence are reflected in the words of a young mother, who shares her views of discipline with family violence researcher Suzanne Steinmetz:

> I've heard that you shouldn't spank when you're angry, but I can't agree with that because I think that's the time you should spank; before you have a chance to completely cool off, too. I think that the spanking helps the mother or dad as well as impresses the child that they did something wrong, and when they do something bad, they are going to be physically punished for it. You don't hit them with a stick or a belt, or a hairbrush, but a good back of the hand. . . . they remember it (Steinmetz, 1987:729).

Think about what this mother is saying. In part, you spank your child because it is a "catharsis"—it helps the mom or dad get the frustration out of their system (legitimate-expressive). You also spank because you want to impress upon the child that they have done something wrong (legitimate-instrumental). This mother also gives us an indication of where she draws the line between legitimacy and illegitimacy, by suggesting that some behaviors (spanking with a stick, belt, or hairbrush) are not acceptable (Steinmetz, 1987:729–730).

Remember that each of these cells represents "family violence." Yet, as sociologists studying deviance, we are primarily interested in violence that crosses the legitimacy line—violence that society regards as abusive. This, of course, is the problem. At what point does legitimate violence become illegitimate? The objectivist conception appears not to be able to tell us this. Can the norms of legitimate violence be objectively determined? Of course not. Can the various situations in which a norm may or may not apply be specified? Of course not. In short, the objectivist conception cannot tell us when family violence is deviance.

TABLE 10.1 Four Types of Family Violence

	Legitimacy	
	Legitimate-Expressive This is reflected in the belief that it is sometimes "better to spank a child than to 'hold in' one's anger" (Gelles and Straus, 1979:558).	**Illegitimate-Expressive** This is the most recognized and publicized kind of family violence. Includes child abuse, wife beating, and murder.
Expressive		
Instrumental	**Legitimate-Instrumental** This is the most widely occurring type of family violence. Includes, but is not limited to, physical punishment of children.	**Illegitimate-Instrumental** This is punishment that the parent might claim is "for his child's own good" but that society defines as abuse—e.g., a that bruises a child's face.

Source: Adapted table and examples from Richard Gelles and Murray Straus. "Determinants of Violence in the Family: Toward a Theoretical Integration." *Contemporary Theories about the Family.* Eds. Wesley R. Burr, Reuben Hill, Frank I. Nye, and Ira Reiss. New York: Free Press, 1979, 549–581.

The Subjectivist Conception

What is spouse "abuse"? child "abuse"? sibling "abuse"? parent "abuse"? elder "abuse"? From an objectivist perspective, family "abuse" is violent behavior that violates a norm. However, as we discussed above, the objectivists cannot tell us what the norms are concerning family violence. Nor can they tell us where the norms come from. To understand how these normative boundaries are formed, we must consider the subjectivist conception of family violence. From a subjectivist perspective, family violence—abusive violence—is behavior that is labeled "abusive." Abuse is a category of deviance that is created by social audiences. Societal reactions, then, represent the key definitional ingredient. No societal reactions, no deviance.

THE SOCIAL DISTRIBUTION OF FAMILY VIOLENCE

As we mentioned above, a great many behaviors have in recent years come to be known as family violence. While the majority of scholarly attention has been directed at child physical abuse, child sexual abuse, and wife battering, considerable attention has also been directed toward marital rape, sibling violence, elder abuse, adolescent-to-parent violence, wife-to-husband violence, violence in dating relationships, child emotional abuse, and child neglect. (For research on these topics, see, for example, Gelles, 1987; Finkelhor et al., 1983; Pagelow, 1984; 1989; Pillemer, 1985; Agnew and Huguley, 1989; Straus and Gelles, 1990; Pirog-Good and Stets, 1989.) Given the sheer size of this literature, it is important that we set some limitations in our discussions here. Therefore, this chapter will for the most part focus on parent-to-child physical violence and marital violence (mostly wife beating).

The Prevalence of Family Violence

Several methodological problems make family violence an especially problematic area of research. The most obvious problem concerns the operational definition of "abuse." We have already admitted that we (and others) do not know what abuse is. Second, and potentially even more problematic, because the majority of family violence is not reported, much of the research discussed in this chapter is based on self-report surveys. Self-report surveys ask respondents to recall their own experiences with family violence (both as offender and victim). Accuracy, of course, depends on whether respondents accurately remember their experiences. By using self-reports, we also risk the potential distortions that are common in retrospective interpretations (Wisdom, 1989). Most problematic of all, if we are to trust our data, we must trust that the respondents have been honest. Even under conditions of anonymity and confidentiality, responds may lie or, perhaps more commonly, they may "minimize the severity of the violent acts (e.g., a brutal beating becomes a few slaps)" (Steinmetz, 1987:730). Yet since the majority of family violence is hidden we have little choice but to rely on self reports.

The two most commonly cited self-report surveys of family violence (and the two surveys upon which most of our analyses will be based) are the 1975 National Family Violence Survey (sample size 2,143) and the 1985 replication of this study, the National Family Violence Re-Survey (sample size 6,002). These two surveys remain the only nationally representative studies of family violence (Straus, 1990a). Each survey employs the Conflict Tactics Scale as its measure of family violence. As the name implies, the Conflict Tactics Scale measures a variety of methods of conflict resolution that family members might use during disagreements and fights. To measure marital violence, one member of a randomly selected couple was asked to recall how many times *during the past year* they had responded to disagreement with a spouse with rational discussion (this category of responses included items such as "discussed an issue calmly"), verbal aggression (this category included items such as "did or said something to spite" the other person), or physical ag-

gression (listed in Tables 10–2 and 10–3). For those households that included a child or children between the ages of 3 and 17, one child was selected at random and the parent was asked a similar set of questions about how they responded to disagreement with that child. This is how Gelles and Straus measured parent-to-child violence (Gelles and Straus, 1985).

Marital Violence. When data from the first Family Violence Survey were published (Straus, Gelles, and Steinmetz, 1980), they made one point painfully clear: marital violence is not uncommon. In fact, the assault rate among married couples was so high (many times the rate of violence among strangers) that some concluded that the marriage license might in many ways be considered a "hitting license" (Straus, Gelles, and Steinmetz, 1980). During 1985 approximately 16 percent of U.S. couples reported at least one of the eight acts of violence listed in the Conflict Tactics Scale as shown in Table 10–2. Rates of more serious abuse were considerably lower, but still high enough to generate concern, with slightly more than 6 percent of the couples reporting "severe" violence (items 4–8 in Table 10–2) (Straus and Gelles, 1986).

The Family Violence Re-Survey data also suggest that, contrary to popular belief, wives hit husbands as frequently as husbands hit wives. More specifically, the rates of overall marital violence during 1985 (items 1-8 in Table 10–2) are actually higher for wives (12.1 percent) than they are for husbands (11.3 percent). In other words, a higher percentage of wives report using violence against husbands than visa versa. The rate of severe violence is also higher for wives (4.6 percent) than for husbands (3.8 percent).

Data that women are as violent as men are a bit unsettling to feminist theorists and others who perceive the "real" marital violence problem to be wifebattering. Critics

TABLE 10.2   Rate of Marital Violence: 1975 Family Violence Survey and 1985 Family Violence Re-Survey

TYPE OF VIOLENCE*	HUSBAND-TO-WIFE		WIFE-TO-HUSBAND	
	1975 (N = 2,143)	*1985* (N = 3,520)	*1975* (N = 2,143)	*1985* (N = 3,520)
Minor Violence Acts				
1) Three something	2.8%	2.8%	5.2%	4.2%
2) Pushed/grabbed/shoved	10.7%	9.3%	8.3%	8.9%
3) Slapped	5.1%	2.9%	4.6%	4.1%
Severe Violence Acts				
4) Kicked/bit/hit with a fist	2.4%	1.5%	3.1%	2.4%
5) Hit, tried to hit	2.2%	1.7%	3.0%	3.0%
6) Beat up	1.1%	0.8%	0.6%	0.4%
7) Threatened with gun or knife	0.4%	0.4%	0.6%	0.6%
8) Used gun or knife	0.3%	0.2%	0.2%	0.2%
Violence Indexes				
Overall Violence (1–8)	12.1%	11.3%	11.6%	12.1%
(used any violent act in the previous year)				
Severe Violence (4–8)	3.8%	3.0%	4.6%	4.4%
(used any severe violent act in the previous year) ("Wife Beating")				

*This table gives the percentage of spouses who used any one act of violence from the Conflict Tactics Scale for a given year.

Source: Murray Straus and Richard Gelles. "Societal Change and Change in Family Violence from 1975 to 1985 As Revealed by Two National Surveys. *Journal of Marriage and the Family* 48 (Aug. 1986): 465–479.

complain that the Family Violence Surveys, and other surveys that use the Conflict Tactics Scale, fail to measure the degree to which "violent" women are actually acting in self-defense. Additionally, these surveys do not measure the serious injuries more often caused by wife abuse (Kurz, 1989). Sometimes the dialogue between the creators of the Conflict Tactics Scale (e.g., Murray Straus and Richard Gelles) and its feminist critics (e.g., Kurz, 1989; 1991; Loseke, 1991) is somewhat heated. Demie Kurz, for example, has been openly critical of Murray Straus because his "use of large amounts of federal money for research whose conclusions have vastly underestimated the harm done to women and greatly exaggerated their responsibility for that violence [and] has provided a distorted picture of this problem to policy makers" (1991:158). Kurz believes the "real" problem is wife abuse.

What is most interesting about this debate is that Straus and his colleagues generally agree. In their initial report on the 1975 National Family Violence data, for example, Straus, Gelles, and Steinmetz wrote that "it would be a great mistake" if the data on wife-to-husband violence "distracted us from giving first attention to *wives as victims* as the focus of social policy" (1980:43). They agree with the feminists: wife abuse is the "real" problem. They give several reasons for reaching this conclusion: (1) husbands report more serious violence; (2) wives report more serious injuries when victims of violence (in large part because men are stronger); (3) husbands are more likely to repeatedly use violence; (4) women are often acting in self-defense; and

TABLE 10.3   Rate of Parent-To-Child Violence: 1975 Family Violence Survey and 1985 Family Violence Re-Survey

TYPE OF VIOLENCE*	1975 (N = 1,146)	1985 (N = 1,428)
Minor Violence Acts		
1) Three something	5.4%	2.7%
2) Pushed/grabbed/shoved	31.8%	30.7%
3) Slapped or spanked	58.2%	54.9%
Severe Violence Acts		
4) Kicked/bit/hit with a fist	3.2%	1.3%
5) Hit, tried to hit with something	13.4%	9.7%
6) Beat up	1.3%	0.6%
7) Threatened with gun or knife	0.1%	0.2%
8) Used gun or knife	0.1%	0.2%
Violence Indexes		
Overall Violence (1–8) (used any violent act in the previous year)	63.0%	62.0%
Severe Violence (4–8) (used any severe act in the previous year)	14.7%	10.7%
Very Severe Violence (4, 6, 8) (used any very severe act in the previous year) ("Child Abuse")	3.6%	1.9%

*This table gives the percentage of parents who used any one act of violence from the Conflict Tactics Scale for a given year.

Source: Murray Straus and Richard Gelles. "Societal Change and Change in Family Violence from 1975 to 1985 As Revealed by Two National Surveys." *Journal of Marriage and the Family* 48 (Aug. 1986): 465–479.

(5) women are in general more economically dependent on men and, therefore, have fewer means of escaping a violent relationship (Straus, Gelles, and Steinmetz, 1980:43–44).

Parent-to-Child Violence   Straus (1991a) estimates that approximately 97 percent of parents in the U.S. have, at some point in their children's lives, used physical punishment to correct misbehavior. While the rates of physical punishment are highest for children ages 2 through 6, approximately one-third of parents of young teens (ages 13 to 16) continue to use physical punishment.

Because definitions of *abuse* and *mistreatment* differ so dramatically from one audi-

ence to the next, estimates of child mistreatment are more complicated. Some moral entrepreneurs would probably prefer that all parent-to-child violence be defined "maltreatment." Gelles and Straus (1988), for example, have argued that spanking should be criminalized (as it is in Sweden).

Despite the operational problems, there are "official" estimates of child abuse. For example, from 1976 to 1987 (the year federal funding for the project expired) The American Humane Association (1987) collected information on all *reported* abuse and neglect cases (i.e., mistreatment that is reported to child protective service agencies). Based on these reports, the American Humane Association estimates that in 1987 approximately 34 out of 1,000 children were physically abused, sexually abused, or neglected. Unfortunately, since the majority of abuse cases are never reported, and definitions of abuse undoubtedly differ from one service agency to the next, it is difficult to know how to interpret these data.

One way to avoid the definitional quandary is to report specific acts of violence between parents and children. This is exactly what Straus and his colleagues (1980) did in the 1975 Family Violence Survey. They report that 3.2 percent of the parents had kicked, bit or hit their child with a fist in the previous year (see Table 10–3), and approximately 8 percent had done so at least once in their child's life. Slightly more than 1 percent had beaten up their child in the previous year, and 4 percent had done so at least once in the child's life (Steinmetz, 1987). Straus and Gelles (1986) operationalize "abuse" as kicked, bit, hit with fist, beat up, and used gun or knife, and conclude that 3.6 percent of the parents from the 1975 survey abused their child in the previous year (see Table 10–3).

Is Family Violence Getting Worse? It is very tempting to answer this question in the affirmative. After all, we hear about the "increasingly serious" problem on the 6:00 P.M. news. We read about it in news magazines. There seems to be more and more discussion of family violence on afternoon talk shows (e.g., "Phil Donahue," and "Oprah Winfrey"). There are television shows and movies on family violence. Who hasn't seen the made-for-television movie *The Burning Bed*, starring Farah Fawcett? Family violence seems to be a worsening social problem.

But we must remember that increasing attention from Phil Donahue, or movie producers, or the news media does not necessarily reflect increasing rates of family violence. We must, therefore, ask the question again: "Is

family violence getting worse?" We can look to history to find a partial answer to this question. Among those who have examined the historical evidence on the mistreatment of children (e.g., deMause, 1974), the general conclusion is that "children are now exposed to less neglect, mistreatment, and violence than at any time in history" (Steinmetz, 1987:732). It is well known, for example, that in colonial times uncontrollable children could actually be put to death (although there is no evidence that they ever were) (Steinmetz, 1987). Even a look at our more recent history will remind us that the "good old-fashioned whipping" that our parents or grandparents likely received when they were young would probably not be considered an acceptable form of discipline today. Given the history of power differences between "man and wife," we might similarly conclude that wives are less likely to be victims of violence that they were in past times.

But what about the more recent trends? In our idealized "Leave It to Beaver" image of the 1950s family, it is hard to imagine abuse. Somehow in today's modern, urbanized, anonymous world, family violence seems more feasible. Abuse, we might hypothesize, seems a natural by-product of the so-called breakdown of the family.

Official data support the belief that the family violence problem—especially the child abuse problem—has been getting worse in recent years. According to the American Humane Association (1987), the rate of *official* child mistreatment (physical abuse, sexual abuse, and neglect) increased by 340 percent from 1976–1987 (from 10 per 1,000 children in 1976 to 34 per 1,000 in 1987). Yet, as we have already mentioned, there are a number of problems with these data. This increase probably reflects increasing rates of reported abuse, not increases in the actual rate of abuse. Teachers, counselors, and pastors are more aware of child abuse than they were 15 years ago. They are educated about the signs of child abuse and are, in many cases, required by law to report suspected cases of child abuse. Indeed, with increasing emphasis on the recognition and reporting of abuse, "it would be amazing if the numbers of reports had not increased since 1976" (Gelles and Straus, 1987:80).

Given the problems with "official" estimates of abuse, such as those reported by the American Humane Association (1987), the best way to estimate changes in the rate of family violence is with the 1975 National Family Violence Survey and the 1985 National Family Violence Re-survey (Straus and Gelles, 1986). Gelles and Straus (1988) have written that when they first looked at the 1985 data, they expected to find few changes in the rates of family violence. What they found, however, was that the rates of self-reported violence had actually *declined*—and dramatically so—during the ten years (see Table 10–2 and Table 10–3).

In 1975, the rate of parent-to-child "very severe violence" (items 4, 6, 8) was 3.6 percent (i.e., 3.6 percent of parents had been abusive during the previous year). In 1985, the rate had dropped to 1.9 percent, a decline of 47 percent. Less serious forms of parent-to-child violence similarly dropped, but, in general, less dramatically.

The Family Violence Survey data reveal a downturn in wife beating as well (Table 10–2). In 1975, the rate of husband-to-wife "severe violence" (items 4–8) was 3.6 percent (i.e., 3.6 percent of husbands reported using severe violence during the previous year). In 1985, the rates had declined by 27 percent to 3.0 percent. The rates of wife-to-husband violence remained essentially unchanged.

Critics of this research complain that because a different survey method was used in the 1975 research (face-to-face interviews) than in the 1985 research (telephone surveys), the results cannot be compared directly. Gelles and Straus (1988) respond that the results cannot be dismissed on these grounds. In-

deed, there is no reason to suspect that the two different methods would yield such dramatically different results. There is a second and potentially more damaging problem with this research; with increasing condemnation of family violence during the late 1970s and the early 1980s, respondents in the 1985 survey might have been more reluctant to report their abusive behavior.

Gelles and Straus (1988) recognize the problems but stand by their findings. Besides, they argue, given the various societal changes during the past decade, family violence should be declining.[3] These change include the increasing age of men and women when they first get married; smaller families; the economic prosperity of the 1970s and 1980s (resulting in a decrease in family worry over finances); a decrease in the economic dependence of women; an increase in the number of shelters for women; an increase in the number of treatment programs for abusers; and a stiffening of legal sanctions against child and spouse abuse.

RISK FACTORS

Risk factors are somewhat more difficult to estimate than they might at first glance appear to be. The problem is that we have no good, representative estimates of severe violence (i.e., child abuse and wife battering). True, the Family Violence Surveys are large, representative samples. Because of their size, furthermore, they provide reasonably good estimates of the level of violence in the U.S. family. But the rates of severe abuse are small enough that the surveys do not provide enough cases of severe violence to accurately describe risk patterns. Straus and Gelles (1986), for example, estimate the rate of very severe violence ("child abuse") to be 1.9 percent. That is, 19 out of every 1,000 children (3 to 17 years old) had been abused during the 12 months prior to the 1985 survey. With only 1,428 parents included in the survey, this means that there were only 27 severely abused children included in the 1985 sample. With so few cases, risk patterns cannot be confidently estimated.

Besides national surveys, the only other option is to rely on official estimates of child abuse and woman battering. To the extent, however, that some kinds of people (e.g., the poor, and racial minorities) are more likely to come to the attention of formal agents of social control (e.g., police, and social service agencies), and, thus, show up in official estimates of family violence, these data must be interpreted with caution. The common assumption is that middle-class families are somewhat more insulated and are more likely to seek help from family doctors, ministers, private counselors, and others (Steinmetz, 1987; Hampton, Gelles, and Harrop, 1989). There is also speculation that violence in poor families is more likely to be officially labeled "abuse" than is violence in middle-class families (Hampton, 1986; Hampton, Gelles, and Harrop, 1989).

Despite the problems, family violence researchers are confident that they have uncovered several important factors that increase one's risk of becoming a violent family member. These risk factors include various social class factors (e.g., income, education, and employment status), age, gender, alcohol and drug use, and family patterns of abuse.

Social Class.   Family violence that comes to the attention of agents of social control is overwhelmingly among the lower classes. If we look only at these "official" data it is easy to accept the myth that family violence is an exclusively lower-class phenomenon. National surveys of family violence, however, suggest that, while it is true that the *rates* of abuse are generally higher in lower-class families than in middle-class families, rich and poor alike can be violent.

Straus, Gelles, and Steinmetz (1980) report that 22 percent of the families with incomes under $6,000 reported child abuse, and 11 percent reported severe marital violence. Only 11 percent of the families with incomes over $20,000, on the other hand, reported child abuse, and only 2 percent reported severe marital violence.

The college educated are also less violent on average than those without college degrees (Straus, Gelles, and Steinmetz, 1980). The only exception to this pattern is that college-educated women, when compared to women without college educations, tend to be somewhat *more* violent towards their husbands. Steinmetz speculates that college-educated women may be "more aggressive, more strong-willed, and/or less likely to automatically take the submissive role in a marriage" (1987:747).

Wauchope and Straus (1990) estimate that the rate of child abuse among blue-collar parents is approximately twice that among white-collar parents. Kantor and Straus (1990) similarly estimate that more blue-collar husbands approve of a husband slapping a wife (18.5 percent) or have themselves been violent in the previous year (13.4 percent) than white-collar husbands (14.4 percent and 10.4 percent, respectively). Rates of wife battering and child abuse are also lower in families where the father is employed full-time (Steinmetz, 1987). Despite speculation that employment of the mother would lead to higher rates of abuse, Gelles and Hargreaves (1990) conclude that working mothers are no more abusive.

Age.   Family violence surveys consistently demonstrate a negative relationship between age and marital violence. That is, as the age of both the husband and wife increases, marital violence decreases (Straus, Gelles, and Steinmetz, 1980; Suitor, Pillemer, and Straus, 1990). There is some debate, however, as to why violence decreases as age increases. The declines may reflect nothing more than the tendency for violent couples to break up. Or, the trends may reflect the more general tendency for the young to be more criminal than the old. Having fewer "stakes in conformity," the young may be more free to be delinquent (Hirschi and Gottfredson, 1983).

Parent-to-child violence also generally decreases with age—both the age of the parent and the age of the child. Rates of physical *punishment* are much higher for young children. The overwhelming majority of the 3-year-olds have been physically punished, but the rates decline dramatically thereafter. Parents apparently assume that very young children are too young to learn from a spanking and older children are either too large to hit (e.g., a mother may be smaller than her 13-year-old son) or might more effectively learn from another method of punishment (Wauchope and Straus, 1990).

Interestingly, rates of child *abuse* are not correlated with the age of the victim. That is, 16-year-olds are as likely to be physically abused as 3-year-olds (Wauchope and Straus, 1990).

Gender.   We have already discussed gender as it relates to marital violence; wives hit husbands about the same amount as husbands hit wives. With respect to parent-to-child violence, most of the research suggests that parents more often use physical punishment on boys than on girls, although the differences are generally small (Straus, Gelles, and Steinmetz, 1980; Wauchope and Straus, 1990). Boys are also slightly more likely to be victims of physical abuse. Wauchope and Straus (1990) estimate the rate of child abuse to be approximately 47 percent higher for boys than for girls. The American Humane Association (1987) suggests that victims in child abuse related fatalities are also more likely to be boys (54 percent) then girls (46 percent).

While boys are slightly more likely to be victims of child abuse, Straus and his colleagues (1980) suggest that women are more likely to be perpetrators of abuse. In a more

recent analysis, however, few differences were found (Wauchope and Straus, 1990). Because of the small number of cases upon which these estimates are based, a more helpful estimate may come from The American Humane Association (1987), which estimates that 56 percent of the perpetrators in child abuse-related homicides are women. This evidence is especially compelling when one considers that the overwhelming majority of homicides are committed by men.

Alcohol Abuse   There is little reason to question the relationship between alcohol use and family violence. Men and women who drink are more likely to hit each other and to hit their children (Steinmetz, 1987). Gelles and Straus (1988), for example, estimate that couples report that alcohol was involved in almost half of all family violence episodes (including marital and parent-to-child violence). In a recent study that focuses specifically on the relationship between alcohol and wife beating, Kantor and Straus (1990) conclude that the rate of husband-to-wife violence is approximately three times higher for "binge" drinkers (19.2 percent) than for abstainers (6.8 percent). They further estimate that alcohol is involved in approximately one out of four instances of wife beating.

There remains considerable debate, however, as to the causal significance of these findings. Does alcohol cause family violence (i.e., a husband drinks, loses control, and beats his wife) or does alcohol serve as an excuse for men who want to take out their frustrations on their wives. This discussion becomes even more intriguing when we remember that the link between alcohol and violence is more cultural than physiological. Recall from Chapter 4 that, in experimental settings, alcohol has no effect on aggression (Marlatt and Rohsenow, 1981). This evidence, along with the fact that the vast majority of men who drink do not hit their wives (Kantor and Straus, 1990), serves to remind us that alcohol is in no way *the* cause of family violence.

Does Violence Beget Violence? The "violence begets violence" thesis essentially suggests that "violence in the family serves as a training ground for children, who as adults are more likely to approve of violence as an acceptable way of solving problems and to use violence both within the family and outside the family" (Steinmetz, 1987:752). This thesis has been examined in a variety of different contexts. (See Wisdom, 1989 for a review.)

There are several ways to examine the "violence begets violence" thesis empirically. Some of the research has focused on the adjustment problems of abused children. In a study of 60 "abused", 30 "neglected", and 30 "normal" children, for example, Green (1978) found that abused children were more self-destructive (including tendencies toward self-mutilation, suicide attempts, and suicide ideation) than neglected or normal children.

Other research has focused on the relationship between family violence and crime outside the family. Patterns of childhood abuse, for example, are common among murders and rapists (Steinmetz, 1987). The Family Violence Surveys similarly suggest that childhood *victims* of abuse are more likely to assault and commit property crimes outside the family. For abused children who also witnessed marital violence, the rates of criminal activity are even higher. Husbands and wives who are victims of family assault are also more likely to commit assaults outside the family (Hotaling, Straus, and Lincoln, 1990). A similar pattern holds for family violence *offenders*. Wife batters are almost four times more likely to have an arrest record than nonviolent men. Men who abuse both their children and their wives are five times more likely to have an arrest record (Hotaling, Straus, and Lincoln, 1990).

Research focusing specifically on the "family violence begets family violence" thesis finds that, compared to nonviolent husbands, husbands who abuse their wives have higher rates of child abuse. Wives who are victims of abuse also tend to be more abusive toward their children, and children who are victims of abuse tend to be more violent toward their siblings (Straus, 1990c).

In a conclusion that is somewhat controversial, Straus (1991a) argues that the "violence begets violence" thesis extends to adults who experienced non-abusive physical punishment (i.e., spanking) as children. He demonstrates that the more parents are physically punished as children, the more likely they are to become physically abusive to their own children (Straus, 1990c), and the more likely they are to become involved in criminal activities as adults (Straus, 1991a).

Despite the seemingly overwhelming amount of evidence that supports the "violence begets violence" thesis, there are reasons to be cautious in our interpretations. Wisdom (1989), for example, points to the many methodological problems with the research. She argues that there has been an overreliance on self-report and retrospective research (e.g., in which violent adults are asked about their experiences with violence as children) and that control groups have been used infrequently (e.g., a comparison group of nonviolent adults who are also asked about their experiences with violence as children). She also reminds us that the data only suggest that children who were abused, or who witnessed abuse, are, when compared to children who were not abused, *more likely* to be abusive adults. Notice what we have said. Children who were abused are more likely to be abusive adults. They are not predetermined to be abusive adults. In fact, the majority of abused children *do not* grow up to be abusive adults (Wisdom, 1989). The significance of this distinction is illustrated by Gelles and Straus (1988), who tell the story of being approached by a young man after one of their lectures on family violence. With tears in his eyes, the young man confessed that, after hearing Gelles and Straus lecture on family violence, he had come to the conclusion that he could never get married. Somewhat shocked that their lecture would evoke this kind of a response, they asked him why he had reached this conclusion. He responded:

> *"You described the factors that are related to abuse. You said that people who are abused grow up to be abusers. Well, I was an abused child. I don't want to get married and grow up to abuse my children, so I will not get married!" (quoted in Gelles and Straus, 1988:49).*

It is easy to see where this young man got confused. However strong the family patterns, it is important to remember that "it cannot be said that the pathway [from childhood abuse to adult abuse] is straight or certain" (Wisdom, 1989:24).

WHAT CAUSES FAMILY VIOLENCE?

There are really two separate theoretical issues here. The overwhelming majority of family violence theories are objectivist in scope. In an attempt to explain behavior, they ask the question, "Why do they do it?" This emphasis is understandable. If we hope to stop family violence, we have to know what causes family violence. There are, however, a small number of scholars who concentrate on societal reactions rather than behavior. These subjectivist theorists attempt to explain the social, economic, and political origins of deviance categories.

Objectivist Theories

Many objectivist theories of family violence, especially those that are more individualistic in scope, begin with the assumption that "intrafamily violence is abnormal and grows out of some social or personal pathology" (Gelles and Straus, 1979:549).

Macro-Objectivist Theories. Macro-objectivist theorists generally approach the issue of family violence from a different perspective. Given certain social and cultural conditions, family violence may in fact be a "normal" (i.e., common, culturally approved) part of family life. The task of the macro-objectivist theorist is to identify those structural factors which can explain violent family behavior.

If we are to understand what causes family violence, we must come to understand the cultural context out of which family violence arises. Violence is, in many ways, an accepted, encouraged, and even glorified form of expression in our society. Football is our favorite sport. Arnold Schwarzenegger, Clint Eastwood, and Sylvester Stalone are among our favorite movie stars. Violence, or at least aggression, is clearly "in." This cultural context takes on special importance within the family. Parents in the United States still overwhelmingly support the use of corporal punishment (Straus, 1991a). During the late 1960s the U.S. Commission on the Causes and Prevention of Violence reported that 87 percent of those surveyed said that a child needed "strong" discipline and more than 70 percent thought that it was sometimes necessary, normal, or good to slap a 12-year-old (Straus, Gelles, and Steinmetz, 1980; Gelles and Straus, 1988). The most recent estimates are that at least 97 percent of parents in the United States have used physical punishment at least once in their children's lives (Straus, 1991a). Violence between spouses is also accepted, although generally not to the same degree. Straus and his colleagues (1980) have reported that 28 percent of husbands and 23 percent of wives agree that under some conditions couples "slapping each other" is normal.

Our culture at least implicitly encourages

the use of violence, and there are also a number of structural characteristics that "tend to make the family a conflict-prone social group" (Brinkerhoff and Lupri, 1988:411). These factors include the "time risk" of spending a disproportionate amount of time with family members. A second factor is that emotional investment and love are sometimes one-sided. An emotionally invested partner is more vulnerable, especially if the spouse remains uninvested. A third factor, one that feminist scholars have been especially mindful of, is that family relationships are characterized by discrepancies between power and dependence (on both age and gender continuums). Conflict emerges "naturally" out of these power differences. Finally, the family is the most private and, in many ways, the most isolated social group in society. Public displays of family violence—a mother drags her child by the arm into a restroom, a husband slaps his wife as they argue in the mall parking lot—are often dismissed as "family matters." Family privacy norms also dictate that families should be able to solve their own problems, whether they are prepared to do so or not (Brinkerhoff and Lupri, 1988:411–412).

These cultural and social structural factors "set the stage" for us, but they really tell us very little about why some families are more violent than others. To address these issues we turn specifically to three macro-objectivist perspectives: feminist theory, strain theory, and the subculture-of-violence theory.

Feminist Theory. Feminist theory is much like neo-Marxism. Like neo-Marxism, feminism focuses on how the powerful—in this case men—exploit the powerless—women, and to a lesser degree, children. Like neo-Marxism, feminism focuses on both deviance (acts) and definitions (labels). In this section, we will consider how feminism offers an explanation of deviance (acts).

The hierarchical model upon which families have traditionally been based dictates that men have power and control over women and that parents have power and control over children (Dobash and Dobash, 1979; Kurz, 1989; Brown and Bohn, 1990). In this country, for example, legal marital violence was at one time dictated by a "rule of thumb," whereby a wife could be beaten with a stick no larger than a thumb (Yllo and Straus, 1990). Laws also reflected the powerlessness of children. Puritan parents could actually put their own unruly children to death (Gelles and Straus, 1988).

But that was then and this is now, right? After all, men are no longer permitted to beat their wives, and parents are no longer permitted to kill misbehaving children. It is true that the laws have changed, but it would be a mistake to assume that norms of control and dominance are dead. Indeed, from a feminist perspective, "As long as women are responsible for domestic work, child care, and emotional and psychological support and men's primary identity is that of provider and revolves around work, . . . the wife becomes an 'appropriate victim' of physical and psychological abuse" (Kurz, 1989: 496). Of course most sexist men do not physically abuse their wives. At the same time, there can be little doubt that patriarchy has contributed to the current level of family violence in this society.

Looking specifically at woman battering, feminist scholars Dobash and Dobash (1979) maintain that contemporary patriarchy involves both *structural* and *ideological* elements. *Structurally,* women have less status than men and are therefore more likely to be dependent on men. *Ideologically,* patriarchy means that male dominance is seen as legitimate and "natural."

Do these separate components of patriarchy impact the level of family violence in U.S. society? Concerning *patriarchal structure,* we would hypothesize that women who, because of their low status are especially dependent on men (i.e., women with few financial resources, little work experience, and low self-esteem) will have few alternatives to marriage and will "be more tolerant of negative treatment from their husbands, including physical abuse" (Kalmuss and Straus, 1990:369). For the most part, the data support this hypothesis. That is, women whose "objective dependence" on marriage is high (women who do not work outside the home, earn 25 percent or less of the family income, and have young children at home) and women whose "subjective dependence" on marriage is high (women who perceive that they would, compared to their husband, be more hurt by a divorce) tend to experience more violence than women whose dependence is low (Kalmuss and Straus, 1990).

Despite this evidence, the more important causal factor is probably *patriarchal ideology*: "the values, beliefs, and norms regarding the 'legitimacy' of male dominance in all social spheres" (Yllo and Straus, 1990:384). The evidence on the relationship between patriarchal ideology and family violence is convincing. First, historical data illustrate the degree to which women have been viewed and treated as property (Dobash and Dobash, 1979). There is also considerable interview data suggesting that abuse is often a husband's attempt to force his wife to abide by his wishes. These interviews also reveal that men often believe their violence is justified (Dobash and Dobash, 1979; Kurz, 1989). Finally, survey research suggests that husbands who espouse patriarchal beliefs and attitudes are especially likely to be violent toward their wives (Smith, 1990).

There is also considerable research on the balance of power within the family. In their analysis of the 1975 Family Violence Survey, Straus, Gelles, and Steinmetz (1980) reported that only 3 percent of the women in egalitarian relationships (i.e., where major decisions were shared equally by the husband and wife) experienced severe abuse in the previous year. In families where the husband assumed the most power to make important decisions, the rate was considerably higher (11 percent).

In a recent attempt to examine the simultaneous role of patriarchal structure and ideology, Yllo and Straus (1990) ranked 30 states (the smaller states were not included in the analysis) on a variety of economic, educational, political, and legal indicators of the status of women (*patriarchal structure*)[4] and on the degree to which residents of the states were "sexist,"—that is, they believed that husbands should dominate wives (*patriarchal ideology*). As a dependent variable, they calculated the rate of violence in the 30 states. Consistent with their expectations, wife abuse rates were approximately twice as high in "sexist" states as in "nonsexist" states. The result concerning the status of women, however, were somewhat more mixed. Consistent with expectations, they did find that states in which women had the *lowest* status (scoring 1 on a 1 to 5 status scale) did have comparatively high rates of wife abuse. Contrary to expectations, however, states in which women had the *highest* status (scoring 5 on a 1 to 5 status scale) also had high rates of wife beating.

These data would seem to lead to two contradictory conclusions. Rates of abuse are high in low-status states because "women in these states have fewer alternatives to violent marriages" (Yllo and Straus, 1990:394). Rates are also high in very high status states because "these are the states in which husbands may feel most threatened" (Yllo and Straus, 1990).

To attempt to resolve this contradiction, Yllo and Straus (1990) consider the simultaneous effects of structure (status) and ideology (sexist norms) on rates of abuse. They conclude that in general rates of wife beating are highest in sexist, low-status states. Importantly, however, wife abuse rates are also very high in sexist, high-status states. In the words of Yllo and Straus:

*Wife beating is most common where woman's status in economic, educational, legal, and political institutions is relatively high but where prevailing norms favor their subordination within marriage. We suggest that this is true because of the conflicts inherent in the **inconsistency** between the relatively equal structural status of women and the attempt to maintain a traditional patriarchal power structure within the family (Yllo and Straus, 1990:398). [emphasis in original]*

Recognize what Yllo and Straus are saying. We can fully expect wife abuse to decrease as the status of women increases and patriarchal norms subside. However, to the degree that the status of women increases but sexist norms persist, we might expect rates of abuse to actually increase.

Strain Theory. Strain theories (more often referred to as social structural theory or structural theory in the family violence literature) begin with the recognition that rates of family violence are higher in lower-income families. Strain theorists argue that the unequal distribution of opportunities produces greater levels of frustration in lower-class families (Gelles and Straus, 1979). In lower-class families, financial worries, larger families, and crowded living conditions contribute to frustration levels. This frustration sometimes results in aggression. And the aggression is sometimes directed at innocent, yet convenient, victims (i.e., children and spouses). Psychologists sometimes refer to the tendency to displace anger onto innocent victims as the frustration-aggression hypothesis, or scapegoating theory (Howell and Pugliesi, 1988; Webster, Goldstein, and Segall, 1985). When our goals are blocked, we are seldom in a position to take out our frustrations on the actual person (or situation) responsible. As a replacement, we will look for a scapegoat. The assumption, then, is that "frustration and/or strain experienced as a result of structural contingencies can result in aggressive actions towards others, such as a spouse"

(Howell and Pugliesi, 1988:17). This theoretical expectation is empirically supported by research that demonstrates a strong link between stress and family violence (Straus, 1990b; Seltzer and Kalmus, 1988).

In addition to experiencing greater levels of stress, lower-class families are likely to have access to fewer alternatives as they attempt to cope with their frustration. That is, they generally have comparatively less access to community support and services, less time away from family members, and fewer social support ties (Webster, Goldstein, and Segall, 1985).

Subculture-of-Violence Theory. Another theory that attempts to account for the comparatively high rates of family violence among the lower class is the *subculture-of-violence* theory (Wolfgang and Ferracuti, 1967). This theory maintains that, within lower-income families (and in the lower class more generally), there is greater cultural acceptance of violence. Violence is a cultural norm into which one is socialized (Gelles and Straus, 1979). Because this perspective does not tell us how violent subcultural values originate in the first place, Gelles and Straus (1979) have suggested that the subculture-of-violence theory might best be combined with social structural (i.e., strain) theories. Structural frustrations produce violence, and "violence becomes codified in the form of values which justify and norms which simplify carrying out the violent acts" (Gelles and Straus, 1979:569).

Micro-Objectivist Theories.

Social Learning Theory. Of all the theories of families violence, social learning theory is probably the most often applied. The reasons for the interest in social learning theory should be obvious. As we have already discussed, people who were abused or who witnessed abuse as children are comparatively more likely to be abusive as adults. At first glance, this pattern makes little sense. Think of a mother whose most vivid childhood memories are of her own mother beating her while she cowers in a corner. Having experienced the pain of physical violence firsthand, surely she has learned *not* to hit her own children. Similarly, we might assume that a man who as a boy watched in fright as his own father beat his wife has learned not to inflict the same kind of emotional and physical pain on his own wife.

Yet this is not the case. Those who have observed abuse or were victims of abuse are more likely to abuse. The question is why. Most likely, violence is rarely directly reinforced. A father may, for example, encourage fighting siblings to "settle it like men,"[5] but for the most part parents do not purposely teach their children to be abusive spouses or parents.

According to Sutherland's *differential association theory,* deviance results from an excess of definitions favorable to violation of law (i.e., norms) over definitions unfavorable to violation of law. In the case of family violence, definitions include acceptance of violence (as a norm) in the family and rationalizations that would justify violence in the family. Children who observe violence in the family, or are themselves abused, learn that violence is an acceptable way (or perhaps even *the* acceptable way) of resolving family conflict and expressing frustration (Steinmetz, 1987). In part, this occurs because we tend to model the behaviors of familiar others, whether we feel especially close to them or not (Bandura, 1973). Indeed, research on modeling has led family violence theorists to conclude that "familiarity with a model is more important than a warm relationship with a model for a behavior to be imitated, which means that children may be equally likely to imitate a feared or hated parent as a loved parent" (Pagelow, 1981:37).

Learning might also occur as a result of *differential reinforcement.* Pagelow (1981) argues that some men believe that it is their right—maybe even their duty—to "own, control, and dominate women and children" (Pagelow, 1981:41). According to Pagelow, men who are socialized to believe that they have the right to control their wives and children and who have observed and experienced violence while growing up will be more likely to use violence as a way of maintaining control. She writes:

> *Traditional ideology calls for men to have and maintain power over subordinates in the family. If a man, believing that to be a man he must have control over his life and the lives of weaker others, finds himself losing control, then he will attempt to regain control by the best resource at his disposal. If he has learned that men gain control of others by force and violence, he will use that method (Pagelow, 1981:43).*

In such cases, violence is reinforcing. Power, control, "manliness" are reinforcing. Violence may even, as Gelles and Straus remind us, increase a man's self-esteem:

> *Being in control, being master (or apparent master) of a situation, increases one's sense of self-worth. For men or parents whose sense of self-esteem may have been damaged or devalued by experiences outside of the home (losing a job, being humiliated by a boss or fellow worker, etc.), control at home is even more important. (Gelles and Straus, 1988:34).*

A wife may also inadvertently reinforce a husband's behavior by assuming the blame for her husband's behavior, or by promising her husband that she will "try harder" next time to keep the house clearer, or to keep the kids quiet, or whatever he claims is the problem. Assuming the blame might further reinforce the husband's feelings of power and control (Pagelow, 1981). While we need to be careful not to blame women for their own abuse, we must nonetheless recognize that violent behavior that "appears to be accepted by the spouse" (Pagelow, 1981:44) is more likely to reoccur.

Control Theory. Most objectivist theories assume that humans are basically "good," or are at least "blank slates" at birth. The purpose of theory, then, is to explain deviant motivations. With family violence theory, this translates into the question, "Why do people involved in relationships, presumably based on love, physically assault each other?" (Williams and Hawkins, 1989:594). *Social bonding* theories, however, suggest that the question might more appropriately be asked the other way around. That is, given a culture that encourages violence, the isolation of the family unit, and the amount of time family members spend together, why aren't all families violent?

This is the approach taken by Williams and Hawkins (1989), who use Hirschi's social bonding theory to explain factors that produce nonviolent relationships. Although this theoretical framework might just as easily be applied to child abuse, husband abuse, or elder abuse, Williams and Hawkins have chosen to focus on wife abuse.

Attachment refers to level of integration of the family into the larger society (e.g., the extended family, church, and community). The higher the level of integration, the greater the visibility of norm-violating behavior and the greater the social costs of violence. *Commitment* refers to the amount of investment in conformity. The greater the investment in conformity, the greater the stakes in conformity. In addition to the variables Hirschi (1969) talked about (e.g., career and educational investments), this might include length of marriage and presence of children. The implication being that the more one has invested in interpersonal relationships, the greater the costs of family violence. Hirschi's bond *involvement* refers to the amount of time spent in conventional activities. While the investment bond has met with little or no success in studies of juvenile delinquency, Williams and Hawkins maintain that men

who spend quality time with friends and family and who are involved in church and community activities should be less abusive, especially if conventional activities also increase levels of attachment. Finally, the more the husband has internalized the *belief* that violence against his wife is wrong, the less likely he is to be abusive. Belief is an especially informative bond as it pertains to family violence because of the normative ambiguity concerning husband-to-wife violence. Some men do not believe that hitting their wives is wrong (Gelles and Straus, 1979).

To provide an initial test of their theory of wife abuse, Williams and Hawkins (1989) examined conformity factors among non-assaulters in the 1985 National Family Violence Re-Survey, and in subsequent follow-up surveys conducted in 1986 and 1987. This research suggests that two social bonds are especially important predictors of conformity: attachments and beliefs. Williams and Hawkins (1989) found that among non-assaulters, interaction with neighbors, friends, relatives, and parents was considered important (the attachment bond). In an analysis of the 1975 Family Violence Survey, Straus (1990b) similarly found that men who were most involved in community organizations (e.g., clubs, lodges, and business and professional organizations) had considerably lower rates of wife assault than did those with no organizational involvements. Those men who attended church regularly also reported lower rates of violence.

The importance of the belief bond is reflected in the evidence that those who approve of hitting children or spouses report higher rates of violence (Straus, 1990c). The non-assaulters studies by Williams and Hawkins (1989) not only believed that hitting a wife is wrong, but they also perceived greater risks of arrest (than assaulters did) of hitting their wives (Williams and Hawkins, 1989).

Deterrence Theory.   Gelles and Straus (1988) sound very much like control theorists when they offer the admittedly overly simplified explanation that family members hit family members "because they can" (Gelles and Straus, 1988:20; Gelles, 1983:157). Their explanation begins with stories of Chet and David.[6] Chet, although mild-mannered and passive on the outside, beats his wife Marjorie. He admits that he often loses his temper, especially when Marjorie does not clean the house to his liking. David is at the hospital with his son, Peter, who is being X-rayed for possible skull fractures. Peter knocked over the family's new television (something he had been told time and time again not to do) shattering the picture tube. In anger, David "lost it" and hit Peter, who fell into the coffee table.

Gelles and Straus (1988) challenge as inadequate and overly simplistic the popular "theory" that Chet hits Marjorie and David hits Peter because they "lose control" of their anger. Why is such an explanation so inadequate? In answering their own question, Gelles and Straus ask us to consider the following scenario:

> *Imagine that Chet is the manager of a medium-size office. The office employs a janitor who comes in the evenings to empty ash-trays, dust, vacuum, and clean the office. David runs an automobile agency. One day, Chet comes to work and finds that although the janitor has been in, there is barely a sign that anything has been changed. That same day, a three-year-old overturns David's television. What is the outcome? Does Chet, finding his office a mess, pounce on his janitor and begin to pummel him? Unlikely. Does David slap, spank, or even beat the wayward three-year-old? Absurd (Gelles and Straus, 1988:21).*

Why is it that Chet and David seem to be able to control their anger at the office but are so quick-fused at home? Because if Chet does "lose" control and decide to pummel the janitor, he is likely to find himself either fired, in jail, or in the hospital (if the janitor is bigger than Chet). Similarly, if David "loses" control and hits the child in his automobile showroom, he, too, is likely to end up in jail, or the hospital, or both.

From this perspective, family members hit family members because there are not sufficient controls to keep them from "losing" control with their loved ones. Although clearly extra-legal controls come into play here (as social bonding theory reminds us), Gelles and Straus (1988) focus most explicitly on *legal* social controls. In this sense, they are offering a *deterrence theory* of family violence. They maintain that, while in general the costs of street violence in our society are quite high, similar costs are "rarely paid by those violent in the home" (Gelles and Straus, 1988:23).

One reason for the relatively low costs is that family violence is, compared to street violence, relatively invisible. As the title of the well-known Straus, Gelles and Steinmetz book suggests, family violence often takes place *Behind Closed Doors* (1980). In addition, victims are often unable (e.g., children) or unwilling (e.g., spouses) to bring charges. Finally, family privacy norms dictate that the family should be allowed to solve its own problems (Gelles, 1983). Taken together, these factors make the *perceived certainty* of getting caught low.

Gelles and Straus (1988) maintain that, even when police receive a report of family violence, they are likely to respond comparatively slowly. They respond more slowly because, first of all, domestic disturbance work is considered low-prestige work (Gelles and Straus, 1988). In addition, domestic disturbances are relatively dangerous. Although the dangerous nature of intervention in domestic disputes is often exaggerated in the media, there were 69 officers killed responding to domestic disturbances between 1972 and 1984; this represents 6 percent of the total killed in the line of duty (Gelles and Straus, 1988).

Police intervention is unlikely to result in the arrest of the perpetrator. Domestic violence has historically been viewed as a family matter, and police have generally been trained to encourage husbands, wives, and parents to get help (Eigenberg and Moriarty, 1991). Cases in which children are beaten are more likely to be turned over to Child Protective Services than to the criminal justice system (Gelles and Straus, 1988). Based upon results from the family violence surveys, Gelles and Straus (1988) estimate that the number of police interventions that result in arrest is somewhat less than one in ten. Finally, if an arrest is made and put before the courts, judges are put in the no-win position of either ignoring the problem or breaking up the family, something they have been very reluctant to do (Gelles, 1983:159). In short, "the criminal justice system holds very little threat of costs for the average violent family member" (Gelles and Straus, 1988:24). In the language of deterrence theory, this means that there is little *perceived severity* of punishment.

This is the bad news. But there is good news. The legal costs of family violence are growing rapidly. In recent years, many states and cities have passed laws requiring arrest in domestic disturbances. Others have left some discretion in the hands of the police, but have still mandated that arrest should be made (Ferraro, 1989; Eigenberg and Moriarty, 1991). Similarly, a badly bruised child today is less likely to escape the watchful eye of his or her teacher (who is now required by law to report the suspected abuse). From the standpoint of deterrence theory, we would hypothesize that as the legal costs of family violence increase, the rates of family violence should decrease. We might further hypothesize that recent declines in family violence (Straus and Gelles, 1986) might, in part, be attributed to the increasing legal costs of family violence.

There remains, however, considerable debate over whether such expectations can be justified empirically. The debate centers primarily around a series of studies on the specific deterrent effects of arrest. The first, the Minneapolis Domestic Violence Experiment (Sherman and Berk, 1984), remains a pioneering study on specific deterrence. With the help of the Minneapolis Police Department, Sherman and Berk devised a system by which suspects in domestic disturbances would be randomly assigned to one of three methods of police response: mediation (counseling the parties involved), separation (suspects were told to leave the residence), and arrest. Deterrent effects were estimated in two ways. First, victims of the domestic disputes were interviewed six months after initial contact. Second, researchers examined police records to see if suspects had been arrested for additional domestic violence. Analysis of the data showed that suspects who had been arrested were less likely to re-offend than suspects in either of the other two intervention groups.

The Minneapolis Experiment had an immediate impact on the criminal justice community and many police departments began to mandate arrest in domestic violence cases. The social scientific community, however, was much more cautious. Social scientists (including Sherman and Berk) maintained that more research would be needed before definitive conclusions on the deterrent effects of arrest could be reached. The call for more research was answered quickly by the National Institute of Justice, which funded replications of the Minneapolis Experiment in six cities. These replications have for the most part produced very disappointing findings. Researchers examining date from Omaha (Dunford, Huizinga, and Elliott, 1990), Dade County (Pate and Hamilton, 1992; Berk et al., Campbell, Klap, and Western, 1992), Charlotte (Hirschel, Hutchinson, Dean, Kelley, and Pesackis, 1990), Colorado Springs (Berk et al., 1992), and Milwaukee (Berk, 1992; Sherman, Smith, Schmidt, and Rogan, 1992) found no overall reduction in assault as a result of police arrest. Results from the Atlanta replication have not yet been published.

The results from the replication experiments are seemingly as discouraging as the results from the Minneapolis experiment were encouraging. The news, however, may not be all bad. First, criminal sanctions appear not to increase the risk of new violence (through retaliation), which has been a concern of victim advocate groups (Ford, 1991; Dunford, Huizinga, and Elliott, 1990). Second, and even more importantly, while the overall deterrent effects of arrest have been insignificant in each of these studies, two more subtle patterns in the data may lead researchers to a greater understanding of when domestic violence can be deterred. Remember that social bonding theory and deterrence theory refer to different kinds of social controls. Social bonding theory refers to extralegal social control, what Hirschi (1969) called "stakes in conformity" (attachment, commitment, involvement, belief) and deterrence theory refers to legal social controls (the certainty and severity of criminal punishment). The data from the most recent replications suggest that when stakes in conformity are low (e.g., the offender is unmarried and unemployed), arrest actually leads to an *increase* in the rate of assault (ironically, this lends support to a labeling theory of domestic violence). When stakes in conformity are high (e.g., the offender is married and employed) arrest significantly *reduces* the rate of assault (which supports deterrence theory). (Sherman, Smith, Schmidt, and Rogan, 1992; Pate and Hamilton, 1992; Berk, Campbell, Klap, and Western, 1992).

Social Exchange Theory. Another micro-objectivist theory, one that we have not as yet introduced in this book, is *social exchange* theory. Social exchange theory is similar to deterrence theory in its most important assumption, namely, that humans, being rational and self-serving, will engage in behaviors for which they perceive the potential rewards to outweigh the potential costs. With deterrence theory, of course, this principle is applied specifically to the relationship between the individual and the state. With social exchange theory, the reward/cost principle is applied to relationships between people. There are any of a number of rewards people might exchange; money, love, self-esteem, security, recognition, admiration, and so on. The assumption is that, always in search of a profit, we will only enter into relationships and only stay in relationships, if we perceive that the rewards outweigh the costs.

Marriage is, of course, guided by social exchange principles. In general, we enter into marriage because we assume it will make us "happy." That is, we assume the rewards will outweigh the costs. Our expectations of the kinds of rewards and costs marriage should bring come from many sources: we watch our parents, friends, or even television and movies. Whatever the source, the key is that we have certain expectations of the rewards and costs when we enter into a marriage. When these expectations are not met, we may perceive the relationship to be inequitable. Even in a patriarchal society such as ours, in which men usually get more than they give in marriage, some men might perceive the relationship to be inequitable because it has not provided the rewards that they expected.

Remember that social exchange theorists argue that inequitable relationships will be terminated. Inequitable marriages, however, are complicated by a couple of factors. First, often only one spouse perceives the relationship to be inequitable (Brinkerhoff and Lupri, 1988). Second, the inequitable relationship cannot be easily broken off. Divorce is an option, but it involves considerable effort (i.e., costs). Therefore, when a spouse does not receive the reward he or she expects, and perceives few alternative options, we would expect frustration and resentment. Violence may, therefore, be a rewarding expression of this frustration (Gelles and Straus, 1979; Gelles, 1983). While social exchange theory cannot tell us why spouses in inequitable relationships choose violence (as opposed to another response), it seemingly provides insights into important antecedents to violence (Gelles and Straus, 1979).

Child abuse can also be viewed from a social exchange perspective. Not all parents perceive the rewards of parenthood to outweigh the costs. And the parent-child relationship is next to impossible to terminate (Gelles and Straus, 1988). Lacking alternatives, a parent may deal with the dissatisfaction of parenthood with violence. This theoretical perspective might help us explain the evidence that rates of abuse are higher for sick, handicapped, premature, ugly, and demanding children (Gelles, 1983).

Subjectivist Theories

Macro-Subjectivist Theories. Macro-subjectivist theories focus on the social and political origin of words such as *maltreatment, abuse, neglect* or even *violence*. These terms are social labels, and they are defined by social audiences. As social audiences change, boundaries of inappropriate behavior change. Consider, for example, how quickly we have accepted the importance of infant car seats. As discussed by Garbarino (1989), not long ago babies commonly traveled on mommy's or daddy's lap. Infant deaths were tragic, but unavoidable. In recent years, such deaths have been reinterpreted, first as "preventable accidents" and most recently as "neglect related." In a recent, highly publicized case in Florida, for example, Ramiro de Jesus Rodriguez, a recent immigrant to the United States from Nicaragua, was tried and acquitted of vehicular homicide in the death of his three-year-old daughter Veronica. Veronica who had been sick and vomiting, sat in her mom's lap while Ramiro drove them all to a grocery store to get medicine. On the way back from the store, Veronica was killed in an accident. Despite the increasing use of car seats in this country—according to *Newsweek* (Jan. 14, 1991), in 1979 only 15 percent of kids sat in car seats, today 81 percent do so— such deaths are not uncommon. Yet Florida decided to prosecute the case, hoping to prevent future tragedies by making an example of Rodriguez (*Newsweek*, 1991; *Time*, 1991).[7]

Did Rodriguez kill his daughter? Was he guilty of child maltreatment? In this case, the courts found that he was not guilty. But you get the point. The boundaries between abuse and non-abuse, or between neglect and non-neglect are not objectively given. They are, as Gelles and Straus remind us, defined by social audiences:

> *Twenty years of discussion, debate, and action have led us to conclude that there will never be an accepted or acceptable definition of abuse, because abuse is not a scientific or clinical term. Rather, it is a political concept. Abuse is essentially any act that is considered deviant or harmful by a group large enough or with sufficient political power to enforce the definition. . . . Unfortunately, there is no one set of objective acts that can be characterized as abusive (Gelles and Straus, 1988:57).*

Interest Group Theory. Despite the fact that Gelles and Straus tend to adopt an objectivist view of family violence (focusing on theories of violent family behavior), they nonetheless recognize the importance of an interest group perspective in coming to understand definitions of child abuse and spouse abuse. Interest group theorists remind us that deviant labels emerge as moral entrepreneurs successfully gain enough social or political power to bring their particular "causes" before the public eye.

Woman Battering as a Social Problem. The interest group perspective is strongly influenced by feminism, especially as it relates to spouse abuse. Feminist scholars have focused on how power differences influence the creation of laws that give men the right to hit women. The most extreme view, which is held by radical feminists, is that spouse abuse is an example of the "victimization of a gender-oppressed class. In a socially produced, male-dominated, and sanctioned pattern of interaction, the abusive husband is simply an expected product of his society. Only by eliminating socially instituted sexism can women reduce their victimization" (Steinmetz, 1987:749). From this perspective, men use violence against women to maintain patriarchal order.

Whether we agree with this more extreme view, there can be little doubt that, while the treatment of women has differed from culture to culture, women have generally been dominated and controlled by men (Dobash and Dobash, 1979). With respect to the family, early marriage laws actually gave men the legal right to hit their wives. In summarizing the research of Dobash and Dobash (1979) and O'Faolain and Martines (1973) on the legal status of wives throughout history, Pagelow argues that early Roman marriage laws "spelled out the rights and obligations of husbands and wives, which were heavily weighed to insure husband's *rights* and wives' *obligations*." (1984:281). Pagelow continues:

> Husbands' rights to judge, control and punish their wives were written into law, legitimating their subjugation through force. Whipping was reserved for minor offenses, but wives could be, and were, put to death for drinking their husbands' wine or for infidelity. On the other hand, wives were forbidden to reprimand or even touch their husbands as punishment for the latter's infidelity (Pagelow, 1984:281).

According to Sigler (1989), English Common Law also held that women were inferior to men. A woman had no legal existence apart from her husband. She was owned and controlled by her husband. The propertied status of women was reflected in early English rape laws. The law held that when a women is raped, restitution should be paid to the husband (or if the women is unmarried, her father) for damage done to his property (Sigler, 1989). Men were also held responsible for their wives' behavior. Since the man was expected to control his wife, the law allowed him a degree of latitude in the use of force. As we mentioned earlier, the "rule-of-thumb" law gave the husband the right to hit his wife with a rod no thicker than his thumb (Sigler, 1989).

In this country, laws against wife battering were first enacted in North Carolina in 1871. With the North Carolina law it became illegal to "beat a wife with a stick, pull her hair, choke her, spit in her face, or kick her to the floor" (Pagelow, 1984:284). In 1921 when Mississippi instituted a similar law, every state had passed legislation that classified wife beating as assault (Pagelow, 1984).

The first organization of the battered women's movement, called Chiswick Women's Aid, began in England in 1971.[8] Originally the purpose of the organization was to share with battered women information about welfare and legal rights. However, it became apparent that women needed a place to escape violent husbands, so the house was opened to overnight guests (Pagelow, 1984). Erin Pizzey, one of the founders of Chiswick's Women's Aid, was the most outspoken advocate of victimized women during these years. With the 1974 publication of her book *Scream Quietly or the Neighbors Will Hear*, and the radio and television exposure that came with it, the battered women's movement was gathering considerable momentum. In 1976, over 2,000 women from 33 countries attended the International Tribunal on Crimes Against Women. By the end of the 1970s, there were over 170 battered women's shelters in the United Kingdom alone (Pagelow, 1984).

Pagelow (1984) traces the roots of the battered women's movement in the United States to a 1976 study published by the National Organization for Women (NOW), which indicated that wife abuse was occurring at a rate faster than was commonly assumed. With increasing urgency, shelters began to open up in this country the way they had in Europe, and by 1980 there were over 150 shelters across the country (Pagelow, 1984). Concern about domestic violence has continued through the 1980s and into the 1990s. Today, in addition to the many shelters and domestic violence hot lines, there are numerous organizations committed to the elimination of woman battering. Among the more prominent organizations are the National Coalition of Domestic Violence, the Displaced Homemakers Network, the National Association of Women and Law (in Canada), the National Organization for Victim's Assistance, the National Clearing House for the Defense of Battered Women, and the National Council on Child Abuse and Family Violence.

From an interest group perspective, it is important to remember that these organizations not only respond to the domestic violence problem, but they are also important players in the battle to define the domestic violence problem. While it would be wrong to assume that each of these organizations has the same social and political agenda, it is probably safe to assume that each is committed to convincing us (the public) and them (the politicians) that the domestic violence problem is more significant than it has to this point been perceived it to be.

Child Abuse as a Social Problem. Interest group theorists who study child maltreatment similarly remind us that children have not always been valued, loved, and protected. Much of history, for example, is marred by the practice of infanticide—the killing of infants soon after birth.[9] Especially vulnerable have been girls, abnormal infants, and unusually featured infants (Pagelow, 1984).[10] DeMause (1974) describes in great detail the considerable maltreatment children have been subjected to. Sometimes this maltreatment has come in the name of adult amusement, as in the case of the brother of Henry IV, who was tied up and tossed about like a sack of potatoes, only to be dropped and killed (Pagelow, 1984). Sometimes this maltreatment has come in the name of "discipline."

U.S. efforts to protect children from maltreatment can be traced to the early 1700s, when the first orphan asylum opened in New Orleans. During the 1800s, with increasing concern about the terrible conditions in early almshouses, there was a push to place children in homes. However, unlike the current foster care and adoption practice of placing "needy" children with "loving" parents, these early indenture programs were essentially a form of slavery, whereby children "worked for a specific number of years for only their food and lodging, and if they were lucky, they were treated reasonably well" (Pagelow, 1984:157).

The first laws giving the government the authority to respond to abused and neglected children were introduced in the early 1800s. While these laws are most often interpreted as an altruistic attempt by the government to protect children from harm, some social scientists maintain that the government was actually interested in protecting its economic interests. For example, Anthony Platt (1969), who adopts a neo-Marxist view of government attempts to protect children, argues that the government was mostly interested in getting "trouble" (i.e., lower-class) children off the streets. Stephen Pfohl agrees that child protection was primarily directed toward the poor when he asserts that "preventive penology, not child protection" was the underlying purpose of government protection (1977:313):

> The virtue of removing children from their homes was not to point out abuse or neglect and protect its victims, it was to decrease the likelihood that parental inadequacies, the "causes of poverty," would transfer themselves to the child and hence to the next generation of society . . . Thus . . . the whole nineteenth century movement towards institutionalization actually failed to differentiate between abuse and poverty and therefore registered no social reaction against beating as a form of defiance (quoted in Pagelow, 1984:159).

Through the 1900s, concern for children continued to escalate; and in 1962 when C. Henry Kempe introduced the "battered child syndrome" to the American Academy of Pediatrics, child abuse was officially discovered as a social problem. In 1963, Colorado passed the first child abuse laws requiring physicians to report suspected cases of child abuse. The 49 other states quickly followed suit. Eleven years later, in 1974, the federal government took its first official stand on child abuse, passing the Child Abuse and Prevention Act and establishing the National Center on Child Abuse and Neglect (Pagelow, 1984:161).

In the years since the passage of the Child Abuse and Prevention Act, concern about child maltreatment has continued to escalate and several organizations have emerged to combat the problem. National organizations include the National Committee for the Prevention of Child Abuse, the Family Resource Coalition, the Children's Defense Fund, the National Center for Missing and Exploited Children, and the Child Welfare League of America. Once again, interest group theorists remind us that these organizations play an important role in defining the child abuse problem.

Social Scientists as an Interest Group. One of the most important interest groups in the construction of family violence as a social problem is the social scientists themselves. For the most part, family violence researchers recognize their role in exposing the family violence problem, not their role actually constructing the family violence problem. (For an exception to this statement, see Gelles, 1987, Chapter 3.) For example, well-known family violence researcher Suzanne Steinmetz correctly argues that "Historical evidence suggests that family violence is not a new social problem; rather it has only recently been identified as a social problem by researchers, journalists, social planners, and the judiciary" (1987:729). Yet, in the process of "exposing" the family violence problem, family violence researchers are in essence creating the boundaries between what is and is not deviance.

In their popular book *Intimate Violence*, Gelles and Straus (1988) give Steinmetz credit for "discovering" the sibling violence problem. Gelles and Straus recall that, when Steinmetz first began to examine violence between siblings, she "had some difficulty persuading parents to discuss sibling violence— not because they were embarrassed or thought such violence wrong, but because *it was so routine they did not think it worth mentioning*" (1988:60, emphasis added). This represents a good example of how social scientists actually "create" new categories of deviance. Gelles and Straus are suggesting that sibling fights are so common that parents do not perceive the fighting to be a problem. But Gelles and Straus do perceive sibling fighting to be "a problem." As influential advocates of non-violence in the family, they no doubt believe that they have a responsibility to convince the rest of us that sibling violence is a real problem.

What we need to remember is that social scientists do have a vested interest in the phenomena they study. Much of the attention directed toward Murray Straus and Richard Gelles, for example, has come because they have successfully defined family violence as a major social problem. Indeed, there can be little doubt that Gelles and Straus (as well as many others, of course) have capitalized on the popularity of family violence as a social problem. In no way do we mean to suggest that Gelles and Straus have primarily been motivated by a search for fame and fortune. We are quite convinced that nothing could be further from the truth. In fact, we have tremendous respect for Gelles and Straus, not only as social scientists but as passionate spokespersons for a cause that we, too, believe is very important.

What we are saying is that they (and many others) perceive it as their "calling" to uncover the depths of the family violence problem. If this means speaking out against sibling violence, they will speak out against sibling violence. If this means speaking out against corporal punishment (see Gelles and Straus, 1988; Straus, 1991a), they will speak out against corporal punishment. Remember, however, that as they work to create increased awareness of family violence, and new categories of family violence, they are essentially creating new categories about which new research is needed. This means more articles, more books, more speaking engagements, and so on. As the size of the problem expands, the need for their services expands.

Another way to conceptualize the interest group perspective on family violence is to consider the debate among social scientists about what should or should not be considered an important problem. Consider, for example, the dialogue between Murray Straus (e.g., Straus, 1991a; 1991b) and feminist scholars (e.g., Kurz, 1989; 1991; Loseke, 1991) over the Conflict Tactics Scale. What the combatants are really arguing about is what the "real" deviance is. Straus and his colleagues agree with feminist scholars that wife abuse and child abuse are very serious; but they argue that the problem is larger than just wife abuse and child abuse—it is a problem of

family violence (which includes everything from "spouse" abuse to corporal punishment). Feminist scholars, for example, criticize Straus's emphasis on "spouse abuse," (as opposed to wife abuse) arguing the real problem is powerful people taking advantage of powerless people. In the words of feminist scholar Demie Kurz (1991:158), "women do not commit 'spouse abuse' the way men do."

Straus (1991a) also touched a sensitive cord in his recent presidential address to the Society for the Study of Social Problems, in which he argued that the violence problem in our society begins with corporal punishment. From his perspective, research should focus on the effects of corporal punishment and social policy should focus on the elimination of corporal punishment. In a somewhat angry response, Loseke (1991) complains that incorporating physical punishment into the "child abuse" category incorrectly equates violence that causes no injury with violence that causes injury.

Once again, what is most interesting about this dialogue is that both sides accuse the other of doing the same thing, namely, ignoring (or at least moving beyond) the evidence in order to advance a particular political or moral agenda. Loseke resents Straus's (1991) call for the elimination of corporal punishment arguing that he is using scientific rhetoric to advance his moral agenda:

> This is social problems talk lodged within the academic talk advancing the Cultural Spillover Theory. Social problems talk is political talk encouraging readers to take practical action—in this case, to "stop physical punishment" (Loseke, 1991:163).

Says Straus of Loseke's charge that he offers nothing more than a call for "practical action":

> Is Loseke taking up a call for "value free" sociology? Obviously not; rather she is again expressing her opinion that ending physical punishment by parents is not high in her priorities. (Straus, 1991b:189.)

Straus also responds to feminist critic Kurz (1991), who maintains that a social policy that focuses on corporal punishment will inevitably neglect the real source of the problem—gender inequality:

> I infer that what Kurz means is that the theoretical argument and the empirical data suggesting the importance of physical punishment do not convince her. Of course, she is entitled to that opinion and she might even be correct. However, I believe that attempts to advance a moral agenda by denigrating the efforts of those who have a slightly different agenda is a zero sum approach that is likely to be self-defeating. . . . ". . . . I believe that the real problem is neither that I ignore gender nor that my theory and data are wrong but that some of my findings on gender and violence are not "politically correct" (Straus, 1991b:182).

From an interest group perspective, the point is not who is right. The point is that these battles, at least in part, determine what is and is not defined as deviance.

SOCIAL POLICY AND SOCIAL CONTROL

Child advocacy groups ask the question. Churches ask the question. Feminists ask the question. Law-enforcement officials ask the question. Social scientists ask the question. The media ask the question. How, they all want to know, do we stop family violence? As you might well imagine, there are any of a number of ways this questions might be addressed.

Change Culture?

Richard Gelles and Murray Straus have been very outspoken in their claims that the most important first step in the elimination of family violence is eliminating "cultural norms and values that accept violence as a means of resolving conflict and problems in families" (1988:194). The elimination of norms and values that encourage violence will result in "in-ternal controls so that family members will not resort to violence as either a first or last resort in expressing themselves or dealing with conflict or stress." Social control, therefore, begins with the "cancellation of the hitting license in families" (Gelles and Straus, 1988:194).

How, according to Gelles and Straus, do we cancel the hitting license in families? Criminalizing corporal punishment. Straus maintains that violence begets violence through "cultural spillover," arguing that "violence in one sphere of life tends to engender violence in other spheres" (Straus, 1991a:137). Straus empirically demonstrates that physical punishment (both the physical punishment experienced by the respondent and respondent approval of physical punishment) is positively related to child abuse, spouse abuse, assault, and homicide. He admits that he cannot prove that corporal punishment is causally significant. For example, perhaps " 'bad' children are hit, and these same bad children go on to have a higher rate of criminal activity than other children" (Straus, 1991a:147). Or perhaps troubled or abusive parents are more likely to spank and to raise troubled children. At the same time, he seems confident in his conclusion that "although physical punishment may produce short term conformity, over the longer run it probably also creates or exacerbates deviance" (Straus, 1991a:147).

Many social scientists believe that, if social policy focuses on the elimination of physical punishment, we miss the "real" causes of family violence, namely, poverty, unemployment, racism, and most importantly for the feminists, patriarchy (Kurz, 1991; Loeske, 1991). Indeed, for feminist theorists, "the pathway to the use of violence by adults is heavily linked to gender" (Kurz, 1991:159).

Straus and his colleagues, of course, do not suggest that corporal punishment is the only cause of family violence. Other cultural culprits include society's implicit acceptance of violence as evidenced by capital punishment and the glorification of violence in television movies, and children's toys (Gelles and Straus, 1988). They also agree with feminists and many social scientists who believe that norms of inequality in the family must also change. Promoting equality in the family will ultimately lead to lower rates of violence.

A Legal Response to Family Violence

In Chapter 3, we introduced the research of Donald Black (1972) who has argued that, other things being equal, police are more likely to make an arrest when the victim and the suspect are strangers. Black found that arrest is especially unlikely if the victim and suspect are family members. Police have, in fact, historically been encouraged to diffuse violent family situations rather than to arrest violent family members (Eigenberg and Moriarty, 1991). But with the 1984 publication of the Attorney General's Task Force on Family Violence Final Report, the practice of police non-intervention began to change. The Attorney General's Report recommended that family violence be treated like other criminal violence. It also called for increasing efforts in prosecuting domestic violence cases (Ferraro, 1989; Forde, 1991).

Domestic Violence and the Law. Why the change in policy? In part, the change occurred because of increasing public concern about domestic violence. The plight of women trapped in domestic violence was painfully illustrated in many highly publicized cases, including but not limited to the Francine Hughes case with which we began this chapter. Even more important, however, was the Sherman and Berk (1984) research demonstrating the specific deterrent effect of arrest in domestic violence cases. Prior to the Sherman and Berk (1984) research, social policymakers were concerned that increasing legal sanctions might create more marital vio-

lence (e.g., angry husbands would "take out" their anger on their wives). With evidence that arrest would deter rather than increase domestic violence, social policymakers responded quickly. Ten days after the results from the Sherman Berk study were published in the *New York Times*, the New York Police Commissioner initiated new rules that required New York City police to make arrests in domestic disputes. In September of the same year the Attorney General's Report was published (Gelles and Straus, 1988).

The need to recognize and respond to domestic violence as crime was further reinforced in June of 1985 when Tracy Thurman won a $2.3 million civil suit against 3 Torrington, Connecticut, police chiefs and 29 police officers.[11] Tracy's case is tragic. She had been repeatedly beaten by her husband, Charles. Unable to get protection from the police, she went to live with friends. When Charles came to visit in June of 1983 she called the police. By the time the police arrived (25 minutes later), Charles had stabbed Tracy repeatedly and had broken her neck. In court, Tracy successfully claimed that the Torrington police violated her constitutional right for equal protection. If she had been attacked or threatened by a stranger, she argued, she would have been given more protection (Eigenberg and Moriarty, 1991; Gelles and Straus, 1988).

By the late 1980s, most states were either requiring arrests (as of mid-1992, 12 states had mandatory arrest laws) or were strongly encouraging arrests when probable cause exists (generally interpreted as meaning either the presence of a witness, or injuries, or property damage) (Ferraro, 1989). In addition, most states began to allow police to make arrests for misdemeanor assaults (most family assaults are misdemeanors). Connecticut, the site of the Thurman case, serves as a useful example. In 1986, the state legislature passed the Family Violence Prevention Act; among other things, it included (1) mandatory arrest with probable cause; (2) increased accessibility and use of protective orders; and (3) victim assistance and notification of rights by police (Lyon and Mace, 1991). While mandatory arrest laws such as this clearly limit the discretion of police and the discretion of victims (who many times might choose not to press criminal charges were they given the choice), observational research by Kathleen Ferraro (1989) on Arizona's mandatory arrest law suggests that police continue to exercise considerable discretion in their decision of whether to arrest.

Given the most recent research on the limited deterrent effects of arrest (Sherman et al., 1992; Pate and Hamilton, 1992; Beck et al., 1992), one has to wonder about the appropriateness of mandatory arrest policies. After all, "If arrest deters only those who have something to lose (e.g., a job), that fact must be taken into account when policies are established" (Pate and Hamilton, 1992:695). The legal world will likely be forced to confront this question as findings from the recent research are circulated in the criminal justice community.

Concern over wife battering has contributed to another legal debate which has attracted considerable popular media attention recently (Gibbs, 1993). Should women who kill abusive husbands be held responsible for their actions? From a legal standpoint it is often difficult to make a defense for women who have killed abusive husbands. Yet, many people believe that battered women should be forgiven for their actions. At present count, 26 states have joined a national clemency movement and have commuted the life sentences of women convicted of killing their husbands (Gibbs, 1993). Others are likely to follow. Critics of the clemency movement maintain that however horrifying the abuse may have been, murder cannot be condoned.

Child Abuse and the Law   Several factors make the legal control of child abuse even more problematic. The most glaring problem,

once again, is that there is no agreed upon definition of abuse. By the mid-1970s all 50 states had adopted legal definitions of child abuse. While definitions vary, most states have adopted versions similar to this from the National Center of Child Abuse and Neglect, which defines abuse as

> . . . *the physical or mental injury, sexual abuse, negligent treatment, or maltreatment of a child under the age of eighteen by a person who is responsible for the child's welfare under circumstances which indicate that the child's health or welfare is harmed or threatened thereby* (Gelles and Straus, 1988:57).

Some states have attempted to further clarify these ambiguous boundaries. The state of Washington, for example, modified their statute (which is very much like the above definition), stating that the child abuse law "should not be construed to authorize interference with child-raising practices, including reasonable parental discipline, which are not proved to be injurious to the child's health, welfare, and safety" (Title 26 RCW, p. 80). Of course such modifications do little to clarify the muddy legal waters; in the end, the boundaries will continue to be worked out in the courts.

A second obstacle in the legal control of child abuse is that children are almost always beaten "behind closed doors." Children often cannot speak for themselves. In an effort to force child advocacy, all states during the mid-1960s passed laws requiring professionals to report suspected child abuse and neglect cases.[12] While historically the rate of reporting has been low (generally less than 50 percent), with the increasing attention given child abuse, and increasing awareness of the signs of child abuse, reporting rates have increased in recent years (Wurtele and Miller-Perrin, 1992).

A final complicating factor in the legal control of child abuse is that every time a child is removed from the home, a family is broken up. Many states remain committed to a policy which, whenever possible, keeps families together. According to the state of Washington, for example, "the bond between a child and his or her parent, custodian, or guardian is of paramount importance. . . (Title 26 RCW, p. 79). Washington's commitment to protecting the rights of parents and keeping the family together produced tragic results in 1988 when three-year-old Eli Creekmore was removed and returned to his home on three different occasions, despite evidence that he was being abused. When Eli was killed by his father, public outry resulted in a change in the law. The law now states that if the child's rights and the parents' rights conflict, the child's rights should be considered more important. The new law also allows social workers to intervene when they believe the child is at risk, regardless of whether the child has been substantially harmed.

As with domestic violence, the overall trend in recent years has been to treat child abuse as a crime. Like other violent attacks, child abuse is assault and the criminal justice system has increasingly been treating it as assault.

SUMMARY

Family violence is perhaps the most tragic form of deviance we will study in this book. Family members hitting family members—it makes so little sense. But as we learned in this chapter, from a sociological standpoint, family violence is more understandable than it might at first appear to be.

Those who approach family violence from an objectivist perspective focus on behavior that violates a norm. *Violence* is defined as "an act carried out with the intention of, or an act perceived as having the intention of, physically hurting another person" (Steinmetz, 1987:729). This definition is so inclusive, however, that it does not allow us to distinguish between normative and nonnormative violence. In other words, the objectivist conception cannot tell us when family violence becomes family abuse. Those who approach family violence from a subjectivist perspective are especially quick to remind us that *abuse* cannot be objectively defined. From this perspective, family violence is defined by social audiences.

Family violence is a very broad topic that includes not only marital and parental violence, but violence between siblings and abuse of the elderly as well. Also generally included under the family violence umbrella are sexual abuse and neglect within the family. Because we could not examine the entire family violence issue in this chapter, we primarily focused on *marital violence* and *parent-to-child violence*. Because most family violence is not reported, much of the research on the social distribution of family violence is based on self-reports. The only nationally representative surveys are the *National Family Violence Surveys*, conducted in 1975 and 1985. Each survey employs the *Conflict Tactics Scale* as its measure of family violence. As the name implies, the Conflict Tactics Scale measures a variety of methods of conflict resolution—including violence—that family members might use during disagreements and fights. Concerning marital violence, research based on the National Family Violence Surveys suggests that each year approximately 16 percent of U.S. couples experience at least one instance of violence. Somewhat surprisingly, wives hit husbands slightly more frequently than husbands hit wives. Most everyone agrees, however, that husband-to-wife violence is more serious. Estimates of parent-to-child violence depend even more directly on how one chooses to define violence. If we define spanking as violence, then 97 percent of children have experienced violence at least once. Only about 2 percent of the parents from the 1975 survey had been physically "abusive" (kicked, bit, hit with fist, beat up, and used gun or knife) in the previous year. Finally, a comparison of the 1975 and 1985 surveys suggests that, contrary to popular perceptions, and contrary to official estimates, rates of family violence are actually decreasing.

There are several important factors that increase one's risk of being a violent family member. Rates of violence are higher among the lower class, the young, alcohol and drug users, and those who grew up in violent homes. The relationships are far from perfect, however, as many high-risk people are not violent and many low-risk people are violent.

Macro-objectivist theories, which focus on structural explanations of violent family behavior, begin with the recognition that our culture accepts and even glorifies some violence. In addition, the amount of time we spend with family members, the emotion shared in family relationships, the power differences that often characterize families, and the privacy norms that surround the family, should make the family especially prone to violence. Objectivist scholars who approach violent family behavior from a feminist perspective demonstrate that when women have less status than men (*patriarchal structure*) and when norms legitimize male dominance (*patriarchal ideology*), rates of woman battering are especially high. Strain theories maintain that the higher rates of family violence among the lower classes result from the chronic stress associated with "hard living."

The most common micro-objectivist theory is social learning theory, sometimes referred to as the *violence begets violence* thesis, which maintains that children who observe violence in the family, or are themselves abused, learn that violence is an acceptable way (or perhaps even the acceptable way) for resolving family conflict and expressing frustration. Violence may be directly reinforcing for men who want to be in control or who want to assert their "manliness." Consistent with social bonding theory, men with strong attachments (with friends and extended fam-

ily) and beliefs that violence is wrong are less likely to be abusive. Deterrence theorists maintain that, as long as the legal costs of family violence remain low, rates of family violence will remain high. Research is mixed, with one very significant study finding that arrest deters marital violence, but with the more recent studies suggesting that it does not.

Some have argued that the elimination of family violence begins with the elimination of societal norms and values that encourage violence. How to change culture remains a matter of considerable debate. Some maintain that society should curtail violence on television and in the movies and eliminate children's toys that encourage violence. For others, the change begins with promoting nonsexist ideology in the family. For still others, change begins with criminalizing corporal punishment, or eliminating capital punishment. Another strategy for eliminating family violence focuses on legal controls. In recent years, most states have begun to "get tough" on family violence. Twelve states have adopted mandatory arrest laws and most others are encouraging police to make arrests. States have also become increasingly aware of the need to protect children and to prosecute abusive parents.

GLOSSARY

Abuse Objectivists and subjectivists alike agree that there is no single definition of abuse. For subjectivists, the meanings of words such as *abuse, maltreatment*, and even *violence* are created by social audiences. Objectivist attempts to define abuse are more likely to focus on the variation of norms across culture and across time.

Conflict Tactics Scale The scale used on the Family Violence Surveys. It measures a variety of methods of conflict resolution that family members might use during disagreements and fights. It includes items on rational discussion (items such as "discussed an issue calmly"), verbal aggression (items such as "did or said something to spite" the other person), and physical aggression (the actual use of violence).

Marital Violence (Domestic Violence) A term some scholars purposely choose to make explicit the fact that women hit men as often as men hit women. Other scholars prefer terms such as *woman battering* and *wife abuse* to make explicit their belief that the real problem is men hitting women.

National Family Violence Surveys The only nationally representative studies of family violence: the 1975 National Family Violence Survey (sample size 2,143) and the 1985 replication of this study, the National Family Violence Re-Survey (sample size 6,002).

Patriarchal Ideology Sexist values, beliefs and norms whereby male dominance is seen as legitimate and "natural."

Patriarchal Structure The relatively low status of women and the financial dependence of women on men.

Violence "An act carried out with the intention of, or an act perceived as having the intention of, physically hurting another person" (Suzanne Steinmetz, 1987:729). This is a very broad definition that includes both normative behavior (e.g., spanking) and nonnormative behavior (e.g., murder).

Violence Begets Violence A thesis essentially suggesting that "violence in the family serves as a training ground for the children, who as adults are more likely to approve of violence as an acceptable way of solving problems and to use violence both within the family and outside the family" (Steinmetz, 1987:752).

SUGGESTED READINGS

Dobash, R. Emerson, and Russel P. Dobash. *Violence against Wives: A Case Against the Patriar-* *chy.* New York: Free Press, 1979. This is the most significant feminist statement on woman battering.

Gelles, Richard, and Murray Straus. *Intimate Violence.* New York: Simon and Schuster, 1988. This is a very readable book written by the two premier researchers in family violence. Gelles and Straus effectively combine data from their Family Violence Surveys with personal experiences and interviews. This book is written for a popular audience.

Lloyd Ohlin, and Michael Tonry, eds. *Family Violence.* Chicago: University of Chicago Press, 1989. This is a collection of commissioned articles that reviews the current research on the social and legal issues involving family violence.

Pagelow, Mildred. *Family Violence.* New York: Praeger, 1984. This book explores all the major forms of family violence. Pagelow's approach is descriptive (including the history of concern for family violence), empirical, theoretical, and practical (including intervention and prevention strategies).

Straus, Murray A., Richard T. Gelles, and Suzanne K. Steinmetz. *Behind Closed Doors: Violence in the American Family.* New York: Doubleday/Anchor, 1980. Based largely on the 1975 Family Violence Survey, this book was the first comprehensive empirical examination of the family violence problem in the United States.

REFERENCES

Agnew, Robert, and Huguley, Sandra. "Adolescent Violence toward Parents," *Journal of Marriage and the Family* 51 (Aug. 1989): 699–711.

American Humane Association. *Highlights of Official Aggregate Child Neglect and Abuse Reporting.* Denver: American Humane Association, 1987.

Bandura, Albert. *Aggression: A Social Learning Analysis.* Englewood Cliffs, N.J.: Prentice-Hall, 1973.

Black, Donald J. "The Social Organization of Arrest." *Stanford Law Review* 23 (1971):1087–1111.

Brinkerhoff, Merlin B., and Eugen Lupri. "Interspousal Violence." *Canadian Journal of Sociology* 13 (1988): 407–434.

Brown, Joanne C., and Carole R. Bohn, eds. *Chris-*

tianity, Patriarchy, and Abuse. New York: The Pilgram Press, 1990.

deMause, L. *A History of Childhood.* New York: Psychotherapy Press, 1974.

Dobash, R. Emerson, and Russel P. Dobash. *Violence against Wives: A Case Against the Patriarchy.* New York: Free Press, 1979.

Dunford, Franklyn, David Huizinga, and Delbert Elliott. "The Role of Arrest in Domestic Assault: The Omaha Police Experiment." *Criminology* 28 (1990); 183–206.

Eigenberg, Helen, and Laura Moriarty. "Domestic Violence and Local Law Enforcement in Texas: Examining Police Officers' Awareness of State Legislation," *Journal of Interpersonal Violence* 6 (Mar. 1991), 102–109.

Ferraro, Kathleen J. "Policing Woman Battering." *Social Problems* 36 (Feb., 1989): 61–74.

Finkelhor, David, Richard Gelles, Gerald Hotaling, Murray Straus, eds. *The Dark Side of Families: Current Family Violence Research.* Beverly Hills, Calif.: Sage, 1983.

Ford, David A. "Preventing and Provoking Wife Battery through Criminal Sanctioning: A Look at the Risks." *Abused and Battered: Social and Legal Responses to Family Violence.* Eds. Dean Knudsen and JoAnn Miller. New York: Aldine De Gruyter, 1991, 219–261.

Garbarino, James. "The Incidence and Prevalence of Child Maltreatment." *Family Violence.* Eds. Lloyd Ohlin and Michael Tonry. Chicago: University of Chicago Press: 1989, 191–209.

Gelles, Richard. "An Exchange/Social Control Theory." Eds. Finkelhor, Gelles, Hotaling, and Straus, 1983, 151–165.

———., ed. *Family Violence.* Beverly Hills, Calif.: Sage, 1987.

Gelles, Richard, and Eileen Hargreaves, "Maternal Employment and Violence Toward Children." Eds. Straus and Gelles, 1990, 263–277.

Gelles, Richard, and Murray Straus "Determinants of Violence in the Family: Toward a Theoretical Integration." *Contemporary Theories about the Family.* Eds. Wesley R. Burr, Reuben Hill, Frank I. Nye, and Ira L. Reiss. New York: Free Press, 1979, 549–581.

———. "Is Violence Toward Children Increasing." Ed. Gelles, 1983, 78–88.

———. *Intimate Violence.* New York: Simon and Schuster, 1988.

Gibbs, Nancy. "Till Death Do Us Part," *Time.* (Jan. 1993): 38–45.

Green, A. H. "Self-Destructive Behavior in Battered Children," *American Journal of Psychiatry* 135 (May 5, 1978):579–582.

Hampton, Robert L. "Race, Ethnicity, and Child Mistreatment: An Analysis of Cases Recognized and Reported by Hospitals." *The Black Family: Essays and Studies.* Ed. Robert Staples. Belmont, Calif.: Wadsworth, 1986, 172–184.

Hampton, Robert L., Richard Gelles, and John Harrop. "Is Violence in Black Families Increasing?: A Comparison of 1975 and 1985 National Survey Rates." *Journal of Marriage and the Family* 51 (Nov. 1989):969–980.

Hirschel J. David, Ira Hutchinson III, Charles Dean, Joseph Kelley, and Carolyn Pesackis. "Charlotte Spouse Assault Replication Project: Final Report." National Institute of Justice, Washington, D.C. Unpublished Report, 1990.

Hirschi, Travis. *Causes of Delinquency.* Berkeley, University of California Press, 1969.

Hirschi, Travis, and Michael Gottfredson. "Age and the Explanation of Crime," *American Journal of Sociology* 89 (1983):552-584.

Hotaling, Gerald, Murray Straus, Alan Lincoln, "Intrafamily Violence and Crime and Violene Outside the Family." Eds. Straus and Gelles, 1990, 431–470.

Howell, Marilyn J., and Karen L. Pugliesi. "Husbands Who Harm: Predicting Spousal Violence," *Journal of Family Violence* 3 (1988):15–27.

Kalmuss, Debra S., and Murray A. Straus. "Wife's Marital Dependency and Wife Abuse." Eds, Straus and Gelles, 1990, 369–382.

Kantor, Glenda, and Murray Straus. "The 'Drunken Bum' Theory of Wife Beating." Eds, Straus and Gelles, 1990, 203–224.

Kristof, Nicholas. "Where are China's Baby Girls?" *Seattle Post-Intelligencer.* June 17, 1991, A1, A4.

Kurz, Demie. "Social Science Perspectives on Wife Abuse." *Gender and Society* 3 (Dec. 1989): 489–505.

———. "Corporal Punishment and Adult Use of Violence: A Critique of 'Discipline and Deviance,'" *Social Problems* 38.2 (May 1991): 159–161.

Loseke, Donileen. "Reply to Murray A. Straus: Readings on 'Discipline and Deviance.'" *Social Problems* 38 (May 1991): 162–166.

Lyon, Eleanor, and Patricia Goth Mace. "Family

Violence and the Courts: Implementing a Comprehensive New Law." *Abused and Battered: Social and Legal Responses to Family Violence* Eds. Dean Knudsen and JoAnn Miller. New York: Aldine De Gruyter, 1991, 167–179.

Marlatt and Rohsenow, 1981 "The Think-Drink Effect," *Psychology Today* (Dec. 1981):60–69.

Newsweek. "Did He Kill His Daughter?" Jan. 14, 1991:43.

O'Faolain, Julia, and Lauro, Martines. *Not in God's Image: Women in History from the Greeks to the Victorians.* New York: Harper and Row, 1973.

Pagelow, Mildred. *Woman-Battering: Victims and Their Experiences.* Beverly Hills, Calif.: Sage, 1981.

———. *Family Violence.* New York: Praeger, 1984.

———. "The Incidence and Prevalence of Criminal Abuse of Older Family Members." *Family Violence.* Eds. Lloyd Ohlin and Michael Tonry. Chicago: University of Chicago Press, 1989, 263–214.

Pillemer, Karl. "The Dangers of Dependency: New Findings on Domestic Violence Against the Elderly." *Social Problems* 33 (Dec. 1985): 146–158.

Pirog-Good, Maureen, and Jan Stets, eds. *Violence in Dating Relationships: Emerging Social Issues.* New York: Praeger, 1989.

Platt, Anthony M. *The Child Savers: The Invention of Delinquency.* Chicago: University of Chicago Press, 1969.

Pfohl, Stephen J. "The Discovery of Child Abuse." *Social Problems* 24:310–323.

Pizzey, Erin *Scream Quietly or the Neighbors Will Hear.* Short Hills: Ridley Enslow, 1974.

Seltzer, Judith A., and Debra Kalmuss. "Socialization and Stress Explanations for Spouse Abuse." *Social Forces* 67 (Dec. 1988):473–491.

Sherman, Lawrence, and Richard Berk. "The Specific Deterrent Effects of Arrest for Domestic Assault." *American Sociological Review 49* (Apr. 1984):261–272.

Sherman, Lawrence, Douglas Smith, Janet Schmidt, and Dennis Rogan. "Crime, Punishment, and Stake in Conformity: Legal and Informal Control of Domestic Violence" *American Sociological Review* 57 (Oct. 1992):680–690.

Sigler, Robert T. *Domestic Violence in Context: An Assessment of Community Attitudes.* Lexington, Mass.: Lexington Books, 1989.

Smith, Michael D. "Patriarchal Ideology and Wife Beating: A Test of a Feminist Hypothesis" 5 (1990), 257–273.

Steinmetz, Suzanne K. "Family Violence: Past, Present, and Future." *Handbook of Marriage and the Family.* Eds. Marvin B. Sussman and Suzanne Steinmetz. New York: Plenum, 1987, 725–765.

Straus, Murray. "The National Family Violence Surveys." Eds. Straus and Gelles, 1990a, 3–16.

———. "Social Stress and Marital Violence in a National Sample of American Families." Eds. Straus and Gelles, 1990b, 167–180.

———. "Ordinary Violence, Child Abuse, and Wife Beating: What Do They Have In Common." Eds. Straus and Gelles, 1990c, 403–424.

———. "Discipline and Deviance: Physical Punishment of Children and Violence and Other Crime in Adulthood." *Social Problems* 38 (May 1991a), 133–154.

———. "New Theory and Old Canards about Family Violence Research." *Social Problems* 38 (May 1991b), 180–197.

Straus, Murray, and Richard Gelles, eds. "Societal Change and Change in Family Violence from 1975 to 1985 As Revealed by Two National Surveys." *Journal of Marriage and the Family* 48 (Aug. 1986): 465–479.

———., eds. *Physical Violence in American Families: Risk Factors and Adaptations to Violence in 8,145 Families.* New Brunswick, N.J.: Transaction, 1990.

Straus, Murray A., Richard T. Gelles, and Suzanne K. Steinmetz, *Behind Closed Doors: Violence in the American Family.* New York: Doubleday/Anchor, 1980.

Suitor, Jill J., Karl Pillemer, Murray Straus. "Marital Violence in a Life Course Perspective." Eds. Straus and Gelles, 305–317.

Time. "He Had Been Punished Enough." May 13, 1991:54.

Wauchope, Barbara, and Murray Straus. "Physical Punishment and Physical Abuse of American Children: Incidence Rates by Age, Gender, and Occupational Class."Eds. Straus and Gelles, eds., 1990, 133–148.

Webster, Rhonda L., Jay Goldstein, and Alexander Segall. "A Test of the Explanatory Value of Alternative Models of Child Abuse." *Journal of Comparative Family Studies* XVI (Autumn 1985):295–317.

Williams, Kirk R., and Richard Hawkins. "Controlling Male Aggression in Intimate Relationships." *Law and Society Review* 23 (1989):591–612.

Wisdom, Cathy Spatz. "Does Violence Beget Violence?: A Critical Examination of the Literature." *Psychological Bulletin* 106 (1989):3–38.

Wolfgang, Marvin, and Franco Ferracuti. *The Subculture of Violence: Towards an Integrated Theory in Criminology.* New York: Barnes and Noble, 1967.

Wurtele, Sandy K., and Cindy L. Miller-Perrin. *Preventing Child Sexual Abuse: Sharing the Responsibility.* Lincoln, Neb.: University of Nebraska Press, 1992.

Yllo, Kersti, and Murray Straus. "Patriarchy and Violence against Wives: the Impact of Structural and Normative Factors." Eds. Straus & Gelles, 1990, 383–399.

ENDNOTES

1. Interestingly, with recent legal changes in the insanity defense (today it is more difficult to get an acquittal with an insanity defense) and increasing concern for battered women, this case would probably be tried today as self-defense.

2. Throughout the book we will use terms such as *marital, spouse, husband,* and *wife,* but most of this research refers to couples, whether they are married or not. There is considerable research comparing violence between married and cohabiting couples (e.g., see Pirog-Good and Stets, 1989), but space limitations do not allow us to consider such research here.

3. It is interesting to note that, while Gelles and Straus (1985) freely admit that the declines caught them by surprise, they are quick to offer post hoc explanations for why the trends make sense.

4. States where the overall status of women was relatively high included, for example, Alaska, Colorado, Connecticut, Washington. States where the overall status of women was relatively low included, for example, Alabama, Louisiana, Utah.

5. For example, one of the stories that surfaced in the media about 1992 presidential candidate Pat Buchanan was that, while he was growing up, his father made him "hit a punching bag 400 times a week and cheered when Pat bloodied the nose of a first-grade bully" (*Time,* Feb. 17, 1992:28).

6. Following is a paraphrased summary of Gelles and Straus (1988:20–22).

7. Many maintain that Florida chose to make an example of Rodriguez because he is an immigrant who speaks no English. There were 81 similar cases in the previous four years that Florida chose not to prosecute (*Time,* 1991).

8. The following section on the battered woman's movement is a summary of Pagelow (1984:261–267).

9. The following section on the history of child maltreatment is a summary of Pagelow (1984:147–163).

10. Interestingly, infanticide is not simply a practice of the past. There is some speculation, for example, that infanticide is still common in some remote villages in China. Motivated in part by a strong traditional preference for sons and limited by China's 12-year-old "one child policy," Chinese villagers may be killing unwanted girl children. This practice may, in part, explain the five percent of infant girls who are unaccounted for in China's 1990 census (Kristof, 1991).

11. After an appeal, she later settled out of court for $1.9 million.

12. Defined by the state of Washington as "any practitioner, professional school personnel, registered nurse, social service counselor, psychologist, pharmacist, licensed or certified child care providers or their employees, employee of the department, or juvenile probation officer . . ." (Title 26 RCW, p. 81).

Chapter 11

Rape

RAPE: JANE DOE AND STEVEN LORD

Early one November morning (3:00 A.M.), 1988, "Jane Doe" was abducted by Steven Lord from the lot of a Fort Lauderdale, Florida, restaurant. "Jane" had just stepped out of her car when she felt a knife against her back. The man, Steven Lord, instructed her to cross the lot and get into his car. Leaving the parking lot, Steven Lord headed north on Interstate 95. He raped her repeatedly during the five-hour trip north. On one rape, he cut her hand in retaliation for her resistance. On the final rape, he hit her on the head. Semi-conscious she could not recall how he got her back in the car. She regained consciousness after Steven Lord had run into another car. She seized the moment, ran to another car and pleaded for help. The police were notified and they took her to a hospital.

Upon release from the hospital, she returned home. She stated that she had received no sympathy, no instruction, and no counseling. She no longer wanted to prosecute. To ensure her testimony, the police received a "rite of attachment" which is simply an order to bring her to court. The police misinterpreted the "rite of attachment" as a warrant for her arrest and put her in jail. She remained in jail for five days without a charge or explanation. On the fifth day in jail, the police obtained her testimony. Her confinement was later described by the judge who ordered the "rite of attachment," as "just an error in the system."

On October 4, 1989, a jury of three men and three women found Steven Lord not guilty of rape. The foreman of the jury stated, "We felt she asked for it for the way she was dressed. The way she was dressed with that skirt, you could see everything she had. She was advertising for sex." A female jury member commented, "She was obviously dressed for a good time, but we felt she may have bit off more than she could chew" (Associated Press, *Daily News-Record,* 1989). The "Jane Doe" vs. Steven Lord case raises many questions concerning the incidence of rape and the official processing of rape. Consider the following:

- Are typical victims of rape like Jane Doe— young, single, provocatively dressed females alone in public places?
- Are typical rape offenders like Steven Lord— young, single, male drifters who use physical force to abduct and rape their victims?
- Are some rapes "victim-precipitated"? For example, did "Jane Doe" positively and directly contribute to her eventual fate?
- In most rape trials, is it the victim, not the suspect, who is on trial?

These and other important questions are addressed at various points in this chapter. Before we address these issues, however, we feel it useful to begin with an examination of competing definitions of rape.

WHAT IS RAPE?

The Objectivist Conception

According to the objectivist conception of deviance, rape is behavior that violates social norms regulating sexual intercourse. The most familiar objectivist definitions of rape are rape laws. Not all objectivist definitions of rape, however, are legal. Feminists expand the definition of forcible rape to behaviors not included in the criminal law definition of forcible rape. A comparison of legal and feminist definitions of rape reveals important issues that divide scholars, lawmakers and the public alike as to what behaviors constitute forcible rape.

Legal Definitions of Rape. Legally, there are two distinct types of rape: *statutory rape* and *forcible rape.* Statutory rape laws specify inappropriate opposite-sex partners (under-aged partners). Traditional forcible rape laws define rape as illegal sexual intercourse with a female by force or the threat of force.

Statutory rape laws criminalize sexual intercourse with a female who is younger than a statutorily defined age; typically sixteen or eighteen years of age (Field, 1983). Her consent does not negate her partner's criminal liability. However, the under-aged female who consents to sexual intercourse is not criminally liable for her behavior. In *Michael*

M. v. Superior Court of Sonoma County, 1981, the Supreme Court ruled that states have the right to exclude females from criminal liability for statutory rape. The Justices' reasoned:

> Because virtually all of the significant harmful and inescapably identifiable consequences of teenage pregnancy fall on the young female, a legislature acts well within its authority when it elects to punish only the participant who, by nature, suffers few of the consequences of his conduct. It is hardly unreasonable for a legislature acting to protect minor females to exclude them from punishment. Moreover, the risk of pregnancy itself constitutes a substantial deterrence to young females. No similar natural sanctions deter males. A criminal sanction imposed solely on males thus serves to roughly "equalize" the deterrents on the sexes (Gardner, 1985:361).

In some states, however, a mistake with respect to a minor female's age is an acceptable defense against statutory rape.

Forcible rape is an act of sexual intercourse without female consent. Victims are women of all ages, offenders are men, and female consent negates male criminal liability. The FBI defines forcible rape as "Carnal knowledge of a female forcibly and against her will" (*Uniform Crime Reports*, 1992:23). The FBI includes attempted rapes in its forcible rape totals. The FBI definition of rape is also used by the *National Crime Survey* (NCS), which is a national victimization survey aimed at discovering the extent of unreported crime.

Feminist Definitions of Rape. Feminists argue that the traditional criminal law definition of forcible rape is inadequate for two reasons. First, traditional criminal law limits rape to the act of sexual intercourse which is often narrowly defined as penile penetration of the vagina. Therefore, forced anal and oral penetration or penetration of the vagina by an object other than the penis is assault rather than rape. Feminist Susan Brownmiller (1975:378) argues, "All acts of sex forced on unwilling victims deserve to be treated in

concept as equally grave offenses in the eyes of the law, for avenue of penetration is less significant than the intent to degrade." Her argument has not fallen on deaf ears. Many states have replaced their traditional rape statutes with a more comprehensive package of sexual assault laws. An important component of the new sexual assault laws is an expanded definition of sexual intercourse to include vaginal and anal intercourse, oral sex, or any other intrusion by any object into the genital or anal opening of another person (Gardner, 1985:360). A detailed comparison of traditional rape laws and the new sexual assault laws is presented later in this chapter.

Second, feminists advocate a shift from the law's focus on "without the victim's consent" to "coerced by the offender" (Box, 1983:123). This shift is evident in feminist definitions of rape as any act of sexual intercourse where the female's "genuine affection and desire" (Tuttle, 1986:270) is absent. According to this view, where there is no female desire, there is male coercion and, thereby, forcible rape. For example, if a women consents to sexual intercourse out of fear of losing her job, promotion, or raise, or for fear of losing a relationship or angering a spouse, she is responding to male coercion which constitutes forcible rape.

Rival objectivist definitions of rape (legal v. feminist) present a dilemma. Either rape is relatively infrequent (legal) or very frequent (feminist). In practice, lack of consent is difficult to legally establish, especially where physical violence is absent. On the other hand, the requirement of "genuine desire" could in effect criminalize, at some point, virtually all males.

In addition to being beyond judicial capabilities, the requirement of genuine desire could, for many, trivialize rape. Still others might see rape as a figment of a woman's imagination and, therefore, argue that "true" rape does not exist. Recognizing this dilemma, Box offers a definition of rape that broadens the nature of violating a woman's physical integrity and, yet, provides for a more inclusive category of behaviors. He defines rape as ". . . sexual access gained by any means where the female's overt genuine consent is absent" (Box, 1983:125). His definition treats several acts of sex (anal, oral, vaginal) as rape. Also, "overt genuine consent" is absent where verbal or physical refusal has been ignored or where social threat is used to gain sexual access. For example, sexual access of a woman who has said "no" constitutes forcible rape. Also, sexual access gained by word or deed of social coercion (i.e. loss of job, threat to discontinue relationships or services) constitutes forcible rape.

Whether you agree with the traditional legal definition of rape or the feminist definition, it is important to understand that sexual intercourse is only one of a variety of sexual violations. Forced sex often occurs by other than physical means. Currently, rape laws are being reformed in many states. The intent of these "new" laws is to emphasize the offender's act rather than the victim's experience and to direct attention to the violent rather than sexual aspects of the crime (Searles and Berger, 1987).

The Subjectivist Conception

From the subjectivist view sexual aggression by one against another is rape only if social audiences define it as such. The rapist is one to whom that label has been applied. The audiences that label one as "rapist" includes the victim, the offender, legal authorities, juries, and the public. Similarly, the victim of rape is one who these same audiences judge to be a victim. For these audiences, social characteristics of the victim, the offender, and the social situation of a sexual encounter determine whether one will be defined as "victim."

For the moment, recall that Steven Lord abducted "Jane Doe" at knife point. Forcibly

and against her will, Lord had sexual intercourse with "Jane Doe." Was "Jane Doe" raped? According to objectivists, yes. With or without conviction, Steven Lord's *behavior* constitutes rape. For subjectivists, however, rape is a *definition* that is applied by others to a particular sexual encounter. In the case of "Jane Doe," for at least one important audience, the jury, Jane was not raped.

If Jane had been of higher social standing in the community, if she had been married, or if her dress had been less provocative, would her sexual encounter with Steven Lord have been defined as rape? If she had been abducted at 3:00 PM rather than 3:00 AM, or, if she had been abducted from her home rather than a public parking lot, would she have been raped? Or, if the composition of the jury had been different (for example, younger jurors, more female jurors), would Steven Lord have been found guilty of rape? These and other questions relating to the characteristics of the various audiences who define a particular sexual encounter as deviant or criminal are central to the subjectivist's view of rape.

THE PREVALENCE OF FORCIBLE RAPE

How Much Rape Is There?

The answer is difficult to obtain because traditional methods of discovery such as the *Uniform Crime Reports* (UCR's), the *National Crime Survey* (NCS), and self-report studies have notable weaknesses. For example, in 1991, the *Uniform Crime Reports* reported 106,593 forcible rapes, constituting a rate of 42.3 per 100,000. Eighty-six percent of those reported rapes were completed rapes and 14 percent were attempted rapes. However, the NCS reveals that only 54 percent of completed and attempted rapes are reported to police (U.S. Department of Justice, 1992).

Why do so many rapes go unreported to police? Some of the reasons for not reporting one's rape to the police are:

1. A woman may not know that she has been raped. Some women may come to share the assailant's definition of his sexual assault as an act of love, or come to view themselves as "conquered property" and continue intimacy with the conqueror (Russell, 1975).
2. Some women may blame themselves, or fear that their loved ones will doubt their innocence believing that "nice girls do not get raped."
3. The victim of rape may be too ashamed, embarrassed or humiliated to report having been raped.
4. Some women fear reprisal by the offender or wish to protect the attacker who may be a friend, relative or husband.
5. Many women may believe that the police will not take their complaint seriously. Also, they may desire to avoid the trauma of getting involved with the criminal justice system. Some women may fear that they, rather than the offender, will be on trial.

Given these reasons for not reporting rape, what affects a woman's decision to report her rape to police? From the *National Crime Survey*, Lizotte (1985) found three factors that significantly affected the reporting practices of rape victims. First, the more familiar the rapist was to the victim, the less likely the victim was to report the rape. Similarly, a study of victimization surveys over a ten-year period revealed that only 45 percent of non-stranger rapes were reported to police whereas 60 percent of stranger rapes were reported. Second, Lizotte found that rape victims were more likely to report to police if the rapist had no right to be where the rape took place. Third, if the victim was seriously injured, the rape was more likely to be reported.

The reporting practices of rape victims may also be important for understanding increases or decreases in the rate of rape as reported by the UCR's. In 1991, reported rapes increased 3.9 percent from the previous year. Reported rapes have also increased 13 percent since 1987, and over 40 percent since 1977 (FBI, 1992:269). Have rapes really increased so dramatically since 1977, or do the reporting practices of rape victims account for much of the increase? There is evidence to suggest that increased reporting does account for much of the increase. There are four bases for this suggestion. First, the NCS studies conducted over this same period of time shows a decline in rape victimization rates. Second, legislative reform in the definition of rape and changes in what is admissible evidence in rape trials have occurred. As previously mentioned, many states now include oral and anal sex as forcible rapes, and newer definitions of rape focus more on the offender's use of force or threat of force than on the victim's resistance. Also, *rape shield laws* that restrict or limit evidence of the victim's prior sexual behavior as a defense against rape are now common. Third, some established rape crisis centers claim to have been successful in increased victim reporting. Finally, changes in people's sex-role attitudes away from more traditional views such as "a woman's place is in the home" have been found to increase victim willingness to report rape. For example, Orcutt and Faison (1988) found a strong relationship between a decline in traditional sex-role attitudes and an increase in non-stranger rapes reported to police.

NCS data reveal that there are almost twice as many attempted and completed rapes as are reported to police. However, the actual number of rapes may be higher. For many of the same reasons rape victims do not report to police, they may not report their rape even to an anonymous interviewer. In addition, NCS interviewing techniques undermine rape disclosure by victims. Koss and Harvey (1991:17–22) note that subjects are asked to reveal violence or attempted violence by a family member or relative who often is present at the time of the interview. Also, NCS interviews are not specially trained to handle sensitive issues, and they are not matched with subjects by gender or race. You can imagine how difficult it would be for a woman to disclose her rape to a male interviewer. Further, NCS interviewers never use the word rape. Rather they ask a series of questions on physical harm. This strategy assumes that the respondent will conceptualize her experience as rape.

Given the limitations of national estimates of the prevalence of rape, many researchers have done independent studies to better estimate the number of women who are victimized by rape. These studies, however, are difficult to integrate. Often, samples are unrepresentative of the general population and researchers do not use the same definition of rape. In order to obtain meaningful and comparable figures on the prevalence of rape, Koss and Harvey (1991:23–29) reviewed only those studies that used scientific samples and a legal definition of rape. These studies included samples of adolescents, college students, adult women, and special populations including the elderly, ethnic groups, prisoners, and psychiatric patients. The cumulative findings revealed that approximately 20 percent of women have been victimized by rape. This figure is about 50 times greater than rates based on the NCS. Koss and Harvey (1991:29) conclude, "These findings transform rape from a heinous but rare event into a common experience in women's lives."

How many rapes occur each year is unknown. Rape is vastly underreported to police. The NCS also greatly underestimates the prevalence of rape. What is known, however, is that many women are the victims of attempted and completed forcible rape every year, and that any one woman faces a significant probability of being a victim of an attempted or completed rape in her lifetime.

What about men who are raped? As you have learned, the FBI definition restricts the victims of rape to women. Also this definition is adopted by the NCS. However, the reformed rape laws in many states are sex neutral. Despite the sex neutrality in these laws, rape remains a penetration offense. Therefore, a woman cannot rape a man by sexual intercourse. As Koss and Harvey (1991:4) point out, where a man is coerced by a woman to have sexual intercourse with her the victim penetrates the offender, but rape is penetration of the victim by the offender. Where an offense of penetration occurs to men the perpetrator is virtually always another male (Koss and Harvey, 1991). How frequently does this occur? No one knows for certain, but vast underreporting is suspected. It is "unmanly" for a man to share or complain about injury, or to otherwise admit that he cannot take care of himself. Male reporting is further compounded by the fact that his victimization was of a homosexual nature. However, Risin and Koss (1988) provide some insight to the prevalence of male rape. Their victimization study of male sexual abuse included questions on attempted and completed penetration incidents. From a national survey of 2,972 college males 2 percent had experienced at least an attempted penetration. Over 81 percent of all sexually abused males did not report their abuse to anyone.

Given our limited knowledge of male rape, this chapter focuses exclusively on female rape. Now let us turn to the types of rape identified in the literature. Our discussion of the prevalence of rape will then examine the male offenders and female victims of rape and the victim-offender relationship with special attention to date and marital rape.

Types of Rape

Given our limitations in measuring the extent of rape, our generalizations about the nature of rape are cautious. There is, however, reasonable consensus in the rape literature about various types of rape. Sociologists have distinguished types of rape by offenders motivations and methods of rape. Steven Box (1983:127–9), for example, has identified five types of rape: sadistic rape, anger rape, domination rape, seduction turned into rape and exploitation rape.

Sadistic Rape   is the infusion of aggression and eroticism. The rapist's goal is to become aroused by the aggression. His sexual gratification sometimes requires the victim's physical resistance. His brutality is often manifested in ritualistic acts such as bondage. Objects such as bottles, pipes or sticks are often instruments of sexual assault. Ritualism for the sadistic rapists may be reflected in his selection of victims who share a common characteristic regarding their appearance or vocation (Groth, 1983:1353).

Anger Rape   is the sexual release of anger and rage. Very often the rapist applies more violence to subdue his victim than is necessary for sex. His goal is to punish—not to gain sexual gratification. His punishment is a means to retaliate for his perception of having himself been wronged by others. He acts on impulse and his rapes are episodic. His anger is bottled until it explodes on impulse (Groth, 1983:1353).

Domination Rape   or "power rape" is sexual conquest. The rapist's intent is to dominate her sexually rather than to degrade or hurt her. Rape is the means to establish potency, and to reaffirm his masculinity. Although motivated by sexual desire, his sexual encounters are non-consenting and his method is capture and conquest. He desires the women to welcome his physical embrace. Her reaction seldom meets his fantasy and, therefore, he does not find his assault sexually satisfying. His sexual assaults are planned and his victims selected as opportunity arises.

Seduction Turned Into Rape   is seduction carried too far. For men and women to maneuver toward one another in a seductive manner is to some extent an acceptable strategy for the communication of sexual interest. If the victim previously or at sometime during the encounter (flirting, foreplay, non-coital sex) decides to stop short of coitus but coitus does occur, seduction has turned into rape. Here, the rapist seldom employs physical force beyond his body weight and firm embrace. Rather he "pursues and pressurizes, cajoles and bullies, and ultimately 'persuades'" (Box, 1983:128). That is, he is persuaded because he believes that she is supposed to say no; but if he takes charge in the pursuit of his pleasure he will ultimately bring pleasure to her. His motivation is a combination of sexual desire and assertion of manliness (Box, 1983:128).

Exploitation Rape   is motivated purely for sexual pleasure. The opportunity for exploitation rape arises out of men's superior social, economic, and political position in society. It is endemic to our society. Where women must depend on men for their livelihoods, their sexual favors are easily exploited. Box notes:

> . . . given her relatively weak position, the female often makes a rational choice that the alternatives to coitus are even more personally harmful; her consent though is not an expression of her desire, either for sexual pleasure or to please and physically comfort her male partner, nor is it genuine because the conditions under which it is given—conditions of economic or social vulnerability created by relative inequality—are not those under which consent can be said to exist (1983:129).

Other forms of exploitation rape may be institutionalized. Cross-cultural studies reveal that men sometimes subject disobedient women to rape (Sanday, 1981). Similarly, the sale of women as concubines and sex from enslaved women are exploited rapes.

The five types of rape and their probable

recognition by law are presented in Table 11-1. These five types provide insight for understanding rape behavior (objectivist explanations). They also serve to remind us of the severe limitation of legal definitions of rape and of the data gathered by legal agencies.

Who Are the Men Who Rape?

The preceding review of the extent and nature of rape in our society has pointed out a number of measurement problems that limit our knowledge about rape. Clearly, these problems also impede an accurate identification of the social characteristics of men who sexually assault women. As we have seen, at best, only about one-half of all rapes are reported to the police. Of the rapes that are reported, slightly over one-half are cleared by an arrest. Therefore, the official portrait of men who rape more accurately reflects the characteristics of those who were caught than those who raped. Box (1983:136) suggests, for example, that the physically violent rapist who is unlucky and lacks the intelligence or resources to avoid arrest comprises the majority of official rapists.

The problem to which Box refers is difficult to overcome because self-report studies have seldom been used, and victimization data about the men who rape is limited to the victim's perception of offender characteristics. Where the victims is willing to describe her assailant, her description is limited to estimates of age and race. However, age and racial characteristics of rape assailants as perceived by victims are similar to those who are arrested for rape.

Of those arrested for rape in 1991, 44 percent were under 25 years old. Offenders between 18 and 24 accounted for 29 percent of the rape arrestees (FBI, 1992:223–224). The majority of rapists reported in the *National Crime Survey* are also perceived by their victims to be over 18 and under 30 (U.S. Department of Justice, 1992). Blacks, who comprise about 12 percent of the U.S. population, are overrepresented among those arrested for rape and those who are identified by rape victims. Forty-four percent of those arrested for rape in 1991 were black (FBI, 1992:231). Similarly, 26 percent of the lone offenders rapists in the National Crime Survey were perceived by victims to have been black (U.S. Department of Justice, 1992:303).

In addition, according to rape victims most rapists acted alone, attacked a single victim, and seldom used a weapon. In the *National Crime Survey* (U.S. Dept. of Justice,

---

TABLE 11.1   Types of Rape and Their Recognition by Law[1]

TYPE OF RAPE	PRIMARY TYPE OF POWER EMPLOYED TO COERCE VICTIM	OFFENDER'S PRIMARY MOTIVES	PROPORTION OF VICTIMS RECOGNIZED BY LAW
sadistic	physical (actual)	aggression/sex	all[2]
anger	physical (actual)	aggression/revenge	most
domination	physical (threatened/actual) emotional/social/some	sex/conquest	many
seduction	physical	sex/manliness	few
exploitation	economic/organizational/social	sex	none

[1]*Source:* Steven Box. *Power, Crime and Mystification.* New York: Travistock, 1983, p. 162.

[2]Many are transformed into murder charges.

1992:303–305), a lone assailant was reported for 85 percent of the rapes; a lone assailant and a single victim accounted for 75 percent of the rapes; and offenders used a weapon in 26 percent of the rapes. When more than one offender was reported, the rapists were perceived to be younger. In twenty-eight percent of multiple offender rapes, all offenders were under 21 years old, and another 21 percent of the multiple offender rapes involved at least one person under 21 (U.S. Dept. of Justice, 1992:303–305).

Who Are the Victims of Rape?

All women are at risk of being raped. Young, single, black women from low-income families, however, are disproportionately the victims of attempted and completed rapes. This is the profile of rape victims that emerges from the *National Crime Survey* (U.S. Dept. of Justice 1992).

The highest victimization rates for attempted and completed rapes are among 16 to 24 year-olds. Women in this age range are about three times more likely to be victims than women as a whole. Rape victimization rates decrease dramatically with increasing age. Females 12 to 15 years old are about as likely to be raped as women 25 to 34 years old, but they are about 5 times more likely to be raped than women 35 years old or older (U.S. Dept. of Justice 1992). The age distribution of attempted and completed rape victims was similar for whites and blacks. However, black women had a higher rate of victimization in almost all age ranges (U.S. Dept. of Justice 1992).

Women from low income families, unemployed women, divorced or separated women, and women who live in the central city were also more likely to be victimized by attempted and completed rape (U.S. Dept. of Justice, 1992). The social characteristics of attempted and completed rape victims were similar. There were, however, some personal characteristics that differentiated attempted from completed rape victims. Personal characteristics that were associated with independence were central for avoiding rape (Swift, 1985). For example, women of greater physical stature (taller, heavier, and physically active) and who were less dependent (employed, never married, and more educated) better avoided rape than women who were smaller and more dependent.

There was also evidence that women who responded aggressively to an attacker were more likely to avoid a completed rape. Women who offered no resistance or opted for a less forceful response such as, crying or pleading were more often the victim of a completed rape than women who offered physical resistance such as running, kicking, or screaming (Bart and O'Brien, 1985; Swift, 1985; Kleck and Sayles, 1990). The most effective form of resistance was resistance with a weapon (Kleck and Sayles, 1990).

Most forms of resistance were not related to an increase in victim injury. Unarmed threats or arguing with the attacker was the only form of resistance related to a high risk of victim injury. The most serious injury to the victim was the rape itself. In only about three percent of rape incidents was there an additional serious injury (Kleck and Sayles, 1990).

Victim/Offender Relationships

The victims and offenders of attempted and completed rapes are relatively similar in age and race. Seventy percent of all rapes involve persons of the same race (FBI, 1992). Both UCR's and the NCS suggest that to the majority of rape victims, the assailant was a stranger. This, however, may be largely a reflection of victim reporting practices. As we have previously stated, rapes by non-strangers, especially intimates such as in date rape and marital rape, are often not reported to police or survey interviewers.

Date Rape.   Behind the blue dot that 3.2 million viewers saw on their TV screens was the face of Patricia Bowman, a single mother of a 2-year-old daughter, who accused William Kennedy Smith of raping her. How could this be? Was Mr. Smith the "date" who Ms. Bowman described as "a very nice man," a medical student who she trusted and enjoyed because he could talk to her about problems she had experienced with the premature birth of her daughter? Or, was he the "rapist" who Ms. Bowman claimed threw her to the ground, pulled up her blouse, pulled off her panties, penetrated her, and warned her, "No one will believe you" (Booth, 1991:31). The defense claimed that he was the "date" who Ms. Bowman had described, and that she invited sex by removing her panties before strolling the beach with William Smith. The prosecution claimed that he was the "rapist," and that police and medical reports demonstrated that Patricia Bowman sustained injuries suggestive of rape (Lacayo, 1991:31). In December, 1991, William Kennedy Smith was acquitted by a jury of rape and battery charges. Was their sexual encounter consensual? Or, was it forced; and just as William Smith had told Patricia Bowman, "No one will believe you"?

In July, 1991, former heavyweight boxing champion, Mike Tyson, was charged with rape. Tyson's alleged victim was an 18-year-old beauty pageant contestant for Miss Black America. This time, however, a jury did not blame the victim for her own predicament (Oates, 1992). On February 10, 1992, Tyson was found guilty of rape and sentenced to 6 years in prison. Presently, Tyson is serving time at the Indiana Youth Center. He is appealing the verdict.

The celebrity of Smith and Tyson has brought public attention to an all too common situation—a date ending in an alleged rape, a woman claiming to have been sexually assaulted, and a man insisting that he has done nothing wrong. For most persons, the words "date" and "rape" are incompatible. "Rape" brings to mind the image of a deranged stranger who attacks in streets and alleys under cover of darkness. "Date" implies trust, companionship, and commitment. These perceptions of rape and date, however, do not fit the facts. Research on rape repeatedly demonstrates that by doing what is socially accepted and expected—dating—women put themselves at risk.

From a survey of 930 women in San Francisco, Diana Russell (1984) found that the majority of rapes were perpetrated by a man known to the victim. The prevalence of attempted and completed rapes by the victim/offender relationship from Russell's study is presented in Table 11–2.

Only 16 percent of the rapes were perpetrated by a stranger. An equal percentage of these incidents were perpetrated by a date. Russell's findings on date rape are consistent with other surveys. From a survey of students enrolled in 32 institutions of higher education in the U.S., Koss (1988) found that 15.4 percent of college women had been raped. In 84 percent of these rapes, the perpetrator was a close acquaintance or date. Others have estimated that as many as 20 or 25 percent of all co-eds have been victimized by attempted or completed rape (Meyer, 1984; Koss, Gidycz, and Wisniewski, 1987).

Seldom, however, are these rapes reported. In Koss's (1988) survey of college campuses, only five percent of these co-eds who had been raped reported it. Often female students are too ashamed, embarrassed, or frightened to report their rape. Many victims, however, do not report because they do not view date rape as "real rape." This view is shared by the men who rape them. Only 4.4 percent of the men in Koss's survey admitted to behaviors that legally constitute rape. Yet, only 1 percent of these same men believed that they had done anything wrong. Ac-

TABLE 11.2   Attempted and Completed Rapes by Victim/Offender Relationship

VICTIM/OFFENDER RELATIONSHIP	PERCENT OF ATTEMPTED/ COMPLETED RAPES
Acquaintance	23
Date	16
Stranger	16
Husband or ex-husband	10
Lover or ex-lover	8
Authority figure	8
Friend	7
Boyfriend	4
Other relative	4
Friend of family	2

Source: Derived from Diana E. Russell, *Sexual Exploitation: Rape, Child Sexual Abuse, and Workplace Harassment* (Beverly Hills, California: Sage Publications, 1984) pp. 61–62.

cording to Koss (1988), even when men use physical force, they see their behavior as congruent with consensual sexual activity.

The perception that "rape" and "date" are inconsistent is shared by females and males alike. Their perception is reinforced by traditional rape laws which focus on "consent by the victim." Where there is female consent there is no rape, and dating is a consensual relationship.

Marital Rape. The words "marriage" and "rape" appear even more inconsistent than "date" and "rape." Doesn't a wife by marriage consent to having sex with her husband? Today, twenty-eight states in the U.S. allow husbands to be prosecuted for rape of wives with whom they are living. Forty-nine states permit the prosecution for rape of husbands who are separated from their wives. Alabama is the only state that exempts a husband from rape of his legal spouse (Gelles and Straus, 1988).

The extent of marital rape is difficult to determine due to vast underreporting. However, some estimates have been given. For example, in Russell's (1984) survey of 930 San Francisco women, 10 percent had been raped by husbands or ex-husbands (Table 11-2). However, wives and ex-wives were victimized by their husbands and ex-husbands more often than what appears in the Table. The figures in Table 11-2 are percentages of the total incidents. Many of the sampled women had never been married and, therefore, could not have been victimized by a husband or ex-husband. When recalculated for married women only, attempted/completed rapes by a husband or ex-husband increases to 12 percent. Another two percent of married women were forced by their husbands or ex-husbands to engage in other sex acts such as anal or oral sex. Married women were more than twice as likely to be victimized by their husbands/ex-husbands than by a stranger. Two other studies found the proportion of marital rape to be similar to that reported by Russell. Finkelhor and Yllo (1982) found that 12 percent of wives had been raped by their husbands. Holmstrom and Burgess (1983) estimated 14 percent of wives had been raped by their husbands.

The distinction between wife-rape and wife-beating is an issue of disagreement for social scientists. Yllo and Finkelhor (1985) point out that several scholars argue that wife-rape occurs primarily in violent marriages. For these researchers wife-rape and wife-beating are both aspects of domestic violence. This view of marital rape is challenged by Yllo and Finkelhor (1985). They point out that some wife rapes are indeed connected with wife beating, what Yllo and Finkelhor refer to as "battering rapes." On the other hand, there are wife rapes that are not associated with wife beating. Yllo and Finkelhor call these "force-only rapes." In "battering rapes" the husband's motivation was anger. His intent was to inflict harm rather than sexual satisfaction. In "force-only rapes," the husband's motivation was dominance. His intent was to achieve sexual satisfaction through conquest rather than to inflict harm (Yllo and Finkelhor, 1985).

EXPLANATIONS OF FORCIBLE RAPE

Macro-Objectivist Theories

Rape varies cross-culturally. There are "rape-prone" and "rape-free" societies (Sanday, 1981). Also, the incidence of rape varies between groups within societies. In the U.S., for example, UCR's and the NCS suggest higher incidences of rape among young, low-income, single, minority group members who live in large urban areas. Macro-objectivists attempt to explain these patterns of rape behavior. There are three prominent macro-objectivist approaches for explaining rape: opportunity-structure theories, subcultural theories, and gender inequality theories.

Opportunity Structure Theory. At least three opportunity structure theories of rape can be identified. Chronologically, we begin with VonHentig's (1951) demographic strain explanation of rape. VonHentig argues that rape results from a sex-marital imbalance.

Where there is a surplus of unmarried males relative to unmarried females the opportunity for legitimate sex partners is strained. This leads to rape as a means to obtain sex partners. However, from a study of forcible rape in Philadelphia, Amir (1971) did not find the marital demographic structure to explain the extent to which males commit rape.

Anthropologist, R.A. LeVine (1959) provides an opportunity explanation of rape similar to VonHentig's. From a study of sex offenses among the Gusii, LeVine suggests that four salient factors are associated with rape. They are:

1. Severe formal restrictions on the nonmarital sexual relations of females
2. Moderately strong sexual inhibitions on the part of females
3. Economic or other barriers to marriage that prolong the bachelorhood of some males into their late twenties
4. The absence of physical segregation of the sexes

These factors imply that rape results from blocked access to women. According to the theory, then, if men are denied access to women, men will resort to force in order to secure sexual partners. According to Sanday (1981:22), LeVine's work suggests the following hypothesis: "Sexual repression is related to the incidence of rape." From her survey of 95 societies, Sanday (1981) found no significant relationship between sexual repression and rape. This finding challenges all opportunity theories of rape because all opportunity theories explain rape as an expression of sexual repression.

Another opportunity explanation of rape is a theory developed by Clark and Lewis (1977). These writers argue that men perceive sex as a commodity controlled by women. Therefore, men have a right to bargain for or buy female sexual favors. Men resort to many forms of coercion when bargaining for sex. Lies, promises, gifts, threats, and even physical force are the coercion strategies used by men. The type of coercion varies according to the personal and economic assets a particular man possesses. So, too, does the value of particular women vary. Simply stated, some women have a higher property value than others, and some men have the assets to bargain while other men, who lack assets, must take sex from women by force. Clark and Lewis (1977:131) state, "Within the technical [that is, legal] limits of the term, rape will always be an inevitable consequence of the fact that some men do not have the means to achieve sexual relations with women, except through physical violence." Clark and Lewis's emphasis on the lack of assets to bargain for sex, especially for higher valued females, suggests a relationship between social class and forcible rape. Men from low socio-economic backgrounds more often commit forcible rape. Also, men from low socio-economic backgrounds "frequently choose middle-class women as their victims" (Clark and Lewis, 1977:130). By way of summary, where the lack of resources to obtain opposite-sex relationships is greatest, forcible rape is most likely to occur.

Evidence that men from low socio-economic backgrounds are more likely to commit rape must be viewed with caution. As previously noted, rapes committed by social, economic, or political coercion are less likely to be perceived and reported as forcible rapes than are rapes committed by means of physical force. Lacking the assets of middle-class men, lower-class men may more often resort to physical coercion rather than having a higher propensity for committing rape. Also, there is no evidence that lower- or working-class men frequently rape middle-class women. In fact, given our knowledge of victim/offender relationships and the context within which rape often occurs (that is, dates and marriages), rape may more often occur between persons from similar class backgrounds.

Subculture of Violence Theory. Wolfgang and Ferracuti (1967) attribute high rates of criminal homicide among young, lower-class, black males to a subculture of violence. According to this theory, violence is in the lifestyle, socialization process, and interpersonal relationships of a subculture whose members share norms that condone violence. Amir (1971) extends the subculture of violence theory to explain rape. Amir claims that in lower-class, black communities, violent behavior and sexual exploitation are adaptations to poverty that have become a normal way of life. Amir states:

> *The Negro male's aggressive sexuality seems . . . due to the strong need to overcome problems of masculinity and of sexual identity. This is because of the Negro family structure (mother-based family) and the need to overcome general social disadvantages, by substituting sexual aggressive masculinity for failures as a man in the economic and social status spheres (1971:330).*

The subculture of violence theory locates the source of violence, homicide, and rape in a deviant culture where aggression has become the norm. Again one must ask, is rape concentrated in lower-class black communities or is it here that this type of sexual aggression (sex by means of physical force) is most often acknowledged by both victims and officials. As previously noted, where the offender's motive is aggression, the proportion of victims recognized by law increases.

Some sociologists, however, do not believe that one must belong to a subculture to acquire values and rationalizations supporting forced sex. Rather, the dominant culture itself legitimates sex by force. These sociologists prefer a gender inequality explanation of forcible rape.

Gender Inequality Theory. Gender inequality theory holds that rape results from a cultural tradition of male social, political, and economic dominance (Brownmiller, 1975;

Schwendinger and Schwendinger, 1983). Male dominance creates and maintains a view by men that women are property. Therefore, men possess, dominate, and demean women in interpersonal relations including sexual relations. From this perspective, rape is perpetrated for power and domination rather than for sexual gratification.

Gender inequality theory, however, is vague on how inequality impacts on rape rates. Some theorists predict that greater inequality increases rape rates, while others suggest that lesser inequality cause male frustration and, thereby, increases rape (Ellis, 1989). Studies of gender status inequality at the community and society level support the male frustration version of gender inequality theory. That is, a reduction in gender status disparities is associated with a slight increase in rape rates (Ellis, 1989).

The strongest evidence in support of gender inequality theory is provided by Sanday (1981). She examined the key factors suggested by rival theories of rape in 95 tribal societies. Sanday concluded,

> The correlates of rape . . . strongly suggest that rape is the playing out of a socio-cultural script in which the expression of personhood for males is directed by, among other things, interpersonal violence and an ideology of toughness. (1981:24).

In tribal societies the status of women is associated with fertility and the status of men with aggression. In "rape-free" societies, fertility and aggression are valued equally. In "rape-prone" societies, masculinity is accorded more prestige. Where masculinity is more highly valued than femininity, Sanday argues, the sexual aggression against women is a way for men to demonstrate their maleness and it reinforces the superiority of male status.

Sanday's (1981) findings represent a major advance in gender inequality theory. She extends the link between rape and cultural concepts of masculinity and femininity to the status of women relative to men in the larger society. Further, her findings provide insights for understanding and reducing rape in our own society. As Sanday puts it:

> Rape is not an integral part of male nature, but the means by which men programmed for violence express their sexual selves. Men who are conditioned to respect the female virtues of growth and the sacredness of life, do not violate women. It is significant that in societies where nature is held sacred, rape occurs only rarely. The incidence of rape in our society will be reduced to the extent that boys grow to respect women and the qualities so often associated with femaleness in other societies—namely, nurturance, growth, and nature. Women can contribute to the socialization of boys by making these respected qualities in their struggle for equal rights (1981:25–26).

Sanday's (1981) findings and recommendations are in the opposite direction of the frustration version of gender inequality theory. That is, as the status disparity between maleness and femaleness decreases, rape also decreases. The direction of gender inequality and rape remains an important issue for gender inequality theories of rape. Similarly, in a state-level analysis of gender inequality and rape, Baron and Straus (1989) concluded that rape rates in the U.S. are higher in states in which gender inequality is greater.

Micro-Objectivist Theories

Unlike macro-objectivist theories which concentrate on rates of norm-violating behavior within and between societies, micro-objectivists focus on the social structures and processes that explain individual deviant behaviors. The central question is what social forces motivate certain individuals to engage in deviant acts. There are three prominent micro-objectivist explanations of forcible rape: gender socialization theory, interpersonal dominance theory, and victim-precipitation theory.

Gender-Socialization Theory. In several ways gender socialization theory resembles gender inequality theory. Both theories view learning as largely responsible for rape. Also, both theories associate learning with cultures like our own where male exploitation of women is a deep-rooted social tradition (Ellis, 1989). They differ, however, in that gender inequality theory emphasizes structures of socio-economic dominance, whereas, gender socialization theory focuses on attitudes and interpersonal interactions that lead to sexual aggression. Also, gender socialization theory is less emphatic about rape as a nonsexual behavior (Ellis, 1989). The premise of gender socialization theory has been clearly stated by Scully and Marolla, who note:

> . . . *deviant behavior is learned in the same way as conforming behavior, that is, socially through interaction with others. Learning not only includes the techniques of committing the crime, but also motives, drives, rationalizations, and attitudes that are compatible with the behavior (1985:306).*

This is not to suggest that men learn to value rape per se. Rather, men and women have learned that masculinity entails aggression and domination. This pattern of masculinity is evident among men in many aspects of life including the work place, recreation, and interpersonal relations as well as sexual relations.

There is considerable evidence to support the view that rape is expressed through traditional gender roles of male domination and female subordination. As you have learned, many, perhaps most, rapes occur in the context of acceptable and expected male/female relationships such as dating and marriage. Also, one study found that 50 percent of the men believed that it was "acceptable for a man to force a girl to have sexual intercourse when she initially consents but then changes her mind, or when she has sexually excited him" (Shortland and Goodstein, 1983:221). This finding helps us understand why men

who rape often do not believe they have done anything wrong. Indeed, as you will recall, 4.4 percent of male respondents in a survey of campus rape admitted to having committed a rape. However, only 1 percent of these men saw their behavior as criminal.

Men often justify their behavior with traditional myths such as "nice girls don't get raped" or "when women say no they really mean yes" (Scully and Marolla, 1985). Such myths pervade our culture. Several studies have demonstrated that males who accept these myths are more likely to sexually assault women (Burt, 1980; 1983; Rapaport and Burkhart, 1984). Also, men who accept these rape myths are more likely to blame the victim of rape (Lottes, 1988; Brady et al, 1991; Blumberg and Lester, 1991).

Male attitudes favorable to sexual aggression are reinforced by male peers. For example, Alder (1985) found one's perception of peers' sexual aggression was the best predictor of personal acts of sexual aggression. Also, Schaeffer (1992) found that men who live in all male dorms as opposed to co-ed dorms have more traditional beliefs about female sex roles and are more likely to hold to rape myths.

Interpersonal Dominance Theory. Thomas and Hepburn (1983) locate the source of violent behavior, including rape, in the structural features of asymmetric relations. Asymmetric relations are the superordinate and subordinate positions that often develop in enduring relationships, such as among family, friends, and acquaintances. In enduring relationships, interpersonal violence is a strategy used by the superordinate to maintain social dominance, or a strategy used by the subordinate to reduce dominance. Where asymmetry is high, as in male-female relationships—especially in husband-wife and boyfriend-girlfriend relations—violence is most often initiated by the superordinate (men.) This is because it is more appropriate for the superordinate to make more and a wider range of demands on the subordinate with less accountability than the other way around (Thomas and Hepburn, 1983:276).

Research on rape is consistent with the association between asymmetric relations and violence suggested by Thomas and Hepburn. As we have seen, many rapes are acts of aggression and domination rather than strong-arm means of achieving sexual gratification. Further, the patterns of rape are similar to those of homicide and assault. For example, rape most often occurs among persons of like age, social class, and race; and many rape victims are intimates or acquaintances of the offender. However, direct evidence of disruptions in the asymmetric structure of social relations as the cause of rape, homicide, or assault does not exist. Also, Yllo and Finkelhor (1985) suggest that one type of wife rape, "battering rapes," is an act of aggression and dominance, but another type of wife rape, "force-only rape," is intended to achieve sexual gratification. Felson and Krohn (1990) suggest that many rapes are sexually motivated. They argue that rape victims are targeted because they are young and presumably attractive. The offenders are young males who seek sexual gratification and, therefore, are less likely to injure their victims beyond the rape itself. Whereas, older offenders seek dominance and, therefore, are more likely to physically injure their victims. This is contrary to Thomas and Hepburn's assumption that all rapes, including wife rapes, are strictly acts of aggression and domination.

Victim-Precipitation Theory. Unlike interpersonal dominance theory, victim-precipitation theory assumes rape to be a violent means to secure sexual gratification. It is suggested that the victim has expressed, verbally or symbolically, that she is available for sex. For example, Amir (1971:266) defines victim-precipitated rape as "those rape situations in which the victim actually, or so it was deemed, agreed to sexual relations but retracted before the act or did not react strongly enough when the suggestion was made by the offender." Similarly, Curtis (1974:600) defined victim-precipitated rape as "an episode ending in forced intercourse when a female agreed to sexual relations or clearly invited them verbally or through gestures, but then retracted before the act."

Several sociologists have strongly objected to the notion of victim-precipitated rape (Brownmiller, 1975; Clark and Lewis, 1977; Schwendinger and Schwendinger, 1983; Box 1983). Opponents have raised two major objections to victim-precipitated rape.

First, victim precipitation is based solely on the offender's perception and interpretation of what the victim may have said or done, rather than on what she actually said, did, or intended. To illustrate this problem we present Box's (1983) objection to Nelson and Amir's (1975) suggestion that hitch-hike rapes are victim precipitated. Box asks:

> By what stretch of the imagination can getting into a car with a stranger be construed as "clearly inviting" sexual relations or "deeming" to agree to them? Is accepting an offer of a lift a "gesture" that sex is available? A sexual encounter may be what the driver wants; it may be an option he perceives to exist; it may well be he interprets all female hitch-hikers' actions and utterances as clear evidence that they are "asking for it." But these are his wants, perceptions and interpretations; they are not the victim's. She was merely asking for, and prepared to accept, only a lift (1983:132).

Applied to any type of rape, victim precipitation relies on the rapist's perception and interpretation of the victim's behavior as an explanation of rape. Therefore, Schwendinger and Schwendinger (1983:66) argue that victim-precipitation theory takes "sexual judgments and rationalizations at face value and converts them into a causal explanation of rape."

The second major objection raised by opponents is that victim-precipitated theory shifts blame from the rape offender to the rape victim. The victim is at fault for having aroused the offender to a point where he could no longer contain himself, or she was at fault for having placed herself in that position to begin with. Blaming the victim, opponents suggest, has negative legal, sociological, and policy implications.

Legally, victim precipitation diminishes the culpability of the offender and, in effect, places the victim on trial. In our opening recount of Jane Doe and Steven Lord, the jurors' statements clearly suggested victim precipitation to the point of exonerating the offender.

Sociologically, explanations that focus on the victim divert attention away from the motivations of the offender. Such explanations also minimize the role of structural and cultural conditions that foster rape. No less problematic is that victim explanations of rape may provide credible rationalizations for men and reinforce self doubts for women.

Preventive practices based on the notion of victim precipitation have the potential for two negative effects. First, practices to alter or confine a woman's dress, demeanor, and activities reinforce the idea of "a woman's place." Second, such practices may infringe on women's civil liberties and their right for self determination.

Macro-Subjectivist Theories

Macro-subjectivist theories focus on the social processes by which certain behaviors are defined as deviance and persons as deviant. Among these theories are interest group theories and organizational theories. Interest group theories assume that various groups in society, with divergent values and special interests, vie for power to translate their interests into official norms. Organizational theories identify the informal norms that emerge within organizational settings that explain how social control agents process cases and, thereby, produce official deviants and official rates of deviance.

Interest Group Theories. A feminist-conflict theory that explains official reactions to rape has emerged from the works of several feminist writers (Griffin, 1971; Wood, 1973; Brownmiller, 1975; Smart, 1976; Sanders, 1980). According to this theory, rape laws "protect the property rights of males in the sexual and reproductive functions of women" (Myers and LaFree, 1982:1283). Official reactions (for example, reactions on the part of the criminal justice system) to rape reinforce male property rights by only protecting "valuable women." Valuable women are those who conform to traditional sex-roles or who are valuable sexual property, for example virgins, the young, and married women (Myers and LaFree, 1982:1283). The oppressive purpose of rape laws is demonstrated by the selective application of sanctions to men who sexually violate "valuable" women.

Feminist-conflict theory is both logical and plausible, but conceptual and research problems are apparent. Conceptually, LaFree (1980:834) argues that several feminist theorists ". . . have been partisan, relying on untested assertions, anecdotes and analogies to justify their theoretical claims." Also, Schwendinger and Schwendinger (1983) note that at least one prominent feminist writer, Susan Brownmiller, fails to escape sexist thinking. Schwendinger and Schwendinger (1983:84) state ". . . she rejects the sexist stereotyping of women and accepts only the stereotype of men." Thus, she remains "a prisoner of a traditional sexist framework."

Also, research in support of feminist-conflict theory (Clark and Lewis, 1977; Holmstrom and Burgess, 1978; Burt and Albin, 1981) lacks methodological rigor. Myers and LaFree (1982) point out that previous research has focused exclusively on the prosecution of rape. Comparisons to other crimes are rare. Research has also focused exclusively on victim characteristics. Defendant and offense characteristics have been ignored.

Myers and LaFree (1982) overcome the limitations of previous research and provide a rigorous test of feminist-conflict theory. These researchers compare court decisions for sexual assault defendants with the court decisions for defendants of other violent crimes and serious property crimes. Their findings did not support feminist-conflict theory. Myers and LaFree (1982:1297) found that victim characteristics did affect court decision making, but the impact of victim characteristics was not different or greater in rape cases than other non-sexual felonies. Also, indicators of sexual property value and traditional sex-role behavior did not affect rape cases differently from other non-sexual felonies.

Organizational Theories. Organizational theories highlight the activities that produce a particular deviance definition within an organization of social control. An organizational theory of rape seeks to explain the official processing of rape cases.

Our focus here is on the criminal court. To be more precise, the "bureaucratic court." The central figure in the bureaucratic court is the prosecutor (Blumberg, 1967). The prosecutor must process crimes, including rape, efficiently. Efficiency is maximized by processing cases in a routine manner. Routine processing of rape is accomplished by the prosecutor's practice of viewing a new case of rape as similar to previous rape cases. This process of typification results in a construct of rape as a "normal crime" (Sudnow, 1965). Rape as a "normal crime" consists of the prosecutor's stereotypes of the kinds of victims, offenders, and social situations typical of most rapes. Rape, then, comes to be defined

by the kinds of women, men, and social situations typical of rape, rather than by the actual behavior that occurred.

Processing rape as a "normal crime" allows the prosecutory to offer "standard deals" to the defendant in exchange for his guilty plea. According to George Cole (Associated Press, 1991:7), a scholar on the administration of justice, most rape cases are plea-bargained, and cases are adjudicated every few minutes. The "L.A. Law" scenario or the William Kennedy Smith and Mike Tyson trials is exceedingly rare.

Many studies of the court processing of rape cases find that the social characteristics of the victim and the offender determine the outcome of the case (for example, Clark and Lewis, 1977; Holmstrom and Burgess, 1978; Feldman-Summers and Palmer, 1980; Sanders, 1980; LaFree, 1980). LaFree (1980:834), however, notes that most research on the official processing of rape has "methodological shortcomings" and has "emphasized the intentional biases of processing agents." LaFree argues that a theory of rape processing must recognize two inherent difficulties in processing rape cases: the absence of witnesses and the distinction between forcible (criminal) and consensual (noncriminal) sexual acts. Without witnesses and with blurred distinctions between "persuasion, seduction, and coercion" court officials make decisions based on rape typifications rather than on intentional biases (LaFree, 1980).

Rape typifications are also influenced by prosecutors' concern about how rape is likely to be defined by juries. For example, a Denver district attorney stated "If we could prosecute every case where we believe the victim, our filings would be three or four times what they are now. The first thing I ask is, do I believe the victim? Then I ask, is this going to be prosecutable?" Also, a prosecutor in Atlanta characterized jurors as "the clog in the system. They want you dragged off the street and raped in front of a TV camera" (Mansnerus, 1989:20).

Research by LaFree, Reskin, and Visher (1985) demonstrates that where "consent" is the issue rape victims are on trial. In such cases, jurors are influenced more by the victim's character than by measures of evidence. If the victim reports having sex outside of marriage, or reports a history of drinking or drug use, or was acquainted with the defendant, jurors were less likely to find the defendant guilty. However, in cases where the issue is the "identification of the defendant" as the assailant, evidence such as eyewitnesses, use of a weapon, and injury to the victim were more important than victim characteristics (LaFree, Reskin, and Visher, 1985). These findings are also consistent with the outcome of the rape case that began this chapter. In the case of "Jane Doe," consent was the issue. Steven Lord admitted having had sexual intercourse with "Jane," but argued that "Jane" consented. In the "Jane Doe" case, victim characteristics appear to have determined the outcome. Similarly, one might ask what role victim characteristics played in the outcome of the William Kennedy Smith and Mike Tyson trials. Was Patricia Bowman the "imperfect" victim—an unwed mother who had been drinking and dancing with the defendant prior to the alleged rape? Was Desiree Williams the "perfect" victim—an 18-year-old beauty who was a member of her church choir and college scholarship recipient?

In sum, rape typifications explain official reactions to rape. Rape typifications are social constructs of the kinds of victims, offenders, and social situations perceived by prosecutors as typical of rape. These stereotypes of rape are shaped by the demand for efficiency, the perceived probability of success and difficulties inherent to rape cases. If a rape goes to trial, characteristics of the victim are most important to judges and jurors in cases where lack of consent is the issue.

Micro-Subjectivist Theories

Micro-subjectivist theories explain how various audiences define a sexual encounter as rape. Rape is a judgment (definition) imposed by others, and often independent of whether an actual rape has occurred. We have already discovered some important factors that influence a jury's definition of rape. Here, we examine the social definitions of rape by social audiences outside of the courts. We will also examine the question, does the official label "rapist" leads to subsequent rape behaviors by those who are so labeled?

Audience Definitions of Rape.   Valuable insights into factors determining differing social definitions of rape are provided by two important studies. In one study (Klemmack and Klemmack, 1976), a sample of women were asked to define rape from seven hypothetical examples of sexual aggression. All examples legally constituted rape, but, only slightly more than half of the women surveyed defined these examples as rape. The education, employment status, tolerance of sex before marriage, and view of women's roles among the respondents affected their willingness to define situations as rape. Women with a higher education were more likely to believe that rape had occurred. Employed women were also more likely to judge these examples of sexual aggression as rape. Women who were tolerant of sex prior to marriage, too, were more likely to define situations as rape. However, if the victim and offender were known to have any relationship prior to the sexual encounter, less than half of the respondents were willing to define the cases as rape.

In another study of public definitions of rape, Williams (1979) examined the effect of sex-role attitudes on rape definitions across ethnic groups. Sex-role attitudes were measured as views of traditional male-female sex roles and views about women's liberation. Rape definitions included the respondent's willingness to define a sexual encounter as rape, the respondent's assessment of the victim's fault, and the respondent's willingness to prosecute the assailant. The major research question centered on whether respondents'' sex-role attitudes explain definitions of rape independent of the respondent's social characteristics (age, sex, education, income), and does this vary between ethnic groups (Anglos, African Americans, and Mexican Americans)?

The findings demonstrated a link between sex-role attitudes and definitions of rape. Both, less traditional sex-role beliefs and behaviors, and women's stronger liberation beliefs and behaviors were significantly related to defining situations as rape. These sex-role attitudes were also related to the respondent's not faulting the victim. These findings held for all ethnic groups. Sex-role attitudes, however, were not related to respondent's willingness to prosecute the assailant. Rather, willingness to prosecute alleged rapists was related to the respondent's inclination to define a sexual encounter as rape.

However, the sex of the respondent affected assessment of fault or willingness to prosecute differently between ethnic groups. Black males were more likely to assess female fault and less willing to prosecute assailants than black females. Mexican-American males were also less willing to prosecute assailants than their female counterparts. Anglo men, however, were less likely to assess female fault than were Anglo women. The differences between minority men and women on assessment of fault and willingness to prosecute is, perhaps, explained relative to their threat of rape. Minority women are disproportionately victims of rape. Minority men, however, are more likely to be falsely accused of rape, especially interracial rape, and subject to unequal treatment by criminal justice officials (Williams 1979:84). Therefore, Williams (1979:84) suggests, ". . . minority women see prosecution of the assailant as 'justice' while minority males see it as a threat and even as 'injustice'." But, why would Anglo men be less likely to assess female fault than Anglo women? Williams (1979:84) suggests that because they are on top of the sexual and racial hierarchy, Anglo men have a "paternal responsibility (which goes with respectability and power) to protect their women from 'outsiders'." Also, because of their respectability and power, Anglo men are less threatened by false accusations and official bias in prosecution. Therefore, Anglo men ". . . can afford to be liberal and even tolerant in their judgments of females who are involved in rape" (Williams, 1979:84).

In sum, research demonstrates that public definitions of rape do not necessarily coincide with behaviors that constitute legal rape. Also, to some extent, rape is in the "eyes of the beholder." As a matter of definition, rape is influenced by the social characteristics of the observer and by pro-feminist attitudes about sex roles and women's liberation. Williams' overall finding that more traditional attitudes about women's roles and women's liberation was linked to faulting the victim and defining forced sexual encounters as rape has been consistently reported in the literature (Lottes, 1988).

Labeling Theory. The labeling theorist views the deviant (rapist) as one to whom the official label (convicted rapist) has been successfully applied. Once labeled, the "convicted rapist" may acquire a new deviant identity, now imagining himself as a sexual abuser. His deviant, abuser, self-image pervades in subsequent sexual encounters with women. His use of force in subsequent sexual encounters reinforces his abuser self-image.

Studies of convicted rapists do not suggest the emergence of a sexual abuser self-image. To the contrary, convicted rapists often justify their sexual violence as legitimate, arguing that their victims were teasers or that their victims would eventually relax and enjoy the encounter (Scully and Marolla, 1985). Also, the view that forced sex is appropriate behavior does not appear to be the product of official labeling. Shortland and Goodstein's (1983:221) study of perceptions of rape in dating situations found that 50 percent of males who had not been formally labeled as sexual abusers believed that forced sex was appropriate when the female had changed her mind or if she had sexually excited the male.

SOCIAL POLICY AND RAPE

The history of rape policy in the United States has occurred within the context of the women's movement. The philosophy of rape policy is the protection of women's rights. The objective is the right of self-determination. The tasks of rape policy are: rape law reform, aid to the victims of rape, and a reduction in the instance of rape.

Rape Law Reform

For the past two decades the destruction of traditional rape laws has been a major objective of the women's movement. The success of the women's movement in creating a new definition of rape is apparent from the enactment of *sexual assault* laws which began in the mid-1970s and continues. These statutory changes are indicated in Table 11–3.

Traditional rape statutes and rules of judicial evidence demonstrate a general distrust of women. Evidence of a woman's prior sexual history and the requirement of corroborating evidence for the traditional offense of rape reflect the system's distrust for women (Field, 1983). Both have been the target of feminist criticism, and significant changes in rules of evidence have occurred.

During the 1970s, the federal government and 46 states enacted *rape shield* laws. These laws prohibit or limit the use of evidence pertaining to a victim's sexual history. However, rape shield laws contain exceptions which vary by jurisdiction. In practice, then, a woman's sexual history remains admissible under certain conditions. In some states, inquiry into a woman's sexual history is at the discretion of the judge. Other exceptions include instances where the prior sexual conduct was with the defendant, or where the defendant argues that someone else is the source of the physical evidence, such as pubic hair or semen. Also, some states allow evidence of prior sexual conduct for the purpose of discrediting the witness, but not as evidence of victim consent (Field, 1983:1359).

Rape shield laws are an improvement, but given their exceptions, they often continue to reflect a general distrust of women. However, the repeal of the statutory requirement of corroboration is a major feminist victory. Prior to rape law reform a victim's testimony had to be corroborated to sustain the charge of rape. Corroboration, however, can be particularly difficult to obtain in the case of rape. For example, women who are overcome by fear or the power of the assailant may not physically resist and, thereby, avoid the bruises, abrasions and torn clothing that would corroborate force. Seldom, too, is a victim's first thought to get a medical examination to verify penetration. In fact, her first response may be to get clean and, thereby, wash away corroborating physical evidence. Further, eyewitnesses that may be able to corroborate the identity of the accused are rare or reluctant to come forth (Field 1983:1360).

Through rape law reform, feminists have broadened the definition of rape to the category of assault. They have eliminated much of the legal institution's distrust of women as, for example, in the passage of rape shield laws, the repeal of corroboration, and the reduction of the penalty for rape. To reduce the penalty for rape may appear odd, at first, but it is aimed toward increasing rape convictions.

TABLE 11.3   Traditional Rape and the New Sexual Assault Laws

OLD COMMON LAW RULES REGARDING RAPE	STATUTORY CHANGES ENACTED IN MANY STATES
Only females can be the victims of rape.	Any person (male or female) may be a victim.
Only a male could directly commit the crime.	Any person (male or female) can directly commit the crime.
A husband could not rape his wife (under the common law, however, the husband could be charged with assault and battery).	A husband can be charged with the rape of his wife under the law of states that have made this change from the old common law.
Rape was defined in one (or at most a few) degree.	A variety of degrees of criminal conduct are defined in more specific language.
Rape was defined only as the insertion of the penis into a vagina by force and against the will of the female.	"Sexual intercourse" is broadly defined not only as vaginal intercourse, but also "cunnilingus, fellatio, anal intercourse, or any other intrusion, however slight, of any part of a person's body or of any object into the genital or anal opening of another, but emission of semen is not required" (Section 940.255[5] [c] of the Wisconsin Criminal code).
Common law rape did not include the crime of "offensive touching" (however, this could be charged either as disorderly conduct or assault and sometimes battery if there was an injury.	Many modern sexual assault laws include the offense of "offensive touching" in that they forbid "sexual contact" (intentional touching of an intimate part of another person's body without consent).
As consent by the victim was a total defense, the common law tended to focus on the resistance offered by the victim in determining this issue.	The new statutes focus on the degree of force threatened or used and the degree of harm done in determining the issue of consent.
Rape was classified as a crime against sexual morality.	Sexual assault is more often classified as a crime against a person.

Source: Thomas Gardner, *Criminal Law: Principles and Cases,* 3rd ed. West Publishing Company, New York, NY, 1985, p. 360.

Rape law reform reflects the interests of feminists at many levels. Beginning with the statutory definition of rape to the evidentiary rules of procedure and ending with the penal sanctions prescribed by law. If effective these rape law reforms could advance both long-term and immediate objectives of the woman's movement. In the long-term, national legislation may become our children's morality. However, for now, do rape law reforms increase the reporting, prosecution, and con-

viction of rape offenders? Currently, research on the effect of rape reform has fallen short of expectations. For example, Caringella-MacDonald (1985) found that rape victims are still more likely than non-sexual assault victims to have their credibility challenged in court, and offenders are still receiving significant sentence reductions for a plea bargain. Also, Berger, Searles, and Neuman (1988) reported that court officials and the public remain slow to accept rape law reform and are especially reluctant to punish non-consensual sex that is not physically forced.

Rape Crisis Centers

The inception of the rape crisis center is rooted in the contemporary woman's movement. From the ranks of women's rights organizations a small contingency of "radical feminists" took action on rape. They formed anti-rape squads. These squads took the initiative to publicly speak out on rape, instruct women in self-defense, and encourage "Sisters-Give-Rides-to-Sisters" campaigns (Largen, 1985:4). The anti-rape squads paved the way for the rape crisis center.

The first rape crisis center, the Bay Area Women Against Rape (BAWAR), appeared in Berkeley, California, in 1972. The earliest centers were created by feminists and run exclusively by volunteer women. These early centers were formed to provide crisis intervention services for rape victims and promote social change through community education and action. Eventually, financial needs and volunteer turnover required many centers to hire professionals and staff who were acceptable to public and private funding sources. This organizational change reoriented rape crisis centers. The primary feature of the centers had become victims' services. The social change component had faded for most centers. These changes, however, could not sustain the rape crisis center movement. Many centers folded; others severely cut services. In 1981, Congress approved federal funding for rape crisis centers. Federal funding guaranteed rape crisis center survival and transformed rape victim assistance into a national commitment (Largen, 1985:8–9).

Today's rape crisis centers are diverse; and few resemble the early feminist prototype. Most centers provide direct services and community education and action. Direct services include: emergency assistance, crisis intervention, and counseling. Community education and action include: public education, the training and monitoring of control agencies that treat and process rape victims, lobbying for legislative reform, and political action work, i.e., rallies, protests, boycotts (Gornick, Burt, and Pittman, 1985:254).

From a national sample of 50 rape crisis centers, Gornick and her colleagues (1985:264–67) identified four general types. The first type is independent and closely resembles the early feminist prototype. They are run as collectives, have small budgets and staff, operate via a telephone service, have little physical space, and are usually politically active. The second type is structured to a more mainstream social service program. Some are independent, others are affiliated with large service programs such as YWCAs, family service programs, or some local government agency. These "agency type" centers are service-oriented and less feminist. The third type is affiliated with a large social service agency, typically a mental health agency. They provide scheduled counseling rather than crisis intervention and seldom participate in community action. Their administration and staff are not separate from the main agency. The fourth type of rape crisis service is the hospital/emergency room-based program. Like the mental health agency-type, they are administered and staffed by hospital personnel. These programs receive a large number of cases, but their personnel is large enough so that individual staff see few rape victims. This type of program is crisis intervention oriented. Several of these programs include systematic follow-up counseling. These programs provide minimal community education and are not politically oriented.

Given the diversification of rape crisis centers, an evaluation of their effectiveness is difficult. However, some general successes and failings have been noted. Based on self-report information from a national survey of rape crisis centers, King and Webb (1981) conclude that centers have been effective in providing immediate services to rape victims. They found, however, follow-up counseling to be problematic. Sixty-two percent of the rape victims received only one follow-up contact. The suggested reasons for this counseling deficiency include lack of funding, the stigma attached to counseling, and the center's reluctance to acknowledge the need for counseling (King and Webb, 1981:100–101). An evaluation of the community education and action component is difficult. There has been, however, some success for a few exemplary rape crisis centers (Koss and Harvey, 1991:142–154).

The evolution of rape crisis centers has been a process of struggle. Rape crisis centers have evolved to the many different models. Few resemble the prototype centers of the early 1970s. The most important factor in their transition from agents of social change tovictim aid service agents was the influx of government monies. Diverse ideologies, structures, and functions encumber a comprehensive policy. A few evaluation studies have reported success, especially in providing immediate aid to rape victims at a few exemplary rape crisis centers (Koss and Harvey, 1991).

SUMMARY

According to the objectivist conception of deviance, rape is behavior that violates social norms regulating sexual intercourse. The most familiar objectivist definitions are rape laws. The law distinguishes between two types of rape: statutory rape and forcible rape. *Statutory rape* is sexual intercourse with an under-aged person. Forcible rape laws vary from state to state. However, the FBI provides a standard definition of forcible rape for law enforcement agencies throughout the nation. According to the FBI, *forcible rape* is: sexual intercourse of a female by force or threat of force and against her will. Alternative objectivist definitions of forcible rape have been offered by feminist scholars. One such definition of *forcible rape* is: sexual intercourse where the female's genuine affection and desire are absent. The intent of feminist definitions is to direct attention to the offender's violent act and away from the victim's sexual experience. According to the subjectivist conception of deviance, rape is a definition applied by social audiences to some but not all sexual encounters.

The prevalence of forcible rape in the United States is difficult to determine. Both the *Uniform Crime Report* and the *National Crime Survey* greatly underestimate the extent of rape. Independent studies discover that the majority of rapes are not reported to police and that as many as one of every five women is raped. This rate is about fifty times greater than is the NCS rate.

Five types of rape can be drawn from the current rape literature. They are: sadistic rape, anger rape, domination rape, seduction turned into rape, and exploitation rape. *Sadistic rape* involves the connection between aggression and eroticism where offender sexual gratification depends on victim resistance. *Anger rape* is the impulsive release of anger where the offender's intent is to subdue and punish the victim in retaliation for his having been wronged by others. *Domination rape* is a sexual conquest over the victim for offender's gratification and affirmation of his masculinity. *Seduction turned into rape* evolves out of an intimate encounter where the offender pressures, cajoles, and persuades his victim beyond non-coital sex. *Exploitation rape* involves the offender's use of social, economic, or political advantage to exploit victims for sexual favors. Sadistic and anger rapes are most clearly recognized as rape by victims, offenders, and the law and, therefore, more likely to be reported.

The offenders and victims of rape are similar in age and race. The majority are under

25 years of age and African Americans are overrepresented in rape incidents. In the vast majority of rapes, the victim and offender are the same race. According to the UCR's and the NCS, the majority of rape offenders were strangers to the victims. However, independent research suggests that for many, perhaps most, rapes, the victim and offender are known by one another. Very often they are intimates such as dates and spouses. For example, 20 to 25 percent of all co-eds are raped by a date or college acquaintance. Marital rape, too, is more common than national data sources indicate. Researchers consistently find that about 12 percent of married women are raped by their husbands. Two types of marital rape are identified in the literature: battering rapes and force-only rapes. *Battering rapes* are motivated by anger, and the husband's intent is to injure. *Force-only rapes* are motivated by dominance, and the husband's intent is sexual gratification through conquest.

Competing objectivist explanations of rape behavior were presented. Three macro-objectivist theories were examined: opportunity theory, subculture of violence theory, and gender inequality theory. Presently, the weight of empirical evidence supports gender inequality theory.

Three micro-objectivist theories were also examined: gender socialization theory, interpersonal dominance theory, and victim-precipitation theory. There is considerable evidence in support of the gender socialization view that rape is expressed through traditional gender roles of male domination and female subordination. There is also some evidence that the interpersonal dominance theory may be relevant for some types of rape, but not for rape in general. Victim-precipitation theory has been strongly opposed by a number of sociologists who do not believe it to be an appropriate explanation of rape.

Competing subjectivist explanations of rape definitions were presented. Feminist-conflict theory is an interest group theory which purports that rape laws protect male property rights by selectively punishing rapists who sexually violate "valuable women." This theory is not supported by recent research. However, organizational features of the court do influence court officials' definitions of what constitutes rape. The demand for efficiency and perceived probability of successful prosecution influence court officials' definition of an alleged sexual assault as rape. Where consent is the issue, the social characteristics of the victim affect court officials' definition of a sexual encounter as rape.

Micro-subjectivist theories explain rape as a judgment that is made by various audiences who define a particular sexual encounter as rape. Research suggests that social audiences differ in their willingness to define particular sexual encounters as rape. Also, attitudes about appropriate sex-role behavior are related to one's willingness to define an incident as rape. There is, however, little evidence to suggest that, once one is labeled as a rapist, he develops a deviant identity or engages in subsequent sexually aggressive behavior as a consequence of having been so labeled.

Current rape policy in the United States has been influenced largely by feminist efforts to reform rape laws and to assist the victims of rape. Many states are substituting other terms for rape to draw attention to the violent rather than to the sexual aspects of the crime. One example is the sexual assault laws. *Sexual assault laws* are gender neutral and replace rape with multiple degrees of sexual assault and battery. Another legal reform has been federal and states' enactment of rape shield laws. *Rape shield laws* prohibit or limit the use of evidence pertaining to a woman's sexual history. Feminists have also been instrumental in the establishment of rape crisis centers. *Rape crisis centers* provide direct services (e.g. crisis intervention and psychological and legal counseling) to rape victims and community education and action (e.g. public education, training for agents who handle rape victims, and lobbying for legal reform). The effectiveness of rape crisis centers remains an empirical question.

GLOSSARY

Anger rape   A physically aggressive assault where the offender releases anger by punishing the victim.

Battering rape   A marital rape motivated by anger where the husband intends to inflict pain on his wife.

Domination rape   A sexual assault where the offender seeks to affirm his masculinity by sexual conquest.

Exploitation rape   A sexual assault where the offender uses his social, political, or economic advantage to coerce sexual favors from the victim.

Force-only rape   A marital rape motivated by domination where the husband seeks gratification by conquest of his wife.

Forcible rape (FBI definition)   Sexual intercourse with a female by force or threat of force and against her will.

Forcible rape (a feminist definition)   Sexual intercourse where the female's genuine affection and desire are absent.

Rape crisis centers   Agencies (often volunteer) that provide direct assistance to rape victims (e.g. crisis intervention, counseling, and legal assistance) and community education and action (e.g. public education, training for agents who handle rape victims, and lobbying for legal reform).

Rape shield laws   Statutes that prohibit or limit the use of evidence pertaining to a woman's sexual history.

Sadistic rape   A physically aggressive assault where the offender seeks sexual gratification from the victim's resistance.

Seduction turned into rape   A sexual assault where the offender pressures, cajoles, and persuades his victim into sexual intercourse.

Sexual assault laws   Reformed legal statutes that are gender neutral and replace the term rape with multiple degrees of sexual assault and battery.

Statutory rape   Sexual intercourse with a person who is below the legal age of an adult.

SUGGESTED READINGS

Burgess, Ann W. *Rape and Sexual Assault*. New York: Garland, 1985 (New Edition *Rape and Sexual Assault II*, 1988).

These two volumes contain a comprehensive collection of readings on forcible rape and other sexual assaults. Topics include: definitions of rape, types of rape, rape victims and offenders, victim response, official processing of rape cases, and rape prevention.

Groth, A. Nicholas. "Rape: Behavior Aspects." *Encyclopedia of Crime and Justice*. Ed. Sanford H. Kadish. New York: Free Press, 1983, pp. 1351–1356.

A brief summary of measures of rape, motivations of rape offenders, types of rape, and theories of rape. It is written in a nontechnical style and intends to provide general information about rape to novice readers.

Ellis, Lee. *Theories of Rape*. New York: Hemisphere, 1989.

Three theories of rape are extracted from the literature: feminist theory, learning theory, and evolutionary theory. These theories are tested relative to existing research on the causes of sexual aggression.

Koss, Mary P. and Harvey, Mary R. *The Rape Victim*. Newbury Park, CA: Sage, 1991.

This book provides a brief review of the crime of rape including legal definitions, types of rape, prevalence of rape, and causes of rape. Emphasis, however, is on the clinical and community intervention strategies that treat rape victims and prevent rape.

LaFree, Gary, Reskin, Barbara, and Visher, Christy. "Jurors Responses to Victims' Behavior and Legal Issues in Sexual Assault Trials." *Social Problems* 32 (1985): 389–407.

Methodologically, the most rigorous analysis of legal and extralegal factors that affect jury trials of rape. Where consent is the major issue, victims are put on trial.

Sanday, Peggy Reeves. "The Socio-Cultural Context of Rape: A Cross Cultural Study." *Journal of Social Issues* 37 (1981): 5–27.

A rare examination of rape between societies. This study tests three macro-level theories of rape, and provides empirical support for gender inequality theories of rape.

REFERENCES

Alder, Christine. "An Exploration of Self-Reported Sexually Aggressive Behavior." *Crime and Delinquency* 31 (1985):306–331.

Amir, Menachem. *Patterns in Forcible Rape.* Chicago: University of Chicago Press, 1971.

Associated Press. "Televised Smith Trial Makes Little Change in Public Perception." *Daily News-Record.* Harrisonburg, VA: December 20 (1991):7.

Baron, Larry and Straus, Murray A. *Four Theories of Rape in American Society: A State Level Analysis.* New Haven, CT: Yale University Press, 1989.

Bart, Pauline B. and O'Brien, Patricia H. *Stopping Rape: Successful Survival Strategies.* Elmsford, NY: Pergamon, 1985.

Berger, Ronald, Searles, Patricia, and Neuman, Lawrence W. "The Dimensions of Rape Reform Legislation." *Law and Society Review* 22 (1988):328–349.

Blumberg, Abraham S. *Criminal Justice.* Chicago: Quadrangle Books, 1967.

Blumberg, Michelle L. and Lester, David. "High School and College Students' Attitudes Toward Rape." *Adolescence* 26 (1991):727–729.

Booth, Cathy. "Behind the Blue Dot." *Time.* December 16 (1991):31.

Box, Steven. *Power, Crime, and Mystification.* New York: Tavistock, 1983.

Brady, Eileen C., Chrisler, Joan A., Hosdale, Christine D., Osowiecki, Dana M., and Veal, Tracy A. "Date Rape: Expectations, Avoidance Strategies, and Attitudes Toward Victims." *The Journal of Social Psychology* 131 (1991):427–429.

Brownmiller, Susan. *Against Our Will: Men, Women, and Rape.* New York: Simon and Schuster, 1975.

Burt, Martha R. "Cultural Myths and Supports for Rape." *Journal of Personality and Social Psychology* 38 (1980):217–230.

———. "Justifying Personal Violence: A Comparison of Rapists and the General Public." *Victimology* 8 (1983):131–150.

Burt, Martha R. and Albin, Rochelle S. "Rape Myths, Rape Definitions, and Probability of Convictions." *Journal of Applied Social Psychology* 11 (1981):212–230.

Caringella-MacDonald, Susan. "The Comparability in Sexual and Non-Sexual Assault Case Treatment: Did Statute Change Meet the Objective?" *Crime and Delinquency* 31 (1985):206–223.

Clark, Lorenne M.G. and Lewis, Debra J. *Rape: The Price of Coercive Sexuality.* Toronto: Women's Educational Press, 1977.

Curtis, Lynn A. "Victim Precipitation and Violent Crime." *Social Problems* 21(1974):594–605.

Ellis, Lee. *Theories of Rape.* New York: Hemisphere, 1989.

Federal Bureau of Investigation. *Uniform Crime Reports.* Washington, D.C.: United States Government Printing Office, 1992.

Feldman-Summers, Shirley and Palmer, G. C. "Rape as Viewed by Judges, Prosecutors, and Police Officers." *Criminal Justice and Behavior* 7(1980):34–36.

Felson, Richard and Krohn, Richard. "Motives for Rape." *Journal of Research in Crime and Delinquency* 27(1990):222–242.

Field, Martha A. "Rape: Legal Aspects." In *Encyclopedia of Crime and Justice.* Ed. Sanford H. Kadish. New York: Free Press, 1983, pp. 1356–1364.

Finkelhor, David and Yllo, Kersti. "Forced Sex in Marriage: A Preliminary Research Report." *Crime and Delinquency* 28(1982):459–478.

Gardner, Thomas J. *Criminal Law: Principles and Cases.* 3rd ed. New York: West, 1985.

Gelles, Richard J. and Straus, Murray A. *Intimate Violence.* New York: Simon and Schuster, 1988.

Gornick, Janet, Burt, Martha R., and Pittman, Karen J. "Structure and Activities of Rape Crisis Centers in the Early 1980's." *Crime and Delinquency* 31(1985):247–268.

Griffin, Susan. "Rape: The All-American Crime." *Ramparts* 10(1971)26–36.

Groth, A. Nicholas. "Rape: Behavior Aspects." *En-*

cyclopedia of Crime and Justice. Ed. Sanford H. Kadish. New York: Free Press, 1983, pp. 1351–1356.

Holmstrom, Lynda L. "The Criminal Justice System's Response to the Rape Victim." *Rape and Sexual Assault*. Ed. Ann Wolbert Burgess. New York: Garland, 1985, pp. 189–198.

Holmstrom, Lynda L. and Burgess, Ann W. *The Victim of Rape: Institutional Reactions*. New York: Wiley, 1978.

———. "Rape and Everyday Life." *Society* 20(1983):33–40.

King, Elizabeth H. and Webb, Carol. "Rape Crisis Centers: Progress and Problems." *Journal of Social Issues* 37(1981):93–104.

Kleck, Gary and Sayles, Susan. "Rape and Resistance." *Social Problems* 37(1990):149–162.

Klemmack, Susan H. and Klemmack, David L. "The Social Definition of Rape." *Sexual Assault*. Eds. Marcia J. Walker and Stanley L. Brodsky. Lexington, MA: D C Heath, 1976, pp. 135–148.

Koss, Mary P. "Hidden Rape: Sexual Aggression and Victimization." *Rape and Sexual Assault II*. Ed. Ann Wolbert Burgess. New York: Garland, 1988, pp. 3–25.

Koss, Mary P., Gidycz, Christine A., and Wisniewski, Nadine. "The Scope of Rape: Incidence and Prevalence of Sexual Aggression and Victimization in a National Sample of Higher Education Students." *Journal of Consulting and Clinical Psychology* 55(1987):162–170.

Koss, Mary P. and Harvey, Mary R. *The Rape Victim*. 2nd ed. Newbury Park, CA: Sage, 1991.

Lacayo, Richard. "Trial by Television." *Time*, December 16 (1991):30–31.

LaFree, Gary D. "Variables Affecting Guilty Pleas and Convictions in Rape Cases: Toward a Social Theory of Rape Processing." *Social Forces* 58(1980):833–850.

LaFree, Gary D., Reskin, Barbara F., and Visher, Christy A. "Jurors' Responses to Victims' Behavior and Legal Issues in Sexual Assault Trials." *Social Problems* 32(1985):389–407.

Largen, Mary Ann. "The Anti-Rape Movement Past and Present." *Rape and Sexual Assault*. Ed. Ann Wolbert Burgess. New York: Garland, 1985, pp. 1–13.

LeVine, Robert A. "Gusii Sex Offenses: A Study in Social Control." *American Anthropologist* 61(1959):965–990.

Lizotte, Alan J. "The Uniqueness of Rape: Reporting Assaultive Violence to the Police." *Crime and Delinquency* 31(1985): 169–190.

Lottes, Ilsa L. "Sexual Socialization and Attitudes Toward Rape." *Rape and Sexual Assault II*. Ed. Ann Wolbert Burgess. New York: Garland, 1988, pp. 193–220.

Mansnerus, Laura. "The Rape Laws Change Faster Than Perceptions." *The New York Times*, February 19 (1989):20E.

Meyer, Thomas. "Date Rape: A Serious Campus Problem That Few Talk About." *Chronicle of Higher Education* 29(1984):15.

Myers, Martha A. and LaFree, Gary D. "The Uniqueness of Sexual Assault: A Comparison with Other Crimes." *Journal of Criminal Law and Criminology* 73(1982):1282–1305.

Nelson, Steven and Amir, Menachem. "The Hitch-Hiker Victim of Rape: a Research Report." *Victimology: A New Focus, 5,* Ed. Isreal Drapkin and Emilio Viano. Lexington, MA: D C Heath, 1975, pp. 47–64.

Oates, Joyce C. "Rape and the Boxing Ring." *Newsweek*, February 24 (1992):60–61.

Orcutt, James D. and Faison, Rebecca. "Sex-Role Attitudes Change and Reporting of Rape Victimization, 1973–1985." *The Sociological Quarterly* 29(1988):589–604.

Rapaport, Karen and Burkhart, Barry R. "Personality and Attitudinal Characteristics of Sexually Coercive College Males." *Journal of Abnormal Psychology* 93(1984):216–221.

Risin, Leslie I. and Koss, Mary P. "The Sexual Abuse of Boys." *Rape and Sexual Assault II*. Ed. Ann Wolbert Burgess. New York: Garland, 1988, pp. 91–104.

Russell, Diana. *Sexual Exploitation*. Beverly Hills, CA: Sage, 1984.

———. *The Politics of Rape*. New York: Stein and Day, 1975.

Sanday, Peggy Reeves. "The Socio-Cultural Context of Rape: A Cross Cultural Study." *Journal of Social Issues* 37(1981):5–27.

Sanders, William B. *Rape and Women's Identity*. Beverly Hills, CA: Sage, 1980.

Schaeffer, Ann. *Rape Supportive Attitudes: Effects of On-Campus Residence and Education*. Harrisonburg, VA: James Madison University Honors Thesis, 1992.

Schwendinger, Julia R. and Schwendinger, Herman. *Rape and Inequality.* Beverly Hills, CA: Sage, 1983.

Scully, Diana and Marolla, Joseph. "Rape and Vocabulary of Motive: Alternative Perspectives." *Rape and Sexual Assault.* Ed. Ann Wolbert Burgess. New York: Garland, 1985, pp. 294–312.

Searles, Patricia and Berger, Ronald J. "The Current Status of Rape Reform Legislation: An Examination of State Statutes." *Women's Rights Law Reporter* 12(1987):25–43.

Shortland, Lance R. and Goodstein, Lynne. "Just Because She Doesn't Want to Doesn't Mean It's Rape: An Experimentally Based Casual Model of the Perception of Rape in a Dating Situation." *Social Psychology Quarterly* 46(1983):220–232.

Smart, Carol. *Women, Crime, and Criminology: A Feminist Critique.* Boston: Routledge and Kegan Paul, 1976.

Sudnow, David. "Normal Crimes." *Social Problems* 12(1965):255–270.

Swift, Carolyn F. "The Prevention of Rape." *Rape and Sexual Assault.* Ed. Ann Wolbert Burgess. New York: Garland, 1985, pp. 294–312.

Thomas, Charles W. and Hepburn, John R. *Crime, Criminal Law, and Criminology.* Dubuque, IA: Wm. C. Brown, 1983.

Tuttle, Lisa. *Encyclopedia of Feminism.* New York: Facts on File Publications, 1986.

U.S. Department of Justice. *Criminal Victimization in the U.S.* Washington, D.C.: Bureau of Justice Statistics, 1992.

VonHentig, Hans. "The Sex Ratio." *Social Forces* 30(1951):443–449.

Williams, Joyce E. "Sex-Role Stereotypes, Women's Liberation and Rape: A Cross-Cultural Analysis of Attitudes." *Sociological Symposium* 25(1979):61–97.

Wolfgang, Marvin and Ferracuti, Franco. *The Subculture of Violence: Towards an Integrated Theory in Criminology.* London: Tavistock, 1967.

Wood, Pamela L. "The Victim in a Forcible Rape Case: A Feminist View." *American Criminal Law Review* 11(1973):512–525.

Yllo, Kersti and Finkelhor, David. "Marital Rape." *Rape and Sexual Assault.* Ed. Ann Wolbert Burgess. New York: Garland, 1985, pp. 146–158.

Chapter 12

Criminal Homicide

CRIMINAL HOMICIDE: TED BUNDY, PATRICK PURDY, AND JEFFREY DAHMER

On February 9, 1978, 12-year-old Kimberly Leach was kidnapped from the grounds of her junior high school. Three months later she was found dead—her body had been discarded in an abandoned pigsty. Three weeks prior to her abduction two Florida State University co-eds were found dead in their rooms, skulls crushed. These victims were linked by a common murderer, Ted Bundy. Bundy confessed to murdering as many as fifty women, many of whom he had raped and mutilated. Described as "the all-American boy murdering all-American girls" (Gelman and Gonzalez, 1989:66), Bundy was one of the most competent serial killers of our time.

On January 17, 1989, Patrick Purdy opened fire on a crowd of elementary school children in Stockton, California. Within minutes, over one hundred rounds had been fired from his AK-47 rifle. After the horrifying episode, five children were dead, 30 others had been wounded, and Purdy was dead by a self-inflicted bullet from his nine-millimeter pistol. Purdy was described as "an embittered drifter seemingly obsessed with war" (Church, 1989:23).

On July 22, 1991, Tracy Edwards, a young gay male, told police of his escape from a man who he described as a "freak . . . crazy." A man, Edwards told police, who had a human head in his refrigerator. The police arrested the alleged "freak" who told them that he had salted, peppered, tenderized, and used A-1 steak sauce on the body parts of three men he had killed and dismembered. "Like filet mignon," he told police (Mathews and Springer, 1992:31). Is this a scene in a movie sequel to "Silence of the Lambs?" Is this the confession of "Hannibal the Cannibal?" Unfortunately, the answers are no. The incidents described are real, and the confession is that of Jeffrey Dahmer. A jury found Dahmer to be sane, and he has received multiple life sentences for some of at least 15 known victims.

Killings by Ted Bundy, Patrick Purdy, and Jeffrey Dahmer were highly publicized. Most homicides are not. Rather, they are typically reported in the local news sections of the daily newspaper. However, highly publicized killings do affect public opinion and even the social policies that at-tempt to reduce the number of criminal homicides. Therefore, we will return to Ted Bundy, Patrick Purdy, and Jeffrey Dahmer in our discussion of two major policies aimed at reducing criminal homicides—the death penalty and gun control.

WHAT IS CRIMINAL HOMICIDE?

The Objectivist Conception

For objectivists, homicide is the killing of one human by another. Homicide includes a variety of behaviors that may be either non-deviant or deviant. In most societies killing to protect oneself or others is not deviant because these behaviors do not generally violate social norms. Killing is deviant only when it violates a society's norms. In societies that are regulated by law there are two forms of homicide—noncriminal and criminal. Both noncriminal and criminal homicide include legally specified subtypes.

Noncriminal homicide includes excusable and justifiable homicide. **Excusable homicides** are accidents or misfortunes where neither negligence nor unlawful intent are involved. For example, hunting accidents are often classified as excusable homicides. **Justifiable homicides** are killings that result from necessity or lawful duty to protect oneself or others. State executions and the killing of a suspect by a police officer in the line of duty are justifiable homicides. Killing in self-defense may be either excusable or justifiable homicide depending on specific state statutes and the circumstances surrounding the killing as perceived by legal authorities.

Criminal homicide includes murder and manslaughter. **Murder** is "the willful (non-negligent) killing of one human being by another" (FBI, 1990:8). Murder is punishable by life in prison and sometimes by death. Another type of murder is **felony murder.** Felony murders are killings that occur in the commission of a felony such as rape or robbery. These murders are often not premeditated, but the law treats them as if they were.

Offenders convicted of felony murder are punished the same as those who are convicted of murder.

Manslaughter may be non-negligent or negligent. **Non-negligent manslaughter** is an intentional killing that lacks the "malice of forethought" of murder. "Heat of passion" killings are common examples of non-negligent manslaughter. A "heat of passion" killing requires that the offender is adequately provoked by the victim and that the killing occurs before the offender's blood cools (Weinreb, 1983; Gardner, 1985). **Negligent manslaughter** is an unintentional killing that takes place during the commission of a misdemeanor such as reckless driving. For example, negligent manslaughter was the charge brought against the director and two workers of the movie *Twilight Zone* for the death of actors Vic Morrow and two children that resulted from a helicopter crash during the filming (Gardner, 1985).

Criminal homicide according to the FBI in the *Uniform Crime Report* includes murder and non-negligent manslaughter. Attempted murders are classified as aggravated assault. Objectivists frequently use the *Uniform Crime Reports* for the study of criminal homicide (rates, patterns, and trends). The *Uniform Crime Reports* also contain information about those who are arrested for criminal homicide, their age, sex, or race.

The Subjectivist Conception

Subjectivists would argue that the taking of another's life is criminal only when social audiences label it as such. From this perspective, even willful killing is not inherently murder. For example, consider the soldier's duty to kill. Few would regard the soldier's conduct as murder. The reason is that in war the definition of willful killing has changed. And after the war, definitions of what constitutes murder as opposed to approved killing may change again. The point is that even in

the case of an act such as killing the enemy in times of war, it is ultimately social audiences who will determine whether the act is legitimate or murder. Indeed, Galliher (1989:56) suggests "It may well be that if the Axis powers, rather than the Allies, had won World War II, instead of the Nuremberg trials, there might have been Washington trials to sentence Generals MacArthur and Eisenhower for war crimes and President Truman for genocide in ordering atomic bombings of Japan. Had this happened, it is likely that U.S.-born children would be learning different definitions of these men and their acts."

Consider one further illustration of criminal homicide as a definition rather than as a quality of behavior. From Colonial America to today, some women have chosen to terminate their pregnancy by abortion. Under British common law, abortion up to the late fourth-early fifth month of pregnancy, was a Colonial woman's right. For nineteenth-century U.S. women, the identical behavior was defined as non-negligent manslaughter. Today, U.S. women have the right to an abortion, given that it occurs in the first trimester of pregnancy. Definitions of abortion have ranged from a "woman's right" to "criminal homicide," even though the behavior is the same.

THE PREVALENCE OF CRIMINAL HOMICIDE

The ratio of reported criminal homicides to the actual number of criminal homicides is believed to be quite high. Therefore, the *Uniform Crime Reports* are the most widely used data for identifying the extent and patterns of criminal homicide.

Variations by Nation, Region, and Community

Criminal homicides are relatively rare crimes. Criminal homicides comprise only

1 percent of the total violent crimes in the United States. Yet, in the United States there is one criminal homicide every 22 minutes. In 1991, there were 24,703 reported criminal homicides, or 10.0 per 100,000 population. The number of criminal homicides reported increased 4 percent from 1990. The 1991 murder total increased 19 percent from 1987 (FBI, 1992:14).

How does the rate of criminal homicide in the United States compare with that of other nations? Differing definitions and methods of classification are limitations when comparing different societies as to the extent of criminal homicide. Even so, United Nations data provides useful information for cross-cultural comparisons. Table 12-1 contains the rate of "homicide and injury purposely inflicted by others as a cause of death" for nations reporting to the United Nations in 1983 and 1984.

The rates presented in Table 12-1 confirm the previous findings of high homicide rates in Latin American countries and low homicide rates in Northern and Eastern European countries (Wolfgang and Ferracuti, 1967; Clinard and Abbott, 1973; Archer and Gartner, 1984). Further demonstrated in Table 12-1 is the fact that the United States has a high criminal homicide rate compared to other industrial nations.

Criminal homicide rates vary within the United States by region and community. Historically, the Southern states have reported the highest criminal homicide rates. In 1991, the criminal homicide rate in the Southern states was 12 per 100,000; for the Western states, 10 per 100,000; 8 per 100,000 in the Northeastern states; and 8 per 100,000 in the Midwestern states (FBI, 1992:14). Explanations for the South's high rate are presented with other objectivist theories later in this chapter.

In 1991, metropolitan areas reported a rate of 11 per 100,000; cities outside of metropolitan areas reported a rate of 5 per 100,000; and

for rural areas, the rate was 6 per 100,000 (FBI, 1992:14). The growth of cities, however, does not inevitably generate higher criminal homicide rates. Japan, for example, is highly urbanized but criminal homicide rates are relatively low. Also, despite urban growth, Egypt, Ireland, the Maldives, and Turkey have reported declining rates of criminal homicide (Mueller, 1983). However, certain social conditions within a city may generate high criminal homicide rates. Historically, within urban communities criminal homicide has been highest in densely populated, physically deteriorated areas predominantly populated by racial minorities. Criminal homicide in Washington, D.C., "murder capital of the United States," and other large metropolitan areas is similarly located in the densely populated, physically deteriorated inner city where racial minorities are most highly concentrated. However, "the new U.S. murder capitals" are cities with populations under one million. Murder rates are rising faster in the medium-size cities than in the largest cities. A sample of medium-sized cities and their percent increase in murders from 1985 to 1990 include: Milwaukee, 126 percent; New Orleans, 101 percent; Jacksonville, FL, 84 percent; Memphis, 71 percent; Charlotte, 60 percent; Baltimore, 43 percent; Kansas City, MO, 38 percent; Cleveland, 23 percent (McCormick and Turque, 1991:17).

Criminal Homicide Offenders and Their Victims

Criminal homicide is more prevalent among certain populations (age, sex, race, and social class) within a society. In modern nations, criminal homicide primarily occurs among the young, minorities (racial, ethnic and religious), and males (Wolfgang and Zahn, 1983). Who are the criminal homicide offenders in the United States, and who are their victims?

Criminal Homicide Offenders.   The young, males, African Americans, and the poor are

TABLE 12.1   Homicide and Injury Purposely Inflicted by Others as a Cause of Death. Rates per 100,000 People, 1984 and 1989

COUNTRY	RATE PER 100,000	YEAR
El Salvador	39.9	1984
Puerto Rico	13.1	1989
United States*	8. 9	1988
Costa Rica	4.0	1988
Bulgaria	2.5	1989
Hungary	2.9	1989
Canada	2.1	1989
Israel	1.3	1987
Australia	2.4	1988
Austria	1.1	1989
Poland	2.1	1989
Portugal	1.5	1989
Hong Kong	1.2	1987
Belgium	2.1	1986
New Zealand	2.0	1987
Czechoslovakia	1.2	1989
France	1.1	1989
German Federal Republic	1.0	1989
Japan	0.6	1989
Netherlands	1.0	1989
Greece	1.1	1988
England/Wales	0.6	1989

*This is the FBI Uniform Crime Reports rate for murder and nonnegligent manslaughter and is not reported in the United Nations statistics. It is provided here for comparative purposes.

Source: United Nations, *Demographic Yearbook 1990.* New York: United Nations, 1992, pp. 454–473.

significantly overrepresented among criminal homicide offenders. This has been a consistent pattern for more than a decade (Riedel and Zahn, 1985). Eight-six percent of those arrested for criminal homicide are over 18 years old, with 55 percent under the age of 25. Ninety percent of arrestees are males. African Americans comprise 55 percent of those arrested for criminal homicide (FBI, 1992: 223–224). Although the *Uniform Crime Reports* do not contain information on the social class background of arrestees, studies using police data consistently find offenders to be poor and uneducated (Wolfgang, 1958; Swigert and Farrell, 1976; Williams, 1984).

Criminal Homicide Victims. Victims of criminal homicide, like their assailants, are most often young, male, black, and poor. The victims are slightly older than their assailants. Eighty-eight percent of the victims are over 18 years old. The high-risk group are aged 20 to 34 with 48 percent of all victims in this age range. This is true for both men and women, and African Americans and whites. With the exception of victims aged 4 and under, the majority of victims of all age groups die as a result of a gunshot wound. The majority of those aged 4 and under are killed by personal weapons, such as hands, fists, feet, and so on (FBI, 1992:18).

Seventy-eight percent of criminal homicide victims are males. Most often (87 percent of single victim/single offender situations) men are killed by other men. Men are also the primary victims of women who commit criminal homicide. Eighty-three percent of women's victims are men. Yet, 90 percent of all female victims are killed by a man (FBI, 1992:17).

African Americans constitute 50 percent of the criminal homicide victims. Criminal homicide is clearly intraracial. Ninety-three percent of the African-American victims are killed by African Americans and 85 percent of the white victims are killed by whites (FBI, 1992:17). The lifetime risk of becoming a homicide victim is far greater for African Americans than whites. For African-American males between the ages of 15 and 24, criminal homicide is the leading cause of death. Although homicide victims and offenders are primarily male, the percentage of African-American female homicide victims between 15 and 29 years of age is about three times greater than that of white males of the same age (U.S. Department of Health and Human Services, 1990:170–193).

Victim-Offender Relationship

The above information on the offenders and victims clearly suggest that criminal homicide is largely a same group phenomenon. That is, the young are slain by the young; men by other men; minorities by the same minorities; and both victim and offender generally share a low social class position.

Table 12-2 contains the percentage of murders by victim-offender relationships. Relatives, friends or neighbors, and acquaintances account for 47 percent of the known victim-offender relationships. The offender and victim were strangers in only 15.0 percent of known murders. Some researchers, however, suggest an increase in criminal homicides committed by strangers in the past

TABLE 12.2 Murder by Offender-Victim Relationship[1]

OFFENDER-VICTIM RELATIONSHIP	PERCENT OF TOTAL HOMICIDES
Immediate Family	10.7
Other Family	1.8
Acquaintances	26.0
Friend or Neighbor	8.1
Stranger	15.0
Unknown	38.4

[1]Derived from Department of Justice, Uniform Crime Reports, 1991. (Washington, DC: Government Printing Office, 1992 p. 19)

decade (Riedel, 1987; Zahn and Sagi, 1987). This increase may in part be reflected in the changing circumstances for murder. Table 12-3 contains the percentage of homicides by circumstance for the years 1987 through 1991.

The data in Table 12-3 demonstrate that arguments of various kinds continue as the most frequent circumstance for murder. Also evident in Table 12-3 is a slight decrease in argument murders and a slight increase in felony murders. Felony murders are more likely to involve strangers than any other murder circumstance. Therefore, the slight increase in felony murders and slight decline in argument murders may, in part, account for the increase of stranger murders observed by researchers. However, arguments between persons who are related or otherwise known to one another account for most murders.

Arguments are an important aspect of victim-precipitated homicide. Victim precipitation refers to the homicide situation in which the victim initiates an altercation, physical or verbal, that results in his or her death. Studies by Wolfgang (1958) and Curtis (1974) find about one-fourth of criminal homicides are victim-precipitated. In a small sample study (70 cases) of victim-offender interactions prior to homicide, Luckenbill (1977) reported nearly two-thirds as victim-precipitated. We

TABLE 12.3   Murder Circumstances, 1987–1991[1]

	PERCENT OF TOTAL HOMICIDES				
CIRCUMSTANCE	*1987*	*1988*	*1989*	*1990*	*1991*
Total	17,963	17,971	18,954	20,045	21,505
Percent[2]	100.0	100.0	100.0	100.0	100.0
Felony Total:	19.6	19.0	21.4	20.5	21.3
Robbery	9.3	8.3	9.1	9.2	10.2
Narcotics	4.9	5.6	7.4	6.5	6.2
Sex offenses	1.4	1.2	1.1	1.1	.9
Arson	.9	1.0	.9	.8	.6
Other felony	3.0	2.8	2.9	2.9	3.3
Suspected felony	1.1	1.3	.8	.7	.9
Argument total:	36.8	34.5	35.2	34.5	31.9
Romantic triangle	2.0	1.7	2.0	2.0	1.4
Property or money	2.6	2.7	2.9	2.6	2.4
Other argument	32.1	30.1	30.3	29.9	28.0
Miscellaneous non-felony types[3]	17.6	18.9	19.0	19.5	19.7
Unknown	24.9	26.3	23.7	24.7	26.0

[1]*Source:* Department of Justice, Uniform Crime Reports, 1991 (Washington, D.C.: Government Printing Office, 1992 p. 19)

[2]Because of rounding, percentages may not add to totals.

[3]Includes murders committed during brawls while offender was under the influence of alcohol and/or narcotics.

will discuss victim-premeditated homicide later as a micro-objectivist theory of homicide.

Our review of criminal homicide offenders and victims does not suggest "mayhem on the streets" by the diabolical or the deranged. Rather, real-life killers and their victims are most often persons who loved, or hated, each other—spouses, relatives, friends, and acquaintances. Where offender and victim were strangers, the offender's intent was often to commit another crime, such as robbery or assault. Also, the offenders and victims are most often among the most vulnerable in society—the young, the poor, the uneducated, and racial minorities.

But, what about the Ted Bundys, Patrick Purdys and Jeffrey Dahmers who systemati-cally kill over an extend period of time or go on a shooting spree? Who are they? Who are their victims? Why do they kill? Studies of multiple murder are sparse, and limited by small samples and weak methodology. However, a brief review of these studies provides some insights.

Mass and Serial Murder

Before we begin let us define our terms. Mass murder refers to the killing of a number of persons in one instance or in a relatively short period of time, perhaps minutes or a few hours. Patrick Purdy, who in Stockton, California, killed 5 children and wounded 30 others within minutes was a mass murderer. Serial murder refers to the killing of separate victims over a period of time with "cooling off periods" between victims (Busch and Cavanaugh, 1986:6). Ted Bundy, who killed 19 to 36 persons, and Jeffrey Dahmer, who killed at least 15 persons, were serial murders.

Busch and Cavanaugh (1986) provide a comprehensive review of the literature on multiple murder. They review 11 studies of multiple murder. Nine of these studies are an analysis of but one murderer. Another study has a sample of 8. However, included in their review is the exceptional study by Ressler and his colleagues of 36 multiple murderers. This sample size is significant given that the FBI estimates that there are about 45 multiple murders in the United States at any given point in time (Busch and Cavanaugh, 1986). Similarly, Levin and Fox (1985) estimate that about 35 multiple murders are presently operating across the U.S.

Who are mass and/or serial murders? Ressler and his colleagues report the following characteristics (cited in Busch and Cavanaugh):

> *male*
> *white*
> *average to bright average I.Q.*
> *poor academic performance*
> *unsteady employment history*
> *instability in family structure and family residence*
> *psychological or physical abuse as children (75%).*
> *(1986:14)*

Beyond these general characteristics, mass and serial killers come from diverse backgrounds. Seldom are they mentally ill. Levin and Fox (1985:47) suggest that they are more "evil than crazy." They are sociopaths who demonstrate little feeling for others or remorse for their behavior.

Ressler and his colleagues distinguish mass/serial murderers as disorganized offenders (66 percent of their sample) and organized offenders (33 percent). **Disorganized offenders** have fathers with unstable employment histories, were treated with hostility as children, have sexual problems (inhibitions, ignorance, or aversions), live alone, commit their crime close to home, and are frightened and confused at the time of their crime. **Organized offenders** are intelligent and skilled workers; have precipitating stress (financial, psychological, employment); are angry at the time of their murder; follow the events of their murders in the media; and change jobs or leave town (Busch and Cavanaugh, 1986:14-15).

Holmes and DeBurger identify four types of serial killers:

> Visionary killers *are often psychotic and respond to voices or visions of the types of persons to be killed.*
>
> Mission-oriented killers *seek to rid the world of undesirable persons, such as prostitutes or homosexuals.*
>
> Hedonistic killers *kill for thrill and excitement. For some, murder gives them sexual gratification.*
>
> Power/Control-oriented killers *seek pleasure by physically overpowering and dominating other persons (1988:58-59).*

Who are their victims? Research on mass or serial murder has failed to systematically identify any specific victim characteristics. However, serial killers very often seek victims who share particular physical or emotional characteristics. They also often prey on persons particularly vulnerable to attack, such as the young, runaways, hitchhikers, and prostitutes (Levin and Fox, 1985). According to Busch and Cavanaugh (1986), organized offenders kill more persons on the average than disorganized offenders (1.75 victims versus 4.04 victims). Also, disorganized offenders are more likely to know their victim prior to committing murder.

Research on mass and serial murder is rare, less specific, and less methodologically sound than is research on criminal homicide in general. To date, data "do not suggest a specific relationship between multiple murder and any particular psychiatric diagnosis or theory of criminology" (Busch and Cavanaugh, 1986:17).

However, beginning with Wolfgang's (1958) classic study of homicide in Philadelphia, research on homicide has been regular and systematic, and has produced relatively consistent findings on the patterns of criminal homicide. From this research tradition criminologists have developed alternative theories of criminal homicides. Here, we will review the prominent objectivist and subjectivist explanations of criminal homicide.

EXPLANATIONS OF CRIMINAL HOMICIDE

Macro-Objectivist Theories

In the United States, criminal homicide varies significantly by location and among different groups. Rates of criminal homicide are highest in large urban areas throughout the nation and in the South. Criminal homicide is also higher among young, African-American males of low socioeconomic status. The victim and offender are generally acquainted. Macro-objectivists attempt to explain these patterns of criminal homicide. Structural and cultural theories are the prominent theoretical traditions of the macro-objectivist approach. Structural theories explain differing rates of homicide between groups by their position (class, social status, authority, power) in the social structure. Subcultural theories examine the shared values and norms of a region or by group members that support violence to explain different rates of criminal homicide. We will examine two structural theories, external restraint theory and structural inequality theory; and two subcultural theories, subculture of violence theory and southern subculture of violence theory.

External Restraint Theory. Henry and Short (1954) and Gold (1958) offer compatible theories to explain social class differences in criminal homicide. Although their theories identify concepts suggestive of micro-objectivist social control theory ("external restraint" for Henry and Short) and social learning theory ("socialization" for Gold), both link criminal homicide to social organization. The motivation for violence is structurally induced frustration, and the degree of external restraint or type of socialization are determined by social class position. Therefore, these theories are most compatible with macro-objectivist strain theories (see Chapter 2).

Henry and Short (1954) argue that homicide is a distinct type of violent reaction to frustration. Suicide is another violent response to frustration. The strength of external restraint (the degree to which one must abide by the expectations of others) explains the direction of violence, murder or suicide. Where external restraint is high, others are seen as the source of one's frustration. Thus, violent responses are directed toward others (criminal homicide). If external restraints are weak, one's own inadequacies are seen as the source of frustration. Here, violent responses are directed inward (suicide).

According to Henry and Short, the degree of external restraint is determined by social class position. Without resources, power, authority, or status, persons in a low socioeconomic position are more externally constrained. Therefore, they are most likely to direct their lethal behavior outward. Henry and Short maintain that the degree of external restraint can also explain differing homicide rates for males and females and African Americans and whites. That criminal homicide rates are higher in the lower class and for African Americans supports their theory. Although other factors, such as physical stature and socialization, may account for low rates of criminal homicide for females, males do have much higher rates of suicide than females. This, too, is consistent with Henry and Short's external restraint theory.

Henry and Short also maintain that criminal homicide rates change for middle and lower class groups with fluctuations in the general economy. In times of economic recession, middle class persons are more likely to lose social status and authority than lower class persons. The loss of social standing leads to frustration for middle class people. They attribute their losses to external restraints imposed by economic recession, rather than to their own inadequacies. As a result, criminal homicide increases within the middle class during economic recessions. In contrast, lower class people experience relatively less loss during a recession and are therefore less frustrated. Criminal homicide within the lower class, then, decreases in recessionary periods.

On the other hand, economic prosperity results in an increase in criminal homicides within the lower class and a decrease in criminal homicides within the middle class. This pattern is also attributed to increased or decreased frustration due to the external restraint of economic prosperity. Middle class people are equipped with education, skills, and the material resources to take advantage of economic prosperity. Whereas, lower class persons are not; and therefore, their position relative to others worsens during economic prosperity. Losses or the failure to gain during economic prosperity creates heightened frustration for lower class people and, consequently, their anger is directed outwardly.

The major problem with external restraint theory is that correlations between broad social categories (class, race, gender) and rates of norm-violating behavior (criminal homicide, suicide) are merely suggestive. There has been no test of external restraint, per se, on murder or suicide.

Similarly, Gold (1958) attempts to explain the correlation between low socioeconomic status and high rates of criminal homicide. Elaborating on Henry and Short's theory, Gold identifies parental punishment as a type of external restraint. The type of punishment

is related to a person's social class position. For lower class children, physical punishment (spanking, hitting, slapping) is a form of external restraint. Their source of frustration is others (parents). Therefore, lower class children are socialized to direct their violence outward. Central to Gold's differential socialization argument is that types of punishment, external (physical) versus self-induced (guilt), are related to social class. However, not all studies on the use of physical punishment and social class find significant class differences (Thomas and Hepburn, 1983).

Structured Inequality Theory. The Thesis of structured inequality theory is that socioeconomic inequality is the source of much criminal violence (Blau, 1977; Blau and Blau, 1982; Blau and Schwartz, 1984). Where inequality is great, people become frustrated and develop feelings of relative deprivation. Relative deprivation means that individuals evaluate their position relative to others, and they see others are better off. This leads to frustration because they believe there is little they can do to improve themselves relative to others. Relative deprivation is particularly acute when socioeconomic inequality is rooted in an ascribed position, for example, race. When socioeconomic inequality is linked to an ascribed status, people view their low status position as inescapable, and feelings of relative deprivation are intensified. Racial inequality, then leads to "diffuse feelings of hostility" that manifest themselves in "impulsive acts of aggression" (Blau and Golden, 1986:15). Impulsive aggression is often expressed as interpersonal violence against convenient targets, such as family, friends, and among those who share residential, work, and leisure environments.

According to structural inequality theory, race-income inequality rather than poverty or racial composition of the population is the source of high rates of criminal violence. From an analysis of the 125 largest metropolitan places in the United States, Blau and Blau

(1982) found race-income inequality to be positively related to high rates of criminal violence. Furthermore, poverty and racial composition were not significantly related to high rates of criminal violence when the effect of race-income inequality was controlled. Blau and Blau (1982:126) concluded, "aggressive acts of violence seem to result not so much from lack of advantages as from being taken advantage of, not from absolute but from relative deprivation." In a follow-up study using these same data, but a different methodological procedure, Blau and Golden (1986) did not find the relationship between race-income inequality and high rates of criminal violence to be as strong as originally suggested. In addition, Blau and Golden (1986) found that a higher proportion of African Americans in metropolitan areas was significantly related to high rates of criminal violence.

More recent, Crutchfield (1989) examined the income inequality, relative deprivation relationship to high rates of criminal violence at the neighborhood level. That is, he tested the inequality hypothesis within a city, Seattle, Washington, rather than between cities. Furthermore, he argued that because employment is related to income, the relationship between income inequality and rates of criminal violence is a result of employment characteristics (unemployment rate, percent of full-time workers, and percent employed in low-paying jobs) rather than income inequality per se. When employment characteristics were controlled, the relationship between income inequality and violent crime rates was reduced. However, the relationship between income inequality and murder rates remained significant. Also recent, Balkwell (1990) found ethnic inequality to be a strong predictor of high homicide rates in metropolitan areas even after controlling for poverty, general income inequality, regional culture, race composition, and social disintegration.

The findings from cross-national studies of homicide rates also support Blau's structured inequality theory. The most consistent finding is that homicide rates are highest for countries with the greatest income inequality (Krahn, et al., 1986). However, Steven Messner (1989) discovered that economic discrimination was more strongly related to national homicide rates than income inequality. That is, countries with "intensive and pervasive" economic discrimination against social groups with ascribed characteristics (race, religion, ethnicity) have comparatively high homicide rates. Messner (1989:597) concluded that it is the "structuring of economic inequality on the basis of ascribed characteristics" that is the source of a society's high homicide rate. Messner's (1989) findings give strong support to Blau's (1977) thesis that where income inequality is rooted in ascribed positions, relative deprivation is acute and rates of interpersonal violence are high.

In sum, structured inequality theory suggests that income inequality is the major source of criminal violence. This is especially true where income inequality is based on ascribed characteristics. Research within the United States and between nations supports structured inequality theory, but suggests that income inequality better explains high murder rates than criminal violence in general.

Subculture of Violence Theory. Subcultures of violence are subgroups within a society whose members share values and norms that condone or demand violent behavior (Wolfgang and Ferracuti, 1967). Violence is a valued response to physical, symbolic, or verbal challenges. These values are learned and transmitted through socialization.

The subculture of violence explains variations in homicide rates between regions and groups in society. For example, Wolfgang and Ferracuti (1967) attribute high homicide rates among young, lower-class, African American males to a subculture of violence. Among this group, violence is "a part of the lifestyle"; it is "the theme of solving difficult problems or problem situations" which will "arise mostly within the subculture" (Wolfgang and Ferracuti, 1967:159). Official data on rates of criminal homicide, offender-victim characteristics, and victim precipitation are suggestive of a subculture of violence. However, studies of attitudes that condone violence do not support the subculture of violence thesis. Ball-Rokeach (1973), from a national study of adult males and a group of incarcerated felons, discovered a weak relationship between attitudes that condone violence and actual violent behavior. Also, Doerner (1978) reported that whites are more tolerant of assault and more likely to have been assaulted than African Americans. Yet, African Americans are more involved in homicide. The relationship between violent attitudes and violent behavior, and to homicide in particular, has not been established.

Southern Subculture of Violence Theory. Some authors claim that norms condoning violence are more prevalent in the South (Hackney, 1969; Gastil, 1971; Ayers, 1984). Gastil (1971) attributes the south's high homicide rates to a "violent tradition" in Southern culture. This violent tradition may condone killing for a variety of situations, or it may indirectly raise criminal homicide rates because of the value placed on weapons possession or the acceptance of hostile family and class relations, which in turn lead to criminal homicide. Regardless of its content, Gastil attributes the relatively high homicide rates in the United States to the spread of Southern culture, "Southernness." Gastil provides evidence supporting the relation between southernness and criminal homicide rates.

The most recent version of the Southern culture of violence theory is Ayers' (1984) "culture of honor" thesis. The culture of honor is "a system of values within which you have exactly as much worth as others

confer upon you" (Ayers, 1984:13). Confirmation of worth, then, requires a constant assertion of self through aggressive behavior. Honor, a cultural trait inherited from English aristocracy, was originally the sole possession of adult white men. However, by the twentieth century, the economic and industrial transformations of the south provided conditions for the evolution of "dignity," the cultural antithesis of honor. Dignity "the conviction that each individual at birth possessed an intrinsic value" (Ayers, 1984:19) is expressed individually by self-control rather than self-assertion. This is expressed socially by a preference for impersonal justice (formal legal system) rather than personal justice (vengeance or vigilante violence). In today's South, as elsewhere, honor dictates norms of conduct among those groups most removed from economic and political rewards, and where impersonal justice is suspect. Among the most representative of these groups are young, African-American, lower-class males.

Several researchers have criticized Gastil's methodology and attribute the South's high homicide rates to structural factors, such as poverty, socioeconomic, and racial-income inequality (Loftin and Hill, 1974; Blau and Blau, 1982; Parker, 1989; Balkwell, 1990). Ayers has been criticized on similar grounds (Carter, 1986). Also, the South does not differ significantly from other regions on the ownership of handguns, which is the principle firearm used in criminal homicide. Rifle and shotgun ownership account for the South's higher rate of firearm ownership (Wright, Rossi, and Daly, 1983).

However, some researchers continue to find a relationship between southernness and homicide rates (Messner, 1983; Huff-Corzine, Corzine, and Moore, 1991; Lester, 1991). Ellison (1991) provides a major insight to the issue of southernness and the approval of interpersonal violence. He found that native southerners condone violence in defensive and retaliatory circumstances more than natives of nonsouthern areas. He also found attitudes that condone defensive or retaliatory violence where related to the Old Testament theology that stresses moral judgment and divine punishment. Such a theology is popular in much of the South. There are two major problems regarding Ellison's findings and southern homicide rates. First, he only measured approval of low-level violence, such as beatings, not killing. Second, he only examined attitudes toward violence directed against strangers, not family, friends, or acquaintances. It is, therefore, incumbent on future research on southern violence to differentiate between types of violence and targets of violence (Ellison, 1991:1234).

Two main difficulties remain with subcultural theories of violence. First, subcultural theorists devote considerable attention to describing those who share the subculture and to the consequences of subcultural affiliation. But, scant attention is paid to defining the subculture's content or demonstrating its existence. Second, theorists infer violent norms from high rates of violence among certain groups or regions, and then explain the high rates of violence as products of violence-supporting norms. This circular reasoning is a *tautology* (something true by virtue of its logic alone and, therefore, untestable) and scientifically unacceptable. A subculture of violence must be identified independent of, and established prior to, its consequence (high rates of homicide) if it is to become a valid explanation.

Micro-Objectivist Theories

Micro-objectivist theories center on the properties of social relationships and social interactions that account for the emergence of homicide episodes. Here we will review two micro-objectivist theories: asymmetric social relations theory of violence and victim-precipitation theory. Asymmetric social relations theory attributes violence to the hierarchical

structure of interpersonal relationships. Victim-precipitation theory locates the source of violent episodes in the dynamics of social interaction.

Asymmetric Social Relations Theory. The hierarchical structure of dominance (superordinate and subordinate) in established personal relationships (family, friends, and acquaintances) is viewed by some sociologists as a source of violent behavior (Straus, Gelles and Steinmetz, 1980; Ball-Rokeach, 1980; Thomas and Hepburn, 1983). Superordinates direct violence against subordinates to maintain their dominance. Subordinates direct violence against superordinates to reduce dominance. Violent behavior, then, is a maintenance or change maneuver depending on one's position in the relationship (superordinate or subordinate). The probable direction and motivation for violence depends on the degree of dominance in the relationship. For example, Ball-Rokeach (1980) suggests that the greater the dominance, the greater the probability of violence by the superordinate against the subordinate. As the degree of dominance lessens, superordinates use violence to regain their position and subordinates use violence to reduce dominance.

The relationship between gender and criminal homicide fits the probable maneuvering suggested by Ball-Rokeach (1980). Men are accustomed to superordinate positions and, therefore, are more likely to maneuver to keep their superordinate position or maneuver to reduce dominance where they are subordinates. Also, in male/female relationships, men are generally superordinates. When women (subordinates) are victims of homicide, nine times out of ten they are killed by a man. Remember, the theory predicts that where dominance is high (as in male/female relationships), violence is by the superordinate against the subordinate (Ball-Rokeach, 1980). On the other hand, when women (subordinates) kill, they generally kill men (superordinates). According to Ball-Rokeach's theory, this suggests a maneuver within an established relationship to reduce dominance.

Victim-Precipitation Theory.   Homicide situations where the victim initiates an altercation that results in his or her death are termed victim-precipitated homicides (Wolfgang, 1958; Curtis, 1974; Luckenbill, 1977). Briefly stated, Luckenbill identifies a six-stage process characterizing the typical murder:

1. *The victim challenges the offender, either physically, symbolically or verbally.*
2. *The offender interprets the victim's action as offensive or threatening.*
3. *The offender retaliates to "save face."*
4. *The victim then retaliates. At this stage, the audience often encourages violence, increasing the potential for violence.*
5. *Victim and offender are now committed to violence, having passed up "outs" that were earlier available.*
6. *The victim is dead or dying. The offender flees, waits for the police, or is restrained by others until the police arrive* (1977:179–85).

Not all episodes of interpersonal violence result in death. The first five stages of Luckenbill's victim-precipitated homicide are common for many non-lethal assaults. Research is needed on victim and offender characteristics and audience reactions that distinguish between interpersonal assault and victim-precipitated homicide. For example, Luckenbill (1977) found that in about one-half of the victim-precipitated homicides the victim and offender had had a previous altercation. Many victim-precipitated homicides, then, may not be as episodic as they at first appear. Previous altercations might influence the offender's interpretation of the victim's present behavior as offensive. What victim and offender now perceive as appropriate "saving face" maneuvers or appropriate "outs" may be affected by previous altercations. Similarly, present audience reactions may, in part,

hinge on their knowledge of previous altercations.

Further research on victim-precipitated homicide found that the victims were more likely to engage in evasive action and actually attacked less often than the offenders (Felson and Steadman, 1983). Victims, perhaps, often do not share with offenders the values supporting lethal violence as an appropriate response to "saving face." This finding suggests that *intra*personal properties, such as values and norms, are important factors influencing the motivation, direction and consequence of *inter*personal violence. Identification of *intra*personal properties that structure the *inter*personal processes leading to victim-precipitated homicide may be an important direction for future research.

In sum, micro-objectivists focus on the structure of interpersonal relationships and the dynamics of interaction that lead to episodes of homicide. Micro-objectivists have not provided a general theory of homicide. Rather, they have attempted to explain certain homicide situations. Here, we reviewed two important homicide situations. They were (1) homicides within established personal relationships, such as families and friendships, and (2) victim-precipitated homicides.

Macro-Subjectivist Theories

Interest Group Theories.   Interest group theories focus on the social, economic, and political processes from which definitions of deviance are created. The question to be addressed by interest group theories is "how does killing become criminal homicide?" The answer according to interest group theory is to be found in the process by which legal definitions are made. Here, we will discuss the neo-Marxian argument that the definitions of criminal homicide protect the interest of the powerful. Also, we will present a case history of abortion laws in the United States to illustrate how special interests translate events into legal definitions which create crime and criminals.

Class Bias in the Definition of Criminal Homicide. According to neo-Marxists different types of violent behavior occur in capitalist societies. The types of violence follow distinct class lines, and the laws that regulate these violent behaviors reflect class interests. Neo-Marxists identify four types of violence: interpersonal, organized, state, and systematic violence (Michalowski, 1985:278–79).

Interpersonal violence is comprised of reactive personal expressions of frustration that are seldom planned but instead occur in immediate situations. Victim-precipitated homicides and killings associated with the commission of some other "street" crime such as robbery are examples of interpersonal violence.

Organized violence consists of planned acts by one or more individuals who use violence as a means to "resolve a problem, achieve a goal, or make a public statement" (Michalowski, 1985:278). Acts of organized violence range from gang "turf" wars to terrorism. Most organized violence is symbolic and victims are impersonal such as the killing of rival gang members or "pigs."

State violence is "politically authorized violence" (Michalowski, 1985:279). The use of violence, even killing, by police and national guard in the line of duty is state violence. State violence is legal. A killing by a police officer in the line of duty is "justifiable homicide."

Systematic violence encompasses the "violent outcomes" that result from the institutions and enterprises that support the economic arrangements of capitalist society. Included as systematic violence are the profit-seeking actions of decisionmakers within established institutions that result in disability, disease, and death. The purposive manufacture of unsafe and potentially lethal products as well as the exposure of workers to unhealthy and potentially lethal work environments by industry are two examples of systematic violence.

Interpersonal and organized violence are disproportionately committed by persons in the lower socioeconomic classes. When these behaviors result in death, the majority are legally defined as criminal homicides (murder and non-negligent manslaughter). Systematic and state violence, on the other hand, are committed by state officials and economic elites.

In terms of the number of deaths, killings by the powerful far exceed the number of deaths that result from murder and non-negligent manslaughter (Michalowski, 1985:279). Killings by the police in the line of duty are legally "justifiable." But who do police kill and how often? In most instances, their victims are those whose actions oppose oppressive social, economic, or political arrangements, or those who resist the repression of police force. Also, deaths resulting from established industrial or business practices are seldom defined as murder or non-negligent manslaughter. In the legal sense, deaths resulting from industrial and business practices generally are considered to lack criminal intent. Corporate structures, for example, are complex organizations that make the connection between the kind of specific intent (premeditated or deliberate) required for criminal homicide and its consequence (death) distant and complex. Most often there is no "smoking gun." Rather, death most often results from rationally calculated decisions to maximize profit.

According to the neo-Marxist perspective, state officials (police and national guard) kill to protect political and economic arrangements that serve the interests of the powerful. Economic elites kill in the pursuit of profit. Systematic and state violence is more widespread and no less evil than the interpersonal and organized violence committed by members of the lower class. Rather, criminal homicide laws as written and applied label the violent among the lower class as murderers. It is by the same law that state officials and economic elites elude criminal labels for their killing.

Abortion: A Case History.   Mohr's (1978) historical analysis of abortion laws illustrates how and why abortion became criminal homicide. British common law was the rule regulating abortion in early America. According to common law, a criminal destruction of the fetus could occur only after quickening (fetal movement). Quickening generally occurs late in the fourth or early in the fifth month of gestation. The crime of abortion, as the expulsion of a quickened child, was different from intended killing and punished much less severely. The first U.S. abortion laws emerged between 1821 and 1841. These laws attempted to regulate methods for inducing abortion and persons who performed abortions. The laws did not attempt to dissuade women from having abortions and prescribed no punishment for the woman herself. Mohr (1979:43) characterizes these early laws as "malpractice indictments" because they were an effort by legislators and physicians to control the practice of medicine.

In the early nineteenth century, abortion was viewed as a desperate act by desperate women. It was an unmarried woman's means of saving her reputation. By the mid-nineteenth century, abortion had become more widespread and increasingly used by middle-class, white, married, Protestant women as a means of limiting family size. These changes were occurring at a time when a new class of professional physicians was emerging. Under the auspices of the American Medical Association (AMA), a physician's crusade against abortion was launched in the late 1850s. The crusade culminated in laws that made killers of those who had or administered abortions. These strict anti-abortion laws were enacted throughout the United States between 1860 and 1880, and remained unaltered in principle until the Supreme Court decision legalizing abortion in 1973 (*Roe* v. *Wade*).

Physicians' interest in anti-abortion legislation was both professional and personal. Professionally, anti-abortion laws provided legal punishment to healers and midwives who would practice abortion. Legal punishments also facilitated control over medical practice by organized physicians. Since any healer could practice medicine, the AMA's code of ethics was unenforceable. Expulsion from the profession did not prohibit a healer from the practice of medicine. Unable to police themselves, physicians were unable to elevate the practice of medicine to a profession. The anti-abortion campaign provided public support for the organized physicians' portrayal of abortion as a practice of hacks, quacks, and immoral profit seekers. Anti-abortion laws provided state power which enabled a new class of emerging professional physicians to control the practice of medicine. The anti-abortion campaign also provided organized physicians an opportunity to regain their historical position as society's policymakers.

Personal interests too motivated organized physicians to crusade for anti-abortion laws. Most physicians were, in fact, morally opposed to abortion (Mohr, 1978). Mohr (1978) suggests that physicians, more than others, realized the "quickening" had no significance in indicating a stage of gestation. Nativism was another personal reason shared by most organized physicians. These physicians were mostly white, native-born, and Protestant. The rise of abortion among white, married, Protestant women was contributing to a significant decline in native birth rates. Mohr (1978:167) notes, ". . . Protestants' fears about not keeping up with the reproductive rates of Catholic immigrants played a greater role in the drive for anti-abortion laws in nineteenth-century America than Catholic opposition to abortion did." Also, in their "blatant nativism" organized physicians became one of the "most defensive groups" on women's suffrage. Although many physicians blamed men for driving the "weaker sex" to abortion, most physicians sought to prevent women from putting society at risk by denying their "biologically determined social imperative" (Mohr, 1978: 169–70).

The physicians' abortion crusade of the mid-nineteenth century created definitions (legislation) of abortion that transformed a woman's right into an act of intentional killing (manslaughter). The resulting abortion legislation revoked the quickening doctrine, made killers of those women who had abortions, and criminalized the advertising of abortion and abortion products.

Today powerful interest groups are actively lobbying for legal reform in abortion laws. Pro-Choice advocates believe the abortion laws must protect a woman's exclusive right to make the abortion decision. Pro-Life advocates believe that abortion laws must protect the unborn by criminalizing most, if not all, abortions. Given the composition of the Supreme Court at present, many are predicting new abortion laws that will criminalize most women who choose an abortion (Kantrowitz and Carroll, 1991). Will history repeat itself? Will a woman's right once again be transformed into an act of criminal homicide? Cases to overturn Roe v. Wade are already in the pipeline.

Organizational Theories. According to these theories, organizational structures and policies affect the routine activities of control agents who define lethal acts as criminal homicide, process alleged homicide offenders, and produce official rates of criminal homicide. One example may be found in the organization of the nation's court system. Organizational theorists suggest that the bu-

reaucratic organization of the criminal court may influence how a particular killing is defined (murder, non-negligent manslaughter, justifiable homicide, and so on) more than the actual *behavior* that occurred.

According to Blumberg (1967), the organizational imperative of the bureaucratic court is *efficiency*. Efficiency is maximized by cooperation in plea bargaining. Guilty pleas maximize the efficient processing of cases and benefit both prosecutors and defense attorneys. "Success" for the prosecutor is minimization of time and expense, and a certain conviction. These are guaranteed by a guilty plea. Also, defense attorneys persuade their client that they have received a "special deal" in exchange for their plea of guilty. For example, the defendant may plead guilty to a lesser offense or have some of the charges dropped.

The negotiation of guilty pleas by attorneys and prosecutors is streamlined by the practice of viewing any particular offense as a "normal crime" (Sudnow, 1965). Normal crimes are ". . . those occurrences whose typical features, e.g., the ways they usually occur and the characteristics of persons who commit them (as well as the typical victims and typical scenes), are known and attended to by the P.D. (public defender)" (Sudnow, 1965:212). Details of the act and actor are used by the prosecutor to place the present case into a category of "events of this sort" or "such cases" (Sudnow, 1965:130). Once defined as typical of "events of this sort" the prosecutor can offer a "standard deal" for the particular case at hand. Standard deals are efficient for processing a large number of cases with assembly-line speed.

Many criminal homicides are normal crimes, for which standard deals are exchanged for guilty pleas. The characterization of homicidal events may vary by prosecutor and court jurisdiction. However, convictions for criminal homicides are often preceded by a negotiated plea of guilty. The main participants in the bargain, prosecutor and defense attorney, deal according to the organizational demands of efficiency. Adherence to organizational norms guides control agent's placement of a particular act of killing into specified legal categories, for example, murder, non-negligent manslaughter, reckless homicide, self-defense, and so on. According to the organizational theorist, official rates of criminal homicide reflect the practices of control agents more than actual nature and extent of criminal homicide.

Micro-Subjectivist Theories

Micro-subjectivists focus on the social processes by which others (the public, witnesses, police, juries) define some acts as murder and label some actors as murderers. From the micro-subjectivist point of view, murder depends more on who the actors (victim and perpetrator) were than on the act itself (premeditated or deliberate killing). The central research question is: Do those who define murder focus more on who the victim and/or perpetrator were than on quality of the act? If so, what characteristics of the victim, perpetrator or defining agents themselves produce a definition of murder and the label of murderer? Micro-subjectivists are also concerned with the effect of deviant labels on one's self-identity and subsequent behavior. Does the label murderer produce future acts of violent aggression on the part of those so labeled? This question is central to a labeling theory of violence.

Audience Definitions of Murder. To date, micro-subjectivists have not identified the properties of the process by which others come to define an act of killing as murder. Nor have they identified the social characteristics of victims, perpetrators, or defining agents that affect the definition of murder or the label murderer. However, some real-life cases can be used to illustrate the micro-subjectivist view, i.e., murder is not murder until

it is defined as such by others and, "murderers" are people so labeled. For example:

On April 26, 1989, Rudy Linares disconnected his 15-year old son from his life support system and held hospital workers at gunpoint until his son died. Rudy Linares was charged with murder. The grand jury would not indict Linares for murder. On May 18, 1989, the state prosecutor's office announced it would not prosecute Linares for murder. Linares' behavior was "inappropriate under law," but "understandable from the standpoint of a parent," commented State's Attorney Cecil Partee (Associated Press, 1989:1).

Legally euthanasia (mercy killing) is murder. Mercy is not recognized by the law as a mitigating circumstance for killing. In the case above there was *behavior* that legally constituted murder, but there was no *definition* of murder. Also, there was a perpetrator whose intent (behavior) was premeditated or, at least, deliberate, but there was no criminal label of murderer.

To appreciate the micro-subjectivist point of view, imagine yourself as one of the grand jurors in the case above. Now ask yourself, if the perpetrator had been a friend of the victim rather than his father would you define what happened as murder? If not, ask yourself, what if the perpetrator had been a sympathetic hospital worker who mercifully chose to end the victim's and family's suffering? Is it now murder? In these questions, the act has remained the same. Only the actor (perpetrator) has been changed. Does changing the actor cause you to alter your view of what happened? Could what happened depend on the actor (perpetrator) more than on the act itself?

These questions are, of course, rhetorical. They are intended to illustrate the subjective process by which social actors define an act as an example of a general kind of behavior, in this case, how a killing becomes murder. Murder is not inherent in an intended act of killing, as objectivists suggest it to be. Rather, micro-subjectivists view murder as a meaning created by social actors to understand what happened. And, murderers are persons so labeled. The label murderer itself implies the meaning of an evil and dangerous person. Central to the micro-subjectivist view is that the created and imposed meanings of murder and murderer depend more on the characteristics of actors (victims, perpetrators, and defining agents) than on the nature or consequence of acts of killing.

Labeling Theory. The effect of official labels, for example, convicted murderer, on one's further criminal behavior is the cornerstone of labeling theory. The logic is as follows: (1) once actors have been labeled murderers, they see themselves and are seen by others as violent and dangerous; (2) a set of behaviors consistent with the actor's new identity (as violent and dangerous) emerge; and (3) further violent behavior results from the actor's new identity.

Studies on the law violations by paroled first degree murders to not suggest a dramatization of evil. On the contrary, convicted murders are much less likely to violate parole than non-murderers, and rarely do they again engage in lethal violence (Waldo, 1970). Colin Sheppard (1977:77–8) provides substantial evidence of this. In a 9-year study of 342 California murderers, only 10.8 percent violated parole. Only one murdered again. In Michigan, 4 of 175 murderers violated parole over a twenty-five year period, and none killed again. A thirty-one year study of 63 New York murderers on parole reported 3 parole violations with no killings. In Ohio, 15 of 273 paroled murderers violated their parole over 20 years, and no one killed again.

These studies do not provide a direct test of the effect of labeling. Such a test would require a measure of behavior prior to the label. However, these studies fail to support the notion that the label murderer is related

to a career of confirming behavior, that is, subsequent killings.

SOCIAL POLICY

Those who commit criminal homicides comprise a diverse group of individuals. How then do we identify potential killers? If we cannot identify potential criminal killers, perhaps, we can control the circumstances that lead them to kill. But, the most typical circumstances of criminal homicide is interpersonal conflict between intimates, friends, or acquaintances. What legislation would you suggest to regulate interpersonal relations?

In the absence of answers, there has been a reliance on two fairly traditional approaches to the problem of criminal homicide. The first is the death penalty and the second is gun control.

The Death Penalty

To the tune of "On Top of Old Smokey," spectators sang: "He bludgeoned the poor girls/ all over the head/Now we're all ecstatic/Ted Bundy is dead." In celebration, signs were held high and proud: "This Buzz is for You," "Roast in Peace," "Thank God It's Fryday," "Too Bad/So Sad/You're Dead Ted" (Gelman and Gonzalez, 1989:66).

The celebration of Ted Bundy's execution was an exception, but for many Americans there is something "right" about the execution of murderers. Arguments for or against the death penalty are heated. These arguments sway between science and morality; and they are often intended to persuade or dissuade others.

Here, we make no attempt to persuade or dissuade on the use of capital punishment. Rather, we focus on the effectiveness of the death penalty. Its effectiveness depends on its purpose. Not all agree on the purpose(s) of the death penalty. However, arguments that the death penalty deters murder or that it is a just dessert can be dissected by scientific evidence.

Deterrence suggests that the execution of convicted murderers will deter others from committing murder. The deterrent effect should result in decreasing murder rates. At best, "the current evidence on the deterrent effect of capital punishment is inadequate for drawing any substantive conclusions" (Blumstein, Cohen, and Nagin, 1978:62). At worst, the death penalty may increase murder rates (Bowers and Price, 1980b; Bowers, 1984). This is known as the *brutalization effect*. However, the most consistent finding from research over the past six decades is that the death penalty has no measurable effect as a deterrent to murder (Peterson and Bailey, 1988).

Some proponents of the death penalty counter the findings of no deterrent effect by arguing that the way the death penalty is administered negates its effectiveness as a deterrent for murder. One argument is, if the death penalty is to deter murder, then, executions should be highly publicized. Indeed, Stack (1987) reported a decline in the rate of murder during the month following a highly publicized execution. Less publicized executions were not followed by a decline in the rate of murder. However, Stack only investigated the effect of publicity on murder rates during a period of time when the rate of executions were declining and murder rates were increasing (1950–1980). Therefore, Stack's investigation did not examine changes in murder relative to changes in executions and their associated publicity. Stack also overlooked three highly publicized executions that occurred during the 1950s (Bailey and Peterson, 1989). A more systematic investigation of the effect of execution publicity on murder rates was done by Bailey and Peterson (1989). These researchers extended the years examined to include periods when execution rates were increasing and murder rates were decreasing (1940s and 1980s). They also added the three highly publicized executions that Stack had overlooked. Bailey and Peterson (1989) found no evidence that execution publicity influenced murder rates during the time that Stack had originally investigated (1950–1980) nor during the extended time of their investigation (1940–1986).

Proponents of the death penalty have also argued that the death sentence is given too seldom to act as a deterrent. The relationship between the number of death sentences and murder rates has been investigated. Contrary to the deterrence argument, Peterson and Bailey (1988) found that as the number of death sentences increased, the murder rate increased.

However, the majority of those who support the death penalty would continue their support even if it had no deterrent effect (Ellsworth and Ross, 1983). For many, the death penalty is simply *just desserts*. Effective just desserts, however, requires a fair (consistent) imposition of the death penalty. Is execution just desserts if imposed in an arbitrary and capricious manner?

One attorney described the imposition of the death penalty as a "crooked lottery." He noted, "If you have ten convicted murderers and pick three names out of a hat, then eliminate one because he is white and one because the murder victim is not white, we cannot say that the remaining murderer, who is executed, has gotten his just desserts" (Brunk, 1983:27). The selection of a handful of persons for execution from the thousands of convicted murderers is arbitrary (Bowers and Pierce, 1980a; Bowers, 1983; Bedeau and Radelet, 1987). Those awaiting execution cannot be distinguished from those sentenced for life by the seriousness of their crime. Also, accomplices in the same murder may receive different sentences (one life, the other death). Discrimination, too, occurs in death penalty sentences. People who kill whites are more likely to receive the death sentence than are those who kill African Americans (Paternoster, 1983; Gross and Mauro, 1988). The greatest chance of receiving a sentence of death occurs when an African American kills a white (Baldus, Pulaski, and Woodworth, 1983).

The death penalty is ineffective for reducing criminal homicide rates, and its arbitrary and discriminatory imposition renders it ineffective as just desserts. According to Gallup Poll surveys during the past decade, the death penalty is supported by about 75 percent of Americans. Also, executions have increased steadily during the 1980s (Bailey and Peterson, 1989) and few, if any, constitutional challenges appear on the horizon. Today, there are over 2,000 people awaiting execution. Since 1976, more than 120 people have been executed in 36 states in the United States (Greenfield, 1990).

Aside from the question of the effectiveness of the death penalty, there is controversy concerning the execution of juvenile offenders.

The Execution of Juveniles. Terry Roach, seventeen and mentally retarded, was sentenced to die in the electric chair for his involvement in the murder of two teenage youths. Attempts for clemency failed. At age twenty-five, Terry Roach was executed. David Brunk, an attorney for Terry, recounts the horrifying realities surrounding Terry's final hours:

I read to him in his cell, and it was like reading to a child at bedtime. When his family minister came, Terry asked which prayers would work best at getting him into heaven. That was the mental level on which he was operating. Justice and retribution were concepts beyond his grasp. There was no moral component to his thinking, and that's what immaturity is. It made very real to me that putting an immature person, a kid, into that inexorable process of death is very different from doing it to an adult. It's very dehumanizing to do it to anybody, but it's

something else again to do it to a kid. (Seligson, 1986:6)

In the United States 281 juvenile offenders have been put to death (Bartollas, 1990). As of October 1986, thirty-three juveniles were awaiting execution throughout the United States. The execution of juveniles raises important moral and legal questions. Equally important is that, "America may be alone in the world in executing its young" (Seligson, 1986:5). However, it was not until 1989 that the U.S. Supreme Court ruled directly on the constitutionality of executing juveniles. On June 26, 1989, the Supreme Court rules that the execution of 16 and 17 year olds does not constitute "cruel and unusual punishment" *(Stanford v. Kentucky and Wilkins v. Missouri).* This ruling means that it is now up to the individual states of the United States whether to execute juveniles or not.

Gun Control

The Stockton massacre where Patrick Purdy fired into an elementary schoolyard, killing five and wounding 29, with an AK-47 assault rifle started a new wave of city and state gun control legislation. Within months of the Stockton massacre, President George Bush placed a temporary import ban on semiautomatic assault rifles (AK type weapons and Uzis).

Clearly, there is an association between firearms and criminal homicide. According to the *Uniform Crime Reports* (FBI, 1992), 64 percent of all criminal homicides involve the use of a firearm. This percent has remained about the same for the past five years. Handguns are the preferred firearm for murder. In 1991, 77 percent of all firearm-related homicides were committed with handguns. This statistic also has remained the same over the past five years (FBI, 1992).

The number of Americans killed by handguns is staggering. Thus, it is not surprising that some researchers attribute increased homicides to the increasing number of handguns (Fisher, 1976; Farley, 1980; McDowall, 1991). What is surprising is the finding that the availability of guns has no effect on the victim's probability of death in threatening or hostile encounters. Kleck and McElrath (1991) report that, in hostile interactions, gun possession reduces the probability of an attack; and, in the case of an attack, reduces the probability of injury. If injury does occur, gun possession increases the probability of death. However, Kleck and McElrath (1991: 688) conclude: "The effects of guns, however, are very small when one assesses the overall impact, both positive and negative, at all stages of violent incidents."

The strongest gun control laws impose mandatory sentences for unlawful possession of a firearm or for the use of firearms in the commission of a crime. Massachusetts' Bartly-Fox law requires a one-year jail sentence for anyone in possession of an unlicensed firearm. A Boston study of murder and robbery following the Bartly-Fox law reported a reduction in homicides with firearms. The researchers, however, did not attribute this reduction to the mandatory sentence. Rates for similar crimes (homicide and robbery with firearms) also dropped in cities with no gun control laws during that time (Pierce and Bowers, 1981). In subsequent evaluations of the Bartly-Fox law, researchers have concluded that gun control laws have little preventive effect on homicides (Wright, Rossi, and Daly, 1983; O'Carroll, et al., 1991).

A mandatory prison sentence for those who commit a crime with a firearm is also unsuccessful for reducing firearm related homicides. Studies of mandatory sentencing in Michigan and Florida have not found a relationship between these laws and a decline in firearm related homicides (Loftin and McDo-

wall, 1981, 1984). A mandatory prison sentence added to a sentence for criminal homicide which is already long and harsh is not likely to be perceived by an offender as threatening (Loftin, Heumann, and McDowall, 1983).

SUMMARY

There are both objectivist and subjectivist definitions of criminal homicide. Objectivists prefer legal definitions of criminal homicide. Legally, there are criminal and noncriminal homicides. Criminal homicides include murders and non-negligent manslaughters. *Murder* is the willful killing of one human by another. *Non-negligent manslaughter* is an unpremeditated killing that lacks the criminal intent of murder, for example, a *heat of passion* killing. Heat of passion killings require that the offender is adequately provoked by the victim and that the killing occurs before the offender's blood cools. Noncriminal homicide includes excusable and justifiable homicide. *Excusable homicide* is a killing that results from an accident or misfortune. *Justifiable homicide* is a killing that results from lawful duty to protect oneself or others. Subjectivists argue that the killing of one human by another is criminal homicide only when social audiences label it as such. The murderer is one who is so labeled. The social characteristics of those it has been alleged have committed criminal homicide (the young, males, African Americans, the poor) reflect the labeling activities of others, rather than revealing the true identity of those who kill.

Criminal homicides comprise only one percent of America's violent crimes. However, the U.S. homicide rate is high compared to other industrial nations. The highest rates are reported in Latin American countries.

The rate of criminal homicide is highest in the South and in the metropolitan areas of the United States. The young, males, African Americans, and the poor are more often arrested for criminal homicide than are other groups. Their victims are also most often the young, males, African Americans, and the poor.

The vast majority of murders involve a single victim and offender, and many of these are victim-precipitated. *Victim-precipitated homicides* are homicide situations in which the victim initiates an altercation that results in his or her death.

Mass and serial murders were also discussed. *Mass murder* refers to the killing of a number of persons in one violent episode. *Serial murder* refers to the killing of separate victims over an extended period of time. Four types of serial killers are identified. *Visionary killers* are often psychotic and respond to voices or visions of the types of people to be killed. *Mission-oriented killers* seek to rid the world of these persons who they perceive as undesirables. *Hedonistic killers* kill for risk and adventure. *Power-Control-oriented killers* seek pleasure by physically overpowering their victims.

Macro-objectivist theories attribute criminal homicide to social structural conditions or subcultural traditions. Structural theories explain the differing rates of criminal homicide between groups by their position (class, social status) in the social structure relative to others. Subcultural theories explain differing group rates of criminal homicide by group members shared values and norms that condone violence. The correlations between social groups and criminal homicide rates support structural theories. Structured inequality theory is well-supported by empirical research on homicide rates at community, national, and cross-national levels of analysis. Subcultural theories are difficult to test, and research has not identified a subculture of violence independent of the high rates of violence that the subculture is supposed to explain. This logic is tautological. A *tautology*

is something that is true by virtue of its logic alone, and, is, thereby, untestable.

Micro-objectivist theories explain criminal homicide relative to the structure of social relationships within which homicides occur, or by the social interactions the precipitate homicide. Micro-objectivists provide major insights for homicides that occur between intimates (family, friends). They do not, however, provide a general theory of criminal homicide.

Macro-subjectivists theories focus on how interest groups and organizational agents create definitions of criminal homicide. Neo-Marxists identify four types of violence: interpersonal violence, organized violence, state violence, and systematic violence. *Interpersonal violence* is comprised of reactionary, impulsive acts of frustration that occur in immediate situations. *Organized violence* consists of planned acts by one or more persons who use violence to resolve a problem or achieve a goal. These acts range from local gang wars to national terrorism. *State violence* is politically authorized violence. These acts range from police and national guard violence against citizens to war. *Systematic violence* consists of violence that results from profit-seeking activities of institutions and enterprises that support the economic arrangements of modern capitalism. Neo-Marxists argue that law defines as criminal homicide the acts of violence of powerless individuals (interpersonal and organized violence), but excludes killings by the powerful (state and systematic violence).

We also examined the nineteenth-century movement by physicians to legally prohibit abortion. This culminated in legislation defining abortion as criminal homicide. In so doing, a woman's right was transformed into an act of intentional killing, and a new class of murders was created.

Also, examined was the organizational demand of the bureaucratic criminal court. The demand for efficiency often leads prosecutors to define a killing in a way that best produces a guilty plea and certain conviction.

Micro-subjectivists focus on the social characteristics of the victim, perpetrator, or defining agents that produce a definition of murder and label of murderer. Real-life illustrations of the effect of labeling killings as criminal homicide and perpetrators as murderers are evident. However, micro-subjectivists have not yet systematically identified the individual properties that affect definitions of murder or of the label murderer.

Also, micro-subjectivists have not examined the effect that the label *convicted murderer* (definition) has on that person's subsequent *criminal activity* (behavior). However, studies of paroled murderers find them seldom involved in any future crimes, especially not in another criminal homicide.

In the United States, we have relied on two traditional policies to reduce criminal homicides: the death penalty and gun control. Several arguments have been posed for the death penalty, but many of these arguments rest on matters outside the realm of scientific inquiry. However, the argument that the death penalty deters others from murder has been the subject of considerable research. Some researchers have reported that the death penalty has a *brutalization effect.* The brutalization effect is that the death penalty increases the number of criminal homicides. However, the most consistent finding from such research is that the death penalty does not deter criminal homicide. Also, gun control laws, many and varied as they are, have not been proven effective in reducing criminal homicide rates.

GLOSSARY

Brutalization effect　Increased homicides that result from the death penalty.

Excusable homicide　A killing that results from an accident or misfortune.

Heat of passion killing　A homicide situation

in which the offender was adequately provoked by the victim and the killing occurred before the offender's blood cooled.

Hedonistic killer　A type of serial killer who kills for risk and adventure.

Interpersonal violence　Violence that results from impulsive acts of frustration and occurs in immediate situations most likely between persons known to one another.

Justifiable homicide　A killing that results from the lawful duty to protect oneself or others.

Mass murder　The killing of a number of persons in one violent episode.

Mission-oriented killer　A type of serial killer who seeks to rid the world of persons he or she perceives as undesirable.

Murder　The willful killing of one human being by another.

Non-negligent manslaughter　An unpremeditated killing that lacks the criminal intent of murder.

Organized violence　Planned acts of violence perpetrated by one or more persons to achieve a goal, such as gang wars and terrorists acts.

Power-Control-oriented killer　A type of serial killer who seeks pleasure in physically overpowering others.

Serial murder　The killing of many separate victims over an extended period of time.

State violence　Politically authorized violence most likely perpetrated by legal authorities against citizens.

Systematic violence　Violence that results from profit-seeking enterprises that support modern capitalism.

Tautology　A statement that is true by virtue of its logic alone and, therefore, untestable.

Victim-precipitated homicide　A homicide situation in which the victim initiates an altercation that results in his or her death.

Visionary killer　A type of serial killer who

is psychotic and responds to voices or visions of the type of people to be killed.

SUGGESTED READINGS

Balkwell, James W. "Ethnic Inequality and the Rate of Homicide." *Social Forces* 69(1990):53–70. An empirical test of structured inequality theory from a sample of 150 metropolitan areas in the United States. The results show ethnic inequality to be a strong predictor of high homicide rates even after controlling for the effects of poverty, economic inequality, region, race composition, and social disintegration.

Ellison, Christopher G. "An Eye for an Eye? A Note on the Southern Subculture of Violence Thesis." *Social Forces* 69(1991):1223–1239. A study of norms that condone interpersonal violence under defensive or retaliatory circumstances. Results indicate that native southerners support violence under defensive or retaliatory circumstance more strongly than nonsouthern natives. Also, the legitimacy of interpersonal violence is linked to aspects of southern religious culture.

Holmes, Ronald and DeBurger, James. *Serial Murder.* Newbury Park, CA: Sage, 1988. A comprehensive study of serial killers. These authors identify four types of serial killers: visionary killers, mission-oriented killers, hedonistic killers and power-control-oriented killers. They also provide a selected sample of serial killers from 1900 to 1990.

Kleck, Gary and McElrath, Karen. "The Effects of Weaponry on Human Violence." *Social Forces* 69(1991):669–692. An assessment of the impact of weapons on three types of hostile interactions: situations that escalate to physical attack, attacks resulting in injury, and injury resulting in death. Results suggest that availability of guns does not increase homicides.

Levin, Jack and Fox, Alan. *Mass Murder.* New York: Plenum Press, 1985. A study of 156 mass murderers. They conclude that mass murders are not biologically or psychologically abnormal. Rather they are more "evil than crazy." There is generally a reason for their attack.

Peterson, Ruth D. and Bailey, William C. "Murder and Capital Punishment in the Evolving Context of the Post-Furman Era." *Social Forces* 66(1988):56–70. An examination of the impact of the death penalty on state homicide rates from 1973–84. Consistent with previous research, they find no evidence of deterrence.

Weinreb, Lloyd L. "Homicide: Legal Aspects." *Encyclopedia of Crime and Justice.* Ed. Sanford H. Kadish. New York: Free Press, 1983, pp. 855–866. A nonlegalistic discussion of the legal aspects of homicide. Types of homicide, degrees, and penalties are defined.

Wolfgang, Marvin E. and Zahn, Margaret A. "Homicide: Behavioral Aspects." *Encyclopedia of Crime and Justice.* Ed. Sanford H. Kadish. New York: Free Press, 1983, pp. 849–855. A nonjargonistic review of cross-national and national patterns of criminal homicide. Sociological theories are also reviewed in light of empirical evidence.

REFERENCES

Archer, Dave and Rosemary Gartner. *Violence and Crime in Cross-National Perspective.* New Haven, CT: Yale University Press, 1984.

Associated Press. "Father Cleared in Comatose Son's Death." Harrisonburg, VA: *Daily News-Record* May 19(1989):1–2.

Ayers, Edward L. *Vengeance and Justice: Crime and Punishment in the 19th-Century American South.* New York: Oxford University Press, 1984.

Bailey, William C. and Ruth D. Peterson. "Murder and Capital Punishment: A Monthly Time-Series Analysis of Execution Publicity." *American Sociological Review* 54(1989):722–743.

Baldus, David, Charles Pulaski, and George Woodworth. "Comparative Review of Death Sentences: An Empirical Study of the Georgia Experience." *Journal of Criminal Law and Criminology* 74(1983):661–678.

Balkwell, James W. "Ethnic Inequality and the Rate of Homicide." *Social Forces* 69(1990):53–70.

Ball-Rokeach, Sandra. "Values and Violence: A Test of the Subculture of Violence Thesis." *American Sociological Review* 38(1973):736–749.

———. "Normative and Deviant Violence from a

Conflict Perspective." *Social Problems* 18 (1980):45–62.

Bartollas, Clemens. *Introduction to Corrections.* New York: Harper Collins, 1990.

Bedeau, Hugo A. and Michael L. Radelet. "Miscarriages of Justice in Potentially Capital Cases." *Stanford Law Review* 40(1987):21–179.

Blau, Judith R. and Peter M. Blau. "The Cost of Inequality: Metropolitan Structure and Violent Crime." *American Sociological Review* 47 (1982):114–129.

Blau, Peter M. *Inequality and Heterogeneity.* New York: Free Press, 1977.

Blau, Peter M. and Reid M. Golden. "Metropolitan Structure and Criminal Violence." *The Sociological Quarterly* 27(1986):15–26.

Blau, Peter M. and Joseph E. Schwartz. *Crosscutting Social Circles.* Orlando, FL: Academic Press, 1984.

Blumberg, Abraham. *Criminal Justice.* Chicago: Quadrangle Books, 1967.

Blumstein, Alfred, Jacqueline Cohen, and Daniel Nagin. *Deterrence and Incapacitation: Estimating the Effects of Criminal Sanctions on Crime Rates.* Washington, D.C.: National Academy of Sciences, 1978.

Bowers, William J. *Legal Homicide: Death as Punishment in America, 1864-1982.* Boston: Northeastern University Press, 1984.

———. "The Pervasiveness of Arbitrariness and Discrimination under Post-Furman Capital Statutes." *Journal of Criminal Law and Criminology* 74(1983):1067–1100.

Bowers, William J. and Glenn L. Pierce. "Arbitrariness and Discrimination under Post-Furman Capital Statutes." *Crime and Delinquency* 26(1980a):563–635.

———. "Deterrence or Brutalization: What is the Effect of Executions?" *Crime and Delinquency* 26(1980b):453–484.

Brunk, David. "Condemned to Death: The Capital Punishment Lottery." *The New Republic.* December 12(1983):26–28.

Busch, Katie A. and James L. Cavanaugh. "The Study of Multiple Murder: Preliminary Examination of the Interface Between Epistemology and Methodology." *Journal of International Violence* 1(1986):5–23.

Carter, Timothy J. Book Review: "Vengeance and Justice: Crime and Punishment in the 19th

Century American South." *Contemporary Crises* 10(1986):218–221.

Church, George J. "The Other Arms Race." *Time* February 6(1989):20–24.

Clinard, Marshall B. and Daniel J. Abbott. *Crime in Developing Countries: A Comparative Perspective.* New York: Wiley, 1973.

Crutchfield, Robert D. "Labor Stratification and Violent Crime." *Social Forces* 68(1989): 489–512.

Curtis, Lynn A. "Victim Precipitation and Violent Crime." *Social Problems* 21(1974):594–605.

Doerner, William G. "The Index of Southerness Revisited." *Criminology* 16(1978):47–56.

Ellison, Christopher G. "An Eye for an Eye? A Note on the Southern Subculture of Violence Thesis." *Social Forces* 69(1991):1223–1239.

Ellsworth, Phoebe C. and Lee Ross. "Public Opinion and Capital Punishment: A Close Examination of the Views of Abolitionists and Retentionists." *Crime and Delinquency* 29 (1983):116–169.

Farley, Reynolds. "Homicide Trends in the United States." *Demography* 17(1980):177–188.

Federal Bureau of Investigation. *Uniform Crime Reports.* Washington, D.C.: U.S. Government Printing Office, 1990.

Felson, Richard B. and Henry J. Steadman. "Situational Factors in Disputes Leading to Criminal Violence." *Criminology* 21(1983):59–74.

Fisher, Joseph C. "Homicide in Detroit: The Role of Firearms." *Criminology* 14(1976): 387–400.

Galliher, John F. *Criminology: Human Rights, Criminal Law, and Crime.* Englewood Cliffs, NJ: Prentice Hall, 1989.

Gardner, Thomas J. *Criminal Law: Principles and Cases.* 3rd ed. New York: West, 1985.

Gastil, Raymond D. "Homicide and a Regional Culture of Violence." *American Sociological Review* 36(1971):412–427.

Gelman, David and David L. Gonzalez. "The Bundy Carnival." *Newsweek* February 6 (1989):66.

Gold, Martin. "Suicide, Homicide, and Socialization of Aggression." *American Journal of Sociology* 63(1958):651–661.

Greenfield, Lawrence. *Capital Punishment, 1989.* Washington, D.C.: Bureau of Justice Statistics, 1990.

Gross, Samuel R. and Robert Mauro. *Racial Dispari-ties in Capital Sentencing.* Boston: Northeastern University Press, 1988.

Hackney, Sheldon. "Southern Violence." *American Historical Review* 39(1969):906–925.

Henry, Andrew F. and James Short. *Suicide and Homicide: Some Economic, Sociological and Psy-chological Aspects of Aggression.* New York: Free Press, 1954.

Holmes, Ronald and James DeBurger. *Serial Mur-der.* Newbury Park, CA: Sage, 1988.

Huff-Corzine, Lin, Jay Corzine, and David C. Moore. "Deadly Connections: Culture, Pov-erty, and the Direction of Lethal Violence." *Social Forces* 69(1991):715–732.

Kantrowitz, Barbara and Ginny Carroll. "Tipping the Odds on Abortion." *Newsweek* July 8 (1991):23.

Kleck, Gary and Karen McElrath. "The Effects of Weaponry on Human Violence." *Social Forces* 69(1991):669–692.

Krahn, Harvey, Timothy Hartnagel, and John W. Gartrell. "Income Inequality and Homicide Rates: Cross-National Data and Criminologi-cal Theories." *Criminology* 24(1986):269–295.

Lester, David. "Mortality from Suicide and Homi-cide for African Americans in the USA: A Regional Analysis." *Omega* 22(1991): 219–226.

Levin, Jack and Alan Fox. *Mass Murder.* New York: Plenum Press, 1985.

Loftin, Colin, Milton Heumann, and David McDo-wall. "Mandatory Sentencing and Firearms Violence: Evaluating an Alternative to Gun Control." *Law and Society Review* 17(1983):287-318.

Loftin, Colin, and Robert H. Hill. "Regional Sub-culture of Homicide: An examination of the Gastil-Hackney Thesis." *American Sociological Review* 39(1974):714–724.

Loftin, Colin and David McDowall. " 'One with a Gun Gets You Two' Mandatory Sentencing and Firearms Violence in Detroit." *Annals of the American Academy of Political and Social Sci-ence* 455(1981):150–167.

———. "The Deterrent Effects of the Florida Fel-ony Firearm Law." *Journal of Criminal Law and Criminology* 75(1984):250–259.

Luckenbill, David. "Criminal Homicide as a Situa-tional Transaction." *Social Problems* 25 (1977):176–186.

Mathews, Tom and Karen Springen. "He Wanted to Listen to My Heart." *Newsweek* February 10 (1992):31.

McCormick, John and Bill Turque. "Big Crimes, Small Cities." *Newsweek* June 10(1991): 16–19.

McDowall, David. "Firearm Availability and Ho-micide Rates in Detroit, 1951–1986." *Social Forces* 69 (1991):1085–1101.

Messner, Stephen F. "Regional and Racial Effects on the Urban Homicide Rate." *American Jour-nal of Sociology* 88(1983):997–1007.

———. "Economic Discrimination and Societal Homicide Rates." *American Sociological Review* 54(1989): 597–611.

Michalowski, Raymond. *Order, Law, and Crime.* New York: Random House, 1985.

Mohr, James. *Abortion in America.* New York: Ox-ford University Press, 1978.

Mueller, Gerhard O.W. "The United Nations and Criminology." *International Handbook of Con-temporary Developments in Criminology.* Ed. Elmer H. Johnson. Westport, CT: Greenwood, 1983, pp. 63–81.

O'Carroll, Patrick W., Colin Loftin, John B. Waller, David McDowall, Allen Bukeff, Richard O. Scott, James A. Mercy, and Brian Wiersema. "Preventing Homicide: An Evaluation of the Efficacy of a Gun Ordinance." *American Jour-nal of Public Health* 81(1991):576–581.

Parker, Robert Nash. "Poverty, Subculture of Vio-lence, and Type of Homicide." *Social Forces* 67(1989):983–1007.

Paternoster, Raymond. "Race of Victim and Loca-tion of Crime: The Decision to Seek the Death Penalty in South Carolina." *Journal of Criminal Law and Criminology* 74(1983):754–785.

Peterson, Ruth D. and William C. Bailey. "Murder and Capital Punishment in the Evolving Con-text of the Post-Furman Era." *Social Forces* 66(1988):56–70.

Pierce, Glenn L. and William J. Bowers. "The Bar-tly-Fox Gun Law's Short-Term Impact on Crime in Boston." *Annals of the American Acad-emy of Political and Social Science* 455 (1981):120–137.

Riedel, Marc. "Stranger Violence: Perspectives, Is-sues, and Problems." *Journal of Criminal Law and Criminology* 78(1987):223–258.

Riedel, Marc and Margaret A. Zahn. *The Nature and Patterns of American Homicide.* Washington, D.C.: U.S. Government Printing Office, 1985.

Seligson, Tom. "Are They Too Young to Die?" Richmond, VA: *Richmond Times-Dispatch (Parade),* October 19(1986):3–6.

Sheppard, Colin. "The Violent Offender: Let's Examine the Taboo." *Crime in America.* 2nd ed., Ed. Bruce J. Cohn. Itasca, IL: F.E. Peacock, 1977, pp. 72-81.

Stack, Steven. "Publicized Executions and Homicide, 1950-1980." *American Sociological Review* 52(1987):532–540.

Straus, Murray A., Richard J. Gelles, and S.K. Steinmetz. *Behind Closed Doors: Violence in the American Family.* Garden City, NJ: Doubleday, 1980.

Sudnow, David. "Normal Crimes: Sociological Features of the Penal Code in a Public Defender Office." *Social Problems* 12(1965): 255–276.

Swigert, Victoria L. and Ronald A. Farrell. *Murder, Inequality, and the Law.* Lexington, MA: D.C. Heath, 1976.

Thomas, Charles W. and John R. Hepburn. *Crime, Criminal Law, and Criminology.* Dubuque, IA: Wm. C. Brown, 1983.

United Nations. *Demographic Yearbook, 1990.* New York: United Nations, 1992.

United States Department of Health and Human Services. *Vital Statistics of the United States 1988.* Hyattsville, MD: National Center for Health Statistics, 1990.

Waldo, Gordon P. "The Criminality Level of Incarcerated Murders and Non-Murders." *Journal of Criminal Law, Criminology and Police Science* 61(1970):60–70.

Weinreb, Lloyd L. "Homicide: Legal Aspects." *Encyclopedia of Crime and Justice.* Ed. Sanford H. Kadish. New York: Free Press, 1983, pp. 855–866.

Williams, Kirk R. "Economic Sources of Homicide: Reestimating the Effects of Poverty and Inequality." *American Sociological Review* 49 (1984):283–289.

Wolfgang, Marvin E. *Patterns of Criminal Homicide.* Philadelphia: University of Pennsylvania Press, 1958.

Wolfgang, Marvin E. and Franco Ferracuti. *The Subculture of Violence.* London: Tavistock, 1967.

Wolfgang, Marvin E. and Margaret A. Zahn. "Homicide: Behavioral Aspects." *Encyclopedia of Crime and Justice.* Ed. Sanford H. Kadish. New York: Free Press, 1983, pp. 849–855.

Wright, James D., Peter Rossi, and Kathleen Daly. *Under the Gun: Weapons, Crime and Violence in America.* New York: Aldine, 1983.

Zahn, Margaret A. and Philip C. Sagi. "Stranger Homicides in Nine American Cities." *Journal of Criminal Law and Criminology* 78(1987): 377–397.

Chapter **13**

Corporate Crime

IMPERIAL FOOD PRODUCTS, INC.

On September, 3, 1991, 25 people died and 56 others were injured in a fire at a chicken-processing plant in Hamlet, North Carolina, owned by Imperial Food Products Company of Cummings, Georgia. On December, 30, 1991, the company was fined $808,150 by the North Carolina Department of Labor. The survivors and victims' relatives were outraged by the "slap on the wrist" fine (Smothers, 1991:A12).

Not one time in the plant's 11 years of operation had state safety officials inspected the plant. After the fire, however, investigators discovered 83 safety violations; 54 of which were willful and serious violations. Paramount among these violations were "locked exit doors, unmarked exits, inadequate emergency lighting and work stations too far from exit doors" (Patterson, 1991:A3). On March 12, 1992, the president of Imperial Food Products, Inc., an operations manager, and plant manager were each charged with 25 counts of involuntary manslaughter. In September, 1992, Emmett Roe, President, Imperial Food Products, Inc., was sentenced to 19 years and 11 months prison term. This sentence was part of a plea agreement that also dismissed the involuntary manslaughter charges against the co-defendants (Grossman, 1992:A10).

FORD MOTOR COMPANY, INC.

Is corporate violence limited to relatively small companies, like Imperial Foods, that struggle for economic survival in a world of corporate giants? Are employees the only victims of willful corporate violations that likely result in death? The answer to these questions is—no. Large corporations routinely and unknowingly endanger the lives of consumers, and the public. The now "classic" Ford pinto case illustrates the malice aforethought of corporate cost cutting that often results in widespread injury and death to unsuspecting consumers.

In 1972, on a Minneapolis highway, the driver of a Ford Pinto entered a merge lane where her Pinto stalled. She was struck from the rear by a vehicle traveling approximately 28 miles per hour. The Pinto's gas tank ruptured. A spark ignited the gas vapors, and the Pinto immediately burst into flame. In agony, the driver died within hours of the fiery crash. Her passenger, a thirteen year boy, survived but his face was burned beyond recognition and most of his body is badly scarred.

Low-speed rear-end collisions are common, but a fiery crash resulting in death and disfigurement is not. Was this a freak accident? The answer is no. Ford Pintos were regularly involved in fiery crashes throughout the 1970s. By 1977, 500 people were burned to death in Pintos. Was Ford Motor Company surprised by the Pinto-related burn deaths and injuries? No. Did Ford act swiftly to correct the Pinto's defective fuel system? Again, the answer is no. Ford's better idea was to pay for the deaths and injuries rather than to pay the $11.00 per car alteration that Ford officials estimated could have saved 180 lives a year.

Ford chose not to make the Pinto safer because the Company's "cost-benefit analysis" showed no financial benefit in preventing human death and injury. The cost-benefit analysis demonstrated that 180 burn deaths, 180 serious burn injuries and 2,100 burn vehicles would have cost $49.5 million. Whereas, to recall the Pintos and make the $11 per car repair would have cost $137 million. Ford decided that a safer Pinto was too costly (Dowie, 1977:24).

In August, 1978, three Indiana teenage girls were burned to death when their 1973 Pinto had been struck from the rear and burst into flames. In September of that year, Ford Motor Company was indicted for reckless homicide in Elkhart, Indiana. Ford Motor Company became the first corporation ever to be charged with a criminal homicide. Later, Ford was acquitted by a jury. The trial judge played a key role in the jury's acquittal. The judge was a former law partner of Ford's co-defense counsel. He did not allow the prosecution to present as evidence Ford's internal memos. He also ruled as inadmissible crash test data that showed that the Pinto's gas tank would rupture if struck from the rear at moderate speed. The judge reasoned that the crash test data involved a 1969 Pinto, whereas the Indiana teenagers died in a 1973 Pinto. The fuel systems on the 1969 and 1973 Pintos were identical (Michalowski, 1985).

Just prior to Ford's indictment for reckless homicide, Ford was ordered to recall and repair all Pintos produced between 1970 and 1976. In 1977, Ford's new Pinto incorporated a one-dollar, one-pound metal baffle that prevented the gas tank from rupturing. This baffle was on one of the only modified Pintos to ever pass a crash test nearly ten years prior to its inclusion on the 1977 Pinto (Dowie, 1977).

As was true of the Pinto, widespread death, injury, and destruction resulting from corporate rational calculations to maximize profit is not unusual. What was unusual about the Pinto case was the widespread media coverage, consumer awareness, and a criminal indictment. As you will learn from this chapter, corporations do kill, injure, and steal; but their actions are seldom discovered or seldom labeled as crimes. Now, however, we need to examine what it is that sociologists term *corporate crime*. There are rival objectivist definitions and a subjectivist definition of corporate crime.

WHAT IS CORPORATE CRIME?

The Objectivist Conception

According to the objectivist conception of deviance, corporate crime is comprised of behaviors that violate norms. What kind of norms? A major question for objectivists is: Should the study of corporate crime be limited to behaviors that violate legal norms or should study be extended to all behaviors that cause social harm?

Are Corporate Crimes Violations of Law or Acts of Social Harm? This question began when Sutherland (1940) introduced the term *white-collar crime*. White-collar crime challenged the conventional view that crime was concentrated in the lower classes. This view, Sutherland maintained, resulted from criminologist's use of official measures of crime, like the FBI's *Uniform Crime Reports*. Official measures focus on "street crimes" such as robbery, burglary, and larceny, which are primarily committed by the lower classes. Crimes committed by persons in the higher social classes such as bribery, tax evasion, price-fixing, and restraint of trade are not included in official measures. Also, violators

are often handled by civil courts and government agencies or commissions, rather than by criminal courts. Therefore, Sutherland (1949) argued that all "socially harmful" behaviors proscribed by law are crimes. These include many misconducts that are not violations of the criminal law, but are punished by the state through civil and regulatory law. Although Sutherland extended the definition of crime beyond the criminal law, he kept criminology's focus on legal norms. Sutherland's position that white-collar crimes are crimes regardless of the law proscribing them—criminal, civil, or regulatory—has been adopted by several contemporary scholars of corporate crime (Clinard and Yeager, 1980; Blum-West and Carter, 1983; Box, 1983; Coleman, 1989). These scholars restrict corporate crime to behaviors that violate legal norms. For example, Clinard and Yeager (1980:16) define corporate crime as "any act committed by corporations that is punished by the state, regardless of whether it is punished under administrative, civil, or criminal law." This definition is particularly appropriate given that most corporate wrongs violate both criminal and civil law, and the decision to pursue a case in a criminal or civil court is based primarily on extralegal grounds (Blum-West and Carter, 1983).

Other contemporary objectivists, however, are not content to limit the study of corporate crime to legal norms. Rather, they extend Sutherland's notion of social harm to acts whether or not these acts are prohibited by the state. For these objectivists, crime is an intrinsic quality of behavior, not a behavior proscribed by law. Quinney (1980), Young (1981), and Michalowski (1985) all view harmful behavior, rather than the law, as the defining criterion of corporate crime. For example, Michalowski (1985:324) defines corporate crimes as "actions that are either prohibited by law or that knowingly lead to social injury, taken by official representatives of legitimate business to facilitate capital accumulation within those businesses." The focus on social injury provides a behavioral definition of corporate crime rather than a legal definition.

Defining corporate crime as a social harm rather than as a legal violation allows for the inclusion of wrongdoing by multinational corporations that is missed by strictly legal definitions. As Michalowski and Kramer (1987) note, multinational corporations have more assets and resources than do entire Third World nations. They can, therefore, greatly influence the laws that are or are not enacted to regulate their activities.

Are Corporate Crimes White-Collar Crimes?
Another question raised by objectivists is: are corporate crimes and white-collar crimes the same thing? Sutherland (1949:9) defined white-collar crime as "crime committed by a person of respectability and high status in the course of his occupation." This definition, however, would include crimes committed by corporate employees against the corporation, for example, embezzlement and computer crimes. Also, this definition excludes crimes that are committed by the corporation as an organizational unit, rather than by specific individuals within a corporation. You may ask, how is it possible for a corporation to engage in criminal behavior? Ermann and Lundman identify three ways in which corporations produce deviant behaviors.

> *First, the limited information and responsibility characteristic of positions within large organizations can produce a situation where no individual has been deviant but the combination of their work-related actions produces deviance.*
>
> *Second, organizational elites can indirectly initiate deviant actions by establishing particular norms, rewards, and punishments for people occupying lower-level positions.*
>
> *Third, elites at or near the top of an organization can consciously initiate a deviant action and explicitly use hierarchically linked positions to implement it (1982:7).*

We began this chapter with the highly publicized Ford Pinto case. This case illustrates how corporate elites can indirectly initiate deviant actions. Ford's president, Mr. Lee Iacocca put forth a plan to rush the Pinto into production in two-thirds of the normal auto production time. Therefore, tooling, design, and testing of the Pinto were going on at the same time. Mr. Iacocca further insisted that the Pinto not cost a cent more than $2,000 to produce, and that the Pinto not weigh an ounce over 2,000 pounds. Given these constraints, safety was given a low priority. In the words of one Ford engineer, "Safety wasn't a popular subject around Ford in those days." In fact, Mr. Iacocca often stated, "Safety doesn't sell." "So, even when a crash test showed that that one-pound, one-dollar piece of metal stopped the puncture of the gas tank, it was thrown out as extra cost and extra weight" (Dowie, 1977:25–26).

Mr. Iacocca did not order that an unsafe product be produced, and no Ford executive, engineer or worker intended to kill or injure anyone. Rather, an iron-clad rule of production and delegated responsibility throughout a chain of decisionmakers and operators resulted in the production and sale of an unsafe product. Where would you place the blame, on Mr. Iacocca, his coalition of executives, the engineers, assembly line operators, or Ford Motor Company?

Contemporary objectivists agree on the shortcomings of Sutherland's original definition of white-collar crime. However, they disagree as to the usefulness of the concept of white-collar crime. Clinard and Quinney (1973) drop the term white-collar crime. They divide the crimes by respectables in the course of their business activities into two separate types: occupational crimes and corporate crimes. Occupational crimes are "offenses committed by individuals for themselves in the course of their occupation" and "offenses by employers against their employees." Corporate crimes are "offenses committed by corporate officials for their corporation and offenses of the corporation itself." (Clinard and Quinney, 1973:188). These definitions separate what Sutherland had joined together—crimes by respectable persons to enhance themselves and crimes by respectable persons for the benefit of the corporation. Also, Clinard and Quinney's definition of corporate crime recognizes that crimes can be attributed to corporations themselves, and not solely to corporate actors.

Coleman (1989), however, is opposed to dropping the term white-collar crime. Rather, he argues that the distinction between occupational crime and corporate crime is useful only if they are seen as subtypes of white-collar crimes. Thus, Coleman broadens Sutherland's original definition so as to include a wider variety of crimes committed by respectables, both individuals and groups. Coleman (1989:5) defines white-collar crime as "a violation of the law committed by a person or group of persons in the course of an otherwise respected and legitimate occupation or financial activity." This definition requires that actors hold a respectable position, but not necessarily occupy a high social status. Also, white-collar crimes can be attributed to an organization. Furthermore, financial crimes that are not part of one's occupation, such as tax evasion, are included as white-collar crime.

Objectivists no longer use white-collar crime and corporate crime interchangeably. However, there remains disagreement among objectivists as whether to distinguish corporate crimes from other crimes committed by respectable persons, groups, or organizations or to fuse all crimes committed by respectables. Those who favor the former conceptualization offer a specific definition of corporate crime. Whereas those who prefer the latter conceptualization retain white-collar crime to designate all forms of crime committed by respectables.

Unfortunately, disagreements over how to best define corporate crime "cannot be resolved purely on logical and empirical grounds; they are unavoidably political, and prospects for resolution are dim" (Shover, 1990:307). Fortunately, however, these disagreements have not impeded empirical studies of corporate crime that are "grounded in a variety of working definitions" (Shover, 1990:370).

The Subjectivist Conception

From a subjectivist point of view, deviance and crime are created by social audiences who come to define particular activities as such. Deviance is not a quality of the act, rather it is a label attached to particular acts or actors by others (accusers, sanctioning agents, and interested publics). Subjectivists define corporate deviance as "an organizational act . . . widely labeled and responded to as deviant . . . " (Ermann and Lundman, 1982:13). Ermann and Lundman (1982:13) argue that the label deviant or criminal "depends in large part on the power of accusers as compared to that of the organization."

To illustrate the subjectivist view of corporate deviance Ermann and Lundman (1982:11-13) describe the Chisso corporation's dumping of hazardous wastes in the Minamata Bay of Japan. Chisso is a chemical factory in Minamata, Japan. From the beginning, 1907, Chisso dumped its chemical wastes into the Bay. By 1925 Chisso was paying fishermen for damages resulting from their wastes. In 1932, Chisso began dumping mercury into the Bay. By 1975, mercury poisoning was verified in 798 victims, 2,800 more were awaiting verification, and over 100,000 people residing around the Bay had been affected by mercury poisoning. As early as 1959 and 1960, Chisso corporation knew of research that attributed mercury poisoning to their dumping. Chisso ordered their physician to stop his research, blocked outside researchers from obtaining mercury samples, and paid victims to sign a document which stated, "if Chisso were later proven guilty, the company would not be liable for further compensation" (Ermann and Lundman, 1982:12). In 1968, Chisso stopped dumping mercury into the Bay.

The facts are that Chisso dumped known dangerous chemicals in the Bay, covered their activities, intimidated victims, and concealed evidence of the hazard from the public. Are Chisso's actions deviant? According to the subjectivist view, "No action, not even Chisso's dumping of poison into Minamata Bay, is intrinsically deviant" (Ermann and Lundman, 1982:13). Where labels and responses to actions as deviant are absent, there is no deviance. Both of the objectivist definitions (legal vs. social harm) would consider the actions of the Chisso corporation as deviant.

Would subjectivists consider Ford's sale of the Pinto as deviant? Yes! Ford was widely labeled and responded to as deviant. And, although a jury did not find Ford guilty of homicide, adverse publicity and threat of a formal hearing by the National Highway and Traffic Safety Commission pressured Ford to voluntarily recall all 1971 through 1976 Pintos (Fisse and Braithwaite, 1987).

THE PREVALENCE OF CORPORATE CRIME

How much corporate crime is there? No one knows for certain, because corporate crimes are largely "hidden" crimes. However, government estimates and sociological studies suggest that corporate crime is widespread; and that corporate crime is the most costly form of crime in America. Here, we will first examine why corporate crimes are largely *hidden* crimes. Second, we present sociological data on the extent of *official* corporate crime. Third, we present government and sociological estimates concerning the physical,

economic, and social costs of corporate crime. Finally, we identify and discuss the forms of corporate crime.

Corporate Crime as Hidden Crime

There are several reasons why so much corporate crime remains hidden. We will identify five. First, corporate crimes are perpetuated in "suits," rather than in the "streets." This private planning and execution of acts conceals corporate wrongs and corporate wrongdoers from public and official scrutiny. Second, the public and officials (police, prosecutors, judges, and juries) know little about the nature and extent of corporate crime. Most Americans are unaware of the extensive and serious injury to the community and persons caused by corporate actions. Also, there are no established "images" of corporate crimes or "stereotypes" of corporate criminals (as there are for street crimes) to facilitate audience interpretations, definitions, and labels. Third, the victims of corporate crime are most often unaware of their victimization, or, they lack a readiness to define corporate actions as crimes. On the one hand, they may not know that anything happened to them. On the other hand, victims may view what happened as: "just one of those unfortunate things," "an accident," "you get what you pay for," and so on (Box, 1983). Fourth, the cause-effect relationship between corporate acts and their consequences are blurred by the distance in time between them (Ermann and Lundman, 1982:20). For example, workers who have been exposed to dangerous toxins on the job may not develop illnesses, handicaps, or die until years after they have left their jobs for other jobs or retirement. Or, symptoms may appear in the children of workers who themselves have never stepped foot in the plant. Therefore, assigning responsibility to a particular exposure is difficult. These exposures are seldom known, unless the illness is extreme and many people are affected (Ermann and Lundman, 1982). Government regulators, too, who themselves often embrace business values, often attribute responsibility everywhere except to the exposure in question. This is evident from the statement of Othal Brand, a member of the Texas pesticide regulatory board, who noted: "Sure, it's going to kill a lot of people, but they may be dying of something else anyway" (Newsweek, 1990:17). Fifth, federal regulatory agencies, not the criminal justice system, are the primary investigators of corporate crimes. What corporate actions they choose to investigate or not are not known to the public. Only their sanctions become public information. As you will see later in this chapter, regulatory agencies most often apply administrative sanctions, and criminal sanctions least often to corporate offenders. In effect, regulatory agencies hide corporate actions from public view, and administrative sanctions insulate corporate offenders from criminal labels.

The Extent of "Official" Corporate Crime

The most comprehensive studies of the extent of corporate crime are limited to official actions that are taken against corporations. The authors of these studies recognize that the criminal activities that they discover and record are only the "tip of the iceberg" of total corporate violations. Nevertheless, these studies reveal corporate violations to be frequent and repetitive.

The first large-scale study of law violations by large corporations was done by Edwin Sutherland (1949). Sutherland studied seventy of America's largest corporations. For these firms he reported a total of 980 law violations between 1892 and 1942. Each of the seventy corporations had at least one violation, and 97 percent had two or more violations.

However, the most comprehensive investigation of corporate crime was conducted by Clinard and Yeager (1980). These researchers investigated 582 of the largest publicly owned corporations in America. They focused primarily on the 477 largest manufacturing corporations. Also investigated were 18 wholesale, 66 retail, and 21 service corporations. Sixty percent of the total number of corporations had been charged with a law violation within just a two-year period, 1975 and 1976. Among these, 50 percent were charged for a serious or moderately serious law violation. The largest corporations were the most frequent violators. Of these, the most frequent violators were concentrated in three industries: oil, auto, and pharmaceutical. The oil industry accounted for one of every five legal cases between 1975 and 1976. The auto industry accounted for one of every six legal cases; and the pharmaceutical industry accounted for one of every ten (Clinard and Yeager, 1980:113–120).

Moreover, a large number of corporate violators are repeat offenders. Sutherland (1949) found that the average corporation had 14 enforcement actions taken against it between 1892 and 1942; and that 97 percent of the 70 corporations studied were repeat offenders. Clinard and Yeager (1980) found a similar pattern. Approximately one-half of the 477 manufacturing corporations were repeat offenders during 1975 and 1976. And, 18.2 percent of these corporations had five or more enforcement actions taken against them in the two year period. Corporate recidivism (repeat offenders) is as high or higher than recidivism for ordinary "street" crimes. The recidivism rate for ordinary crime varies from about 25 to 60 percent (Clinard and Yeager, 1980:26–27).

The Costs of Corporate Crime

Scholars generally speak of the costs of corporate crime relative to three broad areas: economic costs, physical costs, and social costs. In all of these areas the costs of corporate crimes far exceed the costs of "street" crimes.

The economic costs of corporate crime are difficult to calculate precisely. However, over a decade ago, the Senate Judiciary Committee on Antitrust and Monopoly estimated that faulty goods, monopolistic practices, and other violations costs consumers between $174 and $231 billion a year (Kramer, 1984). The Justice Department estimated a $10 to $20 billion annual loss to taxpayers from corporate violations of federal regulations (Kramer, 1984), and the Internal Revenue Service estimated $1.2 billion unreported corporate income on annual tax returns (Clinard and Yeager, 1980). Similarly, Green and Berry's (1985) estimate of the annual economic costs of corporate crime approaches $400 billion. Green and Berry (1985) offer the following estimates: price fixing and other market restraints, up to $265 billion; commercial kickbacks and bribery, up to $10 billion; cleaning up illegally dumped toxic wastes, up to $100 billion. By comparison, the current annual cost from all robberies, burglaries, larcenies, auto-thefts, and arsons put together is about $17 billion (FBI, 1992).

The physical costs of corporate crime are also staggering. Each year, as many as 10 million workers are injured on the job, 100,000 die from job-related diseases, 390,000 contract new job related diseases, and 6,000 die in accidents while on the job (Cullen, Maakestad, and Cavender, 1987:67). Many of the 2 million workers disabled and 14,000 killed each year in industrial accidents result from corporate working conditions in violation of federal law (Kramer, 1984:20). For example, Messerschmidt (1986:100) estimates that from 35 to 57 percent of accidents on the job result from safety violations. Air, water, and soil pollution in violation of federal standards contributes to hundreds of thousands of deaths annually. One hundred and forty thousand deaths a year are attributed to air pollution, much of which is in violation of federal standards. Consumers experience 20 million serious injuries yearly from unsafe or defective products. Of these injuries, 110,000 result in permanent disabilities and 30,000 in death (Kramer, 1984:19–21). By comparison, over the past ten years the number of all murders and non-negligent manslaughters has averaged approximately 20,000 a year (FBI, 1992).

The social costs of corporate crime for some observers, are more damaging than the economic and physical costs. The Presidents Commission on Law Enforcement and Administration of Justice (1967:5) stated that corporate crimes are "the most threatening of all—not because they are so expensive, but because of their corrosive effect on the moral standards by which American business is conducted." Many sociologists agree with this statement (Sutherland, 1949; Conklin, 1977; Kramer, 1984; Moore and Mills, 1990). Moore and Mills identify three areas of potentially significant social impact:

1. Diminished faith in a free economy and in business leaders
2. Loss of confidence in political institutions, processes and leaders
3. Erosion of public morality (1990:414).

In addition, corporate crime may increase crime among the general population. For example, Conklin (1977:8) identifies four ways in which crimes at the top are connected to crimes at the bottom. First, corporate crime "sets an example of disobedience" for the rest of the population. Second, crimes committed by those in high places "serve as rationalization for the lower classes to justify their own criminal behavior." Third, the mild punishments that corporate criminals receive causes bitterness among ordinary crime offenders who by comparison receive more severe punishments. Fourth, corporate crimes contribute to social unrest. For example, Conklin (1977:8) attributes consumer fraud and exploitation as an "underlying cause" of the ghetto riots during the 1960s.

Types of Corporate Crime

In the literature, sociologists have devised a variety of schemes to classify types of corporate crime. From this literature we have identified four types of corporate crime according to who the victim is. They are: crimes against owners, crimes against employees, crimes against customers, and crimes against the public-at-large.

Crimes Against Owners. Crimes against owners are violations committed by corporate executives, managers, or officials against stockholders. Violations against stockholders include falsifying financial reports, accounting irregularities, falsely inflating stock, or selling fraudulent stock. From 1964 to 1973, the Equity Fund Company sold a packaged deal of life insurance and mutual fund investment. Mutual fund share-holders were encouraged to borrow from their shares to pay for their life insurance policy. Equity began by exaggerating its assets by more than $6 million in order to attract potential stockholders (Ermann and Lundman, 1982:42). Equity employees also created phony mutual fund holders who borrowed from non-existent mutual shares to purchase phony insurance policies. This created phony profits which falsely inflated stock prices. In 1973, a former Equity executive exposed the fraud. He was indicted as a co-conspirator. His disclosure revealed that phony share/policy-package holders out numbered real ones by the thousands. Immediately after his disclosure, the stock plummeted in value. Soon after, the Equity Fund Company filed bankruptcy, and many real shareholders suffered severe monetary loss, perhaps, as much as three billion dollars (Blundell, 1978).

A new "hybrid" crime against owners is "collective embezzlement," which is "crime by the corporation against the corporation" (Calavita and Pontell, 1990:322). "Collective embezzlement" refers to the "siphoning off of funds" from a corporation or business "for personal gain, at the expense of the institution itself and with implicit or explicit sanction of its management" (Calavita and Pontell, 1990:321). The savings and loan crisis provides an illustration of "collective embezzlement." Our review of the savings and loan crisis, its costs, and the crimes committed is taken from Calavita and Pontell's (1990) study of fraud in the savings and loan industry.

The price tag for rescuing insolvent savings and loans (S and L's) is $100 billion for this decade, and from $300 to 473 billion by the year 2021. Fraud was the major factor in 70 to 80 percent of the insolvencies. Three types of fraud occurred: "unlawful risk-taking," "looting," and "covering-up" (Calavita and Pontell, 1990:316).

Unlawful risk-taking became an epidemic following the Gan-St. Germain Depository Institutions Act in 1982. This congressional enactment permitted S and L's to pay as much interest as commercial banks, authorized S and L's to make commercial loans up to 40 percent of their total assets, and allowed 100 percent financing. With the ceiling on interest rates lifted, S and L's began to offer high interest rates to brokerage firms across the country. Brokered deposits brought large amounts of cash to the S and L's. This facilitated and, to some degree, necessitated speculative high-risk loans with a potential high payoff to defray the high interest rates being paid. An added incentive to borrowers was that their high-risk ventures were federally insured—risk-free loans. The growing dependency on brokered deposits in conjunction with high-risk commercial loans pressured many S and L's managers to exceed the 40 percent total asset limit or to violate regulatory laws for making commercial loans.

Looting took many forms and was perpetrated by insiders and by insider/outsider partnerships. S and L's insiders often went on "buying sprees" where bank funds were used to purchase goods and services for personal use. Another insider practice was "excessive compensation" for S and L's directors, executives or managers in the form of large salaries, bonuses, dividends, and perquisites. Insider/outsider partnerships involved a variety of "special deals." One "special deal" was "land flips" which involved "transfers of land between related parties to fraudulently inflate the value of the land. The land is used as collateral for loans based on the inflated or fraudulent valuation. Loan amounts typically greatly exceed the actual value of the land" (U.S. Congress, House Committee on Government Operations, quoted in Calavita and Pontell, 1990:324). Another insider/outsider deal was the "daisy chain." This special deal involved the exchange of a loan for a large deposit. The borrower then defaulted on the loan. The borrower got the cash with no intention of repayment, the S and L's inflated its assets, and bank executives received large bonuses for the large deposit.

Covering up was also widespread among insolvent S and L's. One common cover-up strategy involved setting up a special account from which to draw interest payments. For example, a loan of $500,000 is extended to $750,000 with $250,000 in a special account to draw interest payment from. This makes the loan appear current even if the loan has failed or was phony to begin with (Calavita and Pontell, 1990:327). However, Calavita and Pontell, (1990:327) report the most common cover-up was to keep two or three sets of books to conceal law violations and violators.

How many fraudulent schemes have gone or remain undetected is uncertain. The billions of dollars lost from such fraudulent ventures is impossible to calculate accurately. It is doubtful, however, that Equity and a few insolvent S and L's stand alone or are the only businesses to create fictitious customers, fabricate policies, or exaggerate assets. The motive to maintain or increase the market value of a company's stock is as real today as it has ever been, and the probability of detection remains relatively low.

Crimes Against Employees. Occupational health and safety violations and violations of labor laws are corporate crimes against employees. Labor law violations cost American workers unknown millions of dollars, but health and safety violations costs 100,000 lives and 390,000 disabilities every year. As many as 20 percent of all cancers result from polluted work environments. As many as 20 million workers are exposed to dangerous chemicals at work each year (Simon and Eitzen, 1986:109–110). The substances that the largest number of workers are exposed to are: asbestos—1.6 million exposed; lead—835,000 exposed; arsenic—600,000 exposed; benzene—600,000 exposed; cotton dust—600,000 exposed; and coal dust—208,000 exposed (Simon and Eitzen, 1986:111).

Why do so many workers die, or become disabled in their work environments? The answer appears to be that a safe workplace cuts into corporate profits. In 1972, for example, Johns-Manville, the largest manufacturer of asbestos products in the United States estimated that it would cost $17 million to install and maintain dust-control equipment. Whereas, Workmen's Compensation for workers killed or disabled by asbestos dust would cost $1 million a year (Ermann and Lundman, 1982:70). Thus, Johns-Manville maintained their 30-year policy of not informing workers of the potential health hazards from asbestos dust. Company executives did not, however, anticipate the long-term costs. By the late 1970s, class action suits against Johns-Manville were estimated at $12 million a year and rising.

More recently, there has been a dramatic development in possible sanctions against corporations whose employees die as a result of unsafe working conditions. Corporations and their executives may now be found guilty of criminal homicide.

On February 10, 1983, Stephan Golab, and employee of a Film Recovery Services, Inc. factory in Elk Grove, Illinois, collapsed and died while stirring tanks containing sodium cyanide. His cause of death was determined to be cyanide poisoning. After his death, the Occupational Safety and Health Administration (OSHA) inspected the plant. The inspection found 20 safety violations. OSHA fined Film Recovery Systems, Inc. $4,555. However, the Cook County State's Attorney's Office brought criminal homicide charges against Film Recovery Systems, Inc. and three of its executives. In what proved to be a precedential ruling, three company officials were found guilty of murder and were sentenced to 25 years in prison. The company was found guilty of manslaughter and fined $24,000 (Harvard Law Review, 1987:535).

Crimes Against Customers.   Crimes against customers are many and varied. Among others, the production of unsafe products, price-fixing, and consumer fraud are widespread.

The production of unsafe products can result from honest oversight, but often it is willful and, once discovered, consciously covered up. We began this chapter with the Pinto case, perhaps the most highly publicized instance of the production of a product known by corporate officials to be unsafe. However, the Pinto is not an isolated case in the auto industry. Before the Pinto, there was GM's Corvair. Ralph Nader's 1972 publication of *Unsafe at Any Speed* showed Corvairs to be particularly susceptible to overturning. Several other Corvair defects were noted by Nader, including a heater that vented carbon monoxide to the driver and passengers. GM's response was to cover-up any evidence confirming Nader's allegations, and to publicly discredit Nader (Simon and Eitzen, 1986:98). After the Pinto,

there was GM's x-body cars (the 1980 Chevrolet Citation, Pontiac Phoenix, Oldsmobile Omega, and Buick Skylark). GM's x-body cars had a serious defect in their brake system. By 1983, the government had received 1,700 complaints about brakes locking, including fifteen deaths resulting from cars that were thrown into dangerous spins after their brakes locked. GM documents indicated that company officials were aware before production of the problem. The Justice Department charged GM for not correcting the defective brake system and for concealing information about the x-body cars from government authorities (Simon and Eitzen, 1986:99).

Unsafe products are by no means limited to the auto industry. A sample of companies sanctioned over the two previous decades includes: Goodrich Tire and Rubber, Beech Aircraft, McDonnell Douglas, Richardson-Merrell, Hormel Company, Bassett Furniture, Advance Machine Company, Inc., and Pittway Corporation (Ermann and Lundman, 1982:84; Michalowski, 1985:338). How many more have gone undetected? How many people have died or been seriously injured by unsafe products? And, how many of you will be killed, disabled or injured by products known by corporate officials to be hazardous to life?

Price fixing is an agreement between supposedly competing companies to set and maintain uniform prices. Price fixing may cost each customer very little but generate billions of dollars for the companies involved. Sutherland's (1949) pioneer study of corporate violations and Clinard and Yeager's (1980) more recent study of violations by the largest 582 U.S. corporations showed price fixing to be widespread among a variety of industries. Clinard and Yeager (1980:141) further found that "Corporate executives themselves indicate price fixing is widespread." The most famous case of price fixing in the United States was the agreement among manufacturers of heavy electrical equipment. This agreement cost customers about $2 billion a year. Despite the magnitude of this conspiracy (General Electric, Westinghouse, and 27 other companies) and the massive cost to customers, seven defendants were each sentenced to thirty days in jail and fines totaled approximately $2 million (Geis, 1967). More recent fines have increased; for example, Shell Oil agreed to a $180 million settlement for violations of crude-oil and refined-product price controls (Wall Street Journal, 1987:11). However, government support for trust-busting, according to a veteran congressman, "is a mile wide, but only an inch deep" (Clinard and Yeager, 1980:140).

Consumer fraud generally involves deceptive advertising, overcharging, and promising services that cannot or will not be delivered. Perhaps, the fastest growing and largest consumer fraud, today, is in the health care industry. Fraud and excessive health-care field costs range between 50 and 80 billion dollars a year (Witkin, Friedman, and Guttman, 1992:34). In health care, "cartel-type frauds" involving several providers and suppliers are increasing. Also, electronic claims filing eliminates a paper trail for investigators, and outpatient care disperses the location of fraud making it tougher to pin down the source of fraud (Witkin, Friedman, and Guttman, 1992). Two new and ingenious kinds of health care fraud, as reported by Witkin, Friedman, and Guttman (1992: 34–38), are "rolling labs" and "equipment sales."

Rolling labs are companies that perform unnecessary and fake tests on patients and then bill the insurance company or Federal government. One such operation involved 1,000 companies that between 1986 and 1988 filed one billion dollars in false claims. In this operation, telephone sales people offered comprehensive physical exams to persons, mostly elderly, with private insurance and/or Medicare. After the customers filled out a medical-history form, company officials doctored the form, previously signed by a physician, with false information of a current illness. The insurance companies or Medicare were then billed for bogus tests. For just one patient, the bogus bill was $7,500 (Witkin, Friedman and Guttman, 1992:35).

Equipment sales have become a "high-tech, modern medicine show" for dishonest marketers who now sell lift chairs, oxygen concentrators, and home dialysis systems instead of "snake oil." In one scam, telephone sales people would obtain Medicare numbers over the phone, then they would make medical diagnoses for expensive "high-tech" equipment while on the phone and insure customers that Medicare would provide 100 percent coverage. Orders were then placed on medical forms that doctors had signed before they had been completed. Of course, medicare beneficiaries were actually obligated to pay 20 percent and Medicare 80 percent for the unnecessary and unwanted equipment. In addition, outrageous prices were charged. For example, a $28 piece of bed-size foam became a "dry flotation mattress" that sold for $900. Equipment companies also took advantage of regional differences in Medicare payment rates. For example, "Medicare pays $41.93 for a wheelchair seat cushion in Tennessee, but pays $248.96 in Pennsylvania for the very same item. Not surprisingly, lots of suppliers have set up 'branch offices' that are little more than mail drops in high-priced states" (Witkin, Friedman, and Guttman, 1992:37).

These are just two examples of fraudulent schemes in "a world of plenty." Home-care providers bill for more hours than are provided, and charge nurses rates for aides time. Also, mental health facilities are paying "bounty hunters" to bring in patients who are temporarily hospitalized, often against their will, and given treatments to maximize insurance payments (Witkin, Friedman, and Gutt-man, 1992:42–43).

Crimes Against the Public-at-Large. Corporate crimes against the public generally involve public health and safety violations such as polluting the environment. There have been many highly publicized instances of massive environmental harm for which corporations have been liable such as the Santa Barbara oil spill in 1969, the dumping of Kepone, a toxic insecticide, into the James River of Virginia in 1976, and the Exxon Valdez oil spill in Prince William Sound of Alaska in 1989. However, other corporate violations against public health and safety have had a more direct and devastating impact on human life. The events in Buffalo Creek, West Virginia, and Love Canal, New York, illustrate the devastating impact that corporate violations can have on human life.

On February 25, 1972, in Buffalo Creek, West Virginia, a dam illegally maintained by the Buffalo Creek-Pittston Coal Company burst. The 20 to 30 foot tidal wave destroyed 16 communities, 1,000 homes, and 125 people were killed. Most of the residents settled for the property damage initially offered by the Pittston Coal Company. The approximate 600 persons who did not immediately settle were later awarded a total of $13.5 million by Pittston (U.S. Congress, 1980:3).

From 1942 to 1953, the Hooker Chemical and Plastics Corporation dumped toxic chemical wastes in the Love Canal near Niagara Falls, New York. In 1953, Hooker donated the Canal to the local school board. The school board used part of the Canal for the construction of a school and sold the remainder to a developer who constructed 200 homes on the site. As early as 1958, Hooker executives knew that children were exposed to chemical burns and toxic fumes. Hooker executives, however, chose not to notify school board officials of the hazards for fear of legal action that would necessitate an ex-

pensive clean-up. For residents of Love Canal, the odds of cancer were one in ten. Residents also had unusually high rates of chromosomal abnormalities. Eventually, Love Canal was declared a federal disaster area. New York State sued Hooker for $635 million, and the Environmental Protection Agency sued for $124.5 million for four Hooker chemical dumps in Niagara Falls (Simon and Eitzen, 1982:4–5).

EXPLANATIONS OF CORPORATE CRIME

Macro-objectivist Theories

Macro-objectivist theories focus on broad societal arrangements in seeking explanations for norm-violating behavior. These theories attempt to explain the distribution of norm-violating behaviors across various social groups or strata. Strain theory and neo-Marxist theory are two types of macro-objectivist explanations. Both strain theory and neo-Marxist direct focus on the social structural arrangements that give rise to the criminal behaviors of corporations and corporate actors.

A Strain Theory of Corporate Crime. Box provides a strain theory of corporate crime. The source of strain is the contradiction between corporate *goals* and *environmental needs*. Corporate goals include profit, growth and market control. Environmental needs include the needs of competitors, the state, employees, consumers, and the public. The contradiction between corporate goals and environmental needs creates a corporate anomie (see anomie theory, Chapter 2). Criminal acts are corporate adaptations to anomie. For example, the contradiction between corporate profit-seeking and the political needs of the state may result in illegal campaign contributions by corporations to political parties or candidates. Examples of the types of crimes that result from the contradictions between corporate goals and environment needs are listed in Figure 13-1.

Corporate anomie is a necessary condition for corporate crime, but corporate anomie alone is not sufficient to explain why corporate actors perpetrate crimes. Corporate actors must have certain individual characteristics (unlimited ambition, shrewdness, moral flexibility) and a motive for corporate crime. These individual characteristics reflect the "situational demands" of corporate organization, and they are "learnt in association with other corporate executives." "Anomie of success" is the term Box (1983:64) applies to these individual characteristics. The motive for corporate crime is the "rational solution to problems created by contradictions between corporation and environment" (Box 1983:64). The motive for corporate crime is easily transformed into actual illegal corporate acts where three broad societal conditions accommodate their occurrence: ideology, law enforcement, and opportunity. The U.S.'s free enterprise/business ideology is a higher morality from which corporate crimes are made respectable, or, at least, from which corporate illegalities are inferred to as something less than criminal. Also, law enforcement seldom applies criminal labels to corporate illegal acts. Finally, opportunity exists where there is little surveillance, hidden behaviors, and the power to shape laws and reject criminal labels.

Box's strain theory of corporate crime (Figure 13-1) has not been tested as a unified causal explanation of corporate crime. However, Box's theory integrates the two essential components of a causal explanation of criminal behavior (motivation and opportunity). Also, his theory is consistent with sociological research on corporate crime. From a review of research on corporate crime, James Coleman (1989) identifies components of motivation and opportunity that closely resembles Box's theory of corporate crime.

Also to Box's credit is his theoretical incorporation of the process of socialization. The individual characteristics of unlimited ambition, shrewdness, and moral flexibility are learned from association with other corporate executives. Corporate socialization through association was first identified by Sutherland (1949).

Neo-Marxist Theories of Corporate Crime. Central to neo-Marxist explanations is their conceptualization of the capitalist state. In Chapter 2, you learned that many neo-Marxists view the state as a coordinating agency responsible for administering the affairs of capitalist society. The chief administrative activities of the state are essentially two-fold. First, the state must protect and contribute to the process by which wealth in capitalist society is accumulated. Second, the state must maintain political legitimacy by regulating the process of accumulation on behalf of us all—rich and poor. For example, the state must create opportunities for industry to accumulate profits and markets. But, the state must also protect laborers, farmers, children, and other sectors of the population from the brunt of industry's accumulation, if the process by which we accumulate (capitalism) and the state itself are to survive. To properly perform its functions of accumulation and legitimation, the state must regulate capitalism. Therefore, the state has interests of its own (survival) that preempt the interests of the wealthy. State regulation, then, is the source of corporate crime.

According to T.R. Young (1981) there are three characteristics of the capitalist state that create an environment in which corporate crimes become necessary. They are as follows:

1. Ordinary practices of private business come to be defined as illegal. Labor practices, marketing practices, pollution practices and fiscal practices enter into

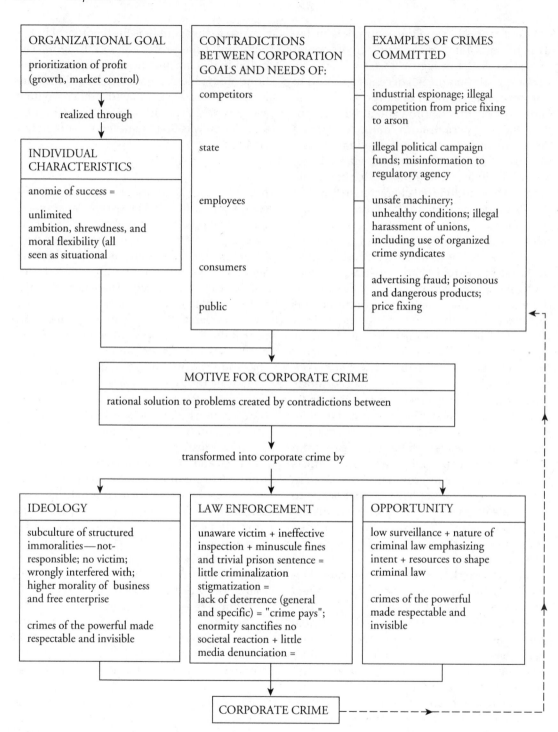

FIGURE 13-1.   A Strain Theory of Corporate Crime

Source: Box, Steve. *Power, Crime, and Mystification.* New York: Tavistock, 1983 p. 64.

deliberations on the criminal code and become proscribed by law.

2. The state sets such hard conditions for producing and selling that the corporation must violate them if it is to survive.

3. The state acts irrationally and infuses private owners with little more than contempt for its stupidity—why obey stupid laws. The state acts irrationality by serving corporate special interests one at a time. This practice results in inconsistent laws (Young, 1981:326).

These three characteristics of the state result from the contradictory tasks (accumulation and legitimation) that the state must perform if it is itself to survive. Given these characteristics, corporate crimes are crimes of survival. Corporate crimes are committed routinely and systematically. Corporate violations are rational business acts by actors who are confronted with irrational regulation—"stupid" and "inconsistent" laws.

The cause of corporate crime, then, is state regulation of capitalist accumulation to insure stability and, thereby, legitimate the long-term investments that are necessary for continued accumulation. In the short-term, however, regulations are obstacles to maximization of profit, therefore, corporations routinely violate state regulations to insure immediate profit-making.

However, this explanation of corporate crime may be limited to a type of capitalism—industrial capitalism. In industrial capitalism, profit-making depends on the production and sale of goods. Some observers, however, believe that the United States has entered a new phase in capitalism—"finance capitalism." In finance capitalism, profit comes from "fiddling with money"; for example, corporate takeovers, currency trading, loan swaps, land speculation, futures trading, etc. What is being produced is capital gains rather than products (Calavita and Pontell, 1990:335–336). In this "casino" economy,

capitalists are no longer constrained by long-term investments and labor relations, and they have little to loose by "reckless behavior" (Calavita and Pontell, 1990:336). Therefore a new and different opportunity structure for corporate crime has emerged. With the advent of finance capitalism, new types of corporate crime are emerging, for example "collective embezzlement," and their cause is deregulation rather than regulation. No longer constrained by the natural laws of long-term investment and labor relations, the decline in state regulatory laws (deregulation) creates new opportunities for financial crimes. Here, "financial crime is confined only to the limits of one's imagination" (Calavita and Pontell, 1990:336). The savings and loan crisis demonstrates all too well what one's imagination can do when unconstrained by the production process and the state.

Micro-Objectivist Theories

Micro-objectivist theories attempt to answer why particular actors engage in norm-violating behavior. These theories focus on the social forces that account for an individual's acquisition and maintenance of deviant behavior. In Chapter 2, we learned that social learning theory and control theory represent micro-objectivist theories. Both social learning theory and control theory have been applied to corporate crime.

Learning Theories of Corporate Crime. Social learning theorists maintain that corporate executives through interaction with corporate superiors and peers learn to define criminal acts as positive or necessary business practices. Edwin Sutherland (1949) provided the first social learning explanation for corporate crime. He argued that corporate crime and ordinary street crime share a common cause—differential association. Sutherland used case studies to demonstrate that corporate criminals learn definitions favorable to the violation of law in association with other corporate criminals. However, Sutherland did recognize differences between corporate and traditional crimes. Unlike traditional crimes, corporate crimes are highly organized, and they lack widespread public condemnation. This meant two things to Sutherland. First, corporate crime is organized crime. Definitions favorable to the violation of law are realized by individual actors through either a formal or informal corporate organization for crime. A formal organization for crime is formed by "gentlemen's agreement," "pools," and "in conferences of representatives of corporations." An informal organization for crime is formed by a consensus among corporate executives to not willingly "bear the burdens of competition" or "permit the economic system to regulate itself with laws of supply and demand" (Sutherland, 1949:219). Second, the corporate organization is not met with a organization of resistance (public condemnation). The lack of organized condemnation for corporate crime means that corporate criminals are not exposed to significant definitions unfavorable to the violation of law.

In sum, corporate crime results from an excess of definitions favorable to the violation of law. Definitions favorable to violation of law are learned in association with other corporated criminals. These favorable definitions are transformed into criminal acts by formal and informal organizations for crime that are internal to corporate structures. And, corporate actors are not exposed to significant definitions unfavorable to the violation of law because there is little external condemnation of corporate crime. Sutherland's recognition that corporate organization shapes learning is central to another, more contemporary, learning theory of corporate crime by Clinard and Yeager. They, however, abandon Sutherland's notion of favorable versus unfa-

vorable definitions, and they do not see associations as the cause of corporate crime.

Clinard and Yeager (1980:298) have done the most comprehensive study of corporate crime ever. These researchers conclude that corporate crimes result form a "corporate way of life." According to Clinard and Yeager, a "corporate way of life" supportive of illegal behavior is most likely where illegal practices are already widespread in a particular industry, the pressure for profit is great, competition is high, and government regulation is uncertain. Given these external forces, corporate executives create and maintain an internal organization for crime. The internal organization for crime consists of business norms that support illegal behavior. These norms are transmitted to individual executives and managers through the process of socialization. That is, corporate actors learn to be criminal as a part of their job. Corporate sanctions or rewards (continued employment, advancement, salary, benefits) insure actor conformity to business norms. These business norms are not specific positive or negative definitions of crime. Rather, they are beliefs and rules that neutralize an actor's commitment to conventional noncriminal norms. One important business norm that neutralizes the constraints of conventional morality is that all legal regulation of business constitutes a violation of free enterprise. Here, corporate actors who engage in illegal violations are conforming to a greater good—free enterprise; and, thereby, they are free from guilt of any "real" wrongdoing.

Neutralizations that free actors from feelings of guilt are, of course, a central component of traditional control theories, rather than social learning theories (see Chapter 2). However, Clinard and Yeager's emphasis is on the learning of a "corporate way of life" that condones illegal behavior through socialization and corporate sanctioning. The content of the "corporate way of life" is business norms that, in effect, neutralize conventional law-abiding constraints. Therefore, it is more a matter of degree than of kind that Clinard and Yeager's work illustrates a social learning theory.

Control Theories of Corporate Crime. Control theories suggest that corporate actors hold the values and norms of conventional society. The central question for control theorists is: "why do corporate actors violate the norms in which they believe?" The answer depends on the particular brand of control theory: social bond, neutralization, or deterrence (see Chapter 2). Concerning corporate crime, neutralization theories and deterrence theories are prominent. Neutralization theories focus on the justifications or excuses that both motivate corporate actors to violate norms and that free corporate actors from feelings of guilt. Deterrence theories emphasize the legal controls that motivate corporate actors to refrain from violating norms. Deterrence theorists assume that prior to engaging in illegal conduct, corporate actors calculate whether such conduct will result in more pleasure (profits) than pain (losses).

Neutralizing Corporate Crime. Simon and Eitzen (1986) argue that corporate crime can be explained by the corporate actors' occupational role which is shaped by bureaucratic structural characteristics. These authors identify three central qualities of structures: "(1) centralization of authority, (2) creation of specialized vocabularies and ideologies, and (3) fragmentation and routinization of tasks" (1986:236).

Centralization of authority secures middle- and low-level corporate actors conformity to the will of corporate elites. The overwhelming power of corporate elites insures the cooperation of nonelites in committing criminal acts. Corporate nonelites have been trained to accept elite corporate power

as legitimate. Also, nonelites know that failure to comply could result in negative sanctions such as being fired, demoted, not promoted, and reassigned or relocated that are less desirable.

Specialized vocabularies and ideologies is the organizational characteristic that allows actors to engage in illegal acts because they do not see their acts as particularly wrong. According to Simon and Eitzen, a "sanitizing ideology" and a "vocabulary of motives" trickle down to nonelites from a subculture of elite behavior that forms at the top of the corporate organization. This subculture of elite behavior "consists of norms and sentiments that make deviance permissible" (Simon and Eitzen, 1986:238). The subcultures ideological content is the "precepts and customs delicately balanced between conventional and criminal (deviant) behavior, as well as objectives that may be obtained through both deviant and nondeviant means" (Simon and Eitzen, 1986:238). Corporate actors filter their illegal acts through this "ideological prism" which sanitizes their illegal acts by giving them the appearance of being noncriminal (Simon and Eitzen, 1986:238). A central part of the "sanitizing ideology" is a "vocabulary of motives." The vocabulary of motives is comprised of a variety of verbal justifications or excuses that motivate corporate actors to engage in illegal conduct and remove any feeling of guilt. These vocabularies are verbal justifications for action—techniques of neutralization. Simon and Eitzen provide examples for four techniques of neutralization.

1. Denying responsibility: The rationalization here shifts blame to sources other than the corporation. Examples include: the consumer "misused" the product, the employee's death was an "accident," or the problem resulted from the government's failure to regulate effectively.

2. Denying victimization/dehumanization: The justification here is that no real person suffers. While millions of people may in fact suffer from corporate bribes of government officials, the act was directed against a government, a competitor, or the market not against persons.
3. Authorization/higher loyalties: Here corporate actors claim loyalty to a superior morality, for example, "business ethics" or "our country's values."
4. Condemning condemners: This rationalization is an attack on those (government) whose regulations interfere with the free-enterprise system. Regulations cause crime not corporate actions (1986:238–240).

Techniques of neutralization free corporate actors to engage in illegal acts while maintaining a respectable self-image. Corporate actors perceive themselves as pillars of their communities, and they view crime as an activity of the lower class.

The final corporate organizational characteristic identified by Simon and Eitzen is "fragmentation and routinization." The fragmentation and routinization of bureaucratic work distances workers from one another and from the consequences of the work. Routine tasks are specialized and compartmentalized to the point where the left hand does not know or want to know what the right hand is doing. Corporate elites prefer not to be informed of the means of underling actors behaviors, only the ends. That is, did they get the job done profitably? Also, corporate elites can hide their own crimes from other workers. Finally, corporate actors cannot associate their fragmented actions with the consequence of the finished corporate product. For example, workers who engaged in the production of dioxin never witnessed the effects on residents of Love Canal (Simon and Eitzen, 1986:240). Nor did Ford Motor Company executives sift through the charred bodies or witness the permanent scars and disabilities that resulted from the Pinto's defective gas tank.

Deterring Corporate Crime. Deterrence theory assumes that humans are motivated to seek pleasure and avoid pain. It is further assumed that human actors rationally calculate whether an act will result in more pleasure than pain. If an actor perceives that his or her behavior will result in more pain than pleasure, then the actor will not engage in that particular behavior. Therefore, deterrence theorists view legal sanctions that are both certain and severe as essential to preventing norm-violating behavior. Certain and severe legal sanctions are necessary to accomplish both general and specific deterrence. General deterrence refers to an instance where others refrain from norm-violating behavior because they are aware of the legal sanctions that were applied to another. Specific deterrence refers to the effects of legal sanctions on the particular individual who was sanctioned.

Corporate crimes are, for the most part, rational and calculative in nature. Therefore, the certain application of severe legal sanctions to corporations and corporate actors should deter corporate crime. The problem, however, is that certain and severe legal sanctions are not applied to illegal corporate acts, and criminal labels are seldom applied to corporate actors who commit crimes that benefit the corporation. Briefly, let us review why this is the case.

Federal regulatory agencies are the primary bodies that create laws and apply legal sanctions to corporate violators. The resources available to regulatory agencies are minimal compared to corporations. Therefore, regulatory agencies can only investigate a small number of selected cases, and cannot afford delays. Delay, of course, is a favorite strategy among corporate lawyers. Corporate lawyers, too, are more skilled in defense than government lawyers are in prosecution. Braithwaite (1979:130) notes, "government lawyers, who must in many ways be all-rounders, cannot compete with the corporate lawyers who spend their whole lives finding out all there is to know about a delimited area of 'legal loop-holers.' " Regulatory agencies are also limited by national boundary in their pursuit of corporate violators. Today's multinational corporations can export their crimes to other countries where there is even less regulation (Box, 1983:46). Corporate decision makers know in advance of their illegal acts that regulatory agencies do not have the resources to discover, pursue, or prosecute them. The deterrence factor of certainty of punishment is all but nonexistent for corporate norm violators.

Severity of punishment, too, is not evident where legal sanctions are applied to corporate violators. The typical sanction applied to corporate illegality is an administrative warning, consent decree, or fine. The fines imposed on corporations are not severe. When these fines are compared to a corporation's gross earnings, they are absurdly low. Corporations often pay a fine that is less of their gross earnings than what individuals pay for a parking ticket compared to their gross earnings. Ermann and Lundman (1982:148), for example, figured the largest corporate fine given in 1961 was the equivalent of $12.30 for a person whose gross income in that year was $15,000. In 1976, the largest corporate fine was the equivalent of $1.80 for a $15,000 annual wage earner.

Given the large profits to be gained from corporate illegality, present legal sanctions are perhaps incentives rather than deterrents for crime. We will return to the issue of deterrence in our discussion of social policies to control corporate crime.

Carter and Blum-West (1984) note a shortcoming in theories of corporate crime that seems appropriate for social learning, control, and deterrence theories. These authors

argue that corporate crimes are permissible, and legal sanctions are seldom applied because "doing business" excuses wrongful behaviors. Behaviors that if committed outside the realm of business would quickly be defined as crimes.

Sutherland came close to seeing this by noting that businessmen viewed their illegal acts as "sharp" business practices rather than as crimes. Similarly, Clinard and Yeager identify a "corporate way of life" and Simon and Eitzen a "subculture of elite behavior." However, these concepts fail to recognize the ubiquity of "doing business." Carter and Blum-West suggest that "doing business" is a cultural concept not a subcultural one. Americans generally do not see business acts, including many illegalities, as a departure from norms. If a departure is perceived, the act will seldom be seen as a "real" crime. Many law-abiding citizens engage in illegal acts in the course of business; for example, not reporting all income. Or what about the home buyer who agrees to pay the points (advanced interest) back to the seller after closing a FHA or Veterans loan. Legally, some points are to be paid by the seller. Or, after selling a used car, how many parents have told their child, "that's not really lying or cheating, it's just business, do you understand the difference?" The public and law enforcers are quick to define those injures that we do to one another more or less directly as crimes, but these same injuries are seldom seen as crimes if committed in the course of business.

This is not simply a lack of public condemnation. Crime seriousness surveys reveal that the public often views corporate crime as more serious and more deserving of punishment than many street crimes (Braithwaite, 1982). Also, there is evidence that public punitive attitudes toward corporate crime are increasing (Cullen, Link and Polanzi, 1982). Rather, once defined as crime, as corporate illegalities are in crime seriousness surveys, with all that the label "crime" implies about evil intent and immorality, the public is more than ready to condemn these acts. What is lacking in real-life cases is the readiness to see corporate offenses as criminal acts. What differs is not the degree of condemnation, but the readiness to define business infractions as crimes (Carter and Blum-West, 1984).

Macro-Subjectivist Theories

Macro-subjectivists focus on the social processes by which certain behaviors are defined as deviance and particular persons as deviant. Among these theories are interest group theories and organizational theories. Interest group theories seek to explain the creation of official deviance definitions (usually laws) as the products of power struggles between various interest groups. Organizational theories attempt to explain the creation of deviance definitions as products of social control agents who process cases within a particular organizational setting. Agents' definitions produce official deviants and official rates of deviance.

Interest Group Theories. Concerning corporate crime, the question to be addressed by interest group theories is: "How do certain business activities become criminal acts?" According to interest group theory, the answer is to be found in the economic, political, or moral considerations that prompt interest groups to create legal definitions.

The U.S. antitrust movement, occurring at the end of the nineteenth century, provides insight into how and why certain business practices ("in restraint of trade" and "substantial lessening of competition") came to be defined as criminal. The legislation that ultimately stipulated these business practices to be criminal is the Sherman Antitrust Act of 1890.

The social, political, and historical forces that culminated in the Sherman Antitrust Act were grounded in the economic conditions

of small farmers in late nineteenth-century America. During the 1870s and 1880s, farm prices were declining but the price of goods and services purchased by the farmer remained fixed. Increasing numbers of farmers fell into debt, tenancy, and ruin. The farmers attributed their worsening condition to the growth of big business "trusts" or monopolies. Midwest and western farmers formed political organizations to force government regulation of big business. Among these, the most successful organization was the National Grange. The Grangers demanded legislation to regulate railroad fees and laws to eliminate the rebates and passes given to big business. The passage of the Interstate Commerce Act of 1887 eliminated the discrimination in railroad fees.

Notwithstanding this important political victory, farmer hostility remained. Farmers formed alliances with small businessmen and urban factory workers. Small businessmen feared ruin from the concentration of wealth and resources of trusts, and urban factory workers feared the loss of their bargaining power. By the late 1880s, these alliances were ready for political action and their targets had expanded to a number of trust industries, such as those in fuel oil, iron/steel, sugar, and agricultural machinery. The public hostility toward big business and the strength of antitrust organizations could not be ignored. In the 1888 presidential election, both the Democrats and Republicans included antitrust planks in their platforms. The Fifty-First Congress was also "determined" to legislate an antitrust policy. In the words of Senator Sherman:

> *"If we will not endure a king as a political power, we should not endure a king over the production, transportation, and sale of any of the necessities of life" (Neale and Goyder, 1980:16).*

In 1890, the Fifty-First Congress enacted the Sherman Antitrust Act. The Sherman Antitrust Act prohibits restraint of trade and monopoly:

Section 1. Every contract, combination in the form of trust or otherwise, or conspiracy, in restraint of trade or commerce among the several states or with foreign nations, is hereby declared to be illegal . . .

Section 2. Every person who shall monopolize, or attempt to monopolize, or combine or conspire with any other person or persons to monopolize any part of the trade or commerce among the several states, or with foreign nations, shall be deemed guilty of a misdemeanor . . . (Neale and Goyder, 1980:3).

The Sherman Antitrust Act of 1890 has been described as a defeat for big business at the hands of mass public opposition in the form of interest group coalitions of independent farmers, small businessmen, and urban factory workers (Stone, 1977; Neale and Goyder, 1980). This interpretation, however, has been challenged; most notably by Gabriel Kolko (1963). Kolko argues that early federal regulation of business including the Sherman Antitrust Act was a victory for big business. Case studies of the major trusts of the era (iron and steel, oil, automobile, agricultural machinery, telephone, copper, and meat packing) shows that the failure of big business to control markets through mergers led big business itself to lobby for federal regulation. Unable to regulate prices, increase profits, and protect themselves from competitors, big business sought to secure their dominant position through federal regulation. Antitrust laws would restrain competition so as to prevent complete control of markets and resources from rival competitors. Federal antitrust laws would also undercut some of the severe and unpredictable antitrust laws of individual states that threatened the dominant business of the time. The Sherman Antitrust Act of 1890 was a significant step toward "political capitalism." Kolko (1963:5) notes "Ironically, contrary to the consensus of historians it was not the existence of monopoly that caused the federal government to intervene in the economy, but the lack of it." Con-

trary to the public view of trusts, there was vigorous competition in all of these industries. Political capitalism is political intervention to achieve stability, predictability, and security that cannot be achieved by business itself in an erratic and fluctuating competitive economy (Kolko, 1963:3). According to Kolko, the real interest group behind the Sherman Antitrust Act of 1890 and subsequent federal regulations between 1900–1916 was big business.

The original and intended purpose of the Sherman Antitrust Act of 1890 remains an issue. The laws' effect, however, suggests a victory for big business. First, a record number of mergers occurred during the decade that followed the passage of the Sherman Antitrust Act (Hofstadter, 1955). Merger movements had failed prior to the Sherman Antitrust Act (Kolko, 1963). Second, the Sherman Antitrust Act defined acts in restraint of trade and monopoly attempts as misdemeanors—punishable by a fine not to exceed $5,000, by imprisonment up to one year, or both. To understand the insignificance of this criminal penalty, we have calculated what the equivalent of this fine would be for an individual wage earner. Suppose a business with annual sales of one hundred million dollars (not large, even by 1890 standards) was fined $5,000. The equivalent for a person earning ten thousand dollars a year (large by 1890 standards) would be only five cents.

Regardless of the source of interest group pressure, the Sherman Antitrust Act of 1890 began the use of criminal law to regulate the economic activities of business. The Sherman Antitrust Act transformed activities in restraint of trade and in furtherance of monopoly into criminal behaviors.

Organizational Theories. Organizational theories focus on the operation of informal norms within a particular agency of social control. Adherence to these informal norms guides control agents' placement of particular business practices into specified deviance categories, for example, antitrust violations. According to the organizational theorist, official corporate deviants and official rates of corporate deviance reflect the practices of social control agents, rather than the nature and extent of corporate misbehaviors.

Government bureaucracies, known as federal regulatory agencies (Interstate Commerce Commission, Federal Trade Commission, Securities and Exchange Commission, Environmental Protection Agency, etc.) label and sanction corporate misbehavior. Unlike the criminal court bureaucracies that label and sanction individual misbehavior, regulatory agencies both create and enforce laws that apply to business. On the one hand, regulatory agencies are themselves interest groups. They must create laws in the face of potential opposition from the corporate sector, small business, labor, and the concerned public. On the other hand, regulatory agencies must investigate and sanction offenders.

The inner workings of these agencies involves a complex set of lawmaking and law enforcement activities. Sociologists have been more interested in regulatory agency lawmaking than law enforcement. However, some research provides insights into the enforcement norms of the regulatory agencies that label and sanction corporate offenders. Inner organization enforcement norms of regulatory agencies are, in part, shaped by outside political pressure and the power of corporations.

Regulatory agencies are subject to outside political pressure, especially from the executive branch of government. Some regulatory agencies are directed by a group of commissioners who are appointed by the President. Other regulatory agencies are directed by an administrative head and staff. The head administrator is appointed by the President (Coleman, 1989). The executive branch of government is clearly not insulated from the power of the corporate sector. Presidential campaigns are largely financed by corporate

contributions, and the President's advisors and cabinet members are often corporate leaders. Thus, regulatory commissioners and administrative heads are persons who embrace the values of the business community. For example, in his review of the Ford Pinto Case, Dowie (1977) noted how Ford easily convinced successive Secretaries of Transportation that safety standards would damage the auto industry.

> *The Nixon transportation secretaries were the kind of regulatory officials big business dreams of. They understood and loved capitalism and thought like businessmen. Yet, best of all, they came to office uninformed on technical automotive matters. And you could talk "burn injuries" and "burn deaths" with these guys, and they didn't seem to envision children crying at funerals and people hiding in their homes with melted faces. Their minds appeared to have leaped right to the bottom line—more safety meant higher prices, higher prices meant lower sales and lower sales meant lower profits (Dowie, 1977:30–1).*

Also, the pro-business years of the Reagan Administration brought a "virtual administrative paralysis" to the federal regulatory enforcement (Coleman, 1989:165). During the early Reagan years (1981–83), the number of antitrust complaints and sanctions by the Federal Trade Commission declined by 56 percent from the three-year period (1977–80) that preceded Reagan (Coleman, 1989).

Another outside force affecting organizational enforcement norms is the "power of accusers" (regulatory agencies) as compared to the power of corporations (Ermann and Lundman, 1987). Corporations have tremendous influence and wealth with which to combat the enforcement efforts of regulatory agencies. The resources (time, money, and staff) of regulatory agencies are easily strained by the superior resources of corporations. The meager resources of regulatory agencies are illustrated well in the Federal Trade Commissions's (FTC) antitrust case against the oil industry. This single case consumed about 14 percent of the FTC's total antitrust budget, and after eight years of investigation the FTC dropped the case because of its "length and complexity" (Coleman, 1989:163).

Regulatory agents who embrace the values of big business, and the wealth of corporations appears to produce two internal regulatory enforcement norms. First, corporate misbehaviors are, for the most part, handled as administrative wrongs rather than as crimes. Second, regulatory organizations pursue small time offenders in order to increase the number of convictions. Administrative sanctions and the convictions of small firms maximize the organizations efficiency.

Regulatory agencies can take administrative or civil action, or they can recommend criminal action against corporate violators. If criminal action is recommended, the Justice Department or a federal district prosecutor will ultimately decide whether or not to bring criminal charges. Administrative actions include warnings, fines, reparation payments, and consent decrees. Consent decrees result from agency/corporation negotiations. In effect, what they say is "the firm has done nothing wrong and it promises never to do it again" (Parenti, 1977:129). Civil actions are fines. In order to maximize efficiency, the majority of corporate misbehaviors are labeled as administrative wrongs and remedied by administrative action. Research on the corporate illegalities of 477 U.S. manufacturing corporations in 1975 and 1976 found that about 75 percent of the 1,529 sanctions were administrative. Twenty-one percent were civil sanctions. Only 2.4 percent were criminal penalties (Clinard and Yeager, 1980). Administrative sanctions are often negotiated settlements between the corporate offender and the regulatory organizations. They are more quickly obtained than civil or criminal sanctions. They also require fewer investigatory resources and, thereby, function to maximize organization efficiency.

Another informal enforcement norm that functions to maximize organization effi-

ciency is, "don't go after the corporate big boys." The power of corporate giants strains organizational resources. Strained resources result in few convictions. Few convictions give the appearance of organizational inefficiency. In order to maximize efficiency, regulatory agencies often pursue less complex cases involving smaller firms. There is convincing evidence, for example, that the Food and Drug Administrative has avoided investigating the large food-producing corporations. Also, the Federal Trade Commission and the Antitrust Division of the Justice Department have concentrated on "small-time" antitrust violators, while avoiding the antitrust practices of multinational corporations (Coleman, 1989).

In summary, political pressure and corporate power shape the informal enforcement norms of federal regulatory organizations. Regulatory agents routinely define corporate misbehaviors as administrative wrongs that can be more quickly remedied by administrative sanctions. Also, regulatory agents concentrate on small-time offenders. These organizational norms maximize bureaucratic efficiency and insulate large corporations from criminal labels and criminal penalties.

Micro-Subjectivist Theories

Micro-subjectivist theories focus on the social interactions that prompt audiences to interpret, define, and label a particular act as a type of deviance and actors as deviant. Before an act can be defined as an instance of deviance, however, an audience must know that the act occurred. Similarly, before an actor can be labeled deviant, an audience must "know of" a perpetrator. In the case of corporate actions, audiences are most often not aware that the act has occurred. There is, then, no social reaction. Therefore, there is often no deviant act or deviant actor. According to the micro-subjectivist, deviance is a definition imposed by others, and the deviant is one who is so labeled. Let us turn to audience definitions of corporate crime; and, then, examine the applicability of labeling theory to corporate crime.

Audience Definitions.   Corporate actions are relatively absent from public and official audience responses that interpret, define, and label them as criminal. Why? The answer is two-fold: (1) corporate crimes are, for the most part, hidden from public view; and (2) corporation have the power to reject the labels of others.

At the beginning of this chapter we identified five sources that contribute to hiding corporate crime from public view. Therefore, here, we will concentrate on the power of corporations to reject criminal labels.

Corporations actively work to defend themselves against criminal labels and redefine their actions as noncriminal. Corporate wealth is the source of a corporation's ability to reject criminal labels once an accusation of criminal wrongdoing has been made. Ford Motor Company's reaction to the charge of homicide illustrates the use of corporate wealth to reject criminal labels. Civil suits, consumer groups, and newspaper editorials brought Ford's culpability for death and injury to public attention. Ford responded by denying that the Pinto was unsafe by providing alternative research and different interpretations of research results to government officials, and by countering with an advertising campaign featuring several well-known celebrities (Ermann and Lundman, 1982: 231–2). Although Ford was eventually ordered by the government to repair the Pinto's unsafe gas tank, Ford's power was successful in rejecting a criminal label. The jury did not label Ford's actions as criminal.

The use of corporate wealth to reject criminal labels is also evident before formal accusations are made. Corporations spend millions of dollars annually to establish good will. For example, Mobil Oil and Exxon are the largest contributors to the Public Broad-

casting System. Why such generosity? In the words of one corporate executive, "to win credibility and . . . to provide access to, and rapport with, key groups and special publics—legislators and regulators; the press; intellectuals and academics" (Ermann and Lundman, 1987:21). Having established their credibility, corporations can provide an alternative view of the cause of particular social problems. For example,

> In the winter of 1980, . . . Mobil sponsored the "Edward and Mrs. Simpson" television series. Each installment was prefaced by a "fable." Each fable was lavishly produced and all had the same message. The corporation was not responsible for the current oil crisis. Rather, the crisis was the fault of clumsy intervention and regulation of big government (Ermann and Lundman, 1987:21–2).

The hidden nature of corporate crime and the power of corporations to reject criminal labels limits and alters the social interactions between audiences (victims and interested publics) who interpret and define corporate acts as crimes and corporate actors as criminal. Therefore, micro-subjectivists who view crime solely as the creation and application of definitions by some to others have focused most exclusively on street crime where criminal stereotypes abound, and the status characteristics of victims, offenders, and interested publics are highly visible.

Labeling Theory.   The central question for labeling theorists is, how do audience reactions—in the form of labels, stigmas, and sanctions—operate to increase norm-violating behavior.

The logic of labeling theory is the opposite of deterrence theory. Labeling theorists argue that formal and informal efforts to control deviance often increase the likelihood of further deviant behavior rather than deterring it.

At least two prominent scholars of corporate crime do not believe that labeling theory applies to corporate crime. For example, Braithwaite and Geis (1982) argue that the labeling of corporate wrongs as crimes would most likely deter rather than increase further norm-violating behavior. Their logic is as follows:

> *Although the labeling hypothesis makes it unwise to use publicity as a tool to punish juvenile delinquents, it is sound deterrence to broadcast widely the names of corporate offenders. Corporations and their officers are genuinely afraid of bad publicity arising from their illegitimate activities. They respond to it with moral indignation and denials, not with assertions that "if you think I'm bad I'll really show you how bad I can be," as juvenile delinquents sometimes do.*
>
> *. . . Corporate crimes are almost never crimes of passion; they are not spontaneous or emotional, but calculated risks taken by rational actors. As such, they should be more amenable to control by policies based on the utalitarian assumptions of the deterrence doctrine (Braithwaite and Geis, 1982:301–302).*

As previously discussed, corporations are quite active in establishing good will in order to avoid accusations of illegality, and they use their wealth and power to reject criminal labels once an accusation of criminal activity has been made. It does appear, then, that corporations are "genuinely afraid of bad publicity," as Braithwaite and Geis (1982) have suggested. While there is little evidence to suggest that corporations are deterred by present sanctions, present sanctions are primarily administrative rather than criminal; and the names of corporate offenders are not "broadcast widely." Therefore, the official and unofficial reactions that are central to labeling theory are notably absent in the case of corporations and corporate actors.

SOCIAL POLICY: CONTROLLING CORPORATE CRIME

Clinard and Yeager (1980) identify a variety of strategies intended to control corporate crime. These strategies can be grouped into three general approaches: (1) voluntary changes; (2) state intervention; and (3) consumer action. T.R. Young (1981) provides a systematic critique of all the corporate crime control strategies proposed by Clinard and Yeager. We will present each of the strategies put forth by Clinard and Yeager and T.R. Young's critique of each. We will conclude our discussion on social policy with a look at the neglected victims of corporate crime.

Voluntary Changes

Development of a Stronger Business Ethic. This strategy assumes that corporations should persuade corporate personnel that they ought not engage in misconduct in the first place—"an ounce of prevention is worth a pound of cure." The development of a stronger business ethic can be accomplished by a three-step procedure (Clinard and Yeager, 1980:300–305). First, individual corporations must develop ethical standards and disseminate these standards to all employees through employee handbooks and policy manuals. These ethical standards, however, must be demonstrated in the deeds, not just words, of management. Second, corporations should work toward general corporate business codes to be endorsed by influential organizations, such as the U.S. Chamber of Commerce, and professional associations like the American Association of Advertising Agencies and the National Association of Purchasing Agents. Third, universities, colleges, and professional schools should require students to take courses on business and profession ethics to reinforce the importance of ethical conduct.

T.R. Young (1981:329) suggests this call for ethical behavior among private corporations to be an "exercise in economic naivete." Young argues that the point in forming a corporation is to avoid personal liability for criminal conduct. In corporate structures, decision making is diffused enough to make it difficult to prove the level of intent necessary for a criminal conviction. For example, what specific person or persons at Ford Motor Company intended to produce a potentially lethal product? Given that corporations are designed to avoid criminal liability, ethics are but words which "bind the moral" and "free the nonmoral" to pursue the compelling goals of private gain (Young, 1981:329).

Corporate Organizational Reform. Another voluntary strategy to control corporate crime is organizational reform. Here too, emphasis is on prevention. Clinard and Yeager (1980:307) suggest two organizational reforms: more control by the corporate board of directors and government appointment of public directors. The point of more control by the board of directors is to reform the present situation where boards of directors function primarily as a rubber stamp for corporate management. This reform, T.R. Young characterizes as "palpable nonsense." His objections are two-fold. First, boards of directors already, in law, have control. Second, there is no evidence that more board control means less crime.

The second organizational reform is to have "general public directors" appointed to the corporate board of directors. Public directors should comprise 10 percent of the total board and should be appointed by federal corporate commissions, such as the Securities and Exchange Commission (Clinard and Yeager, 1980:308–309). T.R. Young (1980:329) argues that historically public directors in capitalist societies "usually means an opportunity for party hacks to extort and to accumulate private wealth." We have already seen how federal commissions and agencies are staffed by persons who embrace the values of the business community.

State Intervention

Federal Corporate Chartering. This reform suggests that federal chartering be required of all corporations instead of the present practice of state chartering. The logic is that public good is better protected by federal control than by individual states. According to T.R. Young, federal chartering simply means more federal police. This, Young argues, ignores the failure of the many federal agencies and commissions that presently exist to control corporate crime. "The primary result of this federal chartering would be to increase the rate of reported crime more than to lower the real crime rate" (Young, 1981:329).

Deconcentration or Divestiture. This reform strategy calls for the break-up of large corporations. Large corporations would be required to deconcentrate and to divest themselves of products and subsidiaries. Federal agencies or commissions would decide what size is too big for a particular industry. T.R. Young argues that there is no evidence to suggest that smaller firms produce less crime or smaller criminals. The motives for crime would remain, and there would be more firms to police. Young (1981:329) suggests that, perhaps, smaller firms would desperately scramble to recapture control of the market by both criminal and noncriminal means.

Larger and More Effective Staffs. The strategy here is to increase the staffs and budgets of existing federal regulatory agencies. We have already acknowledged that federal regulatory agencies are "out-gunned," so to speak, by the superior resources of large corporations. Again, this strategy rests on the premise that more police means less crime. At worst, there is no such evidence. At best, this premise remains an empirical question. Young (1981:330) protests that larger and more effective staffs in no way address conditions that motivate corporate crime.

Stiffer Penalties. The objective of this strategy is deterrence. However, research on deterrence does not demonstrate that harsh penalties will reduce crime. At least this is not the case for street crimes. In the case of corporate crimes, Young suggests that more severe penalties may possible eventuate into more crime. In Young's (1981:330) words, " . . . the firm would spend more money for lawyers and bribes, thus driving up the unproductive cost of business . . . and more corporate executives would be in prison and, presumably, learn more and better ways to evade detection." The problem with Young's critique is that it assumes that what occurs for street crimes is what will occur for corporate crimes. Not all scholars agree with this parallel. For example, Braithwaite and Geis (1982) see corporate crimes, because they are rational rather than spontaneous and expressive, as more amenable to deterrent strategies. However, one part of deterrence research on street crimes that most likely would apply to corporate crime is that the certainty of a criminal conviction may be more important than the severity of punishment. To date, the issue of deterring corporate crime is an empirical question yet unanswered because criminal prosecution is not common for corporate violators. Also, let us not forget that we punish crimes for reasons other than deterrence, for example retribution, incapacitation, and rehabilitation. If the inability to deter were sufficient grounds for not imposing severe penalties whole sections of the criminal code could be abandoned.

Publicity as a Sanction. The logic here is that public scrutiny, degradation, and embarrassment may produce a considerable deterrent effect. Clinard and Yeager's research (1980:318) indicated that the publicity of law violations is "the most feared consequence of sanctions imposed on a corporation." Similarly, Braithwaite and Geis (1982:301) argue that "it is sound deterrence to broadcast widely the names of corporate offenders." Young's (1981:330) criticism of publicity as a sanction is that corporations will simply spend more of their money to counteract the negative publicity and pass the costs on to consumers. He notes that when Coors violated the rights of its workers it increased its advertising budget by eight million dollars and increased the cost of beer to pay for it.

Federal Ownership. Clinard and Yeager (1980:322) suggest federal ownership, or nationalization, as a "last resort" for the "few industries" where competition is not effective. Young (1981:330), on the other hand, recommends federal ownership as a "first resort . . . for all." Young (1981:330) implies that Clinard and Yeager's proposed strategy would culminate in federal ownership of the "lemons of capitalist society." He further argues that socialist states, where there is nationalization of industry, do a better job of providing food, health care, and education for the populace than do capitalist societies. However, Young himself admits that the benefits from federal ownership requires comparative research on capitalist and socialist societies.

Consumer Pressure

Whatever strategy is used to bring consumer pressure on corporations to behave is based on the assumption that socially responsible citizens will reward corporate good behavior and punish corporate misbehavior in the market place. Young (1981:330) refers to this strategy as "puerile" which means silly or childish. Ask yourself, are you willing to pay more for goods and services because they are provided by a moral, law-abiding firm, or are you looking for the best buy available? Even if you are willing to do so, Young (1981:330) appropriately points out that "buying sugar, autos, oil, electrical, air travel, food, and other basic commodities outside the monopoly sector would be difficult indeed."

In the absence of some alternative strategy, it seems that some combination of Clinard and Yeager's suggested strategies is required to control corporate crime. Or, perhaps,

Young (1981) is correct in seeing federal ownership, or nationalization, of industry as a "first resort."

Before we conclude, it is important to mention a policy reform that has not been suggested. It is victim compensation. During the 1980s, there was a surge in victim-rights legislation and victim assistance programs throughout the United States. This victims' movement, however, has ignored the rights of victims of corporate crime (Moore and Mills, 1990). Yet, as you have learned, the human and financial costs of corporate crime dwarf the costs of street crime—a fact that few would dispute. Why, then, have the rights of victims of corporate crime been ignored? Moore and Mills (1990) suggest three reasons. First, victims who presently seek redress from corporate victimization receive little satisfaction in response. Often, they receive little more than the "run-around." Victims of corporate crime must "negotiate a maze of agencies and institutions, most of uncertain jurisdiction and commitment. Often the process produces little beyond frustration and, eventually, angry resignation" (Moore and Mills, 1990:411). Second, programs assisting the victims of corporate crime would impose costs on the business community. Given the current political pro-business, antiregulation climate, legislation that might increase business costs is, frankly, "poor politics." Third, corporations are not easily perceived as criminal offenders and, often, victims are perceived as undeserving. Corporate crime, like rape, raises "double standard issues." Moore and Mills put it this way:

> Both crimes are characterized by widespread ambivalence toward the proscribed conduct, victim involvement, and victim's claims for redress. As a result, many white-collar victims do not "arouse the general sympathy reserved for those who have suffered harm, loss, or injury. Instead, these victims often are viewed with a mixture of skepticism, suspicion, and disbelief" and they are seen as "unworthy of society's protection."(1990:413)

Moore and Mills (1990:416) conclude that the neglect of corporate crime victim rights is "not cost-free." Simply stated, the lack of effort to remedy corporate crime victimization undermines efforts to control it.

SUMMARY

There are objectivist and subjectivist definitions of corporate crime. Objectivists offer competing definitions of corporate crime. Objectivists ask should corporate crimes be limited to legal violations or should they be defined as acts of social harm? Proponents of a legal definition define *corporate crime* as any act committed by a corporation or corporate actor that benefits the corporation and that is punishable by the state. Proponents of a social harm definition define *corporate crime* as an act committed by a corporation or corporate actor to benefit the corporation that is punishable by the state or knowingly leads to social injury.

Objectivists also disagree as to whether corporate crimes are distinct from white-collar crimes or are a type of white-collar crime. For example, Clinard and Quinney (1973) drop the term white-collar and distinguish between occupational crime and corporate crime. *Occupational crimes* are offenses by individuals for their own benefit committed in the course of their occupation and offenses committed by employers against employees. Their definition of corporate crime is similar to the legal definition given above. Coleman (1989), on the other hand, argues that the distinction between occupational and corporate crime only makes sense if they are conceptualized as subtypes of white-collar crime. He defines *white-collar crimes* as violations of law by a person or group of persons in the course of a respected and legitimate occupation or financial activity.

According to subjectivists, *corporate crimes* are organizational acts that social audiences respond to and label as such. The behavior and its relation to the law does not matter, rather reactions define it as corporate crime or not.

Corporate crimes are undiscovered, underreported, and concealed. However, government and sociological studies suggest corporate crime to be widespread. In addition, corporate offenders are very often repeat offenders. What is known for certain is that corporate crimes injure and kill many more unsuspecting persons than do all violent street crimes put together. Corporate crimes also cause more economic loss than all property street crimes put together. Furthermore, it is suspected that corporate crimes erode public trust, undermine authority of legal institutions, and contribute to an increase in street crimes.

We identified four types of corporate crime: (1) crimes against owners, (2) crimes against employees, (3) crimes against customers, and (4) crime against the public-at-large. *Crimes against owners* are offenses committed by corporate elites against stockholders. A new type of crime against owners, "collective embezzlement" was discovered in the Savings and Loan crisis. *Collective embezzlement* is the taking of funds from a corporation for personal benefit with the acknowledgement of the corporate operators. Two types of collective embezzlement in the S and L industry were: "land flips" and "daisy chains." *Land flips* are transfers of land between related parties to fraudulently inflate its value to secure loans in great excess of the actual value of the land. *Daisy chains* are loans that are exchanged for a large deposit which increases bank assets and provides bonuses for bank operators who secured the deposit, and the borrower purposely defaults and keeps the money loaned. *Crimes against employees* are corporate violations of occupational health and safety laws, and labor laws. *Crimes against customers* are corporate violations of production, product, pricing, or advertising standards that cause harm to the consumer. *Crimes against the public-at-large* are corporate violations of public health and safety standards and environmental laws.

Rival objectivist explanations of corporate crime were reviewed. Two macro-objectivist were examined: strain theory and neo-Marxist theory. Strain theory locates the cause of corporate crime in corporate anomie. *Corporate anomie* is the contradiction between corporate goals (profit) and environmental needs (competitors, state interests, employees, consumers, and the public). Neo-Marxist theory locates the cause of corporate crime in the state's regulation of the corporate sector to provide political stability and secure long-term economic interests. However, some neo-Marxist scholars argue that state regulation is the cause of much corporate crime in industrial capitalism, but that we are now in a new economic form—finance capitalism. Under finance capitalism, deregulation, not regulation, is the cause of newly developing corporate crimes, such as "collective embezzlement."

Two micro-objectivist explanations of corporate crime were reviewed: learning theory and control theory. There is evidence that corporate executives learn from corporate peers that willful criminal acts are positive and necessary business practices. Two control theories were presented: neutralization theory and deterrence theory. Neutralization theory focuses on a "subculture of elite behavior" within corporate structures. The *subculture of elite behavior* is a ideology or belief system that "consists of norms and sentiments that make deviance permissible." Adherence to this ideology functions to neutralize the normative constraint of ethics and law and, thereby, frees corporate actors to engage in wrongful behavior. This subculture has not been empirically established. Deterrence theory argues that corporate actors engage in criminal behavior because informal and formal sanctions against it are few and seldom enforced. There is, however, no direct evidence that tougher laws and law enforcement will deter corporate crime. Deterrence theory is hard to empirically assess, especially in the powerful and corrupt corporate world.

Two macro-subjectivist theories were presented: interest group theory and organizational theory. The U.S. antitrust movement culminating in the Sherman Antitrust Act of 1890 illustrates how two customary business practices, restraint of trade and lessening of competition, come to be defined as criminal. However, the legal definitions were implemented so as to protect the interests of "big business." Organizational theories focus on the informal norms of regulatory agencies and agents who ultimately define particular behaviors as criminal or not. There is considerable evidence that political pressure and corporate power shape agencies' definitions and enforcement of corporate misconduct so as to reduce criminal definitions and sanctions.

Micro-subjectivist theories focus on the social audiences that interpret, define, and label corporate misconduct as crime. Criminal definitions of corporate misconduct are relatively absent of public and official reactions because corporate crimes are generally concealed from public view and corporations have the power to reject deviant labels.

We concluded this chapter with an examination of several specific voluntary, state intervention, and consumer pressure policies that have been suggested to reduce corporate crime. None of these appear to be effective strategies. Finally, we noted the absence of any policy to compensate or to assist the victims of corporate crime.

GLOSSARY

Collective embezzlement The taking of funds from a corporation for personal benefit with the acknowledgment of corporate operators.

Corporate anomie The contradiction between corporate goals (profit) and environmental needs (competitors, state interests, employees, consumers, and the public.)

Crimes against customers Corporate violations of production, product, pricing, or advertising standards that cause harm to the consumer.

Crime against employees Corporate violations of occupational health and safety laws and labor laws.

Crime against owners An offense committed by corporate elites against stockholders, including falsifying financial reports, accounting irregularities, falsely inflating stock, and selling fraudulent stock.

Crime against the public-at-large Corporate violations of public health and safety standards and environmental laws.

Daisy chains A type of collective embezzlement where loans are exchanged for a large deposit to increase bank assets and provide bonuses to bank operators who secured the deposit, and the borrower purposely defaults and keeps the money loaned.

Land flips A type of collective embezzlement involving transfers of land between related parties to fraudulently inflate its value to secure a loan in great excess of the actual value of the land.

Objectivist legal definition of corporate crime An act committed by a corporation or corporate actor that benefits the corporation and that is punishable by the state.

Objectivist social harm definition of corporate crime An act committed by a corporation or corporate actor that benefits the corporation, that is punishable by the state, or that knowingly leads to social injury.

Occupational crime An offense by individuals for their own benefit committed in the course of their occupation or offenses committed by employers against employees.

Subculture of elite behavior A corporate ideology or belief system that consists of norms and sentiments that make deviance permissible.

Subjectivist definition of corporate crime An organizational act that social audiences respond to and label as corporate crime.

White-collar crime Violations of law by a person or group of persons in the course of a respected and legitimate occupation or financial activity.

SUGGESTED READINGS

Blum-West, Steve and Timothy J. Carter. "Bring White-Collar Crime Back in: An Examination of Crimes and Torts." *Social Problems* 30(1983):545–554.

This study concludes that "crime" and "tort" are no longer meaningful labels for classifying either the underlying behaviors nor the type of legal actions or social reactions to corporate misconduct. Therefore, the study of organization and causation of misbehavior should be separate from consideration of how the behavior is defined.

Calavita, Kitty and Henry N. Pontell. " 'Heads I Win, Tails You Lose': Deregulation Crime and Crisis in the Savings and Loans Industry." *Crime and Delinquency* 36(1990):309–341.

A detailed examination of the costs, crimes committed, and causes of the Savings and Loan crisis. Importantly, the cause is located in the capitalist infrastructure which is transforming from an industrial to a financial mode of production.

Clinard, Marshall B. and Peter C. Yeager. *Corporate Crime.* New York: Free Press, 1980.

This study remains the most comprehensive empirical study of corporate crime in the "Fortune 500." Special attention is given to the manufacturing sector where violations are routine and many corporations are serious repeat offenders.

Coffee, John, Jr. "Corporate Criminal Responsibility." In *Encyclopedia of Crime and Justice,* Ed. Sanford H. Kadish. New York: Free Press, 1983, pp 253–263.

A non-legalistic review of U.S. laws that regulate corporation. These laws are placed in historical context, and precedential cases are identified.

Coleman, James W. *The Criminal Elite.* 2nd ed. New York: St. Martins, 1989.

A systematic review of the sociology of white-collar crime including its definitions, causes, and consequences. Theories of white-collar crime are assessed relative to empirical studies and case illustrations.

Ermann, David M. and Richard J. Lundman. Corporate and Governmental Deviance. 3rd ed. New York: Oxford, 1987.

A subjectivist approach to understanding corporate crime. A detailed analysis of the nature, types, responses, and control of corporate deviance.

Michalowski, Raymond and Ronald Kramer. "The Space Between the Laws: The Problem of Corporate Crime in a Transnational Context." *Social Problems* 34(1987):34–53.

A strong argument against legal definitions of corporate crime. Multinational corporations exercise great influence in the Third World over the laws that regulate their activities. Therefore, internationally agreed-upon principles of human rights must be applied to standards of corporate behavior.

REFERENCES

Associated Press. "3 Surrender in Plant Fire." *New York Times* March 13(1992):A14.

Blum-West, Steve and Timothy J. Carter. "Bringing White-Collar Crime Back in: An Examination of Crimes and Torts." *Social Problems* 30 (1983):545–554.

Blundell, William E. "Equity Funding: 'I Did it for Jollies' " In *Crime at the Top: Deviance in Business and the Professions,* Ed. John M. Johnson and Jack D. Douglas. Philadelphia: J.B. Lippincott, 1978, pp. 153–185.

Box, Steven. *Power, Crime, and Mystification.* New York: Tavistock, 1983.

Braithwaite, John. "Challenging Just Desserts: Punishing White-Collar Criminals." *Journal of Criminal Law and Criminology* 73(1982): 723–763.

———. "Transnational Corporations and Corruption: Towards Some International Solutions."

International Journal of Sociology and Law 7(1979):125–142.

Braithwaite, John and Gilbert Geis. "On Theory and Action for Corporate Crime Control." *Crime and Delinquency* 28(1982):292–314.

Calavita, Kitty and Henry N. Pontell. " 'Head I Win, Tails You Lose': Deregulation, Crime, and Crisis in the Savings and Loans Industry." *Crime and Delinquency* 36(1990):309–341.

Carter, Timothy J. and Steve Blum-West. "Corporate Crime and Criminal Penalties." *Annual Meeting of the American Society of Criminology*. Cincinnati, OH:1984.

Clinard, Marshall B. and Richard Quinney. *Criminal Behavior Systems*. 2nd ed. New York: Holt, Rinehart and Winston, 1973.

Clinard, Marshall B. and Peter C. Yeager. *Corporate Crime*. New York: Free Press, 1980.

Coleman, James W. *The Criminal Elite*. 2nd ed. New York: St. Martins, 1989.

Conklin, John E. *Illegal But Not Criminal: Business Crime in America*. Englewood Cliffs, NJ: Prentice-Hall, 1977.

Cullen, Francis T., Bruce G. Link, and Craig Polanzi. "The Seriousness of Crime Revisited: Have Attitudes Toward White-Collar Crime Changed? *Criminology* 20(1982):83–102.

Cullen, Francis, William J. Maakestad, and James Cavender. *Corporate Crime Under Attack*. Cincinnati, OH:Anderson, 1987.

Dowie, Mark. "Pinto Madness." *Mother Jones*. September-October (1977):18–32.

Ermann, David M. and Richard J. Lundman. *Corporate and Governmental Deviance*. 2nd ed. New York: Oxford, 1982.

———. *Corporate and Governmental Deviance*. 3rd ed. New York: Oxford, 1987.

Fisse, Brent and John Braithwaite. "The Impact of Publicity on Corporate Offenders: Ford Motor Company and the Pinto Papers." In *Corporate and Governmental Deviance*, Ed. M. David Ermann and Richard J. Landman, pp. 244–262. New York: Oxford, 1987.

Federal Bureau of Investigation. *Uniform Crime Reports* Washington, D.C.: U.S. Government Printing Office, 1992.

Geis, Gilbert. "White-Collar Crime: The Heavy Electrical Equipment Antitrust Cases of 1961." *Criminal Behavior Systems: A Typology*, Eds. Marshall B. Clinard and Richard Quin-

ney. New York: Holt, Rinehart and Winston, 1967, pp. 139–151.

Green, Mark and John F. Berry. *The Challenge of Hidden Profits*. New York: William Morrow, 1985.

Grossman, Laurie M. "Owner Sentenced to Nearly 20 Years over Plant Fire." *Wall Street Journal* September 15 (1992):A10.

Harvard Law Review. "Getting Away with Murder: Federal OSHA Preemption of State Criminal Prosecutions for Industrial Accidents." *Harvard Law Review* 101(1987):535–554.

Hofstadter, Richard. *The Age of Reform: From Bryan to FDR*. New York: Knopf, 1955.

Kolko, Gabriel. *The Triumph of Conservatism: A Reinterpretation of American History 1900–1966*. New York: Free Press, 1963.

Kramer, Ronald C. "Corporate Criminality: The Development of an Idea." In *Corporations as Criminals*, Ed. Ellen Hochstedler. Beverly Hills, CA: Sage, 1984, pp 18–28.

Messerschmidt, James W. *The Trial of Leonard Peltier*. Boston: South End, 1986.

Michalowski, Raymond J. *Order, Law, and Crime*. New York: Random House, 1985.

Michalowski, Raymond and Ronald Kramer. "The Space Between the Laws: The Problem of Corporate Crime in a Transnational Context." *Social Problems* 34(1987):34–53.

Moore, Elizabeth and Michael Mills. "The Neglected Victims and Unexamined Costs of White-Collar Crime." *Crime and Delinquency* 36(1990):408–418.

Neale A. D. and D. G. Goyder. *The Antitrust Laws of the United States of America*. New York: Cambridge, 1980.

Newsweek. "Overheard." April 23(1990):17.

Parenti, Michael. *Democracy for the Few*. 2nd ed. New York: St. Martin's, 1977.

Patterson, Dennis. "N.C. Plant Fined $808,150 After Fatal Fire." *Washington Post*. December 31(1991):A3.

President's Commission on Law Enforcement and Administration of Justice. *The Challenge of Crime in a Free Society*. Washington, D.C.: U.S. Government Printing Office, 1967.

Quinney, Richard. *Class, State, and Crime*. 2nd ed. New York: Longman, 1980.

Shover, Neal. "Introduction." *Crime and Delinquency* 36(1990):307–308.

Simon, David R. and D. Stanley Eitzen. *Elite Deviance*. Boston: Allyn and Bacon, 1982.

———. *Elite Deviance*. 2nd ed. Boston: Allyn and Bacon, 1986.

Smothers, Ronald. "North Carolina Plant is Fined $808,150 in Fatal Fire." *New York Times* December 31(1991):A12.

Stone, Alan. *Economic Regulation and the Public Interest: The Federal Trade Commission in Theory and Practice*. Ithaca, NY: Cornell University Press, 1977.

Sutherland, Edwin H. "White-Collar Criminality." American Sociological Review 5(1940):1–12.

———. *White-Collar Crime*. New York: Holt, Rinehart and Winston, 1949.

U.S. Congress, House of Representatives, Subcommittee on Crime of the Committee on the Judiciary. *Corporate Crime*. Washington, D.C.: U.S. Government Printing Office, 1980.

U.S. Department of Justice. *Uniform Crime Reports: Crime in the United States*. Washington, D.C.: Federal Bureau of Investigation, 1990.

Wall Street Journal. "Shell Oil Co. to Pay $180 Million to Settle Price-Control Issues." *Wall Street Journal*. January 5(1987):11.

Witkin, Gordon, with Dorian Friedman and Monika Guttman. "Health Care Fraud." *U.S. News and World Report*. February, 24(1992):34–43.

Young, T.R. "Corporate Crime: A Critique of the Clinard Report." *Contemporary Crises* 5(1981): 323–336.

Chapter *14*

Religion as Deviance

"THE PEOPLE'S TEMPLE"

To this day, an explanation for the events of November 1978 are somewhat sketchy. There were a few witnesses: people who had somehow escaped the tragedy of Jonestown, Guyana. There were the tapes: most of the significant events had been recorded on audiotape. But for the most part, those who knew most about what happened at Jonestown perished along with the Reverend Jim Jones himself, when they drank (some voluntarily, some at gun point) cyanide-laced Kool-Aid.

The ministry of Jim Jones began innocently enough in the early 1950s when he founded the nondenominational Christian Assembly of God Church, an urban ministry of soup kitchens, day care facilities, and drug counseling for the poor. He preached a unique blend of Christian fundamentalism and social and racial justice. He preached this message, furthermore, in a fairly mainstream religious setting. His original church in Indianapolis, the People's Temple Full Gospel Church, was affiliated with the Disciples of Christ. In 1964, Jones himself was ordained as a Disciples of Christ minister (Bromley and Shupe, 1981).

The first significant event in the church's history occurred in 1965 when Jones received a vision of a nuclear holocaust that would soon destroy the earth. In response to this vision, he moved 100 members of his Indianapolis church to the Redwood valley of northern California where, he argued, they would be spared from the destruction. In California, his message began to change radically, becoming much less religious, and much more political. He encouraged his followers to be politically active, and he himself served as chairperson of the San Francisco Housing Authority between 1976–1977. At the height of his popularity, he was honored by one interfaith group as one of the hundred "most outstanding" U.S. clergy. He received a second award in 1977 when he was named the Martin Luther King, Jr., Humanitarian Award winner (Bromley and Shupe, 1981).

In other circles, however, Jones and his People's Temple were not viewed in such a favorable light. Defectors from the church (Jones called them "traitors") began to share stories of an authoritarian, cruel, "evil" leader. The media enjoyed the developing controversy and devoted considerable attention to the horror stories of the defectors. As

sociologist John R. Hall reminds us, "We do not know how true, widespread, exaggerated, or isolated the incidents reported were. Certainly they were generalized in the press to the point of creating an image of Jones as a total ogre (1990:283). This outside pressure reinforced in Jones a growing sense of paranoia, leading eventually to the mass exodus of the People's Temple to Jonestown, Guyana. In Guyana, Jones hoped to create a utopian socialist community away from the increasing scrutiny he had been under in California. The move, however, only served to intensify the efforts of family and friends concerned about the fate of their loved ones. As pressure mounted, Jones became increasingly attracted to the notion of a "revolutionary suicide" as a dramatic and final statement to the world (Bromley and Shupe, 1981). In the end, over 900 people (including almost 300 children younger than 17 years of age and 200 elderly over the age of 65) lost their lives. The first to be killed were the babies, who had the cyanide squirted down their throats. The majority of the older children and adults drank of the Kool-Aid voluntarily, although some were shot as they tried to escape (Barker, 1986).

Even beyond the tragedy of the suicides, the Jonestown incident is significant because in many ways it marked the beginnings of public fear of deviant religion—or in popular terminology, "cults." (In this chapter, we use the terms *deviant religion*, *cult*, and *new religion* interchangeably.) The Jonestown tragedy resulted in the establishment of several social movement organizations that have taken it upon themselves to find and expose the *next* Jim Jones.

"THEY CALL HER GURU MA[1]"

"I would put nothing past her," said Kathy Schmook, a local author and founder of Network of Friends, a support group for ex-members adjusting to life outside the church. "She has the eyes of a shark—dark and black. She's trying to get them used to getting in and out of their shelters in the same way that Jim Jones got his people used to drinking Kool-Aid" (Conklin, 1990:C3).

Some claim to have found the next Jim Jones in the foothills of the Rocky Mountains, just north of Yellowstone National Park. Her name is Elizabeth Clare Prophet and she, along with her followers in the Church Universal and Triumphant, believe the world is coming to an end—and that it is going to happen soon. Guru Ma, as her followers call her, insists that glasnost is a deceptive ploy and that nuclear holocaust is imminent. To protect themselves, Prophet and her followers, as many as 5,000 people, have spent millions of dollars building underground bomb shelters, complete with enough rice and barley to wait out the nuclear holocaust. Some claim that church members have also collected enough arms and ammunition to protect themselves from the few contaminated survivors who will look to the shelters for food. But Church Universal and Triumphant leaders claim that stories of the stockpile of weapons have been greatly exaggerated (Conklin, 1990; *Newsweek* 1993b).

The Church Universal Triumphant is an interesting mix of Christianity, Eastern mysticism, and right-wing politics. Montana is the seventh headquarters of the church, which was founded in Arlington, Virginia, in 1958. Prophet has predicted that the cataclysm would occur on October 2, 1987, February 15, 1990, March 12, 1990, April 23, 1990, but each date has passed without incident (Conklin, 1990). Yet her followers continue to build shelters, anxiously awaiting the end of the world.

"STANDOFF IN WACO"

The most recent religious leader to attract attention as "the next Jim Jones" is David Koresh of the Branch Davidians. Koresh and his followers attracted worldwide attention in early 1993 when they held off a violent assault from Bureau of Alcohol, Tobacco and Firearms (ATF) agents. The February 28 gunfight at the Waco, Texas compound lasted nearly an hour and left four Federal agents dead. Early reports from inside the compound were that 10 cult members were dead, including a two-year-old girl. Koresh himself was injured (Lacayo, 1993).

David Koresh is the most recent in a long line of leaders of the Branch Davidians, an extremist group which split from the Seventh-Day Adventist church in 1935. After he seized control of the group in the mid-1980s, he began to make predictions about one final confrontation between the Branch Davidians and unbelievers. In anticipation of this prophesied confrontation, the group began to amass weapons (Lacayo, 1993; Newsweek, 1993a).

It was the accumulation of weapons that initially attracted the attention of the ATF. The exact reasons for the attack, however, remain somewhat unclear. Most of the weapons had been obtained legally. Federal officials were apparently concerned that Koresh was planning to convert legal semi-automatic weapons into illegal automatic weapons (Lochia, 1993). Also unclear were the reasons for the dramatic assault. Koresh frequently left the compound and could have been easily apprehended. The ATF might also have tried to negotiate with Koresh before they attacked the compound. Whatever the exact reasons, the attack merely confirmed for Koresh and his followers that the end was near. After all, Koresh had been predicting such an attack for some time. By mid-April, nearly two months after the original confrontation, it became clear that the Branch Davidians were content to wait and see what God had in store for them.

By mid-April, nearly two months after the original confrontation, it became clear that the Branch Davidians were content to wait and see what God had in store for them. Federal officials, however, were not nearly so patient. Frustrated and angered by Koresh's many unfulfilled promises to lead his followers out of the compound, Federal officials began to publicly hint that they might soon force an end to the confrontation. They also began to threaten Koresh: either surrender voluntarily or we will force you to surrender. Early Monday morning, April 19, 1993, Federal authorities did just that. Using tanks, they punched holes into the side of the Waco, Texas compound and then proceeded to fill it with tear gas. Apparently they had hoped that, if nothing else, the tear gas would force mothers to bring their children out of the compound. What happened they surely did not anticipate. Rather than surrender and face prison terms (four ATF agents had been killed in the initial gun battle), the Branch Davidians set themselves on fire, thus fulfilling Koresh's prophecy that they would be "devoured by fire." Dramatically and tragically, the compound burned to the ground in less than half an hour, with an estimated 86 people (including Koresh and 24 children) still inside.

Admittedly, the People's Temple, the Church Universal and Triumphant, and the Branch Davidians are atypical of deviant religious. Most deviant religions are so small and shortlived that we never hear of them. And only rarely are deviant religions violent. Yet consideration of these three groups raises several questions that we will attempt to answer in this chapter. What is a deviant religion? Or in more contemporary language, what is a cult? Who joins deviant religions? Why do they join? Are deviant religions common? Are deviant religions dangerous? Should society limit the religious freedom of such groups?

WHAT IS A DEVIANT RELIGION?

In Chapter 1, we briefly distinguished between the objectivist conception of deviance—deviance as norm-violation—and the "absolutist" conception of deviance—behavior that is inherently deviant. In many ways, the absolutist perspective is reflected in the various medical conceptions of deviant behavior that we have discussed in this book. That is, to the degree that some bizarre behavior is considered to be a manifestation of a disease, its conceptualization as deviance is not dependent on a consideration of cultural norms. Schizophrenia in New Guinea has the same manifestations as schizophrenia in California, just as cancer in New Guinea is as deadly as cancer in California.

There is an absolutist conception of deviant religion as well. For the absolutists, some religion is *wrong,* or perhaps even more descriptively, *evil.* We recognize that there may well be "right" religious groups and "wrong" religious groups. And we certainly recognize that the world is full of people who believe they can tell the difference. But since the absolutist perspective does not reflect the relative nature of deviance, it is of little use to us as we try to understand the sociology of deviant religion. To do this we must once again turn to the objectivist and subjectivist conceptions of deviance.

Objectivist Conception

The objectivist conception is most clearly represented in the traditional distinction between *church* (culturally acceptable religion), *sect* (a break off from a church), and *cult* (new religion). Ernst Troeltsch (1931) was the first to theorize about the differences between church and sect, although recent scholars have made the distinctions more useful (e.g., Johnson, 1963; O'Dea, 1966; Stark and Bainbridge, 1985). In general, churches tend to be characterized by (1) cultural compromise with the values and institutions of the surrounding society; (2) heavy reliance on, and acceptance of, membership based on birth; (3) tolerance of other religious institutions; (4) reliance upon formally trained leadership; (5) acceptance of and respect for formal organization and institutional structure; (6) formalized worship; and (7) more liberal (i.e., less literal) interpretations of religious doctrine (Chalfant, Beckley, and Palmer, 1987; O'Dea, 1966). The sect, on the other hand, is characterized by (1) separatism from and defiance of the values and institutions of the surrounding society; (2) an emphasis on a conversion experience prior to joining; (3) intolerance of other religious institutions; (4) de-emphasis on formally trained clergy, and greater emphasis on the involvement of lay people; (5) de-emphasis on formal organization; (6) less formal, more emotional worship; (7) more conservative (i.e., more literal) interpretation of religious doctrine.

A more parsimonious way to conceptualize church and sect, as suggested by Benton Johnson (1963), is to consider the degree to which the religious organization is in a state of tension with the surrounding society. A church accepts and a sect rejects the social environment in which it exists.

The church-sect continuum has proved useful to sociologists interested in explaining the development of various versions of the same religion in society (in the United States, we call these denominations). In his book, *The Social Sources of Denominationalism* (1929), Richard Niebuhr argued that through time, sectlike organizations tend to take on the characteristics of churches. This transformation leads to discontent among members who feel that the organization is drifting from the ideal. Discontent leads to schism and the forming of a new sect, which will itself be eventually transformed into a church. Thus, there is an endless cycle of sect producing church producing new sect (Stark and Bainbridge, 1985).

Sects, therefore, are not new religions but are instead, at least in the eyes of the followers, a more authentic version of traditional religion. Because sects violate the norms of mainstream religion and question the norms of the secular society, they can, from an objectivist point of view, be conceptualized as deviant religion. Yet, as revivals of traditional religion, sects are less culturally offensive than the more controversial "cults."

Whereas sects represent religious *revival*, cults represent religious *innovation* (Stark and Bainbridge, 1985). In any culture, new forms of religion appear that are not calling for the return of the original, "pure" religion. These organizations, therefore, are non-schismatic; that is, they have not grown out of "parent" organizations. Like sects, cults are in a high state of tension with society, but have the additional distinction of being "new" religions. Therefore, cults are, by definition, deviant religion (Stark and Bainbridge, 1985).

All religious traditions begin as cults (including Christianity). With time, as Stark and Bainbridge remind us, "they may become the dominant tradition, in which case there is no longer much tension between them and the environment, and they become the church or churches of that society" (1985:26).

Students of religion should avoid categorizing specific religious organizations as church, sect, or cult. Sociologists have long recognized the limitations of these distinctions. What is important for our purposes is that some religious organizations tend to have churchlike qualities (e.g., mainline reli-

gious denominations such as Presbyterian, United Methodist, Episcopalian, Lutheran, and Catholic), some have sectlike qualities (e.g., more conservative denominations such as the Amish, Jehovah's Witnesses, Seventh Day Adventists, Pentecostal and Holiness groups, and various independent "Bible" churches), and some have cultlike qualities (e.g., The Unification Church [the Moonies], Hare Krishna, Scientology, Transcendental Meditation, The Church Universal and Triumphant, and various forms of "New Age" religion). Sects, and especially cults, are deviant from an objectivist perspective because they violate the norms of conventional ("churchlike") religion.

Subjectivist Conception

Objectivist scholars suggest that deviant religion can be objectively defined since the norms of conventional religion are objectively given. In contrast, the subjectivist conception defines deviance as a label. "Cult" is a label—a derogatory label. What becomes interesting to the subjectivist is the social process whereby absolutist *moral entrepreneurs* assume the right and responsibility to expose the "evil" religions, and work to create the deviant label "cult." The sociological world was first introduced to the word *moral entrepreneurs* by Howard Becker (1963), who argued that when powerful, credible figures morally condemn a particular behavior, the rest of us may very well accept their definitions of right and wrong. Subjectivists seek to understand the success moral entrepreneurs have enjoyed in making "cult" a "four-letter word," thus generating public hostility toward specific deviant religious traditions. From this perspective, some religious groups may be defined as cults for the purposes of exercising social or legal control over their religious practices.

To review, there are two sociological conceptions of deviant religion (or in popular terminology, cults). First, according to the objectivist conception, cult is a religious movement that violates the norms of convention religion. It is what Stark and Bainbridge (1985) refer to as religious innovation (or "new" religion). It is important to recognize that objectivists like Stark and Bainbridge (1985) use the term *cult* without prejudice. The second sociological conception, the subjectivist conception, defines *cult* as a label. Subjectivists see the word cult as a derogatory label imposed on some unpopular religious groups by powerful moral entrepreneurs. Because subjectivists see the word *cult* as a derogatory label, they prefer not to use the word in their discussions of the deviant religions. Instead, they generally prefer the terms *new religious movements* or *so-called cults*. Both of these sociological conceptualizations challenge the more popularly accepted absolutist perspective, which suggests that cults are religions that are evil, deceptive, destructive, immoral, and unhealthy. For absolutist moral entrepreneurs, the term has proved to be useful in creating a hostility towards various undesirable "evil" and "deceitful" groups.

WHO ARE THE RELIGIOUS DEVIANTS?

This question needs to be addressed at two different levels. The first concerns a description of the deviant religions, and the second, a description of the adherents of deviant religion.

What are the Deviant Religions?

We will limit our discussion to those religious movements that are in the greatest state of tension with the surrounding society. These movements have all been labeled "cults" by society, although from an objectivist point of view some might be better categorized as "sects." While most cults are small and short-

lived, these religions can be viewed as successful by virtue of their relatively large number of members and years of existence. As a direct result of this success, they have received considerable attention in both the popular world and the sociological world. In addition to the religious movements we discuss below, we might also include the People's Temple, the Church Universal and Triumphant, and the Branch Davidians, which we introduced earlier.

The Children of God (The Family of Love). The Children of God, which today is known as The Family of Love, has a history similar to that of the People's Temple. Its founder, David Berg, is an ordained Christian and Missionary Alliance (a conservative, sectlike denomination) minister. The movement began in Southern California in the late 1960s as Teens for Christ, a Jesus Movement coffeehouse ministry filled with long-haired, "hippie," drug culture dropouts (Bromley and Shupe, 1981).

After Berg had a falling out with the Christian and Missionary Alliance, his group became increasingly bitter towards organized religion, staging disruptive demonstrations during local church services. This antagonism led to considerable public scrutiny and hostility, eventually forcing Berg and his followers (numbering 75–100) out of Los Angeles (Bromley and Shupe, 1981).

He divided his followers into small mission groups that dispersed across the country, actively recruiting college-age, middle-class youth. Eventually, these mission groups reunited in Canada. Berg became increasingly radical, referring to himself as "Moses" Berg. By 1972, with the movement now numbering over 2,000 members worldwide, "Moses" Berg commanded his people to leave "Egypt" (i.e., the United States) to establish several colonies around the world. By the 1980s, there were approximately 4,000 to 5,000 Children of God in some 600 colonies (Bromley and Shupe, 1981).

The Unification Church (The Moonies).
Probably the best known deviant religious movement in the United States is the Unification Church. The Moonies were founded by the Reverund Sun Myung Moon in Korea in 1954. The first missionary came to this country in 1959. In 1964, when Moon visited the United States for the first time, the movement was already well established (Lofland, 1977). Moon has revealed his vision in the *Divine Principle,* which is essentially a Bible with several revisions introduced by Moon (Bromley and Shupe, 1981). The *Divine Principle* teaches that we live in "the last days," with God soon to establish His Kingdom on earth (originally predicted for 1967). With the end of the world imminent, Moonies work fervently to prepare the world for the Messiah's return. The *Divine Principle* teaches that the Messiah will likely come in this century and, instead of being Jesus Christ, will probably be South Korean (Lofland, 1977). According to Bromley and Shupe (1981), most Moonies are hesitant to publicly admit that Moon is the messiah of the second coming, yet they undoubtedly see him in that role.

After a rather inauspicious beginning in the 1960s, when there were fewer than 250 western members, the Unification Church did experience considerable growth beginning in the early 1970s (Barker, 1984). However, even during the mid-1970s when the movement was most successful at attracting converts, there were fewer than 2,000 to 3,000 fully committed Moonies (Bromley and Shupe, 1981).

The International Society for Krishna Consciousness (The Hare Krishna). Because of their unique appearance (saffron robes and shaved heads) and interest in public visibility (on urban streets and in airports), the Hare Krishna were perhaps the most visible of all the deviant religious groups in the United States during the 1970s and 1980s. The movement began in the United States in 1965 when His Divine Grace A. C. Bhaktivedanta Swami Prabhapada imported his version of Hinduism from India. Hare Krishna are expected to abstain from illicit sex, intoxicants, and meat, fish, and eggs. In addition, they are to withdraw from all aspects of the material world, which includes a de-emphasis on science, rationality, education, materialism, aggression, and competition. In removing themselves from the material world, Hare Krishna believe they can achieve a complete personal transformation and achieve a state of Krishna consciousness (Bromley and Shupe, 1981; Rochford, 1985).

Scientology.   Scientology, which started out as a psychotherapy called Dianetics, began in 1950 when science-fiction writer L. Ron Hubbard's book, *Dianetics: The Modern Science of Mental Health,* became a best-seller. Dianetics is a psychological "theory" suggesting that painful memories can be eliminated through a process called "auditing" (counseling with a trained Dianetics therapist). In his book, Hubbard claimed that Dianetics could cure people of a variety of psychological and physical problems. The popularity of Dianetics spread rapidly and many "therapists," with no direct connection to Hubbard, began to treat people. With so many new therapists on the scene, Hubbard began to feel as though he was losing control of the movement. Through the early 1970s, he struggled to rid the movement of its "amateurs," "heretics," and "revisionists," eventually gaining "licensing" control over who could and could not claim an expertise in Dianetics (Bromley and Shupe, 1981:48). In 1952, Hubbard gave Dianetics a new wrinkle, renaming it Scientology, and incorporating "reincarnation, extraterrestrial life, and a spiritual dimension missing from the more purely psychological Dianetics" (Bromley and Shupe, 1981:48).

The Rajneesh. The Rajneesh religion, which is today largely disbanded, was a Hindu sect that combined the elements of Eastern religion with pop psychology. The followers of Rajneeshism, or Sannyasin as they called themselves, claimed to be undergoing a change toward personal enlightenment and individual self-realization, hoping eventually to be "deprogrammed" into new beings who would "respond in daily life without resort to norms or patterns" (Carter, 1987:148). Followers were expected to (1) wear "sunrise" colors (orange, red, and purple); (2) wear a necklace of 108 beads with a picture of the leader of the movement, the Bhagwan (blessed one) Shree Rajneesh; (3) use the new Sannyas's name assigned by the Bhagwan; and (4) practice meditation (Carter, 1987).

By the early 1980s, Sannyasin had established meditation centers across Europe, Asia, and North America. The center of the movement, however, remained the Bhagwan's own communal following in Poona, India. After experiencing several legal and tax problems, the Bhagwan fled India, eventually settling his "oasis community," named Rajneeshpuram, on 64,000 acres in eastern Oregon (a move that was not well accepted by the nearby residents of Antelope, Oregon).

The unique practices and beliefs of the movement, the tension Rajneeshpuram caused in eastern Oregon, and the highly visible signs of devotion by the Bhagwan's followers (who reportedly gave the Bhagwan over 90 Roles Royce cars) resulted in considerable media attention during the mid-1980s. The media attention climaxed in 1985, when the Bhagwan, after pleading guilty to violating immigration laws, returned to India. The deportation of the Bhagwan essentially meant the end of Rajneeshpuram and for all practical purposes, Rajneeshism itself ended in 1989 when Rajneesh died.

There are, of course, many other well-publicized deviant religious movements in the United States, Transcendental Meditation, Erhad Seminars Training (EST), The Divine Light Mission, and Nichiren Shoshu Buddhism, to name but a few.

Who Joins Deviant Religions?

Among the general public, and in some social-science circles as well, it is common to assume that those who join deviant religious movements are primarily society's rejects: the "mentally ill" (or at least psychologically disturbed), the isolated, and the social misfits. Yet, as Stark and Bainbridge point out, if cult movements primarily recruit people who are abnormal, then they have "little hope of becoming significant new religions, for they will originate with followers who are so incapacitated and stigmatized that such groups will be forever limited to the fringes of societies" (1985:394). Since many cult movements are now popular and accepted religions, one has to wonder whether the assumptions of psychological abnormality are misdirected (Stark and Bainbridge, 1985).

With a few notable exceptions, the social-science community has concluded that assumptions of abnormality are incorrect. "Normal" people can be attracted to "abnormal" religion. Of course, there is variation in the types of people who join deviant religious groups. For example, cults are more likely to provide answers for people who are seeking solutions to life's major questions. But these "seekers," as they are sometimes referred to, need not be conceptualized as abnormal. In a later section, we will discuss "seekership" and other predispositional factors in cult involvement. For now, however, let us briefly consider the social and demographic patterns of cult involvement.

In general, research demonstrates that cult converts are disproportionately young, middle class, and educated (Snow and Machalek,

1984; Barker, 1984). According to Barker (1984), in the mid-1970s nearly 80 percent of British Moonies were between the ages of 19 and 30; the mean age in 1982 was 28. Rochford (1985) similarly reports that over half of United States Hare Krishna joined before the age of 21. In terms of social class, the distribution of Moonie recruits closely resembles the general population. However, Moonie recruits have somewhat higher levels of education than the population in general (Barker, 1984). For many, joining the cult means dropping out of college. Among the Hare Krishna in Rochford's (1985) sample, for example, 26 percent were attending school at the time they decided to join the cult.

Many cults also tend to be disproportionately female. One reason for this trend may be that, when compared to Christianity, the cults generally offer women more opportunities to be religious leaders (Stark and Bainbridge, 1985). However, female overrepresentation is not typical of all cults. In fact, the Moonies attract nearly twice as many men as women (Barker, 1984).

Some studies indicate that the use of illegal drugs contributes to cult involvement (Wuthnow, 1976; Stark and Bainbridge, 1985). Judah (1974), for example, claims that a very high proportion of Hare Krishna report having been involved in drug use before joining the movement. The Church of Scientology estimates that 62 percent of its adherents in the mid-1970s had taken illegal drugs prior to membership (Stark and Bainbridge, 1985).

Based upon surveys of several contemporary cult movements, Stark and Bainbridge (1985) report that a disproportionate number of cult recruits grew up with parents who claimed no religious affiliation. On the other hand, Barker (1984) and Rochford (1985) report that converts tend to be from homes in which religion *is* important. While there may be some disagreement on this point, there is agreement on the fact that few recruits are

religiously active at the time they come into contact with the cult movements. Surveys consistently reveal that it is the people who claim to have no religious affiliation who are most likely to be attracted to unconventional religious practices (Bainbridge and Stark, 1980).

THEORIES OF DEVIANT RELIGION AND RELIGIOUS DEVIANTS

Macro-Objectivist Theories: Where Do Cults Come From?

Many social scientists contend that as society progresses and becomes more modernized, religion is slowly replaced by "worldly" institutions, and discredited by the findings of science. These "secularization theorists" view religion as an endangered species of sorts. They argue that, since the "gods" are an imaginary creation of humans, scientific knowledge will eventually eliminate the "need" for religion.

No doubt there is considerable evidence in support of secularization theory. Americans, for example, are more likely to look to Darwin and his contemporary disciples than to Genesis for an explanation of the origin of the human species. Similarly, Americans are more likely to visit their doctors than their pastors when they find themselves ill. Secularization theory's predictions seemed to be confirmed further during the 1960s when many of this country's mainstream religious denominations began reporting rather dramatic membership declines. Between 1965 and 1985, for example, the Episcopal Church declined 20 percent, the United Methodist Church declined 16 percent, and the Presbyterian church declined 24 percent (Perrin and Mauss, 1990).

While such trends seemingly provided support for secularization theory, there were other trends during the same time period which secularization theory cannot explain: namely, the growth of sects and cults. Between 1965 and 1985 sectarian movements like the Mormons, Assemblies of God, and the Jehovah's Witnesses more than doubled. Several other more mainstream yet conservative denominations (e.g., Southern Baptists, Nazarenes) also grew (Perrin and Mauss, 1990). In addition, several unusual religious cults never known before 1960 grew during this period.

The success of the sects and cults which continues today, poses a serious problem for those who have been predicting the demise of religion. If science and religion are incompatible, critics of secularization theory argue, why would the religious segment of U.S. society most antagonistic toward science and modernism be thriving? While the mainstream denominations have seemingly made enough accommodations to culture to coexist peacefully with science, sects and cults have remained more antagonistic toward the modern world.

Secularization and Religious Innovation.
The success of sects and cults during the past two decades has led to increased attention from social scientists interested in why modernization *will not* lead to the end of religion. It is true that traditional religions are always becoming more worldly. However, "the result of this trend has never been the end of religion, but merely a shift in fortunes among religions as faiths that have become too worldly are supplanted by more vigorous and less worldly religions" (Stark and Bainbridge, 1985:2)

We have already discussed church/sect theory (Niebuhr, 1929), which is essentially an explanation for how religious revivals, or sects, grow out of organizations that are eroded by secularization. But how does secularization stimulate religious innovation, that is, cults? Stark and Bainbridge contend that religion is capable of offering rewards other

organizations cannot offer. These rewards, furthermore, are attractive to rich and poor alike:

> For example, no one can demonstrate whether there is life after death, but everyone can see that immortality cannot be gained in the here and now, in the natural world available to our senses. But the simple unavailability of the reward of eternal life has not caused people to cease wanting it. To the contrary, it is probably the single most urgent human desire (Stark and Bainbridge, 1985:6).

Stark and Bainbridge argue that, since science is not likely to progress to the point at which it replaces religion in offering a promise of this reward, religion will remain in one form or another. This assumption leads to two postulates. First, as religious organizations become more secularized (and therefore less capable of offering the promise of everlasting life), they will be replaced by less worldly and more vigorous organizations. Thus, sect grows out of church. Second, and even more informative for us, geographic regions that are secularized (thus having few religious organizations that offer the promise of everlasting life) will be fertile ground for religious innovation, or cults.

To demonstrate empirically their theoretical expectations regarding cult development, Stark and Bainbridge examine data from rather unique sources: subscription rates to *Fate* magazine (a popular magazine on parapsychology, the occult, and related matters); listing of "New Age" movements, bookstores, and foodstores in *The Spiritual Community Guide;* and locations of cult organization headquarters. Based on data like this, Stark and Bainbridge (1985) conclude that cults are strongest where traditional churches and sects are weakest. In the "unchurched" belt in the West (Nevada, Alaska, Washington, Hawaii, Oregon, and California), and Canadian West, church membership and attendance rates are particularly low, and cult membership rates are high. In Western Europe, where church attendance rates are much lower than those in the United States and Canada, cults are even more plentiful and successful.

The Stark and Bainbridge theory tells us more about why cults arise than how cults arise. In another chapter of their book, they do provide specific descriptions of cult formation (1985:171–188), but such details are less important to us here. What is important for us to recognize is that cults arise when and where sects and churches fail to satisfy the religious thirst of the people. Thus, cults can be seen as an inevitable and natural by-product of secularization.

Micro-Objectivist Theories: Why Do People Join Cults?

With few exceptions, the question of who joins cults has been approached from a micro-sociological perspective. The focus of this perspective is on the process by which *individuals* come to be recruited and converted into deviant religions.

A Control Theory of Deviant Religious Involvement. In the previous section, we learned that cults attract a disproportionately high percentage of young, single, and religiously unattached people. A *social bond* theorist might interpret these data as suggesting that such people are more free to participate in deviant religions. That is, they have fewer "stakes in conformity" (Hirschi, 1969). Even if a 40-year-old married business executive with three children comes into contact with a Moonie (which is itself unlikely because Moonies do not target such populations in their recruitment), she is not likely to accompany him to a religious gathering. Her husband expects her home to eat the dinner he has cooked at 6:00, and she wants to tuck her children into bed at 9:00. Indeed, she has neither the time nor the freedom to become

a Moonie. Young, single college students, on the other hand, have fewer reasons not to be involved in cults. If nothing else, such individuals have more discretionary time necessary to participate in deviant religion (Snow and Machalek, 1984). In addition, young college students are especially likely to have lost faith in the traditional religions and are probably more aware of culturally unique religious alternatives (Stark and Bainbridge, 1985).

We might provide a similar interpretation for the relationship between drug use and cult involvement. Drug use undoubtedly contributes to a weakening of bonds to conventional society. In summarizing the impact of the drug culture of the 1960s and 1970s on the growth of the cults, Stark and Bainbridge conclude that the young people using drugs "were violating secular norms and defying the opposition to drugs of conventional religious organizations. Associating with fellow deviants and detached from the institutions and social networks that enforce conventionality in most citizens, they were free to experiment with novel religious alternatives" (1985:413).

We might use social bond principles as well to explain why people who are not active in convention religions are more likely to join a cult. It probably goes without saying that an adherent to one faith is generally not available for recruitment into another. This assumption not only has implications for micro-level analyses of why people join cults but is the basis for the macro-level theory we introduced in the previous section concerning where and why cults form in the first place (Stark and Bainbridge, 1985).

Stress, Tension, or Other Predisposing Conditions. Control theory fails to consider variation in the degree to which people are motivated to commit deviant acts. Recall that Hirschi (1969) begins with the assumption that all are sufficiently motivated to commit criminal acts. Such assumptions are particularly problematic with regard to recruitment into deviant religions. Not everyone, it would seem, is equally motivated to join a deviant religious group. Indeed, everyone is not equally likely to ask the questions that deviant religions provide answers to. Historically, this emphasis on motivation has involved an examination of the circumstances that make people particularly *susceptible,* as if being committed to a deviant religion meant one had some kind of disease (Heirich, 1977; Snow and Machalek, 1984). Converts have variously been depicted as weak (Richardson, Harder, and Simmonds, 1972), having a need to be controlled (Gordon, 1974), possessing "addictive" personalities (Simmonds, 1977), and needing to "escape from freedom" (Levine, 1980a).

There is also a tradition of theory in relative deprivation, which, as a version of strain theory, traces its roots to the work of Robert Merton (1938). In the study of deviant religion, however, the focus of strain theory has been more at the micro level and less economic than that conceptualized by Merton. Glock (1964), for example, discusses several other forms of deprivation, including social deprivation (absence of societal rewards such as power and status), organismic deprivation (being physically or mentally handicapped), and psychic deprivation (not feeling satisfied with, or accepted by society). The assumption Glock makes is that people join religions that offer relief from the kinds of deprivation they suffer.

Other researchers have concentrated on various specific forms of tension and stress, such as marital strain, the loss of a family member, and the loss of a job (Snow and Machalek, 1984). However, while such factors have generally been assumed to be important, empirical support is lacking and studies investigating such factors have been plagued by methodological problems (most commonly, the absence of a control group) (see Snow and Machalek, 1984; Heirich, 1977).

This emphasis on tension and strain is rejected in the John Lofland and Rodney Stark (1965) article, "Becoming a World Saver: A Theory of Conversion to a Deviant Perspective." Lofland and Stark observed the recruitment and conversion practices of the early followers of the Unification Church in this country. As a result of their observations, Lofland and Stark developed a "value added" scheme of conversion to a deviant perspective. The model is "value added" because seven factors accumulate successively and are said to be necessary for conversion. Three of the factors involve attributes that exist *within* converts prior to contact with the group. These "predisposing conditions" include (1) acute tension—converts described themselves as suffering from a prolonged state of tension, strain, frustration, crisis, or deprivation; (2) a religious problem-solving perspective—converts tended to look to religion, rather than nonreligious mechanisms (e.g., psychological counseling, political or public service involvement, or drugs) to deal with their problems; and (3) religious seeker attributes—converts defined themselves as engaged in a religious search.

This portrayal of converts as religious "seekers" is reflected as well in the research of Balch and Taylor (1978), who in 1975 joined (as hidden observers) a small cult that offered followers a UFO trip to heaven if they could overcome their worldly attachments and humanly emotions (Balch and Taylor, 1978:44). Balch and Taylor argue that, before joining the UFO cult, members had "organized their lives around the quest for truth" (1978:52). In addition, members of the cult "shared a metaphysical world-view in which reincarnation, disincarnate spirits, psychic powers, lost continents, flying saucers, and ascended masters are taken for granted" (Balch and Taylor, 1978:54).

Learning to be a Cultist.   In recent years, sociologists have increasingly avoided motivational theories such as these. This shift has primarily occurred for four reasons. First, social scientists have increasingly recognized the methodologically problematic nature of concepts like "seeker." While it is possible to demonstrate that Moonies (Lofland and Stark, 1965) or members of a UFO cult (Balch and Taylor, 1978) "seek" answers to unanswerable questions, it is difficult to demonstrate that their quest is qualitatively different from yours or mine. Perhaps they have merely chosen a different avenue in which to satisfy their quest. Perhaps, in concentrating on how they are "different" we are only reflecting our biased assumptions that they should be different. Second, according to Heirich (1977), the interesting question is not *who* will change, but rather, under what circumstances the change will occur. In other words, perhaps we should spend less time trying to identify various motivational factors that could make people "susceptible" to change and more time trying to conceptualize how the change occurs. Third, scholars have increasingly recognized that, while perceived deprivations may predispose people to conversion, these factors do not cause conversion (McGuire, 1987; Stark and Bainbridge, 1980). Finally, in portraying converts as "victims" of structural strain, or "victims" of various psychological problems, and so forth, social scientists are, in a sense, playing into the hands of the anti-cult entrepreneurs who contend that cults prey on certain kinds of weak and defenseless people, "brainwashing" them and rendering them psychologically helpless. Social scientists, the vast majority of whom reject the brainwashing model, are not interested in providing ammunition for the anti-cultists.

Given these concerns, learning theories have become increasingly relevant. Recall that Lofland and Stark (1965) argued that three dispositional factors are necessary preconditions for conversion. In order for conversion to occur, however, four situational factors that occur *outside* the individual are also necessary. These "situational conditions" include (1) a turning point—Moonie converts had reached a point where they recognized the need for a new way of dealing with their problems; (2) the formation of affective bonds—when friendship bonds between the recruit and one or more Moonies did not exist prior to involvement (most often, they did), they were formed at this point; (3) the neutralization of extra-cult affective bonds—as in-group bonds developed, out-group bonds weakened or, in some cases, were severed; and (4) intensive interaction—total conversion came only as a result of intensive and prolonged interaction with Moonies.

In emphasizing networking, the formation of in-group bonds, the loosening of out-group bonds, and prolonged interaction, Lofland and Stark are proposing that one becomes a Moonie in a manner similar to the way one becomes a Presbyterian, a member of a fraternity, or a member of a criminal subculture. In other words, they are essentially offering a theory of *differential association*. Becoming a Moonie probably involves more intense interactions than becoming a Presbyterian (because the Unification Church is a deviant religion), but the process is essentially the same. In interaction with the deviant subculture, one learns beliefs about the nature of God and the universe, values concerning what is and is not important in the subculture, and norms regarding appropriate and inappropriate behavior.

Brainwashing and the Medical Model of Deviant Religious Involvement.   The theory of brainwashing is not a sociological theory of deviant religious involvement. It is, in fact, essentially a medical theory of deviant religious involvement because it suggests that the individual has no control over his or her behavior. Essentially the brainwashing argument is that religious recruits ("victims" in brainwashing terminology) are subjected to psychological coercion by cult members. Over time and with enough coercion, the recruit eventually succumbs to the psychological pressure, giving into the demands of the group ("captors" in brainwashing terminology) and becoming psychologically controlled by the members of the group.

The theory of brainwashing developed out of studies in the 1950s on coercion techniques used by Chinese Communists on Western prisoners of war (Schein, 1961; Lifton, 1961). The term *brainwashing* was meant to suggest that prisoner's brain could be purged of all prior commitments and values and replaced with a new and acceptable perception of self. While several models of brainwashing have been suggested, most have included the following characteristics:

1. Captors have complete control over the lives of the prisoners—when they eat, sleep, go to the bathroom, and so forth. This control, it is argued, will make the victim disoriented and less resistent to change.
2. Only information that supports the ideology is made available to the prisoner.
3. Prisoners are isolated from friends and relatives. When the assault on the old identity begins, the victim has no one around for social support.
4. The prisoner's old identity is destroyed.
5. The prisoner is offered a new and acceptable identity, one that is rewarded by the captors.

Actually, Edgar Schein (1961) and Robert Lifton (1961), the two most significant researchers on the practices of the Chinese Communists, preferred the term *coercive persuasion* over *brainwashing* because they did not believe that external events could completely overwhelm free will, as is implied with the word *brainwashing* (Anthony, 1990):

> *Coercive persuasion is a more accurate descriptive concept because basically what happened to the prisoners was that they were subjected to unusually intense and prolonged persuasion in a situation from which they could not escape; that is they were coerced into allowing themselves to be persuaded (Schein, 1961:18).*

The term *brainwashing* became popular during the early 1970s, when, with deviant religious movements growing, some psychologists (e.g., Singer, 1979; Conway and Siegelman, 1978, 1982) began to compare the practices of the Chinese Communists with those employed by new religious movements. Such comparisons have proved quite controversial. The overwhelming majority of social scientists who study new religious movements have severely criticized brainwashing as a theory of deviant religious involvement. These scholars contend that people join and leave deviant religious movements because they choose to join and leave.

Research has suggested that the brainwashing theory is inconsistent with the findings that most conversions are voluntary and occur in the absence of physical confinements (Richardson, Harder, and Simmonds, 1972; Robbins and Anthony, 1980; Barker, 1983). Both Schein (1961) and Lifton (1961) argued that incarceration and physical maltreatment are what separate coercive persuasion from other forms of group influence (Anthony, 1990). In addition, if the cults do brainwash, they are not very good at it, for even the recruitment practices of the most intense groups are seldom successful. In their research on the notorious "Oakland Family" of Moonies (who are known for their deceptive and high-pressure conversion practices), Bromley and Shupe (1981) estimated that only 1 out of 200 young people approached by the Moonies ended up converting. Barker (1984) similarly concluded that over 90 percent of those attending Moonie workshops did not join the Moonies. Brainwashing is also inconsistent with findings that voluntary defections are relatively frequent (Shupe, Spielman, and Stigall, 1977; Barker, 1984). If religious groups have such control over the minds of their "captors," why are defection rates so high? This is one question that we asked ourselves during the Waco confrontation between the Branch Davidians and federal agents. If, as the popular media led us to believe, David Koresh had "complete control" over his followers, why were there so many defectors willing to talk to the press? It seemed there were more defectors than believers.

Additionally, research suggests that the typical devotee is nothing like the blindly following zombie suggested by the brainwashing theorists. Even devotees who appear to outsiders to be religious fanatics may have little knowledge of (or interest in) the religious doctrines that supposedly dominate their lives. And they may have very rational reasons (which may or may not be religious) for being involved in the group. One Moonie whom Bromley and Shupe interviewed plainly admitted: "The Unification Church offers me a communal way of life, and good communes are hard to find nowadays" (1981:110).

Of course, the cults *do* exert extreme pressures to conform. In fact, this pressure is quite often very important in the success of the cult. We probably would not have heard of the Unification Church if the early Moonies had not been so aggressive. Brainwashing critics, however, contend that whether converts are defined as "victims of brainwashing" or whether they are defined as "religious converts" is largely dependent on the values of those outsiders who are making the observations. As we will discuss in more detail later, the accusation that religious groups are "brainwashing" has become a social weapon to be used against unpopular fringe groups

(Richardson, 1983). In the absence of data that cults are physically coercive, there is little reason to believe that cult practices are qualitatively different from those employed by, for example, the military, or equally intense (but less culturally offensive) sects. Robert Lifton (1961) has himself recognized that *brainwashing* is an ideologically loaded term and has warned of the tendency for moral entrepreneurs to misuse and overuse the theory:

> Behind this web of semantic (and more than semantic) confusion lies an image of "brainwashing" as an all-powerful, irresistible, unfathomable, and magical method of achieving total control over the human mind. It is of course none of these things and this loose usage makes the word a rallying point for fear, resentment, and for a wide gamut of emotional extremism. One may justly conclude that the term has a far from precise and a questionable usefulness (Lifton, 1961:4).

The criticism of brainwashing, as an objectivist theory of deviant religious involvement, is perhaps best summarized by Saul Levine, who, in an article in *Psychology Today* writes:

> Going back to the very beginning, we have seen that the percentage of potential joiners who drop out at each escalation of group pressure also escalates; of every 500 youngsters who are approached, only one actually joins. If recruitment techniques are so sinister, why do they so rarely work? The answer is that very few children are looking for what radical groups have to offer. They don't buy it because they don't want it. Those who do usually get what they want.
>
> This does not mean that radical groups don't use group-pressure techniques to assure conformity. They do. But so do corporations intent on whipping up the enthusiasm of the sales force, preachers who seek generous donations from their congregation and football coaches eager for a winning season (Levine, 1984:27).

Macro-Subjectivist Theories: When Deviant Becomes Evil

The objectivist who uses the word *cult* generally does so without prejudice. *Cult* is merely the term used to designate the new religions in a given society. However, in popular culture the term *cult* has come to mean much more than deviant religion. It has come to mean "devious" and "evil" religion and has come such a popular label for unpopular groups that, as we mentioned earlier, the subjectivists often avoid using the term at all, preferring to speak of the "so-called cults," or the "new religions." If "cult" is a label, then any explanation of cults must begin with a consideration of the social and political process by which that label has been applied. We therefore begin with a discussion of interest group theory.

Interest Group Theory. To the average American, the cults are to be watched and feared. Their purpose, it is assumed, goes far beyond religion because ultimately it is their intent to take over the world. Interest group theorists are quick to remind us, however, that today's mainstream religions were yesterday's cults. Furthermore, we can look to history to see that the hostility directed towards today's deviant religions is similar to that directed towards movements of the past. For example, the Mason movement, which today is a perfectly acceptable fraternal organization, was severely criticized in the nineteenth century (McGuire, 1987). So too were the Roman Catholics who, prior to the American Revolution, had few political rights (Bromley and Shupe, 1981). We could cite a number of other examples—the Mennonites, the Mormons (who moved to Utah to avoid persecution), the Jehovah's Witnesses—who have been persecuted because it was feared they would have some detrimental effect on U.S. society (Bromley and Shupe, 1981). Critics of these and other groups made claims similar to those made against the new religions of today; that these religions exercised too much control over members' lives, demanded total commitment, conducted secret

activities (McGuire, 1987), used deception and coercion in recruitment (the term *brainwashing* was not yet used, but the allegations were essentially the same), and were guided by a corrupt and money hungry leadership (Bromley and Shupe, 1981). To further make the point that the prejudice against new religions is nothing new, Bromley and Shupe (1979) make a fascinating comparison of the conversion and commitment practices of the Unification Church to the now socially acceptable Tnevnoc cult. During the latter part of the nineteenth century, the Tnevnoc conversion and commitment practices, Bromley and Shupe argue, were essentially similar to those employed by the Moonies (i.e., every bit as "devious"). What makes this comparison especially interesting is that, in the end, the authors reveal that Tnevnoc is actually *convent* spelled backwards. Yes, Bromley and Shupe tricked us! They were actually comparing life as a Moonie to life in a convent.

Another similarity between deviant movements of the past and today's cults is that the most damaging allegations have often come from ex-members whose accounts of the practices of the group in question must be convincing and damaging enough so as to mobilize action against them (Bromley and Shupe, 1981).

These lessons from the past are important, for they remind us that "if we grasp the real meaning of the present controversy, it will be more helpful to view it in terms of conflicts of interest rather than as a conspiratorial plot against Christianity, America, or innocent youth" (Bromley and Shupe, 1981:19). Because some groups preach a deviant ideology, moral entrepreneurs (called "anti-cultists" from here on) are quick to label the practices of these groups "evil." If we are to understand the battle over these "evil" religions, we must understand the interest groups involved. At one end, of course, stand the new religions that, although quite different from each other, have often been grouped together by the anti-cultists. At the other end is a loose coalition of "anti-cult" organizations, which we shall call the anti-cult movement (ACM).

The ACM began in 1971 as a response to the Children of God movement. The nomadic, communal, authoritarian life-style of the Children of God, argue Bromley and Shupe, "often made communication between youthful members and their families difficult at best, and parents were frequently confused at their offsprings' sudden conversions and seemingly fanatical commitment" (1981:28). The movement actually began when a retired naval officer and his wife in Chula Vista, California, unsuccessfully attempted to "rescue" their daughter from a Children of God commune in Texas. They soon discovered other angry families who were anxious to "expose" the Children of God (Shupe, Spielmann, Stigall, 1980). These families first met in San Diego in 1972 and founded FREECOG, or officially, "The Parents' Committee to Free Our Sons and Daughters From the Children of God Organization." As stories of other cults circulated, the scope of FREECOG expanded, eventually becoming the Citizens Freedom Foundation. Today this organization is called the Cult Awareness Network, and is the most visible and largest (2,000 members in 20 cities) anti-cult organization (Newsweek, 1993b).

During the past 20 years, several anti-cult organizations have come and gone. The specific agendas of each organization have often differed, but their overriding purpose has essentially been the same. This purpose has included, first of all, the self-proclaimed authority to tell the world what is and is not a cult. It is their job, they feel, to "expose" the cults. The specific criteria used to categorize religious movements as cults often differ from organization to organization. But there is one common definitional component: that religions are cults if they are "destructive." The assumption, it would seem, is that the

distinction between destructive and benign is clear for all to see (Newsweek, 1993b). From a macro-subjectivist perspective, however, such distinctions are never clear. They are negotiated by competing interests. So the interesting question is not which religions are destructive. Rather, it is who is going to tell us which are destructive. It seems that the label "destructive cult" has often been reserved for those nonnormative religious groups whose adherents live their faith too intensely. This point is perhaps best summarized by Meredith McGuire who writes that our society "defines as 'deviant' one who is *too* committed to religion, especially authoritarian religion. The resocialization processes themselves are less of an issue than the legitimacy of the group's religion itself" (1987:68).

ACM organizations have also tried to find and "rescue" family members (Shupe, Spielmann, Stigall, 1980). Because the cults have been allegedly using coercive persuasion and mind control, drastic measures of "rescue" seem justified to the anti-cultists. During the 1970s, the practice of *deprogramming* was developed, whereby an unsuspecting cult devotee would be kidnapped and pressured to denounce his or her religious beliefs ("unbrainwashed"). But kidnapping is illegal. And forcing someone to relinquish their religious beliefs surely smacks of intolerance and disregard for religious freedoms and civil liberties. So it would seem that deprogramming would be illegal. This is where the charge of brainwashing becomes an important legal tool for the ACM. Lawyers have entered the picture (e.g., Delgado, 1980; 1982), arguing that beliefs that result from external manipulation (i.e., brainwashing) are not authentic beliefs and are not offered constitutional protection (Anthony, 1990). Since the cults are coercive in their recruitment and conversion techniques, some argue, the practices of the deprogrammers is legally justified.

There are four broad categories of people who join anti-cult organizations. The most numerically significant category of people (80 to 90 percent) comprises the families and friends of cult members (Shupe, Speilmann, Stigall, 1980). The second category includes ex-cultists who provide important firsthand accounts for why the cults need to be controlled. Third, a small number of deprogrammers, motivated in part by economic interests, have worked diligently to raise public fear of deviant religion. Finally, the ACM contains several religious groups who have mobilized in moral opposition to the deviant religions.

While these are the primary categories of people organized in opposition to the deviant religions, two other constituencies have proved to be important resources for the ACM. The first includes a small number of mental health professionals who have been extremely important in providing legitimacy to pathological and brainwashing conceptions of cult involvement (Robbins and Anthony, 1982). Consider, for example, the following medical interpretations (cited in Robbins and Anthony, 1982) of cult involvement:

Destructive cultism is a sociopathic illness which is rapidly spreading throughout the U.S. and the rest of the world in the form of a pandemic (Shapiro, 1977:83).

Destructive cultism is a distinct syndrome. It includes behavioral changes, loss of personal identity, cessation of scholastic activities, estrangement from family, disinterest in society and pronounced mental control and enslavement by cult leaders. Management of this sociopathic problem requires confrontation, sociologic, psychotherapeutic and general medical measures (Shapiro, 1977:80).

These afflictions [are] physical impairments of thought and feelings, protracted alterations of awareness and personality that can be diagnosed, in the strictest sense, as varieties of information disease *(Conway and Siegelman, 1978:151). [emphasis in original]*

Medicalizing cult membership serves to redefine cult involvement as "induced mental pathology" (Robbins and Anthony, 1982:285) rather than mere religious commitment. Such conceptions, of course, play right into the hands of the anti-cultists. "To the extent that 'sick' persons are the victims of inner pathological process which interfere with normal behavioral functions, their behavior is assumed to be beyond their control" (Robbins and Anthony, 1982:285). In arguing that the "victim" lacks free will, the medical theorists are implicitly endorsing deprogramming. Robbins (1984) even goes so far as to argue that medical conceptions are essential to the anti-cult cause:

The medicalized "mind control" claim articulates a critique of deviant new religions which not only obviates civil libertarian objections to social control but also meets the needs of the various groups which are threatened by or antagonistic to cults: Mental health professionals, *whose role in the rehabilitation of victims of "destructive cultism" is highlighted;* parents, *whose opposition to cults and willingness to forcibly "rescue" cultist progeny are legitimated;* ex-converts, *who may find it meaningful and rewarding to reinterpret their prior involvement with stigmatized groups as basically passive and unmotivated; and* clerics, *who are concerned to avoid appearing to persecute religious competitors. An anti-cult coalition of these groups is possible only if medical and mental health issues are kept in the fore-front and if the medical model is employed in such a way as to disavow the intent to persecute minority beliefs and to stress the psychiatric healing of involuntary pathology (Robbins, 1984:253). [emphasis in original]*

We must recognize that psychotherapies and new religious groups are often competing for the same clients. Indeed, many deviant religions claim to offer psychosocial rewards similar to those offered by psychotherapist. Since the market of people who seek such solutions (and can afford such solutions) is limited, the competition between the deviant religions and psychiatrists and psychologists is predictable (Kilbourne and Richardson, 1984), leading some in the mental health community to complain that the cults offer a fraudulent "substitute for therapy" (Robbins and Anthony, 1982). Despite its considerable power, however, the medical community has not been completely successful in medicalizing deviant religious involvement. Success has been limited, first of all, because the medical community is itself divided, with some psychiatrists being very outspoken in their defense of deviant religions and their criticism of the brainwashing theory (e.g., Levine, 1984). In addition, several interest groups (some traditional religious groups, the ACLU, and many social scientists) have come to the defense of the new religions and have been critical of medical conceptions (Kilbourne and Richardson, 1984).

The second constituency important to the anti-cult movement is the mass media, which is probably the single most significant influence on that attitudes of people toward the deviant religions (Beckford, 1983). In Britain, parents who had generally interpreted their children's conversion experiences as positive, suddenly became worried when they read media accounts of Moonie conversions (Beckford, 1983). According to Richardson, media accounts were especially superficial and misleading following the Jonestown tragedy: "There was a failure to differentiate the groups: the Manson Cult and People's Temple were discussed in articles that also talked about the Hare Krishna, the Children of God, the Unification Church, and other groups. Major differences were not mentioned and any similarity was exploited . . ." (1983:101). Early media accounts of the Jesus Movement and the Unification Church (prior to Jonestown) were generally positive because it was perceived that these groups helped confused youth. However, as youth began to demonstrate their total commitment by moving to communes, sentiment quickly changed (Richardson, 1983).

More recently, it was the Branch Davidians who found themselves the focus of considerable attention. Most of the media coverage was predictably sensationalistic. Consider, for example, this warning from *Newsweek* magazine:

> *Waco is a wake-up call. If the cult watchers are to be believed, there are thousands of groups out there poised to snatch your body, control your mind, corrupt your soul. . . . Warning: do you know where your children are?* (Newsweek, 1993b:60)

This quote reminds us that in their efforts to publicize the atrocities of deviant movements, there is a tendency for interest groups and the media to create the impression that deviant movements are larger and more significant than they might actually be. This is the contention of Bromley and Shupe, who introduce their book *Strange Gods: The Great American Cult Scare* with the following admonition:

> *There is no avalanche of rapidly growing cults. In fact, there probably are no more such groups existing today than there have been at any other time in our recent history. Furthermore, the size of these groups has been grossly exaggerated and almost all have long since passed their peak periods of growth. Much of the "cult explosion" has been pure media hype* (1981:3). [emphasis in original]

A fascinating contemporary example of how the cult threat gets exaggerated is the well-publicized "increase" in satanism and satanic crimes. The satanists, so we are led to believe, are taking over the country, performing ritualistic sacrifices of children, murdering virgins, and mutilating animals. These stories are supplemented by media and police reports that often link certain bizarre crimes (especially murders) to satanism. Scholars who have taken the time to investigate atrocity stories about satanism, however, argue that there is generally little truth to the rumors. Balch and Gilliam (1991), for example, describe the events surrounding the 1974 murder of a Missoula,

Montana, woman, Donna Pounds. Within days of her murder, rumors linking the murder to the initiation process of "devil worshippers" began to spread. According to the rumors, the initiation process would eventually result in three murders: the murder of a Christian woman, a virgin, and a betrayer. Donna Pounds, the wife of a Baptist preacher, was the Christian. The stabbing murder of five-year-old Siobhan McGinnis, which had occurred two months before the Pounds murder, meant that there was one victim yet to come. Not surprisingly, fear that another person would be murdered caused considerable alarm in Missoula. Eventually the murders were solved and police could discover no link to a satanic cult. Yet the rumors of satanic activity in Missoula remain to this day (Balch and Gilliam, 1991).

The rumors and hysteria surrounding satanism are not limited to localized events. In the last few years, for example, rumors about female "breeders" bearing children for satanic sacrifice have become commonplace. These rumors have fueled anti-cult claims that satanism is an evergrowing threat. In many ways, rumors about women being used as "breeders" can be traced to Lauren Stratford's autobiography *Satan's Underground* (1988). In the book, Stratford claims to have been raped by satanists, eventually bearing three children, all of whom were taken from her and sacrificed. Largely as a result of the outrageous nature of her claims, Lauren was a "hot ticket," telling her story on shows ranging from "Geraldo" to the Christian talk show the "700 Club." Stratford also used *Satan's Underground* to launch a successful career as satanic ritual abuse expert and therapist. However, when *Cornerstone* magazine writers Gretchen Passantino, Bob Passantino, and Jon Trott decided to investigate Stratford's story (something "Geraldo," the "700 Club," and publisher of her book had chosen not to do) they

found that the entire story was a "gruesome fantasy." Stratford claims, for example, to have led a fairly "normal" public life, attending high school and college like "normal" girls. Yet, she claims to have had three children during her high school and college years. Passantino, Passantino, and Trott (1989) could not find a single witness, nor could Stratford produce a witness. Passantino and her colleagues found plenty of people who knew Lauren during high school and college, but all claimed emphatically that she was never pregnant.

Rumors such as these have contributed to what sociologists are now calling the "satanism scare" (Richardson, Best, and Bromley, 1991). In what ways is the satanism scare related to an interest group perspective on deviant religion? The answer is that, if interest groups can make the problem (in this case satanism) out to be bigger than it actually is, they can more successfully generate support for their cause. From the perspective of the ACM, for example, the bigger the cult problem, the more easily society can be motivated to do something about the cult problem. By focusing on the alleged atrocities of the satanists, the ACM hopes to generate public fear toward cults more generally. In this way, the ACM has used satanism in much the same way that it used the People's Temple during the 1970s (Bromley, 1991). Fundamentalist Christianity also has much to gain by creating a satanism scare. The greater the threat of satan, the greater the need for Christian solutions. Plus, satanism represents a sensationalist topic some Christian writers have been quick to take advantage of (Richardson, Best, and Bromley, 1991). It would be wrong, however, to conclude that all Christians, or even all fundamentalist Christians, have "bought into" the satanism scare. Indeed, many Christian writers (e.g., Passantino, Passantino, and Trott, 1989; Perrin and Parrott, 1993) have been critical of Christians who have contributed to the hysteria surrounding satanism.

Micro-Subjectivist Theories: Brainwashing or Identity Transformation?

Micro-subjectivists have paid very little attention to deviant religious involvement. There are, in fact, no definitional theories of deviant religious involvement, and the connection to labeling theory is indirect at best. Labeling theory concerns itself with the effect of having a deviant identity forced upon the individual by powerful institutions or individuals of social control. Given the small size and relative insignificance of deviant religious movements, one could hardly consider these cults to be powerful institutions of social control. Additionally, the notion that the identity is forced on the individual is not consistent with empirical evidence that recruits generally join (and leave) the cults freely. At the same time, however, as an interactionist theory of how one comes to accept an identity assigned by others, the social-psychological process that labeling theory is based upon is applicable in the study of deviant religion.

In their study of the Moonies, Lofland and Stark (1965) argued that "verbal converts" only became "total converts" as a result of intense and prolonged interaction with members. The process they refer to, resocialization, or identity transformation, has been a popular area of study for micro-subjectivists. According to the micro-subjectivist theory, the individual is perceived as an ever changing product of outside influences. As social influences change, the "self" and "identity" will change. In the more dramatic cases, the convert gains a completely new sense of who he or she is, gives allegiance to a new authority, adopts new central meanings that contradict the old ones, and reevaluates his or her old identity as wrong or "inferior" (Gordon, 1974:165).

Such changes, which are sometimes described by the convert as having happened suddenly and dramatically, are, from a micro-subjectivist standpoint, more likely to take place gradually. Self-perceptions that have taken years to form are not likely to be radically transformed overnight. Thus, it is best to conceptualize conversion as a process rather than an event (Richardson, 1978; Staples and Mauss, 1987).

The most extreme cases of radical identity transformation (e.g., a fundamentalist Baptist becoming a Hare Krishna) are probably uncommon. Not only are cult memberships rather small, but even those converts who may appear to have experienced a dramatic conversion may not have experienced the internal changes we might assume. Balch (1980), for example, argues that few converts actually experience a dramatic change in identity. Rather, they merely learn a new set of roles. He compared the "front stage" and "back stage" of members of a UFO cult and concluded that converts experienced no actual transformation of consciousness. They had merely learned the special vocabulary necessary to play the part of "convert."

Notice how the resocialization notion of identity transformation is very similar to the concept of brainwashing. Both suggest that others have a profound effect on how we come to see ourselves. There is a significant difference, however, because the term *identity transformation* implies a volitional individual actively in search of (and active in the construction of) a new identity; but *brainwashing* implies coercion, whereby a helpless recruit becomes psychologically bound to a powerful other.

SOCIAL POLICY AND SOCIAL CONTROL

The Deviant Religions and the Law

Religious pluralism owes its existence to the First Amendment declaration that "Congress shall make no law respecting an establishment of religion, or prohibiting the free exercise thereof." But what limits, if any, should be placed on this freedom? Richard Delgado (1980), a lawyer who is critical of cult practices, argues that the First Amendment offers absolute protection for freedom of belief, but not absolute protection for freedom of action. Therefore, according to Delgado, the courts are placed in the precarious position of trying to protect freedom of religious belief while at the same time protecting individuals and society from harm. Recruitment and conversion practices that violate the rights of individuals and cause harm to individuals or society are not constitutionally protected.

Quite obviously, some limitations are necessary. One would be hard-pressed to defend the suicides at Jonestown, even those that were voluntary, as religious practices protected under the First Amendment. And it is doubtful that many would defend the violence of the Branch Davidians. Few controversial religious practices, however, are quite so clear-cut. The problem, of course, is in drawing the line between what is and is not individual or societal harm (Delgado, 1980). Some would argue that all religion is harmful. Karl Marx, for example, is well known for his admonition that religion, especially established religion, is the "opiate of the people." In emphasizing the rewards of the afterlife, religion conceals from the masses their oppressed state in this life. From a Marxist standpoint, therefore, all religions should be criminalized.

ACM attempts to control the practices of the deviant religions generally center around claims of brainwashing, or in less controversial terminology, the use of deception and physical and mental coercion in conversion. Given ACM charges, several questions need to be answered: Do the cults employ some kind of magical mind control method that removes free will from the individual? Do the cults use deception and coercion in re-

cruitment? If so, should legal restrictions be placed on such actions?

The answers to these questions, of course, largely depend on whom one asks. Consider, for example, this impassioned exhortation from anti-cultist (and sociologist) Edward Levine:

> *Prospective members are completely unaware that they are being recruited or that they have unwittingly entered the first phase of what is actually a process of indoctrination. Now enveloped by a process of thought control conducted by the most cunning kind of deception and manipulation, cult recruits are deliberately kept involved in group activities for fifteen hours and more a day. They are never left alone, even when going to the bathroom, lest in isolation they begin to doubt or question what they are doing and being told. Purposely kept fatigued so that their minds cannot function effectively, deliberately not told that they are being proselytized, only gradually introduced to the cult's religion, and constantly kept under peer pressure to accept what they are told, cult recruits are deprived of any opportunity rationally to learn about, examine, and appraise the religious and secular views of the cult (Levine, 1980b:35).*

As we have argued, such justifications for the social control of cult activities are, for several reasons, simply not consistent with the empirical evidence. First of all, the anti-cultists who make such claims have generally conducted no systematic research of their own, and often rely almost exclusively on the accounts provided by ex-members. For the social scientist, however, such accounts are of questionable usefulness because there is a tendency for individuals to reconstruct past actions so that their actions may appear justified (to both self and others). That is to say, ex-members who have difficulty explaining why they joined such a "strange" religion may employ a brainwashing interpretation. As Robbins and Anthony remind us, such interpretations "may be psychologically rewarding for ex-converts by absolving them of responsibility for their involvement" (1982:291). Particularly problematic are the accounts of ex-members who have been deprogrammed. One of the chores of the deprogrammer is to provide for the cult member an explanation for how he or she was "trapped" by the cult. The similarity of brainwashing accounts provided by various ex-members who have been deprogrammed (which anti-cultists cite as evidence that brainwashing occurs) probably has less to do with the similarity of their experiences than it does with the similarity of the interpretations fed to them by deprogrammers. In addition, having left the movement, defectors may have a personal vendetta or a financial incentive (in civil suits) and may exaggerate or even lie about their experiences. The more outrageous the stories, the more likely official actions against the group will be taken.

Bromley and Shupe (1981) argue that when the evidence accumulated by trained anthropologists, sociologists, and scholars of religion is considered (as opposed to the evidence of ex-members), there is little reason to suggest that the deviant religions are, on average, any more coercive and deceptive than more accepted institutions. Of course, there are isolated cases of questionable practices. During the 1970s, for example, the Children of God were well known for their practice of "flirty fishing," whereby attractive women were sent to pick up recruits and, if necessary, sleep with them in order to "bring them to Jesus" (Bromley and Shupe, 1981). The Moonies have also been criticized for targeting young, lonely looking people and inviting them to educational, peace, philosophical (or whatever) workshops. The true identity of the group is concealed from the potential recruit until interpersonal bonds are formed. Bromley and Shupe (1981) contend that the most deceptive stories can often be traced to an especially aggressive branch of the Moonies on the West Coast called the

"Oakland Family" and is not typical of the movement as a whole. Besides, lots of organizations use "hooks." The life insurance salesperson gives a predictable presentation on the importance of financial security before telling you what it will cost. The Jehovah's Witness approaches your door distributing material on the environment. The Mormons sponsor television advertisements on the importance of family.

Beyond a few isolated incidents (e.g., Jonestown), deviant movements cannot be said to be physically coercive. There remains, however, considerable debate over whether the cults are psychologically coercive. Anti-cultists contend the repetitious chanting among groups, such as the Hare Krishna, makes people vulnerable to mind control. Perhaps this is so. Should such practices, therefore, be criminalized? Others are more concerned about high-pressure workshops, such as those sponsored by the Moonies. At these workshops, critics like Levine (1980b) contend, recruits are not allowed to be alone, are deprived of sleep, are bombarded with lectures and other information, and are "love bombed" (showered with love, kindness, empathy, hugs, and eye contact). Notions that such practices make recruits psychologically malleable are given medical legitimacy by mental health professionals who argue that the combination of physical exhaustion and intellectual stimulation leads to a form of "information disease" (Conway and Siegelman, 1978). Conway and Schneider (1978) suggest that recruits who are tired and bombarded with information will "lose it" and "snap." Let us not forget, however, that high school students spending a week at Christian retreat (especially a conservative Christian retreat) might have a similar experience. They, too, are tired (who sleeps at camp?), hear lots of lectures, are seldom alone, and are "love bombed." Are they also victims of "information disease"?

Earlier in this chapter, we discussed anti-cult claims that cult converts become "programmed" robots who, in the words of Levine "automatically obey no matter what they are ordered to do" (1980b:35). There is no evidence that this is true. Cult members are not zombies. They are probably as coherent, rational, and self-serving as the rest of us (Bromley and Shupe, 1981). Besides, it is unlikely that programmed robots could defect at the rates cult members do (Barker, 1984).

It is important to recognize that, while the majority of social scientists may see the brainwashing argument as flawed, court decisions do not always reflect the views of these social scientists. We mentioned above that from a social-scientific point of view, the accounts of ex-members may be of limited usefulness. However, from a legal standpoint, such accounts pull considerable weight and have, with help from the medical community, resulted in some successful suits against the new religions. (For a current summary of the legal debate, see the Winter 1992 issue of *Behavioral Science and the Law,* which is devoted entirely to "Cults and the Law"; or see Robbins, Shepherd, and McBride, 1985).

According to Dick Anthony (1990), the limited success the anti-cultists have enjoyed in court can largely be attributed to the testimony of psychologist Margaret Singer. Singer, who studied coercive persuasion under the tutelage of theorist Edgar Schein, offers the courts her own version of brainwashing, which she calls "systematic manipulation of social psychological influence." Singer has no empirical support for her theory and, in fact, has never published her theory. However, she claims in court that her theory improves upon processes specified by Schein (1961) and Robert Lifton (1961). Singer maintains that the indoctrination practices of the cults are especially successful because co-ercive persuasion is best achieved without the use of threat or force. Such testimony, which is not supported by empirical evidence, directly contradicts the assertions of both Lifton (1961) and Schein (1961), who argue that physical coercion is an essential component to coercive persuasion (Anthony, 1990). Singer also argues that the techniques of the cults are amazingly successful. Evidence on the success of the Chinese Communists, however, suggests that just the opposite is true. Scheflin and Opton (1978) estimate that fewer than 50 out of 3,500 POWs collaborated with the Koreans after the war (Anthony, 1990).

Anthony (1990), who is himself a psychologist, is openly critical of Singer's "pop psychology" and her claims to be representing the views of Schein and Lifton. In Anthony's opinion, Singer is nothing more than a moral entrepreneur hiding behind the legitimacy of her Ph.D. Equally surprising and "scandalous," according to Anthony "is that the courts, and the scientific and professional organizations upon whom the courts rely for advice in technical matters of this sort, have been letting her get away with the presentation in courts of law of simplistic concepts from the worlds of propaganda and science fiction as if they were serious scholarly arguments" (1990:325).

We should note that professional organizations such as the Society for the Scientific Study of Religion and the American Psychological Association have recently mobilized to challenge brainwashing arguments. However, as is evidenced in a recent California Supreme Court decision in favor of two ex-Moonies who sued the Unification Church for brainwashing (*Mokol and Leal v. Holy Spirit Association*, 1988), Singer's arguments have generated considerable legal support. The Mokol and Leal case, in which Singer is the star witness, is currently being appealed to the U. S. Supreme Court. "Should it be affirmed at this level," argues Anthony, "it will likely have the force of law in our country for at least a generation as the Supreme Court is slow to reverse itself once it has made a definitive decision" (1990:325).

Implicit support for the anti-cultists also comes as a result of court reluctance to convict deprogrammers. While the courts have not exactly endorsed deprogramming, judges and juries have often sympathized with family members and deprogrammers who defend themselves as only being interested in the mental health of the cult member and in reuniting the family (Robbins, 1984).

While the legal debate over brainwashing has dominated attempts to control the practices of the deviant religions, there are a number of other social control issues as well. For example, what guidelines should the state use for determining what is (and is not) religion? Because contributions to religions are tax deductible and the property owned by religions is tax exempt, there are obvious financial advantages to being a religion. What limits (if any) should be placed on the fundraising practices of religions? These issues have been, and will likely continue to be important in the legal debate over deviant religions.

The "Treatment" of Religious Deviants

Many mental health professionals contend that cults are psychologically damaging. Maybe this is true. The question, however, is whether the "psychologically damaging" effects of cultism is any more of our business than is, for example, the "psychologically damaging" effects of Presbyterianism. For many (but not all) of those who contend that it is damaging (because the cults deceive and coerce their members), deprogramming is a justifiable and necessary method for restoring the ex-member to a psychologically healthy state.

Psychiatrist Saul Levine (1984), however,

contends that deprogramming is not only ethically wrong, but that the deprogramming may itself be psychologically damaging. He admits that many cults are not psychologically healthy environments, but he strongly defends a person's right to seek solutions to life's dilemmas in these settings. He urges people who have "lost" family and friends to the cults to be patient and to not resort to deprogramming, which could damage already strained psyches and relationships further. Chances are that eventually the loved one will leave the cult under his or her own volition.

SUMMARY

From an objectivist point of view, *deviant religion* is religion that violates the norms established by the culturally accepted churches. There are essentially two kinds of deviant religious movements: *sects* and *cults*. Sects, are religious movements that break off from the traditional churches (*religious revival*). Sects are in a state of tension with the surrounding society and can therefore be categorized as deviant religion. However, as revival of traditional religion, sects are generally less culturally unique (and therefore less controversial) than cults. Cults are new religions—*religious innovation*—and are, by definition, deviant religion.

The subjectivist holds that deviant religion is best conceptualized as a societal reaction rather than a norm-violation. Thus, the focus is on the *moral entrepreneurs* who work to make "cult" a "four-letter word." Both the objectivist and subjectivist conception challenge the more popularly accepted *absolutist perspective* of moral entrepreneurs, which suggests that cults are evil, deceptive, destructive, immoral, and unhealthy religion.

Although there are many deviant religions that have attracted attention, the most controversial contemporary movements are the Children of God, the Unification Church (the

"Moonies"), the Hare Krishna, Scientology, and the Rajneesh. Research on who joins religions like these has concluded that "normal" people can be attracted to "abnormal" religion. This is not to say, of course, that there is no variation in the types of people who join deviant religious groups. Cult members are disproportionately young, middle class, educated, and female. A significant number have also experimented with illegal drugs. Finally, converts are generally not attached to religions prior to joining the cult.

The most accepted explanation for deviant religion represents a modification of *secularization theory*. From this perspective secularization does not necessarily mean the end of religion, as traditional secularization theory holds; it merely means that the form of religion will change. Research has demonstrated, for example, that cults appear where more traditional churches and sects are doing poorly. That is, they appear in the most secular part of this country (in the western United States), and in the most secular parts of Canada (again, the west), and in the most secular parts of Europe (Northern Europe). The relative failure of the more traditional churches means that the religious needs of the people are not being met, thus creating a religious market conducive to cult growth.

There are several theories of cult involvement. From the perspective of control theory, young, single college students with few religious ties and a history of drug use have few stakes in conformity and are thus more free to participate in deviant religions. There is also a tradition of research that looks at the impact of tensions, strains, and other conditions that may predispose one to look to deviant religions for answers. Sometimes this research portrays converts as religious "seekers" who have for much of their lives actively searched for "truth." Other research focuses on learning factors, such as the forming of intra-group bonds, the weakening of extra-group bonds, and intensive and prolonged interaction between the convert and cult members. A competing medical perspective, *brainwashing*, suggests that with enough psychological pressure, unsuspecting recruits can be coerced into joining new religious movements. According to brainwashing theory, converts are psychologically controlled by the members of the religious group. Critics of brainwashing as a theory of cult involvement argue that converts voluntarily choose to join and voluntarily choose to leave deviant religious movements. Critics admit that the psychological pressures to join cults are often intense, but they argue that these pressures are not qualitatively different from those used by more culturally accepted, yet equally intense, institutions (e.g., the military, and sports' teams).

Macro-subjectivists focus on the reactions of others to certain deviant religions. They argue that the charge of brainwashing is nothing more than a social weapon used by *anti-cultists* against unpopular deviant religious groups. From this perspective, the charges made against today's new religions have more to do with deviant ideology than with cult practices. We need only to look to history to see that new religions have often been feared and persecuted. Organized in opposition to the new religious movements is the *Anti-Cult movement (ACM)*, which is composed primarily of the families of cult members, ex-cultists, deprogrammers, religious leaders, and other moral entrepreneurs. Anticult efforts to define as evil certain religious movements have been helped by some mental health professionals who claim that cult involvement is induced mental pathology. Such claims are used by the ACM to legitimize *deprogramming* efforts. Mass-media focus on the sensational and controversial has also been important to the anti-cult cause. Anti-cultists have also been influential in facilitating the perception that the cults are larger and more significant than is actually the case.

The Constitution protects religious freedom in the First Amendment. There is considerable debate, however, concerning when limits should be placed on this freedom. Most social scientists and religion scholars who study the new religions claim that, on average, the cults are no more deceptive and coercive in their recruitment and conversion practices than any of a number of culturally acceptable organizations. However, on the strength of testimony of ex-cultists and a handful of mental health personnel who testify against the new religions, some successful suits have been brought against the new religions. In addition, attempts to prosecute deprogrammers for kidnapping have largely failed, thus providing implicit support for the anti-cult cause.

Family and friends of those who have been "lost" to the cults have often been tempted to hire deprogrammers, who promise to rescue and return their child to a healthy mental state. However, some psychiatrists suggest that deprogramming is not only questionable ethically and legally but that it may be psychologically damaging to the cult member.

GLOSSARY

Absolutist Perspective A non-sociological conception of deviant behavior that assumes that some religions are inherently deviant. For the absolutists, the cults are inherently evil, deceptive, destructive, immoral, and unhealthy.

Anti-Cultists The moral entrepreneurs who have "taken on" the anti-cult cause.

Anti-Cult Movement (ACM) A loose coalition of anti-cult organizations, including most notably the Cult Awareness Network, which attempt to limit the religious freedoms of the deviant religions.

Brainwashing A theory suggesting that converts are psychologically coerced into giving up prior commitments and values, and are forced to accept commitments and values as defined by the group. From this perspective, cult members ("victims") are recruited ("captured") and stripped of their free will. Also sometimes referred to as "coercive persuasion" or "mind control."

Cult A term objectivists find descriptively helpful and use to distinguish new religions (cults) from mainstream religions (churches) and religious revivals (sects). Subjectivists avoid using the term *cult* because they see it as a derogatory label. Instead, they prefer to use the terms *so-called cults, new religions,* or *deviant religions.*

Deprogramming The practice of kidnapping and "un-brainwashing" religious converts. Those who claim that the cults brainwash recruits argue that deprogramming is justifiable and does not violate First Amendment protections of religious freedom.

Deviant Religion Any religious movement that violates the norms of conventional religion (objectivist conception) or is labeled a "cult" by moral entrepreneurs (subjectivist conception). More commonly referred to as a *cult* (and sometimes a *new religion*).

Moral Entrepreneurs Powerful, credible figures who morally condemn a particular behavior and attempt to convince the rest of society to accept their definitions of right and wrong. Generally working from an absolutist perspective of deviant religion, moral entrepreneurs assume the right and responsibility to expose the "evil" religions and work to impose the deviant label "cult" on some deviant religions.

Religious Innovation Any non-schismatic (i.e., it has not grown out of a "parent" organization) "new" religious organization. Also referred to as a *cult.*

Religious Revival. Any organization that attempts to return to the original, pure religion. Also referred to as a *sect*.

Sect Attempts to recreate a more authentic version of a traditional religion in a society. Because sects violate the norms of mainstream religion and question the norms of the secular society, they can, from an objectivist point of view, be conceptualized as deviant religion. Yet, as revivals of traditional religion, sects are less culturally offensive than the more controversial cults.

Secularization Theory A theory maintaining that worldly institutions and beliefs (e.g., knowledge) will eventually eliminate the "need" for religion.

SUGGESTED READINGS

Bromley, David G., and Anson Shupe, Jr. *Strange Gods: The Great American Cult Scare.* Boston, Mass: Beacon Press, 1981.

This book includes a descriptive summary of the more noteworthy new religious movements during the 1970s. More importantly, it examines the empirical evidence surrounding the brainwashing controversy.

Richardson, James, Joel Best, and David Bromley. *The Satanism Scare.* New York: Aldine De Gruyter, 1991.

This collection of papers examines the current concern over satanism and satanic crime. It adopts a subjectivist perspective, arguing that the satanism scare is largely a social construction.

Society March/April: 1980.

This issue of *Society* includes articles from proponents of the brainwashing model of cult involvement as well as critics of the brainwashing model. It is truly fascinating reading.

Stark, Rodney, and William Sims Bainbridge. *The Future of Religion: Secularization, Revival, and Cult Formation.* Berkeley, Calif.: University of California Press, 1985.

The Future of Religion is probably the most significant book on the sociology of deviant religion.

REFERENCES

Anthony, Dick. "Religious Movements and Brainwashing Litigation Evaluating Key Testimony." *In Gods We Trust: New Patterns of Religious Pluralism in the United States.* Eds. Thomas Robbins and Dick Anthony. New Brunswick, N.J.: Transaction Books, 1990, 295–334.

Bainbridge, William S., and Rodney Stark. "Client and Audience Cults in America." *Sociological Analysis* 41(1980):199–214.

Balch, Robert. "Looking Behind the Scenes in a Religious Cult: Implications for the Study of Conversion." *Sociological Analysis* 41(1980): 137–143.

Balch, Robert, and Margaret Gilliam. "Devil Worship in Western Montana: A Case Study in Rumor Construction." *The Satanism Scare.* Eds. James Richardson, Joel Best, and David Bromley. New York: Aldine De Gruyter, 1991, 249–262.

Balch, Robert, and David Taylor. "Seekers and Saucers: The Role of the Cultic Milieu in Joining a UFO Cult." *Conversion Careers.* Ed. James Richardson. Beverly Hills: Sage, 1978, 43–63.

Barker, Eileen. "New Religious Movements in Britain: The Context and the Membership." *Sociological Analysis* 41(1983):137–143.

———. *The Making of a Moonie.* New York: Basil Blackwell, 1984.

———. "Religious Movements: Cult and Anticult Since Jonestown." *Annual Review of Sociology* 12(1986):329–346.

Becker, Howard. *Outsiders: Studies in the Sociology of Deviance.* (1963) New York: Free Press.

Beckford, James. "The Public Response to New Religious Movements in Britain." *Social Compas* XXX.1(1983):49–62.

Bromley, David. "The New Cult Scare." *The Satanism Scare.* Eds. James Richardson, Joel Best, and David Bromley. New York: Aldine De Gruyter, 1991, 49–72.

Bromley, David G., and Anson Shupe, Jr. "The Tnevnoc Cult." *Sociological Analysis* 40(1979): 361–366.

———. *Strange Gods: The Great American Cult Scare.* Boston, Mass: Beacon Press, 1981.

Carter, Lewis F. "The 'New Renunciates' of the Bhagwan Shree Rajneesh: Observation and Identification of Problems of Interpreting New Religious Movements." *Journal for the Scientific Study of Religion* 26(1987):148–172.

Chalfant, H. Paul, Robert E. Beckley, and C. Eddie Palmer. *Religion in Contemporary Society.* Palo Alto, Calif.: Mayfield Publishing Company, 1987.

Conklin, Ellis E. "Doomsday Disciples." *Seattle Post-Intelligencer* Apr. 12, 1990:C1, C3.

Conway, Flo, and Jim Siegelman. *Snapping.* New York: J.B. Lippincott, 1978.

———. "Information Disease: How Cults Created a New Mental Illness." *Science Digest* (Jan. 1982):87–92.

Delgado, Richard. 1980 "Limits to Proselytizing." *Society* March/April:25.

———. "Cults and Conversion: The Case for Informed Consent." *Georgia Law Review* 16.3 (1982):533–574.

Glock, Charles Y. "The Role of Deprivation in the Origin and Evolution of Religious Groups." *Religion and Social Conflict.* Eds. Robert Lee and Martin Marty New York: Oxford University Press, 1964, 24–36.

Gordon, David F. "The Jesus People: An Identity Synthesis." *Urban Life and Culture* 3(1974):159–178.

Hall, John. "The Apocalypse at Jonestown." *In Gods We Trust: New Patterns of Religious Pluralism in the United States.* Thomas Robbins and Dick Anthony. 2nd ed. New Brunswick, N.J.: Transaction Books, 1990, 269–293.

Heirich, Max. "Changes of Heart: A Test of Some Widely Held Theories about Religious Conversion." *American Journal of Sociology* 83 (1977):653–680.

Hirschi, Travis. *Causes of Delinquency* (1969) Berkeley: University of California Press.

Johnson, Benton. "On Church and Sect." *American Sociological Review* (Aug., 1963):539–549.

Johnstone, Ronald L. *Religion in Society: A Sociology of Religion.* 2nd ed. Englwood Cliffs, N.J.: Prentice Hall, 1983.

Judah, Stillson. *Hare Krishna and the Counterculture.* (1974) New York: Wiley.

Kilbourne, Brock, and James T. Richardson. "Psychotherapy and New Religions in a Pluralistic Society." *American Psychologist* 39 (1984):237–251.

Lacayo, Richard. "Cult of Death." *Time* (March 15, 1993):36–39.

Levine, Edward M. "Rural Communities and Religious Cults." *Adolescent Psychiatry* 8(1980a):138–153.

———. "Deprogramming Without Tears." *Society* March/April 1980b:34–38.

Levine, Saul. "Radical departures." *Psychology Today* Aug. 1984:20–27.

Lifton, Robert J. *Thought Reform and the Psychology of Totalism: A Study of 'Brainwashing' in China.* New York: Norton, 1961.

Lofland, John. *Doomsday Cult.* rev. ed. New York: Irvington, 1977.

Lofland, John, and Rodney Stark. "Becoming a World Saver: A Theory of Religious Conversion to a Deviant Perspective." *American Sociological Review* 30(1965):862–874.

McGuire, Meredith. *Religion: In Social Context.* Belmont, Calif.: Wadsworth Publishing Company, 1987.

Merton, Robert. "Social Structure and Anomie." *American Sociological Review* 3(1938)672–682.

Mills, Jeannie. *Six Years With God: Life Inside Rev Jim Jones' Peoples Temple.* New York: A & W Publishers, 1979.

Molkol and Leal v. Holy Spirit Association. 46 California Supreme Court 3d 1092(1988).

Newsweek. "The Messiah of Waco." March 15, 1993:56–58.

Newsweek. "Cultic America: A Tower of Babel." March 15, 1993:60–62.

Niebuhr, Richard. *The Social Sources of Denominationalism.* New York: Henry Holt, 1929.

O'Dea, Thomas. *The Sociology of Religion.* Englewood Cliffs, N.J.: Prentice-Hall, 1966.

Passantino, Gretchen, Bob Passantino, and Jon Trott. "Satan's Sideshow" *Cornerstone* 20(1989):23–28.

Perrin, Robin, and Armand Mauss. 1990 "The Great Protestant Puzzel: Retreat, Renewal, or Reshuffle?" *In Gods We Trust.* Eds. Thomas Robbins and Dick Anthony. New Brunswick, N.J.: Transaction Press, 1990, 152–166.

Perrin, Robin, and Les Parrott, III. "The Satanism

Scare: Are Christians Becoming Demon Obsessed?" *Christianity Today* (1993).

Richardson, James T., ed. *Conversion Careers: In and Out of the New Religions.* Beverly Hills: Sage, 1978.

Richardson, James T. "New Religious Movements in the United States: A Review." *Social Compass* 30(1983):85–110.

———. "Satanism, Religion, and the Courts." Paper presented at the annual meeting of the Society for the Scientific Study of Religion, Salt Lake City, Utah, 1989.

Richardson, James, Joel Best, and David Bromley. *The Satanism Scare* New York: Aldine De Gruyter, 1991.

Richardson, James T., Mary Harder, and Robert Simmonds. "Thought Reform and the Jesus Movement." *Youth and Society* 4(1972): 185–202.

Robbins, Thomas. "Constructing Cultist 'Mind Control'." *Sociological Analysis* 45(1984): 241–256.

Robbins, Thomas, and Dick Anthony. "The Sociology of Contemporary Religious Movements." *Annual Review of Sociology* 5(1979):75–89.

———. "The Limits of 'Coercive Persuasion' as an Explanation of Conversion to Authoritarian Sects." *Political Psychology* 2(1980):22–37.

———. "Deprogramming, Brainwashing and the Medicalization of Deviant Religious Groups." *Social Problems* 29(1982):283–297.

Robbins, Thomas, William Shepherd, and James McBride, eds. *Cults, Culture, and the Law.* Chico Calif.: Scholars Press, 1985.

Rochford, Burke. *Hare Krishna in America.* New Brunswick, N.J.: Rutgers University Press, 1985.

Scheflin, Alan, and Edward Opton. *The Mind Manipulators* New York: Paddington Press, 1978.

Schein, Edgar H. *Coercive Persuasion.* New York: W. W. Norton and Co., Inc., 1961.

Shapiro, Eli. "Destructive Cultism." *American Family Physical* 15(1977):80–83.

Shupe, Anson, R. Spielmann, and S. Stigall. "Deprogramming: The New Exorcism." *American Behavioral Scientist* 20(1977):941–946.

———. "Cults of Anti-Cultism." *Society* March/ April 1980:43–46.

Simmonds, Robert B. "Conversion as Addiction: Consequences of Joining a Jesus Movement Group." *American Behavioral Scientist* 20 (1977):909–924.

Singer, Margaret. "Coming Out of Cults." *Psychology Today* 12(1979):72–82.

Snow, David, and Richard Machalek. "The Sociology of Conversion." *Annual Review of Sociology* 10(1984):167–190.

Staples, Clifford, and Armand Mauss. (1987) "Conversion or Commitment?" *Journal for the Scientific Study of Religion* 26:133–147.

Stark, Rodney, and William Sims Bainbridge. "Networks of Faith: Interpersonal Bonds and Recruitment to Cults and Sects." *American Journal of Sociology* 85(1980):1376–1395.

———. *The Future of Religion: Secularization, Revival, and Cult Formation.* Berkeley, Calif.: University of California Press, 1985.

Stratford, Lauren. *Satan's Underground* (1988) Eugene, Oregon:Harvest House.

Troeltsch, Ernst. *The Social Teaching of the Christian Churches.* New York: Macmillan, 1931.

Wuthnow, Robert. "The New Religions in Social Context." *The New Religious Consciousness.* Eds. Charles Y. Glock and Robert N. Bellah. Berkeley: University of California Press, 1976, 267–293.

Name Index

SUBJECT INDEX